PRAISE FOR OTHER WORKS BY TOBIAS CHURTON

From *Aleister Crowley in America*

"Magician Tobias Churton has successfully cast a spell, transforming his 750-page comprehensive scholarly tome into a gripping and obsessive page turner, leaving one wishing for more."

JAMES WASSERMAN, AUTHOR OF *TEMPLAR HERESY: A STORY OF GNOSTIC ILLUMINATION*

From *Gnostic Mysteries of Sex*

"Churton's scholarship seems to be both deep and broad . . ."

PUBLISHERS WEEKLY, OCTOBER 2015

From *Occult Paris*

"Tobias is as erudite as he is excited and exciting. His scholarship is alive with passion, imagination, humor, and, most of all, humanity."

STEPHEN J. KING (SHIVA X°), GRAND MASTER, ORDO TEMPLI ORIENTIS

"No one can evoke the feel of a place and an era like Tobias Churton!"

CHRISTOPHER MCINTOSH, PH.D., AUTHOR OF *ELIPHAS LÉVI AND THE FRENCH OCCULT REVIVAL*

"Any book by Tobias Churton is a special event. . . . Churton is a world authority on Gnosticism, Hermeticism, and Rosicrucianism. Moreover, he possesses the rare ability to impart his vast knowledge on his chosen subjects in an engaging and accessible fashion."

STEVE EARLES, HELLBOUND.CA, 2017

From *Deconstructing Gurdjieff*

"Churton understands. He has a profound ability to write about complex esoteric subjects in clear, down-to-earth language. . . . There is great wisdom and a uniquely modern perspective in Churton's meticulous thought and prose."

JOHN ZORN, CC

T0322988

OTHER BOOKS BY TOBIAS CHURTON

Aleister Crowley in America:
Art, Espionage, and Sex Magick in the New World (2017)

Deconstructing Gurdjieff: Biography of a Spiritual Magician (2017)

Occult Paris: The Lost Magic of the Belle Époque (2016)

Gnostic Mysteries of Sex:
Sophia the Wild One and Erotic Christianity (2015)

Jerusalem! The Real Life of William Blake (2015)

Aleister Crowley, The Beast in Berlin:
Art, Sex, and Magick in the Weimar Republic (2014)

The Babylon Gene (novel; 2013)

The Mysteries of John the Baptist:
His Legacy in Gnosticism, Paganism, and Freemasonry (2012)

Aleister Crowley: The Biography (2011)

The Missing Family of Jesus: An Inconvenient Truth—How the Church
Erased Jesus's Brothers and Sisters from History (2010)

The Invisible History of the Rosicrucians:
The World's Most Mysterious Secret Society (2009)

Kiss of Death: The True History of the Gospel of Judas (2008)

Freemasonry: The Reality (2007)

The Magus of Freemasonry: The Mysterious Life of Elias Ashmole—
Scientist, Alchemist, and Founder of the Royal Society (2006)

Gnostic Philosophy: From Ancient Persia to Modern Times (2005)

The Golden Builders:
Alchemists, Rosicrucians and the First Free Masons (2004)

The Fear of Vision (poetry; 1996)

Miraval—A Quest (novel; 1989)

The Gnostics (1987)

THE SPIRITUAL MEANING OF THE SIXTIES

The MAGIC, MYTH & MUSIC *of the* DECADE THAT CHANGED *the* WORLD

TOBIAS CHURTON

Inner Traditions
Rochester, Vermont

Inner Traditions
One Park Street
Rochester, Vermont 05767
www.InnerTraditions.com

Library of Congress Cataloging-in-Publication Data

Names: Churton, Tobias, 1960- author.
Title: The spiritual meaning of the sixties : the magic, myth, and music of the decade that changed the world / Tobias Churton.
Description: Rochester, Vermont : Inner Traditions, 2018. | Includes bibliographical references and index.
Identifiers: LCCN 2018004069 (print) | LCCN 2018038318 (ebook) | ISBN 9781620557112 (pbk.) | ISBN 9781620557129 (ebook)
Subjects: LCSH: Religion and civilization. | Nineteen sixties. | Spirituality. | Mythology. | Magic. | Religion and culture.
Classification: LCC BL55 .C485 2018 (print) | LCC BL55 (ebook) | DDC 200.9/046—dc23
LC record available at https://lccn.loc.gov/2018004069

Printed and bound in the United States by McNaughton & Gunn

10 9 8 7 6 5 4 3 2 1

Text design by Virginia Scott Bowman and layout by Debbie Glogover
This book was typeset in Garamond Premier Pro with Birch Std, Gill Sans MT Pro, and Cochin LT Std used as display typefaces

To send correspondence to the author of this book, mail a first-class letter to the author c/o Inner Traditions • Bear & Company, One Park Street, Rochester, VT 05767, and we will forward the communication, or contact the author directly at **tobiaschurton.com**.

*This book is dedicated with love
to the treasured memories of
my brother Victor Churton (1955–2017)
and Jean-Luke Epstein (1952–2017)*

Merovée Sophia Churton

*I also dedicate this book to my daughter,
Merovée Sophia Churton, who may now, I hope, "see"
the Sixties she missed, first time round, and to her
millennial generation and subsequent generations
of boys and girls, that they might know the truth of what
passed before them in a decade that is now and shall
be a signal seed of good things still to come, if
we learn the lessons, and practice them.*

Contents

PART SEVEN

Acknowledgments

This book was first lived, in full, before it was written. In contemporary academic parlance that makes it an "emic" study, written from internal elements of the culture described, that culture being our own, and what has come before it and created it. However, the book is also the fruit of many years of informed reflection, which makes it an "etic" study, that is, a perspective from outside, made by the observer. Happily we do not have to live in an academic universe, and there are grand moments when subject and object fuse into one, and we may glimpse a transcending truth and be accordingly enlightened. In order to create this fusion of perspectives I have drawn heavily on my own memories, reflections, and subsequent studies and experience, a great deal of which has lended itself to this narrative as if born to it. I should here like to acknowledge the names of those persons who have in so many different ways helped to make this narrative possible, and taken me out of myself in the process.

When I decided to undertake the grand search for "the spiritual meaning of the 1960s" I quickly involved myself in long discussions with my dear friend, graphic artist Jean-Luke Epstein. As a designer of album covers, he is perhaps best known for his designs for LPs by the Stranglers (amongst many other top-flight artists), but our discussions focused mainly on the first, now very rare, interview he undertook with members of the Pink Floyd, as they were known in 1967, and his later dealings with designer Storm Thurgerson (1944–2013), who with

Aubrey Powell designed the Floyd's second album cover, *Saucerful of Secrets* (1968), and who together went on to form the famous market leader in album design, Hipgnosis. Discussions moved from analyzing the "image" of the Sixties, to how the power of images has obscured the "real" Sixties, as it was lived and felt at the time. Our last discussions graduated to profound discussions about death, immortality, and the destiny of the soul. The last thing he sent me this year was a song of his own he'd recorded, "The Sound of Your Soul," whose refrain rang "Crying for Home, the Waiting is Over, and the Moment is Now." Shortly after, in May 2017, Jean-Luke died suddenly and prematurely. For me, he will always live in the spirit of this book.

Another active contemporary of London's psychedelic heyday (1966–1969) whose thoughts inspired this book is artist Vanilla Beer, who today dwells and paints in Languedoc, southwestern France. She had firsthand experience of the London art scene in those proverbially "heady" times and is also gifted with a spiritual perspective and clear intellect on the question I undertook to unravel. Thank you, Vanilla, for the time you gave to answering my questions, and thereby contributing authentic fresh perspectives to the book.

I traveled through the decade in question with my mother and father, Patricia and Victor Churton, who gave their three boys everything they possibly could have given us. They kept us opened up, alert, optimistic, informed, and clear thinking throughout. Every year that passes since their deaths makes me see so much more of what they gave freely, and how ever harder it is to go on without their vivid presence in the world. The spirit they projected is alive in the pages of this book, and I am ever grateful for it. I owe them everything.

One thing that helps us carry on through the vale of earthly life when sometimes it seems that all we are doing is losing, is the appearance of new and unexpected friends on the way. Among those new friends I have been fortunate to garner in these latter years stands the figure of author James Wasserman. Jim speaks from experience, from hard effort, from his mistakes, and his personal triumphs. Jim is one of those old souls who truly *appreciates* everything that comes his way, and much of the time can sort out the wheat from the chaff with a wit with an edge. His account of life lived in the full foam of late Sixties drug taking, idealism, and disintegration has made a vital contribution to the comprehensiveness of this investigation into areas gross and subtle. Jim's a survivor, and survivors have the best tales to tell. I was lucky to get his.

An old colleague of Jim's is the publisher of this book, Ehud Sperling. Ehud told me he'd been waiting years for someone to come along and write this book about the Sixties. I was more than happy to oblige, and thereby fulfill a latent dream. Ehud opened my mind to aspects of the story I should surely have missed had he not been there to give his time to explain to me from personal experience his perception of the significance of Hindu god Shiva as animating spirit of the decade's creative-destructive inner dynamic.

In 1985 I was co-writer-researcher of a 100-minute BBC TV drama about the spiritual journey of John Lennon, *John Lennon: A Journey in the Life,* directed by Ken Howard and starring Bernard Hill as Lennon in a production personally assisted by Yoko Ono Lennon. Researching the musical drama with Dalia Johananoff offered privileged access to a large number of people intimately involved with John's extraordinary life in the 1960s. I had the opportunity to meet Roy Orbison, Roger Waters, Screaming Lord Sutch, John Gustafson, G. B. "Zoot" Money, Helen Shapiro, Edwin Starr, Linda Thompson, Carl Wayne, Paul Jones, and Andy Fairweather-Low; they all lent their musical prowess to the production, and they all had stories to tell of the music scene during the period. I also encountered writer, satirist, and actor Peter Cook, actor Victor Spinetti (who performed in three of the Beatles films), John's Auntie Mimi, and many others who played a part in the Beatles story, including Bill Harry, who gave us the phrase "Mersey Beat," and who used to discuss with John spiritual subjects (other than rock 'n' roll) in Liverpool's pubs when a fellow student. This all opened my mind to the inner world of the period, for sure, but perhaps the greatest boon was the extended time I was fortunate to spend talking in depth with former Beatles press officer Derek Taylor (1932–1997). Through Derek's wise, witty, and openhearted vision I felt the ambience of the "inner circle" in a way that could only be communicated "mind to mind," really quite different from the image or collection of images available to the less involved public. Spirituality was a dominant theme of our conversations. This was a man who had spent time with John when "tripping" on LSD and who encouraged John at moments when the harassed Beatle felt depressed and his work of little value.

I also enjoyed the chance of meeting and talking at length to art critic Anthony Fawcett, author of a unique study of John the artist, *John Lennon: One Day at a Time* (1976), and who was John and Yoko's personal assistant in matters of art from 1968 to 1970. This offered me a priceless insider's view of events that were reflected very differently in the world's press. The inner life is what counts.

I also wish to extend my gratitude to William Breeze, who furnished me with a fascinating and amusing firsthand account of Grady McMurtry and the recovery of the O.T.O., as well as many other important details concerning New York's *real* movers and shakers in the Sixties; to Frank van Lamoen, curator at the Stedelijk Museum of Modern Art, Amsterdam, who offered invaluable assistance regarding the life of painter Yves Klein, and other significant artists of the period; to Jon Graham, who commissioned and encouraged this work, and to Mindy Branstetter, who has been my ever charming and helpful editor at Inner Traditions on this project. To you all, my heartiest thanks!

TOBIAS CHURTON
DECEMBER 2017

PART ONE

ONE

The Sixties—*PHEW!* —and Me

Only I see the century as a child . . .
Stormy its birth; its youth, how fierce and wild!
Its end, how glorified!

FROM *CARMEN SAECULARE*,
ALEISTER CROWLEY, 1900

The prophets of the Sixties had died long before they began. Perhaps that explains why few leading personalities of the decade could really interpret what it was they were involved with. William Breeze, editor of the works of one of those prophets,* once asked key Sixties artist, folklorist, and experimental filmmaker Harry Everett Smith (1923–1991) how he had survived the Fifties, a decade Breeze considered appallingly colorless and boring. Smith replied that it wasn't so bad—it was at least possible to know everyone in the USA worth knowing. *How about the Sixties?* asked Breeze. "They were great," said Smith, "if only we'd known what we were doing."[1] If Harry Smith, an artist involved with occult divination and chief advisor to the arguably epoch-marking

---

*William Breeze (b. 1955), international head of the Ordo Templi Orientis, has edited and annotated many of the works of Aleister Crowley (1875–1947).

"Levitation of the Pentagon" demonstration* did not know, who did? The Sixties were combustible, a riot of reaction on all sides. Many were "busking it" or "winging it," flying by the seats of their pants, carried along with the waves, blowing in the wind, wisping down the vales of time along with the elusive answers. Many of the decade's more loveable characters would, *a posteriori,* beg forgiveness in Christian mode: "Forgive them, for they know not what they do" (Luke 23:34).

The press never seems to have experienced any doubt as to what was being done in the Sixties. Providing oracular wisdom on any subject you can name, the media predicts the future, interprets the present, and accounts for the past. The media provides the stuff of today's and of tomorrow's history—which, however regrettable that may or may not be, brings me to what initiated this investigation.

My daughter was born in 2000. At a certain point in her teens she began collecting vinyl records: largely re-releases of "seminal" 1960s music by the Beatles, the Who, the Band, the Byrds, the Rolling Stones, Pink Floyd, Jimi Hendrix, and the Doors. I daresay some of this interest may have come from what Dad had been playing on and off since she was born, but the fact is that she was pursuing this music of her own volition, and somewhat to my surprise. Had I tried to get her interested out of my own concerns, she would doubtless have looked askance on it, for reasons you'll readily understand. She "dug" it because it spoke directly to her in a way much contemporary popular music did not—and the contemporary music she *did*—and does—buy into undoubtedly drew inspiration from the best of Sixties pop/rock. Among my daughter's friends who share her enthusiasm subsists a common belief that "the Sixties" was something they are very annoyed to have missed, even something they might have preferred to have been born into. Still, something of "it" may yet be accessed through music, not out of nostalgia or, obviously, wistful reminiscence, but of immediate delight. The music seems to these young people very "now," fresh,

---

*The "Levitation of the Pentagon" occurred on October 21, 1967, during which event, hippies famously poked flowers down the barrels of young soldiers' M16s on the Pentagon's steps in an effort to "exorcize" its evil spirits (see pages 530–36).

Fig. 1.1. The Rolling Stones circa 1965.

of the moment, even vital and superior. Initial attractions coalesce rapidly, but I cannot help feeling that among the music's many attractions the principal vital component infused into the atmosphere generated by the decade's dominant musicians was that of a tantalizing, heartfelt youthful freedom "to be," the easing of shackles, as well as an unexpected new realism, personal commitment, vivid interiority, sense of foreboding and impatience with loneliness; lightened by a laughter-filled liberty of free imaginative space, with promise of liberating love, color, excitement, magic, surprise—and, yes, something more, something deeper, something (he coughs) *spiritual*.

Precisely what we mean by that much abused word we shall get to in due course, but for now let's just make it clear that the "thing" (which of course it is not) called the 1960s means to my daughter and many others of her age and older, a complete package: an almost lost land of limitless vistas, and yes, also and strangely, *the Sixties* as a singular noun invokes a destination, a place it would be desirable to reach *forward* to. Wherever that perceived spirit is not, people of this sensitivity regard as a turnoff; simple as that. If you want my daughter's vote, you had better have some of that Sixties spirit in you, chum, or forget it: you're a bore, and probably a tool of malevolent forces to boot. Of course, my daughter has yet to face that familiar moral blackmail we call "earning a living"; but then, bathing in the reflected light of characteristically 1960s social realizations, she does not have to "earn" her life. We now readily understand life as a gift, not a loan at interest, despite the incessant demands of capital, and as Jesus taught, unless we share the receptivity of little children, we cannot hope to enter the kingdom of God (Mark 10:13–15); indeed, the richer we become, the more doubtful become our chances. We're getting "spiritual" again, aren't we? Dear, oh dear. I fear I must pass on the news that rumors of the death of God were and are greatly exaggerated, though the assumption of it suits many.

When discussing the 1960s with my daughter, I have been quick—perhaps too quick—to suggest to her that the image of the Sixties garnered from TV documentaries, from the internet, from books in the school library, and of course from listening to records and downloads, often constitutes a culture legend: a potent one doubtless, but historically misleading in many respects. How can one talk meaningfully of a decade, in any case? A decade is a period of time, arguably quite arbitrary in scope, whose dominant personalities were often born long before the decade began, and whose formative experiences predated and often dominated what came after. A decade is a convenient slice from a continuum of unimaginably complicated phenomena involving over three billion human beings (in 1960), and getting on for four billion human beings by 1970. All of these lives, coming and going in the natural universe, were unique, with perceptions relative to each individual, even where suppressed or largely unexplored. Yes, this is all of the nature of cold fact, but "decades" we like nonetheless, and don't seem to be able to do without them. Is it merely convenience? Does it have something to do with our collective hunger for *change?* Faith is void without a future. While we usually divide things up for purposes of measurement, what really does a decade *measure?* Decades are primarily social, not scientific, constructs, often related to the memories of common generations, and related to epochs of fashion, or eras of wars. Few live to a centenary, so decades mark out stages in life, the biblical allotment of life being three score years *and ten* (Psalm 90:10). It is natural then to leap to the conclusion that one man's decade, or a generation's collective decade also has greater historical significance, where temporal history is usually divided, for recording purposes, into centuries.

There is another dimension. Every change in date—especially of years—has some significance, relating our lives to the movement of our planet in relation to other bodies, in particular the sun. We have anciently thought of the heavenly bodies moving—or revolving—in revolutions, and when we add astrological signifiers, we are quickly inclined to think our significant dates carry new dispensations of change (time for a revolution). We hunger for change because we are aware that much needs changing, and because stasis is both boring and an invitation to corruption and decay. When change is experienced as accelerating (as, say, in the late 1950s and subsequent years), we become excited, whether to anxiety or high and hopeful expectation depends on prevailing expectations, fears, and hopes.

One key feature of the decade of the 1960s was how early on people became *decade conscious*. President Kennedy—who himself was a symbol of change—established the time zone. In May 1961, he famously declared that America would put a man on the moon by the end of the decade, as though setting a race marker: first one to pass the post wins the Cold War, sorry . . . Space Race. Of course, losing the Cold War could also have apocalyptic repercussions. The end of the world was posited universally as a distinct possibility; this alarming sensibility— coupled with Kennedy's own baleful assassination—further compressed the popular sense of a significant decade with apocalyptic undertones. The decade was truly heading somewhere; quite literally, it was going to take the species higher and further than had ever been known of or experienced before! And this decade leap in consciousness was going to be *seen*, in real time, by practically everybody at once. The Sixties were being *watched*. A decade could see itself in the mirror of its technology, seeing and believing its own signs. "Do you know we are ruled by TV?" asked a troubled Jim Morrison of L.A. group the Doors at the decade's end. He could just as easily have asked: "Do you know we are ruled by time?" Time and TV had become almost synonymous. TV times were the times to be in, and switched on. TV made the alien familiar. There was even talk of celestial observers of our doings (they could watch us on TV), much as there had been in the first century of the Christian era. Biblical imagery was never far from serious discourse in the 1960s. Martin Luther King could, like Moses before his death, see the Promised Land—and it wasn't Israel.

However, we are primarily discussing the rolled-up lump of decade that is frequently rolled out again, its tired dough sometimes redefined on the breadboard, to succeeding generations. "The Sixties" in general contemporary media speak and media image means sexual liberties, miniskirts, psychedelia, flower power, street demonstrations against the Vietnam War, and of course the "dirty war" itself. The Sixties means the Space Race, Richard and Liz, James Bond, and generally speaking,

Fig. 1.2. Richard Burton and Elizabeth Taylor in Cleopatra, *1963.*

a sizzling, starkly colorful cocktail that is at once a whole lotta fun and a harbinger of perceived decline. Sometimes the decade is itself blamed for subsequent disappointments, social, political, and economic. Nevertheless, as far as my daughter and her friends are concerned, the predominant idea, in visual terms, constellates into bright psychedelic clothing, peace symbols, "Peace and Love, man," long hair, smiles beatific and beautiful people, floral abundance, hard-driving, spacey, and elegant pop music, yeah-baby liberation ethic, freedom from constraint, warmth, rainbows, sunshine, joss sticks, and a whole lotta love, partying, drugs, and rock 'n' roll. That's pretty well the Sixties.

So, to ask anyone acquainted with that collage, "What is the spiritual meaning of the Sixties?" may invite the answer "What spiritual meaning?" or more likely, a verbal replay of the now familiar collage of collective media memory adumbrated above. The spiritual meaning of the Sixties might then be simply the meaning of spiritual *freedom,* or alternatively, with a zeitgeist-aware link of the personal and the political: liberation. This liberation may have many ambiguous or contradictory features, only one of which might be called spiritual. For those who have embraced characteristically "Sixties liberation," the liberation connotes freedom from imperialism, freedom from old men (patriarchy), freedom from racial or religious prejudice, freedom from sexual ignorance and repression, freedom from arrest, and freedom to live a life combining personal and (sometimes) political independence, ecstasy, and freedom from the past: away with the old, and on with the New! In its anarchic, as distinct from its socialistic aspects, the decade seemed to present something like Raymond Foye's concept of a "Temporary Autonomous Zone," or as Mike Myers's telling Sixties (or *Sexties*) spoof, *Austin Powers: International Man of Mystery* (1997), had it: "a consequence-free environment," where even gonorrhea seemed to have been unheard of—though I, and doubtless others, well recall blunt notices affixed to walls of public lavatories regarding VD's prevalence and risks during the period. Our current acronym, STD, for sexually transmitted diseases does not bear the disinfectant-reeking stigma of the Sixties' VD, which might as well have stood for "Victory of Damnation" rather than "venereal disease."

Fig. 1.3. Sean Connery as 007 spy, James Bond

The print media delighted, a little over halfway through the decade, in giving Great Britain's capital the epithet "Swinging London" and that highly exportable adjective with all its gleeful moral ambiguities and checkered geometry of opaque titillation would in due course be extended to cover the entire decade, whether deserved or not; such was the power of the image. And that is very important. During the 1960s, as TV ownership and magazine distribution rocketed, the *power of the image* increased significantly, and powerful images are prone to be worshipped.* And the Sixties is itself an image, quickly evoked from any number of individual shots or takes: the earth from outer space, for example, the smiling hippie girl with flower, the costumed people in San Francisco or Carnaby Street, London, the kaleidoscopic rock poster, the mini car or miniskirt, and so on. The prevalence of near-universal Western image-power, electronically switched-on, made Marshall McLuhan's ambiguous creation "the "Global Village" (1968) an inevitability.

While I have been keen to get over to my daughter the fact that during the decade itself, flower power, psychedelics, personal liberation, and rock music had very little "take-up" until the decade's latter years

---

*Note the contemporary abuse of the words *icon* or *iconic,* arguably twisted from Andy Warhol's part-ironic veneration of the ephemeral commercial image: sole, opaque image of imaginative transcendence for those outside the sacred Orthodox faith experience of the genuine *ikon.*

and were throughout the decade comparatively remote from the direct experience of most of the world's population (even in much of Great Britain), the media's own take on the decade can appear strangely fragmentary. That is to say, if a documentary or news editor wishes quickly to evoke the Sixties we shall see those oft-repeated, even abused snippets of familiar newsreel associated, typically, with 1967. How many times have you seen the girl's head swaying mesmerically from side to side as she sits in a field, gazing with vague intent, and oblivious to the world around her, on some relatively trivial outer object her inner perception has rendered infinitely fascinating, with the word *LOVE* painted in red paisley-style on her face? And I'm sure I've seen those two public schoolboys in velvet suits, cavalier haircuts, and pink round spectacles making their way down Carnaby Street somewhere before. Could it have been on the last repeat show of Sixties rock bands? One can usually expect a girl in a state of partial undress and a topless, bearded man smoking something or other dancing clumsily to music that we cannot hear (for these snippets are usually relayed without original soundtrack). However, if the documentary program is dealing with some other aspects of Sixties history, such as the successful Soviet space program, or the CIA-backed Bay of Pigs disaster in Cuba, or the Cuban Missile Crisis itself, or indeed, TV shows concerned with political independence movements or civil conflicts in the African continent, or the Arab-Israeli Six-Day War, or Chairman Mao's "Cultural Revolution" (a considerably bigger, if hideously manufactured, top-down "youth movement" than anything Britain or America could muster), or the war in Biafra, or the beginning of the "Troubles" in Northern Ireland, we shall find the Swinging Sixties to be nowhere in sight, as if they have fled from the horror of hard news, bombs, napalm, torture, real street anarchy, and grotesque poverty, taking refuge in the nearest cool pad to roll up, light up, sit back, and think good thoughts. Outside the Cool Scene, however, we have another Sixties altogether, and the effect of this fragmentation of images is very much to render, say, the psychedelic politics and lifestyle challenge of the intertwined youth and art movements somewhat secondary, almost like vulnerable annoyances, of ephemeral significance, or even as entertaining scenarios pure and simple. Just how

Fig. 1.4. The Beatles in America, 1964.

threatening these images once were to the establishment status quo has been forgotten, and the sense of it cannot be recaptured.

It is no surprise to anyone to hear that the Sixties has been marketed. It has become a marketable commodity, and indeed, was so in its own time. As we shall see, it took little time between the signal appearance of the distinctive psychedelic "love" vibe in 1965 ("Say the word and you'll be free" in the Beatles' "The Word"), and the 25-cent Loveburger on an oversubscribed sidewalk in Haight-Ashbury, San Francisco, in 1967. No sooner had the Beatles set foot on American tarmac than you could buy a Beatle wig at Woolworths. Fashion is money, and for all money knows, only money knows, for only money *has,* and money is *all* money has, unless we sell our minds as well as our labor.

There is a telling scene in John Schlesinger's rather hyped-up, but very touching buddy movie *Midnight Cowboy* (1969), which at least has the virtue of having been made in the "heat of the night" so to speak. The scene is a bleak, wintry, indifferent New York in the late Sixties.

Joe Buck, a poor white "boy" has come to make his way as a hustler in the Big Apple. Expecting to glide on its surface, he soon slips under the peel and descends unnoticed into its rotten core, receiving naught for his comfort save abuse, rip-offs, and unpaid gay blow jobs. Joe is soon so bereft as to favor the company of a genial rogue, the equally poverty-stricken, crippled street survivor, Enrico Rizzo, unkindly dubbed "Ratso" by his new friend. They have hit rock bottom, with no rock to cheer them. The Sixties, to date, has passed them by. And yet, the director implies, are they too not signs of the times? We see them in their own fragile world, hugging a coffee in a down-market deli, playing tough with one another when a pair of jet-setter "beautiful people" enter to distribute invitations to a hip party somewhere in Manhattan (presumably Greenwich Village), taking the curious pair's photographs in lieu of names for entry to the privileged shindig. Rizzo is convinced this is an opportunity to market Joe's talent for satisfying society women who can afford time and money for zipless carnality, and the two friends duly roll up—that is, turn up—for the party. Mounting a set of unremarkable steps, they enter the archetypal (that is, media-created) Sixties psychedelic happening, with bass-pulsing, synthesizer-driven, LSD-oriented rock music from The Groop, splurges of pulsating blobs projected onto the walls like so many dissolving paisley cravats, and marijuana liberally smoked among the not quite blissed-out partygoers, who all look terribly bored, yet suppressed-glad to be seen, glad to be on the inside. Oblivious to any delight to be extracted from this psychedelic perfumed garden, Rizzo loses patience with all the free love stuff (no profit for a pimp there!) and pulls Joe away from the somewhat hollow, jaded, blatantly superficial (and satirically presented) enticements. In an instant, they are back on the freezing cold, hard, love-free streets again, clutching their chilled bodies and inadequate dress, while the Sixties is left going on behind them, up those stairs, behind the closed door, forbidden to the uninvited, beyond the reach of those who don't make the image. Clearly, the director had the Warhol "Factory" scene in mind. However, the point is that as far as the *core* psychedelic Sixties went, for the most part, it was invitation-only, and if you were desperate to get in, you had to dress the part and play the part, conscious that bad vibes and uncool attitudes—hair or no hair—could be sniffed out (no pun intended; coke was not a predominant '60s drug). "Uniform" might be very broadly understood, but there was a clear distinction between the in-crowd and those on the cold outside, or sitting comfortably at home watching TV, watching the curious antics of pop stars, watching the Vietnam War, watching the detectives. There was of course a great deal of attention given to hair, one way and another. But then, hair has always been a sign, from Samson onward. If we care less about it now, it is thanks to brave pioneers during the decade in question, who until the early '70s risked being beaten up, or worse, for nonconformity in this regard.

In order to surmount difficulties in formulating a true picture (images again!) of the 1960s, I tried to give an inkling of my own personal experience to my daughter. What is interesting is that she found it very hard to believe I was actually *there*. It was as if I had said I'd participated in the chariot race in *Ben-Hur!* Well, I *was* there, and I can remember a great deal about it (the Sixties, that is). It is a self-serving falsehood to say you had to indulge in psychedelic stimulants to have been "there" in the '60s. Indeed, I shall always be ready to assert that my experience of that era was, and is, as valid and meaningful as anybody else's—*and I mean anybody's*—and I grant the same liberty of value to anyone else. To be a child in the Sixties was, if you were so blessed, to be close to the kingdom of God, though I grant that is hardly everyone's experience, even as "little children" whom the one who suffered children to come unto him encouraged genuine aspirants among the adults of his entourage to resemble.

It's been interesting over the years for me to compare different people's experiences, some of them from behind that privileged closed door. I've built up quite a picture in the process, but it can never be even remotely complete. Everybody's story is different. And there are thousands of millions of stories. Mine is one of them, and I've already written my story down, for as someone once wrote: *if it's not written, it didn't happen.*

My Sixties was filled with wonderful, as well as quite mundane, but still memorable stories, and this is not the place to relate them all, except insofar as my experience illuminates the central investigation of this book, which is: There are many people today who believe that there was something peculiarly special about the Sixties, not just in sociological and political terms, nor only in the technical fields of lunar exploration, cinema, and music—much of which must now be so familiar to people—but in the spiritual dimension. Something, it is believed by believers, was *going on.* I don't just mean people at the time self-consciously trying to bring new things and attitudes into the public sphere, the movers and shakers, but *what was actually motivating them;* what were they responding to, deep, deep down, or high, high up? Was it simply material events, or response to ideas heard or read about in books and elsewhere? The hint and more of *spiritual activity* is perceived to be there, however difficult it may be for many of us to grasp that notion rationally.

My daughter finds the era fascinating, involving, for something of a deep and meaningful nature seems to her to have survived the passage of time (half a century stuffed with more and more and more images) and has reached out to her and her friends. Is that simply a result of marketing hype: an illusory Sixties repackaged as CD, DVD, iPhone download, Google, website, and all the rest of the *electroplasmatic* microcosms of our day? Is there any spiritual meaning to the authentic 1960s? Can we even locate an authentic 1960s? If so . . . *What is the spiritual meaning of the 1960s?* When I mentioned this to my daughter as the question I wished to investigate in my next book, she immediately said: "That book I will read." I cannot tell you how surprising that statement was to me. "But will it interest your friends?" I asked, meekly. "Yes, it will. We all want to know."

So for you, my darling, and for all your friends, known and unknown, and for all those in the future who might otherwise be "sold a turkey" on this question, or be subtly or unsubtly deflected from asking it, I am writing this. And I shall start, as is only right, with a little of my own fair experience as best as I can I recall it.

I was conceived in the mild, wet, and stormy winter of late 1959 at a village called Minworth in the English county of Warwickshire (Shakespeare's

Fig. 1.5.
NASA test pilot
Joseph Walker beside
an X-15 airplane,
circa 1961.

county), and born the youngest of three brothers on August 4, 1960, a Leo with Sagittarius rising, in Loveday Street Hospital, Birmingham, just as Joseph A. Walker, test piloting a NASA F-16, became the fastest-ever man in history, at 2,196 astounding miles per hour. "Oh my God!" screamed Walker, stunned by the staggering thrust of rocket power that wrenched him to his seat. I don't know whether my dear mother uttered something similar as I was detached from the mother ship into the shocked air of the sterile world, for I would not have heard a word of it. Little Tobias Alex Churton was born deaf. Stone deaf. The birth defect was later supposed linked to some facial asymmetry, the result perhaps of a heavy-handed caesarian, or possibly the drug thalidomide, offered to expectant mothers as the new decade's latest answer to the time-honored misery of morning sickness.

Despite the concerns of the outside world, little Toby was blissfully cozy in his inner world. He heard nothing of the planetary cacophony until around the end of the harsh winter of early 1963, when the pleasing sharps of the Beatles' first British number one single, "Please Please Me," pierced the fearful hollow of his ear like premature buds of spring.

Such audio as I then enjoyed did not arrive at the stable of my sensorium straightaway, however. I recall a bulbous, tuber-like hearing aid and the echo-laden, tinny sounds of voices resounding within its chamber. Then, one day in '63 I was sitting in the little front garden of our semi-detached house in Park Lane, Minworth, playing with a local gypsy girl. Suddenly, a great whooshing sound washed through my ears and brain like a great wind-rushed wave whose vacuum-smashing storm seemed to clear a curious blockage. *I could hear!* Really *hear.* But I could not speak. I was taught to speak, without an accent, by a National Health speech therapist, who did her job remarkably well; some might say, too damn well! My ear was thus fine-trained, my voice likewise. Little wonder I enjoyed singing to myself so much: other people's tunes, my own tunes, any tunes. Melody is honey for sore ears; harmony is color.

Our plain, redbrick house was a "tied house," that is, it came with my father Victor Churton's job as an engineer at the nearby Minworth sewage works—known familiarly as the Muck Beds—constructed in 1939 by the Tame & Rea District Drainage Board. The Tame and Rea were two little rivers that flowed north through Birmingham. Minworth was then a rather unattractive, mostly brick, insular village, surrounded by fairly flat countryside in the Royal Borough of Sutton Coldfield, a few miles northeast of industrialized Birmingham that in the northwest merged imperceptibly into "the Black Country" or old industrial heartland of the Midlands. Those familiar with the argot of alchemy will understand me when I say that I began life at the *nigredo,* the first, black stage of chemical transmutation, a basic substance sometimes finding its practical analog in the image of raw excreta. Like Moses, I was brought home in a basket. So my elder brother Victor informed me years later, adding that he hated me on sight. He'd had one brother born to threaten his supremacy; two, presumably, was too many—or was it my cross-eyed appearance that caused such disquiet? For in addition to being born deaf, I had an extreme squint that took me into the hospital for isolating eye operations five times between the ages of three and nine. It was probably a good thing these disabilities earned special care because otherwise I might have ended up in a pit, like the young Hebrew patriarch gifted with the many-colored coat. Indeed, one of my first memories was being abandoned by my brothers in a sinking, squelchy bog in a field beyond the house, surrounded by overbearing cows. Very scary. Notwithstanding all that, I was a joyous baby (so my mother told me, and the pictures bear it out), and I grew up loving everybody, even to my elder brother's embarrassment, when I would embrace and kiss his visiting friends without inhibition! I had seen a world positively *made of love.*

My parents, Pat and Vic, had met on a Birmingham Corporation bus and married six weeks later, my mum-to-be breaking off an engagement to a "nice, respectable chap" to do so. Dad's immediate background was respectable working class (if you attend to sociological analyses)—his father Bertie was a railroad engineer (or "train driver" as we call that once-hallowed role in England, when trains, like volcanoes, still ran on steam)—while my mother Patricia's upbringing was comfortably middle class, interrupted by war when her father, chiropodist Donald Stanley, volunteered for the RAF in 1939 and spent the war in Burma and India, apart from his wife and only daughter. Granddad

Fig. 1.6. The author as baby in pram; late 1960–early 1961.
Victor to the left, James to the right.

Fig. 1.7. The child Toby in 1965 after four eye operations to correct a severe squint.

was a medic and participated in the desperate but decisive battles of Imphal and Kohima in March–July 1944, at that time the biggest defeat inflicted on the Japanese army, pushing the arrogant Japs back from India into Burma.

A fourteen-year-old tool-making apprentice in 1941, my father had served in the fire service during the Luftwaffe's Blitz on Birmingham and, after the war, served as a corporal in the British Army Royal Electrical and Mechanical Engineers (REME) during the "Malayan Emergency" against Communist insurgency in Malaya 1948–1953. The point to bear in mind is the enormous, possibly incalculable, psychological, physical, and spiritual influence of World War II and ensuing military and political engagement with Communist internationalism on my parents, their generation, and on our upbringing in the 1960s. The war entered the earliest conversations I can remember. Indeed, when Mum or Dad would say things like, "When we [meaning the Allies] were fighting in the war"—whether discussing the First or Second World Wars—I truly believed that *I* had been with mummy and daddy as a boy *in the trenches* and had, seeing myself there behind a gauze of vague memory in an almost forgotten portion of life, carried arms and fought Germans: such is the power of the word *we* to a child, and of language in general. The image in my mind was only reinforced when the BBC broadcast its TV documentary series *The Great War* at the end of 1964. In my

Fig. 1.8. Mum with her dad the day war was declared in September 1939.

imagination, I had been in the war and in everything I did, I was in my imagination in intuitive touch with what Jung called the unconscious with its subterranean passages to the collective experience of our kind.

For myself personally, the 1960s *was* a spiritual experience, in both the general and the particular senses, so I think I may have something to contribute in investigating and assessing its spiritual meaning, having been, in every real sense, *there.* And its spiritual meaning for me personally I can say in brief right now: It was for me the unfolding discovery of the sovereignty of the individual in society, and the freedom of the individual to accommodate, and be accommodated in, cosmic consciousness, or as I suppose that expression's biblical equivalent puts it: the kingdom of heaven, which is nigh and within us, where God is all in all. And why is it easier for a camel to go through the eye of a needle than for a rich man to enter said kingdom of heaven? Because where your treasure is, there your heart is also. *Ergo,* those whose heart belongs to money, and whose primary attraction is to the material world, will never understand the spiritual meaning of the 1960s, or the spiritual meaning of anything else. It is the *content,* not the body, or outer manifestation, that has spiritual, or ultimate significance.

And that's enough about me, for the time being.

The corollary of the above confession of general relevance is that it should be borne in mind that it was perfectly possible to have a very spiritual 1960s living experience, without the least recourse to pop and rock music, long hair and costume, psychedelic stimulants, or latent, imported, or nascent Hinduism or Sufism. But if you did experience the 1960s spiritually, you will necessarily have been brought to recognize at some point or other that the youth movements of the time were also undergoing a spiritual crisis endemic in Western culture particularly, and that is reflected in many of their attitudes, rebellions, and electric creativity, despite many self-proclaimed Christians' vocal opposition to much of what appeared to them dangerously novel and sinful. The fact is that moderate or radical youth subcultures were by their lights "picking up" on "something" too, and as we shall see, it may be that the best use was not, or was not always made, of whatever that something might have been. Which leads us logically to our next issue.

TWO

Pro and Anti:
The Myth of Progress

The 1960s as a period of cultural innovation has had more than its fair share of critics over the years. One of the earliest and most astute cases for the prosecution was advocated by Cambridge graduate, journalist, and author Christopher Booker (b. 1937). Founder-contributor to Britain's leading satirical magazine *Private Eye* from the early Sixties, Booker wrote comedy for the BBC's prominent and controversial early Sixties satirical sketch series *That Was the Week That Was* and is to this day a powerful defender of the British nation-state, and penetrating critic of the European Union's undemocratic, obscured agenda. Booker has denied any valid spiritual content particular to the 1960s at all, and if there is no spiritual content, there can be no spiritual meaning.

Taking his cue from observing the gaudy commercialism of the late Fifties and early Sixties, and the disturbing (to some) phenomenon of Dionysian (though wine-free) Beatlemania that first appeared in 1963, Booker saw the Sixties succumbing to a "vitality fantasy," a hollowness of mass hysteria whose effects indicated to the pundit's eye an abandonment of Christian values of respect, anti-idolatry, and self-control, and whose source could therefore only ultimately have been evil, however unconscious of that force for spiritual deformation the idols of popular adoration might, in their ignorance, be generously presumed to be. Booker's initial reaction suffered some modification over the decade as some of the idols themselves began to express spiritual interests and began to criticize openly the materialist society that in its enthusiasm had propelled its chosen ones to fame and fortune. The issue then became what kind of salvation might be forthcoming from the assorted optimisms of Sixties counterculture.

In his remarkable book *The Neophiliacs,* first published in 1969, Booker dismissed the decade for perilous superficiality. Rather than being a bright new dawn, heralding unlimited progress, it was, he asserted, a fantasy world, a derangement of imagination and ungrounded utopianism: a "Tupperware" revolution of vacuous, distracting change for novelty's sake—the technological revolution in plastics that accompanied the era typifying its slick, substance-thin, value-free, mass-produced, opaque, and vain meaninglessness: an era in love with the New for no sound reason, all papering over profound shadows of encroaching breakdown of civilization and sundry persistent miseries. Influenced by psychologist Carl Jung, the root of the problem for Booker was that the era galvanized the imagination of the unconscious religious seeker without offering an adequate religion to satisfy the demand. If God had become dead to the mind and heart of the modern idealist, it was an urgent necessity to resurrect him. For Booker, the key event had already occurred nearly two thousand years earlier, and the proper pattern for the Good Life had already been laid down for human beings, a pattern that could never be gainsaid by fashionable but spiritually adrift wishful thinking. The true Good came from the true God.

The United States had its own critics of the period, though after the political demise of Richard Nixon in 1974, the American Right largely left it to Southern evangelicals to declare the case that the Sixties had let something profoundly pernicious, even Satanic, out of the bag. After the Reagan administration established itself as the new norm, the 1980s brought a veritable orgy and bonfire of historical revisionism, peppered with some forty-something embarrassment at the follies of youth. American neoconservative opinion has echoed British conservative views of the Sixties, namely that the decade was distinguished by a general decline in moral values, respect for tradition, nation, religion, educational basics, common sense, and common decency—its vaunted sexual revolution a mere legitimization of a suburban brothel paid for in social costs, if not hard cash. You didn't have to be a believer in the Protestant work ethic to share these views, you could be a discrete atheist or relaxed agnostic: contrary to the explicit teaching attributed to Saint Paul, the love of money was not necessarily the root of "all kinds of evil" (1 Timothy 6:10). Hospitals, schools, art, churches, and sewers all cost money, and the ones who could make the most tended to be those who really loved money, for whatever reasons. The activists of the Sixties (you'd have thought there *were* no voluble conservatives in the Sixties!) were deluded utopians, deliberately out of touch with reality. Few went as far as McCarthy's attacks on sympathizers with Communism during the 1950s, but hostility was real. Nevertheless, there was ambiguity and confusion about the nature of the happiness Americans ought to pursue. Where the drugged "head" might taunt straight society with the view that "Reality is for people who can't cope with dope," bitter experience suggested to the conservative that dope was for people who couldn't cope with reality. Cocaine abuse nonetheless grew apace in the Eighties, a stimulant (or was it anesthetic?) for the aspiring plutocrat. By the late 1980s, hippies and their kin were now the ones definitely "uncool," and the view had become widespread that the counterculture had lost because it was led by, and followed by, *losers.* To the victors the spoils!

Au contraire, retorted Sixties survivors who, unlike the Yuppies, were active at the period being dissed, having operated at the epicenters of change, rather than luxuriating as folk reacting to change, or wallowing in transient new wealth. These older proponents of social, political, spiritual, and psychological "revolution" repeated for those prepared to listen that the apparent, or alleged, "permissive hell" was rather a dawn for an as-yet-unfulfilled libertarian heaven, all but strangled at birth by repressive, reactionary, patriarchal forces (caricatured in the late Sixties as "Blue Meanies" or "the Man"), deeply unsettled by unfamiliar priorities. Proponents of the era's benefits proclaim that the territory of personal liberation had since been colonized by popular capitalism, which in its turn left new generations unsatisfied, even bewildered and vulnerable to manipulation by unscrupulous politics and the insidiousness of commercialization. *They* need to know what they have missed. For many young people, something called "the Sixties" has become groovy again.

In fact, the message of the radical aspects of the decade's rehabilitation appeared quite early, in the year Tom Wolfe's *Bonfire of the Vanities* was published in fact, and appropriately perhaps, in Great Britain, when Granada TV's massive celebration of the Beatles' *Sgt. Pepper's Lonely Hearts Club Band* (1967) received national broadcast in June 1987. Titled *It Was Twenty Years Ago Today,* the elaborate two-hour documentary contained the freshest, most informed treatment—and evenhanded defense—of American countercultural activity ever aired before a mass audience. In it, actor Peter Coyote, formerly of the 1960s San Francisco dissenting group the Diggers, and associates in happening-management such as Peter Berg, David Simpson, Chet Helms, and Ron Thelin (of Haight-Ashbury's Psychedelic Shop; d. 1996) articulated the view, with impressive eloquence, that the 1960s (and the 1967 impulse in particular) deserved to be seen in positively realist-apocalyptic terms as an astounding ingress of spiritual light, or higher inspiration, into a collective materialist darkness of unconsciousness and reactive depression. Even though the door had, in intervening years, been pushed shut by the fearful and the angry, the hint of a transformative light yet remained, and the "door of perception" might yet be nudged open for new generations.

For Paul Kantner (d. 2016) of San Francisco band the Jefferson Airplane, all analysis suffered from the fact that those at the era's centers experienced something that transcended memory (and therefore history); minds were blown, frequently by powerful stimulants, so as he liked to quote: "If you remember the Sixties, you weren't there." Well, he obviously did remember that he was there, though there were clearly gaps in memory and unsureness about details. What of course he meant, more or less, was that the little hole in the great college wall that led into the reserved garden of delights was the psychedelic (soul-expanding) experience of lysergic acid diethylamide 25, whose effects could be, like the vision of Isis in Apuleius's *The Golden Ass,* so extraordinary (on a good day) that language was simply inadequate to express them, nor could the human memory store or recall the most special qualities and wonders of the experience itself, as the sensation of the experience had no long-term registration that could be evoked and expressed by will alone. The ordinary mind had no ready psychological categories to accommodate the experience. Thus, the ordinary mind could be said to have been "blown" and the sense of self unseated, sometimes threatened, depending on the nature of the mind subjected to the drug.

Language, whose world represents our world, being inadequate, what could be said of the LSD experience? How would you describe a hot bath to a being that had never experienced *heat?* It was like the distinction between inspiration and memory, or between the art of genius, and the craft of experience. You had to have the experience, to be *there* to know, and if you were there, and had the experience, you would never be able to remember the experience properly, or be able to relate it effectively to anyone without the experience. Of course, any student of mystical psychology quickly realized that these experiences, at their "best" or highest phases, were either profoundly akin to religious experiences, or *were* de facto religious experiences, even in the tradition of mystical ecstasy or spiritual transcendence. But what might this all mean to the world? The general answer of the time to such a question would be something like: "whatever it means to you." For all the togetherness, subjective relativism still left the perceiver somewhat isolated. If the common dream could be reality, as artist Yoko Ono maintained, could the individual's delusion also be a collective experience? The shadow of the bad trip reared its terrifying head. To counter the pull of oblivion, the new believers needed Good Thoughts to steady the ship on unchartered seas. Under the influence of psychedelic stimulants, writers and artists saw ancient messages in a new light, thus in 1967, the Beatles' conclusion that "All You Need Is Love," while ancient in inspiration, sounded new to many, while to others, it seemed threatening because of the sexual and economic vulnerability of the adult world. "Love one another" Jesus enjoined his disciples. The disciples might have forgotten exactly what it was like to be in the perhaps highly exalted state of mind in which they first heard these words from the liberated soul of their master, but they could at least remember the words. A liberating realization, glowing with interconnectivity and wonder, can in dull sobriety read like a mere ethical injunction, a *must do:* a mere law. In the beginning was the Word, the Voice, the creative will and spark of intelligence, and the Word was with God, not printed in a book. Hence the mystic, or gnostic, sees direct experience as being superior to law, the spirit superior to the letter.

As regards the 1960s today, there are a vast number who neither can remember the decade, nor were there in any other sense, but such is the magnetism of the era's potent legend, many people wish profoundly they had been there, and if they cannot time travel, they would like to see "it" happen all over again, the sooner the better. Many young persons feel they have both missed—and been denied—a legacy perceived as their spiritual and social due. Older persons look back with often self-deceiving nostalgia. For the greater number of celebrants of the legend, it must be said that the era they imagine existed as a composite narrative of colorful freedom, peace, and love is largely a media creation, something of a myth based on sensationalism and the electronic media's ability to magnify, obliterate, and exaggerate detail, obscuring inconvenient facts. Nevertheless, history records real fire at the root of the mythic smoke; extraordinary adventures in mass international communication did occur. One thinks of the moment in January 1967 when promoter Chet Helms announced at San Francisco's "Gathering of the Tribes" event that he had just returned from New York and from London to prophesy to the Human Be-In: "It's happening everywhere!"

What was? We want to know.

Well, quite obviously, one thing that was happening and that constituted a happening in itself, was that people, mostly young adults, were gathering together. For maturing "beat poet" Allen Ginsberg (1926–1997) this coming together in peaceful, if temporary, coexistence signified an end to the 1950s image of the isolated individual, the lonely rebel without a cause, the isolate dreamer, garret artist, drifter beat poet, caught in the embrace of a solipsistic existentialism, the angry young man (or woman) that society did not, could not, would not, understand. Frank Sinatra had, from the mid-Fifties, dignified the loneliness of the long-distance lover in a series of era-defining albums for Capitol: the lonely man who had loved and lost with only a cigarette left for company, knocking back one (more) "for my baby." For Ginsberg, the very act of coming together was a sign of self-transcendence: hope and optimism after despair. Love was free. It did not go unobserved that there were strong biblical parallels to this supposed transition from isolation to togetherness. The story of how Jesus's followers scattered in fear after the Crucifixion was potent. We may think of poor tough guy, failed disciple Peter, alone, skulking among enemies, denying closeness to his arrested master lest he be singled out and arrested, sinking into himself, depressed and in denial as the cock crowed thrice. And then comes the story of how the apostles come together again, though still closed in, afraid, in an upper room, where they suddenly get it: a rushing wind of fire-kissed spirit that turns them into instant communicators, so voluble and outspoken indeed, that they are accused of being drunk, and yet, the message catches on, and the numbers of converted rise. In 1960s terminology, the apostles got "high" and began to share all their things in common with a little help from their friends and to preach openly that the new age had begun.

For critics like Booker, such a comparison might appear both unsettling and impious. But the fact that people did come together across the world has entered folk memory, and is dutifully repeated in form at least at pop festivals today, even though the meaning of it all seems to have been largely lost on the way. In the process, a legend has been born, a kind of dream. The dream may yet encode something of a spiritual drama that calls for the attention of minds that seek satisfaction of profound cravings, often of an undefined spiritual nature (thereby both proving and denying Booker's contention concerning adequate religion and the 1960s alleged lack of it). It is, anyhow, clear that the Sixties legend is more pervasive and persistent than its historic detractors might have imagined. If the dream is not strictly historical, cannot the same be said for the stories of the beginnings of any spiritual movement? Where, after all, does spiritual movement begin?

CHANGE AND PROGRESS

One of the acutely irritating features about growing up during the 1960s I well recall was—in England at least—the oft-repeated phrase "It's *Progress*, isn't it?" The background to this ludicrous statement of faith need not detain us long, but its application during the decade is of signal importance, and was something Christopher Booker observed also as a prevalent delusion of the period, a shibboleth characteristic of the decade as a whole. Booker was sensitive to the idea that the decade seemed to have erected its own Babel: a secular faith, something he (and my father incidentally) believed would eventually come crashing down on its head when the fizz in the optimistic pink draft went flat having bubbled its gaseous way to explode on the superfices, leading inevitably toward a sickly sweet syrup, tasteless and ultimately revolting. The progress of a cancer is a progress of sorts, and the process of dying certainly has a future.

All the dominant religions feel the need to define and ultimately encompass the future; they all claim to know more or less what's going to happen in the end. You can't have a religion without a future. The Sixties had more "future" than any decade could properly handle.

Improvements or refinements in technology have filled many people with "hope for the future." The nineteenth century saw its vaunted enlightenment encapsulated in its sophistication of mechanical industry. The art movement of "futurists" in the first decades of the century permitted all existential doubts to cease as one took a front seat in a fast car, or aircraft. Just watch the world go by, as you go by the world! The fresh breath of science would blow away the cobwebs of doubt. And now, in the Sixties, techno-man had penetrated the threshold of space itself! Clearly, the sheer passage of time had brought visible *progress*. Wrap this up neatly with Darwin's famous analysis of natural selection and you had the evidence for unending progress, so long as we believe it. Note the catch. You have to believe in progress. It might not just happen by itself. It is a secular faith; it accommodates the supposed absence of God, indeed, it may require it. But what happens when you have different ideas of progress? Hitler's idea of progress, say, was very vivid to him and his closest followers, but it was a different idea to most other people's. Well,

Hitler had been crushed, hadn't he? So that was Progress made manifest; we got the guns, we got the numbers. Yes, Progress might be painful, but Progress was progress, and, like the saints, would just go marching on!

The argument, however limited, however scantily clad in common sense or observed fact, was widely employed by educated and uneducated people with a confidence bordering on insanity in the 1960s. Any change that might be questioned, even acts of state-sponsored destruction, or barbarous demolition to sate developers' greed, could be quickly justified by progress. All you had to do was stop thinking about what you might think was right, and replace it with the certainty that change was "for the best." New was good, old was bad. What people wanted was change and they were going to get it—lots of it; resist and you just won't count. So, the Edwardians constructed strong wooden furniture and houses out of mahogany and oak with great craft of carpentry. Who needs it? Here's a nice, modern bit of cheap aluminum or stainless-steel furniture, with some plastic pinned on top. Sure it's flimsy, but it *looks modern*. It's progress. It's new. The past is past. And what of that beautiful stone railway station constructed in grand, classical style at the height of Victorian confidence? Knock it down. Obliterate it; it stands in the way of Progress. What if what replaces it comes to be seen for what it is: ugly, overbearing, cold, uninspiring, and useless? Progress dictates: put up something else, so long as it's cheap, and modernistically angulate, with not a feminine curve—the very beginning of art—in sight. And make sure people don't think too much about what they've lost. Keep them thinking about Progress. And somehow they will progress too: all the way to the grave, but their children and grandchildren will inherit the Future. The future's bright. Progress, racing ahead; progress means catching up. Progress means listening to the new thing. Don't hold on to the past, what you know. Progress means change. Change is progress. Change is the sign of progress. Progress is the meaning of change. Change is the stock-in-trade of the politician. "People are crying out for change!" Whose change? No matter. They will be given some change, or made to pay for it for their own good. Progress is . . . progress, isn't it?

In the end, small change is hailed as Big Progress.

Someone once said the future is a convenient place to store our dreams, but tomorrow never comes. We shall always be closer to the past than to the future. "Take no thought for the morrow," enjoined Jesus to those in search of eternal life.

It should be stated that far from the counterculture itself being addicted to this way of thinking (if that's the right word), the hippies and their multifarious offshoots were often in flat reaction to overbearing change, something they held in common with the Romantic movement that questioned and tried to oppose, or ignore, the industrial revolution and the erosion of spiritual philosophy and of the sacred. As Ian MacDonald observed in his insightful introduction to *Revolution in the Head: The Beatles' Records and the Sixties* (1994), the counterculture of the Sixties actually stood by as a commentary on the social and political whirl of the time, hardly listened to by the mainstream who wanted material progress as fast as possible, and who found its stance bemusing and strange. Far from being a threat to the forces of progress, the authentic counterculture stood more in relation to the bigger picture rather as voices crying in the wilderness; by the 1980s its dream future was promoted not as inevitable, but as an "alternative." By the 1980s the counterculture's symbols had long been repackaged as mere fashion accessories. As MacDonald also observed, when the punks of the late 1970s accused the hippies of a kind of betrayal-by-accommodation, the majority of people had no idea what the fuss was about. They already knew that a hippielike existence was a waste of time leading to squalor and social ostracism, unless enjoyed by long-haired millionaires on gated estates. It was an indulgence, like a Victorian eccentric's delight in Oriental mysticism. An ethic may quickly devolve into aesthetics, matters of taste rather than urgent moral essence.

Nevertheless, there really was a tumultuous concretion of commercialist ugliness and flimsiness during the 1960s that has hardly abated in many places, though the arguments for it now tend to be less optimistic and more pragmatic. You can have some hardwood, but can you afford it? Can the earth afford it? Needless perhaps to say, but *most* "Sixties" architecture imposed on ordinary people's lives had little or nothing of the legendary Sixties aesthetics or imaginative flair about it. It was generally the attempt to do to every town and city of the world what had been done, and what was planned to be done (though it must be said initially by innovative and imaginative minds), in the Berlin of the Weimar Republic: late 1920s and early '30s Bauhaus functionalism in design and "clean" steel and glass, futuristic, science fact not fiction, and straight lines that cut, rather than blended with or complemented space. But the architecture—startling as well as poor—proclaimed one very Sixties thing; it cried out the message: the message of Progress. Things were *changing*. You could see it. And that was Good. Of course it was. Only a poet would deny it.

SEEDS OF '60S CHANGE

In our search for the spiritual meaning of the Sixties, we are confronted constantly by the vividness of change, of the appearance of the new, often interpreted as *signs:* signs of the times. For a long time, there was debate about certain kinds of change. Harold Wilson, British prime minister after 1964, would try to co-opt the Beatles into his idea of change and progress. Their startling visual difference to what went before was drafted in to the cause of progress, though Wilson was not without suspicion of the Beatles' subversive potential. Was this the *right kind* of change? Still, people saw the Beatles as symbols—welcome and unwelcome—of change: change social (working-class opportunity), and change artistic and atmospheric. The group themselves believed in change, were fascinated by novelties, and had their own ideas of what was worth progressing to, and *those* ideas would change quickly too.

The *phenomena* constituting the popular image of the 1960s are well known. We can express them in extraordinary leaps, or changes, from one form to another. These leaps speak eloquently about the pace of obvious change in the decade that at first glance suggests the decade had been given an intravenous injection of amphetamine sulphate from its inception. While this is one way to express the transition from the previous decade to the end of the 1960s, the following leaps tell us little about their meaning:

From Sinatra and Johnny Ray to Led Zeppelin
From *I Love Lucy* to *Star Trek*

From *Bilko* to *Rowan & Martin's Laugh-In* and *Monty Python*

From Jerry Lee Lewis to *Abbey Road*

From Protestantism to Hare Krishna

From crew cuts and Bermuda shorts to *Hair* and Woodstock

From beat poets and folkies to hippies and yippies

From Kennedy to Nixon

From the Boston Strangler to Charles Manson

From Doris Day to Jane Fonda

From *Destination Moon* to *2001: A Space Odyssey*

From *Lawrence of Arabia* to Jean-Luc Godard

From twinset and pearls to the miniskirt

From nuclear family to free love

From Cadillac to beach buggy

From Gagarin and a Soviet dog in space to Apollo 11 "in peace for all mankind"

From middle age to youth

From socially approved student to college dropout

From the Bible to the Bhagavad Gita

From Buddy Holly to Jimi Hendrix

From segregation to civil rights

From British Empire to "Wind of Change in Africa" and Superpower Duopoly

From Ferde Grofé at the Hollywood Bowl to the Monterey Pop Festival

From liquor to psychedelics

From cowboys to Native Americans

From big-game hunting (*Mogambo*) to *Born Free* and the World Wildlife Fund

From pollution to the birth of environmentalism

From Matter to Soul

From uncool to cool

. . . and so on. . . . But none of these transitions *explain* the period.

Do any of these changes have spiritual meaning? You might consider ticking the ones you think may do. Or was it that all these changes were

Fig. 2.1. John Lennon, 1964.

merely superficial? All things must pass. And all things must change. And all changes must pass too. What's left? In 1970, John Lennon, having split up painfully from his fellow Beatles would bitterly opine that all that had really happened in the 1960s in terms of political progress was that a lot of people had grown their hair long, leaving the same "bastards" still in power; the underlying oppressive realities had survived intact. For him, at least in that year of 1970 he vainly dubbed "Year One," the "dream was over" and he largely withdrew into his own personal concerns while putting some residual faith in the confrontational, and more specifically "personal is political" tactical jargon of the New Left, before leaving that behind as well in search of a pre-Beatles identity obscured by subsequent imagery, myth projection, and posturing. The spirit of collectivity had, at least temporarily, gone, and as the Sixties faded, his many fans felt a corresponding deflation and ache of the soul as the so-called Me Decade advanced amid the detritus of broken dreams and the peeling panels of yesterday's progress in decay.

Not surprisingly, the "Progress argument" and the once fervent faith in it, is now considerably muted. Many people are doubtful about the future and predominantly concerned with security: a hard blow after years of promise on promise. In fact, the doctrine of inevitable progress was never any more than an impious hope, a secular faith with feet of clay. There is a spiritual message in this insight if you care to see it, even though it would suggest, in this aspect at least, a key component of Sixties experience and thinking had little or no spiritual meaning at all.

In fact the very stances of conservative and countercultural assessments of the decade *both* belie a superstition of inevitable progress, or that all change, however repellent to some at first sight, is necessarily in some sense a signifier of progress. For while the conservative critic may see the Sixties as a regressive eruption of destructive indulgences, the progressive dissenter sees a regrettable social and psychological deformation insofar as the politics of the Right persists at all. The right wing is castigated for reactionary negativism, that is, its supporters resist or frustrate progress.

While proponents of secular faith (religion free) may still be heard, chiefly on the liberal-leftward side of the political spectrum in Great Britain and Europe, in America at least, there has been a long metamorphosis of the countercultural positions of the 1960s, especially when separated from explicit left-wing commitment, toward a faith in an underlying spiritual evolution. Whether that evolution's progress is inevitable is something of a moot point. No one seriously doubts that human progress, such as we think it, may end in an unspeakable cloud of fallout as a result of human folly, wicked or mindless destructiveness, religious fantasy, or spiritual immaturity, but there is also a faith in a greater order of reality that encompasses not only humankind but all living and existing things, all of which are evolving, adapting, and changing in the time process.

Many ideas entertained by Sixties activist survivors have now coalesced into various strands, one of which of undoubted influence is the Green environmental and earth-conscious movement. Another, intrinsically related, is what the press calls "New Ageism" (which deprecatory characterization tells us very little). There is more respect for ancient sources of "changeless" wisdom today among inheritors of the Sixties counterculture, and we may say that these ideas, and systematic initiatory ideas and structures were not articulated directly in the 1960s because they were little known or, where known, not deeply understood and their application confused. The early counterculture was instinctive, sometimes whimsical with the sense that "one day we must try to tidy all this up but now we're too busy living." Despite the painful ravages of news from Vietnam, there was yet, in much of the media, a persistent suggestion of a holiday atmosphere (albeit enjoyed only by a minority)— thus the *summer* of love, rather than winter or fall. In a qualified sense, there has been progress from the seedling Sixties counterculture itself toward more diverse and tested forms of spiritual engagement. Flower power as such may produce a smile in the aged (though it still appeals to many school-age children, especially idealistic girls) but the deeper *ideas* of flower power—that we can engage political opposition with disarming signs of love; that we need to engage in a better relationship with natural energies and resources, and to respect and love the treasury of the planet that is in our perhaps temporary care—still make sense and are not mere flights from science, but impact on the priorities of scientists, generating a change in attitude that in enlightened quarters puts technology at the service of good intentions rather than simply for political power and private profit. *Countercultured* figures—even late ones such as the late Steve Jobs—have turned out to be exceptional wielders of capital. Money *itself* is not the root of all kinds of evils, but the love of it entails profound spiritual, and subsequently organic and material dangers. It is better to give than to receive.

In this analysis the Sixties in its legendary aspect did not end in 1970 but was a crucial stage in a longstanding development in the human consciousness story. Thus it becomes possible to plant a few words from the late-antique Graeco-Egyptian *Corpus Hermeticum* in our own times and make sense of their spiritual meaning. The Hermetic phrase *mundus imago dei,* for example—so dear to Elizabethan magus-scientist John Dee who died twelve years before the Pilgrim Fathers set sail from Plymouth—has multiple applications today. *Mundus imago dei*: "The world is the image of God," goes the concise Latin phrase.

This may be taken as a simple statement of protoromanticism: "What a wonderful world!" as Louis Armstrong first sang in October 1967(!) but it also has deeper and wider meanings. The world reflects God, that is to say, our state of spiritual being (upward or downward tending) is reflected in the world. Being is seeing. Man's consciousness is reflected in the state of Nature. Thus, in theory, sure, human beings may theoretically cause "climate change" by the *way we think about the world.* If we consider Nature simply as a means to exclusive profits, we shall find ourselves indifferent to polluting and deforming the natural order: changes in atmospheric conditions will be just one outflow of that; poisoning ourselves and other creatures is another. The earth may appear indifferent to us, and perhaps ultimately, it must be, but so long as we are here, we are deeply part of the *holomovement* (to borrow a word from physicist David Joseph Bohm FRS), with a special position in it on account of having access to Mind (Greek: *nous*), and if we wish to "clean up our act," attention to our spiritual condition should be paramount. We cannot buy our way out of that, nor can we trust in progress to do the work for us.

We now need to say something about what we mean by *spiritual condition* and, indeed about what we mean by this discourse about *spiritual meaning.* It dismayed Booker that many people in the Sixties did not seek spiritual meaning in the traditional churches erected, presumably, for that purpose. He may have a case to be scornful of those who spurned inherited forms of religion, but it may equally be charged that the traditional churches had somehow or to varying degrees failed to bring spiritual meaning to the forefront of their appeal to believers and would-be believers in an age of obvious scientific advance. In that sense, Booker might have observed that Christianity's founder found himself unwelcome at his home synagogue and among his familiar acquaintances and perhaps family too. Religious authority—hallowed by time and blessed with political influence—opposed him and his message, and he would be sentenced to death for blasphemy. If Richard Nixon had seen Jesus at a slight distance he would probably have dismissed his savior as a bum.

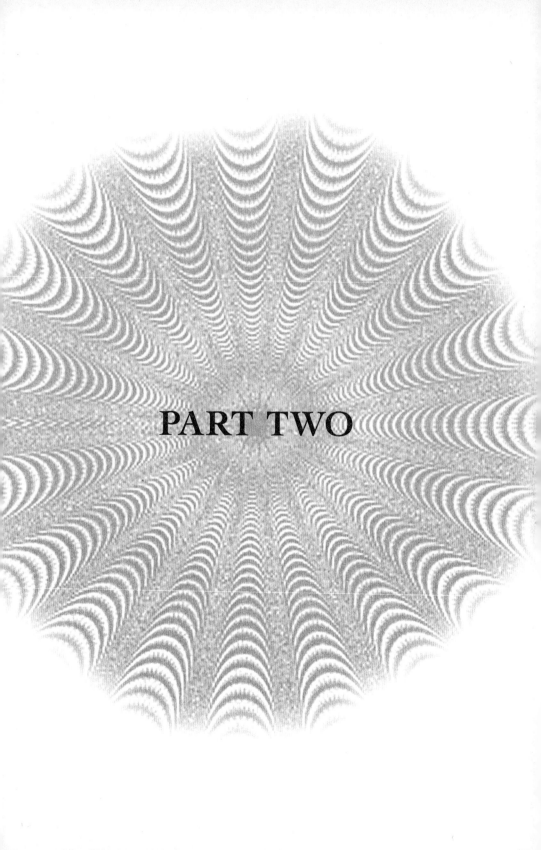

PART TWO

APOLOGIA PRO PHILOSOPHIA SUA

Readers who are perfectly comfortable with the idea of spiritual meaning in relation to a decade, or to anything else, and who have their own clear conception of the idea, may choose to skip the next two chapters (at least for the time being) and go straight to part 3, where they may enter the spiritual story of the decade proper. However, there may be persons either skeptical of, or possibly confused by, the phrase *spiritual meaning*, and who want to know precisely what the author means by *spirit* and *spiritual*. Other readers may be at least curious as to what the author specifically intends by the expression: "the spiritual meaning of the 1960s." In the next chapter (chapter 3) I examine the philosophical and etymological basis for the term *spiritual meaning*, while in chapter 4, I indicate what is meant when we are asked to look for the spiritual meaning of a period of history, and show ways in which the question has been approached by several thinkers in the past. Readers who find philosophical structuring and first-principle rationales tedious or distracting will lose nothing by going straight to chapter 5.

THREE

Defining Terms:
What Does "Spiritual Meaning" Mean?

If I ask what is the meaning of something, the asking straightaway suggests there is something that I do not understand, something I cannot interpret. If it is a phrase, I might have understanding of the individual words, but I may be in the dark as to what the user of those words is really *getting at;* for we use words to *lead us on.* What is the speaker intending to say? What is the *intention?* Do the words—however familiar individually—really mean anything? Meaning—or what is the willed substance and objective of expression—is bound up with intention ("I mean to say . . ."), which begs the question of what is motivating the intended meaning. Meaning is less concerned with the content expressed, and more with what the content signifies: its proper interpretation. We may hear something very clearly, but fail to understand its meaning. Likewise, we may misunderstand what we see.

In matters of translation the issue of meaning is straightforward. If I say the French *la porte* means "the door," everyone knows what I mean. There is an easy reciprocation of meaning; one word means the other. But if I say "the door is a symbol of a rite of passage," it may be more difficult to assess my meaning. One would need to know more about the *context* for a start. We ask the meaning of something when we have difficulty in translating words or ideas into terms that mean something to us, so that we can appropriate the intention behind them and acquire knowledge. So if we ask: "What is the spiritual meaning of the 1960s?" we are asking for a translation, or interpretation of the decade in terms concerning its spiritual content, and that interpretation will most likely employ spiritual terms and be made in terms of spiritual experience.

We are not ultimately asking what is the spiritual content of the decade (the decade *as* spiritual content), rather what, on reflection, having assessed any supposed spiritual content, that content *means*. What does it signify? Does the content throw up signs that help us, or even force us, to see its significance? To find the meaning, we need first to assess the content. What does the spiritual content mean? What is the interpretation of that spiritual content? What does the spiritual content *intend* to express? What motivates this supposed spiritual content? Does the content itself suggest in any sense a coherent spiritual movement, for example, endemic to the decade itself, which may suggest transcendent dimensions to the decade?

Furthermore, such is the potency of the adjective *spiritual* (to repel as well as to attract interest) that we may be asking something more. What is the absolute or essential meaning of the 1960s *as a whole?* We may posit this question on the late-antique philosophical basis (formulated in Neoplatonism) that spirit precedes matter, where matter is that which is manifest to sense perception. How can we interpret the 1960s in terms of its spiritual value? What, as it were, does the spirit intend us to know about the 1960s? What is being shown, or revealed?

Influential German idealist philosopher G. W. F. Hegel (1770–1831) established logically, at least to his own satisfaction, that history represented what he called "Absolute Spirit" (or Mind) becoming conscious of itself through an autoprocess expressed (from our point of view) in space and time. Absolute Spirit (or Mind) is the Ultimate Knower, and the Ultimate Known. Influenced by the Theosophic, gnostic system of Jacob Böhme (1575–1624), history (understood as all existence) is, according to Hegel, Absolute Spirit revealing itself to itself, whereby it might know itself by self-objectification of its own content and potentialities, expressed through temporal and spatial conditions, in which

*Fig. 3.1. G. W. F. Hegel, 1831.
Portrait by Jakob Schlesinger.*

conditions dynamic opposites (the famous dialectical process of thesis and antithesis) are brought progressively into harmonious synthesis, whereupon the objectification process may resolve itself. Everything that can be is the ultimate experience of Mind. Hegel offers the supposition that we are involved in a process of spiritual self-disclosure, a revelation of the Absolute to itself: Spirit's self-revelation or autoconsciousness. The logical culmination of the process must be a restitution of a primal Unity principle (synthesis), but that now knows itself fully, having objectified its contents (or thought itself into manifest being), and is conscious of itself for the first time through its mirror in process. The implication is that Absolute Spirit, like man, learns or acquires consciousness through experience. In other words, and from our point of view, the dualistic nature of being is an interim condition of unity expressing itself, which process of self-knowledge necessarily creates a temporal duality. What we know as history is, according to Hegel's system, the working-out or expression of this process. As for Absolute Spirit, it is *Being* itself, or being in itself. It is the primal postulate; without being, nothing can be.*

---

*Note Exodus 3:14: "And God said unto Moses, 'I AM THAT I AM.' And He said, 'Thus shalt thou say unto the children of Israel, "'I AM hath sent me unto you.'""

So, to ask Hegel about the spiritual meaning of the 1960s would be to invite him to interpret the period in terms of significant indicators of a manifest dialectic of apparently antithetical forces. In particular, Hegel might have seen a process manifested as, say: Establishment vs. Creative Instinct; Preservation vs. Destruction; Change vs. Stasis; Past vs. Future; Tradition vs. Experiment; or Control vs. Liberty; or perhaps Civilization vs. Regression; or Law vs. Liberty; or Force vs. Feeling; Reason vs. Imagination; or Collectivism vs. Individualism—and so on. The ultimate spiritual meaning would be a philosophical example of the ongoing process of Absolute Spirit's dramatic entertainment of its own potentialities for preservation and destruction. Such might constitute the decade's spiritual meaning. One could then explore the ramifications of these dynamics in detail and propose an array of observations on the essential meaning, which observations would constitute secondary or tertiary spiritual meanings. One might continue until satisfied the question was answered. Hegel, however, was an idealist.

You may be relieved to know that I do not intend to impose Hegel's particular metaphysical system onto the decade. I will however, in the next chapter, draw attention to another metaphysical interpretation of history contemporaneous with that of Hegel, one that made an attempt, as we are doing in this book, to understand a recent historic period in terms of its spiritual meaning.

SPIRIT—WHAT DOES IT MEAN?

Now Hegel obviously had a clear enough idea of what *he* meant by the word *spirit*, but such knowledge is not the norm today. If you take a straw poll of what people today mean by spirit, you'll come up with quite a sack of diff'rent critters! Just to give a sense of the range, it's worth noting that the French *l'ésprit* can mean "spirit" as we might mean it (viz: *ésprit de corps*—a kind of fraternal, fighting spirit or energy or hearty willingness) or it may mean "mind," or both simultaneously. With the twentieth-century development of psychology and psychiatry, we tend to identify *mind* with the brain organ and thinking process:

perception, cognition, articulation, nerves, awareness, and so on. But we would not generally say that reasoning or mentation is a spiritual activity, because we have been encouraged to think of thinking as being an organic, rational, even physical or behavioral activity. *Hmm. . . .* All part of the problem. Many people today would associate something as being spiritual insofar as it referred to a deeper experience of interiority: feelings, intuitions, sensitivity to the numinous, profound personal thoughts, sensations of mysterious or imaginative worlds conjured by art, even to the idea of a Jungian unconscious mind with unwilled or imprinted archetypes, accompanied by a panoply of psychological jargon and categories. They might regard their inner dimension as something sacred—at least to themselves—to be respected by others, for they consider their inner life as articulating and reflecting timeless beauty, a sense of truth, goodness, love, aesthetics, mystery, and ethics: in short, *the inner state of being* or core of identity. After the heart, art is considered an avenue or stimulus to this sense, and in this sense people might talk of the spirit interchangeably with the heart, the soul, or subjective experiences of feeling, emotion, perception of truth, or the discovery of a *meaning,* a meaning perhaps of life's mystery or depth, an elusive presence that reason cannot maintain a comprehensive hold on, or be able to contain exclusively.

The word *spirit* commonly denotes the real, even immortal self of a person and may be regarded as distinct from the organic body and ultimately distinct, but not entirely separate from, the organic brain. To the scientific, or arguably pedantic classification-oriented mind, all this sounds dangerously woolly, imprecise, unobjective (subjective), unmeasurable (nonexistent) and therefore unscientific, and therefore, quite possibly, or probably, *unreal*—mere delusions, fantasies of mind, temporary states, comfortable illusions, figures of speech, and so forth. The modernist mind dedicated to the *object* tends to diminish validity to the subject where the subject's mind is not dedicated solely to the object. But what when the object *is* the subject? Tell many a doctor about your personal *feelings* and watch his or her eyes glaze over. Doctors are seldom interested in vague notions, uninformed guesses: is there a pathology present, or not? What are your senses saying? The doctor is primarily concerned with the visible organism. Your state of mind probably reflects your state of body (though a doctor may be less keen on the reverse proposition).

I have often found it both helpful and necessary in assessing spiritual terms to return to the language that first expressed so many of our basic cultural ideas. The New Testament scripture first appeared in *koinē* Greek, that is, the common Greek language written and spoken by persons who were not the most highly educated Greek natives but who shared in the cultural world that followed the conquests of Alexander the Great and his successors in the fourth century BCE.

There are of course a large number of academics today who regard arguably nonspecific words like *spirit* and *spiritual* as being essentially meaningless words, vague words, vague enough to mean anything to anyone and therefore denoting no-thing, or if something, then something merely subjective. Of course, the word *spirit* already meant something that was not a *thing* in the physical sense, which while informing the state or awareness of the five senses, could not be accessed directly by their agency alone. So it has been easy enough to dismiss the word *spirit* as being, from the respectable scientific point of view, meaningless, or simply a fanciful way of referring to being alive, where *being* is identified with physical continuity, and the sense of that being is referred to as consciousness, itself viewed as a product of sense perception. According to this outlook, to ask about the spiritual meaning of the 1960s is really a meaningless question, and my or anybody else's answer to it must also be essentially meaningless, that is, of no interest to science (except perhaps to the realm of psychological or neurological pathology).

Science used to mean knowledge from whatever source. Now it means knowledge known to, or accepted by, scientists, that is, measurable phenomena (objects). Heat was once a feeling, now we think of it as a numbered, graded temperature. What, we may ask, would such a point of view make of, for example, Rudolf Steiner's spiritual science? We may well guess correctly.

Needless to say, science uses symbols. Numbers are symbols. They have no objective existence, being convenient media of measurement of logical sequences, but science necessarily treats numerical relationships objectively, because they *mean* something real (to the logic of science). Case rests.

HOW TO DISCERN SPIRITUAL THINGS

Arguably Christianity's first mystic, and something of a make-do philosopher, Saint Paul had an answer for the above attack of scientism on the spiritual. Paul was himself well used to the opposition of the science of his day to what he perceived as spiritual realities. Athenian pundits summarily dismissed his plea for the resurrection of Jesus, and Paul recognized that his beliefs on this subject were as absurd to Greek philosophers as they were scandalous to most of the Jewish priesthood. Nevertheless, in the terms of the following discussion, he would have found—and his philosophy did subsequently find—Greek thinkers who agreed wholeheartedly with him. By examining briefly Paul's assessment of the spiritual, we shall I think come closer to understanding the meaning of *spiritual meaning* and see why this book's investigation is not necessarily meaningless, unless of course the one asserting such is determined to assert and insist upon a strictly materialist worldview whereby matter (the measurable universe) is sole, supreme reality, where mind is in itself somehow a material, organic event (like the artificial pseudoreality of a projected movie, a magic trick), and absolutely bounded by the known laws of time and space (themselves, I insist, categories of mind!), which *knowledge,* by the way, is far from complete, though I, for one, am willing to assist in expanding the horizon of knowledge.

1 Corinthians 2:14

ψυχικος δε ἀνθρωπος ὀυ δεχεται τα του Πνουματος του θεου; μωρια γαρ ἀυτοῳ εστιν, και ὀυ δυναται γνωναι, ὁτι πνυματικως ἀνακρινεται.

But the psychic [usually translated "natural"] man cannot receive the things of the Spirit of God; for to him [this] is foolishness, and he has not the power [or is unable] to know them, because [they are] spiritually discerned.

This justly famous quotation from Paul provides us with Paul's well-known distinction between the so-called natural man and the spiritually infused man. The difference is a question of depth and scope of perception, and while the ordinary or uninspired man is able to perceive bodily or material things and causal relationships within the compass of his mind, he does not have, for he has not been given, the power to perceive things beyond natural limitations proper to the body. *Spiritual things are spiritually discerned.* The spiritual person knows this; the unspiritual person not only does not know it, but *cannot* know it. One may think of George Harrison's song that goes "When you've seen beyond yourself, then you may find peace of mind is waiting there . . ." ("Within You, Without You," 1967). You must see "beyond yourself" (the ordinary sense of self, or ego) to attain spiritual perception.

The ordinary soul may, however, be capable of an intellectual assent to the possibility of there being more to it than meets the eye as a matter of faith, suspicion, or even of blind hope, but that is nonetheless to admit that one does not have the power of spiritual discernment oneself. It is equally clear that Paul has not abandoned his rational, logical faculties when he has written this; he has not left good sense and simply gone "sky high." Paul's, however, is not an insight derived from unaided reason alone. Spiritual or divine reasoning involves dimensions of awareness beyond those ordinarily experienced by the five senses (or channels to the world, so to speak). Spiritual reasoning *encompasses* ordinary reason, whose capacities though not immediately derived from divine intelligence (being concerned with the known sense-world), are nonetheless ultimately derived from it in principle. Mysticism in all cultures asserts a divine unity that transcends all distinctions.

The reason I have questioned the common English translation of the Greek adjective *psychikos* in this context is because our English translation "natural" for "psychic" in relation to the mind of the "natural man" would not have entirely satisfied later Greek-speaking commentators on Paul's letters. For example, it was common for orthodox Christian pundits like Bishop Irenaeus of Lyon in the second century CE to accuse Gnostic heretics of dividing human beings into three classes, with spiritual salvation reserved (he alleged) to the first class (pneumatics) only.

Gnostic teachers distinguished the powers of the "psychic" man from those of the "pneumatic" or spiritual man. And the Gnostics' justification came directly from Paul in this very passage where psychic is clearly contrasted unfavorably in value to pneumatic. Gnostic writers tended to think of the word *psychic* as meaning people who had soul but who were not in contact with transmundane (world-transcending) *pneuma,* or spirit. The soul suggested emotions, feelings, and sympathies appropriate to the living creature, but Gnostics saw soul as being very bound up with the corruptible body or natural man as natural man, and his material senses, or perceiving sensitivity to *hylē* or "matter." Gnostics protested that those who accused them of being heretics were too materialistic to be able to see what Gnostics, with their claimed spiritual perception, were getting at, and they claimed texts from Saint Paul as justifying their stance. Gnostics were conscious of possessing the spirit-seed, planted in them by the "Sower" who "came to sow."

The translation common to most English Bibles of psychikos as "natural" is really a soft translation, since the word *psychic* would not have been properly understood in the seventeenth century, any more than it would be today. The existing Latin Vulgate Bible translated the Greek as "animalis" where the Latin *anima* refers to the "soul," the *animating* core of the person. Few in the ancient world believed the soul could "save" a person from this world; the idea of transmigration of souls from body to body after death was, however, not uncommon, though Buddhists might regret it. But Paul was insistent it was the Divine Pneuma (the Spirit of God) that was the agent of salvation, and the means of spiritual perception, and the Gnostic, for one, took it that the power of spiritual discernment came directly from the presence of "Spirit of God." Therefore, to be able to discern spiritual things was itself the sign of being saved already, a resurrection or "raising" from the body to divine life having already occurred in and through the *spirit*. It was, according to Gnostics, the natural man that is "crucified" in the world, but the spirit is raised incorruptible from the earth. Paul himself used the metaphor of the seed that must first "die" in the earth before being raised to fulfillment of the seed's ultimate potential (see also John 12:24).

△ △ △

We can learn much from looking at the variant meanings of the Greek words *psychē* and *pneuma,* and see how much confusion we wallow in today when we're really not very sure which words to use. We think of souls being saved (or lost), for example, or people showing spirit. Then there is *soul* music, which is mainly secular or even profane in orientation, and then there are *spirituals,* or gospel music. After death, is it the soul, or is it the spirit that goes to heaven, or elsewhere, or nowhere? Or do we think soul and spirit now mean the same thing? Could we call the Holy Spirit or Spirit of God, the *Holy Soul* or *Soul of God*?

We *don't,* do we? Something of the ancient distinctions—and confusion—remains.

The word *psychē* in Paul's time could mean "breath" as denoting the sign of life. The Latin translation would be "anima," which suggests our word *life* as well as *soul.* Psychē could also mean the life or spirit of man, or soul that survives death. One might think of the departed soul, or ghost (from the Germanic *Geist,* meaning "spirit"). The psychē was essentially distinguished by being *bodiless.* Having no material form, it could be symbolized as a bird or other winged creature since it moved in air, and being bodiless, was itself like air, and flew after death. *And your Bird can sing . . .* *

If you wanted to say something was "of the whole man" you would use the expression *psychē kai* [and] *sōma* where *sōma* means "body"—as we today might say "she tried to keep body and soul together." In Greek mythology Psyche is the mistress of Eros, god of love (carnal love in particular).

To confuse things a bit more, psychē was also understood as the organ of *nous* (that is, the *mind* able to receive divine intelligibility or *logos* = creative mind, or intelligible essence). The combination of psychē and sōma enabled thought and judgment, where *psychē* here means the soul, mind, reason, and understanding. Psychē could also denote the spirit or animating mentality of an author, where the Latin equivalent

---

*The title of a poignant, ambiguous song by Lennon-McCartney on the Beatles' *Revolver* album (1966).

would be *ingenium* or in our looser usage, "genius." In searching for spiritual meaning one might ask then: where was the *genius* of the age?

The Greek adjective *psychikos* can mean "of the soul," or indeed "spiritual," especially when contrasted with *sōmatikos,* which means "bodily." Such a contrast would obviously confuse the sense of Paul's contrast between *psychic,* or natural soul-man, and *spiritual* man capable of spiritual discernment necessary to access divine mind. We must, however, now recognize that Paul was really introducing a new concept into Greek language discourse, because he was importing the Jewish concept of the Spirit of God, hence *Spirit* (when of God) is in *his* context given a capital letter. Greek had no immediate equivalent for the Jewish Spirit of God and it is perhaps not surprising therefore that the Greek-speaking world found it relatively easy to accommodate the idea of the Holy Spirit in terms of a kind of distinct divine being (though such a personification, not surprisingly, would generate philosophical and theological confusion and conflict). Interestingly, it was not only Gnostics who distinguished *psychios* (meaning "alive" or "living" in the sense of natural existence) Christians from *pneumatikos* Christians. The heretical Montanists—late second-century enthusiasts of a charismatic Holy Spirit and supposed precursor of Methodism—called Catholics "psychics" with the sense of Catholics' inability to be freed into ecstasies by the action of the Holy Spirit. In modern parlance perhaps the psychic Catholics were being dismissed as uncool, or in Sixties argot as uptight squares, straights, being unhip or not with it, where *it* in the Sixties context was the spirit or zeitgeist (time-spirit).

When we come to the original meanings of the Greek *to pneuma* (the spirit), we come closer to the range of possibilities inherent in the word *spiritual.* The basic meaning of *pneuma* is "wind," or "air." This translation would doubtless suit opponents of those who adhere to spiritual life! Is not this discourse about spirit all empty wind and hot air? This would have been how Catholic authorities regarded Montanist charismatics—all gas and no gaiters. But we soon see that the emphasis on wind and air (equivalent to the Hebrew *ruach,* which may also be translated as "psyche" in Greek, or "wind" or "breath"—as in life—in

English) is a means of denoting something *that cannot be seen,* but that nonetheless acts, and is real, however invisible, even the essential reality (breath of life), having the power to penetrate and animate. Just think of wind in sails, which our ancient forebears saw much of, for that was the sole way of traversing great seas without oars. The vibrant air is there unseen, until you raise a sail and lo, you can see it, and it *moves.* Would you tell a becalmed sailor that what is not seen does not exist? He looks above for his salvation. Ah, but we can *feel* the wind; yes, but to feel the air, we have to run and to breathe, and to see it, we need a suitable medium. Then we find the evidence of things not seen. We have to be, and to act; our actions denote what we are, that is, the invisible being is rendered visible in act. As above, so below.

Pneuma is then, the unseen motivator, it animates and it drives. It is, as we would say today, a driving force, albeit an invisible driving force. The Latin translation of pneuma is *spiritus,* or *anima*. When breathing ceases, some still speak of a person "giving up the ghost": that which animates, or rather has animated, the now deceased. The body is what is left, and we dispose of it appropriately, remembering the departed. Pneuma is strongly linked to breathing and to respiration, and therefore also to the power of the word, of speech, and we may think of this in terms of our written traditions of God speaking to his prophets, and the divine influence of God on men and affairs generally: the logos or manifest utterance (vibration—note the Sixties allusion!) of invisible being.

Pneuma may also refer to an afflatus, or to the inspiration of poets. The Greeks would have seen such inspiration as poets enjoyed as being derived from a divine source, a god or goddess, the breath of the poet being sweetened by the divine breath whose flower would be experienced as music: that which inspires, or inspirits. One thinks equally of Orpheus's ability to calm the savage beast by his voice, or of Jesus commanding the waves, quelling the storm by the power of the *source* of wind or breath. Again, Greeks could use *pneuma* interchangeably with *psychē* to denote the spirit or soul of man, so in a sense, Paul's distinction of the psychic and pneumatic man is not one Greeks would necessarily recognize. Obviously not a polytheist, Paul seems to imply that spiritual discernment of the things of God can only come from the Spirit of God and not, say, the spirit of the poet in general, however inspired in the ordinary sense. This interpretation might make the ambition of discerning the spiritual meaning of the 1960s somewhat challenging, or even impossible!

In Romans 2:29, Paul uses the term *pneuma* in terms of the highest and deepest, noblest part of the person, that which reaches to God, saying that the true Jew is one whose circumcision is "inward," a circumcision or dedication of the heart, "in the spirit" "whose praise is not of men but of God." In this context the spiritual meaning of a decade would concern itself with the meaning of the deepest and highest impulses active in the period.

During John Lennon and Yoko Ono's famous peace campaign, John Lennon told *Daily Express* journalist David Wigg in 1969 that "John and Yoko are like the wind. You can't see it but when it passes the trees bend." This example of afflatus was perhaps intrinsically connected to Lennon's sudden announcement to old school pal Pete Shotton the previous year that he, John, was "Jesus Christ," perhaps—who knows?—understanding this in himself in the Gnostic sense. The announcement was presented the following day to close colleagues at Apple (the Beatles' business wing) as Lennon's "thing" to be greeted with a silence from which the somewhat surprising claim never emerged again.*

A curious episode, no doubt, but one that may perhaps bring us to some of the less exalted Greek words linked to pneuma, and that may also be of relevance to the 1960s. For example, we find the verb *pneumatiaō* means to be "possessed by a spirit." This may not necessarily mean a bad spirit as we think of possession today. Saint Paul, after all, was in Greek terms possessed by the spirit or mind of Christ (John Lennon too perhaps may have thought so for a short spell, perhaps after a few days of recreational psychedelic ingestion in the company of his friend). Then, also of interest to us we find *pneumatizō,* meaning "to fan by blowing." This relates to *inflation,* being blown by the wind. We may think not only of Bob Dylan's famous song, and of minds being

---

*The account of this phenomenon was made in Pete Shotton's personal account of his memories of his school friend. *John Lennon: In My Life* (1983).

blown, but also excessive pride, overinflation, or inflated, grandiose, vain expectation. In this regard, one recalls a famous announcement made from the stage of the Woodstock Festival in August 1969 to a supposed 400,000 wet and hungry present: "We must be in heaven, man!" This unexpected observation popped out of a stage announcer's mouth after the throng had been enjoined to "pass it on"—not joints, you understand, lest they bogart them, but *food*. "Keep feeding each other," was warmly intoned before the biblical parallel of the "Feeding of the Five Thousand" suddenly occurred (with the speaker presumably on the Mount), before the embarrassing afflatus was swiftly and coolly self-corrected with the too-wry explanation: "There's always a little bit of heaven in a disaster area." Yes, *but that's not what you were really getting at, was it?* The announcer had set himself up, and revealed where his head was probably "really at." *Apocalypse Now,* man. There is a case for saying the decade, in particular its active counterculture, got high on itself: a balloon that kept rising, with the threat of the end of the world—or conversely its ultimate fulfillment—so close to the psyche of the period; to break beyond the bonds of fate; to "break on through to the other side" and so escape the feared conflagration, expressed so eloquently to a cheering crowd at the decade's end by Jim Morrison with the promise: "I don't know what's gonna happen, man, but I'm gonna have my kicks before the whole shithouse goes up in flames! All right!" Cue: music.

Ah . . . the mix gets richer. We have *pneumatios,* meaning "windy," or a portending wind. There was plenty of that in British Prime Minister Harold Macmillan's speech to the South African parliament on February 3, 1960, when he declared a "wind of change" was blowing through the African continent. Bob Dylan, meanwhile, was watching from his watchtower. Then we have *pneumatokēlē,* or flatulent hernia, which contrasts with *pneumato-ergos,* a creator of spirits, and *pneumato-kinētos,* one moved by the Spirit.

Finally we have *pneumatopoieō,* which occurs in the Aristotelian text *Problems,* and means "to turn into air; to dissolve," and we may naturally leap to the mind of Shakespeare and the end of the magic show of one of his last plays, *The Tempest* (how appropriate for the decade!) where magus Prospero refers solemnly to the vanishing of the dream, comparing the fading of its lights to the vanity of human life. "Our revels now are ended," Prospero confesses that the great vistas he has conjured are the works of imagination, a "baseless fabric." The "insubstantial pageant faded" with a celebration of love and harmony, Prospero drowns his magic book in "fathoms deep," then resignedly concludes that *we* "are such stuff as dreams are made on, and our little life is rounded with a sleep." Theater speaks down to life and life condemns theater to death. If the best of the Sixties was indeed a magic show, the rite had to end sometime, though the real play continues, and if anyone should say it was naught but baseless fabric, a mere insubstantial pageant, then they condemn themselves and current obsessions likewise, for nothing Man makes will last, and every man's play on this earthly stage ends, and, graced with this fact, we crave spiritual meaning, even in and through this tempest of a decade.

FOUR

As Above, So Below

Models of Spiritual Meaning in History

That which is below is like that which is above
and that which is above is like that which is below
to do the miracles of one only thing.

ISAAC NEWTON'S TRANSLATION FROM LATIN
OF THE *SMARAGDINE TABLE OF HERMES TRISMEGISTUS*,
AN ALCHEMICAL TEXT THAT FIRST APPEARED IN ARABIC
BETWEEN THE SIXTH AND EIGHTH CENTURIES CE

In many respects, the question of the spiritual meaning of a period of time is a distinctly modern problem. While the Christian world—not uniquely—relied on regular spouts of prophecy and astrological prediction for over seventeen hundred years, notably accelerating with the Reformation, there was, until the so-called Age of Enlightenment or Age of Reason in the eighteenth century, a supraencompassing spiritual theory of history that gave meaning to all events that occurred under its supposed divine dispensation. God created the world; he would at some point bring about its end, and would then enact the first creation's spiritual fulfillment in restoring his original purposes. All human activity during the limited period of earthly existence was lived under the eye and judgment of God the Father and Son, and could be appropriated in its meaning as being either sinful, against God's purposes, or righteous, that is, in accordance with God's purposes; the purposes: salvation for the righteous, damnation for the wicked, perfection of the Plan. Bad happenings could be attributed to the latter, good happenings to the former. Thus, a great storm at sea that wrecked the Spanish Armada's plan to spearhead an invasion of England in 1588 was spiritually meaningful: "God blew, and they [the Spanish] were scattered," as the commemorative coin struck to celebrate the event stated succinctly. *As above, so below.* God's will was mirrored on earth. Man was free to go with the divine wind or face the consequences.

The only "history" that *really* mattered was in the Bible already, and so it was quite normal to see everything happening on earth as having a heavenly (as above) principle behind it, and a more or less direct biblical correlate. Thus, the Knights Templar, for example, were dubbed by Saint Bernard of Clairvaux—who wrote their Rule in the twelfth century—the "new Maccabees": righteous warriors, cleansing the Temple and restoring right worship in Jerusalem, just like Judas Maccabaeus and his holy army in the first and second books of Maccabees in the Catholic Bible. *That* would have constituted the essential spiritual meaning of the Crusades. It didn't matter that some thirteen hundred years of history separated the Maccabees from the Templars: God's Word was eternal. Time was simply the space between beginning and end.

After the Reformation, pious Protestants lived their lives in the light and form of biblical precedents. To leave the Church of Rome was to be like the Jews in exodus from Babylonian captivity, or like Moses outwitting Pharaoh in quest of Promised Land; and the Promised Land could be Massachusetts, or across the wide Missouri, in Utah, or the Transvaal of South Africa. In the 1960s, arguably, the Promised Land might be the fulfillment of Martin Luther King's civil rights prophecy, or journeying "in peace for all mankind" into outer space. As Kennedy put it when launching his push for the moon: "Whatever mankind must undertake, free men must fully share." Transposed into the humanism of the period, the resonance still has that biblical sense humming beneath it.

It therefore begins to make sense why in the eighteenth century, a disquiet hung over attempts to understand human events in a supposed Age of Reason. The authority of Catholic dogma was being eroded in Europe as confidence in man's own reasoning powers grew apace under the long influence of Renaissance philosophy and science. Then, when Hegel was but a student of nineteen years at Tübingen in Württemberg, a mighty explosion knocked the world for six.

In 1789 the French Revolution erupted to pose a direct and violent challenge not only to the Catholic Church as an institution, but to all preexisting conceptions of man's place in history based on scripture. Its gathering tumult, confusion, and regicidal savagery would eventually be crowned by the elevation of a Corsican who regarded himself as the man of will and destiny, who at his imperial coronation in 1804 seized the laurels of his emperorship rudely from the hand of the pope in an epoch-marking gesture. Napoleon Bonaparte was he whose authority lay neither in lineage nor sanction of religion, but in his self-belief. *He* was the spiritual meaning of his life, and history was his.

During and after the astounding shift in emphasis that came with Enlightenment, Revolution, and Bonapartism, it became a profound problem to assess the spiritual meaning of anything, never mind whole periods or segments of history.

It has long fascinated me that attempts were nonetheless made, though they are still neither common knowledge, nor the kind of things students learn about in academic history or in conventional accounts of philosophy or the history of ideas. Looking at what I consider the most significant post-Enlightenment attempts to find spiritual meaning in historical periods may help us to assess the spiritual meaning of the 1960s.

LOUIS CLAUDE DE SAINT-MARTIN (1743–1803)

Initially a follower of Martinès de Pasqually's Illuminist Freemasonry,* Louis Claude de Saint-Martin (1743–1803) called himself the "Unknown Philosopher," a designation still appropriate. Unknown he largely is, but

---

*See my book *The Invisible History of the Rosicrucians* (2009).

he remains nonetheless, in my view, well worth knowing. Best represented by his book *Des érreurs et de la vérité, ou les hommes rappelés au principe universel de la science* (Of errors and of truth, or men recalled to the universal principle of science, 1775), Saint-Martin's thought maintains that man's ultimate aim is to recover the lost faculties of the first Adam before the Fall. The book bravely confronts the secular Enlightenment's concept of reason. True enlightenment does not come from the senses or the calculations of the brain, asserts Saint-Martin. Like religion, enlightenment is a divine gift. Religion is a means of transmitting wisdom to such as can perceive it. The True Cause of all is capable of things unimaginable and incalculable to unaided reason. Reason knows only what it knows.

Man's existential plight and the yearning and frustration of his mind to understand and know a world beyond him is evidence of a primal fall of man, the Fall, which according to Saint-Martin, may be overcome; the process of overcoming the Fall accounts for the vagaries of the

Fig. 4.1. Louis-Claude de Saint-Martin (1743–1803).

historical process. The scattered and fragmented faculties of humans are like a mirror broken by the Fall's impact. The faculties cannot reflect the true light accurately until reunified by regeneration. This rectification of the dignity of humankind is made possible through the virtue of the sacrificial act of the figure he calls the *Réparateur*. Christ the Word is the Repairer, the mender of the rupture that separates humankind from its primal state of man-God. Physical nature, which has also fallen, is not immune to the *Réparateur's* work. The physical world will also be regenerated when the universe reattains the Edenic condition. Saint-Martin believed man's lost faculties, characterized by direct spiritual perception, constituted the true rights of man. Mere changes in administration will not restore them; rather it is that improvements in systems allowing greater access to the primal faculties are indications that reparation is being effected.

On July 4, 1790, Saint-Martin, having discovered the revelation of Jacob Böhme (1575–1624), asked his name be removed from Masonic registers. Saint-Martin concluded from Böhme's work that it was the

Fig. 4.2. Jacob Böhme (1575–1624).
Portrait by Christoph Gotlob Glymann.

divine Sophia (Wisdom, personified as a feminine reflection of God) who enables us to be reborn to the true life. Böhme's 1624 collection *The Way to Christ* directly influenced Saint-Martin's book *Ecce homo* (Behold the man, 1792), which emphasized imitation of Christ as the sole route to spiritual regeneration.

Saint-Martin developed the idea of the man-God, cooperator and minister of the divine will, charged with a mission of salvation. He advocated a government of people chosen by God to lead humanity. Furthermore, Saint-Martin may be read in terms of a progressive social evolution of humanity, advancing toward an age of the Holy Spirit or Paraclete.

So, if you asked Saint-Martin about the spiritual meaning of the 1960s, he might answer that it could be seen in terms of whether it assisted or promoted, or was itself the manifestation of the process of reparation and reintegration, with its graceful parergon, or by-product, in the social evolution of humanity. While the ultimate aim was purely spiritual, or concerned absolute reality, the process was also world trans-forming. This allowed for the possibility that within this process, world events had real meaning.

Saint-Martin lived through and was indeed lucky to survive the events of the revolutionary Terror that came in the wake of the French Revolution. Nevertheless, he was willing to analyze the bloody tumult in terms of its spiritual meaning. Saint-Martin considered the French Revolution to be something that could be decoded as a terrestrial hiero-glyph of spiritual value. According to his analysis, the events of the Revolution, despite their often chaotic and undeniably savage and morally wayward character, nonetheless in the greater picture embodied the quest of humankind for *right order* according to the inner drive for reconcilia-tion and reintegration with God's will. This quest for a divine economy of justice and goodness was what was at the root of even the many per-versions of that idea by frightened or selfishly ambitious and tragically misguided men. Even the revolution's violence served as a sign of the pun-ishment for past indifference to the True Cause. Thus the historical revo-lution represented a foreshadowing of a far greater liberation of humanity still to come: it was a profound and painful lesson, a sacrifice.

It was not the task of individuals, however, to take this interpretation as a justification for their own ambitions. The important thing for the individual was to seek the light by which a cosmic amnesia could be overcome, by attending to the residual fragment of the divine image that, Saint Martin believed, still exists in the human being. According to his scheme, this residual light will mark the first steps toward reorienting our wills with the divine will, thus restoring to fullness the original divine image and likeness. A new kind of human being should emerge from this process that is at once suprahistorical—like the assembly of the perfected—and historical, in that the reconciliation takes place within the processes of life on Earth.

Saint-Martin praised the *hommes de désir* ("the men of desire"), the people who desired the drawing forth of divine life out from under the bondage of the fallen condition. Such people imitated Christ and thus incarnated consciousness of the divine Word and Wisdom; they expiate the world through their sacrificial suffering. I am sure we shall, if we look, find men of desire and women of desire within the scenario of the 1960s.

Saint-Martin called for the people of desire to participate willingly in the Great Work of Reintegration. When the call was heeded, humanity would be showered with divine mysteries that the rationalist, so-called Enlightenment rejected outright. Was *this,* in late '60s-speak, the dawning of the Age of Aquarius?

The 1960s saw the growth of consciousness that has flowered in the environmental movement. Saint-Martin foresaw the reintegration of the eternal Nature. His work *De l'ésprit des choses* (Of the spirit of things) was of great interest to German *Naturphilosophie* (nature philosophy), whose spirit came alive again in the imagination of some West German "Greens" during the 1970s and 1980s, many of whom had begun their political rebirth at the time of the revolutionary events of 1968 in France and West Germany.

According to Saint-Martin, "The imagination is the spiritual part of humanity that possesses the vision of all things. . . . Through imagination we grasp the spiritual unity of the universe"—a statement that would have been welcome daubed on the walls of the Sorbonne in Paris in May '68. Imagination was key to the counterculture of the 1960s and would have been seen by Saint-Martin as a critical aspect of its spiritual meaning. Saint-Martin would also have been intrigued, I'm sure, by the power of poetry evinced in the 1960s, in which era it was still customary to regard songwriters whose work went further than "moon 'n' june" rhymings of banal romances, as *poets,* significant messengers with something to say worth hearing. There is a famous fragment of Granada TV film of the Beatles, having just arrived in the United States in 1964, being chauffeured to their hotel, with Paul McCartney holding a transistor radio to his ear listening to a somewhat overexcited disc jockey—Murray the K—announce an imminent interview wherein the group would talk about "their poetry." McCartney, wary perhaps of the stigma of pretension, says flatly: "But we ain't written no poetry!"—all part of the group's disingenuous charm, no doubt, and an indication that the Beatles were well on the way to a rapid confluence with the folk singer who took his moniker from Welsh poet Dylan Thomas, while the best of the period's popular music eschewed banalities to embrace poetry's imaginative power. And with Bob came imagination's stimulant of choice, cannabis.

Saint-Martin—who as far as we know got his "highs" from mystical contemplation of the truth—was also concerned with theory of language, aware that a great gulf separates humankind from the original Adamic tongue of legend, which by vibrated words could summon the essence of a thing itself from within its being. Limitations of language often suggested limitations of doctrine. For example, if we say "kingdom of heaven," do we mean the literal translation from the Greek Bible, which would suggest a realm of the daytime sky and outer space ruled by an emperor? It was obvious to Saint-Martin that words represented a simile and metaphor for a spiritual reality, only partly decoded through our fallen language. The spiritual reality might be inferred imaginatively from concentrating on the limitlessness of what our eyes present to us. Our eyes do not reveal the whole truth. There is another language, a language of symbol, but this is seldom grasped, and the poet's gift to unify the poetic vision with words is not appreciated universally.

Christ is the Word, the original vibration of creative mind made audible and visible. To become fully reconciled to the Word is simultaneously to obtain a new tongue, a new language. Saint-Martin saw such a new tongue prefigured in the biblical story of Pentecost, when Jesus's disciples suddenly received linguistic gifts so extraordinary that onlookers mistook them for drunkards. Indeed, the apostles had enjoyed a taste of the wine of the new kingdom: divine spirit. According to Saint-Martin's understanding, the Pentecost story may be seen as a slice of history valued for the divine signs it encodes. The more the people of desire are reintegrated into the pleroma (fullness of God), the more of the divine signs they are empowered to decode, the greater their grasp of the original language of creation. When they fully embrace their Sophia (spirit of Wisdom), they are gifted with the fullness of the Word. In Saint-Martin's view, note, historical events are symbolic of, not instruments of, the reintegration of humanity. When the job is done, there will be no scroll to roll up; the end will be in its beginning (*in principio*).

It must be said that the poets of the 1960s—when not employing imagery to describe things that upset, amused, or delighted them—were of an unusually playful, often whimsical, sometimes conceited and facetious nature, and wiser counsel, armed with clear esoteric understanding, might have been able to offer a higher, systematic direction and ultimate purpose to those on the artistic barricades hastily assembled in those proverbially heady, often confusing, gaudy times. But everyone was in a hurry, without realizing perhaps that they would have to decide for themselves what the "end" of it all might be; *it wasn't just going to happen.* But people thought it was: *progress* suggested it was "just going to be great." There was more belief than gnosis, but you can go a long way with belief—but all emissions of energy have limits, and the time comes when you really have to *know* what you're doing, and know what you are being: a tough task when you're hungover.

ANTOINE FABRE D'OLIVET (1767–1825)

Fabre d'Olivet was influenced by Saint-Martin after encountering the Unknown Philosopher's followers in the early years of the nineteenth century. Largely obscure until Symbolist movement artists and occult

Fig. 4.3. Antoine Fabre d'Olivet (1767–1825).

enthusiasts in the 1880s and 1890s recognized him as a kind of spiritual pagan before his time, d'Olivet, between 1813 and 1824, composed a remarkable series of Illuminist works. These included *Les vers dorés de Pythagore* (The golden verses of Pythagoras, 1813), *La Langue hébraïque restituée* (The Hebraic language restored, 1816), *Caïn: Mystère dramatique de Lord Byron* (Cain, the dramatic mystery of Lord Byron, 1823), and the *Histoire philosophique du genre humain* (The philosophical history of the human type, 1824).*

In *The Hebrew Language Restored* d'Olivet claimed he had discovered Hebrew's esoteric meaning, normally reserved for initiates; he was not simply referring to traditional Kabbalah. From his theosophical decoding of the Hebrew text he created an all-encompassing theory of human destiny, superior, he believed, to any written history.

D'Olivet saw historical records as a kind of deaf-mute, unable, as it were, to hear what made them tick, or give *voice* to what was secreted between the lines. Mere evidence from records constituted events without much real meaning. They were spiritually void and ultimately depressing. In a conventional history book, its fundamental account—however accurate externally (dates and so on)—will always be false to

---

*For more information on d'Olivet and his importance to Rosicrucianism, and to the French Occult Revival, please consult *The Invisible History of the Rosicrucians* (2010) and *Occult Paris* (2016).

the truth of life because written without true knowledge of the principles that govern life and the cosmos. This was d'Olivet's view: there was far more to history than mere history.

If humankind was to be restored its proper place in the hierarchy of being, metaphysical facts concerning humanity's spiritual nature must be grasped. Applying his principles to his own time, d'Olivet felt equipped to take on and defeat one of the most famous philosophers of the period.

Immanuel Kant (1724–1804) had argued that spiritual truths were not knowable to reason. That is to say, spiritual truths could not be justified by reason alone. In effect, this argument, however reasonable it might sound—and was intended to sound—nonetheless suggested that to a rational thinking person, belief in the revelation of the Bible, for example, was not consistent with rationality. Kant himself, however, did not conclude from this that revelation was irrational, only that philosophy was not equipped to decide on the truth value of revealed statements. In practice that could be taken to imply a divide between matters of faith and matters of reason. Such division left the issue of *truth* in an ambiguous place. Common discourse would and should take place where reason could be demonstrated. Religion was, in effect,

Fig. 4.4. Immanuel Kant (1724–1804).

being edged out of science. For men like d'Olivet, this was the poisoned work of the Enlightenment, betokening a general darkness; its progress would entail a reversal for the cause of humanity. Among others of his time, d'Olivet saw through what was, in fact, a battering ram into the citadel of Western European religious and philosophical life. Kant, d'Olivet reckoned, had simply misunderstood the facts of human nature.

It was obvious to d'Olivet that Kant was not in touch with what d'Olivet called "the Tradition": spiritual knowledge that had supposedly held sway in a civilization or state of grace that preceded known civilizations, whose Tradition yet survived, transmitted in broken parts in symbols and words that had lost their meaning, or that had been turned from their root. Had Kant been familiar with the Tradition, he would have recognized the ancient tripartite nature of man, according to which, man is body, soul, and spirit. Kant, d'Olivet declared, had confused rationality with the higher reason.*

According to d'Olivet, rationality and reason were to be distinguished on the grounds that while rationality corresponds to the soul, reason corresponds to the spirit. Another word for d'Olivet's "reason" is *intellect,* where the Latin *intellectus* corresponds to the Greek *nous.* While *nous* may be translated as "reason," it is better understood in Neoplatonic terms as "the higher mind" or "higher reason." According to d'Olivet, the true intellectual faculty is a spiritual faculty derived from the intelligible nature and source of the logos-inspired universe; active *nous* is a mirror of heaven, enabling humankind to receive higher knowledge surpassing unaided rationality. This higher knowledge transcends mere ratiocination's ability to order information, a faculty based on experience of the senses (body), commonly called empirical knowledge. Interestingly, the distinction adumbrated here is fundamental to the psychological theory of yoga, whose traditional eight limbs mount toward an *unrational* identification of subject and object.

The soul (the human passions) can rationalize, but the soul is not the source of reason itself; it cannot comprehend the source of

---

Cf Plotinus: "*basileus ho nous,*" the higher reason is king.

intelligibility. That faculty belongs to the spirit, which is of the higher unity. Kant was wrong, asserted d'Olivet, because he confused rationality with intellectuality, failing to grasp the spiritual nature of reason proper.

Neatly, d'Olivet shows that Kant's philosophy results only in stripping humanity of its spiritual faculties through a vain attempt to get an inferior faculty to comprehend its superior. Spiritual truths transcend rationality. (This is a kabbalistic insight too, where the three supernals are above the abyss.) D'Olivet declared not only that Kant failed in his attempt to subject the superior to the inferior, but compounded the folly by concluding that spiritual truths were unknowable: Kant was in error.

Fabre d'Olivet understood reason as an intuitive faculty capable of grasping the ontological Absolute. This ability was also one ascribed to the kind of history generated from the spiritual intellect, rather than the mere cataloging of instances of human passion, temporal sequence, and apparent change (conventional history). Thus, once understood, the Bible's storytelling was far superior to what might have been a conventional chronicle. The book of Genesis in particular related mighty truths concerning humankind that only spiritual reason could grasp.

Fabre d'Olivet described a restored narrative of the book of Genesis. He was obliged to do this, he believed, because its essential inner truth had been hidden by the Essenes for fear of breaking faith with the demands of the Tradition. The time had come to reveal the truth. D'Olivet's Illuminist drama of Genesis is a child of its master and his time, played out in a Behmenist universe flowing with divine powers, with Adam as a spiritual being of great power.

D'Olivet examined the story of Cain and Abel, sons of Adam and Eve, and showed how the biblical story concealed amazing facts of human nature and destiny. He identified unfallen humanity with Will, which, alongside Destiny and Providence, was one of the Tradition's three cosmogonic principles. Human history, in its highest perspective, concerns the interplay of man, who is a fourth kingdom after the animal, the vegetable, and the mineral, with Will, Providence, and Destiny. How history turns out depends on how man responds to each principle.

Man—Will—Providence—Destiny

Man is body, soul, and spirit, which three, when developed, form and comingle into a fourth life, the life of Will. How may the will be kept truly free? Again, this depends on man's interaction with Destiny and Providence.

If man plays his cards right, as it were, he may, through the exercise of the full volitive life, rise from his fallen state to reattain his former status. This achievement will, eventually, harmonize Will, Providence, and Destiny.

In d'Olivet's book on Cain, we read how Adam's posterity divided his former integrated nature. Cain represents Will; Abel, Providence. Thus d'Olivet identified two races: *hommes volatifs,* relying on their own powers, and *hommes providentiels,* trusting in God's love for humanity. Had the human will submitted to Providence, humanity could have been saved. Lucifer intervened, however. Lucifer is a kind of embodiment of Will (the rebellious angel), and persuades Cain to kill his brother. Thus, Will annihilates Providence. It is not that Will is all bad, but that he is literally out of order; he does not see, being blinded by willful rebelliousness, his proper reliance on his brother: "Am I my brother's keeper?" Yes indeed, asserts d'Olivet.

Responding to the crisis, Adam and Eve give life to Seth, who is for d'Olivet the embodiment of Destiny or blind fate. Thereafter, history may be seen as a conflict between the sons of Cain, who champion anarchic liberty, and the sons of Seth, who submit to necessity and work with nature through science. This conflict is ruinous and agonizing for humankind.

Good works are forever done and undone in miserable succession. Humanity calls for Providence but—alas—save for the few like Moses, Orpheus, and Buddha, the *hommes providentiels* no longer walk on earth. However, Providence still works, but indirectly. Providence uses the willful intentions of humanity to effect an ultimate redemption, an *apocatastasis,* or reintegration of Adam. There is something of potential value in humanity in spite of the great disasters. Since, according to Fabre d'Olivet, the will of a being corresponds with its essence, he uses the image of a seed. The seed contains the being's full potentiality.

This can only be activated fully by effort of will. One is reminded of Aleister Crowley's aphorism that a flower achieves beauty by trying to grow. This conception gives us an idea of what d'Olivet meant when he said he had found the true meaning of the original Hebrew.

The first word of Genesis is *bereshith.* D'Olivet asserts that its usual translation, "in the beginning," is superficial. Its essential meaning is *in principio,* or in principle, in potential. God created the potential of the universe, the elements to be: the seed. Human beings are necessary to enable its potential to be fulfilled. The creation brought about potential being. Each person has this potential being within him or her, literally *in potentia.* Man can actualize, realize, that is, *make real,* the potential that is his formerly unknown and unrealized being.

The naturalist or ordinary doctor sees only the incomplete being. The good doctor aids its completion, the fulfillment of its potential. This was a radically different notion from current educational practice, which tended to see a person as a vessel that had to be filled with information and acculturated externally.

We then return to the idea that history is the unfolding of what was there in essence, the fulfillment of potential being in space and time. Metaphysical principles are played out in time and space. D'Olivet distinguishes allegorical history from positive history. *Positive history merely records events without spiritual significance.* On the other hand, allegorical history arranges events that may never have happened into a dramatization of the spiritual destiny of humanity.

According to Fabre d'Olivet, only allegorical history is worthy of study. Humanity is at first subject to destiny, but when the spark or germ (seed) of God, or divine will, develops, the being reacts against Destiny, manifesting as an opposing volitional force whose essence is liberty. D'Olivet observed a constant struggle between will and destiny. Should human beings yield to Destiny, years of miserable suppression and decadence will ensue, whereas *Will joined to Providence* leads them to perfection.

While we may see in d'Olivet's ideas something of the optimistic apocalyptic undercurrents that began to emerge after 1967 into the dreams of many, we may even usefully apply some of his categories as a kind of test of how his ideas might have played out had he witnessed the Sixties himself. Might we see among the "childish" "free" tribes that flowered (literally) in San Francisco as the late winter of 1966 ended, an example of the person who embraces, or tried to embrace the principle of Providence, whose innocent trust in love is a scandal to the world and the worldly—but is yet insecure in relation to Will? Might we see the blindness of surrender d'Olivet calls Destiny in the uncritical embrace in China of the so-called Cultural Revolution with its reliance on forceful coercion spurred by Mao Zedong's thoughts in a little red book, which, unlike Manfred Mann's of 1965, did not contain a single girl's telephone number, with promise of love? And the men of Will—do we not see them in Richard Nixon, Charles de Gaulle, and in the new demagogues of the wind-changed "Born Free" African continent?

It makes you think, or should do.

Was this the dawning of the Age of Aquarius? In the ideal social structure, according to d'Olivet, the full development of the volitional germ or spark constitutes the restored Will of Universal Man. Once he is restored to pristine dignity, Destiny and Providence are then harmonized into a fourth principle: the Mirror of Divinity.

D'Olivet saw Christianity's promise of a new kingdom of heaven as being bound up with the time process. He did not believe Christianity had actually changed anything fundamentally on the religious plane. Salvation being an ongoing process, there was no once-and-for-all salvific act of redemption through which all humankind might be saved. Jesus's death and resurrection were *signifiers* of the process, showing what is possible when the will of humanity combines with the will of Providence. This knowledge Fabre d'Olivet wished to revive as an aspect of the primal Tradition. Humankind must eventually attain that which Christ demonstrated, by the exercise of will in trust of Providence. One thinks of John Lennon in conversation with *Daily Express* journalist David Wigg during his peace campaign in 1969: "We're all Christ, and we're all Hitler. We're all potentially divine, and potentially evil. We all have everything within us." Wigg asked about an interview where the pop star seemed to have said that he was God. *Did he believe that* *he was God?* "Not *the* God, not *the* God," corrected Lennon, "But we're all God, and we're all potentially divine, and potentially evil. We have everything within us. And it's no good blaming God for war because you can use the H-power, the atomic power, whatever it is, to light a room, or you can kill people with it with a bomb."*

It's now time to leave the philosophy behind and get down and into the period, and being in the spirit of the times, let's start at the end—or nearly the end.

---

*John Lennon was not at the time an Unknown Philosopher, but he was certainly, at the time, unknown *as* a philosopher.

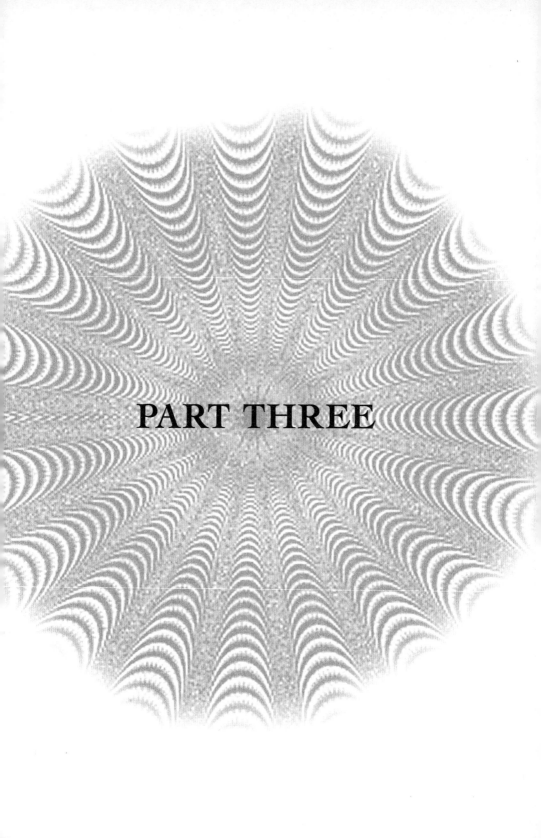

PART THREE

FIVE

Watertown

The end of hope . . . an imaginary place reflected in the puddle of a real one. *Watertown:* the setting for a near-silent little tragedy given voice through word and music. Watertown is in the far north of New York State, on the Black River, not far from the Canadian border. That is the real one, where the name came from. But the Watertown of art we see in a pen-and-ink drawing on the cover of a vinyl record planned in 1968 and recorded the following year. It is small-town America, a rural town. Our vision tapers to the horizon along an old single railroad track on scarred sleepers. In the distance we see the dot of a steam train whose smokestack casts a black plume that fades into a haze of morning drizzle. Watertown's little railway station with its water tower like a stilted dovecote is like so many old upstate railroad stations, mostly gone now, that once hugged the tracks that stretched northward from New York to the lakes and mountains beyond the urban experience: single-story brick, with quaint old chapel-like windows, gently pitched tiles, all cozy and human-size. To the left of the station, a little empty car park glazed with rain, square and tidy, and soon we are on Main Street, with three old cast-iron gas lamps standing polite sentry, aloof from the times that are "a-changin'." Though not all that fast, it might appear, in Watertown. As the title song tells us, there isn't much happening down on Main. If you want action, you've come to the wrong place. The people of Watertown like it like this.

Hugging close to a little deli with its nice striped canopy collecting

Fig. 5.1. The album cover for Watertown.

rain is a tiny fire station built in 1903 in a Spanish style. Now there's a brick, and there, a colonial-style house. A left turn brings us to the church with its modest spire, unassumingly calling for a blessing, but attracting only lightning. A few trees try lazily to match it for height. There's nothing taller in Watertown. Farther down Main, a hotel, bar, and restaurant combine in a sedate chalet, more trees, and what looks like a little Victorian school. Then . . . the hills, and you can smell the wet wood, vaporous leaves, steaming bark, and spice of wet fern and moss, as the steady downpour splatters and echoes. At the center of the scene, two children, very small, gaze at a distant figure standing opposite them in a raincoat, carrying something. Has the figure come off the train, or is the isolated figure attending on it? Is this a man, a woman, mother, father—or a ghost? The space between them betokens a void of pain and loneliness. That is the cover of *Watertown*.

Released on the Reprise label in March 1970, Frank Sinatra's impeccable, emotional, truly moving enactment of the music and lyrics of Bob Gaudio and Jake Holmes, respectively, failed to break into

Billboard's Top 100, and like many works of genius, received mixed reviews. There was nothing flashy about this beautiful record, no glossy snap of Sinatra socking it to the people, just the heart of America calling from a plain record cover, matte and gray, a quiet, unassuming work of art. In some respects, it is hard to believe, but nonetheless salutary to observe, that the deft orchestral accompaniment sessions recorded in New York for the album were completed precisely one week before the greatest out-of-this-world event of the decade: Apollo 11's gloriously successful, impossible-made-possible, faith-fulfilling landing on the moon's Sea of Tranquility. It looked to everyone as though things could never be the same again. Everyone could see there was tranquility in space, but precious little on Earth. Even in Watertown, tranquil and spacious as it might appear, softened by summer rain, there was melancholy anguish, storm of emotion, a tempest of longing and regret searing the soul that cut to the quick the dreams of the 1960s. And the TV-vivid Vietnam War is not alluded to at all.

What is the story, originally conceived in eleven songs with artful, but unmistakably Sixties melancholic-optimist sonic textures of violins, viola, oboe, piano, electric bass, spare electric rhythm guitar, horn, classical guitar, and what sounds like that late Sixties conceit: the harpsichord timbre of elegance and nostalgia. The story, however, is tough, and yet banal, too personal for national attention, the arrangements' spacey realism constantly severing the romantic feelings struggling to rise with the strings. Something's desperately wrong. Something's happened to Watertown. But nothing's obvious in the drizzle.

Listen . . .

Opening song "Watertown" sets the scene. We learn that this step-off-the-train-onto-old-wood community is a place where people settle who want to settle because they are settled. There's a lot of killing time; "no one's going anywhere." But no one's really lonely in "the shelter of familiar faces." Someone, however, is standing in the rain, someone for whom Watertown is going to be a very lonely place. We hear the grinding pistons and groaning boiler of the train that takes people away, and sometimes brings them back.

We now flash to a scene in a coffee shop with cheesecake and apple pie: the past. But this is no movie, with strings and blazing sunset to mark a romantic crisis. Normal life is passing as a man's life is ripped to shreds, quietly, with barely a word: "She reaches out across the table, looks at me, and quietly says goodbye." They avoid each other's eyes, "one still make-believing, one still telling lies." The woman says he shouldn't blame himself. The man cannot express what he feels. His soul slams shut, like a coffin, with the word that gives the song its title: "Goodbye (She Quietly Says)."

Lyricist Jake Holmes (b. 1939) explained what he was getting at in an interview for a 1995 CD rerelease:

> People are sitting in a coffee shop and devastation has happened. They don't articulate their feelings. Instead, they are putting sugar in their coffee and spooning cake. They are having a quiet conversation but meanwhile life is coming apart.[1]

In the next scene, we see (or hear via the song "For a While") how the stricken man tries to cope: the mask he puts up. The melody has an almost breezy rural charm to it, optimism tainted with melancholy and a hint of resignation, but the message is agonizing. He loses himself, or tries to, in the "day to day," a laugh here, a "kind hello" from there. Some small talk allows him to forget for a while that he's not "over you." He is actually addressing the absent love of his life, composing, as it were, a letter in his mind while he offers an "easy grin" to those he knows, while trying to concentrate on his work. And then he forgets, for a while, that he's *not* over her. Then he realizes he's gone a few days without feeling empty. Then it comes back. Jake Holmes explains the feeling:

> I've always felt that there is that moment in your life, when you forget about something that is really terrible. For five minutes the sun is shining and everything is beautiful. Then all of a sudden you realize that the person you cared about is gone, and it all comes back. It is one of those horrible things about grief—one of those little holes in grief when it becomes even more painful.[2]

People tell the man he needs company. If he's got some time, why not drop in and see a friend? But they too have forgotten that he's not "over you," and won't be "for a while" yet.

We now learn the terrible truth that *she* has abandoned him and their two sons, the mute subjects of "Michael and Peter." A family has been shattered. This pain will reverberate across more lives and lifetimes. He's composing another message to her, clearly hoping against hope that his evocation of their lives will stir in her a longing for her family as great as his longing for her and the forlorn completeness of the lives they once knew. He tells her that Michael has her eyes. Does she remember? And Peter is "like me," except when he smiles, and when you look at the two boys, they (the parents) are both of them. Come and share my vision, he is saying; come be a part of the whole once more: restore the shattered picture.

Spring was wet, he tells her, but summer was dry and the roses they planted last year have now ascended the wall. The house needs freshening up. Her mother's a "saint." She takes the boys out when she can, but "she sure needs a man." The obvious question goes unasked: "Doesn't *she?*"

Or has she found one?

For year on year he's been working for "Santa Fe." Another year without a pay raise and he's leaving. You can guess he's said that before, or meant to. But the air of Watertown "still has a country smell," and "you'll never believe how much they're growing." How can she *not* want to witness the children before they've changed forever?

Old "John Henry" came to cut the lawn and "asked where you'd gone." He's been told before but the old fella can't accept it. Well, that's the news, or at least, it's all he can say. Maybe "the words will come my way, tomorrow."

It's no good, "I Would Be in Love (Anyway)" announces that even if the man had known what was to happen, he'd still have fallen in love, and even if he'd known, he wouldn't have changed. For to have changed would have changed the man who loved her, and that love was the most precious reality he ever knew. And he wouldn't, couldn't change, if it meant losing that. And even though he knows "you'll never be with me" and "there are no words to say" he'd still be in love, anyway.

We now learn her name: "Elizabeth," and in the song of that name he glorifies her memory. She was "dressed in dreams for me," a dream come true. And now "a dream has to end," but it was real "not pretend." As far as he knows, she is what she used to be . . . *Elizabeth.* The name is repeated thrice in an effort to reach her, to conjure her back. Then he reflects on her (to him) mysterious character: "What a Funny Girl (You Used to Be)." We are in the soul of his dreaming, brought as close to his personal memory as a song could ever do. He knows how special she was. Can't she see how he knew how special she was? "I never met a person more sincere." She was a creative listener, and though a little naive, she was all he could ever want. What a "funny girl" she used to be.

Now, now we get a hint that maybe there was another involved. Maybe he's got to forgive something she's done. And maybe, if he can forgive, then it might just . . . "What's Now Is Now" is the lonely man's declaration that "just one mistake is not enough to change my mind," for what's now is now, and he'll forget, he tells her, he'll forget "what happened then." He's trying to say that he's been through the mill now, and he has accommodated what has happened, and he, anyway, is ready for a new start, with new understanding.

Something happens. She writes to him. He tells the children what's in the letter. She's sleeping well, has lost some weight. She's seen some shows. Lyricist Jake Holmes imagined that maybe the absent wife had talent and "wanted to be an artist or singer. He was a hometown person. His whole orientation was family and business. . . . She was more restless—a more contemporary woman. She wanted to do other things. She wasn't liberated enough to tell him, and she didn't think he would understand. He was basically a good guy, but she wanted more. She abandoned her family and went for a career."[3] The song is sung with virtually no accompaniment, and the voice is matter-of-fact. The fact is neither he, nor the children, now trust what Elizabeth is conveying in the letter. Each statement is preceded by the phrase "She says": "She says the city's strange." But what does that mean? Does she like its strangeness; does she want it? The weather's been cold in the city, and while there's been some rain "she says there's lots to see." "She hopes we're fine. So she says." "The price is high, High as the sky." And then the clincher, delivered with no joy: "She says she's comin' home."

The last song of the original selection of ten, "The Train," really tells the whole story, and delivers its dramatic climax. He's waiting at Watertown station. The sun has just broken through; he's hopeful. He can't have her coming home on such a rainy day! The children are on their way home from school, and now her train must have left "Ellensville"; one more stop! The excitement is palpable. There've been so many changes since she went away, and he's got so much he wants to say. She'll want to stay this time because he's spent nights working it all out—he even took a dive and went out and bought the summer cottage she fancied. Soon they'll be close, and they'll talk about the part of her he never understood. They're going to be like childhood sweethearts again, and he'll never let her cry. She'll know that he wrote many, many letters to her, a drawerful, but could never bring himself to post them.

We realize he's never really communicated with her.

The platform begins to fill with passengers for Allentown. He thinks he can see the train. The sun's now gone again, and his face is wet with heavy rain. Then the carriages fill for the next stop, and he's static on the platform. But he can't see her "anyplace" and he knows he'd recognize her face, however much she might have changed, but she's not there. Not there.

Never will be.

Devastating. The rerelease version of the album restored a final song, cut from the original. "Lady Day" reflects on the state of mind of the woman who just couldn't make it back up the line. There was just "too much pain," "too much to say"; "it's too late to say goodbye."

Frank Sinatra entered a Los Angeles studio for the recording of vocal overdubs to the music on August 25, 1969, precisely one week after Jimi Hendrix closed the Woodstock Music and Art Fair on the cool Monday morning of August 18. The long weekend Woodstock event at Max Yasgur's dairy farm at Bethel in Sullivan County, forty-three miles from Woodstock proper, brought an estimated 400,000 people

Fig. 5.2. Frank Sinatra, circa 1969.

together peaceably tolerating appalling conditions of cramped sitting, rain, mud, traffic jams, and poor sanitation to hear some of the finest rock acts in the Western world. Michael Wadleigh's movie would seal, even embalm Woodstock as a seminal event of the Sixties, a kind of sign of what was possible when young people of good will assembled. "No rain!" they chanted; "No war!" but neither the rain nor the war stopped on command. And on Monday they all went home. To paraphrase George Harrison's song "It's All Too Much" (released in late 1968), they were shown that they were everywhere, and then went home for tea (or coffee).

I rather imagine the rain that saturated the Woodstock Festival fell from the same dark clouds that overhung the imaginary "Watertown" further north in upstate New York, whose melancholy droplets covered the lonely man's face with nature's tears.

Unlike the *Woodstock* movie and album set, released two months after *Watertown,* Sinatra's album passed by virtually unnoticed, but today has signal relevance. The spirit of the new life the frustrated wife seeks in the city away from her traditional role spells a spiritual void for those left behind (perhaps she attended Woodstock with her new friends in the music-entertainment business). *Wartertown* tells a poignant, realistic story of the dichotomies and anguish at the human heart of arguably the most astounding decade in human history. Its adult protagonists undergo precisely opposite spiritual experiences of the same phenomenon: the apparent freedom of the one means lonely imprisonment in grief for the other. *No* grieving soul is free. The children, as ever, are caught in the middle. A sign more resonant to my mind than Woodstock, *Watertown* exemplifies the difficulties in seeking the spiritual meaning of the Sixties.

It depends on where you were.

SIX

1960: Dawn of the Era

To read histories of the 1960s, one might conclude that, at least to start with, everyone in 1960 was somehow in the same place, seeing the world from the point of view of the storyteller. The people of the world appear as receivers of news, organized by the powers that be. Of course that is not really the case, but history has an inherent tendency to flatten people out, even to make people mere spectators of great events of which journalists have been invited to make copy, while the consumers of news are forced to react this way or that by whoever wields the grip on levers of power and influence. If the world is a show, someone's got to watch it.

What kind of things were people finding on the front pages of newspapers or leading bulletins of radio and TV in 1960? Well, there wasn't, as we say, "a lot to write home about." Euphoria over the end of World War II in 1945 was short-lived. Great Britain, for one, was exhausted by the expense, and the weight of war was felt in households (and the national exchequer) even after the end of rationing of meat and bacon in 1954—a decade after D-Day. One feels in retrospect a great weight of black-and-white politics, monochrome images, and black-and-white attitudes. Gore Vidal once opined that Dwight D. Eisenhower's presidency proved that America could be run without a president. Real power in America seemed, to many, to be wielded by shadowy figures, obscure powers (all men), a determined plutocracy supporting by one means or another, what Eisenhower famously dubbed the "military-industrial complex." As war had released huge amounts of capital into the American economy in 1941, the economic value of extensive military capability was well grasped by unelected powers and their public spokesmen, justified by old-style appeals to patriotism and, of course, as always, employment, and the threatening stick of its withdrawal. The world "out there" was deemed a very dangerous place and Communism was assumed to be a cancer of evil that fully necessitated the tactical position of "mutually assured destruction" (MAD) in the event of outright hostilities. The "Bomb" kept the big war (USA vs. USSR vs. China) pleasingly cold, as the Italian proverb has it, like the dish of revenge preferred by people of taste.

So as the Sixties opened, the world's (theoretically) most powerful man was the same man who had commanded the Allied forces at D-Day in 1944. Had the war ever really ended in the minds of military men of Eisenhower's generation? One wonders. Certainly, maintenance of peace required threat of war, so large-scale war was never far away from politics or from the memories of most people of working age or in retirement. It cast a giant shadow.

The solution to the threat posed by "commies" to the Western world—and to the Far East as well—was a distinctively American idea of "freedom." That meant cash, enterprise, and "democracy" for all. Churlish perhaps to point out that the word never appears in the U.S. Declaration of Independence, democracy had come to mean, not mob rule as classically educated men of the eighteenth century had understood it, no, democracy was now a universal panacea for peace and prosperity, never mind that much of that prosperity came as a result of preparedness for war. "Praise God and pass the ammunition." In the light of American determination to widen democracy's compass, Great Britain and France were soon made to feel the heat. Eisenhower's predecessor at the White House, Harry S. Truman, had made it known that America had not assisted in the defeat of Nazi Germany so that the British Empire could make a comeback, even under the benign, paternal guidance of Sir Winston Churchill. With American rhetoric throughout the late Forties and Fifties encouraging self-governing democracy in the colonies and former colonies of Britain and France, political cadres pushing for independence flourished across Africa and the Far East at the very time British and French economies found themselves least able to stem the rising tide. Emerging new powers beheld an awkward choice between the jostling of superpower Soviet Communist "assistance," or superpower American capitalist-democratic "generosity." By the end of the 1950s, especially in the wake of the embarrassment of the British, Israeli, and French retreat from the armed attempt to retake the Suez Canal from Egyptian President Nasser (who had welcomed Soviet advisors and construction expertise) in the Suez Crisis of 1956, it looked even to conservative government in Britain and France that the great, once lucrative game of empire had had its day. This was seldom a welcome message to those who had fought and suffered to fight two world wars against a Germany determined to destroy or subdue any empire but its own. Those memories were vivid in 1960.

On January 21 of that year, French president de Gaulle sacked General Jacques Massu, commander of the Central Algerian Region. The popular Massu had criticized de Gaulle's Algerian policy, fearing Algeria's settlers, who had been "top dog" under French rule, would have to accept rule over them by majority Arab Algerians. White Algerians began to organize resistance. On February 10, insurgents surrendered, but the setback for resistance to de Gaulle was temporary, and quickly went underground.

The issue of Algeria's future bitterly divided French political opinion and that division threatened de Gaulle's idea of the unified French nation. Thirteen days later, British prime minister Harold Macmillan, having just been taunted as an imperialist on a visit to Nigeria, only to be baited for sympathizing with African nationalists in Rhodesia (now Zimbabwe), referred without bombast to a "wind of change." The South African government ought, Macmillan asserted, take into account the strength of African nationalism. With hindsight, Macmillan was serving notice that white minority rule in the continent was no longer inevitable. Britain herself had the fallback position of the "Commonwealth," a crown-capped prodemocratic international experiment to "cover" any psychological shock of empire loss while, positively, trying to moderate change, temper extremes, and with any luck, forestall Soviet and Chinese authoritarianism from gaining ground in what had been Britain's imperial possessions and dominions.

In general though, despite foreign disappointments, the British people by 1960 were feeling quite good about themselves, and there was a general expectation that despite winds of change elsewhere, overall things weren't bad and were arguably getting better as living standards visibly improved, so long, that is, as the leaders of the United States and USSR could relax their bellicose rhetoric and eventually abandon their ultimately destructive mutual sparring. Young people began to feel hints of that springtime sense that they were now "heirs" to the old, or rather new world, and began to feel, to varying degrees, freer to voice their views and create a rumpus from time to time. Similar feelings were manifesting around the world. Most people were fed up with living under the shadow of war, and more war. Whatever had happened to *fun?*

Youth ought to exist to remind us of this.

Fun, however, was not regarded officially in 1960, broadly speaking, as an unalloyed good, or even entitlement, especially of the young adult. At the end of January 1960, the new pope, John XXIII, opened his first synod in Rome with a warning concerning Roman Catholics' moral and spiritual health. They should resist temptation to watch "unsafe" movies and TV shows. Official religion and sexual energy were antipathetic; therefore, visual images of sexual allure were nothing to celebrate, only to deplore as deliberate attempts to subvert the physical and moral equilibrium of the believer: spiritual salvation was at stake. It was *that* serious. Glamorized aggression was also deemed a spiritual risk for believers, though scenes of killing, especially if stylized, were generally more acceptable than sexual scenes. There were many Catholics serving in armed forces and police roles. Sex was more subversive of Roman Catholic order than violence. The Catholic female ideal, of course, was the nun: totally buttoned up and absolutely desexualized, and the Mother of God whose breast was reserved for the infant Savior. Surrealists had subverted such images before, back in the 1920s, and would do so again, vividly, and to much wider audiences, in the 1960s with sporadic easing of censorship and broadening tolerances.

The Christian Bible sanctioned violence enacted by lawful authorities. Saint Paul advocated the Pax Romana of the old Roman Empire be ordained as consistent with God's purposes. Order had to be maintained for everyone's mutual benefit, and Caesar's administrators and armed forces were accomplishing God's will for human welfare even if those powers did not know it themselves. You weren't asked to like your oppressors, just love them. They too must eventually recognize Christ's lordship. Translated into the twentieth century, that meant that a civil power that recognized the Roman Catholic Church was not, in most circumstances, to be condemned absolutely by the Church. The implications of this fact, especially in South America, would be very great.

On March 11, 1960, in the Belgian Congo, riot police were present, but did not intervene when nationalist Patrice Lumumba spoke publicly for the first time in favor of Belgian handover of power in Africa. A little over three weeks later, demonstrations against the apartheid-imposing government of South Africa so unnerved the country's Boer administration that Prime Minister Hendrik Verwoerd at first relaxed some of the vexatious laws. However, when thousands of black South Africans demonstrated outside the police station at Sharpeville against a law on compulsory carrying of ID passes, government forces resorted to bullets. Machine guns were fired into the front ranks of the demonstrators, the ensuing carnage leaving an official count of fifty-six people dead, and a country in a declared state of emergency. Images of a bleeding child being carried by a traumatized parent fleeing from government guns shocked the world, drawing liberal sympathy to black nationalism and much opprobrium upon white minority rule.

The essentially left-wing usage of the word *liberation,* suggesting a collective breaking of chains, rather than the consumerist and American-style, individualist implications of freedom, entered the wind of rhetoric that whirled about Africa and through the news services, around the world. *Liberation* could have a strictly political meaning, but it carried a spiritual dimension as well: the formerly suppressed energy and hopes of those human beings who formerly had been kept down, or people who were still being kept down. The scope of the word would be extended as the decade marched on, when a collective dream would become an individual preoccupation. Technology, after all, could liberate people from manual work. Aye—and from their jobs too! It began to look like the bottle could no longer hold the genie. Glass would have to break.

The claim of would-be free peoples to govern themselves even insinuated itself into that old Hollywood staple, the biblical epic. On April 5, 1960, director William Wyler's magnificent *Ben-Hur,* starring Charlton Heston as the Jewish hero fighting a wicked empire—and himself—was awarded a record ten Oscars. They really don't make 'em like that anymore! While General Lew Wallace's original novel emphasized the spiritual transformation of Judah Ben-Hur from angry young man, so to speak, into a follower of Jesus's path of forgiveness of enemies, with bitter and utterly comprehensible hatred overcome by love, the script, credited to Karl Tunberg, and Heston's great performance, gave enormous punch to the hero's profound desire for "his people" to throw off the yoke and "stain" of Rome. It was clear that the zealous nationalism

Fig. 6.1. The movie poster for Ben-Hur, *1960.*

Fig. 6.2. Marina Berti and Charlton Heston in Ben-Hur.

that motivated Jewish revolt in the first and second centuries CE was alive and kicking throughout the contemporary world. *Ben-Hur,* nonetheless, while taking fully on board the "cry for freedom" that the hero declared so forcefully would be heard about the world when the wicked empire of Rome finally fell, still carried a powerful antidote to armed insurrection, political violence, and vain sacrifice against overwhelming odds: spiritual liberation from hatred and self-righteousness clothed in the Good Cause. A love that had been forged through spiritual ordeal, as firebrand Ben-Hur suffered, was no sentimental emotion, but a diamond-hard love that could transform not only himself and his family, but, by implication, the nature of political engagement too. Real love is the true sign of liberation. Love cannot live with fear and hatred: a tough doctrine.

One of my first childhood memories was feeling miserable, aged three, on a dark, rainswept morning inside our little house at Minworth during the school holidays, finding that because Mummy was ill, we couldn't go, as planned, to a special holiday showing of *Ben-Hur* at a cinema in Birmingham. Oh the disappointment! Having seen some stills from it in a magazine—the chariot race of course—even then my brothers and I knew we were really missing something very special. Combined with concern over Mummy's sudden inability to look after us, that shadowy, overcast morning would never be forgotten. I wouldn't see *Ben-Hur* until summer 1970 when it went round British cinemas for the last time. It was worth waiting for.

A fortnight after *Ben-Hur* wowed the Academy Awards in Hollywood with unforgettable images of the first Easter, when the bloody self-sacrifice of the Crucifixion generates a miracle for Ben-Hur and his family, Easter 1960 saw over five thousand people quit East Berlin for freedoms to be enjoyed in the "island" that was West Berlin, then geographically isolated in the middle of Communist East Germany. Such a large-scale exodus from East Germany would lead to the first erections of the Berlin Wall in August of the following year: a sign that the Communist bloc at least had every intention of keeping the genie strictly inside the bottle, however much it hurt. Communists believed their creed provided all the liberation the human race had any right to wish for: lose yourself in the alleged joy of the mass, for whom, if not *by* whom, the state was run. Socialism was in theory a realized nirvana in which the soul could be happily absorbed, with all bodily needs taken care of by brother and sister working for brother and sister proletarians, comrades all, free from envy, free from strife. *Ah!* Even leftist Anglican theologians, succumbing to "Christian socialism" would write in the Sixties, as if with divine authority, of the "hell of the unsocialized soul," reducing a metaphysical hell to a social-ist category, on the basis that individualism is just selfishness: one of those half-truths that can be so very dangerous. The notion of the indi-vidual finding absolute fulfillment in the "joy" of the group or collec-tive would be a dominant idea and subtext of the 1960s—sanctioned by numerous Christian theologians, Protestant and Catholic—that gave Communism, despite the facts of what Communist societies were actu-ally like, a persistent caché to some idealistic young people seized more by ideas than material realities, convinced that "real" Communism could work so long as it was done right! There aren't many voluntary communes left, but still plenty of voluble politicians who'd like to turn the world into one.

Fig. 6.3. A West Berlin police officer stands in front of the concrete wall dividing East and West Berlin at Bernauer Strasse as East Berlin workers add blocks to increase the height of the East German barrier, October 7, 1961. (Associated Press)

Fig. 6.4. Defecting East German soldier leaps over a barbed wire barricade at Bernauer Street sector into West Berlin. (Peter Leibing)

On October 22, 1959, the wizened alienist of Bollingen and Küsnacht, Carl Jung (1875–1961), was subjected to close-up interrogation by John Freeman for the BBC's *Face to Face* TV program. Unthreatened by Freeman's coldly analytic interview style, Jung spoke up for the mind and mysterious being of the individual. When Freeman suggested that it seemed the individual would find his fulfillment in absorption into a greater society, with echoes of Teilhard de Chardin's pseudomysticism—for was not that the way things seemed to be going?—Jung gently and smilingly insisted that, to the contrary, the individual would not, and should not allow himself to be swallowed up in some illusory greater whole, losing his soul. The individual, in the face of extinction by the mass, would refuse to be snuffed out; there was more to man than met the social theorist's eye, something remarkable in the being of the animal. The soul was a living thing, not a social receptacle. Jung was singularly prophetic here of a mood that came out of the Sixties but in terms of what appeared to be going on on the surface, was fairly muted during them. Jung's exciting and truly spiritually liberating prophecy of the vindication of the individual would only find sterling representation in the epoch-marking TV series *The Prisoner,* in 1967 and 1968: a series that at the time touched me more inwardly than any other, before or since. Jung got it right, and dogmatic socialism persists, even after all its failures, in getting it wrong. Perhaps the key spiritual issue of the Sixties concerns essentially the spiritual nature of the human individual. Jung's appearance on *Face to Face* was of course the famous interview in which when asked by Freeman if he believed in

*Fig. 6.5. Carl Gustav Jung
(1875–1961).*

God, Jung replied, bright-eyed and full faced: "I do not need to believe. I *know*." Jung had seen the century—and the light at the end of the tunnel.

Two realities, or one? Eleven days before Britain's Princess Margaret married society photographer Anthony Armstrong-Jones on May 6, 1960, ten black Americans were shot in Mississippi's worst race riot to date after "Negroes" gathered on a "whites only" beach. Six days later came another reminder of the pressures on young Americans, black and white. The *Frank Sinatra Show* decided to welcome the acceptable white face of rock 'n' roll, Elvis Presley, back from his crew-cut stint in the U.S. Army. Having done his "patriotic chore" Elvis was warmly welcomed by Frank amid hysterical screams of girls in the audience that hardly abated as the two men harmonized on "Love Me Tender." Now far from his mid-Fifties subversive image, post-army Elvis would be content to enter the heart (and what a heart!) of the U.S. entertainment mainstream, making a string of reasonably successful, undistinguished movies that added nothing to his kudos, but kept him and his entourage in home comforts through the disturbances of the decade.

It was perhaps more than hair that was cut short when working-class Elvis was drafted into a U.S. Army that many college students and professionals found ways to avoid, or flee from. By 1960 the limited U.S. draft was restricted to two years' service in a steady draft intake that would only accelerate by the mid-Sixties with deeper involvement in the Vietnam conflict. In the U.K., by contrast, conscription into the armed services declined steadily after 1957 and ended officially on December 31, 1960: a key event of the decade, and in retrospect, decade defining. This meant effectively that once a young person left school (between fourteen and sixteen for most pupils) the state had no grip on them, so long as they obeyed the law. The word *free* acquired a fresh aspect. Those pressed into the armed services in their late teens tended to have the "nonsense" knocked out of them and, however much they might resent it, had to acquire, at least for the duration, the habit of obedience. This would often make "civvy street" more challenging than it might otherwise have been, and would of course erect a psychological barrier between those who'd been through the military mill and those who had not. How many times was it said in the '60s and '70s: "He should've been in the army!" All that youthful energy and questioning of authority had to go somewhere. Unquestioning obedience would become for many young people an incomprehensible thing of the past. On the other hand, a number of people who'd experienced National Service in the armed forces would go on, partly in reaction, to develop anarchic brands of humor, transforming entertainment with more satirical and surrealist bite, while others (such as Britain's ex-National Serviceman and composer John Barry) would so relish his newfound, "demobbed" liberty as to pour enormous energy into musical innovation in jazz and rock-influenced pop music. Others who had "suffered enough," and found themselves sufficiently well placed, would become godfathers to prickly new talents in the 1960s and open doors to individuals who in the past would have had either to conform strictly, or leave the scene. Sixties artists needed such godfathers, and they appeared, usually unsung (to this day), to give a step onto the ladder to people who wouldn't have stood a chance in another class-ridden, conformist era.

What is even more critical to realize is that with so many young people freed from acculturation into "disciplined" armed services, not only did young people avoid the strictest forms of social conditioning, but it meant that they had little or no direct experience of war or serious conflict. Consequently, when wars were fought and conflicts erupted, such scenarios began to seem remote, strange, even surreal and bizarre, circumstances imagined, not experienced, their protagonists "off the wall" and possibly "insane." Conflict interrupted another conception of how life should be lived altogether.

One form of war, however, was somewhat more intimate in its character, being so indiscriminate, overarching, and fundamentally intimidating. Nuclear war was no empty threat. On May 26, 1960, a Big Four summit of world powers broke up when Moscow reported that a U.S. U-2 spy plane had been downed over the Soviet Union. Soviet foreign minister Andrei Gromyko charged the Americans with bringing the world to brink of war by its "military espionage and sabotage against the Soviet Union." Somewhat ludicrously, American ambassador Henry Cabot Lodge declared Gromyko's was a "fantastic allegation," while the State Department at first insisted there was no spy mission. This left poor pilot Francis Gary Powers in an uncomfortable position since he was the principal evidence. Powers would gain his freedom from Soviet incarceration in a spy swap on February 10, 1962. With Britain's Harold Macmillan as go-between, this spark that narrowly avoided the powder keg was snuffed out when Eisenhower canceled U-2 flights, while on June 30 Macmillan saw fulfillment of his "wind of change" prophecy when at Leopoldville, Belgium's King Baudouin participated in a ceremony to end Belgian dominance of the Congo as that country gained its independence. As so often in Africa, however, settlement was soon overtaken by disruption.

On August 4, as previously stated, I was born into this black-and-white world. Three days later, Fidel Castro, Cuba's leader since the previous year's revolution, seized American-owned property on the island, claiming justified retaliation for U.S. sanctions against his regime. That same day, unnoticed by news, in Hamburg's red-light district of St. Pauli, Liverpool club owner Allan Williams (1930–2016) introduced Indra Club owner, Bruno Koschmider (1926–2000) to the latter's new house band, delivered across the North Sea from England in an old van. They were John Lennon, Paul McCartney, Stuart Sutcliffe, George Harrison, and drummer, Pete Best. They were called the Beatles, and their first

Fig. 6.6. The Beatles in Hamburg, 1960.

gig at the tiny dock-area club was to back a German stripper to an audience of old wankers. The Hamburg experience would make the group the hottest band in Britain by 1963, and after that . . .

On September 14, 1960, while Liverpool's young rock 'n' rollers gradually ingratiated themselves into the comforts and contortions of Hamburg lowlife, cocooned from the world's attention and criticism, the Congolese army's chief Col. Joseph-Desire Mobutu arrested Premier Lumumba and President Joseph Kasavubu in a coup. The cause went back to Congolese independence in June when only eleven days after the ceremony, the copper-rich province of Katanga led by Moïse Tshombe seceded from the new country. When Lumumba dispatched troops into Katanga, Kasavubu sacked him for failing to consult. The Congolese army had already staged a mutiny only six days after independence in reaction to senior military positions being given to Belgians. When Col. Mobutu saw Lumumba sacked by Kasavubu, the coup took place, initiating a civil war whose reverberations continue today.

There was more wind of change on October 1 when Nigeria, Britain's largest African colony, became independent. By the decade's end, Nigeria would also find itself embroiled in civil war with a breakaway province.

Four days before Nigerian independence, American TV audiences in the millions saw presidential candidates John F. Kennedy and Richard M. Nixon face each other in a close-fought TV debate. Come the election result on November 9, Kennedy won the popular vote by less than half of 1 percent. By 3:20 a.m. Kennedy had thirty-one more electoral votes than he needed to win the election. JFK became president-elect of the United States.

Fig. 6.7. John F. Kennedy and Richard M. Nixon debate, 1960.

Kennedy's election came at just the moment when so much not only seemed to have been changing, but so much really was changing, though initial signs might have appeared small at the time. A week before Kennedy's victory, in London, a jury decided in a landmark case that D. H. Lawrence's novel *Lady Chatterley's Lover* (first published in 1928) was not obscene. The novel contained sex scenes, an erotic tryst between an upper-class lady and a working-class man, while the words *fuck* and *cunt* printed within its private editions had kept the book from public bookshelves until this year when Penguin boldly brought it before the public. Prosecution counsel did not help the case when he asked the jury whether they would let "their servant" read the book. What was good for the aristocratic goose was not acceptable for the working-class gander. The comment exposed a social division, and a profound attitude of distrust, that made the case extraordinary in the annals of British legal history. If obscenity was art or literature it was not obscene. This would open many doors for the release of previously controversial material, though it would take more than the decade to bring the greater panoply of censorship of public works down. But the seed was sown, and publicly so. D. H. Lawrence gained a belated fan base.

Another interesting comparison of changing attitudes, mores, and tolerances can be seen if we compare two records released while the obscenity trial proceeded in October 1960. October saw Frank Sinatra's beautifully crafted album of ballads *Nice 'n' Easy* top the Billboard charts. Meanwhile Sinatra himself was strutting his stuff with fellow members of the so-called Rat Pack: Peter Lawford, Sammy Davis Jr., Joey Bishop, and Dean Martin in Las Vegas. Their audiences were mostly fully adult to middle-aged and older, and the humor fairly sophisticated, risqué, sometimes race oriented, and colorful on the subject of booze, which was consumed on stage, as the men sparred with each other with cavalier liberty of movement and speech: alpha males on a bender. At the core of the entertainment bubbled brilliant skills in song and dance, perfected and honed over several decades of tough, professional gigs, public controversy, and high life.

By contrast, October 28 saw the release of one of the first British long-playing soundtrack albums. This was *Beatgirl,* and the composer was twenty-six-year-old producer and arranger, John Barry, born in York in 1933. The movie was a mildly scandalous tale exploiting gathering social fears about wayward teenagers—the concept of "teenager" having been imported from America along with Marlon Brando and James Dean, leather-clad attitudes.

Fig. 6.8.The Rat Pack (left to right): *Frank Sinatra, Dean Martin, Sammy Davis Jr., Peter Lawford, and Joey Bishop.*

In *Beatgirl* the drama erupts when the teenage daughter of a middle-class family starts hanging out (as we say today) with "beatniks," working-class lads who wear unconventional clothing, favoring Brylcreemed rocker haircuts, leathers, and spending much time drinking soda while dancing in loosely coordinated manner in London's Soho milk bars. There is an element of Soho crime involved in the story too, but for all that, the film technique itself, even in its day, was quite old-fashioned. The music, however, was something else. Determined to make a splash, John Barry harnessed Vick Flick's super twanging, moody electric guitar (already reaching for the distinction of the "James Bond Theme" that Barry would arrange in his own sweet, creative way in 1961) to some powerful jazz riffs and dramatic brass arrangements. Barry, ever prolific, also composed a number of rebellious-sounding, sweet and sexy songs for pop artiste Adam Faith and others to sing, all coalescing into an album of drama and attitude that still "kicks ass" today. John Barry would of course go on to become the greatest new influence in film music of the decade and shape our memories of many of the best cinematic moments of the period, and well beyond "the beyondness of things." And while *Beatgirl* was by no means his first record release since completing National Service in 1955, it marked a watershed in his career, and arguably marked a musical sign of the times. The Beatles, remember, were still between gigs in Liverpool and Hamburg, unknown utterly to the wider world, with no record deal in sight, and a whole lotta trouble with Bruno Koschmider and the Hamburg police to keep them occupied. They in fact resembled the beatniks that so worried the adults of *Beatgirl,* but that would change. The "beatgirls" of the famous Beatles would in just over two years turn out to be the polite, unthreatening daughters of all classes. They did scream though, which invited the accusation of "mania," but then, so had Frank Sinatra's bobby-soxers in the Forties. Screaming can be erudite when it comes to spotting talent.

And as if saying goodbye to a fast-vanishing entertainment landscape, Clark Gable, arguably the free world's greatest cinema heartthrob for over thirty years, died at the age of fifty-nine on November 16, 1960.

The Sixties had begun.

SEVEN

Plastic Fantastic

Many readers should recall the opening scenes of Mike Nichols's celebrated film *The Graduate,* starring Anne Bancroft and Dustin Hoffman. Hoffman plays Benjamin Braddock, a young man fresh home from college with all his future before him, *if only he could decide what to do with it.* Premiered in London on August 8, 1968, the film straightaway plunges us headfirst into young Ben's personal dilemma. A middle-aged business colleague of his father's—a "suit"—is confident *he,* a "successful man," has the answer to Ben's dilemma. At an outdoor pool party organized for Ben's homecoming, the avuncular businessman puts his arm round a nervous Ben's shoulder and, looking at him intently, tells his young charge with all seriousness that he has only one word to say to him. As though uttering the very secret of the world and Ben's future with it, the man's eyes widen as the word passes his greedy lips: *Plastics.*

Plastics.

Yup, that's where the bread is. Ben, however, does not feel himself raised in spirit to envision the plastic "City on the Hill" presented to him, for the glib imparter of this wisdom little understands that to a certain kind of young person whose kind had multiplied by the late Sixties, the word *plastic* had already acquired unfortunate connotations: soullessness, inauthenticity, unreality, hypocrisy, a repellent opacity, slipperiness, of things or people superficial, or meaningless, all betokening a spiritual void disguised beneath an illusory, shiny coating of alien cheapness.

Lamenting in 1966 following the famous "Beatles are more popular than Jesus now" controversy with its chilling consequences worldwide, that he now felt pressured *not* to tell the truth because it was so unwelcome in the world, John Lennon wished he could just say the truth without, as he put it, "all the plastic reaction" that left him standing "naked and truthful," alone, instead of being valued for his contribution to understanding, and free to go out on a limb with an intuition of truth because "it'd be worth it." *Plastic reaction* was clearly intended to be understood to mean the learned, automatic, unfeeling reaction of a phony world, where words were hollow and society was erected on a superficial opacity of false values, governed by unspoken rules that stifled life and truth and change and much else.

But what wrong had *plastic* done to be so implicated as symbolic or actual antithesis to spiritual authenticity, spiritual meaning, trustworthiness? Was plastic really guilty?

One of my very earliest memories was of going to someone's house in Birmingham when I was about three and seeing a large Huckleberry Hound figure. Huckleberry Hound was a blue-colored dog with a red bow tie, who stood up like a man and had a Southern (American) drawl, a cartoon character (voiced by Daws Butler) whose first show was launched by ubiquitous Sixties animators Hanna-Barbera in 1958, but whose detective adventures could be seen on TV throughout the Sixties in many countries. The inplastication of this figure was about half my size and quickly seized my appreciative attention. Its owner must have noticed he would make a nice friend for me, and "Huck" was given to me as a present. Huckleberry Hound was as plastic as he was hollow, and I loved him. What I find interesting in retrospect was that I had another toy. It was a gaudy tinplate dragon, or flying moth, in garish red and gold with a convex base that rocked like a rocking horse, and could take a child's weight for a ride in the imagination. Many toys had been made of tinplate throughout the century until the "last war" had curtailed tin supply to the industry, though Japan had regalvanized the tin toy trade until the late Fifties, though often with less finesse than prewar German toys. As I recall, the old tin rocker rather lost my interest when seen next to shiny Huckleberry Hound, whose relative newness

Fig. 7.1. Cartoon character Huckleberry Hound

was attractive, but so also were the clean lines and definite features of Huck, precise and identical to the image on the TV screen. Also the color: Huck was clear blue, while the image on our unstable screen was, of course, gray. The tin creature, by contrast, was indeterminate as a character. Neither was exactly soft to the touch. Plastic had precision, and this was just one reason why it would dominate, even "cover" or laminate the era with its unspiritual sheen. The Sixties was *the* age of plastics, push-button immediacy, robots, good and bad, and of course the Space Race, and all these elements melded into a startling, futurist aesthetic that pervaded every aspect of tactile reality, and that also precipitated a distinct spiritual reaction.

Through my child's eyes, however, I must say I never glimpsed any foreboding in all of this, and household objects that were so viscerally modern were not unwelcome. I think of myself in 1963, in our, I suppose, cold front room (no central heating in those days) between the tin bathtub on the wall that would be taken down and filled with hot water from the kitchen stove on Sunday nights for a bath, and the big, hot, valve-driven, aromatic television set with its frequently wavy images and annoying buzz, on which I would be captivated by Gerry and Sylvia Anderson's puppet series (in "Supermarionation," emblazoned before the titles) *Fireball XL5*. This superb production enlivened by Derek Meddings's realistic special explosive effects, first broadcast in the U.K. in October 1962 (in which month new group the Beatles entered the British Top Twenty with "Love Me Do"), concerned a brilliantly designed rocket, Fireball XL5, that could fly like a plane or zoom into uncharted space. It was commanded by a pop-star quaffed blond male hero called Steve Zodiac, supported by Marilyn-like Miss Venus and other willing assistants-on-strings, including a captivatingly transparent Robert the Robot with cool synthesized voice, alongside winsome alien creature Zoonie who today looks like a prototype for the sinister Gollum in the Peter Jackson–directed *Lord of the Rings* films.

Fireball XL5 was taken on whole by NBC in the States for their Saturday-morning children's programming between 1963 and 1965, introducing American audiences to the English pop theme "Fireball XL5" sung by Don Spencer, who crooned many a child's dream of the time: "I wish I was a spaceman, the fastest guy alive; I'd travel round the universe in Fireball XL5!" Its combination of R & B pop, aliens, robots, push-button plastic controls, all-modern glamour, and space technology makes it an archetypal TV series that meant, at least for children, that the decade's tense Space Race all looked pretty much business-as-usual, pleasantly gratifying to us even as it happened, for we "kids" (dreadful word), that is, we children, were already living in the futuristic universe and flying from star to star in handsome and untypical company, albeit with strings attached. There was now a reality divorce in the home: what was on TV *in* the home was like nothing in the home. So, anything that entered the home that resembled something attractive on TV was welcomed without question. New was good. New meant things were getting better, and the sky was, well, it was no longer the limit. Why, we could fly with Steve Zodiac to who cared where? The lid had come off the world. Alleluia!

THE GREAT PLASTIC, PUSH-BUTTON, ROBOTIC SPACE RACE

In 1948 the lid came off the first Tupperware storage products when Earl Tupper's company, founded in 1946, introduced its all-plastic kitchenwares to the general public, in particular to those wives and mothers targeted to profit from organizing Tupperware parties, garnering orders direct from friends and neighbors through the 1950s and beyond. When my family emigrated to Australia in 1966, and cash was in short supply, the kitchen was dominated by translucent Tupperware products: cheap, easy to clean, soft, modern, practical; how many sandwiches have been grabbed by hungry children from Tupperware tubs—that familiar sensation of white bread and smooth plastic alerting nondiscerning taste buds?

With oil in abundance, plastic usage rocketed after the war. While Tupper set up his business in 1946, U.S. inventor James Hendry's screw injection machine initiated new strides in the sophistication of injected and molded plastic. Polymer research brought low-density polyethylene to Tupperware and polyurethane to DuPont's "Lycra" invention. The 1950s witnessed plastic developments that would change the look of the world, not only in textiles and fashion, but toys and any number of domestic appliances and objects, including car bodies and furniture, that we today take for granted: the ubiquitous polyethylene bag, for example.

In 1950, Britain's ICI* factory at Redcar gave the world its first feel of Terylene, and in 1953 people experienced the drip-dry and no-iron textiles that stemmed from commercializing polyester fibers. Research into ABS (acrylontile-butadeine-styrene) copolymers led in 1954 to the Dow Chemical Company's invention of polystyrene foam.

In 1957 Knerr & Medlin of the Wham-O Toy Co. reinvented the hoop as the "Hula Hoop," giving the old toy a fashionably Hawaiian twist, if you'll forgive the pun. Danish company Lego patented its still-thriving toy-building system in 1958, its elements made first of cellulose, then later ABS polymer. Bang on time to woo the dreams of Sixties girls and girls thereafter, Mattel launched Barbie, the glamorous, affectionate, malleable plastic doll at the American International Toy Fair of 1959, right on the cusp of the new decade. Barbie was made for the Sixties, and women of all ages would be made up in her image. One wonders what the market would have been for a full-sized version.

---

*Imperial Chemical Industries.

Fig. 7.2. Barbie, the most popular fashion doll of the 1960s.

As the Sixties got into their stride the extra toughness and durability in high temperatures of polysulfones or thermoplastic polymers extended the plastics empire, with General Electric commercializing PPEs (poly [*p*-phenylene ether] thermoplastics) in 1960, while the introduction of aromatic polyesters and polyamides into textiles, carpets, sportswear, and the automotive industry carried plastics ever further into daily life.

All this innovation went hand in hand with a consumer boom that got going in the 1950s (though much later in the United Kingdom than the United States) and the appearance of the consumer: commercial target number one. The catch was always the same, more or less: cost and convenience. Tired of war, and most willing to forget about war's khaki drabness, the embrace of the modern felt to many an automatic survival impulse. The whole dream of intense labor-saving, push-button, in-your-face brightness all seemed in harmony with the color, light, and sunshine of the new nuclear-family, radiant, smiling, carefree, vacation-punctuated new era. On the horizon: robotics, the tease of a labor-free domestic life assisted by soulless mechanical-electric slaves. If the new domestics had no feelings, why should people need them? The era could have gone in an altogether colder direction than it did, for something would intervene into the progressive march of the robots.

I remember very well in the Sixties how my mother and father often complained about the adjective *fantastic* being applied to all kinds of people, experiences, and objects. I was regularly reminded that *fantastic* had always meant something quite unreal, a fantasy, vaporous, something essentially vain, dreamlike, or fanciful in nature. For example, if someone claimed to have encountered a being from another time that chatted in the garden, one could dismiss the tale as being evidently fantastic, without any hint of pleasure or surprised delight. Not any more; the idea now seemed to be that the dream could be a reality, and one could have one's expectations overturned any second by the latest new thing that proved progress was occurring and carrying everything along in its wake. *Fantastic!* This febrile respect for novelty let loose the over-brisk hyperbole of the adman into ordinary speech. Suddenly, quite commonplace suggestions were *great* and ordinary objects became *fantastic,* meaning pleasant or amusing. Another word that changed its meaning was *terrific.* I recall the first episodes of CBS TV's enjoyable, off-the-wall comedy *Mister Terrific* in early 1967, starring Stephen Strimpell as a government agent with extraordinary Superman-like powers. Whereas *terrific* had meant terrifying, it now meant, well, fantastic, and of course *amazing,* a word that originally entered the vocabulary from descriptions of the effect of Jesus's miracles in the Gospels. This all pumped up the overblown, hyped-up Sixties universe, as experienced in the ordinary domestic sphere, though frowned upon by beat and folk poets and their aficionados. The criticism, which we shall come to in due course, was by no means baseless. Emphasis on the objective material universe is bound to promote a spiritual deficit, for spiritual realities rely on essential substance and inner meaning: the rock that doesn't move, so to speak.

"WE'RE ALL GOING ON A SUMMER HOLIDAY . . . "

The aping of human characteristics by automatons has a long history, chiefly associated with toys and amusements, but futurists speculated on the idea that evolution of our own "intelligence" (or was it sheer laziness?) might make certain human characteristics effectively redundant, being replaced by mechanical, more "reliable" strike-free counterparts. No trade unions for robots! Why, they might even save us the trouble of thinking! Leisure was the promise. Holidays galore!

In 1954 George Devol invented a manually programmable and operated robot, the "Unimate." Devol's patent for the first robotic arm of its kind initiated the modern robotics industry. Sold to General Motors in 1960, Unimate was put to work in their Trenton, New Jersey, plant, lifting hot metal from die-casting machinery for stacking. Unimate never complained: always a good boy!

During the Sixties, such was the association in the public mind of plastics, robotics, and the space race that their developments now seem to march forward together as though joined at the hip. In 1960, DuPont launched ethylene-vinyl acetate copolymers (EVAs) to compete with rubber and vinyl products in flexibility. Everyone is now familiar with finding EVA foam in the packaging of sports equipment, and as a coating ingredient in water-based paints. Fast-drying water-based acrylic paints, launched in the early 1960s, would see the plastics revolution enter the world of fine art and bring contemporary opacity to canvases by Mark Rothko, Bridget Riley, Andy Warhol, Roy Lichtenstien, and Robert Motherwell, among many other artists working in the dominant genres of the 1960s. Yves Klein (1928–1963), for example, who looked kindly on the spiritual Rosicrucianism of Max Heindel, even developed International Klein Blue (IKB) in collaboration with Parisian art supplier Edouard Adam, with a polyvinyl acetate developed and marketed at the time under the name Rhodopas M or M60A by French pharmaceutical company Rhône-Poulenc as a synthetic resin used in the binder. Perhaps in part inspired by a surrealist take on robotics, in March 1960 ever-inventive Klein found he could distance himself from the act of painting by remotely directing models splashed in his patented color, turning the painting act itself simultaneously into what we only now familiarly call performance art.

While certain artists inspired by spiritual priorities explored inner space, outer space received the mechanical children of futuristic aesthetics. On April 12, 1961, Soviet news agency TASS reported that twenty-seven-year-old Yuri Gagarin had orbited the earth in Vostok; his revolution of the planet taking only 89.1 minutes—just about time for a long bath. We tend to think of the space race as science meeting politics, but we may also consider it as unintended art, since the exploits of the new astronauts also combined abstract, surrealist, Hermetic, and performance art: floating in space directed remotely by voice and push button. It would not be long before some astronauts reported having spiritual experiences to their friends while in the vacuum of interstellar space. The Apollo program was frequently described in biblical tropes.

Emphatically not to be entirely outdone (though it did look at the time that the "darn Ruskies" had won the space race and the propaganda competition), Alan Shepard was launched from Cape Canaveral on May 5 and became the first American in space. In order to have a second crack at the space race, President John F. Kennedy upped his modern-man credentials on May 25, 1961, by announcing the United States would put a man *on the moon* by the decade's end. That gauntlet would define the era, with unforeseen, and not entirely happy, consequences. Three days later, JFK backed his conviction that the future of the earth (and space) belonged to "free men" by approving the expansion of the U.S. Military Advisory Group in South Vietnam in response to North Vietnamese infiltration through Laos. As NASA went into space, the military-industrial complex went back to the jungle, with a vengeance.

On February 26, 1962, Lt. Col. John H. Glenn Jr. became the first American to orbit planet Earth. From his Mercury spacecraft *Friendship 7* (the name reference was to the mystique of the god, not the planet), Glenn addressed Congress after millions witnessed the launch on TV. Meanwhile, DuPont launched polyimide films and varnishes. Enhancing the burgeoning electronics industry, polyimides would find application in cables and spacecraft. More mundane enhancements, though in some expectation of gravity defiance, 1962 also saw saw the launch of silicone gel breast implants. Barbie, however, passed when it came to additional injection molding. Size didn't matter *that* much— not yet at least.

*Fig.7.3. The crew for the Mercury Seven spacecraft
(Courtesy of NASA).*

Less than five months after Glenn's orbit, the U.S. Telephone &
Telegraph ground station at Andover, Maine, received seventeen minutes of signals from the Telstar communications satellite on July 11. A
$50 million project from AT&T, the next day would see the first broad-
casts from Europe to the United States via Telstar, the satellite that gave
its name and achievement to Margaret Thatcher's favorite pop record,
an instrumental recorded in London by Joe Meek and the Tornados,
which topped the Billboard Top 100 in December 1962. If Sixties
"Progress" had a tune, this was it: thin-sounding, electronic, spacey,
clean, driving, optimistic.

Top of the U.S. charts on June 16, 1963, was Japanese crooner
Kyu Sakomoto's performance of "Sukiyaki," whose first lines translate

as "I look up when I walk," and well Sakomoto might have done, for above him—and every other living soul on Earth—floated Valentina Tereshkova, the first woman in space: a triumph for the USSR and for women everywhere. Many an American husband would have loved to see his wife achieve similar heights, but perhaps stay up there even longer, that is, if we accept the provocatively hilarious rhetoric of the contemporary popular Jack Lemmon and Terry-Thomas comedy on chauvinism, *How to Murder Your Wife* (1964).

Developed to help handicapped patients at the Rancho Los Amigos Hospital in Downey, California, the "Rancho Arm" robotic limb was purchased by Stanford University in 1963. The following year Gene Amdahl and team's IBM System/360 computer was announced. Heralded as a major leap in speed and power from its predecessors, it brought serious computer power into business settings. The year 1964 would also see artificial intelligence research laboratories opened at MIT, Stanford Research Institute (SRI), Stanford University, and the University of Edinburgh, Scotland.

On June 3, 1965, Major Edward White took a fourteen-minute walk in space: a first for America, but not the world, Soviet cosmonaut Alexey Leonov having stretched his legs in that dimension on March 18. Nine months later, American astronauts secured the extraordinary feat of bringing Gemini 6 and Gemini 7 to within ten feet of each other while in orbit, an achievement followed up on June 3, 1966, with the landing and taking off from the moon of an unmanned U.S. spacecraft.

Fig. 7.4. Commemorative stamp of Soviet cosmonaut Alexy Leonov on the first spacewalk, 1965.

On August 18, NASA received the first pictures of our planet from the moon's orbit.

The year 1967 began badly for the protagonists of the Space Race. On January 27, three U.S. astronauts were burnt alive in a shocking flash fire while Apollo 1 was still on its launchpad. Just under three months later, Soviet cosmonaut Vladimir Komarov was killed when his spacecraft crashed after reentry into Earth's atmosphere. Undaunted, both sides redoubled efforts to win the glittering prize, while public interest in the space race intensified. By the end of May 1967, seven million people had visited the world-renowned Expo '67 in Montreal, Canada, the U.S. lunar exhibition being one of the most popular attractions of the massive show. Meanwhile, the burgeoning psyche-delic sensibility seemed to have definitely touched plastics development when Scolari, De Pas, and Lomazzi unveiled their polyvinyl chloride (PVC) "Blow" chair. This bubbly inflatable armchair, manufactured by Zanotta in a variety of very bright colors, soon became the "in" furni-ture for any scene vying for cool modernity. Glowing color photos of exceptional vividness promoting the chairs showed Veroushka-like long-legged models wearing "space-age" costumes, with very short skirts, draped over the airy objects in different natural and interior settings, as though the far-distant future had already arrived: a common illusion of the time, and one very sadly surrendered as the years went by.

Offering no visual competition to the fantastic(!) models of the era, Marvin Minsky's Tentacle Arm of 1968 was computer controlled, with twelve "stoned-free" joints operated by hydraulics.

The end of 1968 was suitably graced with the return of three U.S. astronauts who had become the first human beings to orbit the moon on the Apollo 8 mission, experiencing its real "dark side" before Pink Floyd ever ventured there. I well recall the Bible reading of Genesis 1:1–10 (God's Creation) in the King James version the astro-nauts gave to their global audience on Christmas Eve 1968, along with the moving wish that we "on the good Earth" had a merry Christmas with God's blessing. We wished them the same, and hoped they'd return quickly to end the suspense their adventure precipitated in the sensitive. And I remember the snow started falling on Christmas Eve outside our flat in Sutton Coldfield, the first snow my family had seen in some three years, having emigrated to Australia two years earlier. Ah! But what a time!—a promise of biblical fulfillment almost tangible in the crisp night air.

And soon it was 1969, with high expectations. In that year, mechanical engineering student Victor Scheinman gave the world its first electronic, computer-controlled robotic arm, dubbed "the Stanford Arm." It made old Unimate, with his instructions stored on a magnetic drum, look positively antique. In this aspect, 1969 was not the end, but the beginning of an era. Between 1968 and 1972, the then Stanford Research Institute perfected "Shakey," a robot that could, using a vision system of TV cameras, sensors, and laser rangefinders, allied to an external computer system, reason about its surroundings and respond accordingly. One of the development by-products was the A* search algorithm, now essential to internet services. Shakey's prototype first appeared in the *New York Times* in 1969.

Over at Japan's Waseda University in that year, Professor Ichiro Kato gave WAP-1 to the future, the first biped robot, replete with air bags that stimulated artificial muscles.

Using only his own, Neil Armstrong took a "small step for man" 238,000 miles from home, yet seen in real time by 600,000 TV witnesses on July 24, 1969. His colleague, 33rd-degree Freemason Edwin "Buzz" Aldrin, took Communion on landing, with scripture read off-air. Coming "in peace for all mankind," the astronauts saluted Old Glory amid the "stark beauty" of the lunar surface. Appropriately, the U.S. flag was made of nylon.

Christmas 1969 was one of the most memorable of my life. I was home, too briefly, from boarding school and was thrilled when I was given what I had asked for: a space capsule of my own. This was not a NASA castoff, but a superb toy made by Palitoy for their exceptionally brilliant range of "Action Man" equipment that, in those days, was distinguished by a remarkable range of products with impressive authenticity of fabric and design, all made possible by the plastics revolution, which brought real history into the hands and imagination of every boy who had the good fortune to possess the glorious fruits of Action

Fig. 7.5. Astronaut Edwin "Buzz" Aldrin on the moon, 1969.

Man's ever-expanding catalog. The Space Capsule, in which my astronaut Action Man could enter and go to the stars, was completely plastic, could "splash down" in my Sunday night bath, and take off as far, and for as long, as I could hold it aloft. I had joined the Space Race, which, at the time, looked like it still might never end, despite America's having plainly won the contest of the decade "for all mankind."

And at this point I simply must make the case for the use of plastics in toys, especially during the 1960s, for while plastic has undoubtedly acquired connotations of cheap tackiness in many areas including the decidedly unmagical toy industry of today, a good, loved toy is a talisman. It is a link to another world. It stimulates the one essential faculty that joins us to the spiritual world. William Blake described poetry, painting, and music as the "three powers for conversing with Paradise that the Flood [of time and space] did not sweep away." These are three avenues to the Divine Imagination, the life of God in us. Great toys enabled me to travel infinitely in time and space, envisioning and participating in my own mythologies of life and action. Why, I even composed my own music, music I would sing to myself while immersed in what adults call "games" and "playing" but really can be as eloquent and as meaningful as ritual, and a precious realm that is one's own in a world that eventually claims everything.

Many of my happiest early memories are in some way connected with the late, much-lamented lost temple of toycraft that was Gill's Toyshop, on the Parade of Sutton Coldfield, Warwickshire, England, a palace of impending joy that had stood there for some decades, run by the legendary, elusive Mr. Gill, who had built up a shop to rival Hamley's in London's Regent Street, or FAO Schwarz, New York, and that I preferred to either of those, or even to Australia's now vanished Tim the Toyman in Melbourne, at whose altar I had also regularly communed in 1967–1968.

I remember Gill's so well, with its name in big red, lyrical script flowing across a muted green background as though just signed by the giant hand of its originator. I remember the detailed layout, upstairs and down. How did they contrive to get so much in?—the books, the model soldiers, the model cars, the plastic zoo and farm animals, the "floral garden" kits of incredible detail, the construction kits of every imaginable kind, the model airplanes, the dolls, the *Doctor Who* Daleks of every size, even life-size, the Action Man section, copious, always surprising, the model paints and glue department, the board games and multifarious card games, the joke items: every child's dream had its correlate there. Very heaven sparkled throughout that shop, whose holy day was Saturday when clutching our pocket money we would go to its collecting plate and exchange our shillings and pennies for joys untold, and not a word of condemnation. How one hates a world that can let such things pass away, replaced by the dull round of parasitic mediocrity. Let there be Magic. Unless ye be as these little children, ye cannot enter the kingdom of heaven.

While I craved Action Man above all (I had my first Action Man in 1964 from I believe the first British batch from America, as a gift on emerging from an eye operation at the hospital in Lichfield), my brother Victor, five years older than I, was particularly attached to the exquisite craftsmanship of the Britain's Ltd. "Swoppet" series. His favorites in this line of now-rare collector's items were the American Civil War figures, and the fifteenth-century knights. These figures (the mounted knights were the size of the average index finger) all had detachable components, including the colored "favors" flowing from helmets, swords, daggers, metal scabbards, crossbows, heads and bodies that twisted, and many other beautifully molded details, such as the Tudor roses on pennants, or daggers in exquisite metal and painted scabbards. In 1965 and 1966 the BBC showed a series of Shakespeare's plays under the collective title *The Wars of the Roses* and the Britains knights range received a leg up in free publicity. We were all fascinated by the history that went with the toys and read in *Ladybird* illustrated children's books about the medieval *Warwick the Kingmaker* (from our county) and *Henry V,* and got a sense of our own county's and country's history and what things had taken place in a past that now seemed incredibly vivid to us. Play? Toys? I don't think so. These were gateways to understanding, part of the foundation of our developing minds. And we joyed in it all out of our own initiative.

Whenever I hear Sir William Walton's setting of Joseph Canteloube's *Songs of the Auvergne* entitled "Touch her soft lips and part" from Olivier's *Henry V,* I am reminded of those toy soldiers and the old, leafy Warwickshire, of which our town of Sutton Coldfield was once a part, before party politics tore it away and conglomerated its unique flavor in a conurbation called the West Midlands in 1972 with the usual utter lack of imagination or spiritual sensitivity, or indeed any other virtue, such things being unknown to politicians, planners, developers, and the rest of the barbarians who have despoiled our, and practically every other modern nation. For the love of money is the root of all kinds of evils. Did Britains Ltd., make these wonderful figures for money? Aye, but not for money alone, you see. They wanted to show how new plastic technology could really improve on what had gone before, with artistry, dedication, and imagination. They wanted to be the best. Couldn't they have done it more easily, cheaply, as toy manufacturers now do, so blithely? They were for profit all right, but not at the price of pride in craft, the honor of the name, the faith of the purchaser, the decency of the maker: the love of God and the fellowship of the Holy Spirit. Amen.

Certainly, many of the toys made in the Sixties do not deserve the negative connotations that began to accrue to the word *plastic*. And though to describe a woman as a "Barbie doll" is not necessarily the kindest remark one could make, it does not necessarily reflect on the value of the doll itself. Indeed, when people talk of someone as a "Barbie" they are probably emphasizing the aspect of cosmetics, and when we talk of a change being merely cosmetic, we know very well what we are talking about. The smoothing over of natural skin with chemically synthesized unguents in pursuit of what is oddly called "beauty," in terms of "beauty products," is hardly a feature of women-oriented marketing peculiar to the Sixties. And yet it would sometimes seem so. This was largely due to the reaction against plasticity associated with youth movements of the mid- to late Sixties, when hippies rejected the uniform of the mass-market culture, opting for what would also become something of a new uniform of certain kinds of dressing up, or dressing down, in response to which a famous cosmetics firm in 1969 launched a facial make up for women that was *invisible!* Yes, it still looked as if you had your own natural skin, but now it was natural skin somewhat "improved"(!) by the new paste; distinctly contrary to the beauty ethic of going *au naturel,* with all the suggestions of long-haired Edenic innocence and unselfconscious nudity: free from both sin and responsibility (wishful thinking perhaps!).

It was a wonderfully clever stroke of Mike Myers's Swinging Sixties spoof movie *Austin Powers* (1997) to combine the malevolent, sinister image of 1960s robotics (viz: the Cybernauts of TV series *The Avengers;* the Cybermen of the BBC's *Doctor Who*), with the cosmetic, "plastic" image of the Barbie doll in Myers's take on 007's enemy Blofeld, Dr. Evil's latest weapon (designed by Nazi leftover Frau Farbissiner), the "Fembot," who in PVC miniskirt and hairsprayed-to-death blond bigwig, advances in formation with sister Fembots to the tune of

Nancy Sinatra's 1966 hit "These Boots Are Made for Walking" before showering enemies with rapid-fire bullets emitted from machine-gun barrels, doubling as erect nipples protruding from silicone implanted breast emplacements. They just slayed 'em. *And all because . . .* well, it wasn't for the lady who loved *Milk Tray,* it was the launch of Barbie on the world in 1959.

In the poetic mythology of William Blake, opacity is always identified with the figure Urizen, a blind demiurge, false god who is abstracted Reason whose blind (spiritually blind), egotistical logic bounds the universe, whereas the universe of the imagination is unlimited and

Fig. 7.6. Urizen in William Blake's watercolor etching, The Ancient of Days

boundless. Opacity is always covering something, and of itself, has no *depth,* therefore little *meaning,* being only surface, however attractively shiny or reflective it might be. We normally associate shine and glow with something within that is projecting life, light, heat, or plain energy: a pink face glowing with health, unbound by cosmetic enhancement. A star glows because it is the light of a fire within. Plastic shininess is all mirror reflection of alien light on a superficial screen. Opacity suggests unreality, and in an era where the unpleasant aspects of plastic were quickly exploited—fake leather for example billed as "leather-feel" or such euphemisms, or "plastic wood," formica, and the like, made to look *like* wood—plastic soon entered the firing line of the person who wanted spiritual genuineness, authenticity, that is, truth: love, not a manufactured smile, however superficially seductive. Hippie philosophy challenged the *face* of the modern world, and as such was a correlate of the spiritual critique of human hypocrisy.

In truth, something was being covered. It was, amongst other things, past history. In the Fifties many had a deep need to cover over bitter, painful memories of war and loss. Coats of paint were needed everywhere, even the face, if necessary. But many young, sensitive people, postwar children, growing up in the opaque world of comforting superficialities became, understandably, and with some prodding by hallowed culture figures, increasingly irritated. *What was behind the image?* One thing that was behind the image, and the surface, was a war in Vietnam where real people were getting mangled, crippled, shriveled, vaporized, and in many other ways, killed. By 1967, there were something like half a million Americans involved in the war, while opposition to it had moved from purely moral objections to war itself and the justification for America's part in it, to a greater awareness of self-interest as new arrivals at colleges and universities, keen to embrace the sunny love vibe emanating from pop music, felt the chill prospect of the draft, despite the fact that the greatest number of draftees came from black working-class homes. In the light of this, the persistent opacity worked both ways. Images of opacity and superficiality were pervasive, but also seductive. If you chose to inhabit the new, modern plastic techno-advantageous environments, one could soon imagine that the war (in this case World War II) was more "past" than it really was; people were thus apt to be misguided, led on by futurist dreams of progress, led away from uncomfortable truths that some young people, and older pundits, were only too happy to expose, unpleasantly peeling away the Elastoplast from the unhealed wounds of yesteryear. Faced by TV news with more images of actual war as America's involvement in Vietnam deepened after JFK's assassination in 1963, the new era's visible and visceral modernity clashed rather violently, and also in surreal fashion, with images and realities of a war that in too many respects didn't seem to have changed since the days of Korea in the Fifties and Guadalcanal and Iwo Jima in the Forties. More choppers beat the humid air of course, the war's oft-repeated aural analog. But in the main, the Far East war did not look very modern or stylish; it looked alien and messy, even intrusive on the consumer party. While the patriotic motive for military service was compelling for many, there was a burgeoning dissonance between traditional values of duty and much else, and a growing sense of questioning and mutual identity among the young, inspired by a growing popular culture that passed many parents by. The surrealist aspect of juxtaposition was captured both on TV at the time to some minds, and in much later reflective movies such as Francis Ford Coppola's *Apocalypse Now* in 1979, where in one scene a TV news director "captures" the taking of a Vietcong stronghold by Airborne Cavalry on film, while telling soldiers passing the lens not to look at the camera, but to "look like you're fighting!" One might conclude that the media was not "capturing the war" but rather its participants, and its meaning. Adding the music of the Doors and the Rolling Stones only made the "trip" appear more absurd, but which?—the movie or the Real Thing?—which observation brings us not to Coke, that well-established beverage of peculiar properties, or to what French director Jean-Luc Godard called "the children of Marx and Coca-Cola" (referring to Sixties youth in France), but to Frank Zappa's contemporary observations on what he saw was actually happening in President Lyndon B. Johnson's vaunted Great Society—the Great Society being LBJ's USP (unique selling point), voiced at his second inauguration on January 20, 1965.

Johnson's big sell was an inclusive vision of a national society

Fig. 7.7. Frank Zappa (center) and his band, The Mothers of Invention.

working together as a whole and valuing all members of whatever race, creed, or color. In practice this meant government-promoted housing developments, money into education and training, infrastructure investment, and jobs, and a progressive ethic of nondivisiveness. Unfortunately, much of this would be undone by LBJ's other policy of expanding U.S. commitment to combatting Communism in Vietnam, where the generous social contract boiled down to lump sums paid to poor black parents of sons killed serving their country.

Frank Zappa, a remarkable individual in many respects, and despite his long hair, individual appearance, and free-thinking intelligence, was emphatically *not* a hippie, but rather a "freak," and while the designation was an obvious reversal of a poorly focused society's judgment of the unusual, it was also a positive flag of identity. Freaks were individualists, thinking for themselves, expressing themselves, and feeling free to comment on all groups who, in the view of the freak, suffered from collective myopias and lack of insightful analysis into the demented world about them. Freaks had individual minds, out of step with conformities, the kinds of minds progressive psychologists saw as ideals to combat previous generations' tendency to fall unconsciously in line with fascistic dictators or fundamentalist give-it-to-me preachers.

The word *plastic* clearly gripped Zappa's conception of what he was up against, views emitted in the lyrics to "You're Probably Wondering Why I'm Here" on his July 1966 debut LP release, *Freak Out:*

> *You boogied all night in a cheesy bar*
> *Plastic boots and plastic hat*
> *And you think you know where it's at?*
> *Yeah!*

Zappa's dismissal of the plastic insincerities of the world around him (including the youth scene) was even more explicit on his album *Absolutely Free,* released on May 26, 1967, where in the song "Plastic People" he addresses his "Fella Americans," including the president of the United States, in uncompromising terms:

> *A fine little girl*
> *She waits for me*
> *She's as plastic as she can be*
> *She paints her face*
> *With plastic goo*
> *And wrecks her hair*
> *With some shampoo*
> *Plastic people*
> *Oh Baby now You're such a drag.*

Of course, to hear this as it was intended, you'll need a piece of plastic called a vinyl disc, which, like the society Frank Zappa described above, had a hole in the middle. Turn it on and watch the revolution.

EIGHT

Psychology

Our thesis is that self-actualization is a more generic term for what Heilbroner refers to as "self-indulgence" and the uttering of "extravagant and heretical thoughts." We need not assume the cataclysms and consequent future of Heilbroner and others who have made similar predictions to appreciate how great is the wealth needed for a society to provide for the physical conditions of self-actualization for even a small proportion of its people. Americans forget that they are, in terms of wealth, the upper upper class of the world. The college campuses and youth culture in the United States in the last two decades have shown all the frivolity and arrogance of the courts of the ancien régime. Like the French court, but on a larger scale, there has been in them little awareness of the fragile basis for the prosperity being enjoyed and of its dependence on people living far away. Instead it is seriously proposed that self-actualization be a universal ethic for a future that is likely to raise the question of sheer survival. By comparison, "Let them eat cake" shines as a statement of compassionate realism.

Paul C. Vitz,

Psychology as Religion:
The Cult of Self-Worship, 1977,
"Selfism and Today's Society," 63

Obviously, one could write several volumes on "Psychology in the 1960s" and it would undoubtedly have its interest and its audience. Psychology is still taken very seriously, and lots of young people choose it as a territory for their higher education, my wife at one time having been among that number. So if you've just started or finished your thesis on some critical aspect of this subject, you will probably find this little chapter exceedingly slight, undoubtedly subjective, and might conclude that the author should keep his ill-informed snout out of a near-sacred arena. Well, the spiritual meaning of the 1960s would certainly be lacking something in its exposition if I sidestepped this particular mantrap altogether. And I am not ashamed to say that I still hold with my medieval forebears the conviction that "Theology is the Queen of the Sciences" and thus entitled to its purview on any subject. Of course, Dame Theology did not rule alone, but with her sister Wisdom, the essential root of philosophy, which is, after all, the love of wisdom, which has also, I'm afraid, been the root of a number of evils.

The advance of psychology might be considered one of the great success stories of the twentieth century. It began, you may recall, with a number of very bright students, working in special hospitals, mainly in Europe's capitals, studying the clinical problems of the insane, which, for our purposes, means in this context people whose behavior rendered them an intolerable burden upon those around them. Naturally, many theories had grown up over the centuries to account for the odd and frequently alarming conduct of the "mad." Usually there was a type or types of behavior over which the mad person could not exercise control. Where this conduct made life dangerous or intolerable either for the sufferer or those around him or her, restraints or incarceration became necessary. One may remember the madman of Gadara (Mark 5:1–20), who, whenever bound or chained, was able to loosen himself and howl to the distress of those about. When Jesus casts out the legion of demons that had possessed him, the spiritual creatures take refuge in swine that promptly hurl themselves from a cliff. Behind this account is a whole theory of the nature of insanity in terms of "possession," much of which was held with due seriousness by doctors and lawyers for a great many centuries.

The widely regarded founder of psychoanalysis, the Austrian Sigmund Freud (1856–1939), studied medicine and neurology in Vienna, and drew many of his case studies from women deemed "hysterical" or women who considered themselves in some way disturbed and unable to lead contented lives. There were in the late nineteenth century competing ideas to explain very different mental states, and there was much debate about the role of the *spirit* and the whole question of the nature of the *psyche,* a word whose origin we examined in chapter three.

Freud's distinction lay in the extraordinary lengths to which he was prepared to go to propose and insist upon an unsparingly rational approach to the human mind within the sensible natural order, holding that the human psyche could be objectified and its character classified according to intellectually agreeable psychological categories. To Freud we largely owe the now common usage of words like *ego, superego, id, transference,* and *libido.* The ubiquitous *neurosis* goes back at least to the eighteenth century and referred to disorders linked to the nervous system. Freudian *neurosis* generally refers to some mental distress or discomfort, though without any loss of reality contact, or any hallucination (the latter symptoms would indicate *psychosis*). As Yoko Ono put it succinctly on the album *Milk and Honey* (1984): "Psychotic builds a castle, neurotic lives in it." Neurotics might, however, be unable to make accurate judgments, being driven by fears of one kind or another. Nevertheless, a neurotic is able to talk about symptoms of what may be an imaginary rather than pathological disorder. However, of course, the moment we make such distinctions as *imaginary* and *pathological* we enter into a philosophical quagmire. That is, if mind may be seen as a manifestation of matter, cannot the reverse be held with equal conviction? We can only fairly conclude that we have a mind, and we perceive matter.

Enthusiasts for Freud's work flourished between the world wars and particularly after the last war. People were in some need of explanations as to what had happened to humanity; how could we explain it all, if, that is, one had found traditional religions inadequate to the purpose. Freud's particular conception of the "unconscious" was attractive (a psychic cellar for secreting away—consciously or otherwise—unwanted, embarrassing, repressed, or taboo knowledge, fears, and memories), as was his psychological treatment of human tendencies to violence and sexual drives. He also allowed people to take their dreams more seriously as indices of unexpressed wishes, symbolic self-messages, and even life guides. However, there can be little doubt that in popular understanding what distinguished Freud, and gave him the seductive patina of modernity, was the liberation of sex from an automatic discourse of sin and punishment. "Guilt" was understood as derived from something we put above ourselves, and then subject ourselves to, for the "God" of tradition in Freud's view was an ancient fantasm that haunted our species. Freud attempted to uncover the origins of religions in psychological experience. This was all a very long way from the very useful dedication to curing the pains of the insane. Most people who got involved with the works or followers or commentaries on Freud were likely to come away with the idea that human beings are all to some extent mentally ill, and incapable of an ideal "sanity" (that is, psychological cleanliness and freedom from disabling psychological defects). If we were sick, we needed doctors, and guess who the doctors of our newly diagnosed sickness might be? Yes, Freudian analysts. We could, with expert guidance, make a lifetime's effort to "talk it all out." The end would be guilt-free acceptance of "reality." Reality is of course the fundamental problem of psychology. By the 1960s it was held with a jolly sense of conviction that "normalcy *is* neurosis," a curious conclusion for the (presumably neurotic) psychologist to make, not really so far from the pessimistic Christian confession that "there is no health in us."

It was commonly held by those touched with the argot of psychology when I first attended university that civilization itself was the *result* of neurosis. So much for the classics! A theological colleague at university informed me one day that Saint Paul was a neurotic, and that pretty well summed it all up—and once told, one never forgot it.

Many of these ideas had taken firm root by the time of the 1960s, elaborated upon, or disputed fundamentally by any number of big-name psychologists and analysts, among which coterie I may be forgiven for excluding some favorites when I name but the following predominant lights of the field: Carl Jung (1875–1961), Alfred Adler (1870–1937), Otto Rank (1884–1939), Karen Horney (1885–1952), R. D. Laing (1927–1989), Wilhelm Reich (1897–1957), Erich Fromm (1900–1980), Abraham Maslow (1908–1970), Rollo May (1909–1994), Carl Rogers (1902–1987), Arthur Janov (1924–2017), and Ernest Becker (1924–1974; more a cultural anthropologist than strictly a psychologist). They all emerged from the first Freudian splash.

By the end of the 1960s it was commonplace to hear in films, often comedies, the phrase "My analyst said . . . " or "I told my analyst . . . " The analyst had become father confessor to the urban sophisticate prepared to admit some neurotic tendency he or she was pretty sure was shared by many others. Nobody minds admitting to having a mole on the back. Many poor jokes on the subject abounded, such as: "Yesterday I told my analyst I was suicidal. So *he* says: 'From now on, you pay in advance.'" Or: "I told my analyst my brother thinks he's a chicken. So the analyst says, 'Why don't you tell him he's wrong?' 'I can't,' I told him, 'I need the eggs.'" And so on. They seemed funny at the time.

Yes, quite an achievement. By the end of the century the psychiatric wards of the world were still populated by poor souls suffering from the many manifestations of what has long been designated (if not understood) as "schizophrenia" (personality breakdown) or other "psychotic" disorders, and the best thing that can usually be offered, other than patience, is a range of suppressant narcotics, which, should they fail, may mean close incarceration. It seems talking it out just doesn't get to the root of the seriously serious cases. Meanwhile, psychology, while failing to cure the diseases of the grievously afflicted, has managed to persuade many that ordinary human sanity with its ragbag of old, familiar sins is somehow suspect, and we are all suffering from some psychological disability, though of a fortunately, or relatively mild form that might be treated by any number of therapies, just so long as we can free ourselves from the allegedly deleterious effects of repressions, which may only lead to worse neurotic and behavioral entanglements. Common, established disabilities range from the inferiority complex of Adler to its antithesis, narcissism, egomania, numerous addictive syndromes or "manias," and the like, while the novel cult of political correctness also psychologizes its perceived sins to the extent that even customary language may stand condemned in the dock, once tarred with pseudopsychological notions such as patriarchy or cultural imperialism among a host of allegedly socially grievous new sins. With the "cool" salvation from these conditions comes a new language, and anxiety about not using it, ring-fenced from those wicked, forbidden, incorrect concepts. Baptism in the cult generates conformity of mind, and that is the intention: seeds of these questionable developments may arguably have been sown in the 1960s when psychology began to stray into the argot of political theory. People have become word sensitive in a manner analogous to Pavlov's famous dogs, reacting automatically, and unthinkingly, to external stimulus, whether justified or not. Behavior is thus adjusted, the kind of treatment once reserved by psychologists for the criminal.

Everyone knows the almost placebo effect of talking things out or that, as we still believe, "confession is good for the soul." And here's the nub of the issue. The 1960s saw for many educated people a world where traditional religion and any sense of the sacred was giving way, and must give way to its "scientific" successor. The successor was presumed to be psychology. Why? Well, because religion talked about sin and guilt and repression of "natural instincts," (or bodily lusts) and all of these apparently stopped people from experiencing . . . their *True Selves!* These true selves were held, by suppositions prevalent at the time, to be really *very good;* like the French Encyclopedist era's "enlightened" leaders had believed in the purity of the noble savage. Man was—*if only he could be made to realize*—good at heart and root; it was *society* that was to blame. (So let's change *that!*) There was really nothing to be ashamed of. Or afraid of: it was all perfectly normal, that is, explicable by psychological doctrine. People just needed, well, love and care: a nice, liberal, equable society where everything was fair and good, and anyone who disagreed could be "treated" and persuaded rationally to accept the new socializing process while exploring his or her creative individuality within socially utilitarian bounds. And, perhaps, if it helped, then, er . . . drugs, *medicinal of course,* prescribed by an expert, that is, a scientist, and failing that, a trained psychologist.

So, perhaps even without having realized it, having exchanged religion for psychology, people obtained a new set of "sins," and some of these sins would not be forgiven. In the Sixties, the sin might be fascism, or egotism: the individual had not accepted his or her proper place in society, and might be suffering from neurotic tendencies that could turn into a psychosis! Answer: repress these people. Make them feel bad about themselves, or just ignore them. It would not take very long before a whole new array of sins (psychologically disabling prejudices) would be lined up against the, er . . . guilty individual. Racism, sexism, ageism, imperialism, politically incorrect—stop me before I incriminate myself! Every year, new sins are being uncovered. All man-judged, including, of course, the sin that can never be forgiven, the one against the Holy "Society," aka "the People," which abstraction had become a deity. My perhaps facetious point should be clear enough. The concept of sin has not been eradicated, nor has guilt, nor the attitude of judgment. A person stricken with the new failings must make full public confession, some reparation, and then just might be permitted to, as they say, *move on*, because we should not want their lives to be racked with guilt for past crimes against the supposed absolute equality of "humanity."

These tendencies to psychologize sin began quite a long time before the Sixties got going, but they certainly received hothouse conditions for blooming amid the social and educational tumults of the decade, a decade that, in many respects to its credit, welcomed experimentation. Psychology is without doubt fundamentally experimental, and theoretical. As a basis for guiding our social life as a whole, the world of psychology is simply inadequate for any number of obvious reasons, not the least of which is that few of the ideologues of the movement can agree with one another, so that we now must ask "Are you Freudian, or Jungian?" And that's only for starters. Schools of thought, and competing sects of disciples, abound.

Interestingly, Carl Jung grew to greater prominence in the late 1960s because his mature psychology accommodated mysticism, gnosticism, magic, and spiritual symbolism. He understood that the essential problem of many "patients" with psychological difficulties was the loss of religious belief or a spiritual context in which to make sense of their lives. Jung recognized his task as aiding the sufferer to recover out of his or her own inner experience a numinous sensitivity to the sacred and divine, a context in which our difficult natures most often find meaning, that is, find ourselves intentioned rather than alienated as random beings. And if we are to condemn the decade as giving birth to much that is judged by opponents to be antitraditional and destructive of the mind and ethical foundations of the modern, it must also be recognized that in Jung, religion found a profound friend.

It has been argued that all fundamental argument is essentially argument about traditional religion in relation to its heresies, and like so many sweeping statements does gather up in its sweep something of a half-truth. At least in the West, our centers of higher learning were still learning, as is only right. The problem was that the century had seen an expansion of specialization. Given the growth of the knowledge bases and reclassifications of sciences, this was understandable, but it necessarily meant that during the three or four years spent in higher education by most students, it was quite possible to avoid the very universalism that gave the university its name. A college is not strictly the same as a university. It was perfectly possible for a person's worldview to differ quite fundamentally depending on which institution, or which lecturers were on offer.

Nevertheless, by 1960 there were a number of presuppositions that had, over the previous century, settled down into a range of received and often unchallenged ideas. We mentioned a principal one in chapter 2 where we discussed the notion of ineluctable progress. Principal among these ideas is that line of thought that stems from the work of German theologian Ludwig Feuerbach, a "left-wing" follower of Hegel. In *The Essence of Christianity* (1841), Feuerbach announces what he takes to be something of a revelation, namely, that the entirety of Christianity can be expressed in the social relations of human beings. There is no need for God at all. If we love one another, we have reached our highest potential and fulfillment, for selfless love is salvation. Feuerbach asserts that "Man—this is the mystery of religion—projects his being into objectivity, and then again makes himself an object to this projected

Fig. 8.1.
Ludwig Andreas Feuerbach
(1804–1872).

image of himself," adding: "God is the highest subjectivity of man abstracted from himself." The ethical consequences mean that "My fellow man is *per se,* the mediator between me and the sacred idea of the species. *Homo homini Deus est* [Man is God to man]."[1] The highest law must be man's love for man. On accepting this, world history will turn, declares Feuerbach.

Well, Feuerbach leaves his readers striving for the "true man" who is capable of expressing selfless love of his fellow in society. Marx and his followers aimed to fulfill through economic analysis, social engineering, and revolution what clearly individuals alone could not do, since individuals only reach their meaning, according to this still pervasive idealist theory, through society. Communist societies soon discover that some are more equal than others and there is always a transcending (if not any more transcendent) principle above the benighted individual— nothing metaphysical, you understand, just a power, a power whose claim to lord it derives, allegedly, from its representing man's "true being." The individual's life in such a context quickly becomes meaningless, his or her death, merely quantitative, statistical. No philosophy or religion that does not take fully into account the complete life, including decline and death, and the terrifying issues these facts of all life raise, is doomed. There is more to man than meets the eye of man (or as we have been enjoined to say these days [*by whom?*]: humankind).

Nevertheless, with the removal of metaphysics and abolition of the spiritually transcendent, a terminal decline, or at least, total reevaluation of Christianity, had become implicit to much academic discourse in the West by the 1960s. Its effects would be considerable.

Bright students emerging from college and university into the modern world of the 1960s would in many cases be aware of the idea of "the death of God." Many would "take it as read." Its absorption would mark off many a freak or hippie or yippie-to-be from his or her parents' generation, especially if the parents had not gone through the psychological baptism of tertiary education in arts subjects.

God is dead. . . . It is not necessarily a difficult doctrine to grasp when you have your whole life ahead of you, but it does leave the sensitive with the nagging issue of *meaning.* Interestingly, the coiner of the idea himself was concerned with just this very issue when he introduced his somewhat colorful phrase into Western philosophy. Friedrich Nietzsche (1844–1900), who has been accused of so many things, did not relish the idea of God's annihilation—far from it. If we look at section 125 (appropriately titled "The Madman") of his book *The Gay Science,* we shall see that he accuses prevailing culture of the act of murder:

> God is dead. God remains dead. And we have killed him. How shall we comfort ourselves, the murderers of all murderers? What was holiest and mightiest of all that the world has yet owned has bled to death under our knives: who will wipe this blood off us? What water is there for us to clean ourselves? What festivals of atonement, what sacred games shall we have to invent? Is not the greatness of this deed too great for us? Must we ourselves not become gods simply to appear worthy of it?[2]

There is no intention on the writer's part to inform readers of any literal expiration of the deity. It is simply the exercise of a powerful, intended-to-shock metaphor, to wake his readers up to the full implications of what people would lose were they actually to discard religion utterly. They would be without moral direction and without *meaning.*

What then? His point is that *that* is the very direction of the culture, and the movement toward this very obliteration is the unassailable tendency of his times. Prophesying, he wishes to avoid chaos, not cause it, though he can see little to garner from the future, and the present, but impending nihilism, which if accepted, could be very fatal. The idea seems to be that if people no longer truly believe in God and accept the essential message that has held a semblance of civilization together for so long, through thick and thin, then it may as well be as though God does not exist, for God demands belief by nature, and to not-believe is effectively to snuff his existence out from our experience. Nietzsche was not blind to the dangers of nihilism but remained haunted by the vision of a godless, trackless world. How would one cope? One would have to be . . . a superman! Perhaps, but to see the necessity of what it would take, man would have to face the implications fully and with his whole mind at once. But that is as rare as a true Don Quixote.

Allied to the frequently ersatz grasp of Nietzsche came the vogue for existentialism that took off in the 1950s among European students, derived principally through works by J.-P. Sartre and Albert Camus, following a path first beaten by Søren Kierkegaard (1813–1855), with Camus unable to see why Nietzsche should have been concerned by the absence of supreme spiritual authority. Existentialism in its easy-to-digest form advocated that the individual, in the face of the meaningless nature of the world, its nothingness (without God or Spirit to animate it meaningfully), would have to create, with boldness and courage perhaps, or sheer survival instinct, nothing less than his or her *own meaning*, and live "as if" it was the case. This meaning might still be an apparently conventionally religious one of course, or one of acceptable hue to the existence-experience of the (semi?) believer. As an announcer put it at the Woodstock Festival in August 1969 in another context: "It's your trip, so be my guest." *Meaning*, as it were, could not be given; it would have to be somehow earned through immediate senses of value in lived experience. And it would be subjective, that is, of little value to anyone else; one would in fact be subjecting oneself to oneself, which of course must mean becoming an object, or what Blake would call "a little root, outside of himself"—adrift in a world drained of meaning, a being Orson Welles would in 1973 dub the "poor, forked radish" that is contemporary man: alone, in a universe deaf to his music, blind to his art, with cessation absolute its end, an end as cold as its inception was hot. Its last testimony: *ash*. What this might mean in practice, other than beckoning suicide or depression, was always vague, though some existentialists would find their meaning in embrace of art, and some in socialist politics, others in oblivion, or even crime. Ian Dury would sing, in his Seventies paean to Sixties hedonism: "Sex and drugs, and rock 'n' roll, is all my body needs"—and what of his soul? What did that need?—or had he no need of one, cocooned in the body of sensation?

When we add these anarchic and quasi-anarchic tendencies to the general vogue for psychology, we can soon see why those psychologies that favored the self as the proper subject to be embraced by patients were going to be most welcome. The "selfists" (to use Paul Vitz's quite appropriate phrase), among whom he counts Maslow, Fromm, May, and Rogers, suggested that the self could be unglued from social expectations around it and remade in the self's own image. The emphasis was on liberation of the self from social conditioning and automatic response, and the glorying in that new life, whatever it might be. For man, stripped of false projections, was a good being, capable of love with capacity for enjoying "oceanic" or mystical-like experiences, courtesy of the mysteries of the organism. It all added to the colorful life of the engaged, awakened self. This was a hell of a lot to place on the shoulders of the self, and it must be said, that the 1960s self-actualizer with this tendency had generally not got to the bottom of this barrel by the decade's end. There was much collectivism and communal pleasure and commitment to be worked through first, but I do sometimes wonder, that is, when we try to explain what went "wrong" at the end of the decade for those expecting imminent utopia, when the dreams turned sour and the gold became dross, was it somehow a collective experience silently intuited that at the bottom of the search for the authentic self (devoid of God), there just might be a nasty, cold mess lying in wait for the nihilist-to-be? Had the time come to "get it all back together" before the barrel—in the absence of a Houdini—tumbled over Niagara to a foaming, meaningless, doom?

⚠ ⚠ ⚠

Meanwhile, back in the psychiatric wards, where psychology was, in some respects, first born, life went on pretty much as before. At least, so we might think from Ken Kesey's stunning novel *One Flew Over the Cuckoo's Nest*. Published in 1962, and well received, it became a famous film with Jack Nicholson and a fine cast in 1975 under Milos Forman's direction. The implication was the same, however, despite the thirteen-year gap in which the Sixties had come and gone. Psychiatric wards were control centers, not places of self-discovery.

Ken Kesey (1935–2002), who would of course go on to play such a stimulating and stimulated role in the U.S. psychedelic movement came to the subject of his novel while a student of writing at California's Stanford University (where the robotic Rancho Arm was acquired around the same time). While also taking part in CIA-directed experiments in the use of LSD, psilocybin, and DMT, Kesey worked night shifts at the Menlo Park Veterans' Hospital where he took time to talk to the patients, often himself under the influence of psychedelic drugs, kindly provided by America's secret government.

Fig. 8.2. American author Ken Kesey.

Kesey concluded—as British psychologist R. D. Laing would also in the Sixties—that the people he spoke to were not insane. Rather they had been rejected by society and pushed out, and were wounded, because they did not express themselves in the same way as conventional people. The implication was clear enough. Convention was "mad" not to understand the potential and beauty of these individuals, and had no right to judge what was, and was not, to be taken as sane behavior. The incarcerated characters in Kesey's novel were harmless (and certainly less destructive than the legal-safe city-plot property developer), and were above all, creative, spontaneous beings. Greater tolerance, relaxation of automatic condemnation and neurotic(!) insecurity, and realization that we are all a bit mad would, Kesey suggested powerfully, help to constitute a better society for all. One thing Kesey did not suggest for "his" patients, however, was that they register with a psychologist, Freudian or otherwise! They were really all right as they were. It was the attitudes of their paid "protectors" that looked decidedly suspect. The paid guardians of the "mad" were, in Kesey's fictional judgment, monstrous, and they held the keys to the kingdom: liberty.

If the guards at the asylum were not to be trusted, who was to govern the governors?

Kesey would leave Stanford to test the limits, and the limitlessness, of personal freedom on the principle, You don't *have* to conform. Indeed, but if you don't, don't be surprised when the guardians of "freedom" come for you. They came for Kesey.

Oh, and as for the "spiritual meaning" of all this—where in the above chapter would we expect to find Jesus? Neither on the analyst's couch, nor his chair, but rather, one suspects, strapped to his bed, forcefully sedated with the patients in the "cuckoo's nest." You can visit him on Sundays, if Nurse Ratched is agreeable.

NINE

Apocalypse Then

There had been various groups in the middle 1950s campaigning against atomic and nuclear weapons. Those groups were effectively brought together by Canon Collins and Kingsley Martin, editor of the [British political journal] New Statesman. *The articles that set it off were written by J. B. Priestley and Bertrand Russell in autumn 1957. Many of us assembled at Canon Collins's house where we had a discussion about amalgamating the groups that already existed and initiating a campaign on the basis of Russell's and Priestley's articles. There was a march which had already been fixed for the subsequent Easter which became associated with the C.N.D. [Campaign for Nuclear Disarmament] and from that moment onward C.N.D. became the movement that swamped all the others. It became much bigger much more swiftly than anybody had imagined. There were a number of people in the House of Commons who were associated with it; it certainly did reflect the mood of the time and I believe that it did have a very powerful effect on the government. This is revealed in Eisenhower's memoirs. Not many people read Eisenhower's memoirs, but if anyone does they will find a description of the talks between Macmillan [British prime minister] and Eisenhower, with Macmillan using the fact of the great protest movements in this country about nuclear weapons as the lever on Eisenhower to try and get him to move toward a [nuclear] test ban. I think that C.N.D. led the way to the test ban. Without the C.N.D. the veil of secrecy would never have been torn aside and without the veil being torn aside there would never have been the movement toward the test ban, which is the one great victory for sanity in international affairs in the last twenty years.*

MICHAEL FOOT (1913–2010), LABOR PARTY POLITICIAN,
LEADER OF THE OPPOSITION 1980–1983,
FROM ALAN THOMPSON, *THE DAY BEFORE YESTERDAY,* 200

Ordinarily speaking, God makes sense to people. The idea is grasped by children with no difficulty, not infrequently with delight and fascination, and remains with many of them henceforth in varying degrees. We know well the kind of things that can turn people away from, or that obscure, belief in God. They run the gamut from incomprehensible and irreconcilable personal tragedies of loss, to extreme self-centeredness, narcissism, unwanted sense of guilt, confusion over competing religious claims, abuse at the hands of religious figures, betrayal of trust, hypocrisy in religious authority figures, and of course educational encounters with value-free territories of modern scientific method, and personally awkward, even fundamentally disappointing philosophical questions encountered toward the far end of formal education during the late formation period of adult identity. Reason itself can in principle accommodate belief in God, as well as the reverse proposition.

One question has occurred to people of all thinking ages throughout history without any stimulus from tutors or external authorities, that is: "When and how will it all end?" We all know the tale of Chicken Little; he doesn't need much of a hint to leap to the conclusion that the sky is falling.

As far as we know from extant evidence, belief in apocalypse, a morally meaningful "end of the world" scenario enacted as God's will, derives from a period of crisis among literate Jewish believers toward the end of the first half of the second century BCE. The idea of the personal God who must be found to be righteous in dealing with human conduct became an extremely critical issue for persons who, on the one hand, witnessed again despoliation of their territory and religious traditions at the hands of foreign invaders (the Seleucid Greeks being only the latest in a succession of invaders, from the Egyptians, the Philistines, the Assyrians, the Babylonians, and the Persians), and on the other, were faced with the inherited belief that their God Yahweh actually cared about innocent suffering of his followers and would vindicate faith in their covenant with him. "Shall not the Judge of all the earth do right?" (Genesis 18:25).

Apocalypse comes from two Greek words meaning: "to bring out of hiding," in the sense of revealing secrets. The word does not actually mean the "end of the world," though we are now accustomed to thinking of it in this sense, because the alternative title of the "Revelation of Saint John the Divine," commonly called the book of Revelation, or Revelation, is the "Apocalypse of Saint John." An apocalypse was simply a book that contained what purported to be the secret story of God's plans for the human race, not infrequently dealing with the origins of man and his plight on earth, and a revelation in symbolic or in coded terms of God's timetable, if you like, for wrapping up the whole catastrophic, but ultimately God-vindicating exercise. "If you're concerned, just read this! It will set you straight and restore faith; it's going to be all right *in the end.*"

Such works have always enjoyed enormous appeal for those either suffering from the conditions of real life in one way or another, or for those curious about the "endgame." But it should be borne in mind that, unlike their modern equivalents in conspiracy tales, apocalyptic works were composed neither to alarm, nor to induce fear, but rather to comfort the afflicted with knowledge that their sufferings would pass with the dramatic disposal of their perceived enemies. As things turned out, every nook and cranny of these apocalyptic accounts has been interpreted and used to account for all manner of events, as seen from the time period of observers. It is often regretted that obsession with apocalypses, and the end of the world, has for many become the predominant substance of the religious life of believers, who wait in earnest expectation for a redeemer, and can think of little else, there being, according to the logic of the case, little point.

Apocalypticism received its high-water mark in Jewish culture at the time Jesus is believed to have walked the earth, and the conception of a revealed end and judgment is frankly inseparable from the understanding of God's dealings with his creation in this period. Consequently, the Christian Church, in particular, has suffered periodic crises where apocalyptic expectation has overridden any other inherited wisdom as regards our relations with God. The world has not ended, but a perennial disquiet remains, and is of course an inherited portion also of Islamic belief, where Muslims also look to a final Judgment, the separation of good from bad, the expected defeat of Satan.

One thing in all this story that is frequently overlooked by many common ideas of apocalypse is the more optimistic strand of apocalyptic prophecy that holds that before any eventual rolling up of the scroll of time, there will be a period of revelation of God's secrets of Nature, and that a reign of the Holy Spirit on earth (sometimes supposed at a period of a thousand years) would precede the final end of the created order, with which idea we are more familiar. In that time (the Last Light), the world would be exposed to innumerable discoveries of hitherto secret aspects of Nature's powers, and their application would, in the universal diffusion of the Holy Spirit, constitute a Golden Age to surpass all former golden ages. Such a scenario had been a widespread European apocalyptic belief in the seventeenth century when apologists for the Rosicrucian movement declared that scientific advance stemming from the Renaissance was a sign of the "New Age." Spiritual and scientific enlightenment would, it was hoped, go hand in hand under the patronage of Lady Wisdom. As things transpired, only the latter enlightenment seemed to have properly got off the ground, with the vaunted spiritual enlightenment becoming the often confused possession of esoteric orders, which, by the end of the nineteenth century, were widely suspected by mainstream science, though by no means by all individual scientists.

It is this inherent duality in the inherited apocalyptic schemes that ought to arrest our attention when we consider the spiritual meaning of the 1960s, for in that decade we see, to a certain degree, a curious transformation of one aspect of apocalypticism, to another. Fearfulness and hopefulness were juggled in the winds of the times, with, for a brief but influential period, it looking like the hopeful, startling, and even miraculous revelation of a New Age was coming out on top. "We must be in heaven, man!" as we may recall our announcer declaring at Woodstock in '69, (before adding the codicil: "There's always a little bit of heaven in a disaster area.").* This spontaneous exclamation expresses something of that dichotomy quite well.

BAN THE BOMB

The Sixties opened with widespread anxiety over the survival of the human race. The quotation at the head of this chapter refers to the British Campaign for Nuclear Disarmament, which received widespread support from many quarters, including churchmen of different denominations who, while accepting that God might bring the world's end at a moment of his choosing, did not accept the implication that humankind had the right to preempt such a possibility. Canon John Collins (1905–1982) was an Anglican clergyman who had been radicalized by experience in the RAF (Royal Air Force) during World War II. A prominent CND founder, Collins was quickly associated with the slogan "The Church says *Ban the Bomb*," and was joined by concerned Christians from across the theological spectrum, some of whom might have been disposed to consider that should it come to pass that humankind be the author of its own violent end, then such would indeed constitute a "last judgment" upon our stupidity and sinfulness. It would then be true to say we had brought it on ourselves. Christians, however, were called upon to insist that acquiescence in nuclear arms racing was a sin that could be avoided by exercise of sense, consideration for others, and such free will as could be mustered to a godly cause. Few really

---

*See page 52.

believed that the Judge of all creation had a hand in creating nuclear weapons as a means of effecting his grand designs, though the idea was doubtless dallied with by fringe sodalities or Protestant sectarians with little or no interest in ecumenical activism. One could always find an appropriate quote to back up supposed fulfillments of prophecy. Indeed, here's one that just came to me:

> A wicked and adulterous generation seeketh after a sign; and there shall no sign be given unto it, but the sign of the prophet Jonas. And he left them, and departed. (Matthew 16:4)

Jesus seems to be saying that only the faithless unrepentant seek for a sign; if they knew where they stood, they wouldn't need one. Such a state as they're in is already a sign, for those who can see (like Jonah). However, in our context, when we seek the spiritual significance of the 1960s we are right to seek out the signs that force us to see our object through its significance (to borrow Brice Parain's intriguing aphorism).

Those of an apocalyptic cast of mind have never been short of signs to pin their ultimate hopes and fears on, and the ambiguous, but important, quotation from the gospel above might suggest that the "sign of Jonas"—being Jonah's warning of the imminent judgment of Nineveh from whose proclamation prophet Jonah cannot escape—applied well to the gathering insanity of the nuclear arms race that threatened not only everybody on Earth, but the unborn as well. Nineveh could only be saved by repentance, the sign of a *changed heart,* a turning to God. What right had even a very sinful generation to condemn the future of which they had no rightful part? The Islamic religion has to date at least been especially emphatic on the idea that the future is not for man to dispose of, or even predict, being God's sole possession; extreme fundamentalists on all sides rupture this principle, having appropriated God's prerogative. Many women joined the CND movement with a profound thought of loving care to the unborn children inside them and those to be born, eventually, of their children. Other persons' freedom to live is not our own to dispose of; arguably it is rather our mutual duty to ensure it.

Consideration of young people and their children's right to a future free of war was a particularly powerful motive of the Sixties. Young people themselves also had the sense, when alerted, of an entitlement to much better than politicians and military adventurists were offering them. If there was little taste for sacrifice it is because young people intuited or knew too well what use had been made of sacrifice in the twentieth century's earlier wars. There are crosses in every English village, covered with names of the fallen, to testify to that. The names of the dead may not be forgotten, but the people to whom the names refer are well dead, leaving lives of promise unlived. The principle of sacrifice had been perverted; war, or so concluded many who thought about the issue seriously, was not the highest God's means of solving problems. Governments should rather devote their extraordinary resources to good works, not evil ones. "Return your sword to its place, for all who will take up the sword, will die by the sword" (Matthew 26:52).

There were abundant signs of the times observed throughout the Sixties, generally with alarm by those who imagined they could interpret them correctly: miniskirts, long hair, beat music, romantic kissing in broad daylight. One of the first, and rather obvious ones, and one whose ubiquity flourishes to this day is that which in America is generally known as the "peace symbol."

This sign—it is not really a symbol, and is more akin to a logo—was the work of Gerald Holtom, undertaken in 1958 to project the CND's acronym in an unforgettable form, which it does most successfully, for apart from the semaphore letters *C, N,* and *D,* one can also see an arrow pointing upward made of a Christian cross whose arms have become something like rocket, or jet wings, along with something of a road to be traveled to a horizon (the suggestion of a march), a mountain (an ideal and a destination), while overall constituting a figure whose circular symmetry evokes religious and philosophical symbols, from the Chi-Rho to the yin-yang. It also resembles government road signals, indicating attention or alarm, and more pertinently, the ionizing radiation symbol common to the U.K. and the United States to indicate extreme hazard. Nowadays the CND sign is taken as a straight symbol

Fig. 9.1. Two versions of the peace symbol (a) the CND symbol (b) John Lennon's "Imagine" wall in Prague, Czech Republic, painted after Lennon's assassination in 1980.

for peace, with the visual inference of a unification of opposites in a single ascending purpose. It was certainly a "sign of the times" in itself. And when this sign appeared, one naturally thought of resistance to an impending doom. Others might of course see the sign as simply one among many that indicated the apocalypse was imminent. It was impossible to avoid at practically every student demonstration of the decade and was frequently sewn into clothing or worn as a button.

The fundamental intention of the sign was to promote awareness, expanded awareness of what was *really* going on. This message seems to have had a slightly different resonance in Great Britain because in that country, the nuclear program of the government, in its relation to the United States and to NATO had been shrouded in secrecy through the 1950s, and people had very little clear idea of what had been going on, even beneath their feet as elaborate underground bunkers were constructed for government officials and security forces all over the country. In the United States, on the other hand, government policy under Eisenhower had been in fact somehow to "normalize" the idea of nuclear conflict. The bombs were just somewhat larger than folk were used to, and they might be dropped in parts of America where bombs had not been exploded before. Remarkably, from a British point of view, people in America were invited to see warheads exploded in the deserts of western states, while children(!) were given visual advice through safety films of what to do if they happened to be in the classroom and an atomic bomb went off in the vicinity. The hideous dangers of radioactivity, never mind the real destructive force of nuclear weapons, were all muted so as not to alarm the public, while keeping them informed of the necessity for nuclear war if Communist intentions threatened the United States directly. Few people were familiar with the research undertaken into the long-term effects of the obliteration of Hiroshima and Nagasaki in August 1945.

British audiences were supposed to get a take on what the Real Thing might be like with the screening of Peter Watkins's fifty-minute docudrama *The War Game* on October 7, 1965. The film showed with extraordinary, unembellished realism what a Russian nuclear attack on Britain would be like from the point of view of ordinary people. The BBC pulled the film at the last minute, the reason given being that it was was too horrifying for broadcast. This put it cleverly in the category of a "horror" movie, and, at the time, many horror movies were X-rated films, restricted to persons under eighteen. The essential problem was that it was too realistic and would likely have political implications, as well as social ones, so its cancellation was effectively censorship. Nevertheless, anyone who has seen the film has testified to its truly disturbing character. But then, one might expect a nuclear attack on human beings to be rather more than disturbing. In the event *The War Game* won the Academy Award for best documentary feature in 1966, but did not receive a U.K. TV showing until thirty years after it was first scheduled for broadcast.

Three months before the intended broadcast, pop singer Barry McGuire had already "warned" pop audiences of what might be coming their way with his "Western movie" sounding, folk-pop version of P. F. Sloan's 1964 Dylanesque "Eve of Destruction," a dramatic, catchy, but very depressing song that piled up images of bullets and explosions spreading from the Middle East toward rioting in the States, with all the blood and mayhem and threat to youthful life and limb being but a prelude to a great, evidently nuclear, destruction but a short time away. In spite of the big production, it was considerably less effective in my view than Bob Dylan's sonically basic "Masters of War" on *The Freewheelin' Bob Dylan* album, released on May 27, 1963, the album that turned the Beatles on to Bob big-time with its range of lyrical salvos aimed at the world around him. "Masters of War" promised a dire end, or wished-for demise for those profiting from the war industry. Bob served them notice he'd be standing over their graves when they were dead, just to make sure, for their betrayal of humanity.

The album's pioneering cover photograph showed a warmly smiling, well-fed Bob making his way through a wintry West Village arm in chilly arm with beautiful Suze Rotolo. One had the feeling one might bump into Bob anywhere; certainly he was more visible through most of the decade than the "Masters of War" who, he tells us, always hide behind a mask. Winter, incidentally, was a recurrent theme in the upper echelons of mid-Sixties American pop. I think of the Mamas & Papas *California Dreamin'* "on such a winter's day," and any number of numb-fingered strums from Paul Simon and Art Garfunkel. I can't help feeling that this winter metaphor applied to the Sixties troubadours' sensibility that the world of their feelings, emotions, loves, and yearning only rarely found their correlative in the real "outside world." "A winter's day, in a deep and dark December . . ." sang Simon and Garfunkel, gazing from their window to the streets below. The loneliness of a generation, shut in, keen for the sun, but for the time being, sheltering with only love to cover the nakedness of foreboding. This is all in marked contrast to the original troubadours of Languedoc in the twelfth and early thirteenth centuries, who sang of the "fine love," the *enormous* love of the Lady that drove them to heights of lyrical invention unparalleled afterward for centuries, and all rubbed out by a Church crusade and the repressions of the mighty who took the land and torched its heroes and heroines. In the original *cansos* of the troubadours, the *fin'amor* was always celebrated in springtime and summer, and the sun was always warm, and the cheeks, soft, blooming, moist with love, and there was never a "hard rain"—or thought of that greatly feared, beyond a chill, "nuclear winter."

God damn the masters of war.

Five months after *The Freewheelin' Bob Dylan* brought the Beatles up with a creative jolt, Orson Welles's remarkable movie version of Kafka's *The Trial* was premiered in London. And it *was* Welles's version. Kafka had had no idea his tale of a victimized individual, stuck like a cypher in a bureaucratic hell, would end with a nuclear explosion that destroyed everything. "He's guilty as hell!" Welles informed lead character Joseph K's impersonator, actor Anthony Perkins. Kafka had presented Joseph K as a victim of an incomprehensible bureaucratic system that had no place for the individual soul. Welles's Joseph K may be improperly persecuted in a destructive system that does not accept free will, but, according to Welles, K is guilty because he has not challenged that system. Until the powers come for him, he is proud of his little bureaucrat's position, and the bit of power he extends to subordinates, such is the compass of his free will. And finally, in asserting his ego against the system, K goes to even greater extremes and proceeds to judge everything and everyone, including the universe. If he must go, he'll take everything else with him. It transpires that the *little man,* the apparent victim, has it in him to destroy all human existence, such being his conceit. A truly great man would never play so lightly with the lives of others, regardless of his own feelings. Beware, warns Welles, of the dangerous "little man." At the end of the film, K tosses his executioners' dynamite into a crater whose blast becomes that of a nuclear mushroom cloud that envelopes everything to the tune of Albinoni's funereal *Adagio,* a piece that will be resurrected for apocalyptic usage on the Doors' 1975 posthumous release of Jim Morrison's poetry (*An American Prayer*).

Welles's idiosyncratic warning is ultimately more astonishing, and singularly more profound than the catalog of errors that leads to the nuclear holocaust in the black comedy *Dr. Strangelove, Or How*

I Learned to Stop Worrying and Love the Bomb, starring Peter Sellers in a string of bravura caricatures, directed by a talent-struck Stanley Kubrick. It was released in London in January 1964, three months after Welles's *The Trial,* and enjoyed considerably larger audiences than Welles's magisterial work.

There may be a warning here too. The current president of the United States has expressed a particular "germophobia," and displays acute sensitivity to foreign bodies coming into the body of the nation from the outside, though less concerned he seems to be with those kinds of pollutions that generate considerable profits (or should I say jobs) inside the stockade. One observes that the hidden architect of nuclear annihilation in *Dr. Strangelove* is a frustrated, bellicose, outspoken general (played with commendable brilliance by Sterling Hayden) whose concern at the "Commies" allegedly getting into the nation's water supply and polluting his "precious bodily fluids" became intimately apparent to him on failing to satisfy expectations during the "act of love." There are many warnings intended for the future in the 1960s; they did not, as it were, live only for their own time. Sometimes the works of that decade ask us again to examine more closely what they *meant* to say: things oft not appreciated at the time of release.

A good number of fine films, and less than fine films were made with the apocalypse in mind. One of the earliest to emerge might surprise those familiar with its very accessible epic and heroic mass-entertainment qualities. I refer to Samuel Bronston's production of that intelligent epic *El Cid,* starring Charlton Heston and Sophia Loren, directed with élan by Anthony Mann, which, like all great epics, never lets the spectacle supersede the human interest. It helps of course when you use real people, not CGI, which does turn movies effectively into animations without the human characteristics of, say, Disney's *Bambi.*

You may recall how *El Cid* begins with Arab leader Ben Yusef (played to the hilt by Herbert Lom) declaring holy war—that's jihad, my dear—on the kingdoms of Spain and on his morally lax fellow Muslims who are having the temerity to make peace with the infidel and indulge themselves in music, science, philosophy, and other life-enhancing activities, when what they should be doing is Ben Yusef's notion of the "will of Allah," that is: killing, and being killed. After which announcement, Ben Yusef personally beheads the prisoners placed before him in the name of the "merciful and the compassionate." Of course, the subtext in 1963 when the film came out (I went from Minworth to Birmingham to see it with my family; finishing late, we missed the bus and had to walk many miles home in the dark, a trek for my little legs I remember to this day)—pardon the painful digression—the subtext was that Ben Yusef represented the Communist threat from the East and Far East, and that the only thing that would ensure its triumph was that Christian nations allow themselves to be disunited and fail to honor agreements with their allies. In the case of the movie, those allies were presented as friendly, as well as duplicitous Muslim powers. *Now,* of course, we may see the movie with the same subtextual narrative, but with rather different names, being now faced, remarkably, with dark-age forces of jihad driven once more by a Dark Age–born creed, the like of which Europe has not seen since the Battle of Vienna served to contain the besieging Ottoman Empire in 1683. The warning however is still remarkably vivid and most appropriate. You cannot isolate yourself from a threat of this magnitude; you must unite and be generous with allies, for your own good. Yes, we can "change the world," or at least prevent its destruction, if we open up and work together. Retreating into one's shell is, like fear, failure.

Fig. 9.2. Herbert Lom as Ben Yusef in the movie El Cid, *1963.*

⚠ ⚠ ⚠

One must recall of course that throughout the Sixties there always existed the background hum of old-fashioned biblical apocalyptic, with its message of imminent judgment, or, in the case of the Jehovah's Witnesses, the proclamation of a coming perfect world, perfect for a very limited number of the "saved," preordained to be saved—a mere 144,000 at the last count, I believe, with no hint of realization that this number is utterly symbolic (12 × 12) not literal, and in no wise indicates a body count of righteous witnesses (I'd be surprised if there had ever been as many as 144,000 perfect beings in the history of our rampant species). But then, literalism perpetually obscures the symbol, and its depths. One recalls the lines from the New Testament (Mark 13 particularly) about "wars and rumors of wars," and earthquakes and so on. Well, we've had plenty of those for two thousand years. Then there's the "seven heads" in the book of Daniel. I remember in the 1970s Herbet W. Armstrong's *Plain Truth* magazine advocating this was a sure-fire prophecy denoting the members of the "Common Market" as it was then (well, they didn't number seven for very long), but you can always make a prophecy fit anything you like, as you can interpret a Beatles song likewise if hidden meanings are what you're looking for. Sadly, there is a type of person who looks for little else, and what can one do? Argument with such folk is as useless as trying to convert carriers of *The Watchtower* to your way of thinking on your own doorstep.

There is no doubt apocalyptic foreboding influenced many persons to convert explicitly to evangelical forms of Christianity. After all, if the warning comes from the Bible, you want to be "in" with the people who know the Bible best, and that was not the "in" crowd of Swinging London. At least so considered British pop star Cliff Richard who had so many bright hits with the group the Shadows throughout the decade. A great supporter of Billy Graham's evangelism, Cliff Richard became a confessing Christian in 1964, even though he had been baptized an Anglican as a child. He had the spiritual call to faith that is sometimes called "conversion," feeling that Christ's crucifixion was not a doctrine, but a personal matter, summoning him to devote his moral life seriously to the life of the Gospel. In this, it must be observed that Cliff has always tried to demonstrate maturity and wisdom and has set an example of genuine commitment to his faith, and though certain sections of the media have sneered from time to time, as they generally do at anything godly (other than, oddly, the pope), his has been an exemplary witness emanating from an entertainment world more usually associated with excess and egoistic indulgence.

I shall close this chapter with but three examples of the darker apocalyptic vision that impacted in their different ways upon the Sixties, or at least the rather small listening part of that era, not one of these examples being Christian or Jewish or Islamic or religious in orientation at all, but apocalyptic all the same.

I was first given Kurt Vonnegut's novel *Cat's Cradle* to read in January 1983 by Gerhard Fitzthum, German philosopher and active supporter of the then-innovative political party *Die Grünen* ("the Greens"). Studying Nietzsche at the University of Giessen at the time, Gerhard informed me of a theory he called "the law of the conservation of stupidity," which ran something like this. The more sure you are that you are absolutely right, and the more certainty you feel is yours, the more inclined to dismiss any opposition to your idea, the more likely it is that you are stupid or will act stupidly, and that your idea in the context you wish to express it, is stupid too, and your acts will come to be seen

Fig. 9.3. Author Kurt Vonnegut (1922–2007).

as exemplary acts of stupidity. This is, I think, a very good principle for maintaining sanity and sane action, especially where one is responsible for the lives of others. If only politicians and others understood the weight of this law. As an illustration of the principle, Gerhard recommended Vonnegut's novel, and recommended the American novelist's other novels as well, as being peculiarly sane and philosophically practical, and indeed urgent in their appeal against the mad destruction being visited upon the world by ideologues of every kind, not least of which being those who, to further commercial and self-loving ambitions, employ the lives of others in arms or subterfuge.

First published in 1963, Vonnegut's story tells of a man called John who in the course of enquiries comes to learn of a brilliant professor who developed a substance called "ice-nine." Originally conceived as a means of improving the ground for soldiers making their way over muddy or soaked territory, the substance, when in contact with moisture immediately causes it to crystallize into ice. Unfortunately for the inventor's earnings, ice-nine was deemed impractical and was never employed because it was discovered that there was no way to limit its action. Any moisture contact meant that the ice-nine effect would simply spread and spread, and given the nature of moisture on the planet, very soon all water everywhere would become permanent ice. Of course, good plain sense would demand that in the light of the most awful consequences if the substance fell in to the wrong hands, or probably any hands at all, it should have been immediately neutralized, destroyed, and all knowledge of its constitution immediately destroyed for the sake of life itself, which would of course cease should it ever be suffered to make contact with the tributaries of earthly existence. But of course, that would be to ignore its usefulness as the unused and unusable absolute threat: the ultimate doomsday weapon where *nobody wins.*

Now comes the stupidity. Failing to see the utter stupidity of the latter conception, ice-nine is not destroyed. I think you can guess the rest, in principle, and recognize that here, close to the beginning of the Sixties one brilliant and clear-thinking writer recognized the kind of fault in human brain function and moral turpitude of will that could make the classic apocalypse a permanent reality, with no other meaning at its conclusion than for alien observers to note with a shrug that the very clever professor should not have been so damned stupid. We are free to apply any obvious moral we may draw from the observation inherent to the novelist's dark vision, informed not by fancy, but by attention to human realities.

I am absolutely certain, convinced, and sure that human activities with regard to carbon emissions have no effect on the earth's atmosphere whatever. There is no link at all between human activity and increase in temperatures. I totally dismiss the evident conspiracy of scientists who think otherwise. Yes, I love money. But please, never ever be so stupid as to give me ice-nine.

One cannot use the word *apocalyptic* with regard to the Sixties and avoid at least mentioning Jean-Luc Godard's unforgettable, some would say unforgiveable, movie, *Weekend,* released to a shocked and baffled French public in 1967. There is nothing of Flower Power in this film. The characters portrayed by Jean Yanne and Mireille Darc are a highly disagreeable, intensely materialistic, foul-minded French bourgeois couple who seem to hate one another and are plotting adultery and murder to further their self-centered desires. They set off for a weekend in the country in their fancy car and soon find themselves in what must be the longest tracking shot in the history of the movies. We have already seen on the credits that this work of cinema "was found on a scrap heap," and that this is a film "adrift in the cosmos," and to the cosmos we might wish to go, for the tracking shot goes on, and on, and on. At some point we might realize that the director has cleverly in a movie given us the real sensation of the utter boredom and frustration of a real traffic jam. Traffic jams of these proportions were not normal in France in 1967, but they are now normal everywhere. This is a prophetic film, and its adherence to its premises makes it most uncomfortable, but compelling viewing all the same. For as we finally pass out of an experience that is absolutely modern, though one we somehow never really quite notice—such is our ability to "switch off" like we were TV sets in the hinterlands of modern vacuity—we find that the sense of reality steadily declines and we find ourselves in an apocalyptic breakdown of order and sense, where the banal desires of the man and woman are shown up perfectly for the scrap they are, and the scrap they, like the battered cars that are strewn on every side of the road they encounter, will become.

There is little—very little—love in this film. A man plays a scene that is a dark parody of the "singing narrative" of Jacques Demy's romantic musical *Les Parapluies de Cherbourg* (1964). Actor Jean Pierre Léaud sings intensely down a country phone box to his love, only to be pulled violently away by the man who will stop at nothing to get to his mother-in-law so he can kill her and grab the family loot. The romantic fool soon shows another side of his character when the couple undertake to steal his sports car. He is soon as vicious as they are. Everyone practically from this point exceeds the previous characters in viciousness as a surrealist replay of the French Revolutionary Terror of 1792 is unleashed on modern France. Toward the end of the hideously dissolving weekend the wife finds herself nonchalantly eating her husband, having been, like Patti Hearst in years to come, acculturated into a band of hippie guerillas engaged in a war with another band of hippie guerillas fighting over the remains of a vanished civilization. When a female comrade is shot and mortally wounded, the dying girl in bloodied bandana dies singing a little plaintive song of utter nihilism, before she is left, abandoned as the group goes on to their next group experience of casual murder. Their leader Kalfon announces their Mansonesque justification: "One can only overcome the horror of the bourgeoisie with even more horror." The title informs us (in French of course) "end of cinema," and as far as director Jean-Luc Godard was concerned, it was. He went from the surrealist carnage of *Weekend* to a series of filmed experiments aimed at showing or learning "how to make political films politically." For anyone who wants to engage with the visual semantics of that question, and commit to that revolution Godard dreamt of as coming forth from the evil nightmare of the death of capitalism, they will find much to chew over, and get thoroughly bored with, in Godard's subsequent movies, which came out with the rapidity of quarterly broadsides until he seemed to reach an aphasia after the long wake of May 1968. He would emerge again in the 1980s with an arresting aesthetic that no one has come quite near, but then he appeared to self-immolate in the 1960s in a manner unique and thoroughly troubling. *Weekend,* divorced from its times, may now be admired as a work of art. In 1967, it was a disgrace. It was a disgrace not to recognize its grace-denying ambition and psychic horror. Godard shows a world where the Holy Spirit, or anything remotely spiritual, is wholly absent. Godard wanted to tear up the Sixties and start again with a new language. The effort only proves, to my mind, that if you take away the religious and spiritual dimension, the result is a wasteland of meaninglessness from which one will be desperate to escape, if, that is, one's mind is still alive to the human reality. *Weekend* shows the wasteland to itself, with no supermen to redeem it. Nothing comes from nothing. A "return to zero" is a return to nowhere and the beginning of nothing in particular.

Then came the real "Weekend." In 1969, Hollywood was shocked to learn that insane and utterly irrational killings were taking place, virtually on its doorstep. Charles Manson's "Family" were responsible, and Manson, briefly acquainted with Beach Boy Dennis Wilson and a few other L.A. pop dignitaries, had, in his derangement (the scope of which Wilson and friends were utterly oblivious to), decided to enact an apocalypse of his own, to stimulate a final apocalyptic war in America. According to the accounts of Manson in *The Family* by Ed Sanders, and *Witness to Evil* by George Bishop, that was his plan. Blacks would fight it out with whites, and the "pigs," especially "rich pigs," would be destroyed forever. Hell's Angels would play the part in his psychodrama as avenging angels of all Manson hated most. And this would be accomplished by utter denial of the moral order claimed by the establishment as their possession, the *transcending* of mere social mores like "not murdering," or "heeding the sufferings of others," or any "respecting persons or property." Manson chose war with "pigs," that is, privileged beneficiaries of economic boom, and extruded inspiration from a thoroughly disordered hearing of the Beatles *White Album* of November 1968. That is to say, he took the verbal ambiguities he wanted, and the intermittently fiery force of the sometimes experimental music of that, at its most mysterious, deeply crepuscular double album, and in his psychotic, hallucinatory, demented, evil (and any other words we struggle to find appropriate) state, he extracted from what he heard a meaning that suited his desire to revenge himself on the society he felt had rejected this son of a teenage prostitute and a client known only as "Colonel Scott," and that had incarcerated him for most of his young life, with force of a social structure and evidently (to his egotism) fake set of laws and hypocrisies, that he, Charles Manson, with aid of LSD and much physical sex and imagined "satori" of an absolutist, perverse-Upanishadic character, would destroy. For in him, Manson, Son of Man, the moral component of what we thought, what "good folk" imagined was at the root of humanity, was gone, and well gone, destroyed. In his own mind part-god and part-machine, he was convinced he was utterly free of the world of those who judged him, by the perverted lights of his hallucination that to him was a higher reality, having passed beyond the illusion, or supposed illusion, of ordinary human sensibility, so that what the unenlightened deemed killing was not killing, and being killed was not being killed (the invincible Ātman of Vedanta). He and his drug-insulated "family" having, as they thought, killed their egos (along with ordinary human feelings) felt absolutely free, beyond good and evil in an eternal Now, free indeed shortly after midnight of August 8, 1969, to stab to most grisly death actress Sharon Tate, who was carrying her husband Roman Polanski's unborn child, two weeks from birth, along with four of her comfortably well-off young friends there present. "It felt good," said one of his female followers, commenting on the stabbing.

A warning from history? At the root of it all: revenge.

A week later, Woodstock took place. "We must be in heaven, man."

Fig. 9.4. Actress Sharon Tate (1943–1969)

⚠ ⚠ ⚠

And that would make a nice, journalistic line for the closing of this chapter. But wait, "what light from yonder window breaks?" The fact is that if Manson, a deranged criminal by all accounts, had worked his wickedness on unknown persons in Wisconsin, say, or Tierra del Fuego, we should, if we ever heard of such goings-on, have probably dismissed the matter as an ordinary issue for crime and punishment. In fact, Manson, like so many hangers-on to high-profile or stimulating places and events through time, exploited the L.A. scene and grabbed, through headlines and appalling, pitiless excess, attention to himself. The Manson apocalypse fantasy does not in the slightest detract from the value of the best intentions of the era. The spiritually significant conception that was happening at the time was, in simple terms, the novel idea of a projectable, nondenominational, compelling, indeed arresting imperative for building a society dedicated to Peace and Love, and these were in themselves perfectly good and noble ideals that no demented individual could subtract from by pursuing and enacting their opposites. We should not make dramatic capital out of Manson's personalized apocalypse. Be it remembered, now and ever, that the authentic apocalypse, for what it was worth, was intended as a revelation of the substance of things not seen, a premature revelation, perhaps well intentioned, of the goal of faith, that is, the vindication of divine righteousness or goodness, in the end: a dénouement operated solely by divine, not human agencies. Such was, and is still the case. We cannot blame the era for the oppositional perverters of good work enacted by those who with hearts and minds of insight and good faith attempted to "up" the notch of human ethical and spiritual evolution, well intentioned and energized by a decent belief in life and love in the face of often violent, vulgar, and covert opposition. The image of art is not invalidated because a vandal casts ink across its canvas. Vandals come and go, but truth liveth evermore.

Well, that may not be the end of it. Oxford professor of Eastern religions R. C. Zaehner's inspired book *Our Savage God* (1974), regarded the Manson case, not as an isolated episode concerned only with the criminality of an individual and his acolytes, but as a sign of the times that bore deeper contemplation of its meaning. In a powerful chapter about corruption in the Western world, that is, corruption in the light of the austere spiritual vision of the Bible and the Jesus of the New Testament in particular, Zaehner sees perennial state-prisoner Manson (d. 2017) as having come under the influence not only of the biblical apocalyptic judgment scenario, but also those strands of "spirituality" from the Middle and Far East that speak not of a personal God concerned about our behavior, but of an impersonal "Absolute" wherein all good and evil is transcended, so that, from this "higher" perspective, events on earth, such as murder or death, are of no significance in themselves and their occurrence really a matter of indifference. God-is-the-devil-is-God: depending on how you look at it. Moral absolutes are only relative, goes the theory based on mystical experience of "transcending good and evil." Zaehner puts forth a powerful case that Manson actually *did* what the philosophy of radical Eastern progenitors (Buddhist and Hindu) permitted in theory, once, that is, we understand "love" as being merely the symbol of the union of opposites, for a magical, or willed end, not a commitment of personal affection and warm, unselfish care. I think Zaehner ought to have allowed that Aleister Crowley's ethic of Thelema (which Zaehner held to be a perilous outcome of radical Eastern philosophies) insisted that "true wills" did not conflict, and that no one had the right to interfere with the true will of another (the "true will" being effectively the highest spiritually inherent possibility related to an individual), and Manson should have minded his own business, and that Manson had not transcended his ego but been utterly transcended by it, which in psychoanalytic terms would constitute a psychosis insofar as it engendered a hallucinatory or unreal "reality." Regardless of the claims of relativity of consciousness, you will not obtain a refreshing cup of tea from inside a man convinced he is a teapot.

Zaehner's chapter referring to Manson and Crowley is called "Rot in the Clockwork Orange" and obviously alludes also to the casual murderer "Alex" in Anthony Burgess's novel *A Clockwork Orange* published in 1962 (another Kubrick movie) and his misanthropic escapades, fueled by readily available, self-insulating narcotics. Nevertheless,

Zaehner's stands as a point of view to be reckoned with, and if nothing else, argues implicitly that before we accept religious ideas from hither and thither, we should first understand deeply, and humbly, what those we may have inherited are. Furthermore, we should understand more deeply, and discerningly, the implications of "spiritual" ideas strange to us. In other words, we need guides, and it is one of Zaehner's points that in the rebellious spirit of the 1960s and onward to our own time, traditional guides associated with inherited institutions are more mistrusted than they used to be, often, as Zaehner maintains, because the guides themselves have ceased to believe in the essence of what it is they are expected to extrapolate upon. The underlying crisis might then be termed an anarchy of ideas and a protracted crisis of authority. *Who do you believe? And why?* The human tendency to accept uncriticially what at first appears attractive is exemplified by the following codicil to this chapter, which has as its subject not only the fear of the end of the world, but fear of the world itself.

POSTSCRIPT . . . FAR OUT AND OUTTA SIGHT

We should be missing something in our reflections on secular or quasi-spiritual apocalypses of the Sixties were we to ignore the remarkable impact of Erich von Däniken's book *Chariots of the Gods?* First published in 1968, people are still inclined to omit the question mark put to the bold title of a work that purported to show that ancient civilizations were instructed in the ways of interstellar travel and other technical feats familiar to observers of the Space Race by alien beings who visited this Earth in the distant past. While the author took enormous liberties with the idea of "factual fiction" to produce a compelling and highly influential bestseller, the interest of the book from our point of view is not to assess whether von Däniken's hypotheses concerning alien technology had any basis in fact but rather to observe the manner in which his extremely colorful story was almost immediately interpreted.

Everything we have been discussing about the Sixties had fertilized the imaginative soil into which the "chariots of the gods" idea was cast. Not content with showing some pre-Columbian inscriptions of deities in contexts that—with the benefit of seeing *Star Trek* (which entered production in 1966), and an imagination primed for the purpose— might be seen as resembling spacecraft, a designation also applied to heavenly symbols in Akkadian inscriptions discovered in Mesopotamia, the author attempted a reinterpretation of biblical stories on analogous lines, thus beginning a trend that continues to this day and will doubt- less gather even more moss as the conglomerate base of the fancy refuses to budge, however hard the stone is pushed. For example, the story in the book of Kings concerning the prophet Elijah being assumed to heaven in a "fiery chariot" with horses in a whirlwind (2 Kings 2:3–9) was taken by von Däniken as the way a person of the ninth century BCE might describe a flying saucer, or the like, descending to Earth and tak- ing, or abducting, a human being out of this world. And here is the nub of our point. Elijah (in Greek, *Elias*) was widely believed in Jesus's time to be the herald whose coming to earth would signal the "Day of the Lord" (Yom Yahweh) and the last judgment. John the Baptist was identified with Elijah as messianic forerunner. So if, taking the alien scenario as a framework, Elijah returned by agency of alien spacecraft, that would mean that the apocalyptic scheme discernible in the Bible really promised the coming to Earth in the fullness of time of superior technology from outer space, and such might constitute the new age. Very soon after von Däniken's book appeared, there would appear ear- nest advocates for the "mission" of the "spacepeople," in part inspired by the mythology of Fabre d'Olivet's Tradition (allegedly available to a pre-Egyptian primal civilization).* These benign spacepeople would apparently come and wrap up the mystery of our history and being, especially, it was argued, when our own technology had reached a stage when confrontation with theirs would not cause us to wilt into aphasic terror and helpless awe. Well, our trips to the moon plainly indicated

---

*See onetime Andy Warhol colleague Chuck Wein's chaotic, free-form movie experiment *Rainbow Bridge*, shot in 1970, featuring Chuck himself, model Pat Hartley, Jimi Hendrix, and assorted hippies in Hawaii, and advocates of the mission of the spacepeople who were, they alleged, watching us, communicating with their favored channelers, and would, if we listened, help us to fulfill our planetary destiny. The movie was universally panned when released in 1972; time has not softened, but cemented, that critical opinion.

the imminence of a superhuman, alien apocalypse, at least to such as "bought it" and still buy it. Kubrick's astonishing 1968 movie *2001: A Space Odyssey* suggested quite directly that going to the moon risked encounter with alien intelligence, and at its climax turned psychedelic tripping through special effects (colored lights) into a quasi-spiritual transformative experience, much to the delight of those who saw the movie pre-oriented by exotic or chemical stimulants.

What is even more striking is how this whole quasi-religious scheme plugged in to popular ideas about UFOs as related to fear of nuclear catastrophe. The impressive movie *The Day the Earth Stood Still,* directed by Robert Wise and released in 1951 in the wake of several years of widely publicized UFO scares, had long since popularized the idea that alien superiors wanted us to embrace the ways of peace as advocated by spiritual religion, and had sent a final, Christic emissary called "Klaatu," portrayed impressively by the gentle, meek, and mild (till roused in righteous indignation) Michael Rennie in the film—even endowed with the power of resurrection from the dead, albeit tactfully adjusted to a *temporary* power, for the "full treatment" was, he intoned, the sole prerogative of the "Almighty Spirit." That doubtless calmed the Vatican!—as was the producer's careful intention. So, in the Sixties, we get the peace movement, great expectations, and all, it might be supposed, now required to wrap the whole thing up was a celestial visitation and sanction. Suitable channeled messages were already emanating from "psychics," and their message was pretty consistent: peace and love, share and share alike, and beware of the military-industrial complex! "Repent ye, for the kingdom of God (or alien technology) is at hand." Such was the message of ultrasuperior intelligences beaming from "advanced" planetary systems! You could have got the same message from *Top of the Pops.* Besides, had Klaatu not warned the people of Earth: keep threatening each other with your primitive atom bombs, and the superior aliens will have no choice but to execute a summary end-of-the-world scenario; the choice is yours! Disarm or apocalypse! *Then,* when no one was left to notice, it would appear that the ancient prophecies as regards death and destruction were true. We might even add that as Klaatu was able to take humans aboard his craft, then the kindly aliens might do the same at the End for the righteous. The idea of the "space ark" was launched. In 1970, Canadian singer-songwriter Neil Young would sing with no discernible tongue in cheek about the coming to our stricken world of a "silver seed" that would take the "chosen ones" to a new home, far above and away from the pollutions of Earth ("After the Goldrush").

The issue of alleged alien role in human civilization and ultimate destiny was compounded by a prevalent suspicion that the Earth's destiny was being secretly directed by any number of supposed "hidden masters," in the United States generally identified with secret government. (The creepy 1967 U.S. TV drama series *The Invaders* actually posited the secret takeover of government agencies by aliens indistinguishable from human authorities—how's that for calculated paranoia!) The Cold War had massively intensified the role of covert government activity, and the world can't keep a secret for long. The James Bond novels and films—and countless TV, movie, and book spin-offs—added to the ongoing rage for spying as speculation and popular adventure, with ever a hint of revelation. The word *secret* now easily crosses from power politics to mysticism and religion. Interest in whether our governments actually knew about aliens, but weren't telling us, fed directly into popular Belgian children's visual storyteller Hergé's next project. He decided to incorporate the idea into what would be his penultimate "Tintin" adventure, *Flight 714 to Sydney* (*Vol 714 pour Sydney* in the original French).

Fig. 9.5. Book cover of the Flight 714 to Sydney, *the twenty-second volume in the series The Adventures of Tintin, 1967.*

I well recall, aged eight, seizing on a fresh copy of this book in late 1968 from the shelves of the rather magical Victorian "Athenaeum" private library in Collins Street, Melbourne, Australia, which my family used to visit on Friday nights. Apparently there was meant to be a launch party in Paris in May '68 for Hergé's prescient *Flight 714,* but the epoch-marking events of that month disrupted plans, as students appeared to take over the capital in the name of revolution and anti-Gaullism (and perhaps the justice-seeking spirit of ever-young cartoon hero Tintin too).

Hergé's story has Tintin diverted by criminals to an island south of Indonesia where he accidentally uncovers underground primitive temples where the enormous stone figures strongly resemble astronauts. Tintin starts receiving telepathic messages that draw him farther into the labyrinth. Eventually he encounters a secret scientist, Mik Kanrockitoff, apparently a freelance UFO scientist-enthusiast from the magazine *Space Week,* who is in mental communication with aliens, and who explains how the ancient people of the island worshipped extraterrestrials as gods.

At the climax of the adventure, Tintin and his party are lifted from the exploding island by a flying saucer summoned by Kanrockitoff telepathically. The catch is that everybody but Kanrockitoff is mesmerized into forgetting the experience entirely, thus leaving the question open in (chiefly young) readers' minds. It was all very effective, and one might have thought Erich von Däniken might have had a copyright issue with Hergé's team in Belgium. However, Hergé's biggest influence seems to have been Robert Charroux's "The Book of Betrayed Secrets" (*Le livre des secrets trahis,* 1965) whose account of ancient astronauts identified with the "Watcher" angels who descended to Earth to mate with human women in the apocalyptic book of Enoch influenced the author of *Chariots of the Gods?* to such an extent that Charroux's publisher suggested plagiarism to von Däniken's in March 1968 (Charroux's name would appear in the bibliography of subsequent editions).

Interestingly, Charroux's background was in science-fiction writing (from the 1940s onward), and the inspiration for his ancient astronaut comes from authentic apocalyptic sources (the book of Enoch's extrapolation of the account of Nephilim in Genesis 6:1–4) combined with burgeoning scientific expectations of space travel elaborated in mythologizing fiction. It should be appreciated that for many in the postwar world, to enter into space was already to encroach on the "heavens," that is, the territory of angels and their subordinates traditionally and still widely believed to govern the planetary and stellar systems.

The cunning of all this frankly theosophical theorizing was that just as Theosophy under Madame Blavatsky (she and Colonel Olcott founded the Theosophical Society in New York in 1875) aimed to unite, or reunite, science and religion through understanding of the esoteric and the paranormal, so with the late Sixties new apocalyptic scenario, we are presented with a basically "scientific" interpretation of the mysteries of religion, and a kind of rational scheme of ethics: *do the right thing, or your technology will destroy you.* This apocalypse or alleged revelation of the formerly hidden is simply a materialist fantasy, plus a folk singer's dream, occupying some of the outward forms of spiritual religion, but denuding it of any genuine spiritual substance. To turn aliens into gods according to the ignorant model of the Sandwich Islanders encountering early European explorers, is to deny all respect to the source of spiritual understanding; it is in fact, quite technically, idolatry.

In terms of the further spiritual significance of this novel twist on the apocalyptic, I am inclined to conclude with religious philosopher and poet Samuel Taylor Coleridge (1772–1834) that when we are asked to accept scientific evidence for the truths of spiritual religion, those truths become for us neither spiritual nor true. At the bottom of this whole alien-savior hypothesis is the evolutionary-style narrative that superior technology will carry with it superior ethical development, while all about us may make us aware that something resembling the opposite may well be the case. Besides, technology has no ethical bias, and modern scientific method claims to be value-free, the principal aspect of its hegemony that many find intrinsically disturbing. Its aesthetic is fundamentally cold. The only reason we have not yet witnessed the nuclear catastrophe that still hovers over us is because the protagonists have been quite animal, and crudely tooth-and-claw basic enough to understand that you don't win anything on earth when you're dead. However, a mad person might conclude otherwise. The jihadi fantasist of course believes he has sidestepped this issue of futile destructiveness. As I recall the last part of Arthur C. Clarke's original novel *2001: A Space Odyssey,* is it not the "Star Child," that embryolike image of innocence and newness in Kubrick's interpretation of Clarke's book, that returns to Earth to destroy the nuclear weapons that orbit it? Seems the new innocent has an open-will vista with quite a capacity for violent destruction, albeit in a good cause, as Clarke saw it, taking a leaf, I suspect, from Aleister Crowley's prophecy of the "crowned and conquering Child" (*The Book of the Law,* 1904). Presumably Kubrick had his reasons for omitting this dénouement to Clarke's story, but by doing so robbed the movie of a proper climax in terms of viewer satisfaction. The only mystery about the Star Child's appearance in the movie is that his reason for being there has been removed. One might just as well have put a final title over the screen with the biblical quotation: "And a little child shall lead them"—biblical prophecy again! (Isaiah 11:6). That, at least, would have meant something. It is the case that the French word *aliené,* which gave us the early word *alienist* for a psychoanalyst, meant "mad." Aliens are crazy.

Aliens will not, I think, be of any use to the alienated. And if I may say so, a spiritual man is well content with the symbolic image of a "fiery chariot and whirlwind," and would not be any more impressed, indeed I suspect considerably less so, were it a jumbo jet.

All that techno-excitement and futurist panting for the sky, so pervasive in the Sixties, betokened an almost complete loss of understanding of the meaning of spiritual life: a deficit pertinent to the entire apocalyptic scenario through history, if we are to take the word of a wise man like theologian Johann Valentin Andreae (1586–1654)—himself the co-creator of the "Rosicrucian" mystery—who, when dealing with his closest friend Tobias Hess's apocalyptic future-prognosticating excitements, observed that the mania over such things always occurs when the proper work of the church is slowing down.

That, I think, tells us much about the spiritual meaning of the Sixties. A journey through the unreal is an unreal journey.

TEN

Education:
Loosening the Bonds

Education is about drawing out potential faculties that exist in human individuals. The word comes from the Latin *educare,* which means "to draw out." Strange then that so much of what goes by the name of education consists of stuffing in. In the United Kingdom, if one wishes to prepare quickly for an examination, the usual term is *cramming:* to gobble in as much, largely undigested, information as possible in order to regurgitate it on paper before the capacity and will to retain it are lost to other distractions. "And this is what the British population calls an elementary education!" as Professor Higgins laments in song in Lerner and Loewe's musical *My Fair Lady,* when commenting on the analogous case of accented, colloquial English that, in the professor's judgment, robs spoken language of its higher music and meaning, save in exceptional individuals.

Along with the drawing out comes guidance. We need guides to help us to understand what we are learning, aids to the discernment of truth, value, and sense, as well as the experience of how what we learn can be applied in life outside of the lesson, bearing in mind that while experience is a great teacher, her fees are very high. If we can learn sound principles at an early age, and feel we understand what makes them sound, we can avoid many harsh and ruinous experiences in later life. The person who claims to have gone to the "university of life" for his (or her) education, is just as likely to admit, or be proud of having been to the school of hard knocks. But getting knocked, and avoiding the circumstance in future that led to the pain, is really to become a Pavlovian dog, conditioned externally through suffering. This is not the same as *understanding,* and it is not only limiting but is very unpleasant and leaves a deficit of soreness and bitterness. You can make a dog learn to do many things, but you will never get the creature to understand why he or she is doing them. As Doris Day tells grizzled university-of-life-man Clark Gable in that exemplary comedy *Teacher's Pet* (1958), "Education enables us to spell *experience.*"

There is no doubt that our education shapes us. That is generally the idea. However, that idea has its limits, and the 1960s saw the process of education hit those limits in varying degrees of abrasiveness in different ways throughout the world: far too different to adumbrate in this chapter. A scholarly account of "Education in the 1960s" could happily occupy many volumes, and that is not the compass of my attention. I wish to attend to some aspects of education during the decade with a bearing on the question of the decade's spiritual meaning.

One of the first tendencies we discover as the decade unfolds is a tension over just how much "shaping" ought to be the proper province of the professional educator. This issue gained greater political resonance as a result of Cold War ideological competition between the West and those countries run by authoritarian Communist regimes that systematically transplanted and eradicated traditional institutions among the people under their power. The aim of a Communist state was to produce a different kind of person, a new human specimen. The individual was disregarded except insofar as he or she conformed to an ideal collectivity, such being the terrestrial application of Feuerbach's transcendent ideal of selfless love expressed socially as being the be-all-and-end-all of human idealism. In Communist countries, "selfless love" generally meant having, or being expected to have, no real self at all. Individual willfulness was castigated severely in the USSR and China, and in countries influenced by them, as a symptom of bourgeois individualism, necessarily, it was insisted, dedicated to exploitative competition with and over one's comrade for whom one ought to be striving: an absurd theory in practice. I recall in late-Sixties Birmingham (in some respects the "Detroit" of England) being informed by a blue-collar technician from Britain's largest car firm, influenced by current (Communist-inspired) trade-union doctrine, that "Jesus was a Communist." I had to demur and informed the surprised, kindly, and most loveable mechanic, that on the contrary, Jesus praised some workers over others, especially the one who could capitalize on a gift left in trust. In Jesus's view, "fair wages" were based on an individual's performance offered to his "divine employer," not egalitarian sameness. A disappointing steward might in Jesus's parabolic scheme end up unemployed, with no "shop-steward" to cry to. In the divine vineyard, there were bosses, overseers, and servants: an obvious class system, though social mobility upward was encouraged as the reward for dedicated performance! God sits on a throne, not a committee.

So it made for good policy in the West to increase the educational polity of the individual. In fact, of course, individual responsibility had always been a cornerstone of canon law, that is, Catholic theory in practice, which had informed Western ideas of education since the establishment of civilized education with the fading of the Dark Ages. The aim of Catholic practice had been to justify citizenship in heaven, after due purgation of the individual soul, and the benefit of education on this earth was to extend the empire of Christian influence, though the purpose was ultimately to further divine will, with the ultimate End in sight. Much of the educative effort had therefore been laid on providing the monarchical, lay powers with "educated" administrators of justice, guidance, and management—priests, lawyers, and doctors, the essential "professionals," that is, those persons whose employment required the *professing* of an oath of dedication to higher purpose. Education meant maintaining control, the educator was shepherd, and those fortunate to benefit from his inherited learning were sheep in need of close tending, lest they stray into sin and frustrate the aims of the whole.

What needed to be "drawn out" from the child was first, the "old Adam," that is, the sinful, spiritually unregenerated, willful "natural man," whose carnal will and mind was presumed to be in natural enmity against God, for natural man was in love with the body (nature) and identified itself with the natural urges at the expense of higher calling and spiritual salvation. A man in love, for example, was of no use to philosophy, his mind a storm of instability and inattention. The old Adam was frequently to be uprooted, beaten into submission or quiescence (fear is a sure teacher), its challenge extinguished where possible. After that, what needed to be drawn out, and subjected to strict discipline, were those gifts entrusted by God, by whose assistance the redemptive process could be advanced. The disciplines into which human intellectual and spiritual gifts could be drawn were, in general, aspects of the seven liberal arts of a Roman gentleman's education: grammar, logic, rhetoric (the *trivium*); and arithmetic, geometry, astronomy, music (the *quadrivium*). Over and above these sciences reigned Queen Theology— knowledge of God—and all conclusions stemming from the arts had to be subjected, in the last instance, to the revealed order of divine will, whose depth exceeded human capacity to grasp.

Well, that was the basis for educational theory in the West until the Age of Enlightenment when the proposition that there was knowledge that was divine and beyond human capacity to fathom, and to which the dictates of reason must be subjected, was openly defied. While strictly ecclesiastical education continued largely unhindered in the Catholic and Catholic-influenced centers of education (Italy, Spain, Austria, Bavaria, Poland, and most of South America) strictly rational ideas of education proceeded to develop their own "educational" priorities, with extraordinary results in the fields of politics and science, and with many tumultuous social ramifications. I think of Britain's prime minister, the Duke of Wellington (1769–1852; victor of Waterloo) declaring as a good Tory (Land, Church, and King) that to allow the parliamentary Liberals their whole program would mean taking education out of the hands of the Church of England, which would mean setting loose a tiger in the land! He was right of course, and by the onset of the Sixties that tiger had been tearing into the old system and its principles for over 130 years, only to be joined by another equally rapacious creature:

The child.

DR. SPOCK

Distinguished Yale graduate in literature and history, Benjamin McLane Spock (1903–1998) published his first book on mothering in 1946. *The Common Sense Book of Baby and Child Care* afterward sold over fifty million copies and was followed by five further books on childcare, the last three of which appeared between 1961 and 1965, before Dr. Spock turned his literary attention to support his deeply considered activism against the Vietnam War and his commitment to the Committee for a Sane Nuclear Policy (SANE), which he joined in 1962.

I recall my mother telling me how the American Dr. Spock, who brought psychology into a subject formerly the province of doctors, nurses, midwives, and female family members, had made her think about her approach to my and my brothers' upbringing. How far that went I don't know, enough anyway I think to ameliorate somewhat my father's frequently disciplinarian approach, derived from army experience, social background, and sometimes acute personal frustrations. If I have in any way benefited from some of Dr. Spock's advice, I must be one among millions.

Generally speaking, Dr. Spock threw out the old manual on childcare and, benefiting to some degree from knowledge of psychoanalysis—one senses the presence of Dr. Alfred Adler's "individual psychology"—Spock

Fig. 10.1. Dr. Benjamin Spock (1903–1998).

advocated a more flexible, individual-centered approach to bringing up baby. Basically what he frowned upon was the idea that the disciplining of the adult must begin with the disciplining of the baby. Thus, if baby cried, nannies or mothers often repeated what they had been taught, namely, that responding to a child's cries would make them weak and unfit for the toughness of life. A crying baby should be left alone till they got used to the idea that crying didn't change anything. This was of course no new idea. We see Rhett Butler (Clark Gable) in Selznick's production of *Gone with the Wind* in 1939 dismissing his daughter's nanny (in London!) for just this (to us) callous approach—and that story was set in the 1860s!

What Spock did was to suggest that ordinary harshness or apparent indifference to children, however it might conform to society's expectations, stood as scientifically proven to damage them, and was thus another way of "spoiling" them, and that the future belonged to a progressive, milder, more individual-centered approach. For this, Spock has been blamed for juvenile delinquencies of many kinds, for promoting a "demand-fed" brat who requires instant gratification that the parent—and by extension society—is duty bound to satisfy. So, if young Tom and Annie believe the Vietnam War is a bad, dangerous, horrid thing, then it should be stopped for their benefit at once—*or else they will cwy and cwy and cwy, and thcweam and thcweam and thcweam, and get vewy angwy indeed,* until Daddy in the White House actually eliminates the cause of upset, for which effort he may expect no thanks. One can see of course how all this chimes in with the consumer-led capitalism that bloomed in the 1950s and '60s and whose social consequences were still largely obscure. *I want . . . I must have . . .* soon becomes "I am *entitled* to have." *And if I can't, I'm gonna come lookin' for ya!*—the whole ensuing sorry saga of entitlement. Spock was thus an automatic target for conservative reaction that could neither understand nor wish to understand why so many "intelligent youngsters" were prepared to risk being bashed in the head by irate policemen in the collective desire of "switched-on" youth that the government stop sending young people to the Far East only to be returned-to-sender in bags and boxes.

Furthermore, in the 1950s, children began to be seen as something of a precious investment, not just a biological inevitability, or as responsible heirs as hitherto. It is well known that babies born in or shortly after a war are often indulged, for the very fact of their life, their comparative innocence, and their promise of more life in the face of a period of death and feared annihilation.

Meanwhile, advertising created and reinforced the convenient (to government and capital) idea that the nuclear family was a kind of microeconomic world of its own, where the children were the object of care, spending, even occasional reverence. They were, unlike the benighted "Commies," to be free, that is, free of Communism anyway—but not of consumerism. Of course, one did not wish to spoil them through overindulgence, but the influence of Spock was generally to upset or obscure the fulcrum of just where overindulgence and spoiling them actually lay. Besides, in the progressive scenario expounded earlier, the future was held somehow to "belong" to children. Children were the future, and Spock encouraged the idea that children already had in them capacities to make that future, while it was parents' duty to allow all that out into the world, and the parents, alerted by Spock's literary reminder, would find that they too had these capacities and the will to enact the optimistic vision of bright, healthy, free children turning the world into a glorious panoply of satisfied humanity. Children were *good:* agents of society's salvation. They could quickly become the objects and purpose of life itself. The world must be made "safe" for them. What child wants, child must have. The effect was real enough—and did not sacred scripture foresee something of the kind? Saint Paul had instructed followers not to "overcorrect" their children, while Jesus had reportedly told his disciples to "suffer the little children," their will to approach him should be respected, for they had capacities of receptivity and sensitivity to God's will that sinful adults had lost sight of! Bring on the Flower Children! "God is Love" was a favorite button in hippie-saturated San Francisco in 1967. A return to Edenic innocence could elide gracefully, or disgracefully, into the "sexual revolution." The cover of the second *Woodstock* soundtrack album featured a close-up movie still of naked toddlers toying with the drum kits on the festive stage after the adults have gone: "Here is the future" the cover seems to suggest, though to my mind the image more resembles the closing scenes of Steven Spielberg's *Close Encounters of the Third Kind* (1978) where the childlike aliens mingle in pools of light with the self-directed, understanding, oh-so-very-cute child (played by Cary Guffey) who though apparently abducted, has in essence followed his own route to the (holy) mountain for the alien revelation. And in some respects, the newborn child with his or her new capacities was, post-Spock, on the way to becoming something of an alien. In *2001: A Space Odyssey,* of course, the celestial Child is the agent of apocalypse and his arrival a new beginning for the human species. A young, pointedly long-haired David Jones, auto-rechristened "David Bowie" would click into the alien "society's child" idea in his pop single "Space Oddity," an alienated pun on Kubrick's *2001,* first released to coincide with Apollo 11 in July 1969. Major Tom is out in space all right, far out, and he's on his own, and knows it. *Gone,* not with the wind, but with space.

All this idealism could hardly fail to have its impact on the scope of education, and on the developing behavior of those *in loco parentis,* most particularly those either working in, or aware of, the significant number of "progressive schools" that had been challenging conventional test-based education since the late nineteenth century in Europe, the United States, and other parts of the world, including India and Japan, and which had ascribed more significance to the spiritual integrity and self-motivation of the child than was normally entertained. However, I am quite sure that I am not alone in finding that in my experience of five different schools, and speech therapists, during the 1960s, neither I nor anyone I encountered at school ever felt from teachers any marked reverence for us *as children.* For most schoolteachers, old-fashioned discipline was what they had been taught to administer as a necessity for maintaining order, though this was not resorted to immediately by the more loving (and loved) teachers, albeit the threat was always there, but broadly speaking, the times they were a-changin' nonetheless, and in England, at least, physical punishment was administered with less relish by the majority of teachers than it had been in fairly recent years gone by, though my and my brothers' experience was that teachers of Celtic provenance were often the most severe, coming from communities, one presumes generously, where any form of "weakness" among men was still regarded with horror. There were a few sadists, maybe more, and they could get away with quite a lot still in the Sixties, as parents did want their children, by and large "to respect authority," their own in particular.

Attitudes to violence and cruelty—and the scope of the word *violence*—undoubtedly began to change subtly in many places in the 1960s (though by no means all), but speaking as a child in the 1960s, I must say that though the aesthetic appeal of peace and love and flowers and all that, was obvious in the main, but by no means exclusively so, one's knowledge of, or contact with, radical movements or individuals was really slight to nonexistent. Even teenagers are often quite indifferent to younger children, and I can honestly say that I never received either kindness or attention from a hippie, for example, and was not disposed to regard their activities, as seen on TV, with much more than amusement or indifference, though my father, like so many others, saw them as generally disturbing and probably subversive of sensible conduct. Well, hippies wanted to make a point, and they did so; they were different from the rest, or so they thought.

GAME-CHANGE AT SCHOOL

In Great Britain, the 1944 Butler Education Act, named after Minister of Education Rab Butler, for the first time promised state-provided education up to the age of eighteen based, that is, on the capacity of the individual as judged by examinations, and which individuality the state felt it its duty to recognize. This was a great leap in educational provision, since before the Act, only children whose parents had enough money could ensure their children advanced in line with their intellectual abilities. A problem with the Act was that it enshrined the idea of a test at eleven years old that would be decisive in the child's admissibility to grammar schools (with possible move to universities afterward), or "secondary modern" schools where the chances of obtaining qualifications suitable for university education were slim at best. This starkly two-tier system received its first shocks when the Labor government began to encourage local authorities to prepare for secondary moderns to go over to "comprehensive" systems after 1965, where the intake was not based on prior selection but could in theory take in all ability ranges with provision for very small numbers of the brightest to obtain qualifications suitable for universities. Nevertheless, grammar schools held dominant sway as career makers through the Sixties in the United Kingdom, unlike other European countries where state schools generally took in all pupils, though with a strong conformist ethos and discipline that did not begin to alter until after the May 1968 "events" in Paris, whose ramifications led to a revolution in education in France in the 1970s.

It should be noted that the Butler Act in the United Kingdom insisted not only on the teaching of religious education to all pupils, but also for a religious-based Christian assembly of the school before lessons. These features were practically universal throughout schools in Great Britain. Children sang hymns and said prayers and received the idea that goodness of conduct was sanctioned by God Almighty, and that God cared for children. The appropriation of religion was generally of an external nature, and there was no interest shown in other religions to Christianity or in issues of spirituality in general.

Public education in the United States had advanced steadily since the end of the nineteenth century, with funding widely differentiated in poorer and richer parts of the states, and provision inconsistent. The figure of progressive educator John Dewey (1859–1952) looms large in putting some practical thinking into what went on in school, with greater emphasis on building self-confidence in individuals and preparedness for life, rather than the ingestion of information, often wide of requirements beyond school age.* My father always said American educational science books were far better than British ones since they seemed to wish to engage with the mind of the child rather than exhibiting primarily the scholarship of the author; pictures were more widely

---

*One wonders if John Dewey might have given his name to the character "Dewey Finn" played by Jack Black in the evergreen 2011 movie, *School of Rock,* which also showed in a humorous way how imagination, daring, and thinking outside the box could enhance formal education.

Fig. 10.2. John Dewey (1859–1952).

used in U.S. textbooks than in British ones, and of course, there was less class snobbery in social attitudes in America, where, in theory at least, all were at least created equal and deserved a chance to get to the top or somewhere near it, though the individual was responsible to self, God, family, and country, and should not let any of these interested parties down.

First Amendment principles meant, and mean, that religious education, unlike in Great Britain, was not a responsibility for public schools, and religious education was therefore generally left to faith-based, denomination-based extramural courses and specific colleges, though religion could be discussed in an academic, objective manner. To some this is a vital principle, to others a restriction of what is deemed essential knowledge, as the longstanding debate about creationism versus evolution amply demonstrates. It should be observed that church membership in the United States far exceeds experience of churchgoing among Britain's once nominally Christian population, that is, children baptized in a church, so that if British children had no religious education in schools, they would probably never experience the subject as a meaningful (or meaningless) subject of interest at all. In 1990 the British Broadcasting Act removed the requirement of independent TV to make religious programs, though in our period that is irrelevant because for the 1960s period there was only one independent channel in addition to the BBC, and people were not disposed to receiving information about religion from the TV, though leading religious figures were frequently included in general discussions of public interest, considerably more so in fact in those days than is the case today.

This all means that it is impossible today to formulate a clear idea of what constituted the spiritual lives of people in the 1960s in relation to their formal education, and we must be content with looking at the more visible tendencies available to the historical record and to memory to ascertain spiritual meaning.

EDUCATION IN THE MOVIES

There was always a big market for movies aimed at children and teenagers and "the whole family," but there were perhaps surprisingly few that dealt with actual life in the classroom. I can think of two Sixties movies that dared to go there in particular. The first, *To Sir, with Love,* was released in autumn 1967 and, surprisingly perhaps for a film dealing exclusively with young people, did not present a bunch of hippy-dippy flower children or government-challenging hip radicals. Rather it took as its text the experience of a lone black (or "Negro" as the term of the time had it) American schoolteacher in a fairly tough, working-class district of London. The class he encounters is undoubtedly a class of individuals, and their teenage, adolescent characters are all drawn with individual distinction. One might generalize about "kids," but these kids are not generalizations, they all have their own personalities, gifts, foibles, and sense of promise. However, by and large, they are inclined to be swayed to support the toughest individuals in the class. There is a boredom with learning that we can understand, encountering some of their teachers, and a great hostility to authority, as well as an aggressive impatience to get out into "real life" as they imagine, and have experienced it, to be. There is endemic racism, bad attitudes toward sex and violence, and all manner of things that the adult finds hard to tolerate in young people of that age, or indeed any age. The movie shows Sidney Poitier, who plays the teacher with inspiring force and character (and I mean both the character and his exceptional performance), truly getting to grips with the challenge his young charges present to him. Epitomizing the word *dedication,* he even ends up having a boxing match with the tough one who wants to rough up the outsider he sees as threatening "his" territory.

In the end, with no great Hollywood fanfares, they all make significant steps to understanding one another, having been taken through the mill of their emotions, anguish, violence, and crises with a wise, caring, human man about them. What the teacher is able to bring forth from the troubled souls of the pupils is a capacity for mutual concern and respect they didn't know they had, and an opening of their eyes beyond their hates and petty considerations to what consciously lived adulthood should mean. They emerge with self-respect and a capacity for generosity of spirit. In short, he has educated them, and in the process, they have educated him, and he decides to stick with education and eschew a better-paid job with social kudos. He chooses life—and the young people on the verge of adulthood, love him for it. He has "descended" to their world and redeemed them. Yes, this is considerably more moving a story than a bunch of kids being led to a mountain to be "taken up" to some nowhere galaxy of methane gas and sci-fi fantasy and quasi-religious salvation. To "come down to earth" in this case is to enter the hearts of real people. And that is where Sidney Poitier takes himself. When Judy Geeson and Lulu say and sing that they "love" him at the close of the movie, we know that they really mean it, and though they are at a party in psychedelic miniskirts and dancing to a psychedelic pop group, we know that their love is of the purest hue, the real Real Thing that is truly life changing. *To Sir, with Love* is a true love story and concerns the Love Generation that we might only dream about, for there are not enough teachers of the kind Poitier portrays to go around. I say this is a spiritual film that goes a long way to exhibiting a less-observed spiritual meaning of the Sixties: real engagement with real people, real feelings, real hopes and aspirations to be human, to love, and be loved. And to conclude: the teacher does not assume the address of respect (Sir); in the end, he realizes he has had to *earn* it. Lip service is one thing, meaning another.

△ △ △

Another "classic" Sixties film engages with the classroom, this one very different in style and substance. *If . . .* was released in 1968, and its story of youthful rebellion in a British public school* was very much taken as a reflection of, or even component of, that intense period of student rebellion that exploded in London that year with the Grosvenor Square March on the U.S. Embassy to protest the Vietnam War, and of course with the Paris emergency of May 1968, when the Sorbonne erupted in revolutionary-style demonstrations that very near brought about a complete revolution in the French State.

In many ways however, Lindsay Anderson's film of David Sherwin's play *Crusaders* was not really tuned in to the specific political and sociological rhetoric of the May 1968 student rebellion. *If . . .* was in some respects a quite romantic fantasy with something of Robert Hughes's *Tom Brown's Schooldays* about it. Above all, it is a poetic film, where visual images sometimes segue out of realistic sequence and become poetic symbols "for the sake of it," that is, for the sake of poetry's power of allusive inference. Obviously, in that it deals with a group or cadre of upper-class students (aged around seventeen in the main) who have decided to destroy those running the school that has physically punished them for—we would think—trifling misdemeanors, it is a film that shows relish in the act of rebellion and could therefore be construed as a radical left-wing movie advocating what is good for the public school would be good for the country or the world. However, despite the Cambridge-graduate director's intellectual leftism, the film's rebellious youths could just as easily be enjoyed by a right-wing rebellious individualist spirit, and this is, dare I say it, one of its charms, as a Sixties movie dealing to some extent with a spiritual crisis in the young and those making "radical" films at the time.

The young rebels in the film, led by Michael Travis (played with Luciferian élan by Malcolm McDowell) never spout dogmas about Marxist alienation, or the horror of the bourgeoisie, or class conflict, or any of the other tedious theoretical and now antique preoccupations

---

*Please note in the U.K. a "pubic school" denotes not a publicly funded school, but a private institution, maintained by fees, and usually, much historical tradition.

of vocal leftists of the period like Tariq Ali who led the Grosvenor Square protest that brought out the violent tendencies of some of the "good old" British bobbies who tried to keep them off U.S. territory in London; no, "Mick" and his mates are basically individualist anarchists without a cause, except perhaps, the best cause, as they feel it to be: freedom, freedom they could touch and feel. "Some love England and her honor yet!" declares one of the rebels during a piratical, free-form fencing match. They've been put in this school by their parents at great expense, and they feel they know where it's going to lead, and they don't like it. They can feel the prison bars growing about their growing selves, the invisible ones of job, family, respectability, and they just know, it's not *life* as they intuit life to be.

When one of them puts a color photo from a magazine of a bellicose African almost weighed down by ammunition belts and machine gun, one of them (Johnny) just says: "Magnificent!" It's a pure aesthetic response to an image of strength and imagined heroism, nothing at all to do with the politics of anti-imperialism or race. He just feels kinship with the image, and it's instinctive and very powerful.

Needless to say, the climax of the film, shot in somewhat surreal-realist fashion, involves their quixotic (we can be sure) attempt to blow up the "enemy" on Speech Day, culminating in the shooting of the headmaster who says he "understands" them before dying quite magnificently and disappearing in a puff of smoke.

Before the shooting starts, however, there is a key scene that tells us without a doubt that this film has within it that almost indefinable aching for spiritual substance that one finds in the peripheral areas of many interesting Sixties movies, most effective too when peripheral and most discardable when explicit.

Along the path of their adventures, this time on a brazenly "borrowed" Triumph motorcycle, the young men have encountered a girl (played mesmerizingly by Christine Noonan) at a roadside transport café. After a poetic scene of violent lovemaking between Mick and the girl in the café to the stirring tune and rhythm of the Sanctus from Missa Luba, a Congolese version of the Mass, she becomes something of a collective moll to the group and moves in with them. "I like Johnny," she says meaningfully, in a rare moment of speech, to which nobody objects. She is from the outside world and has obviously turned away from it. She will hand Mick the pistol that brings the pompous headmaster to his end. "You're too intelligent to be rebels," he had earlier told them, mistaking intelligence for passivity in the face of authority.

Shortly before the day chosen for the climactic act of revolt, the group has been given the "real work," as the sanctimonious, pseudoliberal head puts it, of clearing out years of detritus collected beneath the school stage, on which assembled clergy (uniformly rendered as absurd or sexually perverse in the movie) and military dignitaries (woefully out of touch) will make their Speech Day speeches. Searching among the bric-a-brac, Mick and the girl find a moldy old cupboard. They open it, only to find within its cobwebbed shelves a series of laboratory bottles of creatures preserved in formaldehyde, as used in biology lessons long passed. To quite mystical music, we are almost shocked to see that the largest of the bottles contains a preserved human fetus, nearly the size of a full-grown baby, close to final formation. Mick, fascinated, reaches for it. Is he going to destroy it? No, he and she simply look at it in silence, and then look into each other's eyes. The three beings (one "dead" and two soon-to-be-dead—or free) are for a second, a mysterious family. Without a word spoken, the girl gently lifts the bottled fetus from Mick's hands and places it neatly back on the shelf and carefully closes the door, as if they have encountered one, just *one* sacred thing in the whole world, and that must remain secret, and safe.

It is *the child* again, promise of *life,* and it is the future. It is life, and it is sacred, and what makes us know *that* is whatever "spirituality" might mean, and even the imperatives of revolt, as adumbrated in the film, and in the rhetoric of much of the period in which it appeared, have no right to violate that primordial promise passed on by women to men through all time. To live, one must let live. That too, is education.

ELEVEN

Discomfiting Changes in Theology

"And do you believe in the resurrection, Professor Nineham?" Mollie Butler asked. "Of course not," replied Professor Nineham: "Would you please pass the mustard?"

ANECDOTE FONDLY TOLD BY MOLLIE BUTLER, WIFE OF RAB BUTLER, THEN MASTER OF TRINITY COLLEGE, CAMBRIDGE, CONCERNING CAMBRIDGE REGIUS PROFESSOR OF DIVINITY, DENNIS NINEHAM, WITH WHOM SHE SHARED HER BREAKFAST TABLE AT THAT TIME (1964–1969)

We tend to think of the Sixties as a fairly secular place, occasionally interrupted by Hinduism in one of its manifold sects from Maharishi Mahesh Yogi's transcendental meditation to Krishna consciousness, but the fact is that the decade pullulated with Christian pundits of one persuasion or another. Hinduism and psychedelia (transcendence through stimulants) certainly challenged conventional religion, as much as they did materialism, and there was abundant commentary, from the Vatican to U.S. evangelist Billy Graham, on the subjects of sex and marriage. The churches in general found themselves more united on the morals front when faced with what was generally seen as encroaching sexual permissiveness in popular culture, and forced by tradition and conviction into a reaction that separated them from new, or emerging spiritual initiatives, as well as from public attitudes toward liberalizing divorce, use of the contraceptive pill, and acquisitiveness (legalization of homosexuality among consenting adults, and of abortion, in the U.K. in 1967 were not popular measures, but were, the government believed, moral and legal imperatives). There was also, following and during Vatican II (the Second Vatican Ecumenical Council, October 1962–December 1965), a greater tendency toward ecumenism, of the major churches cooperating, or simply admitting one another's existence, as the churches realized, though some slowly, that a large part of their intended congregation was no longer listening to them, and clergy began to feel they might be living in a different world to those outside regular worship, and therefore addressing (if and when they could) a different world. These are of course generalizations and there were many exceptions that by no means proved the rule that Christianity was in some kind of terminal decline, as was then, and is now, often thought to be the case by closed-world commentators in the media. The immense challenge of winning the "good fight" has always had to be fought again in every generation, and is sometimes a battle lost.

Politically, the influence of the Cold War had its effects insofar as atheistic Communism generated a loose unity set against a common enemy for, of course, freedom benefits all but her enemies. This situation was somewhat confused, however, by the liberty enjoyed by theologians in the West to show favor to Marxist estimations of capitalist injustices combined with consciences moved to support or be sympathetic toward socialism.

However, from the point of view of theology, there was a notable Sixties phenomenon that appeared to many both within and without the churches as something akin to theological self-harm. This phenomenon obtained more so with regard to the strictly Protestant Churches, and in the Anglican Communion, than in the Catholic (or certainly Orthodox, Greek, and Russian) Churches where institutional discipline over freedom of theological expression was stricter. The tendency to theological suicide must tell us something about the spiritual meaning of the decade, even though, as we shall see, it was only a notable, if more heavily reported phenomenon, among others of engaging interest of spiritual significance.

We have already observed the power of Ludwig Feuerbach's idea that Christianity could somehow subsist purely in the context of social relations, without God as traditionally understood (*Homo homini Deus est:* the "Man is God to man"). It seems it took a very long time for the implications of this subversive notion to filter into the thinking of Christian authorities in Great Britain, but as it turned out, postwar British universities received a triple impact from European philosophies, and theological students and graduates seem to have been hit as hard as anyone.

First, there was the influence of Marxism, a secular, avowedly atheist creed that seemed to transcend (for some) the church's traditional social teaching with a theory not only questioning the morality of riches—as the church had occasionally done—but showing, apparently scientifically, how "injustice" worked through capital allied to a class system. Hegelian dialectics were employed to make the end of "class conflict" look like a scientific and philosophical principle, which it was not. "Christian socialism" had first been championed by F. D. Maurice (1805–1872) long before, but it seemed to make more sense after the 1930s Depression, the Second World War, and the "new Jerusalem" rhetoric of postwar British socialist government.

The second bolt from the Continent was the philosophy known as "existentialism," associated particularly with atheist Jean-Paul Sartre (1905–1980) and "absurdist" writer Albert Camus (1913–1960) in France, and the *Existenzphilosophie* pioneered by Martin Heidegger (1889–1976) in Germany. The problem approached by this philosophy was one that not many had noticed before its exponents felt oppressed by its despair. The problem, apparently, was "being" and what that might really mean. How could one "be," knowing what we know? Or as Jimi Hendrix once moaned in song: "Existing, just existing . . ." ("Manic Depression," 1967). Existentialism's interest lay in its appeal to psychological experience of being human in an apparently indifferent, or supposed value-free world, which throughout its observed organic and mineral structures displayed, it was held, no obvious knowledge of Christian ideas, or unequivocal interest of a personal, loving God. The anti-natural tendency of all Christian theologies, heretical or orthodox, resonated with this philosophical set of priorities. It seemed humanity was on its own. Well, one might have thought, at least, he had his Bible! *Ah!* comes the retort of Sixties theological radicalism: *not so fast!* Throughout the nineteenth century, those very thorough German fellas in their smart, exemplary universities of Tübingen, Marburg, Berlin, and Heidelberg, had been engaged in very detailed scientific analyses of the Bible text, and of the New Testament in particular. The school of "form critics," among whose prominent figures stood Rudolf Bultmann (1884–1976) and Martin Dibelius (1883–1947), had discovered, to their satisfaction, that the New Testament could not be relied upon as a biographical history of Christianity's founder, and that it had to be understood closely as related to particular needs, priorities, and curious ideas of the early church. This put Jesus at something of a remove from the traditional believer, who had neither time nor expertise to engage in the kind of studies that were now being foisted on theological students beyond Germany.

None of this had much impact on the general public until SCM Press published a cheap edition of the bishop of Woolwich, John Robinson's book, *Honest to God,* in London in 1963. The *Observer* broadsheet published an interview with Robinson under the title "Our Image of God Must Go," which was a shocking title for a serious paper in 1963, and seemed to have been touched by that wind of change that had made Robinson himself earlier in the year support publication of *Lady Chatterley's Lover.* Robinson's main points were that people shouldn't think of God as "up there somewhere" or get attached to traditional imagery of the old man with a beard type, but rather should seek God through the way one lived with others. Robinson liked existentialist-influenced Paul Tillich's idea that God was "the ground of our being," whatever novelty that might suggest. By contrast, German mysticism stemming from Jacob Böhme (1575–1624), had associated God with the *Ungrund* or ground*less*, a limitless depth, though Tillich's interest was clearly more on the word "being" than the ground it stood on. More German ideas came through Robinson's interest in the writings of great German Protestant martyr Dietrich Bonhoeffer (1906–1945), who seems also to have been moved by the idea of God experienced in social relations, so much so as for him to question the idea of religion dominated by institutions. Real witness to Christ was built around the capacity to bring faith action into daily life from the core of being identifying itself with the suffering of Christ in the world. This is a noble idea and one with wide appeal today, but somehow in the context of the times, Robinson's book seemed to suggest to many people that the church no longer held traditional beliefs sufficient unto salvation. Confusion ensued. Even more concerning than the idea that going to church might not be the essential act of worship (what then was the church for?), was Robinson's view that moral beliefs believed to be at the core of faith might be subject to change as people understood better the situations about them. Robinson seemed to be trying to prepare people for an explosion of liberalism that might prove a Pandora's box. The Space Race, we may recall, was already encroaching on ideas of the cosmic heavens inhabited by divine creatures, and few would seriously entertain the idea that Russian or American spacecraft might bump into God or his angels, so Robinson probably considered he was performing a service of explanation that the way forward for traditional Christian beliefs was going to require some basic reorientation.

The problem here of course is that it is to traditional core beliefs that people go when they feel threatened, and the beginning of the Sixties already suggested a great deal of discomfiting change was on the way, despite the optimism of some, while the shadow of universal vaporization was also very much in the air. The other factor that should have disturbed, and did disturb the more alert hearers of Robinson's "honest" views, was that he had also taken Bonhoeffer's idea that we should not be content with a metaphysical God who could only exist in the spaces where we had no scientific knowledge. That is, where scientific laws explained things, there appeared to be no place for God, or no need to think of him. With the way things were going we could end up with no God at all (the famous "God of the gaps" issue). The problem here was that there seemed to be a general acceptance of materialism, and if future Christian life was simply a code of ethics enacted "self-lessly" (in the ideal), then where was spiritual life? Where salvation? By this understanding salvation was simply socialization, and God might as well be "dead."

The notion of a post-Christian Christian theology appealed to the thought of the times. It appeared progressive enough, and tallied with the new architecture and typefaces, and since the sky hadn't exactly fallen on uttering the dread words, maybe here really was the promise of divine fulfillment. On April 8, 1966, *Time* magazine in the United States observed on its cover and in an accompanying article that the new "death of God" theology had crossed the Atlantic and seeded itself in the seething culture of American theology in a time of radical change. American exponents of varying emphases of "theothanatology" in the States included Paul van Buren, Thomas Altizer, Rabbi Richard L. Rubenstein, and Gabriel Vahanian.

Born in France, Vahanian graduated with his master's degree from Princeton in 1958, going on to serve on the faculty of Syracuse University, becoming a founder-director of the American Board of Religion in 1964. Rudolf Bultmann praised Vahanian's 1961 book, *The Death of God: The Culture of Our Post-Christian Era,* as a landmark, though atheist exponents of the "death of God" school have found Vahanian too conservative, as he does not accept that God is literally deceased, but that he cannot be taken for granted; the presence of God is always a mystery. Van Buren (1924–1998), though broadly of the school, disliked the expression "death of God," considering it misleading journalese. The point historically is that whatever the theological nice-ties of the theologians, while they were basically speaking to themselves and theological students, what had got out into the general culture was the idea that even Christian authorities, at the very least, shared the doubts of a generation, as to what exactly to believe. Doubt had, in fact, become morally respectable.

In the same year as *Honest to God* appeared (1963), professor of divinity at the University of London Rev. Dennis Nineham saw his commentary on the Gospel of Mark receive wide notice. Nobody doubted Nineham's scholarship. However, he had been drinking from the form-critical stream to such an extent that, hardly surprisingly, evangelicals were dismayed to find his commentary questioned much of the historical framework of the first Gospel, even giving reason to doubt its authorship, and generally throwing the beliefs and convictions of the writer and first audience of the text into a relativist hinterland full of doubt and complex historical and theological caveats. The "good news" looked very complicated, and it was now no longer a matter of certainty to professional theologians as to what Jesus himself really believed, or even said. There is no doubt Nineham followed the idea of scholarly skepticism to degrees that could hurt the feelings of traditional believers. One gets a sense that theologians, ordained to preach the Gospel, were becoming more and more remote from congregations, reliant on academic-speak rather than straightforward conviction. The other side of this spiritual declivity would be that evangelicals would lose patience with much biblical scholarship they considered unfriendly, and congregations would find themselves in difficulties if they wished to understand more than their pastors were prepared to preach. Criticism and doubt seeped into the citadel of spiritual teaching in the West, and the victim was spiritual knowledge itself. Christianity was bound to suffer in this deformation more than Hinduism and Buddhism, because Christianity has always claimed to be a historical religion and has never shown itself willing to accept that its accounts of events taken from the Bible might be profitably regarded as chiefly symbolic or even mythological, knowing of course that would mean to very many observers that the Bible was, to use the vernacular, a collection of "fairy stories," a conclusion I have heard from unlearned commentators on the Bible many times in my life. "If the sun and the moon should doubt," as Blake observed, "they would go out." And for many the light has indeed gone out. And that seems to have some relevance to the great decline of influence of the mainstream churches, at least in Europe and the United Kingdom, where religion has been most obviously institutionalized.

The year 1966 seems to have marked something of a watershed in this process of theological deformation. Not only did *Time* magazine take notice of the "death of God" school, which certainly impacted on young persons looking for a living deity or deities (and finding something of the kind in the persons of the four Beatles, and subsequently, in their footsteps in India), but the year also saw the first edition of theologian John Macquarrie's *Principles of Christian Theology*. Macquarrie (1919–2007) had been appointed professor of systematic theology at New York's Union Theological Seminary in 1962 and was ordained priest into the Episcopal Church by the bishop of New York in 1965. I had the privilege when I was a theological undergraduate of attending his seminar on "Being and God" at Christ Church, Oxford, and well remember how his discourse followed lines of thinking suggested by Heidegger and Bultmann. The existentialist inheritance was very clear from the way he seized upon a novel twist on the meaning of the name of God ("Yahweh") given to Moses in Exodus: "I AM THAT I AM." Macquarrie took the Name into the twentieth century by expressing it in one significant, existentialistically sound word: *Being*. *God is Being*. One thing God has in common with our ordinary notion of being is that being cannot be studied objectively. We can study beings, but *being* cannot be objectified, it is the absolute given of existence. The observer cannot put him- or herself before it. And from there we go on with Macquarrie's philosophical theology. I recall his talk well. I did not take any notes because everything he said seemed obvious to me. That is a compliment. Nevertheless, I remember coming out into the vastness of Tom Quad after the seminar with the corresponding sense that it had all been curiously vacuous. Strange how "God is being" has never quite caught on, and I don't think caught on much in the Sixties either. For myself, I rather prefer something emblazoned on the back of Eric Burdon's (of the group the Animals) leather jacket in California in 1967: "May the Baby Jesus shut your mouth, and open your mind."

Another important book that appeared in 1966, and that never received the attention outside of Italy that it deserved was sociologist of religion Professor Sabino Samele Acquaviva's *The Decline of the Sacred in Industrial Society*, a detailed study of how both the idea of "the sacred" and respect for sacred places and spaces were both in steep decline in the modern world. Acquaviva bemoaned irreligious attitudes and behavior in his native Italy (traditionally staunch Catholic) and showed how nonattendance at Mass could be correlated to the extension of industrial means of production and the dislocation of traditional "parishes," families, and centers of worship, saints' days, acts of reverence, and so on. It seemed to the professor that the sacred itself might disappear since if no one had space for it, then how could one experience sacredness? The book spoke eloquently, with facts and statistics, of the crisis of religion in industrial society, a general religious crisis. And even, in the last chapter, the specter of "The End of the Sacred?" from which I quote:

> From the religious point of view, humanity has entered a long night that will become darker and darker with the passing of the generations, and of which no end can yet be seen. It is a night in which there seems to be no place for a conception of God, or for a sense of the sacred, and ancient ways of giving significance to our own existence, of confronting life and death, are becoming increasingly untenable. At bottom, the motivations for religious behavior and for faith persist—the need to explain ourselves and what surrounds us, the anguish, and the sense of precariousness. But man remains uncertain whether somewhere there exists, or ever existed, something different from uncertainty, doubt, and existential insecurity.[1]

WE'RE MORE POPULAR THAN JESUS NOW

John Lennon (1940–1980), between American tours with the Beatles, had been getting down to some serious reading, while also experimenting with LSD at Mr. and Mrs. Lennon's secluded English home atop St. George's Hill, Weybridge, in the Surrey stockbroker belt. There, Lennon investigated written guidance on LSD usage penned by Dr. Timothy Leary (1920–1996), formerly researcher into psilocybin mushrooms at Harvard, but in 1966 experimenting widely at the Hitchcock Estate, Millbrook, New York, established as the Castalia Foundation. It seems Lennon was aware of the implications of the theological crisis and sense of foreboding festering within the academic side of the West's Christian confessions, and in 1966 had come in his own sweet way to conclusions very similar to some of those of Professor Acquaviva above.

John Lennon's own religious outlook at the time was somewhat confused. He had been going through occasional periods of depression and was troubled by Christian doctrines of suffering, concerns that emerged in his cunning 1965 song "Girl" whose lines about pain leading to pleasure and a postmortem reward in heaven for pain stoically endured on earth brought out the cynical, but heartfelt question: "Will she still believe it when he's dead?" Inspired to a degree by some knowledge of Buddhist doctrines, he later described his intermittent periods of disaffection from belief in God as his "moral turpentine" and was feeling isolated and distinctly unhelped by the kind of arch theological debate on offer on TV—parodied effectively in his book *A Spaniard in the Works* (1965), wherein a pompous, but benign TV ecclesiastic asks: "'Why, if Griff is so good and almighty, why does he bring such suffering into the world?' And I can truthfully say, Saint Alf chapter 8, verse 5, page 9. 'Griff walks in such mysterious ways, his woodwork to perform.' (And what do we *mean* by perform?)"[2] In this short piece titled "I Believe, Boot . . ." Lennon captured the earnest, bumbling, but basically "Sunday smile" semantics-obsessed tenor of clergy involved with the public debate and showed himself unimpressed by much of what he heard. For all the background influence of existentialism, the debates never seemed to get down to the gritty points people like him wanted to know about: the feeling, *the soul,* wasn't there.

By contrast, American academic renegade Leary advocated that enlightenment seekers avail themselves of properly prepared sessions of LSD ingestion, accompanied by passages derived and transliterated by Leary from the Tibetan Book of the Dead including the psychologically dangerous view, or half-truth, that it was the *ego* that stood in the way of nirvana, the latter equated quite inaccurately with the traditional Christian concept of heaven. (It is the *false* "ego" of the "carnal mind" that is in enmity against God.) Lennon found, like Aleister Crowley before him, an attraction for Buddhism because it seemed, at least to begin with, a more scientific approach to enlightenment. That is, if you did certain things, certain "spiritual" results would ensue, chief of which—and the most desirable to John Lennon at the time— being peace of mind, which had been severely disturbed not only by the tempests of Beatlemania but also by the sudden deaths of his mother in 1958 and of his close friend Stuart Sutcliffe in Hamburg in 1962. Peace of mind, he recognized, could allow the flow of healing love, and with it, creativity: *songs,* and thereby, a future.

Lennon was also struck by the consonance of Buddhist concepts of the illusion of the material world ("Nothing is real") with experiences he had as a child and teenager where in a mirror he would see hallucinatory images of his face, changing and becoming, as he put it in a 1980 *Playboy* interview shortly before his murder, "cosmic and complete." In the process, ordinary worldly perception fragmented into nothingness, a simultaneous alienation and hint of elusive spiritual fulfillment. He saw things in a surrealist and hallucinatory manner that nobody he knew saw. This privileged but isolating knowledge would render him ever rebellious, a kind of spy in a world of unconscious egos, ever dissatisfied with automatic, unthinking, platitudinous explanations of life. The key was in the state of mind; the common illusion derived from inadequate awareness. Around 1966, Lennon concluded that the Jesus whose word was *love* was one of the enlightened, like the Buddha, who while they had come to "turn on" the world to cosmic consciousness and spiritual awareness, had their words nonetheless twisted by inadequate followers passing the message on like a bucket of water that, by the end of the line, hardly had any living water left in it, or, to use another analogy, like a whispered word along a line, that by the end of the line sounds different to that first uttered. This principle of "loss through transmission" was parodied in the Monty Python movie (produced by George Harrison) *The Life of Brian* (1979), where a distant hearer of the Sermon on the Mount ponders on the meaning of a divine beatitude ("Blessed are the peacemakers") that has reached his faraway ear as, "Blessed are the cheesemakers," contenting himself that the blessing surely applied to "all purveyors of milk products!" Such misunderstandings, Lennon believed, characterized the times he was living in, and he felt deeply the need for more, for something else that would make sense of his destiny, a destiny he was aware of but couldn't quite define yet. His own groping for inner freedom found its correlate in everything he heard about the changing world of the Sixties; it too, from Africa to

Mississippi, to his mind in Weybridge was crying for "freedom." How could they achieve it? The Beatles, contrary to many expectations, did not have "the answer," but maybe, if they could find it themselves . . .

Normally, the intellectual Beatle kept the depth of his concerns to his trusted friends (comedian Peter Cook was a regular visitor; he too shared Lennon's interest in religious thought), but in March 1966, Maureen Cleave (b. 1934), a savvy journalist whom Lennon already knew well, and who was apt to tease him about the literary level of his songs—John put "long" words into his song "Help!" to impress her—came to his home and asked searching questions about his way of life for her adult readers in the London *Evening Standard* to read. Lennon seems to have been grateful for an opportunity to let off a bit of pent-up steam in the kind of way he used to pontificate at the Ye Cracke pub in Liverpool when he was a hard-drinking art student back in the late Fifties. Lennon drew some of his conclusions from books he'd been delving into. In the course of a long conversation, he gave his then current views on the religion of the West: "Christianity will go. It will vanish and shrink. I'm right and I'll be proved right. We're more popular than Jesus now; I don't know which will go first—rock 'n' roll or Christianity. Jesus was all right but his disciples were thick and ordinary. It's them twisting it that ruins it for me." Now it would take some time to unpack this dense statement, but certainly in London at the time, nobody in the sophisticated metropolis was concerned with doing so, taking the perhaps flippant words as his opinion, and something they might or might not agree with in general.

However, Beatles press officer Tony Barrow syndicated the Cleave interviews to U.S. teenage pop magazine *Datebook* as a way of showing the Beatles had greater depth and were progressing in their concerns. In late July, *Datebook's* editor put the statement that the Beatles were "more popular than Jesus" on the magazine's cover for effect, and predictably, the effect in the southern United States was explosive. First flaring up in Alabama, the statement was just what right-wing Christian conservatives needed to announce to the world that the Beatles really weren't innocent at all, as they had been asked to believe, but were effectively part of an ongoing Satanic conspiracy to undermine the faith of millions, through appealing to the low desires of children and young people for "love"—and didn't they know what *that* meant? The Beatles were *idols* to the "kids," worshipped and adored, and here was the chance to cast the idols down and smash them and do the Lord's work. The news spread that Lennon claimed superiority to Jesus Christ as if Jesus was competing in the pop charts for popularity. Lennon was judged and found guilty of blasphemy without benefit of trial or any other consideration. Worse, the minds of the young were deliberately hauled into the debate and cajoled to *hate* something about which they knew practically nothing.

In 1985 I spoke to Derek Taylor about the rumpus. In 1966, Taylor was Beatles' manager Brian Epstein's representative in Los Angeles as well as publicity manager for folk-pop band the Byrds. Derek quoted Bob Dylan: "I'd become my enemy in the instant that I preach," as an expression of Lennon's predicament. "Someone lights a bonfire under this thing," he said, "but to see the burning, and hooded people and Ku Klux Klan was quite frightening." He wasn't exaggerating. The Beatles had a U.S. tour planned for August and there were public bonfires of Beatles records organized by radio stations in the Bible Belt, eerily reminiscent of the burnings of books under the Nazis in Germany in the 1930s, while a Klan representative in South Carolina appeared grinning on TV to say the KKK was known as a "religious order," as well as a "terror organization," and they would have about fifty men in robes at a Beatles concert, and they would "stop this thing." Derek Taylor continued: "Though John could sometimes be tactless, he was also quick to apologize, and save the group from embarrassment." John did indeed say he was "sorry" for what he said, or what people thought he'd said, and Brian Epstein gave an ameliorative account of how the words had been taken completely out of context, and that actually, John was very concerned about issues of spiritual life and did not think it was a necessarily good thing that the young were more interested in pop music than in the substance of religion. Lennon, shaken by the by-now global uproar, declared to pressmen on the group's arrival in the States that he had used the word *Beatles* objectively, as though a third party, the way other people saw them, not as a claim for himself. "If I'd said

Fig. 11.1. Burning Beatles albums in Alabama, 1966.

TV is more popular than Jesus, maybe I'd have got away with it," he suggested. He was emphatically not comparing the Beatles with "God as a thing, or whatever 'it' is, or with Jesus Christ as a person," but it had all been twisted and created a mad situation of mis-identity. He emphasized also that it had been a conversation with a friend at home in England and the situation regarding faith might have been more true of Britain than America at the time. "I'm not anti-God, anti-Christ, or anti-religion," John confessed sincerely. He just wished people would react in less of a preprogrammed way when confronted by honest sincerity, and that the whole thing would go away.

Frank Zappa spoke up in Lennon's defense at the time; indeed, looking back, there was much truth in what Lennon had to say. The Beatles "thing" had at the time reached unheard of heights of apparent significance, and churches were particularly aware of it, as were wary governments. The Beatles enthusiasm crossed boundaries like the wind, ignoring customs checkpoints or even barriers of religion, ideology, and language. There were no Beatles records pressed in the Soviet empire at the time, but there were secret Beatles fans holding true to the faith in love and inner freedom (as became evident after the fall of the Wall when long-secreted Russian Beatles fans emerged from silence), while the official Communist Party line in the United Kingdom was that the Beatles phenomenon simply indicated the despair of the working classes! So much for Marxist analysis! Timothy Leary in his New Age enthusiasm would in due course do the band the disservice of calling them "avatars," that is, divine messengers of a free and divine spirit in the Indian mode. They *were* idolized, and it was plain that whereas in the past, religion had been a cause of popular excitement, religion was now embroiled in endless arguments that put many people, especially perhaps young people, off. Anyhow, the furor contributed to the group's decision to cease touring, but curiously, it also signaled a period when the group would find its identity inseparable from spiritual issues, and what would soon appear to be a new, and for many threatening, spiritual landscape.

What appeared as Lennon's personal outburst of course gave anyone who had anything against the Beatles and the extraordinary reaction to them their great opportunity. Lennon's remarks were officially condemned by pro-apartheid South African government and by General Franco's Spanish dictatorship. That should signify something. What kind of authority saw the Beatles as really threatening?

It is clear Lennon had not been moved by the conclusions of Vatican II, which had just ended its tumultuous deliberations on the cusp of 1966. For Catholics, the council had generated far-reaching, globally significant reform. Pope Paul VI, along with his officials, who included all the men who would wield the keys of Saint Peter until and including Pope Benedict XVI, put great emphasis on the Eucharist, asserting that it was the apex and fountain of Catholic worship. Mass was permitted to be said in people's own languages for the first time, with priests actually facing the congregation. Nuns' dress was simplified, and there was given out the feeling that the Roman Church was prepared to address the modern world it had all but abandoned on account of its sinful liberalism at the end of the nineteenth century. Many faithful in the church saw Vatican II's urging for renewal as being more liberal, and more far-reaching doctrinally than it really was. Anyway, it obviously did not give freethinking Anglican John Lennon much pause to modify his views of a declining religion. He had himself heard Catholic priests at his concerts bemoaning the fact that they could not get that many young people to their services; to which Paul McCartney remarked they might do more with the music to encourage participation. Such a realization would lead to the appearance of guitars in church services across the world, an instrument so disliked by many traditionalists—many of whom in the Catholic Communion would object to losing the Latin Mass, believing that a language of which they had little understanding was yet somehow sacred, itself indicating not only an aesthetic response to sound and tradition, but a basic belief in spiritual magic.

Pope Paul VI, having just wrapped up Vatican II, was obviously not amused by Lennon's dark and dispiriting predictions that Christianity was in terminal decline; God's vicar had just put all his energies into what he considered a God-inspired spiritual renewal through sharing the body and blood of Christ. If anything, however, was needed to prove the words issued by popes were *not* infallible it was Pope Paul VI's remarks about Lennon's observations that appeared in Vatican newspaper *L'Osservatore Romano:* "Some subjects must not be dealt with profanely, even in the world of Beatniks." The conflation of beatniks with Beatles was unfortunate and showed the old boy was a bit out of touch, since there was nothing beatnik-like about the well-dressed group from England save the interest in rock music, an interest His Holiness presumably did not share. The Beatles had been lauded as composers, and Lennon had had two books published and received prestigious awards including an MBE decoration from Her Majesty the Queen. He was not a beatnik, though he had absorbed the sensibility of beat poets such as Jack Kerouac (1922–1969). But one can understand why the pope should be miffed that some casual remarks of a wealthy musician should so dominate discourse about religion. As far as the church was concerned, Lennon had strayed into *their* territory. And gone were the days when the inquisitorial Holy Office (renamed amid Vatican II as the Sacred Congregation for the Doctrine of the Faith) could have subjected him to the auto-da-fé for heresy. That grisly office would be fulfilled by the psychotic mania of John's murderer in 1980, the individual who claimed, among other things, to have been incensed by Lennon's 1966 views on fame and faith.

As for the origin of some of those views, particularly Lennon's comments about Jesus's disciples being "thick and ordinary" and getting the message in a twist, we need not look far. Seriously intrigued all his relatively short life about Jesus and Christian origins, John had recently given his attention to Hugh J. Schonfield's book *The Passover Plot: A New Interpretation on the Life and Death of Jesus,* published in 1965. Schonfield (1901–1988) had enjoyed early access to some of the famously influential Dead Sea Scrolls, first discovered by a Jordanian Arab in 1947, which gave insights into contemporary thought among Jewish groups before and during the time when Jesus is believed to have lived. Schonfield's book *Secrets of the Dead Sea Scrolls: Studies toward Their Solution,* had been published in 1956. Influenced by Robert Graves's semi-historical, arguably prescient novel *King Jesus,* published in 1946, Schonfield's own plot dealt with a speculative scenario in which what was taken by early Christians as Jesus's religious ministry for mankind was primarily a plan to secure the throne of Israel for Jesus, the rightful claimant and "Son of David" (messiah), a position for which he was born. Schonfield took his source text from the Gospel of John, which Schonfield believed was more in touch with a secret tradition about Jesus than that available to synoptists Matthew, Mark, and Luke. In this, Schonfield was reversing the view of the German form critics that the latter Gospels were more authentic accounts in origin, being earlier than John. John 6:15 was the text that seized Schonfield:

> When Jesus therefore perceived that they would come and and take him by force, to make him a king, he departed again into a mountain himself alone.

To make him a king. . . . According to Schonfield, it wasn't the king-making that was the problem for Jesus, but rather the timing. The time had to be right for the announcement of Jesus's messiah-kingship, and for that he would need to go through a critical passion ritual of suffering in imitation of the prophecies of Isaiah 53:1–12, which state:

Who hath believed our report? And to whom is the arm of the Lord revealed?

For he shall grow up before him as a tender plant, and as a root out of a dry ground: he hath no form nor comeliness; and when we shall see him, there is no beauty that we should desire him.

He is despised and rejected of men; a man of sorrows, and acquainted with grief: and we hid as it were our faces from him; he was despised, and we esteemed him not.

Surely he hath borne our griefs, and carried our sorrows: yet we did esteem him stricken, smitten of God, and afflicted.

But he was wounded for our transgressions, he was bruised for our iniquities: the chastisement of our peace was upon him; and with his stripes we are healed.

All we like sheep have gone astray; we have turned every one to his own way; and the Lord hath laid on him the iniquity of us all.

He was oppressed, and he was afflicted, yet he opened not his mouth: he is brought as a lamb to the slaughter, and as a sheep before her shearers is dumb, so he openeth not his mouth.

He was taken from prison and from judgment: and who shall declare his generation? For he was cut off out of the land of the living: for the transgression of my people was he stricken.

And he made his grave with the wicked, and with the rich in his death; because he had done no violence, neither was any deceit in his mouth.

Yet it pleased the Lord to bruise him; he hath put him to grief: when thou shalt make his soul an offering for sin, he shall see his seed, he shall prolong his days, and the pleasure of the Lord shall prosper in his hand.

He shall see of the travail of his soul, and shall be satisfied: by his knowledge shall my righteous servant justify many; for he shall bear their iniquities.

Therefore will I divide him a portion with the great, and he shall divide the spoil with the strong; because he hath poured out his soul unto death: and he was numbered with the transgressors; and he bare the sin of many, and made intercession for the transgressors.

In Schofield's imagining or reimagining of what Lennon would in later years call "the Easter heist," the Crucifixion was necessary, and witnessed by the disciples. However, what *they* did not know was that there were, as it were, senior officers operating behind the scenes to secure the desired end: Joseph of Arimathea, and the "beloved disciple." There was also some mystery about the preparation of the "upper room" for the Last Supper, indicating a greater plan in Jesus's purview, to which the twelve were not privy. The Crucifixion then is enacted as a ritual. Jesus's death is only apparent. Pain would lead to pleasure. . . . It was unusual for people to die so soon—as Pilate remarked when request to bury the body was made by the Arimathean—for the point of crucifixion was that it was meant to be death over agonizing days in full consciousness of its end. Schonfield suggested a drug was administered to induce unconsciousness, perhaps on a sponge. The problem may have come when a soldier pierced Jesus's side, which may have shortened his life. Anyhow, the point was that the disciples only had a part of the whole operation, on a "need to know" basis, and they couldn't even understand what that part properly was, as the Gospels also suggest, with bickering among them over primacy and Peter rebuking Jesus at Caesarea Philippi, and so on. "For those that are without, all things are done in parables."

Naturally, theologians could hardly bring themselves to comment on what to them was so preposterous a novelty scenario that held within it propaganda to ruin the faith of millions with a rationalistic story of dynastic ambition mixed with symbolic religion. Lennon's, however, was not the kind of mind that disregards the voice of one condemned by many, and he would be fascinated by his own life in terms of the Christ mystery. He knew certainly what it was to have one's words twisted and to be condemned and rejected of men. He had long felt this way about the wicked world, and his deep friend Stu Sutcliffe had felt the same way. You see, there was John the "clown" for his friends and fans, and there was another John, one they did not see behind the mask. The world, John suspected, was in a kind of conspiracy against truth, especially spiritual truth, and could not be trusted. Insofar as the church accommodated the world, it lost the support of the spiritual.

John's essential spiritual outlook was gnostic, or at least, in 1966, gnostic-in-the-making.

The Sixties saw the first rediffusion, if only on a very small scale, of gnostic material since the Gnostic Church enjoyed its short life in Paris under Jules Doinel's abortive leadership in the 1890s,* a historic phenomenon (condemned in Rome, incidentally) that barely touched either the U.K. or the United States.

Geza Vermes's *Dead Sea Scrolls in English* had brought aspects of the scrolls material before a wide public in 1962, and it initiated and contributed to the suspicion that archaeology and historical investigation might yet reveal things that the church didn't want people to know about. Certainly the cozy Victorian picture passed on at Sunday schools around the world was becoming slowly confronted with a more vivid scenario. Such is evident in popular cinema at the time. *King of Kings,* ably directed by Nicholas Ray in 1961, an intelligent film about the life of Christ, is worlds away from the silent movie of the same name directed by Cecil B. de Mille. Ray's movie (featuring Jeffrey Hunter as Jesus) tries very hard to incorporate hard knowledge of the political realities that were reaching boiling point in Judea in the first century of our era. Barabbas appears not as a kind of theological foil but as a concerned Zealot, a freedom fighter who thinks he can manipulate public interest in Jesus for political ends. The movie is aware that Jesus was not alone with a message of salvation for his people, but that he saw the spiritual message as overwhelming, greater than armies. Barabbas had a moral case, but Jesus has the spiritual one. Which was the more powerful may be judged by Barabbas's being released from captivity by his political enemies.

On February 7, 1960, it was announced that letters from failed messiah Simon Bar Khochba ("Son of the Star") had been discovered in Israel. Bar Khochba had led the last armed revolt against the Romans in the early second century, and his defeat had led to the last Jewish diaspora and the leveling of the Temple Mount by the Emperor Hadrian. The Bar Khochba story is often conflated with the last stand of Zealots

---

*See my book *Occult Paris,* 2016.

at Masada in 73 CE that followed the Roman destruction of Herod's Temple in Jerusalem. Excavated by Yigael Yadin in the 1950s and '60s, Yadin's account *Masada: Herod's Fortress and the Zealots' Last Stand* was published in New York in 1966, and gave even greater sense that the facts behind the Gospel must somehow be found beneath the rubble of real historical events concerning real, human, not supernatural people, who were not at all so different from people to be observed in the world then. That is to say, the new historical material derived chiefly from archaeology was humanizing the myths of religion and bringing the spiritual dimension within the realms of an expanding sense of psychology and a growing sense—even excitement—that wonders lay not "up there" but in *there,* in the mind. This all suggested mysticism, the going within, but it also suggested gnostic dimensions of spiritualization of reality, and the breaking down of the materialist shell, or as Lennon was suggesting, the world's illusion. "Strawberry Fields Forever"—which he wrote in Spain in 1966—celebrated the expanded mind he had known as a child in the woods by the old Salvation Army Children's Home (called "Strawberry Fields") in Liverpool, where he would say to himself, transfixed by experience of seeing, *really seeing* the is-ness and infinity of things: "All this is going on," an epiphany of seeing, and knowing at once—and *knowing* that he was knowing ("No one I think is in my tree").

One can hardly help recalling a logion from the gnostic Gospel of Thomas, namely, that the "Kingdom of the Father is spread out upon the earth, and men do not see it." In 1959, the first English translation of the Gospel of Thomas became available, published with a transcription from the original Coptic by E. J. Brill, of Leiden. The text derived from the now-famous cache of so-called gnostic gospels discovered by Muhammad Ali al-Samman of Al Qasr in Upper Egypt. The other fifty-one texts of the collection would not be published in English until 1977. Had they appeared in 1966, as most of them could have done, they would probably have caused a stupendous storm. As it was, the singular Gospel of Thomas seeped into the thought of the few who could get hold of this pricey academic text. The text opened: "These are the secret words that the living Jesus spoke, and which Judas Didymos Thomas wrote down. He who finds the interpretation of these words will not experience death." The text is full of gnomic statements attributed to Jesus such as that about the Kingdom of Heaven being spread out upon the earth, where men do not see it. "No one I think is in my tree . . . *Strawberry Fields forever . . ."*

There were friendly acquaintances of Lennon and McCartney who did know something about the gnostics.

JOHN "HOPPY" HOPKINS AND THE LONDON FREE SCHOOL

On January 30, 2015, the chief light of the mid- to late Sixties London "underground" died at the age of seventy-seven. A graduate of the University of Cambridge, John Hopkins could have enjoyed a career as a nuclear physicist, but instead chose photography as a way of getting to grips with the real world and its inhabitants. Entering the London scene on New Year's Day 1960, by 1965 Hoppy had become a kind of one-man internet, compiling through his many contacts encountered on his varied photography assignments details of anyone who appeared to be "doing anything" in the fecund world of the London art and music scene. Making a stencil copy of the list, he distributed it to all the names included, thus creating a dynamic context for communication and knowledge, as well as a sense of belonging and common purpose. This was the scientist in him, which made him a practical problem solver, as well as a person who could express his genuine enthusiasm openly. Impressed by something positive, Hoppy would say "Wow!" and that meant what it said.

For our purposes, "Wow" meant the first manifestation of the counterculture as a self-conscious animal. The occasion was a standing-room-only poetry event held on June 11, 1965, at the Albert Hall, in Kensington, West London. Playfully titled the International Poetry Incarnation, Hoppy found common cause with young writer Barry Miles (who would edit *International Times;* b. 1943) and with poet Michael Horowitz (b. 1935) to bring together the "happening" poetry of U.S. poets Allen Ginsberg, Lawrence Ferlinghetti, and Gregory Corso, as well as the British fire of Adrian Mitchell, Alexander Trocchi, and

Christopher Logue. The collective feeling was that poetry was back where it ought to be, in the free pulpit of prophecy.

A couple of months later, Hoppy secured the cooperation of Rhaune Laslett and others to set up the London "Free School" in a Notting Hill basement in West London. The idea was to encourage easy acquisition of useful knowledge and crafts, a utopian place where people with skills could pass them on quickly without institutional hurdles. Out of the energies stirred up in the process came the West Indian showcase, the Notting Hill Carnival (still thriving), the influential underground magazine *International Times* (that so enraged the government), and eventually the famous axle of psychedelia, the UFO Club at 31 Tottenham Court Road, established by Hoppy and Joe Boyd in 1966, which employed the first light shows in rock music. Early experimenters in light and sound were the Pink Floyd who played their first

Fig. 11.2. The Pink Floyd: (front row) *Nick Mason, Roger Waters, Richard Wright;* (back row) *David Gilmour, Syd Barrett.*

benefit show at Notting Hill's All Saints Church to raise money for the Free School, before becoming a regular attraction of the UFO Club, much to government chagrin. A recent BBC film on the history of Pink Floyd included an interview with the Floyd's percussionist Nick Mason who mentioned in passing that you could learn about gnosis at the Free School. This was the word that Storm Thurgerson (1944–2013), the designer of the Floyd's second album *A Saucerful of Secrets* (June 1968), combined with *hip* (as in "aware") to produce the trend-leading company of album design: Hipgnosis.

The London Free School happened in the basement of a house belonging to one of the most remarkable and influential minds to emerge from the Sixties countercultural maelstrom. He was John Frederic Carden Michell (1933–2009). From a wealthy background, having as maternal grandfather baronet Sir Frederick Carden, Michell was educated at Eton College and (like Aleister Crowley) at Trinity College, Cambridge. Michell's Cambridge experience had been asphyxiated, as he saw it, by the prevalence of rationalistic and materialistic orthodoxies, with, it seemed, no way to counter the weight of it all. For Michell, it was the emergence of the UFO phenomenon in the Fifties that gave leverage to opening the mind to new ideas about human origins and our essential nature and mystery.

Before Hoppy got the Free School going, Michell's basement had hosted a gambling club run by Black Power activist "Michael X," whose presence in the Notting Hill community had much to do with getting the festival off the ground. Born in Trinidad and Tobago, controversial Michael de Freitas or "X" (1933–1975) got Michell involved in the Free School. It was the scholarly, but unorthodox mind of Michell that offered courses in UFOs, ley lines (invisible power lines believed to pulse between ancient sites of worship forming "sacred landscapes"), and in traditions attributed to the Gnostics: the *knowers*. Michell's extensive and intricate knowledge of gnostic lore is evident today in his book *The Dimensions of Paradise: Sacred Geometry, Ancient Science, and the Heavenly Order on Earth* (1971).

The philosophy to which Michell adhered most strongly was that aspect of occult philosophy associated with Fabre d'Olivet's concept of the Tradition. The Tradition existed, it was believed, in a pre-Egyptian civilization that understood the relationship of spiritual and created orders, but whose knowledge had suffered a primordial deformation, so that it could only be passed on in fragments, but those fragments could be located as "traditional knowledge" in cultures throughout the world and, with spiritual inspiration, recomposed as a beacon for our transformative times.

For Michell and others, the British Isles held a unique role in the return of traditional knowledge to the world, and in this belief Michell had the support of the spiritual legacy of William Blake, and the spiritual traditions that Blake himself represented in his dynamic psychospiritual myths to the world.* In 1967, Michell's pioneering work in what has become a small industry of New Age Earth mysteries publishing began with his book, *The Flying Saucer Vision: The Holy Grail Restored*, published after his article on flying saucers appeared in *International Times* in 1967, but it would be Michell's 1969 book *View over Atlantis* that would give massive impetus to the spiritual-eco-aware speculations of the world's "alternative" hippie-derived, sometimes gnostic, magical sensibilities from the 1970s to the present time. The Glastonbury Festival "pyramid" stage was first drawn up with Michell advising on proper cosmic dimensions, and Glastonbury and much of what it stands for today represents the symbolic bastion of consciousness that resists global materialism and advocates spiritual harmony, in the U.K. and beyond. And much of the ferment that has been brewed into this pervasive movement came from the light that was John Hopkins in London, in 1965.

DAME FRANCES YATES AND THE HERMETIC TRADITION

I recall reading a line from the many works of my kinsman, Anglican theologian and pioneer scholar of mysticism, William Ralph Inge (1860–1954), where, realizing the limitations of institutional religion,

---

*See my biography of Blake: *Jerusalem! The Real Life of William Blake*, 2015.

he declared: "The prophets of the future will not come from the established Churches. I do not think this is a fact to be regretted."

In 1964, Warburg Institute scholar Dame Frances Yates (1899–1981) brought another "prophet" with a spiritual message once more to the fore. This figure was probably imaginary, certainly legendary, but nonetheless served to express what was presented, from at least the second century CE, as the core ancient tradition of gnosis. This figure was Graeco-Egyptian sage, Hermes Trismegistus, "Thrice-Greatest" Hermes (equated with the ancient Egyptian god Thoth), supposed author of late-antique philosophical tracts first printed in Latin as a corpus in 1460, and of sundry works on astrology, magic, and alchemy that together comprise the Hermetic tradition.

Frances Yates's book *Giordano Bruno and the Hermetic Tradition* (1963) advanced a stunning case for seeing "martyr to science" Giordano Bruno (1548–1600), burnt at the stake in Rome as an impenitent heretic—he believed in heliocentricity and that the universe was infinite—was mostly influenced by the magical, gnostic Hermetic tradition, derived from Hermes.

Hermetic philosophy unfolds from the conception that there was once an intimate link between man and God, and that this link was lost. In order to recover it, it was essential to relocate the presence of the divine in the universe, to cease thinking materialistically and egoistically, obsessed with the body and superficial appearances and feelings, and to rediscover the divine nature of man, who, spiritually reborn, is able to see the universe as the reflected image of God. Yates's book had a tremendous academic impact, for suddenly there was a respectable case for the influence of philosophical magic not only on the origins of modern science, but in the sphere of the arts of the imagination and philosophy. Suddenly, esotericism, which had been smothered by materialism in the nineteenth and twentieth centuries, had something resembling scholarly support for its abiding relevance. In 1965 Frances Yates went on a lecture tour of the United States and the long road to reestablishing esotericism as the study of spiritual movements with Gnostic and more ancient sources began. One of the fruits of that tree is the book you are reading.

⚠ ⚠ ⚠

The theologies emanating from broadly "orthodox" Christian churches in the world of the Sixties had much to say under the aegis of nineteenth- and twentieth-century European philosophies, and much about personal and public morals and church practices, but where the theological mainstream left a massive "gap in the market" was an almost systemic inability to get to grips with far more fundamental questions of spiritual meaning, that is to say, those areas of human experience that are not automatically cut and dried from, and for, rational analysis. Unfortunately, longstanding suspicion and rejection of mysticism in the churches bore its fruit in indifference to the spiritual quest at just the moment in history when large numbers of active and concerned people felt the greatest need for spiritual meaning and experience, and were, perforce, driven outside of the churches in search of it. If, as the churches believed, they did in fact possess the whole store of spiritual meaning for humankind, then they demonstrated a woeful inability to express or understand this possession meaningfully, or make common cause with other opponents of materialism.

The movement away from established religion toward the personal quest is undoubtedly a key aspect of the spiritual meaning of the Sixties, and did we understand the matter better as a culture, would be cause for some celebration and confidence. When the Temple is cleansed as a fit habitation for the whole divine spirit, then the prophecies may be fulfilled that the nations of the world will return to it. Meaning is being.

TWELVE

The Persistence
of the Bible

I think we can probably all agree that the Bible is about communication, and what it is regarded as communicating is meaning. In 1961, representatives of all the Catholic and Protestant Churches of the United Kingdom served as directors to the publication of the first edition of the New English Bible. This was a translation of the Bible in the English idiom of the time, using the best possible source texts, undertaken on the basis that the churches might be somewhat out of touch with modern people because the language of the Bible sounded old-fashioned and might therefore have lost some of its meaning to modern ears. Like many attempts of Christian institutions to catch up with modernity, the publication was not greeted with mass rejoicing in the church. Likewise, many in the Catholic Communion did not like losing their Latin Masses for the vernacular versions. Some objections were simply made on the "if it ain't broke, don't mend it" argument. That is, the existing translations (King James Version, and the Revised Version of 1881) were perfectly adequate for salvation, if read with understanding conviction, and besides, in trying to sound modern, the translators had shown how poor modern English can sound adjacent to its early seventeenth-century counterpart. Did we want Shakespeare in the modern idiom? Compare for example the following two translations from the Greek original.

First, here is Mark 8:36 in the King James Version:

For what shall it profit a man, if he shall gain the whole world, and lose his own soul?

And here's the New English Bible of 1961:

What does a man gain by winning the whole world at the cost of his true self?

Well, judge for yourselves, but I know which I prefer, and which, for its sonority hewed and toned during the golden age of the English language, is the most memorable, and therefore the more communicative and meaningful. Whatever, may I ask, entitled the translators to translate a familiar word like *soul* as a word loaded with secular resonance as *true self*—a combination that simply begged another question, and more confusion?

The essence of the problem gets to the root of what we have seen regarding failures in theological discourse that crystallized with the Sixties. There was a confusion of "fashion" or the sense of the modern (as something real and immediate) with *meaning.* The essence of spiritual meaning is that it is always true, has always been true, will always be true. It *is;* being is meaning. Spiritual meaning gives us our rock or our anchorage in a changing world where with every passing second, there is a massive, inexpressible extension of perceptible being before our very eyes, and at every split second too, and so on to infinity. Life goes on, unfolding and apparently extending like dough under a rolling pin. It just keeps going on, and today's now and modern is gone already. Now is past; the future soon goes the same way. Religion must deal primarily with eternal values, not passing ones. That does not mean it cannot or should not engage with passing values, but that it should do so knowing what eternal values are. This is the service of religion. Eternal values are those of the spirit, and the spirit giveth life, and the letter killeth. The New English Bible killed, or at least maimed, the language of truth, and it did so willingly and knowingly and doubtless with the best intentions. The grace of poetry and the spirit of prophecy were absent. Plain sense inflicts the disservice of opacity upon the mystery. And Jesus himself said that knowledge of the kingdom of God constituted a series of mysteries. Mysteries are the stuff of mysticism, and the abrogation of mysticism has been the downfall of the Christian churches, for only the mystical understanding can withstand attacks from materialist science (or I should say "scientism") and its philosophies. The church does not recover the congregation of the faithful simply by accepting science and pleading for an advisory role in ethical management. The Ten Commandments were issued as the product of a vision of God, or at least of his Will, not the other way around. The churches have no right to preach ethics unless they can substantiate the presence of God. Here, I am reminded of what in 1965–1966 drove Beatle George Harrison into the many arms of Hinduism. It was the idea that if there is a God, one must see him, one must know him, one must experience him. God must be experientially real in the being of the believer. George found his way to "God-realization" through Vedanta and other philosophical and spiritual traditions in the Hindu wisdom experience, but here follows a brief tale of one who did not find his way there, at least as far as I can see.

THE BIBLE IN POPULAR CULTURE

In 1968, art writer Anthony Fawcett introduced John Lennon and Yoko Ono to Fabio Barraclough, who was organizing the Arts Council–backed National Sculpture Exhibition, to be held at Coventry Cathedral in June of that year. Barraclough agreed that John and Yoko could contribute their joint sculpture, so long, that is, as they were not included in the official program. John and Yoko produced their own program to promote their idea. The idea was conceptual and attractive (equally one could say the concept was ideal). The artists would plant two acorns side by side: "John" by Yoko, and "Yoko" by John, and the ensuing oaks would then constitute living sculpture and as they grew, the world might ponder what they symbolized: the coming together of East and West in their own persons and spiritual, organic ideals. Since the exhibition was to take place within the ruins of the ancient cathedral destroyed by deliberate, murderous German bombing on November 14, 1940, the symbolism of a new postwar reconciliation of opposites (Japan and England in the persons of John and Yoko) was even more pertinent. This was, as John and Yoko would explain, "Living Art," and again would make an impact being unseen beneath the earth, surrounded by the forms of more acceptable "modern" sculpture, often cold and self-consciously angular. The union, or eventual union, of the Eastern and the Western mind was also suggested in the Lennon-Ono unfolding concept.

John and Yoko duly arrived for the planting on June 15. Greeted, if that is the word, by Canon Verney of the cathedral, a hard-faced Rev. Verney informed the famous Beatle and his partner, artist Yoko Ono, that the cathedral ruins were still consecrated ground, and therefore he could not authorize there being put within those ruins the product of a union of two people who were "living in sin," whose distasteful relationship (from the "Christian" perspective) had not been legitimized

Fig. 12.1. John Lennon and Yoko Ono planting two acorns at Coventry Cathedral, June 15, 1968.

by the law, or by the church. Therefore the sculpture would not share the welcome accorded to other artists. There followed a blazing row in Canon Verney's office in which Yoko vainly tried to summon up sculptor Henry Moore by phone to their artistic cause, and was only concluded when it was agreed that the John and Yoko sculpture would be planted *outside* of the ruined cathedral walls (did no one see the Golgotha symbolism?).

John probably did. For me, the symbolism of this encounter on a summer's day in the English Midlands speaks volumes about the priorities of institutional Christianity during this period. As a codicil, it should be mentioned that the canon was not satisfied with the acorns being resited and refused to allow John and Yoko's catalog to be distributed to the public, as people might think the sculpture had something to do with the artists' relationship! John sent the canon a letter, according to Anthony Fawcett, ironically thanking him for his "Christian attitude," adding that, in his view, Christ stood for people, and would probably have loved him and Yoko for their contribution.[1]

I cannot be the only person who has reached for a Bible in a hotel drawer during a moment of need, or else the Gideons who perform this great service would not bother placing them there for persons unknown.

My relationship with the Bible began, as far as I can remember, at "infants school." My first school was a brand-new modern affair, a state school with mercifully large windows above navy blue plastic or steel panels, which I first attended aged four, that is, in September 1964. Ley Hill Infants School, Four Oaks, Sutton Coldfield, was an attractive, airy school by a fairly busy road lined with shops and houses, with loving teachers who kept us busy. Days ended with a prayer, a dance, and a song: not a bad way to go out at any time. I recall that one of the earliest projects, after some progress had been made with "Janet & John" reading books, was the class display. Our display was Noah's ark, for which we children joined forces to make a big cardboard ark that was soon populated by Britains Ltd. plastic zoo animals in pairs, where possible, trooping in. I loved the whole thing. The display was surrounded by our written accounts of the Flood, pinned to boards, together with our crayon drawings of the ark, the flood, and of course the rainbow. The story made a strong impression on me, and still does. It is of no interest to me whether there was a Noah or an ark (or two); some people long ago thought there were, and compiled a story about them full of fascinating symbols, applicable at the time the stories were compiled, and applicable today, as some recent movies have amply demonstrated.

Some time between then and 1966, my mother bought for my brothers and me the rather magnificent *Children's Bible in Color,* first published by Paul Hamlyn in 1964, after a successful initial U.S. publication. It was heavily and very remarkably illustrated with vivid representations of Bible stories from the Creation to the New Jerusalem. I spent many hours and many days over those and subsequent years poring over its pages, and became accustomed to the link between words, images, and symbols. The painting of a rusty-colored Satan quitting Jesus in high dudgeon, leaving him on the jagged mountaintop having failed to tempt him was very strong: the *rouge* Satan with horns, cloven hooves, and nasty teeth set against a beautiful azure sky as he flew. Equally able to imprint lasting images were the representations of the "writing on the wall" (a hand from nowhere inscribing divine graffiti before the king: "Mene Mene Tekel Upharsin" as I recall it) to widespread awe. Balaam's ass struck a chord for some reason, as did images of a wounded, bleeding Jesus, rendered matter-of-factly without overgilding the lily.

However, the most striking and influential imagery connected with the beaten and crucified Jesus entered my life when one Saturday afternoon in 1965, while we were all looking at long-playing vinyl recordings at Frost's Chemists on Sutton Parade, Dad announced that we were all going that night to the Odeon cinema to see a special film. It was called *The Greatest Story Ever Told,* and with a title like that, my brothers and I entered the cinema in some excitement. Based on Fulton Oursler's novel of 1949, but substantially reworked with historical knowledge of the Jewish mystical Essenes thrown in (at the time, the Dead Sea Scrolls were thought to be the work of, chiefly, Essenes), director George Stevens wanted to convey his reverence for the figure of Jesus in a motion picture that really grabbed audiences from the inside. Well, in my case he succeeded very well, but I wonder whether he was think-ing of the effect of the film on a mind inside a five-year-old body. It certainly didn't bother me that John Wayne (in a cameo) sounded a bit wooden when he declared at the Crucifixion, dressed as the Centurion, that this was truly the "Son of *Gahd*." For me, this very long film with its disturbing (in the best sense) music by Alfred Newman, filmed—one did not know this of course—in Arizona, Nevada, and Utah, was a highly charged experience that had me gripped. Max von Sydow's per-formance was graceful, commanding, and warmly humane, and, thank goodness, he was not given the wild long hair and bushy beard treat-ment that would have obscured his fine Swedish face and sky blue eyes! But that scene when the sky goes dark, and one sees Jesus nailed to the wet wooden beams, and one knows this is goodness, pure love, that is being nailed down, along with truth, because people listened to the wrong message and couldn't understand what they were doing, well, it stirred a quiet tremor within myself. This was exposing truth, starkly. I know how born-again evangelized persons feel when they're confronted by the whole drama of the Crucifixion. But seeing Jesus up there on the cross just made me want to get him off it! I have always questioned why the church has kept him up there so long—even Pilate didn't object to him being taken down, according to the Gospels. In my memory ever after, the image of the crucified in the rainstorm was somehow superim-posed on those great "Renaissance" skies flung out in Super Panavision, and that *blue*. . . . The blue got me more than the blood. That blue really meant something.

The movie was, to its credit, largely based on the Gospel of John (which accounts for the film's wordiness, otherworldliness, and stiffness), sometimes called the mystical gospel, or, according to German scholar Rudolf Bultmann, who wrote a commentary on John, "the halfway house to Gnosticism." In the Gospel of John, there is no real time. There are mentions of time of course, of festivals coming and going, and times of the day and so on, but the events are not restricted in import by time process; it's suprahistorical. There is linear process but the entire time one is aware of an eternal cycle present at every moment that lifts one off the earth into the cosmic dimension. One is reminded of the Platonic doctrine that "time is the moving image of eternity": or, if you like, heaven's cinema! Is our world then the entertainment of angels? I remember putting this awareness of "blue" (sky blue) to my tutor in gospel studies, Canon Fenton at Christ Church College. I said I had always seen John's gospel as being a blue, heavenly sky blue color. He nodded thoughtfully, and said he could see what I meant. It suggested eternity. I got that blue, I think, from *The Greatest Story Ever Told*. Or else, the blue in the screen matched the blue in my soul. Who can say?

Again, we must confront that these images were as much, indeed more so, "of the Sixties," than the usual ones trotted out as illustrative of the era. Many, many thousands of people entered the dark temples of cinema to see this movie occupy, for a while, all space and time. Critics were divided when the film came out—as befitted the subject. Its technical qualities were widely recognized, but there were concerns over length, the number of distracting cameos, and what the *New Yorker* called a note of "sustained vulgarity" through the film. Any attempt to render the eternal in moving images is going to hit the problem of the solid. However, if they had seen it through *my* eyes, well. . . . Having seen it recently, there is much to admire, but one feels many great opportunities for sublimity were missed (the raw locations were bulging with potential symbolism), probably due to the restraint of script once the juggernaut of moviemaking got going. This problem was not evident in the magnificent black-and-white movie, *The Gospel According to Saint Matthew*, directed by Marxist, atheist, homosexual Pier Paolo Pasolini. This film is probably the best rendition of the Gospel story to date. It took a nonbeliever to make a film you could believe in. First shown in Venice in 1964, Pasolini took a young Nicaraguan unknown nonactor to play Jesus, Enrique Irazoqui, and did us all a favor. The movie, like the gospel it follows pretty well to the letter, moves along at a frantic pace. Everything happens immediately, or suddenly, and there is constant amazement. The lines are delivered with no venerable cadences, but flatly and deliberately. The Gospel as told seems made for cinema. When a man is healed of leprosy, the miracle is done in one jump cut. We see the man's leprous face, we see Jesus, we cut back, and the face is whole. This was the way to do it. Pasolini made the gospel into a film and the film into a gospel. There's no attempt to explain or to tone down the message; it's delivered straight—and it's truly remarkable how the Italian countryside seems a dead ringer for Galilee. While in George Stevens's film, we see magnificent landscapes that appear straight out of Quattrocento idealist painting, with Pasolini we see what appears to be a lived-in, organic landscape, full of juicy grapes, in which the characters are able to move naturally, and supernaturally, so we see reality occasionally transformed: the essence of miracle. One feels that Pasolini looked at his settings carefully before shooting, and got ideas from what he saw around him, so the movie ripples with life at all times. I cannot recommend it highly enough, and only wish I'd seen it at the time it was made; then I could give you an even more pertinent reaction, for unless ye be as little children, ye cannot enter these kingdoms of cinematic heaven.

I also rather wish Dick Lester had seen and inwardly digested Pasolini's art when he made the Beatles's second picture *Help!* with its silly script by Charles Wood and Marc Behm. It came out very successfully (pots of loot, with pot to spare) in 1965 and in its making introduced George Harrison to the sitar, after a curious, vacuous scene in an Indian restaurant in London's West End, and that encounter was the beginning of much for George and his fans, so perhaps we shouldn't complain, *if that's what it took*. The "story" is a facetious load of hokum about a Far Eastern sect reminiscent of the old Kali blood cult known as Thuggee, wiped out in India by Shropshire-born William Henry Sleeman (1788–1856). The film's fictional sect requires human victims for sacrifice to their goddess Kahili (I think that's what they shout when they try to cut off Ringo's "sacrificial" ring-bearing finger). Ringo is "the chosen one" and must die accordingly. The idea of sacrifice gives the writers and director a certain amount of seriously self-satisfied satirical play. At one point Ringo says to their leader Chang: "It's rubbish, really, isn't it? *Sacrifice?*" Chang is clearly unmoved by this modernist, rationalist rejection of the ancient religious principle that without the shedding of blood there can be no redemption. Chang wants blood, because Kahili wants it of her followers and none dare transgress. The director puts Chang in a London tea garden populated by religious authority figures. Was Dick Lester trying to get "in" with John Lennon, though this was *before* the Jesus controversy? There's a Greek orthodox priest there, while Chang discusses theology with what appears to be a pompous Anglican bishop in gaiters only too happy to enjoy a little ecumenism with another "faith community," after all, says Chang, they have "much in common," a nice skit on the idea of comparative religion. Both figures seem to be concerned about how to raise the interest of young people in their faith; Chang thinks some nice public sacrifices should arouse a young congregation! (he has a point). For those who care (and that would not have been the intended audience of Beatle fans) the film is trying to make a link between Christian ideas of sacrifice—the crucifixion-atonement doctrine by implication, and the dead killed in the war who sacrificed their lives for the greater good—and that of the palpably balmy sectarians from the "mystic East." This is an interesting idea, but in the context of the madcap setting, it just seems to suggest that the Beatles are more modern, more liberal, and too instinctively intelligent to swallow such ideas, and regard the panoply of ancient religious belief as a daft joke from which they're trying to escape (hence *Help!*).

This was not really the case. Lennon himself was troubled by the whole idea of pain and suffering as a means of "bliss," and while he was definitely of the cast of mind who saw governments ordering their young people to go abroad and die for their country in state-sponsored war as acts of perverse, ecclesiastically solemnized sacrifice, he would probably have understood such injunctions to teenage death as exploiting, even perverting an original, innocent spiritual idea, troubling as it was.

To sacrifice is to make sacred an offering rendered to something or someone "higher"; blood can be symbolic of the cost, of course. That one must lose to gain, is a kind of truism. The Beatles themselves had made many sacrifices to get to where they were in 1965. Sacrifice seems to be not only a spiritual law or principle—even if we can't really accept it or see why, we do seem to have to suffer to get anywhere or really learn anything—but a principle of nature too, for in the process of evolution and organic transformation, substances give way and "die" to forces inherent in others in the process of life. However, one feels that *Help!* is wildly aimed at some vague notion of a false religion, or outmoded superstition and authority, and exploitation of youthful energy by figures of that authority. Well, that could, if focused, have made an interesting Beatles movie—but perhaps not a very profitable one. Incidentally, we do see John Lennon reading his own book *A Spaniard in the Works* (1965) in one early scene, so I suspect there's something in my hunch about a deliberate effort to inject a note, or a few notes, of what was then fashionable satire in amongst the raucous, if rather cold, youth-oriented pop and roll. The latter-day defense that *Help!* was a kind of precursor of the pop-art style of the TV *Batman* (1966) is neither here nor there. *Batman* had a grip on its style. Richard Lester's first Beatles movie, *A Hard Day's Night* (1964) was considerably better, and it must be said, dedicated in its well-spun story by Alun Owen to showing the kind of sacrifices of time, privacy, temperament, and much else, the Fab Four made in order to satisfy management, media, and public. And what did they get in return? Worship, adulation, cash, and—by all accounts—a long headache. Bliss proved more elusive, and would involve different kinds of sacrifice.

Whether one was on the side of the Bible or inclined to satirize it (Cambridge and Oxford alumni Peter Cook, Dudley Moore, and Eleanor Bron all had a satirical dig at traditional religious ideas on British TV*) the fact is that the more or less ordinary interpretation and presence of the Bible was an essential, tangible, and visible part of the fabric of Sixties life, and should not be disregarded as many contemporary commentators persist in doing when assessing the Sixties. How very different people responded to the almost universal presence of the Bible provides perspective on the decade's spiritual meaning.

---

*Recall the "Is this it, then? Is this Heaven?" sketch on Peter Cook and Dudley Moore's BBC *Not Only . . . But Also . . .* series in the mid-Sixties, and also of course Peter Cook's clever, but by no means superficial, script for Stanley Donen's original movie of *Bedazzled* (1968), which provocatively paints Lucifer in an amusingly sympathetic light.

Fig. 12.2.British comedians Peter Cook and Dudley Moore.

I well remember around 1966 my father being very impressed by two of the novels of Frank G. Slaughter (1908–2001), and I picked them up off his (self-made) shelf and tried to read them, being attracted by the grand cover designs. Mostly forgotten today, and obviously not fashionable in much of his interests, Frank Gill Slaughter sold over sixty million copies of his novels from the 1940s to the 1980s. The two novels Dad kept all his life were *The Crown and the Cross: The Life of Christ* (1959) and *The Land and the Promise: The Greatest Stories of the Bible Retold* (1960), both of which were big sellers in the United States and the United Kingdom and helped to enlighten the spiritual mind and bolster faith. These were serious attempts at bringing biblical concepts to the casual reader. That they were conservative goes without saying, since religious concepts are bound to be somewhat indifferent to novelties of opinion, attitude, and fashion. That's partly why they have lasted. However, being of ancient, even timeless provenance does not mean that the good old stories can't be dusted off occasionally and given a strong, fresh airing in the best idioms of the time. The point I suppose is that the Jewish and Christian material and history contained in these novels was respectfully treated, and *that,* generally speaking, was the attitude brought to bear on religious material throughout the decade, with a few, growing satirical exceptions, and of course, as we have observed, the seeds of and re-sproutings of neognostic spirituality as the decade wore on.

There was a stylistic biblicism that was part of the aesthetic of the era, and whose presence would make the modernisms of pop art, abstraction, and new clothes fashion look even more modern and "way out." Perhaps inspired by Hollywood doing its grandiose bit to stem the tide of a feared youth-oriented iconoclasm, I remember how promotions of biblical wisdom tended to appear inscribed on vistalike illustrations of great mountains, crags, sunsets and sunrises, vast expanses of ocean or lake—the cracking of light in the clouds with hints of a welcome apocalypse, and the glitter of moonlight on Galilee-like seashores. There was a kind of biblical grandeur, mostly stemming I think from the United States. Almost next door to the popular Odeon cinema in the Royal Borough of Sutton Coldfield (where I lived 1960–66) was a very modern (American-backed) Christian Science Reading Room in whose window the latest *Christian Science Monitor* was displayed, appropriate Bible texts (as seen by the management of the establishment) with regard to contemporary issues, and always, big Panavision-style photographs of the type I have described.

This pictorial sensibility and somewhat *How the West Was Won*– Arizona meets Rocky Mountains–Oregon Trail, plus romantic lighting aesthetic was brought stylized to the screen in George Stevens's aforementioned life of Christ, but the film that packed in the whole, grand ethic-aesthetic of mid-Sixties commercial biblicism was a magnificent movie shot in Italy under the auspices of producer Dino de Laurentiis, and director-star John Huston, modestly entitled *The Bible: In the Beginning* (1966). My family was living near Melbourne, capital of the state of Victoria, Australia, when, in 1967, Dad took us all by tram from St. Kilda into the city to see *The Bible* one Saturday evening, now too long ago. If I may quote from my autobiographical account of the Sixties:

Several movies stand out in 1967, as do the first-class cinemas we saw them at. You must understand that Melbourne was a truly

fantastic, old-modern city. In its way, far more uplifting a metropolis of modernity than London, it had cause to be proud. At night it
was something else. The street lighting and fabulous neon advertisements around Collins Street, the Yarra River, Flinders Street Station,
the State Library (a nineteenth-century "Parthenon"), and Swanston
Street were staggering to behold, and all very clean, with men and
women well dressed, smart, not gaudy like Vegas. One had a distinct
feeling of being on "the rim of the Pacific," even though the nearest
ocean was the Indian Ocean. To the northeast you had the Far East,
Japan and so on, but to me, *Australia* was the "House of the Rising
Sun." It rose and set like a great hot cinder off the pungent-smelling
beach at St. Kilda, bigger than life. No less big was one of the first
films we saw in the city at a cinema built into a kind of shopping
mall, and not obviously a cinema from the street, though external
appearance belied a massive, airy interior, perfect for a film that
intended to show audiences the Creation of everything! *The Bible:
In the Beginning* (it was meant to be the first installment!) was very
long, thoroughly engaging, and extraordinarily magnificent as cinematic spectacle. Most films in those days had Intermissions, and
this one *really* needed one so we could get our breath back, having
seen a naked Adam and Eve fall from grace, Richard Harris acquire
the mark of Cain, and, to top the first half, the Great Flood and a
very convincing building and launch of the Ark with John Huston
incarnating the childlike spirit and humanity of Noah, asked to do
something by the God who speaks within him that makes him a
laughingstock before the fashionable, smartass world about him.
But Noah is vindicated and gets to see the first rainbow! Dino [the
producer] never got beyond the book of Genesis—still, that took
in everything from "Let there be Light" (wonderfully intoned by
Huston in magisterial form) to the Patriarchs (George C. Scott
as a moving Abraham). In the second half, we got Peter O'Toole
as three angels simultaneously announcing the end of Sodom and
Gomorrah—the latter clearly based on a low-life L.A. sex party
with poor lighting!—and to cap it all, the out-of-this-world (almost)
erection of the Tower of Babel! Boy, they don't—*can't*—make 'em

like that anymore! CGI is just so boring in comparison; you're completely at the mercy of stylists who for all their "worldwide skill" just ain't in the league of production designers like Ken Adam or Alexandre Trauner. However gifted, computer animations look like what they are, and few animations can achieve the true "epic" touch. *Epic* is not an effect, it's an inner experience. Opticals [optical effects] always look better than nonexistent, nonchemical, digital cyber events. "Call me old-fashioned"—but antiques aren't sought after for nothing![2]

Yes, well, I'll probably annoy someone with the last few barbs (it's only my opinion, folks!), but compare for yourself, and see why the best Sixties movies have a pull on the spirit of our species that many modern commercial films, especially in the epic or historical mold, can't equal. *It was the times* . . . and they cannot be repeated. Come the Deluge, we'll see which movies float!

One that definitely deserves to reach the Ararat of postdeluge artworks proves that you don't have to make an epic to reveal a spiritual vision inspired by the history of the Catholic Church. It is fascinating how arguably the two most penetrating movies that work on biblical themes were both made by atheists. *The Milky Way* (1969), a Franco-German-Italian "road movie" directed by master surrealist Luis Buñuel concerns itself with a number of heresies against Catholic orthodoxy. The structure is a journey undertaken by two vagrants along the pilgrimage route of Saint James of Compostela. If they are pilgrims, they are unwittingly, as they have no particular aim in life other than to live and keep moving. As they do so, they encounter Jansenist nuns, Priscillian heretics, and quite a number of discussions on Catholic doctrines, such as transubstantiation and consubstantiation, and the Christology of the Nicene Creed. These discussions become more surreal and absurd because they take place in all seriousness in the unlikeliest places and concern unlikely protagonists of theological positions.

Lustrous with originality, the movie has considerable charm, and for myself, the most charming aspect is the occasional inclusion of perfectly ordinary scenes of Jesus and his followers. We see Jesus laughing, having a drink with his friends, shaving, and generally behaving with a humanity that theologians have argued about. There's a marvelous scene of Jesus at a trestle table at an inn, drinking merrily (as the Gospel insists he did), sharing hilarities with his entourage, and warm looks to Mary Magdalene. The curious effect of all this, especially from the standpoint of the director who had no Catholic faith, is that the humanity of Jesus—a really "laughing Jesus" unlike the cynical, superior Gnostic version—becomes in itself paradoxically transcendent, when set against the bickering over doctrines, allegedly about "Him." He dominates simply by being honestly ordinary, if also rather personally striking. The pilgrimage road takes us somewhere, and the miracle may be that through absurdity, we glimpse something of the nature of a truth. There are not many works of cinematic art that show us that simply to watch a story is a kind of pilgrimage. Unfortunately, with most movies, arrival at the destination, or end credits, rarely brings us the kind of reward pilgrims might pray, and suffer, for. *The Milky Way* is exceptional.

REPRESSION IN RUSSIA

Pilgrimages took place in western Europe throughout the Sixties, and participants would have had little doubt about their ability to answer the question then of what the spiritual meaning of the time they spent on those pilgrimages might be. In general, people went to become closer to God, to do penance, or to secure through faith the power of God to alleviate suffering. Despite the encroachment of the industrialized nonsacred, and an increasingly materialist popular culture, the historic faith of Europe continued as it had done since late antique times (through thick and thin), albeit with declining numbers, and could be personally enriched through sacrificing time for religious observances, such as pilgrimages, because belief in salvation required it.

In the USSR, however, pilgrimages or gatherings at sacred sites of old were expressly banned by Nikita Khrushchev's *Instruction on the Application of the Legislation on Religious Cults,* approved by the Soviet State on March 16, 1961, which clarified and added to existing draconian antireligious legislation. People had the official right to believe in

Christianity, Islam, or Judaism, and the right to meet for "cult rites" at registered places under strict controls, but any kind of evangelism was forbidden. Article 17, for example, forbade use of religious buildings for anything other than worship, thus putting parish libraries outside of the law, as well as any organized religious education, prayer meetings, study groups, or teaching of the religion in the home to children. Any instruction on the subject of religion was the sole privilege of religious courses created by the citizens of the USSR with the special permission of the Permanent Committee for Religious Matters at the Council of Ministers. Clergy and other ministers of religion were only permitted to operate in the area where members of religious associations lived, close to the "temple." (The language used was intended to suggest religion was basically a superstition harking back to a prescientific past.) Ministers of religion were forbidden to wear clerical or distinctive clothing in public. As the state did everything it could to discourage young people from what the state regarded as superstition for fools and the elderly, attendances fell. Religious belief was not helpful to promotion, to say the very least. And there was a further catch. A temple with less than twenty registered members was not permitted to continue and would be closed, the property sequestrated by the state.

Not surprisingly, all of this meant that any kind of evangelical-style Christianity or desire to witness the faith in full openness transgressed the will of the state. In practice, certain groups whose main drive was to secure converts and conversion experiences suffered harsh penalties of unemployment and imprisonment, or dispatch to mental hospitals, for religion was regarded officially as irrational, and therefore of psychiatric interest. Moving stories of the extent of these penalties tended to seep out beyond the Iron Curtain into evangelical church circles, and throughout the Sixties there were numerous paperback books circulated by church groups in the West telling of the sufferings of Christian believers who put their faith before the law of the state in the USSR. Secularists turned a blind eye. These stories nonetheless contributed to the thought-world and priorities of Christian groups around the world, and perhaps especially in America, where the Soviet Union would become characterized as fundamentally "Antichrist." The passing of

Bibles and religious material being forbidden under Communism, the courage of evangelicals, but not only evangelicals, in the faith spectrum of the Russian Empire under Soviet control could easily be, and was, compared to the courage of Protestant martyrs and evangelists of the sixteenth and seventeenth centuries who risked the perils of the Catholic Inquisition for reading and distributing Bibles in the vernacular, and attending prayer meetings outside of official churches.

Belief in God survived, despite persecution, and in some cases, spread under frightening conditions—for which the many sacrifices inspire respect. When you passed out from West Berlin through East Germany (DDR), under Soviet overview, that simple sign YOU ARE NOW LEAVING THE FREE WEST really meant something, and should not be forgotten. If there is any truth amid nihilist existentialism, and the world really is value-free, then it might be found that spiritual meaning is the *only* meaning. Certainly, men and women have been willing to die for it (not kill for it, note), without coercion, and against what the world would recognize as their "best interests" (*Sauve qui peut*).

Indeed, the Bible witness of Christian believers who were not content to believe only for themselves, but who felt an imperative to secure conversions to "the Lord" was an inescapable part of the Sixties spiritual scene. There was considerable religious enthusiasm, and of course much expectation of apocalyptic fulfillments, as we have discussed earlier. Against the doubts and preoccupations of Anglican and Episcopalian theologians, the Sixties was full of affirmations of straightforward biblical faith and practical charity applied to the issues of the day, visible on notice boards everywhere you went.

There are people who in their assessment of the thing called the "Sixties" might opine that the *Sixties* doesn't really mean *everything* that went on everywhere during that decade (an utterly impossible tale to tell, for sure!), but was really a kind of distinctive set of novel aspects of human society that either appeared and flourished, or that began during the period. Therefore, to discuss conventional religion or evangelism in the context of the spiritual meaning of the decade is not really on, because those aspects of religion existed in more or less the same way before the Sixties (Christian Aid and Oxfam, for example, were founded in 1941 and 1942, respectively, while the Salvation Army was founded in 1865), and were already part of the background landscape, and any discussion of the Sixties must be defined by innovation and uniqueness in terms of significant changes that gave the decade its curiously memorable flavor.

I am sympathetic to this argument, but, as stated, spiritual meaning is not itself defined by time, and it would be as true to say that there are no fundamentally new ideas, though there might be novel twists, developments, and combinations of established ideas (Platonism, color, and geometry in "abstraction" in art, for example). Hinduism was hardly new, but it appeared so for many of those in the 1960s unfamiliar with its range of beliefs and images. I think the record shows that the mainstream and fringe churches did not simply go on as before, but rose to the challenges of distinct Sixties experiences, or simply reacted to them. But they certainly changed, and to take a fairly banal example, we should not today have guitars in churches and pop-music hymn settings without the impetus of the decade. By the decade's end, we see, for example, the appearance of the "Jesus freak," a clear hybrid of evangelical charismatic-influenced identity based on the equation of Jesus as a kind of hippie or spiritual "freak" who had long hair, was non- or even anticonformist (true according to the record), who was "cool" about women, and was into "love," man. There is no doubt the spiritual challenges presented by alternative spiritual paths made many clergy think very deeply about issues of sex, love, mysticism, and marriage, and have led to *some* degree of changed attitudes in practically all churches. Religion may be seen as in some way evolving in relation to the challenges of time, whether for good or ill we can only judge by the fruits, and judgment in the Christian tradition is not really for the faithful to make, though, if Saint Paul is accorded authority, some degree of spiritual knowledge permits some degree of spiritual discernment, rare though its flowering is.

Look deeply into the Sixties, and you can hardly fail to see not only that doors were opened to change and awareness, but that they *had* to be opened. If that is the case, then there must have been something pushing for change. Could that be, dare I say it, *God-in-us,* that which is not content with a lie, or forever burying the truth, something that likes to come clean, and break free? If God is free, are we still in chains?

FROM PILGRIMAGES TO *JESUS CHRIST SUPERSTAR*

There are perils in freedom of course. Some would say the ideas underlying Tim Rice and Andrew Lloyd Webber's retelling of the New Testament's essential drama in their musical *Jesus Christ Superstar* exhibited those perils for plain view.

Regardless of the fact that the album of the as yet unperformed musical did not appear until 1970, the work itself was conceived in the late Sixties, and recruitment for the lead singer was taking place in 1969. The work represents a summation of some of the spiritual and arguably anti-spiritual insights peculiar to young, educated people during the decade. It is undoubtedly a serious work and the product not only of gifted songwriting, but of serious thought on serious matters pertaining to Jesus's alleged divinity and the meaning and contemporary relevance of his ministry and demise on the cross. Its very narrative is peculiar to the times that engendered it. The writers have not simply taken a religious text and re-presented it, as happened traditionally when religious works were set to music; they attempted their own retelling of the essential narrative, then thrust it boldly into a hip, modern format. Clearly, creative doors had been opened, preparing the way for this startling exercise of creative liberty. A new confidence in the power of inspiration and free thinking is signified, as well as a conviction that these novel approaches are quite proper, and that no text, religious or otherwise, should ever so dominate the mind that it cannot be reconsidered or recast by the lights available to the artist. This of course pits the writers of the new narrative against the original author or authors, and undoubtedly constitutes a challenge. *Jesus Christ Superstar is* a challenge. It has picked up on a buzz from the outrageous liberties of the avant-garde, of which there was much in evidence in the West End of London where the composers worked.

Jesus is presented in full contemporary humanity, warts 'n' all, with Sixties hip language: a youth going through a long agony of self-doubt.

There is no vindicating resurrection at its climax. Jesus, like the meaning of it all, is left hanging, suspended like the Christ of Salvador Dalì's famous painting *Christ of Saint John of the Cross* (1951). Rice and Webber's is not a work of conventional faith. What it does is to say, "Yes, this story needs to be thought about, retold. What if we see it this way?" The musical has a lot to say about Sixties *fame* through rock music and adulation of the blind follower, blind to the weaknesses and flaws of the worshipped object. This is Jesus seen as a modern pop-art experience. It challenges, but does not despise faith. It is in no way an antireligious work (save to the bigot, I think), nor does it mock its subject. In many ways it asks the question: "What can this story mean today to people who would rather listen to their favorite rock bands than a clergyman?" One might conclude that the meaning put forward is a poor alternative to the traditional message, but at least there has been an effort of serious, sincere consideration, bearing fruit in a work of art. Whether we are seeing "the truth" is another issue, left to the judgment of the beholder. If nothing else, the musical did make clergymen and preachers address the issues it raised, and encouraged a search of conscience in very many listeners.

For our purposes the musical does seem pervaded by a great sense of disappointment, a jaded fatigue with hopes set too high, already beginning to seep through in the aftermath of the hippie euphoria of 1967. From an optimist flowery culture that was very briefly prepared to believe in miracles, practicing an open culture of loving strangers with a willingness to see the world as a miracle, perhaps it took the technological and imaginative miracle of a photograph of the earth seen from the moon to bring those great expectations firmly back down to earth. It seemed the earth, vulnerable, beautiful, yes, but lonely, was *all we'd got*— and each other, of course. Within a year of Apollo 11, when the whole world saw two Americans walk on the moon by dint of science, guts and great faith, against the predictions of the naysayers, we were presented with a version of Christ's life where it was obvious that a divine man could *not* walk on so much as water (as Pilate goads his captive messiah), and when Mary Magdalene prays for his love, she might as well cry for the distant moon. As Prospero utters sadly at the end of Shakespeare's

The Tempest: "Our revels now are ended." *Jesus Christ Superstar* may be *the* sign the Sixties had ended: a heavy burden for its authors, for sure, but they took up their cross and would have to carry it.

A codicil: In December 1969, gossip had it that Tim Rice and Andrew Lloyd Webber inquired as to whether John Lennon would care to play the part of Jesus in their new musical, a not altogether surprising misunderstanding since Lennon had sung on the Beatles single *The Ballad of John and Yoko* in May of that year: "Christ! You know it ain't easy, you know how hard it can be. The way things are going they're gonna crucify me." However, judging from the glossy booklet of press cuttings John and Yoko included in their boxed set *Wedding Album,* released in October 1969, a similar idea had already occurred elsewhere. A pithy newspaper cartoon was reproduced in the booklet showing a haughty, fashionably attired, trendy, swinging "beautiful person" and girlfriend passing a newspaper stand. On the headline appear the words: "BBC Deny Lennon to Play Jesus"—to which the passing hipster nonchalantly says: "Who's Jesus?"

THIRTEEN

Civil Rights

We'd only been in Manhattan a few hours when producer Steve Segaller called me down for a preprandial snifter in the Mayflower Hotel bar (since demolished) on Central Park West. Despite the time constraint and the jetlag, I'd still managed to get in a freezing stroll through Central Park and up and down 8th Avenue and thereabouts. Feeling rather disoriented in the strange environment, and assailed by the stabbing cold of a dusky late afternoon in icy January, I tried to dispel the feeling in a piping hot bath. Steve's call got me back into my clothes just as I'd started to nod off. After innumerable static shocks from practically every metallic surface in sight (nylon carpets!) I made it via elevator to the ground-floor bar only to find Steve wasn't there. So I did what I normally do when alone in such places and took out my notebook and started to write. Suddenly, there was a tap on my shoulder. Nearly jumping off my stool I turned with astonishment to see the smiling face of Horace Ové. At that time, forty-seven-year-old Horace was Britain's only working black film director, and the last time I'd seen him was some days before in the Red Lion pub in Soho, London, next to the Windmill Theatre, where we used to enjoy the odd liquid lunch and early evenings with mutual friend Graham Whitlock, who was working as editor on Horace's latest Channel 4 TV film. I had never expected to go to New York for the first time only to find Horace standing behind me! He was as intrigued to know what the hell I was doing there too. Seems we were working for the same outfit.

I was in New York that January of 1986 to interview the world's top American scholars of gnosticism, Hans Jonas and Elaine Pagels, for a big Channel 4 TV series called *Gnostics,* and, as it turned out, Horace was researching a TV documentary he would direct about famous jazz saxophonist and composer Charlie Parker (1920–1955). In pursuit of this, Horace had come to interview people who remembered "Bird" and the impact he'd made in his short but dramatic life in Harlem.

Producer Steve Segaller arrived and we all sat down. Horace then asked me if I'd like to join him at a jazz club in Greenwich Village. He'd introduce me to James Baldwin whom he'd arranged to meet there for the evening. I can't say I reacted, but Steve certainly did. But then, Steve, who knew New York well, also knew who James Baldwin was, and I, to my shame, did not. I was informed that this was a great privilege, a unique opportunity, and I should be a fool to miss it.

I can be foolish, but am not, I think, the perfect fool, so I agreed to venture once more into the now dark, refrigerated streets outside and make my way in good company into the unknown. I think we were in the yellow cab heading downtown when I was informed a little about Mr. Baldwin's distinction in American culture and history, that is to say, as a man of literature and a famous light of the civil rights movement. I took it in my stride, I must say. I'd met a lot of famous people working as a TV researcher and quickly became immune to the magnetism of fame, and besides, I take people as I find them, and expect them to do the same. I am not fazed by reputation. As Dad would say,

Fig. 13.1.
Author James Baldwin
(1924–1987).

"They're only people, just like you." This advice stood me in good stead for what proved to be an unforgettable evening.

JAMES BALDWIN

We duly arrived at the club, which, like so many interesting places, looked uninteresting on the outside. Inside, however, was a huge, tastefully appointed ballroom-like space, with a low ceiling, wooden floor, and many groups of people round tables in private parties, eating and drinking without inhibition, all lit from glowing bulbs at the centers of the tables. At the club's far end was a low stage with a solitary microphone, before which was an enticing black grand piano. Nobody was playing at the time, but there was a definite sense of anticipation. I'd never been anywhere quite like this at the time so I was getting into the potential swing of things.

Soon I was seated, and before I knew it was engaged in conversation with the lovely, mobile face of James Baldwin, sharing the moments between gulps of Michelob. I must say he was an absolute charmer, warm, considerate, sensitive, and I liked him immediately. Looking back, there was a rapport that is rare, at least in my experience. In truth it was soul to soul and very nice. I remember Horace wanted to get James going on the subject of Charlie Parker, so I backed off a bit and started looking around the room at the odd collection of people gathered there. I will always remember one group near us: tall African American women dressed in the costume of Egyptian priestesses. They were quite serious about it too, and one of them, a striking lady beneath a serpentine headdress, got up and made invocations to "the mighty goddess Isis" or words to that effect, her salutations echoed by the excited throng about her who clapped with abandon. I turned to James and he smiled back with a twinkle. He noticed I was staring at the piano, and asked: "Do you play piano, Toby?" "Only a bit. But I do my own compositions." "You go and play," he said. "Are you sure?" "Yeah, you wanna play, you go play. It's okay." So I did. I got up and went and sat at the piano and started playing a few moody chords in a kind of John Barry mode, at which there was a murmur of light applause at the front. "Oh God," I thought to myself, "Hell! People are listening—I'd better go on." So I played a simple piece of about three minutes ironically titled "Cool" (I was anything but), at the last fading chord of which the club manager very politely joined me and asked me where I was sitting, and, tactfully, if I wouldn't mind going back there, he'd love to bring me a drink on the house in appreciation of my filling in some time before the main act! What a gent! I rejoined the others. "I told you it'd be all right, Toby." James then turned back to Horace and Steve and they continued a strange, involved conversation about the meaning of the phrase "a nigger in the woodpile." This phrase had rather obsessed James Baldwin at times, he confessed, and he then explained its significance in a story he'd written, or was about to write, I forget which. Finally, Mr. Baldwin turned back to me and asked me what I thought of New York. I said my first impression was that it seemed to have no spatial soul. At this he was fascinated.

I expatiated on the theme and described my feelings walking up 8th Avenue for the first time. I said I thought the effect was partly exacerbated by the echo produced when walking due to the new skyscrapers that came down to the sidewalk and seemed to curve into it. The effect to my ears was like being isolated in a box. I said that it was *all objects,* things and people the same. There seemed no attraction in the air or general aura around people, just hollow space, and the echo of footsteps. They felt completely self-contained, shut off from those around them and moving in their own orbits as if in a vacuum. The feeling was one of loneliness and objectification. There seemed to be no feeling in the spaces as I was used to, even in London on a still and chilly day. Where was the spirit? He seemed to like this theme, and said he remembered exactly the same experience when he, as a youth, began to feel his way around Manhattan and other parts of New York. In order to feel the reality of people, there has to be an existing sense of community or else communication rings hollow. Well, it seemed a simple enough idea, but one can see how an idea that is really important can come from being true to an experience. And that is the key to James's observation-filled writing. So it seems to me. It's just feeling, and knowing what you're feeling, and thinking about it, and being able to express it. Well, we were two writers discussing what we do without realizing it, and feeling that each other's minds were not really so different, at least on this subject. And I only thought about this long after.

He was really interested in the TV series we were making, and asked me what a gnostic was, and how it was different from conventional Christian faith, about which he had had a lot of experience, as his violent stepfather had been a preacher in Harlem,* and he, James Baldwin, had between age fourteen and seventeen been a charismatic junior minister himself at the Fireside Pentecostal Assembly, and had gained much comfort from it, before he became more aware of the mechanics of "spiritual enthusiasm" and how you could play the crowd when you'd got the trick of it. He abandoned the faith at seventeen, thinking his church experience had just been a way of coping with social and familial rejection. Well, here we could really talk, because I had gone to Oxford in expectation of being ordained as a priest, but the Church of England did not, you could say, "like my style," so, rejected, I'd turned to writing and TV and music, trying to find a way through it.

It was clear that he did not believe in church doctrines. He had made it clear in his 1963 book of essays, *The Fire Next Time,* that he felt, despite his close friendship with Martin Luther King, that Christianity had made it harder for black people to express and act upon what they felt about being treated as second-rate citizens, that is, when they were treated as citizens at all. Baldwin believed that Christianity somehow blunted the message, or the true sense of outrage at being oppressed. It made one feel better in one way, but did not remove the cause of outrage, and oppressors of black aspirations for equality and dignity could use the idea of Christian forbearance to calm down feelings that were fully justified and called for expression and action. Christianity could make even slavery seem somehow normal. There are passages in Paul's letters where he instructs masters to show respect for their slaves, not to be too harsh. Paul accepted slavery because "flesh and blood" could

---

*Emma Jones gave birth to son James on August 2, 1924. She left his father on account of his drug abuse and went to Harlem where she met a preacher named David Baldwin, with whom she lived in poverty. David Baldwin had other children with James's mother, but while James had to look after them, his stepfather treated him especially harshly.

not inherit the kingdom, so it didn't matter what your status was in this life. Only "in Christ" were all men children of God. Paul called himself a "slave of Christ" and was willing to undergo imprisonment and beatings for the Christ "in him." But, what if you loved your children, or your friends' children? How could you bring them up knowing that they'd suffer what you suffered, and that you'd done nothing to make it better for them? All that turning of the other cheek could make the other cheek very sore and the person with it somehow maimed. James Baldwin also thought the doctrine of reward in heaven was generally understood as a way of coping with a raw deal in this life, it lowered expectation of this life with hope everlasting, but only *after* this life in the "hereafter." It too often made for hopelessness and resignation in the face of oppression. It got to the point where the "Negro" began to accept what appeared to be, and what he was told was his "lot," and that it was just the way it was. That was the deal, and the cards were stacked against him.

James Baldwin knew of course that Martin Luther King found his texts to justify his and his fellow black people's human dignity in the Bible. He could see how Reverend King brought the "Promised Land" back from the hereafter and into the scheme of a concrete political objective, a dream that would come true, albeit at great cost. James Baldwin knew that the Bible had much to say of the vanity of riches and the folly and narcissism of the rich, and he knew that it was Martin Luther King's encounter with the *practical* politics of Mahatma Ghandi that impressed upon him the effectiveness of nonviolent civil disobedience as a way of achieving the ultimate goal of freedom, and the dream of the people who suffered tyranny and oppression. Martin Luther King believed in a supreme moral order in the universe that would be justified by the effect of passive-positive protest and nonviolent civil disobedience in the face of oppressive laws. James Baldwin had suffered the news of his friend cruelly assassinated on April 4, 1968, and wondered whether any such moral order ever did, or could exist in the universe.

In the very early Sixties, Baldwin had met Elijah Muhammad (1897–1975) of the Nation of Islam movement, who believed that only in Islam could the black man stand truly tall among other men, and as a Muslim would never have to cringe before a white man, because Islam claims the prophet Muhammad "sealed" or completed the prophecies of Jewish and Christian dispensations, and Islam had, allegedly, made no self-prejudicial deal with any empire or power of earth. Nevertheless, Elijah Muhammad (formerly Poole) had developed an idiosyncratic form of the faith, with ultimate black supremacy as its promise, on the basis that the original "man" was black and wicked whites had tricked and supplanted him. Muhammad Ali (formerly Cassius Clay), Malcolm X, and Louis Farrakhan accepted Elijah Muhammad as an inspiring guide, though Malcolm X would split over Elijah Muhammad's extramarital affairs and the latter's suspending Malcolm X for commenting publicly on Kennedy's assassination in 1963. When asked by the leader of Nation of Islam where he, James Baldwin, was "at" in his religion, Baldwin told Elijah Muhammad that he had quit church twenty years previously, and was neither a Christian nor any other religion but had learnt to think for himself alone and write about what he saw.

And did he write! James Baldwin gave us enduring, powerful, eloquent, disturbing, and beautiful works on race, class, and on sexuality (he was gay and championed the gay rights movement) and through it all, remained an individual, unwilling to be classed as "a Negro writer." He counted as his personal friends, not only Martin Luther King but also Marlon Brando, Richard Avedon, Josephine Baker, Miles Davis, Harry Belafonte, Sidney Poitier, Ray Charles, Yves Montand, Medgar Evers, and Malcolm X (the latter two also assassinated, and about which events he wrote in his book *No Name in the Street,* 1972).

I have learned these things about James Baldwin only since our first and only meeting (he died the following year, 1987) but now I think I can see why he was intrigued by what I had to say about the gnostics. I remember saying the whole thing about gnosis as I understood it, was that it was an expansive spiritual experience of the divine within the core of humanity, the highest thing we could conceive of, within us, and if we did not let it flower, in the face of a cruel, blind world, then that potential falling back on itself would destroy us. We had to let it come forth, and so become our own saviors. I saw the light in his eyes. It was only much later that I read that he had said that if one *must* believe in a God, at least let it be something that makes people better and happier, and more real, and not something to be used against other people, or against oneself through guilt at what one was, or pointing the finger judging others. "If the concept of God has any use, it is to make us larger, freer, and more loving. If God can't do that, it's time we got rid of him."[1]

Well, we had a nice conversation. We were just two people exercising our "civil rights," or something better, meeting for the first time in a jazz club, filled with lots of different kinds of people, with music, and laughter, and love, and all the rest. And outside, it was very cold and snowing very hard, and the hollow echo of all those boots and shoes was muffled in the freezing snow that covered everything.

The next day, at breakfast at the Mayflower, Horace Ové came over to the table, looked at me and said: "James Baldwin liked your *head,* Toby"—quite possibly the finest compliment I have ever been paid. Man is made in the image of God. Not black man, not white man. Not American man, not Englishman. Not Russian man. Not Arab man. Not Jewish man. Not Chinese man. *Man.* Man was made in God's image, as God's reflected image (Genesis 1:27). And we fell from that unity, or we lost sight of it, or the image was shattered; it's the same thing. We lost the image. Now it can only be dimly perceived through the dark glass of our skin and mortal body. Such is the message of Genesis (the beginning), and the belief of the New Testament is that that image can be seen again, and made audible, in the person and conduct of Jesus, and *therefore,* if we seek hard enough, *in ourselves,* even by willingness to see God in others.* As Martin Luther King observed when it was

---

*While this figure "Jesus" is inspired by the Gospel accounts and the testimony of Paul's personal spiritual experience, it should be noted that gnostic writings refer to this figure as "the living Jesus" and the *living* Jesus is not precisely identified with the image of any historical figure, but with the awakened spirit of the gnostic. From the point of view of the flesh, the living Jesus is a spiritual ideal, also identified by Gnostics with Seth, the son of Adam whose birth resolved the murderous conflict of Cain and Abel, and, if you understand the figure called "Son of Man" as a person who has *seen* the original unfallen image of God's reflection, then it will be seen that "Seth" symbolizes the progeny or generation of those who remain true to this original image of Man (hence Sethian Gnostics, suppressed and declared heretical by orthodox bishops). It should also be emphasized

suggested to him that Christianity made people soft on the oppressor, we do not have to *like* our enemies or accept or in any way let pass what they do, but we can love them, for they are redeemable creatures of God and we may pray for their enlightenment, as much as for our own. However, for many who had witnessed directly the actual torture and lynching of Negroes in America (as had Elijah Muhammad), that was asking too much, and it should be said that the rejection of love for one's enemies and the seeking of recompense, if necessary by violence, is also pertinent to the spiritual meaning of the Sixties.

Nevertheless, perhaps it took something peculiar to the decade to make so many more people a little more aware of a, let's face it, still elusive *cosmic humanity,* and really get going on this long, rocky road, with all its setbacks and despairs, where we can depend on no external moral power, but only that of knowing ourselves in ourselves, all of us, what is right and proper and good and to do to others what we would have them do to us. Of course, you've got to *know* . . .

Well tricky and tortuous as it may be to locate spiritual meaning from the ordinary human, rationalizable side of reality, we seem to have got somewhere near to seeing aspects of the civil rights movement as being in some sense a spiritual movement, a revelation of the depth and power of divine humanity, as well as an obviously social and political one. Freedom cannot simply be given, it must be self-realized and truly *felt.* And this rather makes me think of Jimi Hendrix, who, like James Baldwin and so very many others, was absolutely hit in the heart by the murder of Marin Luther King in April 1968. After that time, Jimi came under all kinds of pressures, including from militant Black Panthers, to

---

(cont. from p. 235) that human beings in their ordinary condition seldom, if at all, reflect the image of God, and according to this understanding, Feuerbach's personal conclusion that "Man is God to man" cannot obtain since man as we find him in human societies, whatever his or her qualities, is at an abysmal remove from primal Man, made in God's image. A process of return to God, or reintegration, must be enacted. In that process we may encounter enlightenment. It should be said that while Christianity was and is abused by some persons to justify oppression of disliked races, it is also sincere religious experience that has enabled white Christians to overcome social prejudice and work and suffer for their black "brothers and sisters" in the cause of civil rights and vice versa.

identify his music more closely with the exclusively "Black Power" cause. Jimi was very sensitive to his role as a black performer, playing mainly to young white audiences, crossing America with his "freak flag flying" in such a turbulent time in American history. He began to see his concerts and music as what he explicitly called in 1969 "the Electric Church," a way of bringing people together, favoring integration, encouraging spiritual unity and a sense of personal freedom and spiritual liberation across the race divide through his music, which more and more began to address social *and* spiritual issues directly, while simultaneously attempting to draw power down from the "music of the spheres" and interstellar energies, which he perceived and to which his guitar and soul aspired as a contact and emanation point.

So, having an inkling of "spiritual history" we must, to make better sense of what we have discussed above, make note of what Fabre d'Olivet would call "positive history," the kind you get in history books, news programs, and documentaries—otherwise known as . . .

A FEW GENERALLY ACCEPTED FACTS IN CHRONOLOGICAL SEQUENCE

Having, by the late 1940s, despaired of the prejudice against black and gay people in America, James Baldwin spent most of the 1950s in France. Returning to the United States in 1957 while the Civil Rights Act was being debated in Congress, Baldwin was moved by brave attempts made by young people to desegregate schools in North Carolina. Taking account of his interest, the *Partisan Review* commissioned him to go south and report on what was happening. In Charlotte, North Carolina, Baldwin met Baptist minister Rev. Martin Luther King Jr., and a subsequent trip to Montgomery, Alabama, furnished material for Baldwin's essays "Nobody Knows My Name" for the *Partisan Review* and "The Hard Kind of Courage," which appeared in *Harper's* magazine. He then contributed more articles on the ferment in the South for top-drawer New York magazines.

On May 25, 1961, just as President Kennedy declared the United States would put a man on the moon by the decade's end, Montgomery,

Alabama, erupted in violence when "Freedom Riders" who'd boarded whites-only buses were attacked by white segregationists. Attorney General Robert Kennedy ordered U.S. marshals in to protect Reverend King who addressed a mass meeting held in a church amid obscenities shouted from the midst of hundreds of angry white-skinned people around the building.

In 1962, James Baldwin penned yet more important articles about the civil rights movement, while supporting the Congress of Racial Equality (CORE) and the Student Nonviolent Coordinating Committee (SNCC). The South was boiling with tensions. On September 30, protestors in Mississippi failed to prevent the enrolment of the first black student at the state university.

Baldwin undertook a lecture tour in North Carolina and Louisiana in 1963 on behalf of CORE with a message pitched between the militancy of Malcolm X and Reverend King's nonviolent approach, with a hope that socialism might take root in America, and that wealth creation for all would be encouraged and its benefits shared for the common good, so averting the specter of feared race war. On May 17 James Baldwin graced the cover of *Time* magazine, which praised him with the words: "There is not another writer who expresses with such poignancy and abrasiveness the dark realities of the racial ferment in North and South." Baldwin dispatched a cable to Robert Kennedy asserting his view that the crisis in the South was stoked up by J. Edgar Hoover and the FBI, Mississippi Senator James Eastland, and by the unwillingness of the president to make his high office a moral forum. The attorney general invited Baldwin to several private meetings, one of which included Baldwin's chosen delegation, whose number included singers Harry Belafonte and Lena Horne, and other activists. Baldwin, meanwhile, was subject to illegal FBI surveillance.

On August 28, 1963, more people gathered in Washington, D.C., to demonstrate than had ever before been seen at a civil rights event. Numbers in excess of 200,000 swelled the scene by the Lincoln Memorial to hear Martin Luther King deliver his famous "I Have a Dream" speech, gazing with visionary gleam to the apex of the collective aim, when it would be properly understood what was contained in the U.S. Founding

*Fig. 13.2. Martin Luther King Jr.
(1929–1968).*

Fathers' belief that "all men are created equal." Only when the oppressed were "free at last" would white and black men become true brothers. The cry for freedom invoked archetypal biblical narratives of the Exodus, when Moses pleaded with Pharaoh to let his people free, empowered to cross the Red Sea, advance to the life-giving waters of the Jordan, so to gaze in wonder upon, and to take possession of the promised land, blessed by God Almighty.

James Baldwin joined Charlton Heston, Harry Belafonte, Sidney Poitier, and Marlon Brando in lending their weight to the intense call of the occasion: an eloquent summoning of the world's conscience in the spirit of the great ideal. If the definition of a religious or numinous experience is to feel oneself to be in the presence of something bigger than oneself, then certainly the sheer numbers who gathered at the Lincoln Memorial that day might lead to shivers up the spine and tingling at the back of the neck suggestive of spiritual movement, but more importantly, the sense of solemn righteousness invoked by Martin Luther King served, at least for a day, to fuse the spiritual and the political, at an unforgettable pitch: a high point in the ragged spiritual tapestry of the 1960s. What this meant spiritually for the United States, and indeed, to countries worldwide was that to oppose a godly conception of racial justice put the opposition in a position of apostasy from the manifest will of God: an uncomfortable and unenviable position for those who claimed that right and God were on their side. South African government watched events unfolding in the United States with trepidation. That did not mean, of course, that a man of African race was somehow "right" simply on account of skin color. Generalized oppression was no cause for self-righteousness. Reverend King was keen to assert that the whole point of racial equality was that any person should be judged for what they had done, not how he or she appeared to others. Love is a Christian duty, not a legal imperative.

Notwithstanding the enormous publicity gained for the movement, forty-fifth governor of Alabama, George Corley Wallace, called on the National Guard to prevent desegregation of schools. On September 10, 1963, Robert Kennedy stepped in to take the National Guard out of Wallace's control. The decision marked a turning point in the crisis.

Three months after Malcolm X (born Malcolm Little) left the Nation of Islam organization to launch his own "Muslim Mosque Inc.," President Lyndon B. Johnson signed the Civil Rights Act, on July 2, 1964. First proposed by President Kennedy the previous year, the Act outlawed discrimination on the basis of race, color, sex, country of origin, or religion. Three weeks later, New York State governor, Nelson Rockefeller called on the National Guard to suppress race riots in Rochester. On August 4, the bodies of three missing civil rights workers were discovered in Mississippi. Between August 19 and September 20, the Beatles undertook an extensive tour of the United States, playing in New Orleans and in Jacksonville in

Fig. 13.3. Malcolm X (1925–1965).

the South, John Lennon having insisted to the group's manager that they would not tolerate any kind of segregation of audiences anywhere. Many young men inspired to grow their hair long by the Beatles' example suffered beatings and insults.

On February 21, 1965, one month after President Johnson described his notion of a Great Society to replace the divisions of the past, Malcolm X was shot to death in Harlem, so ending a feud with Elijah Muhammad's Black Muslims; the Nation of Islam's leader denied any responsibility for the murder.

On June 6, 1966, James Meredith, the first Negro to be admitted to Mississippi's largest university, known as "Ole Miss" in Oxford, was shot in the back while on a civil rights march. On November 8, Californians elected Ronald Reagan as their state governor, while Edward W. Brooke became the United States' first black senator.

On January 21, 1967, citizens of the Bahamas found themselves with their first black governor. On April 30, twenty-five-year-old Cassius Clay lost his heavyweight title after refusing to serve in the U.S. Army against people he refused to accept were his enemies. His commitment to his conscience and to the religion he had embraced, inspired by Elijah Muhammad, prevented him, he asserted, from acquiescing in the law of the land when its observance suppressed conscience and faith. Pacifist draft-dodging was now a national problem for the state's military machine, and many suffered as a result.

In the midst of the "Summer of Love" declared in San Francisco, a two-page "advertisement" appeared in the London *Times*. It was headlined "An American View" and argued that while the United States administration claimed to be seeking peace in the war in Vietnam, the government was in fact secretly destroying peace negotiations, convinced it could win the war by force of arms outright. James Baldwin signed the document, along with Allen Ginsberg, Noam Chomsky, Henry Miller, Susan Sontag, Philip Roth, Pete Seeger, Mike Nichols, and Sam Wanamaker. It appeared on July 14.

On August 30, 1967, Thurgood Marshall became America's first black man to secure a seat on the Supreme Court.

As 1968 opened, the Vietnam War was uppermost in James Baldwin's mind. He signed the "Writers and Editors War Tax Protest," refusing tax payments rather than seeing his earnings abet the Vietnam War.

On April 4, 1968, thirty-nine-year-old Rev. Martin Luther King was assassinated on the balcony of the Lorraine Motel, Memphis, Tennessee, by forty-year-old James Earl Ray,* fueled by hatred to pull the trigger; he fled the scene. Riots broke out in American cities, and from that point on, it became harder for those suffering inequalities on account of race to look with favor on the moderate, sacrificial approach of Reverend King. Feelings of a terrible conspiracy against truth and goodness were enflamed. Reaction would be to the advantage of extremists, as Reverend King had feared. The mood would get uglier, militancy would increase, and calls for separatism would challenge and fatally maim the idea of a great society, united in brother- and sisterhood. Though for some, the dream was over, for others it lived on; what, after all was the alternative? The road was longer than anyone could have thought.

---

*On June 8, James Earl Ray was arrested en route to Brussels. He was sentenced to ninety-nine-years imprisonment on March 11, 1969.

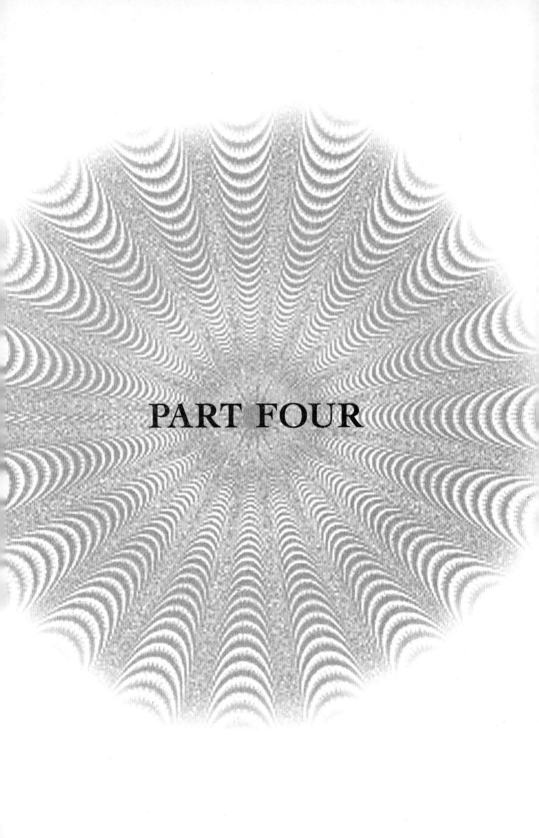

PART FOUR

FOURTEEN

The Party's Over

"The words of the prophets are written on the subway walls," wrote New York singer-songwriter Paul Simon in "The Sound of Silence" (1964). Philip K. Dick remarked that the keynotes of the new or divinely sent signs of the times were to be found in the trash layer the mainstream discards. Such seems to be the case with regard to a remarkable movie directed by Guy Hamilton, now celebrated as director of the third Bond film *Goldfinger* (1964), produced on a monster budget a year later.

The Party's Over was shot in black-and-white in West London in 1963, but on account of its outraging the British Board of Film Censors, was not deemed viewable until 1965, when a cut version received mute critical attention. This is a pity, but not altogether surprising, as the film is "very near the knuckle." Today it looks, at first sight, fairly tame, like an underfunded B-movie effort of determined, skillful enthusiasts. However, within its highly unorthodox story strange powers lurk. Perhaps that is why Marc Behm's thoughtful screenplay attracted movie stars Jack Hawkins and Peter O'Toole as executive producer and coproducer (with Anthony Perry), respectively, to its idiosyncratic cause. Line-producer Perry also managed to plead poverty to secure the genius of budding film composer John Barry, then famous for his stunning recording and arrangement of "The James Bond Theme," his pop- and jazz-oriented music, and the soon-to-be-released highly original and accomplished orchestral soundtrack to the second Bond movie *From Russia with Love.* But the defining stroke that puts *The Party's Over* squarely in the face of the onlooker is the shimmering tremor emitted from Oliver Reed's inspired playing of the young antihero, Moise, acknowledged leader of a group of disparate dropouts, beatniks, and artists who have generated their own subculture with a fairly nihilistic, socially insolent, countercultural attitude. This assembly of itself marks the movie's premise out as prescient, even prophetic.

There is little doubt in my mind that Oliver Reed's dark, brooding, paradoxically intelligent, ever-watchful character's name has been lifted from Moïse Tshombe who, eleven days after Belgium's King Baudouin witnessed Congo's independence in June 1960, declared the secession of breakaway, copper-rich province Katanga, thus igniting a still-unresolved civil war. The Moise of *The Party's Over* is just the kind of troublemaker with the intensity to accomplish something similarly fateful.

Though born in Trenton, New Jersey, in 1925, scriptwriter Marc Behm (who would work on the story and script for the Beatles' *Help!* in 1965), favored French culture and lived in that country after encountering it as a U.S. soldier during World War II. Perhaps exposure to French *nouvelle vague* cinema and literary sensibilities gave Behm the edge with this film of nascent revolution in a collectively and carelessly inhabited house in Chelsea.

After a brief scene at an ill-tempered balcony party, the story begins with the disorganized, disheveled partygoers stumbling over Battersea Bridge to their Chelsea digs after a chill dawn has seen the night's revels turn into a morning hangover (the producers couldn't afford to use the hit song "The Party's Over"). We are soon introduced to the dominating Moise and his pretty girlfriend Libby (Ann Lynn). *Moïse* is French for "Moses," of course, and he is the lawgiver, whose pronouncements the group respects as words from on high.

The gang has made little effort to accommodate a visiting young and beautiful, and rather mysterious American heiress, Melina (well played by Louise Sorel), despite her rebellious wish to escape from a suffocating society dominated by her wealthy father in the States, and willingness to tolerate and muck-in with the rough-and-ready lifestyle of her new, envious, acquaintances. Moise has noticed her, of course, and expresses his interest and feigned disinterest with nihilistic contempt, leaving Melina more isolated and misunderstood than ever. Lost in herself, and the object of mainly carnal attention from the young misfit males around her, she disappears, apparently in the course of a wild jazz party with extravagant twist and freeform dancing and bottle-swigging excess. It's like a rehearsal for what will come later in the decade. Putting it another way, the film shows perhaps a truer, "other side" of the gloss of the Beatles' *A Hard Day's Night,* also shot in West London less than a year later. Lennon had lived such a lifestyle as an art student in 1959–1960, sharing squalid digs with fellow art students and beat poet enthusiasts at Gambier Terrace, Liverpool, in conditions whose abject nature drew the attention of a report in the *People* Sunday newspaper of July 1960 warning of a "Beatnik Hell" threatening the status quo at the fringes of society.

A young American next arrives on the scene and proceeds to interview the members of the group, hitting strong resistance from Moise who encourages the others to shun the handsome but "square" stranger-conformist, who it transpires is Melina's businessman fiancé, Carson (Clifford David), sent by Melina's father, Ben (Eddie Albert), to find his daughter and bring her home. Piece by piece, Carson encounters a picture of guilt and duplicity, of personalities in pieces. However, the film does not make judgments about either their lifestyle or their genuinely pathetic lost-soul-ness. One interesting scene has Carson interviewing short-tempered, apparently Cuban sculptor Geronimo (played by Mike Pratt who would find fame in TV in 1969 with *Randall & Hopkirk* [*Deceased*]). The questioning proceeds amid Geronimo's abstract, distorted, "found" sculptures and mobiles, many of an apparently inane whimsicality that would in a few years find ready buyers keen to cash in on London's world-leading "happening" art scene. The fragmentary and incoherent nature of Geronimo's handiwork mirrors, even edits his moral carelessness and self-delusions, suggesting a coming era of willfulness to evade responsibility in self-incomprehension and group identity.

Eventually, Moise weaves a tapestry of events resembling the truth. We see Moise's story in flashback. Hurt by Moise's exclusively sexual attentions, suffering an emotional crisis, Melina wanders among the drunken group at the fateful party. Amid the loud music, and unbeknownst to all but Moise and the wiser but worried Tutzi, Melina slips on a set of steps strewn with collapsed drunks. Even when discovered "passed out," no one else realizes she has broken her neck. Oblivious to the fact they are manipulating a corpse, some of the throng, male and female, think it amusing to divest the all-too-chic dresser, as they consider her, of her clothes, while one young man, the disturbed Phillip, who has lusted after her, and imagines he loves her, draws on Dutch courage to kiss Melina's still-warm lips. Censors interpreted the scene as one of necrophilia and cut it, at which the director, executive producer, and coproducer insisted their names be removed from the credits on its eventual release.

The ring of investigation begins to close upon the group. Phillip throws himself from the roof to his death, unable to bear the shameful memory of what he did and the gang's having led a macabre funeral procession through the streets in the wee hours before dumping Melina's body with scant, sardonic ceremony. At the end of the movie, Moise plucks up courage to confront Melina's wealthy father, Ben, standing distraught by her very real coffin at Waterloo Station. Moise seems to grasp a chance of redemption. He finds a shared feeling with the father, real loss—and sees and feels, maybe for the first time in his life, a sense of responsibility. The arrogant veneer starts to crack, then slips: a transition played perfectly with great tension by Oliver Reed. He tells Ben that he's sorry. Ben, with restrained dignity, who has also realized his own part in the tragedy, thanks Moise quietly and sincerely. The old man has done what none of the gang could do: put Moise in his place. The arrogant, spoiled, self-loathing narcissist is going to have to grow up, and we see him walk away with tears in his eyes, his pose shattered, with his girlfriend to a new, more ordinary life, shunning the gang.

It is tempting to suggest the story sums up, in advance, one arguable reading for the decade as a whole. The "beatnik" attitudes, regarded as alien in the movie, would be drawn into the magnetic field of fashion and regarded seriously and analyzed. Furthermore, in the microcosm of the establishment-hostile gang we see brought together in a single rejected movie, key aspects of the growing counterculture in art and music. As with Frank Sinatra's *Watertown,* all this rebelliousness comes at a very high price. One feels that Moise is going to spend the ensuing decade embracing a deserved self-punishment, a first unheard voice of regret before the era had even reached its first stammerings of unmediated optimism.

In fact, *The Party's Over* captures the brief period of transition from the Fifties to the Sixties, hence it is jazz music that makes the party wild. In 1961–62, most of the leading British rockers-to-be who would lead the British pop invasion of America from 1964 were at, or had recently quit (due to weight of gig commitments) art school. When John Lennon arrived at Liverpool Art School in 1958 one of the things that annoyed him, he said in retrospect, was the almost universal enthusiasm for jazz, which he hated, along with, apparently, students wearing duffel coats, college scarves, and beards. Lennon dressed offbeat "streetwise" with an outsider's contempt of fashion or convention, an intimidating teddy-boy quaff, sideburns, and drainpipe trousers, and at parties insisted on black leather and sweaty rock 'n' roll: the "Real Thing" for him. Lennon was quite a few years ahead of the game here as regards the musical predilections of the young mainly lower-middle-class boys and girls at art school. This lead would also extend to style in general, thanks to a lucky encounter with German art and fashion students, dubbed "exis" (existentialists) by the Hamburg Beatles. Astrid Kirchherr, Jürgen Vollmer, and Klaus Voormann helped to make the Hamburg of 1960–62 a transformative experience for the Liverpool group. Hamburg mixed with Liverpool sass gave the band the edge that would shake the world.

The leaders of the British rock boom of the Sixties had only two things universally in common (other than a taste for rock). First, they were all brought up in the Fifties (mostly born after 1943), second, all of them had contact, if sometimes slight, with tertiary education, the vast majority, very remarkably, with art school attendance. Look at this:

John Lennon (b. 1940)—the eldest: Liverpool Art College, 1958

Eric Burdon (of the Animals): Newcastle College of Art and Industrial Design, 1959

Charlie Watts (drummer for the Rolling Stones): left Harrow Art School, 1960

Pete Townshend (of the Who): studied Graphic Design at Ealing Art College, 1961 (other students at Ealing included Ronnie Wood and Freddie Mercury)

Eric Clapton: Kingston College of Art, 1961

Jimmy Page: Sutton Art College, Surrey, 1962

Jeff Beck: Wimbledon College of Art, 1962

Brian Jones (founder of the Rolling Stones): applied for scholarship at Cheltenham Art College in 1961; application rescinded due to complaint about his sexual conduct

Keith Richards: Sidcup Art College, 1962

Ray Davies (of the Kinks): Hornsey College of Art, 1962–63

Roger Waters (of Pink Floyd): Regent Street Polytechnic, school of architecture, 1962, along with band members Richard Wright and Nick Mason

Mick Jagger: London School of Economics; studied business, left 1962

Had *When the Party's Over* been made a year or two later, the music for the fateful party would have been provided by ex-art students playing R & B, blues, and rock 'n' roll. Art, even a sprinkling, seems to have spelled the difference. It gave awareness of form, style, fashion, change, revolt, and dynamic ideas: an inner pulse to match the beat.

I spoke to artist Vanilla Beer (b. 1950) about her reflections on the very clear link between art and rock-pop music in the Sixties. Vanilla spoke from experience. Having studied drawing at the Farnham School of Art, Surrey, in 1967, she moved into squalid digs in London in 1968. She quickly became involved in the London music and art scenes while

Fig. 14.1. The Indica Art Gallery, 6 Masons Yard, St James's

attending Walthamstow School of Art, East London. Vanilla received a kiss from Jimi Hendrix at one of his London gigs and found a new boyfriend at the famous all-night, LSD-active "14-Hour Technicolor Dream" happening at Alexandra Palace on April 29, 1967. I think I've seen her there in a scene from the only feature movie* to capture both that authentic counterculture event and the interior and exterior of John Dunbar, Peter Asher, and Barry Miles's Indica Gallery, 6 Masons Yard, St James's, where John Lennon first fixed eyes with Yoko Ono in November 1966 at her first British exhibition, "Yoko at Indica." *Indica,* incidentally, referred to *Cannabis indica,* the popular "pot" smoked liberally for mystical or poetic reasons among the art and music scenes,

---

*The movie, directed by Tinto Brass (*Caligula,* 1979), is now very rare: *Col cuore in gola* ("With heart in mouth"; U.S. title: *I Am What I Am*), released in Italy in 1967, and in the United States in 1969. Starring Jean-Louis Trintignant and Ewa Aulin, it involves long chases from vicious crooks, which take the viewer around that unique London Tinto Brass had heard so much about in Italy. Intended to have been shot in Rome or Paris, Brass believed the most innovative, hip-happening scene in the world was in London, so the Italian crew came to England, in the footsteps of Antonioni (*Blow Up,* 1966), and shot not only inside and out at the Indica Gallery, but a long scene, including drama actually set during the 14-Hour Technicolor Dream event. The Indica scenes show the psychedelic mind-boggling abstracts on canvas and in sculpted plastic exhibited at the Indica in spring 1967. The film gives a fine insight into London street atmosphere in that period; it is *not* like the usual documentaries suggest it was.

where *indica* means "of India" with the added English pun of a sign or something "indicated." The Indica Gallery pointed optimistically to the pleasures and mysteries of the future. Vanilla remembers listening to Yoko Ono giving a talk on her innovative conceptual art at the Guildford Art School around this time, with the use of sanitary towels wrapped round her listeners' eyes, then removed.

As regards the link between the rockers and the art schools, Vanilla observed that the art schools attended (as indicated above) by England's rock-stars-to-be were not the "big names" or establishment leaders in art education in Britain at the time. She recalled that attendance at municipal art schools usually meant some kind of failure academically, and often attracted nervous, edgy people, or what would have been described as "sensitive" people, who were unlikely to find steadiness in a job, or who felt out of kilter with ordinary working life, being driven by creative not pecuniary or practical urges. When Vanilla arrived at art school, she was thrilled, at last, to find herself among *her* people, people who could discuss ideas, enjoy similar things, and who weren't afraid of beauty or new thoughts and experiences. She says she found the tutors often frightening. Above all, she emphasizes, the art scene in London had almost nothing to do with money. Nobody was thinking about how they would use art to make money, or worrying about careers. It was about creativity, with respect to which observation, John Lennon once remarked in an interview of how after first meeting Yoko Ono in late 1966 and subsequently in 1967, he considered her as one going around like a "nun," thinking "everything was spiritual." John, by then, had long been in the school of hard knocks and was all too familiar with base commerciality, though he too was searching for that elusive "something," a goal, a state of being, a direction, a point to living beyond the obvious. He obviously found it liberating to be with a person who didn't think like someone "in the business." For her part, Yoko found it refreshing to meet a real guy different from those she was used to meeting in the art scene. She thought at the time he looked quite conventional but had the gift of pure imagination and a pathos that chimed in with her own troubled psyche. Lennon denied he looked conventional, as at the time he was going through his "psychedelic period" and was sporting way-out multicolored clothing, and looked rather jaded from so many LSD trips, late nights, and bleary mornings.

I asked Vanilla about spirituality in art at the time. She suggested that some kind of an idea of spirituality in art was somehow taken for granted, not openly voiced, in that creativity and art were already an expression of inspiration, or a search for truth out of one's own spirit and deepest experience; and is there a qualitative difference between *deep* and *high*? Overt sense of the spiritual came to Vanilla powerfully through poetry—she attended the Poetry "Incarnation" organized by Barry Miles and John Hopkins at the Albert Hall—and above all, through music. That is, the new music played by the new groups, especially the driving "trippiness" of the Rolling Stones and, after 1966, Hendrix, and "everything else too," though as a Stones fan, she found the Beatles lacking in raw immediacy by comparison: the rebel edge—the Beatles having been inadvertently embraced by many in the Establishment. The Stones were more expressively bluesy and their image, impolite and provocative. Music profoundly moved Vanilla. It was inspirational and made her want to create and live, and feel good about devoting her life to art and a culture of looking and making, ever ready to penetrate beneath the surface. Music touched her so deeply in ways that were "irrational," or just flew over reason and made a beeline straight for the soul. This suggests music had a prophetic character, for were not the first prophets called *nabis* in Hebrew, meaning that they "overflowed"? The early Hebrew prophets used to travel in groups, singing and dancing, overflowing with spirit of God; the devotees of Greek god Dionysios, and of the Hindu Shiva, did likewise.

Singing and dancing: Art.

I asked Vanilla if she was conscious of people in the scene having awareness of seeking for spiritual knowledge. She replied that she and others had an ear for "the search for something spiritual *that wasn't bloody biblical*" (my italics). "Biblical" was what came from home and school, teachers and vicars and nuns; whereas everyone she knew was conscious of having wanted desperately to *get out* of narrow confines, to make your own world, and to make it better. "There must be some kind of way outta here . . ." sang Bob Dylan in "All Along the Watchtower," echoing a common feeling in the frustrated young. No one in the scene doubted the energy of the young really could make a better job of things than their parents or grandparents, whose lives had been permeated by war and politics of domination. Everything seemed to be going in a forward, "progressive" (and permissive) direction. As for God, Vanilla said that people "knew there was *something*." There was a tendency to avoid words like *God* that too easily suggested some ossified, bearded, old, authoritarian, moralistic, and heavy idea of religion: an image of judgment and guilt, a set of self-crushing dogmas, not a mystery or liberating conception. Religion felt like something already *done,* set in stone, not something *yet to be.* What was new in it? Religion was *not* cool, or else, it was felt to be too damn cold: its official representatives could sound so conceited, boring, hesitant, condescending. Was there nothing left that was *exciting* in religion? Where was the magic, the mystery? Things *Indian* looked a lot warmer. Besides, the Hindu traditions and imagery that seemed to be wafting around the whole scene like incense smoke, had a definitely positive, if still obscure, feeling about them. They were pacific and open to sex, for a start, and that was crucial to young people with love on their minds, and tingling elsewhere. In Indian iconography there were goddesses, with breasts, and gods that danced! Sex was identified with the creative instinct, with life, with God: a conception of sex so different from commercialized women in advertising and bad movies and TV, cosmeticized and material-packaged for marriage: plastic. "All romances end in marriage," opined a cynical Sergeant Troy in *Far from the Madding Crowd,* made into outstanding cinema in 1967 by John Schlesinger and Nicholas Roeg, starring "beautiful person" Terence Stamp as Troy, and über-modern free-girl Julie Christie as Bathsheba Everdene, free-spirited antiheroine of Thomas Hardy's novel of fate and love; the latter two doyens of Swinging London supposed immortalized as "Terry and Julie" in The Kinks' magical hit, "Waterloo Sunset," released in May 1967.*

In the art and music scenes (still financially below the movie business

---

*Strange how Moise and Libby leave Waterloo Station arm in arm at the climax of *When the Party's Over;* do they metamorphose into 1967's "Terry meets Julie, Waterloo Station, Every Friday night" in the Kinks' "Waterloo Sunset"? A whimsical cross-reference, nothing more.

in status and outreach), there was an awareness of being up against the money people, the greedy, selfish types with the Big Voice who seemed to have the politicians in their pockets, spinning them lies to bewitch "straight" society, cajoling people into wars and killing. Spirituality was like . . . anything that wasn't like *that*. And there was some awareness that there *was* something to reach for, something out there, or rather, in *here*. Somewhere. Something. That elusiveness opened the mind to the thought of hidden traditions, the occult and many things magical, esoteric, the zodiac . . . space. It was like there was something hovering behind the opacity of the modern.

I asked Vanilla about what she and others were reading. "Oh!" she remembered, "*The Razor's Edge*. Somerset Maugham. That was a big one." Maugham's 1944 novel tells of an American pilot who has undergone traumatic experiences in World War I, and whose values begin to change accordingly after the war. In his search for something transcendent, he realizes how materialistic his ordinary society now looks, and how at a remove from its denizens he has become. The pilot has significant spiritual experiences in India and embraces the Advaita philosophy, realizing God in himself, and looking not to the company of this world but to better company in heaven. The book's closing message is stark: "The sharp edge of a razor is difficult to pass over; thus the wise say the path to 'enlightenment' is hard." Writer Herman Hesse suggested a similar path, ahead of the Fifties beat poets. Hesse also looked to India for spiritual authenticity. His *Siddhartha* (1951, US)—largely about the meaning of Buddhism—was widely read, its precepts admired. Aldous Huxley's *The Doors of Perception* (1954) was also of interest, for Huxley had drawn a link in a scientific and philosophical manner between spiritual experience and his own experimental ingestion of mescaline, a conviction Huxley would take to his deathbed when he chose to die in the psychospiritual embrace of LSD. Huxley's book title was of course from William Blake, who had a growing band of appreciators in the Sixties drawn to his soul-expanding philosophy and his seemingly having through intuition reached high states of consciousness imitated in psychedelic experience and spoken of as the preserve of spiritual initiates. Furthermore, Blake was appreciative of the spiritual value of human sexuality as a gateway to spiritual experience of real being. L.A. group the Doors, whose first stunning album was recorded in August '66 and released in January 1967, would take their name from Blake's "doors of perception," which, "if cleans'd" would enable man to see "all things as they are: infinite." We may appreciate that this positive note is evident on the first track of the Doors' album: "Break on Through (to the Other Side)," while the last track was considerably more fatal, even opposite in import: "The End" constituted an Oedipal apocalypse of sore old scores settled by the young man against his parents. Lead singer, poet Jim Morrison (1943–1971), seized on the vapor rising from the foam of the new psychedelic ocean wave to give voice to an ominously dark side of the still new moon of youthful aspiration.

We may note how in earlier chapters on the Bible and theology in the Sixties, the subject of sex was conspicuously absent from the concerns of authority, except, that is, where it was frowned upon when taking place outside marriage, or indeed, outside, anywhere. This simple factor, which betokens an empire of alternative thought, may explain sufficiently why many sensitive young people turned elsewhere for spiritual understanding. It's not that they didn't want the essential substance of religion (which otherwise appeared fun denying), or were not

Fig. 14.2. Jim Morrison, circa 1969.

interested in spiritual meaning, but music and art were sexy, alive, in the way that an original mind can be sexy and alive. And in the other way too.

So I asked Vanilla for a top-of-the-head answer to what she thought was the spiritual meaning of the Sixties. She replied: "Oh, freedom to think what you like," then paused, as if she'd missed something: "But it is difficult, dangerous, and frightening . . . highly scary!" Was she thinking of "The Void," leapt into by spiritual artist Yves Klein? We shall see.

FIFTEEN

The Spiritual in Art in the Sixties

The Age of Space

A god defined is a finite god.
STANISLAS DE GUAITA (1861–1897)

In terms of consciously working with the spiritual in art in the Sixties, it is arguable that the party was long over, with few concerned to gather the morsels left from the masters' table of a feast last prepared in Paris in the late 1880s, and which had served spiritual fare through the medium of paint with declining publicity from World War I to the Fifties. As Donald Kuspit wrote in his essay "Concerning the Spiritual in Contemporary Art": "The 'spiritual' is a problem concept in contemporary art."[1] Kuspit cites Wassily Kandinsky's vital work *Concerning the Spiritual in Art* (1912) to illustrate how the understanding of abstraction in art had changed almost fundamentally between pioneer abstractionist Kandinsky's time and the changes in postwar art. To be brief, abstract art has in the main become imbued with a basically materialist outlook, eager to present self-contained objects before the onlooker's view. For Kandinsky in 1912, on the other hand, "abstract" art was regarded as necessary precisely *to give expression to spiritual experiences* and thought forms, without impediment of representational, organic forms. Abstraction followed a symbolist ethic of seeking into the essential *idea* of a thing, locating its symbol and giving it form. Abstraction aimed at purifying or refining the form of the secreted *idea*, that is, *what had been abstracted* from the primal idea. The theory was basically Platonist, and had been promulgated with ideal, symbolic representation in mind by art critic and enlightened occultist and aesthete Joséphin Péladan (1858–1918) who pioneered the Rose+Croix Salons and accompanying critical apparatus in Paris during the 1890s (see my book, *Occult Paris*).

Kandinsky had no doubt in his mind that to search for "the abstract in art" in essence constituted a spiritual act in quest of the spiritual.[2] The very *point* of abstraction was to oppose "the nightmare of materialism."[3] Art found its meaning in its relationship with and within the spiritual dimension of experience, that is, the ultimate in experience. Art, wrote Kandinsky, was "one of the mightiest elements" in spiritual life. Expressed in art, this spiritual life could be seen in "a complicated but easily definable movement forward and upward."[4]

Kandinsky's progressive marriage of art and spiritual meaning was no longer generally obvious to the world of art at the dawn of the 1960s, overshadowed as it was by a mingled thought cloud of existentialism and logical positivism. The ground in progressive art had shifted both

Fig. 15.1. Wassily Kandinsky (1866–1944).

stylistically and substantially toward an almost solipsistic subjectivism, a denial of spiritual objectivity, into realms of humanistic psychology and materialism, involving a general indifference to the idea of *correspondence* between levels of being. Correspondence is fundamental to the Hermetic philosophy embraced by spiritual artists at the turn of the twentieth century. The zeitgeist of 1960 *seemed* all against the spiritual in art. Abstract expressionism, in particular, had many followers: the unmitigated splash of the mind's passions and consciousness onto canvas, only bridled by the relish of abstract pattern, the electric brain pulsating via brush to plug into the observer.

It is interesting to see that by the 1960s, a superficial modernism demanded pictures be viewed in very well lit galleries of whiteout neatness in modernist aesthetics, whereas Kandinsky had noted that the idea of the spiritual in art had become most obvious to him when viewing a painting on an easel in crepuscular conditions of indeterminate luminosity, amid shadows and vague furnishings. *Atmosphere* is generally to be sucked from the modern exhibition space as one would filter out a nasty smell. The *poitrine* of art must be well fanned, lest vulgar nature denude the purity of naked air.

We should not be surprised then that a cursory investigation of art in the Sixties might suggest that a lack of spiritual content in art could add to the view that the Sixties as a novel entity was, in this respect at least, devoid of spiritual meaning. However, spiritual things are spiritually discerned, and the penetrating worm of spirit likes to seek deep inside the material to locate the divine signature.

The following list of artists at work in the Sixties who evoked spiritual meanings through their practice of art and whose art at times expresses the spiritual in art, while by no means exhaustive, should serve to arrest those who thought Sixties art was spiritually indifferent or characterized chiefly by ultraminimalist material abstractions, liberating whimsy, or psychedelic swirling of multicolored geometric or organic patterns joined to multidimensional *trompe l'oeil,* exhibiting or suggesting altered states of consciousness. It also suggests there was more to art in the decade than the much-vaunted, in-your-face Pop Art, soft cushionlike sculptures, or Takis's (Panayiotis Vasilakis's) angular creations with random electric light features, that John Lennon inspected at the Indica shortly after encountering the spiritual discourse of Yoko Ono for the first time at 6 Masons Yard, St James's, London, on November 7, 1966.

Here is the list, alphabetically arranged:

Jean (Hans) Arp (1886–1966)	Adolph Gottlieb (1903–1974)	Bruce Nauman (b. 1941)
Michael Ayrton (1921–1975)	Hans Hartung (1904–1989)	Ben Nicholson (1894–1982)
Joseph Beuys (1921–1986)	Wally Hedrick (1928–2003)	Yoko Ono (b. 1933)
Jess Collins (1923–2004)	Robert Irwin (b. 1928)	Mark Rothko (1903–1970)
Marcel Duchamp (1887–1968)	Alfred Jensen (1903–1981)	Harry Smith (1921–1993)
Helen Frankenthaler (1928–2011)	R. B. Kitaj (1932–2007)	Andy Warhol (1928–1987)
Elizabeth Frink (1930–1993)	Yves Klein (1928–1962)	Norman Zammitt (1931–2007)

One must resist any temptation to label any one of these artists as being spiritual artists or of imposing meanings and interpretations upon works that, to the artist, may have embodied thoughts and priorities quite different to those discernible to observers (including this one), but I think we can recognize spiritual aspects of their lives and works that individually, and as an aggregate, help us to understand some little-grasped aspects of the spiritual meaning of the 1960s.

THE ARTISTS

Jean (Hans) Arp (1886–1966) spanned the period from the Belgian, Dutch, and French symbolists all the way to the pioneer conceptual artists of the Sixties. Having by 1900 read the German mystic Jacob Böhme (1575–1624), Arp became a Theosophist. He met Kandinsky in 1912, coming under the influence of Kandinsky's *Concerning the Spiritual in Art*. While World War I raged, Arp immersed himself

Fig. 15.2. Jean Arp's 391, No. 8, Zurich, Switzerland, 1919.

in the thought of medieval German mystics. At the war's end he was producing "Duo-Collages" with Sophie Taeuber, the aim of which was to approach "superior, spiritual reality." In the 1920s Arp shared his interest in Hermetic traditions and alchemy with the surrealists. Such inspired mind games would form a substructure for the daring of Marcel Duchamp. The mind projects into and through the *massa confusa* of matter to volatilize the seed of higher, pure substance: transforming mind. In the Thirties, Arp turned his attention to those pre-Socratic philosophers whose thought had much in common with Hindu Advaita philosophy, locating divinity in nature, where the soul in man is identified with the spirit of God. In the Fifties and Sixties, Japanese admirers introduced Arp to Zen; Arp became a devout Catholic.

Arp completed his *Vers le blanc infini* ("Toward the white infinite") in 1960, a folio of graphics and poems dedicated to his late wife Sophie Taeuber-Arp who had died in 1943. The folio evinces the living presence of Böhme's gnostic Sophia speculation. The divine Sophia (Wisdom) is the mirror of divinity; she emanates the creative vibration. Sophia is also Sophie, now in eternity. Divinity plays upon itself in joy, ecstatic in its reflection, as expressed in Arp's *Jours effeuillés* ("Petal-stripped days," 526):

> But the last time I saw you
> You were a white wave,
> Poised to return forever
> Into the whiteness.

The whiteness is infinitude, space, spirit, purity. It would be a key "color" of the minimalist expressive. It is also death in the sense of absorption or transformation, and what lies beyond without form.

Marcel Duchamp (1887–1968) was by the Sixties something of a grand old man of Art, having pushed Dada into public notoriety decades earlier with his attack on the conventions and expectations not only of what constituted an artwork, but what art actually was. Many will recall his infamous "Fountain" from 1917: simply a public urinal bowl with his name on it, placed on exhibition as if to say: "*There*! That's Art, you fools!" Humor was vital, for humor was, as Duchamp once described it, a kind of dynamite of the spirit, like a match that once struck, caused an effect. Duchamp objected to restraining ideas, one of which was the gallery exhibition itself. One should not have to go into a gallery to see art. Art could and should be seen anywhere because it was the human imagination that gave art its meaning.

Man is creative in essence, unless suppressed. Blake had written in an earlier revolutionary period that imagination was the "divine existence itself," and that is the key to understanding how the art of pure imagination is a divine art. Blake even referred seriously to "Jesus the Imagination," for as Jesus may be seen as the link or path between the human and the heavenly, imagination was the road to the spiritual reality of things; imagination is the creative mind evinced in Genesis. *Fiat lux*: "Let there be light." To quote Blake again: "Poetry, painting, and music, the three powers for conversing with Paradise that the Flood did not sweep away." The "Flood" refers symbolically to the flood of time and space, the limiting conceptions, the bounded and measurable universe, squared by Reason. Spiritual mind is inseparable from imagination. The world of the imagination is unlimited and boundless.

Duchamp, without employing the language of spiritual thinking, thought therefore there was simply too much attention given to art, especially in the forms it was expected to "come" in, and the absurd "values" placed on much of it, which reflected no truthful or immediate and internal conception of value. He hoped to devalue the pretensions of the art business and its greedy materialism by rendering the exhibited art object as meaningless or valueless in itself. Of course, such is the power of money, that his "valueless" works sell for lots of money, and people still go po-faced into galleries full of absurdist works in search of artistic meaning.

The spirit that drives the artist is the essential factor in the Duchamp aesthetic.

Duchamp championed the idea of the "idea." To show the elephant's tail is sufficient for the observer to imagine—or to create in his or her mind—the elephant. The viewer, normally considered passive in the presence of art, becomes active in creating both its form and meaning. The artist's job then is to stimulate the "artist" in everyone. The work is completed by the state of mind of the one engaging with the creative process. Thus a work is not finished until completed satisfactorily in the imagination of the one engaging in it. This was all very much in tune *at root* with the idealist critical theories of Hermetic occultist Joséphin Péladan outlined in the 1890s, and too often ignored, though Kandinsky, among other twentieth-century artists, including Dalì, accepted Péladan's influence. With hindsight, Péladan's critical limitation was that he had the theory of the pure idea, but took it as a given that the abstracted symbol should find ideal form as the artist attained to perfection of that form. He was still thinking, like everybody else, in terms of art as representation, imitative of a nature idealized, but he opened a door, as he'd hoped to do.

By the Sixties, anything as conventional as "representation" was, in the avant-garde at least, regarded as dull, even bourgeois. Abstraction and Dada had liberated the artist from representational verisimilitude, and from nature. Surrealism had entered the subconscious. The next stage on this journey was bound, logically, to be what soon became known as "conceptual art." In the Sixties, pioneer conceptual artists operated in association with Lithuanian-American artist George Maciunas's "Fluxus" collective, founded by him in 1961, and operating to this day chiefly in New York, Germany, and Japan. The collective title "Fluxus" is suggestive of pre-Socratic philosopher Heraclitus's famous adage that "All is flux" or "Everything is strife." The universe of Heraclitus is one of dynamic instability, one step from Chaos, with no absolutely fixed forms, and this conception seems central to Fluxus artists who embarked on new liberties of the creative imagination, *given to* the one engaging with the artistic stimulus. Audience involvement was critical in the quest for meaning. The gallery was the mind.

Apart from composer John Cage who famously invited audiences to listen to silence, the most well-known Fluxus artist is undoubtedly Yoko Ono (b. 1933), who was clearly very inspired by Marcel Duchamp, as well as by the aesthetics of Zen beloved of Jan Arp and Robert Irwin. Yoko's first London exhibition, following many innovative "loft" performances in New York, was held at the Indica in London and subtitled "Unfinished Paintings," where even the word *paintings* was somewhat ambiguous, as the majority of displayed ideas were products not of paint but of plastic construction. One object of art was simply an apple, on sale for £200—very much in Duchamp's humor! You could even see the work as dynamic (as well as fundamentally, temptingly symbolic): stare long enough and it was sure, like all organic matter, to decompose before your eyes. Apples are traditionally tempting. Was it worth the money? Is anything? The works were concepts, or rather were intended to suggest concepts in the minds of visitors. The concept is like a seed. It contains in itself, in its secret structure, its entire growth and development span. Thus we see the conceptual nature of the planted acorns of John and Yoko referred to earlier (see page 209). Show the seed, inspire the wealth of the concept: this was the modus operandi. Some of Yoko's "instructional works" (as evinced in her book *Grapefruit*) involve digging and planting seeds: "Imagine the clouds dripping, dig a hole in your garden to put them in." The sky as a symbol is central to her work, as is wind. Both of these nonformal, nonspatial images suggest infinity and pure being beyond form. In this sense, they are spiritual, alchemical ideas, for they distinguish between the gross and the refined, the material world from the spiritual world. Clouds are frequent actors on the Ono stage; they are form in permanent flux, moved by invisible air. In Greek, "air" is "spirit," and so wind is spiritual movement, the more refined, the more it permeates and changes form. This is an alchemical conception. The Greek feminine *aura* (or breath of air, wind, or soft wind) is in neuter form *to auron,* which means "gold." We see art in quest of the absolute concept: the philosophers' stone. These simple concepts: seed, wind, cloud, sky, lend themselves to a vocabulary of Zen, aimed at higher awareness and inner transformation.

When John Lennon was in Rishikesh, India, meditating under Maharishi Mahesh Yogi's mantra-yoga instruction in January 1968, Yoko sent him a card saying "I am a cloud. Watch for me in the sky." A cloud could be blown from England to India, was free of constraints but the will of the wind. In gnostic symbology, the cloud is the body, obscuring the essence, the spirit. In the Acts of the Apostles (1:9), it is only after cloud has removed Jesus from the apostles' sight that they finally realize the meaning of the words "I am with you everywhere." It is the corporeality that prevents the vision of the light, of eternal presence. One of Yoko's musical compositions (on *Fly,* released in 1971) is called "Body Is the Scar of Your Mind."

The interest in infinity and its spiritual counterpart, eternity, is everywhere present in Yoko's gentle mind-opening and mind-teasing, airy, koan-like works. Her *Eternal Timeclock* is a clock with hour and minute hands removed, hermetically sealed in a transparent, perspex box, whose beat may be heard, like a heart, only with a stethoscope indicating the hidden beat of life. Time is flux; there is no fixed time. Who fixes time? The employer, the government, the oppressor: the one who binds. Yoko's art aims at freedom. Time and space are suggestively abolished. Likewise, Yoko's chess set of all-white pieces and all-white squares speaks much of transcending conflict, differences, prejudices, and even "the rules of the game." Playing this game would exhaust the memory very quickly, wondering which pieces were whose; imaginative players might therefore have to invent their own "new game." The concept is there to be played with. The new game waits to be played; it is a promise: seeds cast in the wind.

One of her most striking Sixties works is the famous *Ceiling Painting* that so caught John Lennon's imagination in 1966. Participants are invited to the presence of a stepladder (itself symbolic of pure ascent) to see something written on canvas that requires a magnifying glass (perception) to be taken in hand. The viewer examines the single inscription on the canvas, to find the word *Yes*. It is as though the canvas knew that its onlooker had a question in his or her mind as he or she ascended, and the canvas-oracle on high knows the answer—and of course, the answer is suitably fulfilling. The "yes" is eternal, amid the chaos of life, the conditions and restraints, and also cheeky, a come-on, a joke. The act of art is an act of faith and knowledge at once, and laughter is an orgasm of the spirit.

These ideas by no means exhaust the dimensions of Yoko's conceptual and spiritual art, much of which has subjective resonance in relation to her personal position as a Japanese woman in a male-dominated, Western-dominated art world. Yoko's central contention revolves around the imperative to imagine, and to reimagine the world we live in. The artist is instructor, bridge builder, a kind of priest or priestess of the real and the actualizable, as Péladan had prophesied back in the 1890s. One should become in oneself a work of art, for that is what one is, and knowing what one is, should make the world ever more consistent with the heights of purified imagination. Being is Seeing. *Mundus imago dei.*

One of John and Yoko's last artworks of the decade was a film titled *Apotheosis,* in which Nic Knowland's camera was attached to a hot-air balloon basket to capture pure ascent through clouds to clear air. *Apotheosis* means both "climax" and the elevation of someone or something to divine status. The alternative is the alternative to white.

White is also symbolic of spiritual absolutes in the work of abstract artist Ben Nicholson (1894–1982), who stayed true to the original call of abstract art. His work is intense; the product of states of sustained attention, which for him seems to have been a religious force of creativity. Nicholson wrote in 1937 that "Painting and religious experience are the same thing, and what we are all searching for is the understanding and realization of infinity—an idea which is complete, with no beginning, no end, and therefore giving to all things for all time. . . . Painting and carving is one means of searching after this reality."[5]

In 1964, 200,000 people visited the Documenta III contemporary art exhibition under Arnold Bode's artistic direction, held at the Museum Fridericianum, the Orangerie, the Old Gallery, and the State Art School at Kassel, in the Federal Republic of Germany. Works by 353 artists were displayed. The roll call included Hans Arp, Robert Rauschenberg, Paul Klee, Yves Klein, Francis Bacon, Paul Cézanne, Georges Braque, Jasper Johns, Kandinsky, Emil Nolde, and Jean Tingueley. Ben Nicholson contributed a large, concrete wall relief to the exhibition. Despite the forbidding material, Nicholson's three-sectioned wall of some 12 feet in height emitted an aura of meditative calm from the simplest elements: to the left, a dark section apparently in golden section to the next, larger section, which featured a large inset circle, and a third plain, clear section, again possibly in golden-section proportion to the midsection, to the right providing resolution. Many similar concretions have graced and disgraced the walls of modern underpasses built in the decade following, but rarely matching Nicholson's for tranquility on the monumental scale.

Mark Rothko (1903–1970) was an artist familiar with the demands of the monumental. In the year Nicholson exhibited his mural in Kassel, John and Dominique de Menil commissioned Rothko to create the meditative space of their proposed nondenominational Rothko Chapel

Fig. 15.3. Dominique de Menil (1908–1997).

in Houston, Texas, to be filled with his paintings. Dominique de Menil (1908–1997) is of critical significance on account of her involvement in promoting the role of spiritual art in the United States. John and Dominique's daughter Philippa was cofounder of the important Dia Art Foundation in New York, out of which emerged the Sufi congregation of Lower Manhattan, of which we shall hear more in due course.

Jean de Menil (Anglicized to John), with money earned from financial services to the U.S. oil industry, was encouraged to invest in modern art. John and Dominique's Catholicism being imbued with Universalist ecumenism, they developed particular interest in that modern art concerned with spirituality. An early modernist collection was supplemented by openness to new, postwar movements; they were keen to patronize works by Max Ernst, Andy Warhol, Mark Rothko, René Magritte, Robert Rauschenberg, Jasper Johns, and Dorothea Tanning, among other modern artists. They were also aware, as were many of the artists they patronized, of the links between classical art, and the art of indigenous cultures, and combined all of this with active support for civil rights in Houston.

Completed in 1971, the Rothko Chapel is, uniquely, a chapel for all faiths and none in particular. Its central space was made a work of art by the presence of Rothko's fourteen black paintings, executed between 1965 and 1967. Each painting is a varied hue of black, of differing textures whose appearance varies with the light at a moment of the day, altogether denoting universality and distinctiveness that is central to the ecumenical vision of faith as a transhuman experience in variant forms. It might be objected that black stands in contradistinction to the "light," associated with white. However, it may be seen that black absorbs light from all sources, suggesting ecumenism. Furthermore, black also suggests depth, while in the language of mysticism, it is oft spoken of the "solitary darkness of God," and, indeed, when the book of Kings describes the removal of the staves that held the Ark in the Holy of Holies of Solomon's Temple, the space is filled with cloud so dense the priests were unable to see, and Solomon explains: "The Lord said he would dwell in the thick darkness. I have surely built thee an house to dwell in, a settled place for thee to abide in forever and ever"

Fig. 15.4. Mark Rothko (1903–1970).

(1 Kings 8:12–13). The Rothko space is intended for prayer and meditation. Outside, Barnett Newman's sculpture, *Broken Obelisk,* dedicated to Martin Luther King, reminds us of what happens when we fail to see the common humanity, and the divine within.

As a boy, Mark Rothko was familiar from Hebrew School with the Talmud and Jewish scripture. After 1913, while living in Portland, Oregon, he went outside his cultural formation to take in the art of Native Americans of America's northwest coast. Around 1936, Rothko met fellow Jewish artist Barnett Newman (1905–1970), pioneer in color-field abstraction, who once said pointedly: "What is the explanation of the seemingly insane drive of man to be painter and poet if it is not an act of defiance against man's fall and an assertion that he return to the Garden of Eden? For the artists are the first men."[6] Newman's work encouraged Rothko's interest in communicating without form, but through pure feeling, abstracted as uninterrupted color fields, juxtaposed with other fields. Rothko met Adolph Gottlieb (1903–1974) in about 1929. Living in Arizona 1937–38, Gottlieb opened himself up to Native "Indian" art and became sharply aware of the spiritual meaning that subsisted beneath or within traditional, formal arrangements of opaque color. Gottlieb's *Deep over Pale* painting of 1964, for example, suggests both primordial creation and cosmic cataclysm.

The power of myth and the capacity to express its symbolism abstractly dominated Rothko's thought in the early 1940s when he allowed Greek and Roman myths to impact upon his evolving aesthetic. Around this time, he and Gottlieb put their names to a letter to the *New York Times,* stating that "We assert that the subject [of abstract painting] is crucial and only that subject matter is valid which is tragic and timeless. That is why we profess spiritual kinship with primitives and archaic art." Gottlieb and Rothko also made plain in a radio broadcast how they were inspired by alienist Carl Jung's spiritual understanding of archetypes, or universal unconscious symbolism, as well as Jung's psychological insight into taking archaic forms and myths seriously. The psychological determinants transcended the historical passages of time and were imprinted on the soul, and could thus be abstracted into art. In 1945, Rothko described his art as an "anecdote of the spirit."[7]

Alfred Jensen (1903–1981) was another artist still active in the Sixties whose work had drawn on ancient cultures and their mythology. In 1960 Jensen read J. Eric S. Thompson's *Maya Hieroglyphic Writing* (1954) dealing with the pictograms sculpted by the Maya civilization of pre-Columbian South America. It was clear that the scripts reflected an intimate experience of the "gods" or formational principles of life, though Jensen was as much interested in Mayan calendrical forms as formal inspiration for painting structure. In the Sixties he moved from abstract expressionism toward the form of the diagram, expressed in works through the Sixties informed by Pythagorean number systems and the mathematical structure of planetary movements. In 1961, he saw the mythic potential of Yuri Gagarin's first manned mission in space and allowed it to inspire a painting series in the same year the Guggenheim offered him a solo exhibition. In 1965 Jensen called each of a series of gouaches, *Hekatompedon* (an ancient Greek temple built on the Athenian Acropolis), the series inspired by rituals practiced in ancient Greece. His works speak of the universal language conveying mind, number, space, time, and meaning, valid today as in the past and for tomorrow. The language representing the science of their day, the diagrammatic form seemed appropriate.

Widely regarded as a German representative of the Fluxus concept with regard to his performance art and imaginative, dislocating installations, Joseph Beuys (1921–1986) came to prominence during his tenure as art lecturer at Düsseldorf's Art Academy in the Sixties, after an already tempestuous life. As a fifteen-year-old Hitler Youth member, he had participated in the Nuremberg rally, and later joined the Luftwaffe. Surviving the crash of his plane while serving on the Crimean front, the occasion served later as an opportunity for self-mythologization. He wove the story that he had been rescued by nomadic Tartars, social outsiders who saved his life by coating his body in fat, then wrapping it in felt. Fat and felt became important experiences for Beuys in his attempt to experience pure thought, united to nature, feelings, intuition, and sensation, without the dominant, materialistic über-rational or coldly analytic intellectual attitude so characteristic of "science" in the Forties, Fifties, and beyond. The instinct to preserve the spiritual freedom of human beings is at the living, warm core of Beuys's art. His interest in free questioning, liberated mind, free spirits, and untrammeled creativity brought him to sympathize with young people being over-molded by educational systems, and thus led him through listening into the world of activist student politics, with commitments to the Green and alternative political youth movements that were such a vibrant part of the new West Germany emerging in the 1980s, out of the freedoms explored in the Sixties. From out of that decade came a desire to harmonize the individual development within a loving society, rather than seeing the individual and society at odds. The social and political problem Germany faced came from the fact that the dominant political thinking in the Sixties was that the Hitler era was the result of pseudo-spiritual ideas, imaginative fantasies, and perverted idealisms of "blood and soil" and race supremacy, unfounded in science. In other words, Germany had been made sick by *irrationality*. The cure then, and the path to ubiquitous *Sicherheit* (or security) was strict rationality, scientific intellectualism, and a social devotion to working a different kind of miracle, a rational economic system based on reason and unexcited labor. This would be hard on a country once known for its intense commitment to art.

Fig. 15.5. Joseph Beuys (1921–1986).
Courtesy of Ronald Feldman Fine Arts.

Beuys had spent much of the Fifties living a hermitlike existence in the Lower Rhineland, with foxes, hares, and other furry creatures for company. At the same time, he was learning from his teachers in art about Rudolf Steiner's anthroposophy movement, a movement with a strong wing in art and science, and their integration into a dynamic, harmonizing spirituality. Though the movement came directly out of Theosophy, its name, meaning the "wisdom of man," and the holistic eclecticism of Steiner's thought, gave the movement a decidedly practical bent, with an accent on *performance.* Steiner emphasized spirit and nature growing together; each responded to the other, and Beuys tried to capture this dynamism in his idiosyncratic art.

In the early 1960s Beuys took part in shamanistic rites to feel the spirit, and the spirit in nature. For his performance *The Chief* in 1963–64, he would remain wrapped in felt for nine hours, with isolation from the material intensifying awareness of the spiritual. In 1960, Beuys created *Bathtub,* using the tub he had been washed in as a child. It was filled with plaster and with fat-soaked gauze, this corresponding to a spiritual experience of transformation from one state to another. For Beuys, fat, whether solid or liquid, represents revival of life, transformation, and change, with nature vitalized and reoriented. In 1965, absolutely against the grain of then-current German rationalism, Beuys performed himself *How to Explain Pictures to a Dead Hare.* Onlookers could view Beuys through a gallery window. Inside, he covered his head with honey and gold and was accompanied by a dead hare. Honey, for Beuys was a living substance. It was also the work of bees, identified by Steiner, following the ancients, as an orderly ideal society. Man is to use his mind to create living substances, new ideas, fresh thoughts. He is not, like the bee, simply to reproduce a system. Gold is the fruit and by-product of spiritual alchemy. These were not dry, abstract propositions, but intended to wrap man up in the reality of nature, with its hidden potential for life, and hope in life force. Man needed to be saved from abstract reason, and he must think and imagine his way out, and create his way out, with fresh paradigms and images, and use what nature has provided, through inner understanding, and genuine encounter with it. This makes Beuys prophetic for our post-Sixties world, grappling with spirit, mind, and the labyrinthine logic of perpetual economics. In 1968, after long battles with academic authorities in Düsseldorf, Beuys would form the German Student Party, a fine performance of making life and art identical. The art is life.

I am grateful to William Breeze for introducing me to the work of Raymond Foye, literary executor for his late friend, poet, and counter-culture Sixties luminary, Allen Ginsberg. Based in New York State, Raymond Foye, author, publisher, editor, and arts curator, has written a superbly stimulating account of the artist, Harry Smith (1921–1993)

Fig. 15.6. Harry Smith (1921–1993). Photo courtesy of James Wasserman.

whose work as painter, filmmaker, folklorist, and occultist attempted a conscious integration of art with the spiritual experience of Native Americans, and with Western Hermetic, alchemical traditions.[8]

Already noted from 1952 for his exhaustive, much valued, and influential aural anthologies of American Folk Music for the Smithsonian Institute, Smith went on to make hand-painted and animated films of abstract art of extraordinary artistry and complexity. Sadly, few of these works have survived (an exception being the mesmerizing *Film No 7*), though sufficient were seen by astonished aficionados to make Smith an inspiration to the U.S. underground film scene of the Fifties and Sixties. Smith was inspired by folk art, medieval and Renaissance magical symbolism (including the magical-musical work of Robert Fludd, 1574–1637), the latter's links to analogous imagery in indigenous cultures familiar to anthropologists, and by trance states induced by what are now commonly called entheogens (to emphasize their spiritual character), or neuroactive stimulants. This work continued through the Sixties and now makes Smith a point of inspiration to contemporary artists.

It is curious that young Mark Rothko had been inspired by Indian art of the Northwest coast when living in Portland, Oregon, in 1913, for ten years later, Portland was the birthplace of Harry Smith. Smith's parents were both Theosophists. Like Rothko, Smith too would come to embrace the songs and ritual survivals of the Lummi and Samish Native Americans, while Theosophy opened Smith's mind to comparative religion and the principle of spiritual universality, located at the esoteric level of all spiritual religions. Smith familiarized himself with Kiowa sign language and Kwakiutl speech. He was able to see the cross-symbolism and persistence of spiritual symbols through the cultural kaleidoscope, leading to a profound, experimental grasp of the integral nature of sound, movement, and image. Inevitably this would inform his sense of the abstract in art. The root of this seems to have come when he devised his own notation for transcribing native dances and music simultaneously. The notation or *diagram* itself (cf. Alfred Jensen) thus formed the base for an abstract art relating to the core *idea* within the performance. What one could see was pure pattern underlying human expression. The pattern comes from a power within: the spirit.

In 1965, Smith told film researcher P. Adam Sitney: "Diagramming the pictures was so interesting that I then started to be interested in music in relation to existence." This practical basis was allied to a childhood and youth among his parents' Masonic accoutrements and the impact of reading Jung on *Man and His Symbols,* and Kandinsky's *Concerning the Spiritual in Art.* The whole field of aural dynamics in relation to color and movement and rhythm and sound and harmony was stimulated in a manner akin to Blake's trinity of "poetry, painting, and music," man's powers for conversing with the infinite, a state of paradise, that is, a garden. We again see the integral nature of the spirit and nature in mutual relation that finds its analog in the dawning earth awareness of the Sixties.

Working in New York during the early Fifties amid the tonal experimentation of Charlie Parker and bebop jazz, which so captivated Smith, he was a welcome visitor to Samuel Weiser's Manhattan-based occult bookshop thanks to Smith's extensive knowledge of Hermeticism, and an enthusiasm for the works of Aleister Crowley, who had died in 1947, but whose ashes still lay in Hampton, New Jersey. Smith's occult interest was recognized by Crowley's Ordo Templi Orientis when its "Gnostic Church" wing made Harry Smith a bishop of that church. Smith's approach to speaking in public about occultism was, in the words of Raymond Foye, a case of "sage denial," eager to dispel any sense of obfuscation in mystical pursuits: "The thing you must understand is that these are not real laws, they're imaginary laws," he once told Foye, pointing to a book on necromancy.[9]

In 1961, Smith ceased work on what Foye describes as "one of the true masterpieces of independent film."[10] Begun in 1959, *Number 12 (Heaven and Earth Magic Feature)* was Smith's remarkable black-and-white animation that was doubly animated insofar as Smith actually added color using filters and slide projection actually *during* projection!—a truly marvelous touch of the magician at work, no longer sorcerer's apprentice but source sorcerer. It is a symbol enfilmopaedia of dazzling devotion, the filmic equivalent of a seventeenth-century alchemical emblem book dancing into life and—when projected—spontaneous color. Max Ernst's collages were a big influence on Smith's unique approach.

According to Raymond Foye, it was Smith's chance meeting with thoroughly ubiquitous Sixties presence Allen Ginsberg that led to Smith's emergence in the Sixties to recognition as an artist in his own right. Unfortunately, the decade would prove a health hazard for Smith. Foye's essay on Smith contains Ginsberg's version of the encounter:

When I was in San Francisco, I heard from a filmmaker, Jordan Belson, about a fabulous magician painter-filmmaker, Harry Smith, who had been a student or descendant of Aleister Crowley, and had Crowley manuscripts. In 1960 I saw this old guy at the Five Spot in New York with black-and-white beard making little marks, listening to Thelonius Monk, and sort of notating something. From Belson's description and from the concentration of his activity and his locale, I decided maybe that's Harry Smith, so I went up and introduced myself. He said, yes, that was his name. I said, "Well, what are you doing there?" He said, "I'm trying to determine where Monk comes in on the beat—before or after, what are the recurrent syncopations, what is the pattern, the mathematical pattern of syncopations in his solos, and how they vary." I said, "Why are you doing that?" he said, "Well, I'm keeping track of his time, because I'm using his music as background to films that I'm making, hand painting frame-by-frame, and collage drawing."

So one thing led to another and we listened to Monk night after night. Then Harry invited me up to his studio. He had a crowded little apartment and the walls were covered with his paintings, which were these amazing cosmic monsters. He'd get me very high on grass, then turn on his little projector and show me these movies, which he had hand painted, frame by frame, some abstract and then moving on into animated collage, then moving on to Tibetan imagery, and finally the *Heaven and Earth* movie, which was an hour and a half at the time. What he had done was set a lot of them, certain ones of them, short ones, to *Misterioso* [an album by Thelonius Monk]. I saw that his point was that the actual frames moved in relation to the music—he had been calculating the frames to the Monk music. It turns out he was a musicologist. He showed me this set of six records, *The Anthology of American Folk Music,* a three-box set he put out way back in 1952, which was on Folkways. He did ethnomusicology studies here in America. So this is now eight years later, and he had gotten into making these films and had already passed through the mixed-media projections.

One day he offered to sell me a rather dark version of the rather long *Heaven and Earth* movie for one hundred dollars. Every time we'd go up there he'd get me high, then he'd ask me for money, because he was starving. Apparently he'd do that with everybody. I got to be scared of going up there because he'd get me tremblingly high on grass and show me these amazing movies. I'd be totally awed and intimidated by the universality of his genius in music and painting.[11]

Being without a projector, Ginsberg took the movie to show Fluxus luminary, Jonas Mekas (b. 1922). Blown away, Mekas asked Ginsberg: "Who is this Harry Smith? He's an absolute genius." Through Jonas Mekas, Smith linked up with the Film-Makers' Co-op and Anthology Film Archives, and, according to Ginsberg, "became with Brakhage and Robert Frank and Warhol, one of the founding fathers of underground film and an influence on subsequent MTV."[12] Ginsberg forgot to mention Kenneth Anger (b. 1927) who would bring his truly amazing Aleister Crowley–inspired films to London in the Sixties and secure the cooperation in making new films of Marianne Faithfull, Donald Cammell, Mick Jagger, and Jimmy Page.*

In 1964, while Smith was away recording a peyote ritual of the Kiowa Indians for posterity, he was evicted in absentia by his landlord for nonpayment of rent. In the process, the landlord got rid of almost all of Smith's oeuvre. Returning to New York, Smith could only locate works that had been already passed into other hands. He started

---

*Anger's most Crowleyan picture was the astonishing *Inauguration of the Pleasure Dome* (1954), which featured Anaïs Nin and Thelemic artist Marjorie Cameron in a dreamlike phantasmagoria assault, and coaxing, of the senses that links straight to the subconscious. Anger's Sixties films included *Scorpio Rising* (1964), *Kustom Kar Kommandos* (1965), and *Invocation of My Demon Brother* (1969): all essential viewing for those in search of the occult spirit of the decade.

drinking and suffered a nervous breakdown. Recovery came slowly with a move to the famous Chelsea Hotel where friend Shirley Clark had a penthouse flat. Staff were kind and in due course Smith's room 731 would be known to Virgil Tompson, Gregory Corso, Arthur Miller, Leonard Cohen, Arthur C. Clarke, William Burroughs, Patti Smith, and Robert Mapplethorpe. Visiting bands from San Francisco such as Jefferson Airplane and the Grateful Dead would give concerts on the hotel roof. In his wild gray beard, Smith became a Chelsea legend.

In the 1960s, jazz would give way to the Beatles for musical accompaniment, and in the late Sixties, Smith worked on film *Number 16,* also known as *Oz: The Tin Woodsman's Dream* (1967), based on L. Frank Baum's famous children's book. It would have been interesting if the Beatles had asked Smith to make their analogous experimental film fantasy *Magical Mystery Tour* (1967), though one doubts whether mainstream criticism could have coped with such a work any better than they did with the Beatles' own. There are only fourteen minutes left of Smith's fantasy, about which he informed film historian P. Adam Sitney: "What I was really trying to do was to convert Oz into a Buddhistic image like a mandala. I can't even remember what those lands were. One of them was 'Heironymus Bosch Land.' All of Bosch's paintings were carefully dissected. Another one was 'Microscopia,' taken from the books of [Ernst] Haeckel, who was the Viennese biological artist and very wonderful. The things he made are just marvelous. He picked out every possible grotesque object there was."[13]

Smith had a lifelong interest in the children's works of Lewis Carroll, the Oxford don with an interest in higher mathematics as the logic of the mystical, and a strong interest in children's stories, a keynote, I think, of his aesthetic. Children's first plays with paint are as abstract as their games. *Unless ye be as these little children, ye cannot enter the kingdom of heaven. . . .*

THE REAL ICON

Sadly perhaps, Smith did not appear in Andy Warhol and Paul Morrissey's 1966 film, *Chelsea Girls,* starring, or anti-starring, Nico and International

Fig. 15.7. The Chelsea Hotel of New York.

Velvet, shot inside the Chelsea Hotel, even though only one of the performers actually lived there. As I recall the movie from a rare screening at the Oxford Film Society back in '78, it had some stimulating split screen work, some stoned sexual dalliances gay and straight, occasional histrionics, and some casual heroin injecting. Andy Warhol (1928–1987) is not a figure one automatically associates with the spiritual in art in the Sixties, but since his untimely death in 1987, Warhol's spiritual beliefs, and the importance to him personally of his religious upbringing have become a little more widely appreciated.

Raised in Pittsburgh, the Warhol family (originally ethnic Lemkos from what is now northeast Slovakia) attended the Saint John Chrysostom Byzantine (or Ruthenian) Church, an experience whose icons, liturgical music, ritual, and vestments left a lifelong impact. Though using the Byzantine Rite of the Eastern Orthodox Church, the Ruthenian Church was fully recognized by the Roman Catholic Church. Warhol attended Mass regularly at the Catholic Saint Vincent Farrer

Fig. 15.8.
Andy Warhol (1928–1987).
Photo by Jack Mitchell.

church in Manhattan, sitting at the back, and volunteered at New York's homeless shelters during the busiest times. I rather think that perhaps *only* a person who had built his inner life on spiritual foundations could have withstood the many outlandish tremors of his "Factory" life in the Sixties and Seventies without going crazy. Andy Warhol had an understanding of sympathy born of spiritual universality, promoting openness to new experience and tolerance of others one might expect to find in a child born on August 6 under the Jovian blessing of a sun in Leo with Leo ascendant.

Warhol's silkscreen diptych *Marilyn* is probably Warhol's most, forgive me, "iconic" work, and was first rolled off the process in August 1962, just after Marilyn died in suspicious circumstances a day before Warhol's thirty-fourth birthday. This might give us a clue to what we ought to mean when we use that very much abused and distorted adjective *iconic.*

Warhol's church experience was one of the richness of Eastern orthodox architecture. The congregation communicants were used to seeing the saints of the church in painted portraits surrounded by ornate gold decoration. The gold represented the nimbus of holiness emanated from the saint in communion with God and the great esteem in which the church held its saints, and held them up for imitation and communion. The paintings were called by the Greek word *icons* (Greek *ikōn,* an "image" or reflection). These images have a special meaning. When one gazes on a religious icon, one is not worshipping the image. That

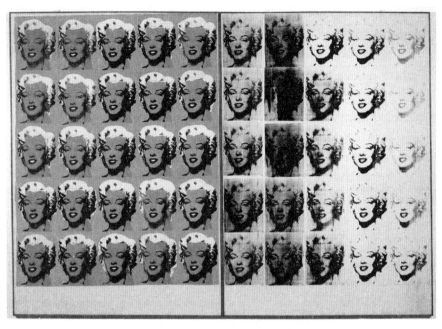

Fig. 15.9. The Marilyn Diptych *by Andy Warhol*

would be idolatry, that is, to place an image before the worship of God. Rather one is enjoined to look spiritually *through* the image, and pray through the image to the spiritual mystery that the image points toward, inwardly toward, as a sign. The sign is the outer manifestation of an inward reality, a reality that is wholly spiritual, eternal. The icon calls us out of this world and toward the kingdom of God. The individual saint is a being who has brought the light of that kingdom to humankind in such a way that their lives have become a sign to the faithful. An icon then, is not simply what we have come to know as an image. It is a visual sacrament.

There seems to me no doubt that Warhol was making an ironic comment, and also a sympathetic, perhaps pitying comment, on the materialism of the predominant culture of the United States, very much in tune with his ironic recognition of commercial art as "art" in the fullest sense nonetheless, if we choose to see it that way. The point about commercial art is that it defies originality insofar as it is mere image reproduced, duplicated, or as we say now "cloned." Duplication of course creates pattern, which has its own artistic value, of limited, though of commercially unlimited dimension.

However, when we come to the silkscreen image of *Marilyn* we are seeing two things. First, we are seeing Andy Warhol's personal response to the undoubtedly tragic demise of the Hollywood "sex goddess," who was nonetheless a living person, a living, enchanting, troubled soul, and not an image at all. He is elevating her memory by turning her manipulated image from the grip of Hollywood image manipulators to art, while also saying that all we have now of Marilyn is an image, what passes in an unspiritual world as an icon, reproducible and disposable. *Life* has been lost, and yet the image of Marilyn will go on and on, reproduced on film, in magazines, in the imagination, and so on. Unlike the unique religious icon, the image has no spiritual life. It is an image of an image. And yet, the image will be worshipped: not an icon, but an idol, which is a projection of the desires of the onlooker, and not by any means a window to God. As an *icon* then, the image is counterfeit; what it points to is absent.

Warhol perhaps has even glimpsed something of the transcendent nature of Marilyn's personal struggle through life. She said shortly before her death that all she and artists like herself wanted was a chance to twinkle, to reveal the inner star, not merely the outer glamour. She felt the *image* of Marilyn as something suffocating. Now the world would be plastered with that image.

Clearly, Warhol has been struck by the inverse resonance of the Hollywood image with that of the *genuine icon*. A genuine icon is a window into heaven. The Hollywood image is a commercial image, superficial, often gaudy, essentially flat, but always spiritually opaque. No light is going to flow through this image to the devoted. The image in cinema is projected *onto* a screen (a silvery or silvered screen to encourage reflection, not penetration).

I think we do the true icon and Andy Warhol immense disservice when we copy the oft-heard word *iconic* and apply it to this and that reproduced picture, object, or individual. As vulgarly employed today, *iconic* is simply a misleading double for *famous* or *well known*, or *powerful* and those are the proper words to describe such images. They are neither worshipped, nor fit for worship. Today we hear about a performance being iconic, a film being iconic, a photo being iconic. They are simply images that are reproduced and commonly familiar, and that was inherent to Warhol's "icons" of the famous. Remember his famous (or was it iconic?) statement on the transience of democratic fame: everyone will be famous for fifteen minutes—the empty transience of the publicly distributed selfie; here today, gone tomorrow. It would only be a matter of time before the "star" him- or herself wanted a silkscreen, not as an ironic comment on their "star value" or fame and cultural prominence, but as a hip *portrait,* as their image turned into art by the magician artist, Andy Warhol. He would be happy to oblige. One can see the wisdom of the act, for spiritual things are spiritually discerned. May we please cease using the word *iconic* for mere images; to do so is to connive in the very facile and destructive idolatry, or false-image making, Warhol was exposing, even profitably and commercially exposing, reflecting modern life back to itself through the artistic prism of genius.

Jerry Garcia, lead guitarist of the Grateful Dead, who graced the Chelsea Hotel roof, always said that there was one school he was proud of attending. That was the San Francisco Art Institute. While I recall Elaine Pagels telling me on a train from Princeton to New York in 1986 that Jerry Garcia was keen on the gnostic tradition, I merely mention Jerry at this point because he studied at the institute with a model for his life; that was Wally Hedrick (1928–2003), a genuine beatnik, 1950s Californian counterculture hero to Garcia. "Wally taught me that art is not only something you do, but something you are," said Garcia.[14]

In 1954 Hedrick had married Jay deFeo (1929–1989), an artist in her own right who has been described as a practicing witch. Together they discussed alchemical imagery and tarot cards, while Hedrick pursued both painting and sculpture. In painting he was working through a "personalized Dada," in sculpture, he pioneered the flattened beer can for abstract-sculpture use. He has also been called a preconceptualist since his work was fundamentally more about idea than finished object with meaning fully expressed. In 1961 he painted *Hermetic Image,* a painted copy from an engraving in *The Philosophical Epitaph* (1673), showing the Hermetic three worlds of terrestrial, celestial, and super-celestial being, with man at the center with access to all worlds, from chaos to heaven and the archetypal world. Probably finding the image reproduced in Seligmann's *History of Magic* (1954), Hedrick regarded its diagram as a self-portrait. Preferring content to form, Hedrick was eclectic in style, exploring the means to the end with the intensity and freewheeling spirit of the beat poet, ever an apostle of Jack Kerouac's *On the Road;* the road was life, and freedom meant change and changing often.

Another artist for whom Native American art held the key to a spiritual world implicit in the being manifested in nature was Norman Zammitt (1931–2007). He was raised on a Mohawk Indian reservation across the river from Montreal, and in youth enjoyed a vision of spirits in snow-covered surroundings. From 1962 to 1964 Zammitt created images on large canvases showing biomorphic shapes and dominated by eyes, and his work showed increasing interest thereafter in the dualities present in the natural world. After 1964, he moved to northern Mexico, continuing a biomorphic style conjoined with geometric forms, such as the honeycomb. Inspired by traditional ritual practices, Zammitt began stringing painted beads into chains thirty to forty feet long. This practice would lead to his distinctive "band" paintings.

By contrast, Bruce Nauman (b. 1941) found his materials shouting to him from the modern experience. In 1965, Nauman stopped painting and created two performance pieces. He then turned to neon, ensuring the light source for his neon compositions was hidden. In 1966 he was reading writings by Robert Morris as well as Frederick Perls's *Gestalt Therapy* (1951), and transcribed Gödel's proof: a mathematical theorem that states any complete system is inconsistent. His 1967 work *Window or Wall Sign* beams forth a paradox of the mystical in the modern. Truly switched on with electricity, the work flickers into stable life in most unnatural blue and peach neon, forming in cursive, friendly script the words: "The true artist helps the world by revealing mystic truths." It would be nice to see such statements making a luminescent splash in Times Square, rather than from purpose-built art spaces. One can but dream. In the late Sixties, Nauman moved on to exhibiting holograms.

YVES KLEIN (1928–1962)—PROPHET

As synchronicity would have it, it was while preparing material for this book that I received an unexpected email from a relative of Yves Klein, one of the great French artists of the twentieth century. I was asked if I knew anything further about accounts that have appeared in several books and studies indicating that the witty standout genius who gave us International Klein Blue and the first performance art paintings had been a Rosicrucian. I must say this was new to me, though not altogether surprising: while for many years it has become customary for some critics subconsciously or otherwise to edit out or to tone down the mystical interests of the chosen few whose names dominate received art history, one finds the spiritual in art is, if one sees it, just as prevalent as the spiritual in artists.

Spurred into action, I proceeded to investigate the question of one of the first modern artists to be involved directly with Rosicrucianism since the heyday of Péladan and the Rose+Croix Salons in the 1890s.

Yves Klein first read Max Heindel's *Rosicrucian Cosmo-Conception* (1909) in a French version in 1947 when living in postwar Nice. Heindel, originally Carl Louis Grashof, a Dane, migrated to the United States and established his "Rosicrucian Fellowship" at Oceanside, California, with ideas largely obtained from listening to Rudolf Steiner's public lectures in Germany, to which he gave his own speculative gloss, emphasizing astrology and visions of spiritual beings inhabiting the planets, and other elements gleaned from existing works.* Rosicrucian astrologer and chemical engineer Louis Cadeaux initiated Klein and his friend Claude Pascal into the society in 1948, whereafter the artist meditated in a cave belonging to friend, Armand Fernandez. Klein painted one of the cave walls blue, for his, the friends had agreed, was the realm of the sky. In 1952 Klein studied Heindel's *Cosmogonie des Roses-Croix* in greater depth through a correspondence course with the Rosicrucian Fellowship in California. The following year he ended his formal membership while still seeking inspiration in Heindel's work, which had

---

*See my book *The Invisible History of the Rosicrucians* (2009).

clearly struck a deep chord within him. It should be said at this point that all Rosicrucian Orders aim at the transformation of the individual along alchemical symbolic lines from a material to a spiritual being, reintegrating the individual into the ideal state of the first, heavenly Adam, before the Fall into materiality and spiritual unconsciousness.

In 1955, in Paris, Klein defended the abstract color-field, that is, the abstract use of large blocks of undifferentiated color, but extended its meaning and applicability. Inspired by mystical sensibility, Yves's "Monochrome" asserted that pure color expressed an absolute unity in an atmosphere of perfect serenity. He appears to have universalized his blue cave experience.

Three years later, on June 5, 1958, Klein chose the apartment of friend, philosopher Robert Godet* to perform the first active stroke of what he called Anthropometry, albeit in private. A nude model was procured. Covered in blue paint, she was requested to roll across a large piece of paper spread over the apartment floor. The result was a unique "monochrome," a word for such works he also took as his new name, for he felt he was birthing the cult of a new epoch. Klein's novel painting method would have to wait nearly two years before being unleashed on the public, when in March 1960 an astonished audience saw Klein's choreographed Anthropometry as art spectacle (action painting), amusing, intriguing, and involving.

The Anthropos is a key figure in gnostic theory, and refers to the primal Man, who in gnostic theory was also called Light whose unseen light should occupy all space, but who fell to matter and unconscious sleep, lost in narcissism. The suffix *metry* means the "measure," (as in geometry = earth measurement) so the word means literally the "measure" or "scope of man," spiritual man. Klein would apply the work to a number of different creative approaches, contrasting them with his remarkable fire paintings produced at the Centre d'Essai du Gaz de France at Plaine Saint Denis where Klein employed massive gas burners from the gasworks laboratories to provide flames that singed the surface

---

*Godet was interesting in his own right in our context. A traveler in the Far East, he was a follower of George Gurdjieff, and shared with Klein an interest in mystical and occult knowledge.

of his giant canvases. Fire elementally feeds on air; air and space become creative fuel of art and life. Klein harmonized the four Aristotelian elements of alchemy into the spark of new creation.

Thomas McEvilly has located some interesting crossovers between Heindel's ideas and Klein's later concerns, even after formal membership of the Rosicrucian Fellowship lapsed.[15] For Heindel, Spirit, or Life, is identical with "space," and is represented by color, especially the color blue. This blue space Spirit is infinitely expansive, and its wholeness is unbounded and without internal division, whereas form is spirit mixed with deforming matter. The origin of this idea is straightforward enough. The Hebrew *ruach* is breath, which God breathed into Adam's nostrils to give the red-earthy creation life, being. The Greek pneuma spirit is also air, invisible, and as far as the ancients were concerned, omnipresent, the ancients having no notion of a vacuous space, or of air as a gas. According to Heindel, air penetrates everything, and all else is transient by comparison, a Hermetic, alchemical conception. According to Heindel's telling of occult tradition, above the world of earthy form are six higher levels, accessed only through transformative initiation. Modern man is obsessed with the form level, with appearances and matter that obscures the higher light from which the essence of man (Life) derives. Heindel promised that the fellowship's purpose was to open the aspirant up once more to awareness of life. The latter phrase has a certain Sixties ring to it, does it not? *Awareness of life. . . .* Also one thinks of Albert Schweitzer's spiritual cure-all: "reverence for life," extending love to all forms of life as a synthesis of nondogmatic spiritual religion. "All you need is love."

Heindel looked at the idea of evolution and concluded that the next stage for humanity must conform to the long-held Rosicrucian and apocalyptic expectation of a forthcoming apocalypse, or revelation, of the "Holy Spirit" (space again!), which though apparently invisible constitutes the true rock of security in the apocalyptic changes to come (as illustrated in Christ's parable of the transient barn in which the fool places his wealth). Man would lose form, so must art, concluded Klein. The true rock is spirit, or in Klein's Heindel-influenced vision, space. So the coming epoch of the Holy Spirit becomes for Klein the age of space. Heindel believed man would have to lose his corporeality and transient solidity to enter what constituted a new element of being. In artistic terms, this meant for Klein the end of the age of form and of matter. Again, pure color negates transient form, and the impurities and fatality of matter.

Klein had a famous photo specially taken of a leap he had made into space himself earlier. It is remarkable, both surreal and spiritual at once. The apparent "nothingness" perceived by the material mind becomes for Klein the rock, the total support, the freedom of the spirit. Space will uphold the transfigured being of the age of space. As Christ said that on this "rock" or "stone" he would build his new assembly of spirit perceivers, so Klein prophesied a new epoch built on space. The act of faith then is to commit to the blue, a color clarion of purity and new values. The signs of the new age of space were clear. Man was straining to leave the earth, even as Klein launched his age of space. The new being of the new era would have to find his being in the infinite, his destiny in the eternal. Art should point the way, should exhibit the leap.

Fig. 15.10. Yves Klein, Leap into the Void. *Photograph taken by Harry Shunk.*

And what it points the way to is the restoration of an Edenic state involving the evaporation of inner and outer boundaries. We may expect to see political, national, and occupational boundaries erased, and a whole train of distinctions dissolving after that, and then inner divisions based on family background, tradition, and tendencies to anything that encroaches on the virtue of new freedom. Nudity was regarded by Klein as a sign of the new freedom, hence the model in blue paint must be nude, without the shell of inhibiting material, able literally to "feel space."

When Klein stood up for blue, he was standing for—or rather leaping for—what he also called "the Void," a kind of abyss through which the art of being human would have to pass to find the spiritual being, symbolized as unbroken space. As McEvilly expresses it: "in confronting an International Klein Blue Monochrome, [the viewer] is staring into the depths of infinite Space/Spirit itself, gazing, as it were, into the coming age of Eden."[16] Yves Klein expressed his challenge in his own person (Heindel had promised a high initiate to lead willing humanity from low-level awareness) to all that came after him even more forcefully: "[Monochromism is] a sort of modern day alchemy practiced by painters, born of the tension of experiencing . . . a bath in space vaster than infinity. . . . It is the only physical way of painting which permits access to the spiritual absolute. . . . My monochrome paintings are landscapes of freedom. . . ." He, Yves Klein, was the messenger of the new epoch: "The void is mine," he claimed, garnering to himself through the alchemy of International Klein Blue Monochrome, the artistic life kingdom of the infinite, the new age of space and the "kingdom of the impossible."[17] In a delightful paradox, Klein has his bold answer to the existential malaise of Sartre, for whom being was pure crisis, *this kingdom stands upon nothingness.*

It would seem to me that Klein launched something more than his own body into the air of the times that would succeed him.[18] The original title of John Lennon's epoch-making psychedelic battering ram "Tomorrow Never Knows" (*Revolver*, 1966), was originally titled "The Void" and the arrangement was first heard in Lennon's imagination as a vast choir of Tibetan monks. A few months later, in "Strawberry Fields

Forever," written while filming Richard Lester's antiwar movie *How I Won the War* in Almeria, Spain, Lennon's dislocated mind would sing that "Nothing is real" ("Strawberry Fields Forever," 1966–1967).

It is arguable that since Klein, the world has been trying to live with a sense of impending void that it has not yet come to grips with: "some consequence yet hanging in the stars." The initiatory gnosis permeated the Sixties imperceptibly, but was there all the same, and it was effected by art and the burgeoning concern with space and freedom.

POSTSCRIPT

I can recall only two visits to art galleries when I was a boy. The first was to the Birmingham Museum and Art Gallery in England. Famed for its Victorian collection of Pre-Raphaelite works, the greater part of the collection consisted of works of classical painting. It was close to the popular gallery housing dinosaurs. The second occasion was a visit to the brand-new Melbourne Art Gallery (National Gallery of Victoria). Recently opened in August 1968 at 180 St. Kilda Road in *best* state-of-the-art Sixties architecture (architect: Roy Grounds); my family visited it shortly before leaving Australia in November of that year, just before the release of the Beatles' *White Album*. The experience remains with me to this day. There was (and is) a huge, thin "wall of water," a massive, permanent waterfall encased thinly in clear glass. Was it a gallery wall or a work of art? It was beautiful. I can still hear the ringing of the water and the touch of the glass. The visit also included my first focused, visual encounter with modern, abstract paintings, circles, spaces, squares, lots of white and yellow, as I remember.

Of the two galleries, without doubt the one that made the greatest impression, and that I loved the most, was the new Melbourne Art Gallery. What I loved most about it was . . . *the space.* A child can become intoxicated on infinity, drunk with the stars in a drunken universe.

SIXTEEN

The Spiritual in Orchestral, Film, and Jazz Music

As I intend to fixate mostly on film music in this chapter, it will make the trip more interesting if I start with a key 1960s soundtrack that is not the work of a film composer at all, but the story behind which gives us a clue to discerning the spiritual meaning of at least some of the Sixties music discussed.

First, I take it that the principle of inspired music is fundamentally spiritual, which is why music transcends reason and can uplift and move us so profoundly. It is rare for the master of abstract logic, the determined rationalist-materialist to come up with a good tune, but they can often construct you an argument to explain why good tunes are unnecessary to music! Music theory is not the same as music, or else music theory books would be bestsellers.

Some consequence yet hanging in the stars . . . Shakespeare's lines from *Romeo and Juliet* might have served as rubric to Kubrick's masterwork, *2001: A Space Odyssey.* The MGM soundtrack released to promote the movie in 1968 featured the works of "classical" composers Richard Strauss (*Also sprach Zarathustra*), Johann Strauss II ("On the Beautiful Blue Danube"), Aram Khachaturian (1903–1978; *Gayaneh*), and the Hungarian composer György Ligeti (1923–2006; *Lux Aeterna,* and *Atmosphères*). Kubrick was of the opinion that no matter how good the best film composers available to filmmakers were, they could never be a Beethoven, Mozart, or Brahms. Surely not, but they could be a Miklós Rózsa (also a "classical" composer, as was Erich Wolfgang Korngold), a Bernard Herrmann, a John Barry, a Maurice Jarre, a Jerry Goldsmith, or an Elmer Bernstein. One wonders whether Mozart could have written as appropriate a score to *The Great Escape* as did Elmer Bernstein! No matter, Kubrick favored already existing, culturally established music to that specially written for the movie by Alex North (composer of *Cleopatra*), whose music was discarded from *2001*'s finished cut.

The point I wish to establish is that the essential theme of *2001*, carried only in part by music, was actually obscured in Kubrick's telling of Arthur C. Clarke's ideas for the movie, and the theme helps us to understand why I think such great film music was written by film composers in the Sixties. The motive driving the inspiration was an *urgency*, sometimes romantic, combined with *life force*.

The film *2001* is about science, and about evolution, the forces that would make the future, as the director sees them. That's all very well, but a movie needs a plot line, and Clarke's plot line combined Kubrick's big ideas with a resolved or partially resolved story whose meaning was reasonably clear.

When we see the protohumanoid ape throw his bone-tool-become-weapon into the air, which by jump cut transfigures into an orbiting craft about the earth, what the movie does not tell us is that the orbiting craft is in fact a missile station, an early model for "star wars," with armed warheads pointing at Earth. In Clarke's imagining, despite the use of science as a tool unparalleled (an evolutionary leap), the "ape" in man is still there, and the tool/weapon has become the means of destroying all life on the planet through nuclear holocaust, against which threat, for all his acquired powers of reason, the ape still feels helpless. How had it happened that a being that had evolved so far could yet find itself in the absurd situation whereby an uneasy peace could only be maintained by the bestial principle of "mutually assured destruction"? This tension is never established in the movie. Indeed, the "Blue Danube" music subverts it; we think we're seeing a utopian future of unbroken techno-musical grace, rather than a pivotal moment of global angst. The real background to Clarke's story idea is the chill of protracted Cold War, combined with postwar optimism for "better relations," producing a creative schizophrenia in Western culture. We are poised for the future at the end of the world, as it were. Maybe, having just made *Doctor Strangelove,* whose *geste* ends in nuclear catastrophe, Kubrick wanted a *way out* of it all. He went very far out to find it, and I am far from convinced his plot transcended the essential dualism of conflict.

Clarke's own solution to the dilemma, taken from an earlier short story about a "Sentinel" found on the moon (this was in tune with Kennedy's vision and NASA's priorities), was that man's glorious future required another evolutionary leap on the scale of that which had made the ape master of his scrap of desert. The polyvalent black obelisk secreted on the moon symbolizes this, while further suggesting extradimensional intelligence. When man is capable of reaching Jupiter (the king of the gods), then initiation to the next level of human development will take place. It will be a rebirth of man as "Star Child," a cosmic-conscious being of undefined dimensions, for whom unlimited space will be his or her natural habitat. Do we not hear the voice of artist Klein amid the technical music of scientific spheres? (. . . and the nascent *Star Trek,* of course).

In Clarke's original telling, the transfigured astronaut-explorer Bowman becomes the means of rebirth. Bowman is reborn as the Star Child who returns, a prodigal, to Earth, and the first thing said prodigal does is to destroy the missile stations that have encircled the planet. What he might do next we may only guess. But NASA associate Clarke has made an evolutionary "step for mankind" before Neil Armstrong and Buzz Aldrin set foot on the real moon's powdery surface.

The global anxiety that fed into the story of *2001* is I believe an energy that brilliant artists transformed into film music that, often in spite of the weaknesses of the films the music was intended to support, manifested as *music of the spirit* independent of the movies themselves. Those in tune with it were lifted above the anxiety to a fresh perception of humanity. The times called for our species to rack its brains, and score its heart and soul for visionary paths beyond the terrible impasse that the ape of promise had finally stumbled upon. Like Bowman, perhaps a Sagittarian figure in Kubrick's movie, man was going to have to shoot his arrow to the "end" of himself; he was going to have to go all the way, beyond the terrestrial, material spheres of traditional cosmology, beyond, into the supercelestial and spiritual realms in search of inspiration. The project was essentially one of saving the world from itself by means of fresh genius.

Hungarian composer Miklós Rózsa (b. 1907) was not exactly a new kid on the block when he carried away a well-deserved Oscar in 1960 for composing the score to *Ben-Hur,* but the inspiration for that score was remarkably fresh. The movie drew on international anxieties for its subtext, proposing love of enemies and sacrifice of hatred as the means to the miracle of new life. Rózsa found his inspiration walking through the ruins of ancient Rome, still standing in the postwar eternal city. The composer's imagination transcended his own troubled times and, through looking back via the prism of present remains, and researching into the music of the past, he was gifted with inspiration for the future. The grand, full-bodied, sweeping, pounding, and swirling gusts of divine music he composed for the epic, seldom bombastic (except where scenes of bombast called for it) or out of touch with humanity

Fig. 16.1. Hungarian composer Miklós Rózsa (1907–1995).

or the source of inspiration, expressed a divine humanity through very great emotion and almost limitless dramatic scope.

Intriguingly, the film opens with the simple blowing of the shofar, the shepherd's ram's horn that Jewish tradition maintains will accompany the appearance of the Messiah on the Temple Mount: the physical meets the spiritual in space and time. From that point, whether it was conveying the proud parade of charioteers, or a desperate sea battle, the spiritual inspiration in Rózsa's music never falters.

By the early Seventies, in provincial England, the soundtrack to *Ben-Hur* had become very hard to obtain. I shall never forget the joy with which I stumbled upon a copy of the soundtrack in a decaying junkshop in Aston, Birmingham, going cheap at 40p, and the difficulty I encountered in pedaling back home ten miles by bicycle trying to support the precious album undamaged between my left arm and the handlebars! For me at the time, *Ben-Hur* was the grail of music.

Aged fifty-three in 1960, Rózsa had come a long way. While his mother had studied music at the Budapest Academy, his father, a successful land-owning industrialist, enjoyed a country estate at Nagylócz, county of Nógrád, north of Budapest, where he exercised his, and his country's responsibilities to the peasants. Ardent patriot Rózsa shared his father's love of country people, recording their music with great care, incorporating it into his later work. Rózsa remembered seeing his father talking to villagers, surrounding him to listen to his account of what he could achieve if he was successful in his political efforts on their behalf (he wasn't). "It was like the Sermon on the Mount," Rózsa wrote—a scene with which he would become very familiar, scoring it twice, for *King of Kings* (1961) and of course, *Ben-Hur*.[1]

Composer of a "Student March" at the age of seven, Rózsa's heart was set on music, but his father thought it better he acquire modern languages and science to ensure success. For eight years Rózsa studied at Budapest's Realgymnasium, an experience whose miseries he could have shared with Sixties stars who'd suffered an equally dispiriting Fifties upbringing. "I was completely and utterly bored," wrote Rózsa of his school days.[2] Leaving in 1925, his father was persuaded to let the musical prodigy attend the Leipzig Conservatory, so long as he also studied chemistry. Coming under the wing of Hermann Grabner, Rózsa would drop chemistry and pursue music, though it promised a hard life. While Rózsa's early classical works would enjoy solid success, there was still no real income from being even a prestigiously published, classical composer. On moving to Paris, Rózsa swallowed his pride and seized an opportunity to write songs for cheap films, and then film music; the big break coming through Hungarian producer Alexander Korda and his brothers, based at Denham Studios in England. With the outbreak of war, Korda moved production of his latest film *The Thief of Baghdad* to Hollywood, and its composer Rózsa followed, establishing himself in the film community with his exceptional gift for fantasy and the dark grit of Hollywood film noir, making friends with other brilliant refugees from Hitler's murderous mania, such as Igor Stravinsky (1882–1971) and Polish composer Alexandre Tansman (1897–1986). By 1943, the Hollywood Bowl could successfully fill its auditorium from an advertisement for Rózsa conducting Ravel's *Bolero,* plus his own suite from the Kordas' *The Jungle Book* (1942).

Distinguished as his movie career was through the latter golden years of Hollywood, Rózsa will remain best known for melodies that reached the general public during the Sixties. "The music of *Ben-Hur* is very close to my heart," he would write in his autobiography.[3] He also recognized that though he, like other classical composers, had only worked in films for the financial opportunities it afforded, that did not mean film composers of his class were not capable of writing some of their best works for the medium. Rózsa himself singled out William Walton's three Shakespeare scores as being on a par with Walton's best concert work, even though movies required a directness that might feel intrusive, sudden, or insufficiently subtle in a classical work. "This directness is a *sine qua non* if film music is to do its job properly,"[4] asserted Rózsa, who was annoyed when it was averred that composing music to very strict time meant somehow a loss for the music. On the contrary, he insisted: "To me, time in music is like space in painting. . . . The discipline of having to compose to a given duration need not affect the quality of the music so composed at all."[5]

Rózsa even allowed himself the rare personal joke within his film music. He was surely not the only composer in the century to resist twelve-tone music, and suffered opprobrium for it among self-conscious modernists. Arnold Schoenberg (1874–1951) had introduced what to the general public sounded "out of tune" tonal values to composition in an effort to break the grip of romantic music and to encourage musical experimentation for a modern world. For Rózsa, *melody* was the essence of music itself, the communication of emotion, not an abstract game with notes. Any cleverness at a composer's disposal should be put to bringing freshness and life into traditional musical values and expression. That did not mean there was no place for dissonance and experimentation, but not *as a rule*. Rózsa's music was almost always adventurous, for example, he introduced the electronic theramin into film music with his score for *Spellbound* (1945), the same instrument Brian Wilson would use to great effect on the Beach Boys' "Good Vibrations" two decades later in 1966. As for twelve-tone, Rózsa used it only once, in his magnificent score for *King of Kings* (1961). When it came to evoking the presence of Satan in the movie, Rózsa, used twelve-tone for a disturbing motif for the Tempter! "For me twelve-tone music is a stillborn idea and 'Father of Lies,'" Rózsa opined.[6] Rózsa's score was somewhat wasted on the finished movie, especially his rousing, bacchanalian "Dance of Salome": cut to ribbons and weakly choreographed. The movie's occasional lapses in quality and taste you would never guess from hearing the magisterial score alone. One feels Rózsa scored an ideal movie in his mind as much as the celluloid one he was paid to write for; the score stimulates enjoyable and intellectually stimulating listening regardless of the film's weaknesses (an exception to the overall brilliance, in my view, would be Rózsa's cumbersome, overblown setting of the "Lord's Prayer" sung by the Choir of the Roman Basilicas and full orchestra). Anyhow, producer Samuel Bronston liked what Rózsa had done, and hired him for his next epic. This was to be one of the great Sixties epics, *El Cid,* directed with color, keen eye, and splendid élan by Anthony Mann on location in Franco's Spain where something of the Middle Ages could still be felt among the castles of Castile. It starred Charlton Heston as Spanish hero Rodrigo de Bivar, and Sophia Loren as his lover, Doña Ximena: both in top form. Politicians and diplomats today might gain inspiration from the film as *El Cid* shows a great man successfully persuading moderate Muslims to make sacrifices for a common cause, though, as averred earlier, the film's subtext in 1961 was clearly the threat of global Communism.

El Cid represented not only a panoramic form of escapism for its audiences, but its making afforded Rózsa and his family something of an escape from Hollywood's decline and the toxic politics of the day. He went to Spain to work with the ninety-two-year-old Ramon Menendez Pidal, Ph.D., the film's historical advisor. Pidal introduced the composer to his massive library where Rózsa found his musical inspiration in the twelfth-century *Cantigas* of Santa Maria, which religious music he combined with exquisite troubadour melodies to generate a symphonic score of enormous depth and emotional range, evoking a time when all that took place did so under the eye of God, of whose interest the players on earth's stage were keenly aware. It is obvious the Protestant-raised, but ecumenically minded Rózsa was upheld in his music by a powerful personal faith, and this communicated itself to mass Sixties audiences. As ancient Rome had informed *Ben-Hur*, old Spain imbued *El Cid*, driving the composer to pose the question: "Where do these influences come from? From the air? The food? The architecture? The people? The music one hears? I don't know, but they were definitely there."[7] Rózsa regarded 1961 as the climax and watershed of his film career, but while Rózsa gained commissions for far fewer film projects in the Sixties—religious epics began to look "uncool" to new studio heads— his big films went round the big cinemas throughout the decade and his albums sold like hotcakes in collections and as individual soundtracks.

Rózsa was in London when the wind of change was brought home to him. In 1963, he composed his last score for MGM, *The VIPs*, starring brilliant media darlings and popular whipping-couple Richard Burton and Elizabeth Taylor, whose marital infidelities, ambitious movie-cum-theatrical initiatives, combined intelligence, and emotional ups and downs kept bourbon-stoked reporters in gleeful anticipation throughout the decade. Arriving in London at 7:00 a.m., Rózsa came upon a crowd of reporters and photographers at the airplane gangway. Flattering himself they might have come to greet three-time Academy

Award winner Rózsa himself, the maestro was surprised to find himself ignored as the press "rushed toward a group of four long-haired men, who turned out to be the Beatles. They certainly beat me in popularity."[8]

Don't worry, Dr. Rózsa, you could have joined the queue with Jesus!

In a BBC *Omnibus* documentary, *John Barry: A License to Thrill,* first broadcast in 2000, Beatles producer Sir George Martin remarked that while orchestral composers had in modern times veered away from melody and what delighted a broader public, composers of the quality and caliber of John Barry were now writing the "classical music" of our day. There is much truth in this observation from one of the decade's key cultural witnesses. From 1963, John Barry (1933–2011) began fully to embrace the possibilities for his film music of the studio orchestra combined with additional, often unorthodox instrumentation where called for. While Barry's first released soundtrack to *Beat Girl* (1960) had relied heavily on a sure touch for pop music combined with distinctive big brass dramatic strokes, October 1963 saw the release of the second Bond movie *From Russia with Love* (a favorite novel of JFK), followed by selections from the orchestral score "composed, arranged and conducted by John Barry," the which album charted in *Billboard* on May 2, 1964, reaching number twenty-seven on August 22, staying in the chart for thirty-four weeks—very impressive indeed for a movie soundtrack (Barry's next Bond score, *Goldfinger,* reached number one in the Billboard 200 later in the year).[9] The year 1963 also saw Barry composing and recording his truly marvelous, wholly original score for the Cy Endfield production *Zulu,* a film about courage, endurance, sacrifice, respect for the enemy, and much else, as well as being the film that gave Barry's close friend Michael Caine *his* first big showcase. Barry's unforgettable music has imprinted itself in the memories and hearts of millions over the more than fifty years since *Zulu*'s startling release in January 1964. Not only was the A-side of *Zulu* a spiritually uplifting sequence of brilliantly orchestrated melodies and timpani-fueled dramatic cues, with all the muscle, discipline, gunmetal, sweat, and spirit of the story, but the B-side showed Barry's superior gift for dance-pop music of arresting power and emotional uplift: a "selection of

Zulu stamps" as the cover notes have it, melodies from the movie played out as South Africa–spun, big-beat stompers, featuring authentically harmonized black voices and Vic Flick's giant electric guitar sizzle and twang, with far better drum kit and bass sounds than George Martin was getting out of Abbey Road Studio One for the Beatles in that or the following year.

Born November 3, 1933, John Barry Prendergast was the youngest of three children of John Xavier Prendergast, entrepreneur of Irish extraction, who had striven hard to become the respected owner of eight cinemas and concert venues in the north of England. Raised in a small house in Hull Road on the outskirts of the city of York, John attended the Bar Convent Catholic Junior School, then Saint Peter's Public School as a day pupil where he suffered prejudice for being a Catholic. At home he heard Sibelius, Ravel, and Beethoven on the family gramophone, but his trips to his father's cinema implanted within him the dream of being a film composer, a most unusual career choice; most film composers coming to the task after pursuing careers in popular music or, as in the case of Rózsa, from cash-starved classical careers. Barry was very aware of the work of Rózsa, as he was of Max Steiner, Erich Wolfgang Korngold, Bernard Herrmann, and the other distinguished composers of the film world. But undoubtedly, Rózsa had raised the bar in quality and meaning, and Barry had no intention of passing beneath it, though with a style and unique ear untrammeled by formal classical music and symphonic orchestration training. Rózsa demonstrated an empire of the possible: film music loved for its own sake, appreciated by listeners for its own sake, musical life and depth of meaning independent of the movie, or the time when the movie appeared. Describing himself as a "musical dramatist," Barry's job was to locate and give expression to *the spirit* of the film's drama. In doing so, it was usually the case that Barry gave the films their spirit, disembodying the soul he discerned in them through power of imagination. While in general it is a cardinal principle of film music that it be felt, but not heard, Barry's music was both felt *and* heard, without ever overdominating or subduing the film; rather it brought forth dramatic meaning. At its best, we may pass

*Fig. 16.2. John Barry
(1933–2011)*

through Barry's music into the heart of the film, at which point we are no longer observers, but joined inwardly to the film's meaning. This is spiritual art.

Barry had special advantages, apart from his innate gift of musical genius and peerless melodic and dramatic sense. Not the least of these was direct personal experience of popular music and public taste, through his father's entertainment circuit, which hosted world stars of the caliber of Louis Armstrong. Barry was a big jazz fan, with a special love for bebop, Chet Baker, and Stan Kenton's band, but young Barry also had a hotline into the burgeoning, but largely unexplored territory of rock 'n' roll and rock-influenced pop music. To cap that, Barry's father had secured the support of Francis Jackson, Ph.D., master of music for the Anglican cathedral, York Minster. Jackson taught a young, quiet, studious Barry rudiments of harmony and counterpoint, giving in the process a love for choral music that remained with Barry throughout his life, to be revitalized magically for the public ear in his outstanding Oscar-winning score for *The Lion in Winter* (1968) set in twelfth-century France, but whose jaw-dropping music, dripping with stunning harmonics, vibrant emotional scope, pace, and tension could only have been written by John Barry in the late Sixties. Nobody before had combined the choral sound of an Accademia Monteverdiana with a Moog synthesizer, fresh from its inventor's lab to a sock-it-to-'em big brass beat plus faux-medieval fanfare. But that's genius.

Signing up for three years in the British Army in 1952, Barry, based in Cyprus and in Egypt, raised his sights even further by paying hard-grafted dollars for a superb correspondence course titled "Composition and Orchestration for the Jazz Orchestra" offered personally by Bill Russo in Chicago, orchestrator and arranger for Stan Kenton's experimental, avant-garde jazz band. Among much else, Russo gave Barry a handy mathematical formula for creating harmonically stable countermelodies. Barry's skill in employing this musical clue combined with his own experimentation and superwide listening would in time distinguish already superb melodic arcs with emotional "otherness," suggestive of an elusive spiritual dimension that hooks the full attention of persons "with an ear."

Most who have listened closely to Barry, or just as relevantly, *felt* his presence in the context of the more than hundred movies he scored, will have been aware of a certain magical, and often tragic melancholy and psychological gloom, combined with a transcending, if subtly pained optimism and life spirit of purified romanticism that colors this princely musical dramatist's oeuvre. There is, as biographer Eddi Fiegel has observed, a real "darkness" in Barry's music, a quality that has prevented easy dismissal of his accessible music, for it is heartfelt, profoundly emotional, lonely, expressed with artistic force by a number of subtle and often highly original musical techniques. The medium of film gave Barry's music a directness, economy, and sense of display that many orchestral composers could only envy, or ignore.

There is a depth of melancholy, a profound sense of loss, that can, to the determined soul, release a sense or wave of the spiritual, at the same time as an outpouring of emotion of grief, or nostalgia, at something from which time and space have set us inexorably, painfully apart. I am reminded of a poster I made for myself when aged about twelve. On a canvas on which were the words "Creation is the product of Pain," I placed a devotional crucifix. This dynamic of the highest creation emanating from the deepest sorrow is vividly present in the Valentinian Gnostic myth favored by the *pneumatikoi* or "spirituals" of the Gnostic movement in the second century CE.

Gnostic teachers such as Valentinus (fl. 160 CE) saw themselves as an esoteric elite of the Catholic Church. In Valentinus's myth, or significant story, before time began, the "Father" God dwells in eternity with his feminine or masculo-feminine reflection, called Sophia, that is, Wisdom—a relationship based on Jewish wisdom literature's speculation on the book of Genesis. In the myth, such is Sophia's ungovernable desire to know the unknowable depth of the Father, that from her tangible passion, she auto-conceives, in a kind of phantom pregnancy and delivery, a principal but unbalanced creative act of her own, as a copy of what she knows by reflection of the ineffable Father. This, in the myth, is the origin of the universe of our senses, especially the catastrophic outpouring downward of the material universe, in which her substance (divine pneuma) is scattered as spiritual seeds, caught in the web of dark, crafted matter. The pneuma is aware that it is somehow out of touch with its source, and yearns nostalgically, but in the darkness of the creation, is driven into a kind of amnesia by a false or copy god, ego of the material realm, sometimes called the "Demiurge" or Ialdabaoth, craftsman and to Gnostics, "fool." He is a projection perhaps of the false ego, or unenlightened soul. The pneuma or spirit can only await the arrival of the one anointed to reintegrate pneuma with its formerly unknown source in the Father. This is the spirit's account of its own predicament in the world.

Gnostic traditions understand the spiritual nature of the most intense emotions, and aim to join them to their spiritual origin. Music can serve this link with imagined paradise, offering momentary glimpses in this overshadowed life of something beyond us, for which we may yet entertain a mysterious nostalgia. It is significant in this regard that one of Barry's last, and best-received works, was an album of music titled *The Beyondness of Things* (1997), with a cover photo of Barry by the ocean's depth, on the shore, alone. Our awareness of tragedy may paradoxically release a sense of transcending hope.

And hope and tragedy are the pillars of the Sixties.

Eddi Fiegel's biography of Barry gives us just a couple of historical clues into the pain of John Barry's inner life experience, something that drove him to make some of the most memorable and important music of the Sixties, and that colored that music in tones we feel now as unmistakably Sixties in feeling, though universal in meaning. Behind the pizzazz of the Sixties, is an enormous, tragic sense of loss.

◬ ◬ ◬

Barry received his Catholic education at the Bar Convent School in York: "It was the most severe Catholic teaching ever, and I hated it," confessed Barry to Fiegel. "You were surrounded by nuns who asked you questions like, "Who do you love more—God or your mother and father?" And I used to say, "My mother and father," and they'd say, "Oh, if that's the case you're sure to go to hell." Despite this arguably sinister assault on natural sensibilities, Barry found something in Catholicism he would not, or could not, do without. "I hated it, but you know it gets so ingrained in you, that kind of thing. I'm still a very strong Catholic. There's something awful about the faith, but there's something terribly good about it as well."[10]

An event occurred while attending the convent school that would color the deeps of his imagination forever. From April to June 1942 Adolf Hitler and his German commanders decided they could demoralize England, devastate its spirit, by bombing the country's ancient cathedrals and historic cities. On April 28, 1942, John was still at school when he heard air-raid sirens—curious because raids normally took place at night to add to their terror. John's parents came to the school to pick him up and take him home. The nuns pleaded with them to let John stay and use the school bomb shelter, saying, "This is the safest place on earth." At around 11:00 p.m., the raid on York began. That night, seventy-nine people were killed outright as the city's narrow medieval streets erupted in flames, singeing the sky red and melting everything that would melt in its path. By morning it became clear that German bombs had fallen right through John's convent school; five of the nuns were dead, and a wing of the school was obliterated. What became intolerable for young John was that nobody ever talked about it. There was no outlet, a reticence compounded by traditional Yorkshire attitudes at keeping feelings covered. Grief unexpressed or made unspeakable generates a lasting dark cloud within the psyche, and to this Eddie Fiegel attributed a portion of the darkness permeating some of John Barry's most characteristic music. Creation is the product of pain. And ambition, for ambition is—as has been recognized—the salve of unhappiness. John's dominant father could not express love for his son directly.

What one must also recognize is that with all the effects of war and the threats and privations experienced during the 1950s, came a corresponding urge for life, light, love, and bright-skied adventure, and in the early Sixties, and especially with the arrival of the famous contraceptive pill, available in Britain through the National Health Service from 1961, this urge for life was magnetized by the lure and pleasure and risk of sex, a particularly hot outlet for lusty Catholics. John loved sex, and love and sex and money and fame all came together in the early Sixties as the champagne cork of the era exploded into a pleasure fest for young men and women turned on by the sense of inheritance to the daylight of freedom: time to cast away the old and the heavy and the doctrinaire and to embrace life with a swing and a flair and a joy of being young, bright, and randy.

All of the qualities suggested above can be found in great, stirring abundance, not only in all the Sixties James Bond music, from and including John's breakthrough score for *From Russia with Love* (plus hit song by Lionel Bart, arranged by John and sung by stylish British crooner Matt Monro), but also in the pathos and fresh, life-filled optimism of *Born Free* (an archetypally huge Sixties hit, also sung with gusto by Matt Monro), and the darker, more nuanced scores to *The Knack* (1965), *The Whisperers* (1967), *The Lion in Winter, Petulia* (1968), *Midnight Cowboy* (1969), *Boom* (1968), and the lush romance and yearning major sevenths of *On Her Majesty's Secret Service* (1969), and *You Only Live Twice* (1967) where Barry seems to have taken the whole world for his oyster, as seen from conflict-filled space, blended with an explosive, orange-crimson bloom of immense rising sun burning on the Pacific horizon, with koto-plucked melodies Debussy or Satie would have appreciated. *Ah*! In a world gone cold, Barry—and, by implication, Bond—were romantics, and hot as hell.

Miklós Rózsa and John Barry did not have it all their own way when it came to Sixties film music that conveyed spiritual meaning. I often say to my daughter that to get a better idea of what the current media image presents of popular music in the 1960s it is helpful to look at the inner sleeves of old albums from the time, when record companies would display their top wares to entice the public to buy another album next payday. A very different picture emerges from that suggesting it was all a question of the Beatles and British and U.S. rock bands and soul and R & B classics. Pop music in the Sixties was amazingly eclectic, and hip bands like the Beach Boys were sat next to show music; Ray Conniff, His Orchestra and Singers; Esquivel; Herb Alpert and his Tijuana Brass; and idiosyncratic vocalists like Yma Sumac on the inner sleeve territory where true pop eclecticism lies hidden. The emphasis generally was on fun, liveliness, rhythm, and romance. Indeed, the more imaginative rockers could somewhat spoil the party with their realism, psychogames, and tendency to isolated gloom (amazing how many top rock songs of the period feature the songwriter sitting in an upstairs room looking out the window or into themselves). Some of the most experimental music came not only from among the top rock bands (usually copying the Beatles, or later, Jimi Hendrix), but was also to be enjoyed, and was enjoyed by most people, with albums such as *One Stormy Night,* where the Mystic Moods Orchestra played very movingly some obscure and not so obscure popular romance melodies to the sonic backdrop of a U.S. lightning-smacked thunderstorm and downpour of rain echoing amid the ghostly horn of a distant steam train to create an experimental pasture of great emotional power and nostalgic surprise. Particularly outstanding was Wayne Shanklin's mysterious "A Dream" that kicked off side one of Leo Kulka and Brad Miller's aural brainchild in perfect mystic mode. Record company Philips's top-selling album of 1965, *One Stormy Night* is highly evocative, and not a little magical, to this day. Curiously, in my own memory this music is joined to the scene of the Crucifixion in *The Greatest Story Ever Told.* Something in the gathering fare of heavy sheets of elemental rain, black skies, and eerie storm suggest greater powers than ours that thwart our intents, if I may paraphrase Avon's Bard.

So, we should not be at all surprised to find the spiritually uplifting soundtrack to *The Sound of Music* (also from that amazing year 1965) outsold anything the Beatles produced that year, and not without reason. *The Sound of Music* remains one of the biggest selling albums of all time (up there with *Sgt. Pepper*), and I can only imagine that practically everybody has heard this record. It has its spirituality built-in, of course. It is about a nun and some naughty children who find harmony through harmony. It is also about love, sacred and profane, and the fusing of the duo in the grace of a second chance for two misfits amid tragedy and loss, personal and political. Written by Richard Rodgers and Oscar Hammerstein II, two of the songs were penned by Rodgers after Hammerstein's death in 1960: "I Have Confidence" and "Something Good" both deeply moving. Julie Andrews provides a heavenly, creamy voice that descended if not from heaven, then from at least the high Alps to a thirsty earth, but for me the key aspect of the alchemy of this all-permeating album lies in the extraordinary harmonic skills of orchestra and Broadway musical arranger Irwin Kostal (1911–1994). Kostal enjoyed a unique gift for taking the melodies of Rodgers and adding just the right kind of transcending harmonic color, depth, line, detail, and eagle-like sweep to render them into heart-tugging spiritual messages that have the power to overcome all possible opposition. Only churls and automatic cynics resist. This skill is not only evident on nearly every cut from the album (most especially perhaps on "My Favorite Things" with its time-blasting, childhood-blessing harp and pizzicato harmonies), but positively envelops the already strong melodies of Robert M. and Richard B. Sherman's fab songs for another of the very biggest selling albums of 1965, Walt Disney's *Mary Poppins*. This is vital Sixties spiritual soundtrack music. *Mary Poppins* even has the added benefit of providing in one extraordinary, innovative "family film" a veritable guidebook in true occult magical thinking, the power of magical imagination laid bare, can you but see it and step into a pavement picture and "love to laugh" with the inviting protagonists. *Poppins* creator P. L. Travers was famously upset that Disney had denuded her stories of their G. I. Gurdjieff-inspired message, but I am not so sure. If someone asked me where to start in the path of learning magic, I should be inclined to recommend viewing the film and memorizing the soundtrack as a perfectly reasonable and palatable entrée. Irwin Kostal may only have put the glitter and glamour on already powerful structures, but the nimbus is what brings us to the icon.

Fig. 16.3. French composer Georges Delerue (1925–1992).

We must not forget the French. Georges Delerue gave his remarkable talents to a number of François Truffaut pictures, most notably *Jules et Jim* (1962), with its haunting, bittersweet melodies of a doomed ménage à trois played out in Henri-Pierre Roché's semiautobiographical story set at the tail end of the Belle Époque. Delerue's delicate, wistful music matches the sense of a decadent poetry and gets into the heart of a romantic melancholy that only the French seem to be able to capture in its humanistic fullness without cloying sentimentality. Delerue's contrasting score to Jean-Luc Godard's avant-garde swipe at the vile materialism of the movie business starring Brigitte Bardot and Michel Piccoli, *Le Mépris* ("Contempt," 1963) reveals a depth of despairing melancholy that is at once poetic (and in the French sense *spirituelle*) and utterly hopeless, and if one could ever speak meaningfully of a "spirit of nihilism," Delerue has captured it in string passages of overwhelming spiritual abjectness, in spite of himself. Godard spent the decade hitting himself constantly at the brick wall of materialism, but his existential nihilism only permitted redemption from nothingness in the form of Far Leftist politics, a poor substitute in my opinion for what I always felt he had in him, and that only began to emerge in his curious fashion in the late Eighties and Nineties. The perhaps ultimate materialist one-liner emerges from the lips of vulgar film producer Joshua Prokosch in *Le Mépris,* played in prickly fashion by Jack Palance, who says, without any sense of irony, "Whenever I hear the word *art,* I reach for my checkbook." Perhaps Godard's lost career was in satire.

A constant of English school holidays in the late Sixties and Seventies consisted in the many repeat showings of the remarkable Franco-London TV series, *The Adventures of Robinson Crusoe,* with Robert Hoffman as Crusoe and Fabian Canalos as Man Friday, syndicated in the States in 1964 and first shown in the United Kingdom in 1965. It was a most loveable black-and-white version of Defoe's 1721 classic of a Christian man marooned alone on an island for years, with, eventually, only an ex-cannibal for company. A great deal of the charm came from the unforgettable theme tune and truly haunting score written and arranged by Robert Mellin and Gian-Piero Reverberi. Directed by Jean Sacha, the film series contained a series of implicit messages for its mainly young audiences, with lots of adventure and drama to make the invisible lessons palatable. There is without doubt a strong spiritual aspect to the down-to-earth (very!) story that comes over in fascinating ways, such as when Crusoe's beloved dog Dick dies, and a notable scene where Crusoe prays to Almighty God before enjoying a feast made up of the plunder of treacherous pirates who have killed and destroyed the lives of many, only for their spoils to be ultimately enjoyed at a rich table laid before Crusoe, his parrot, a goat, and Dick the dog. The music to this scene with its intriguing piano countermelody and harp refrain perfectly captures the simplicity and beauty of Crusoe's tried faith and the presence of a divine spirit upholding the lonely man. "May I never say," prays Crusoe, who appears to have done everything to survive the elements with his own hands, "that the work of my hands alone was the sole source of these blessings." Mighty, dignified stuff, and beautifully told with some of the finest music ever laid next to celluloid's ribbon of dreams. Children are not granted this level of inspiration via TV anymore, with all too obvious consequences.

It was young French composer Maurice Jarre (1924–2009) who gave David Lean's spectacular epic of inner struggle played out on the global stage, *Lawrence of Arabia* (1962), much of its flavor and evocative power, beyond Freddie Young's matchless photography, and Peter O'Toole's utterly compelling performance as Col. T. E. Lawrence, the young officer who used the Arab Revolt of 1915–1918 to try to resolve inner, spiritual conflicts while performing extraordinary services for the large number of Syrian and Hejazi Arabs he encountered before and during World War I, as an Allied intelligence officer. The use of the electronic Onde Martinot by Jarre added much of the mystique of the desert to the film, as well as to a certain, heterodox mysticism to Lawrence's character. Churchill called Lawrence "one of the greatest beings alive in our time," and spoke of Lawrence's "profound faith" with some awe. The nature of this faith is partly explored in the movie, and it is clearly far from a conventionally religious kind, though we do learn that Lawrence was a puritan as regards "the gospel of bareness in materials," loving the desert, as Robert Bolt's script puts it, "because it's clean."

Lawrence is presented as a prophet of will, and willpower, very successfully dramatized in music in a cue on the soundtrack called "Miracle" where amid drifting sands, scurrying up a dune in serpentine fashion in a chill dawn wind, we see Lawrence imagining the tides of men swept up like stars by his will into a great military movement that would descend from nowhere like the will of God on Aqaba's Turkish stronghold and change the course of the war. "Greater love hath no man than this, than that he will give his life for his friend" says the Gospel of John, and this act of sacrifice Lawrence goes to the brink in undertaking when he returns to the initiatory hotplate of the "Sun's Anvil" to rescue Arab comrade, Gasim, and carry the despairing warrior back to the camp when he has been forsaken. Against his kismet-obsessed comrades, Lawrence declares: "*Nothing* is written." Man has the spiritual will to transcend what appears inevitable, a condemnation of the God of Fate suggesting blasphemy to his Islamic comrades in arms, though they are prepared to make exception for the exceptional Englishman who has become their true friend. "Rescue of Gasim and Bringing Gasim into Camp" expresses a spiritual joy that is a highpoint of the film and the vindication of the faith of youth in true fellowship and a guiding star.

My last example of Sixties film music notable for its spiritual relevance and meaning is very different from what we have seen hitherto. *Wonderwall* (released in January 1969) was a curious little film of childlike approach, directed by Joe Massot and produced by Andrew Bronsberg, starring a highly eccentric wild-haired Jack MacGowran and

Fig. 16.4. John Barry with wife, actress-singer Jane Birkin.

Mrs. John Barry, that is, model, singer, and actress, Jane Birkin, soon to head off to France as lover of Serge Gainsbourg to add her heavy breathing and voice of seductive innocence to Gainsbourg's lines about "intestines" in the sex-positive and sex-heavy French language hit, "Je t'aime . . . Moi non plus" (1969).

The music to *Wonderwall* is attributed to George Harrison of the Beatles. Harrison traveled to EMI Bombay, India, in January 1968 to enjoy the Indian musical talents of Mahapurush Misra (tabla), Shambu-Das (sitar), Shiv Kumar Shermar (santoor), S. R. Kenkare (flute), Rij Ram Desad (harmonium), and other skilled practitioners of a music with which Harrison had been in love since 1965. The soundtrack was the first album issue of the Beatles' own record label, Apple, and was a worthy addition to the Sixties tapestry of daring and innovation (I have a much-cherished original pressing). Apart from showcasing Harrsion's work with the Indian musicians, the point of the album, and the film's simple story to some extent, is revealed on the attractive album cover designed by American Bob Gill, along with John Kelly and Alan Aldridge. The Magritte-inspired design shows a straight duality. On one side of a brick wall is a Westerner in dull black and white, carrying an umbrella and wearing a bowler hat and raincoat. On the other side of the wall we can see a bevy of Indian maidens enjoying each other's company in a blissful lake in a rural setting of verdant growth and trees on which hang their discarded saris. Above the man on the left of the design, George Harrison suggested one brick be taken from the wall that otherwise divides the two worlds. There is some hope that East may meet West and some understanding of each other's cultures might take place. Clearly, the sympathy of the creators is with the rich spiritual color of Indian philosophy of flesh-friendly (to a point) God realization, as opposed to the flat colorless world of the uptight, wrapped-up, straight, "tight-assed" Westerner, who, if he but knew it, had all this color bottled up inside him. We see he is leaning slightly eastward. The music likewise pits Western tracks, including an excellent Beatles manqué instrumental called "Party Seacombe" featuring John Barham (piano), Colin Manley (guitar), Edward Antony Ashton (organ), Philip Rogers (bass), and Ron Dyke (drums), against the sparkling, moody, erotic, sometimes meditative, simply conceived Indian tracks. The album grows on you and is easily loved, though at the time it is to be suspected there was little appetite for George apart from the other fab three, and little faith in George as a "film composer." Such is the judgment of the world, but if we look into the spiritual meaning of the Sixties, we can hardly avoid this brave vinyl outpost of a movement that still resonates strongly, namely, the absorption into the West of spiritual philosophies from cultures the West once regarded with suspicion, hostility, even fear. *Wonderwall,* the album at least, is a lighthouse in this respect. The film is enjoyable too. Where else will you see Jane Birkin accoutered in beauty like the night as Botticelli's *Primavera?* Well worth the price of a ticket, if you don't mind climbing a wall first.

One interesting feature of *Wonderwall* is that there is little attempt at fusion of Indian and Western styles, as Harrison and Lennon and McCartney implied on "Norwegian Wood" (1965) in that the song's refrain is played by Harrison on sitar, while "Love You Too" (on *Revolver,* 1966) is a fusion piece played on Indian instruments. Indian scales would affect Harrison's guitar style in its rhythms and microtonal glissandi, emphasized with "slide" playing in years to come, but the conclusion musically in *Wonderwall* seems to be "never the twain shall meet" or very seldom anyway, as the album cover implies, with, yet, an optimistic hint of a future when they would.

Fusion was always risky. It would be jazz trumpeter and composer Miles Davis (1926–1991) who would undertake some of the most daring fusion music in the decade, a road first embarked upon in hints on Davis's much-loved album, *In a Silent Way,* released in July 1969. The album wasn't jazz as jazz fans were used to. It didn't swing and was dominated by electric sounds: electric piano played by Chick Corea and Herbie Hancock, John McLaughlin's electric guitar, and the organ of Joe Zawinul. Today it is easily accommodated as superbly inventive, even spiritually meditative ambient music, or even "chill-out" bliss. Davis seems to be trying to find a way of expressing in music the spiritual quality of silence, abstracting from that deep silence its music, rendering the music a symbol of that idea. At the time its still-lake rippling coolness divided critics. Some jazz critics resented the electric sheen and wave in a manner akin to folkies who despised Bob Dylan's switch to raucous electric guitar in 1965, while rock critics recognized the significance of a leading jazz innovator opening an ear to the soundscapes of rock in a *jazz vs. rock* cold war that had become entrenched on "never the twain shall meet" lines. Arguably, this already betokens a new spirit coming into the music scene, a relaxation of genres and of musical snobbery in a growing mood of universality and common awareness. *The twain must meet. . . .* The mean interpretation, however, was based on the fact that sales of jazz and swing records had slumped to relatively pitiful levels in the wake of the British pop invasion that began in 1964, and Davis's tolerances might look to determined jazz purists like capitulation to market trends, in a similar manner to great middle-of-the-road arrangers such as Ray Conniff and Percy Faith having to mine some of the weaker pop compositions in order to keep their orchestra and singer albums abreast of the market.

In a Silent Way still garners substantial fans, so it would appear Davis's faith in the new direction has been vindicated. Music wins. The album is often praised for its spiritual qualities, though it is difficult to divine what this might really mean. Davis himself was not a "believer" though he said on one occasion that Islam seemed to him at the time a religion that made sense, a view that one can hardly separate from the race politics of the period and the religious commitments of fellow musicians. However, spiritual music need on no account be denominational; indeed, in the late Sixties, the idea of *spiritual fusion* was already in the air. Jimi Hendrix, who was making an impact on jazz's avant-garde on account of his virtuosity, imaginative range, and cool-ness, was talking about his "Electric Church" to inspire universalist, and God-aware transreligious togetherness in 1969. Going to the moon was raising sights. Miles Davis's ambition in this direction would in late '69 reach its apogee with his no-holds-barred fusion double-album ses-sions for *Bitches Brew,* released in 1970, whose powerful sound feels like a new decade has been born out of its predecessor, like the Egyptian god Set, in the form of a desert hare tearing himself from his mother's womb with eyes wide open in the night.

Perhaps Miles Davis's sympathy for what he knew as Islam had something to do with a considerably more directly spiritually inspired album, that of John Coltrane's *A Love Supreme,* released in early 1965, a major moment in Sixties jazz, and the musical incarnation of a pro-found spiritual experience of redemption. In 1957, Coltrane had left Miles Davis's outfit to join Thelonious Monk's band where he extended his saxophonic ecstasies to new heights, but was unable to surmount his addictions to smack and booze. In 1964 Coltrane experienced a direct, personal vision of God that truly swept his soul clean of sickness and doubt, and he went to work on his solo work *A Love Supreme* as a testi-mony to that experience.

Coltrane's epiphany has been linked to the Ahmadiyya sect, as much as to his Methodist upbringing. The sect bases its beliefs on the appearance in the likeness of Jesus, as followers believe, of Punjabi Muslim, Mirza Ghulam Ahmad (1835–1908). Ahmad declared him-self the promised Islamic redeemer to herald the end of time by reveal-ing the spirit of authentic, primitive Islam as a peaceful community, dedicated to eradicating fanatical beliefs and misconceptions, ending religious wars, and sowing the seeds of a truer understanding of the faith, which new understanding would anathematize bloodshed and promote justice and good moral living. Ahmadi missionaries reached U.S. cities, and after World War II numerous jazz musicians embraced Ahmadi Islam. When Coltrane arrived in Philadelphia in 1943 he was struck by Islam's presence among the musicians. His drummer on *A Love Supreme,* McCoy Tyner (Suleiman Saud) was one of a number of Muslims Coltrane played with. Coltrane's prayer to the "gracious and

Fig. 16.5. John Coltrane, jazz saxophonist extraordinaire, 1963.

merciful" God on the liner notes has suggested to Muslim commentators a Koranic idiom. Coltrane's wife, Naima Grubbs, was an observant Muslim, so he had plenty of opportunity to absorb Muslim devotional inflections.

In the four movements of the thirty-two-minute piece— "Acknowledgement," "Resolution," "Pursuance," and "Psalm"—*A Love Supreme* expressed Coltrane's new vision, a vision that had broken his drug and alcohol dependencies and brought him into the light of the love of the supreme God. It is surely significant that the power of the message of *A Love Supreme* should express the supremacy of Love, not of any specific denomination. People of all faiths, and none, can find faith in the love celebrated by the music of John Coltrane. A universalist spiritual vision is surely a component in the spiritual meaning of the 1960s.

By the mid- to late Sixties, at least in terms of sales and popularity, rock had seen off jazz as surely as Cain had slugged Abel. Young

Fig. 16.6.
Leonard Bernstein (1918–1990).
Photo by Jack Mitchell.

audiences just weren't taking to it; jazz critics became defensive, or proudly remote. Similar remarks may be made of the unbridgeable chasm that divided rock, jazz, and orchestral classical music, which—with very notable exceptions such as Leonard Bernstein who in 1967 publicly confessed admiration for the *best* of pop,* as well he might after the youth-oriented triumph of his 1957 musical *West Side Story,* brought to the screen in 1961—simply looked the other way, or looked down their noses a very long way on "three chord wonders" and their untrained, ungroomed, teenage-daughter-threatening ilk. On national television, Bernstein taunted his generation (he was born in 1918) for being square and putting their bigoted heads in a sand that was inexorably shifting in pop's creative direction. Middle-of-the-road popular orchestras needed no strictures from the New York Philharmonic's star conductor. They could not afford to ape the snootiness of the conservatory snobs, as we shall see in the next chapter. They had to embrace pop, even some of its weaker, shallower strains, or else lose out.

Sir George Martin's comments above about John Barry being the "classical music of today" in Barry's adherence to orchestrated melodic

---

*Bernstein made his point eloquently on the CBS News Special *Inside Pop: The Rock Revolution,* broadcast in April 1967 where he quoted Bob Dylan's jibe that ordinary Americans did not know what was really happening, *"Do you,* Mr. Jones?" Respected composer Bernstein particularly singled out Brian Wilson's "Surf's Up" as worthy of comparison with the musical inventiveness of Mozart: a remarkable coup for the Beach Boys, and pop in general.

Fig. 16.7. Brian Wilson of the Beach Boys, circa 1964.

values might suggest new compositions of "pure" orchestral classical music had died the death in the Sixties. That is not entirely the case, of course.

Leonard Bernstein's busy conducting career left him little time for composition in the Sixties, but he still found cause to write the Kaddish Symphony (1963), dedicated to the late president John Kennedy, and based on a synagogue prayer uttered at services for the dead. Bernstein wrote his own text that grappled with the threat to his faith the assassination posed. First performed in Tel Aviv by the Israel Philharmonic Orchestra on December 10, 1963, the Kaddish Symphony brings music from the edge of despair, while Bernstein's *Chichester Psalms,* also Jewish in inspiration, invokes more serene moods of traditional faith as the voice of the boy treble or countertenor is intended as that of the boy David, and conveys his clear relationship with God. Though commissioned for the Southern Cathedrals Festival 1965, in England, it received its first performance in New York in July of that tumultuous year.

Igor Stravinsky (1882–1971) enjoyed a final decade with uncharacteristic interest in music with an explicitly spiritual textual source.

He would have earned no marks from his old friend Rózsa, however, for Stravinsky employed what to Rózsa was a mode of the devil, dodecaphony (or twelve-tone techniques) and other modernist innovations both for his *A Sermon, a Narrative and a Prayer* (1961) and *The Flood* (1962), which combines texts from England's York and Chester Mystery Plays with passages from Genesis.

Herbert Howells (1892–1983), England's Anglican composer of chiefly choral works, gave the Sixties a choral masterpiece in the form of the motet *Take Him Earth, for Cherishing*. He who was to be cherished was John F. Kennedy and the work was first performed by the choir of St. George's Cathedral, Kingston, Ontario, as a tribute to the late president on November 22, 1964.

English composer Benjamin Britten (1913–1976) did not lack ambition. In his youth, he wished to be the fourth *B* after Beethoven, Bach, and Brahms, and with the passage of time, his reputation as a composer in the first class now seems assured. Britten composed a number of religious-sounding works in the 1960s, that is, the themes are taken from the realm of the Bible and liturgical practice, though the musical interest of Britten seems to be predominantly concerned with formal

Fig. 16.8. Benjamin Britten (1913–1976).

beauty and personally expressive musical development rather than conveying any explicitly spiritual message of the composer's experience. However, if Plato is right that we find the divine in truth, beauty, and goodness, then Britten's music may well open a path to spiritual experience for listeners through such beauty, truth, or goodness that may be located in Britten's works.

Britten wrote three *Parables for Church Performance. Curlew River* (1964), based on a Japanese Noh play was turned by William Plomer's libretto into a Christian parable concerning an Abbot, the Spirit of a Boy, a Traveler, a Ferryman, and a Madwoman. The Ferryman does not wish to carry the Madwoman across the Curlew River but in the conflict over who may travel, the Madwoman reveals the loss of a son, who it turns out was buried nearby, leaving a message of faith and hope of remembrance.

The work was for a small ensemble, including harp, horn, viola, organ, double bass, and flute, and the voices of the protagonists. Likewise, *The Burning Fiery Furnace* (1966) tells the story of the Hebrew boys whom the Babylonian king Nebuchadnezzar sends to the fiery furnace in the book of Daniel. Like *Curlew River,* a homosexual subtext has been discerned in Britten and Plomer's treatment of the story, as might also be present in the third parable, *The Prodigal Son* (1968) for the son who leaves the father, taking his inheritance, does so to satisfy his most "secret longings," and having lost his inheritance, returns and is forgiven his folly.

Leonard Bernstein observed that within Britten's music was something very dark. He seemed in the depth of himself to be in a place without spiritual light. Who can say? One cannot leave Britten in the Sixties without referring to his attempt to convey the *Songs and Proverbs of William Blake,* a song cycle composed in 1965 and consisting of the words of one of the most obviously spiritually enlightened artists of all time. Premiered in a performance featuring Dietrich Fischer-Dieskau given at the Aldeburgh Festival in England in June 1965, *Times* music critic William Mann (who had recognized Lennon and McCartney as the best songwriters of 1963) reckoned Britten's approach would in time be judged his best "and most subtle" song cycle, while the *Daily Telegraph*'s John Warrack felt Britten, through confrontation with Blake, had come to terms "with the darkness and sense of cruelty" that had always stalked his art. Opinions, naturally, differ.

It was a great shock to hear the news in November 2013 that Sir John Kenneth Tavener, born in 1944, had died, for it did not seem at all long since the twenty-four-year-old composer had been hailed in 1968 as a young musical prodigy. The British *Guardian* called him "the musical discovery of the year," an opinion lent extra force by a *Times* critic who declared Tavener "among the very best known and regarded composers of his generation." And it was not only the established press who sat up and took notice of this composer dedicated to spiritual values and tradition. When Beatle Ringo Starr heard Tavener's 1968 choral and orchestral composition *The Whale,* he enthusiastically recommended it to the group's Apple label, securing Tavener's first record contract and record release—in 1970.

My wife, Joanna, recalls how during her childhood when her parents ran the Seaford Head Hotel on England's south coast, by the famous Seven Sisters cliffs, John Tavener would arrive in flowing clothes, with his long Renaissance hair and a group of beautiful young women who would gather round him as he sat at the hotel piano, composing and entertaining all fortunate enough to be present.

Fig. 16.9. Composer John Tavener (1944–2013).

The Whale, a cantata loosely based on the biblical story of Jonah and the Whale, was first given its full treatment at London's Queen Elizabeth Hall on January 24, 1968. In August 1969 it was heard at the Albert Hall Proms. There was a blend of whimsical amusement and some powerful choral passages that marked out an original composer whose first inspirations came from Mozart's *The Magic Flute* and Stravinsky's *Canticum Sacrum,* which he heard aged twelve.

In 1961 Tavener's unwavering sense of the presence of God found outlet as choirmaster and organist at the church of Saint John, a Presbyterian church in Islington, London (he would convert to the Russian Orthodox Church in 1977). While Tavener's greatest spiritual, religious works lay ahead to be unfolded from his inner scroll from the 1970s onward, his sensibilities were undoubtedly touched by the liberties of mind to be enjoyed in the Sixties. Tavener was perhaps unusual in that he found he could find the liberty of spirit he sought, not primarily in imported or exotic spiritual traditions, but in a deep feeling for the spiritual Christianity planted in the British Isles since the time of the Celtic church, which church, curiously in tune with nature, emerged while civilization was battered by the violence and ignorance of the Dark Ages. Tavener recognized that in his own time a new "dark age" was raging, that of spiritually blind materialism, and he resolutely set his genius for music against the tide. In this sense perhaps we can see why he asked his listeners to think of the great old monster of the sea, the whale, who, surrounded by the dark terror of the waves, gave home and comfort to the Lord's reluctant prophet, Jonah. Tavener's cantata is not reluctant to give a very scientific and commercial list of all the material products that are now extracted for money from the great whales, sentinels of the ocean's divine mystery.

The Whale was not Tavener's first work. In 1961, aged seventeen, he had written a musical setting for the Credo, the basic statement of Christian belief. *Genesis* followed in 1962, the same year in which he set *Three Holy Sonnets of John Donne* to music. Dean of Saint Paul's in the time of King James I, the spiritually minded Donne gave us the line "No man is an island, entire of himself." In 1965 Tavener wrote his first cantata, *Cain and Abel.*

John Tavener sought spiritual meaning in the 1960s, and he found it in spiritual traditions of devotion and of composition; he found it in himself, and in his gifts, and I think also, he found it in the buoyant, playful spirit of his times, despite its many warning shadows and erosions. For him, I suspect, the spiritual meaning of the Sixties would be no more than what had given spiritual meaning to human beings through all time, awareness of God, and the freedom Tavener believed God has given us to create, and to create freely, whether striving with God's mystery on land, or in the belly of the whale.

SEVENTEEN

What the World Needs Now Is Love

The Spirit in Pop Music

Where do I begin? Well, not with "Where Do I Begin?" for a start! Andy Williams's version of Francis Lai and Carl Sigman's song only hit the top ten with the success of *Love Story* in 1970, so just misses our boat (and trains and planes), though it's unlikely the writers realized the "Sixties" were over, such was the momentum accrued during the previous decade of romantic hits, and "Where Do I Begin?" is very much in the neo-troubadour mode of the period, close cousin to Oscarwinning "The Windmills of Your Mind" composed by Michel Legrand with symbolist-surreal lyrics by Alan and Marilyn Bergman, sung memorably in deadpan fashion by Rex Harrison's handsome son Noel in polo-neck sweater, hipster drainpipes, and Chelsea boots in 1968. *Ah!* Now we're getting it. . . . There was *something* about pop music in the Sixties, wasn't there? *Something even nonbelievers can believe in?* So went Hal David's elevated lyric to "Alfie" (1966). And the moment I write Hal David, I invoke his partner, Burt Bacharach.

When I began making notes for this chapter on the Spirit in Sixties pop, the first thing I wrote was: "Anything by Burt Bacharach!" I sometimes think this wondrous star of modern music was behind the whole thing. Burt Bacharach (b. 1928) and Hal David (1921–2012) are

Fig. 17.1. Burt Bacharach and Hal David

indelibly part of some of my, and perhaps your, earliest and happiest memories.

I remember being taken into the big city of Birmingham (England) in the sunny spring of 1964. The city center was being knocked down and rebuilt in the unremitting modern style. It seemed there were cranes and busy builders and buses everywhere. It all felt dizzyingly new. I recall pointing out to my lovely mummy (I was not yet four) the first man in a turban I'd ever seen; such were rarities in those days! Despite destroying a fine railway station and some grand Victorian buildings, the atmosphere amid demolition and construction was strikingly uplifting. It really was. It felt like there was a great cleansing going on, all upbeat and skyward, bright and hopeful, as if the shadows of the last war were at last finally fleeing from the skies like film from our eyes. Away with dark, blackened sites, covered with soot and grime, and up with skirts rising in accordance with Mary Quant's inspiration and London fashion's futurism. Despite recent political scandals wherein two exceptional whores, just by being themselves, had shown up the seediness and banality of Britain's post-Suez goulash of an establishment,* the confidence of working people was rising; they had a bit more buying power, with expectation of more. There was practically full employment. All of this fresh, bursting optimism, with barely a tinge of cynicism, would soon

---

*The "Profumo Scandal" of 1963, in which a senior British minister was discovered to have been sleeping with a girl who was also sleeping with an official of London's Soviet Embassy. The scandal was a factor in the 1964 election victory of the Labor Party and a return to socialist dogmas after thirteen years of Conservative rule.

have its own song. Petula Clark would sing and swing to Tony Hatch's super-buoyant, super-catchy "Downtown" in November. Hatch got his inspiration that autumn in Manhattan, seeking new songs and heading downtown toward Battery Park, buzzing with a pulsing, positive atmosphere (akin perhaps to that I felt in distant Birmingham). Hatch recalled standing on the corner of 48th Street when the melody hit him: "When you're alone and life is making you lonely, you can always go . . . Downtown!" There was hope, even on the streets, and nothing quite like this thoroughly modern, secular, sexy atmosphere had been felt since Berlin bloomed briefly into modernism in the late Weimar period 1928–1931.

I recall distinctly getting off the Midland Red bus at the trip's end outside a big pub called the Fox & Dogs in Four Oaks, Sutton Coldfield, and looking into a brown paper bag in which was secreted Mum's principal purchase, made in one of those great old record stores in Corporation Street where you could hear the music in a private booth as a prelude to possible purchase. It was a 45-rpm recording with a garish red and yellow label, topped by the words *Pye International*. Burt Bacharach and Hal David's hit "Walk On By," backed with the sublime "Any Old Time of the Day," was released in the United States and the United Kingdom in April 1964 and made the top ten in both countries. Mum was one of the first to delight in the fabulous melody and exquisite voice of Dionne Warwick, a devotion to top-flight quality

Fig. 17.2. Singer Dionne Warwick (b. 1940).

that lasted to the end of Mum's life, and which enlivens mine today. Mum adored that stylish, sophisticated, tuneful, original, and very *black* sound. Was it the music, the lyrics, the singing, backing harmonies, the trumpet solo, the insistent piano refrain on the chorus? It was everything. It was new and it was great. And it had something other songs of the time just didn't have. It had Hal David's feel for a spiritually meaningful, clearly expressed lyric and Burt Bacharach's depth of musical knowledge, experience, and God-given originality.

One only has to look at the chords to see the difference. It starts with a minor seventh. The first refrain of the plaintive cry (that really means its opposite) "Walk on by" takes us from a major chord to another minor seventh, sad enough one might feel, until the killer moment, when on "I break down and *cry*," we fall from a strong C-major down to a yearning, grieving, melancholy, nostalgic F-major seventh, up to a flattened major chord, then back down, defeated, to the bittersweetness, happiness-robbing major seventh. "Don't stop" cries Dionne, wishing he, the man she loves, *would* stop. Or the pain would stop, but to lose the pain, would be to lose the feeling, and it's the sense of loss that keeps the love alive. Despite the rich, dark bluesy harmonies, this almost hopeless love is not the kind of love you find in regular blues songs; the subtleties are French, very French, and while the poetic lyrical background evokes the Languedoc troubadours of the twelfth and thirteenth centuries, the musical background takes us right back to the Occult Paris of the late 1880s and early 1890s when Claude Debussy and Erik Satie were baptized in gnostic Hermetism at Edmond Bailly's *Librairie de l'Art Indépendant* in Paris's Rue de la Chaussée d'Antin.*

Born in Kansas City, raised in Forest Hills, New York, but truly coming alive in the presence of music, Bacharach studied music for three years at Montreal's McGill University. Biographies of Bacharach tend to stress Bacharach's huge interest in the happening jazz of Charlie Parker and Dizzy Gillespie in New York in the 1940s and early '50s, frequently attributing Bacharach's chordal harmonies to extensive use

---

*See the chapter "Satie and Debussy: Moved by the Gnosis" in my book, *Occult Paris: The Lost Magic of the Belle Époque.*

of sixths, dominant sevenths, minor sevenths, and ninths in modern jazz, that is, the "cool" sounds of laid-back and swinging romance with the ample allowance for the improvisation such chord progressions and alternations suggest. But the critical components of Bacharach's musical universe constellated principally in the presence of two remarkable teachers.

The Czech Bohuslav Martinů (1890–1959) taught at the Mannes School (or conservatory) of Music from 1948–56, while French composer Darius Milhaud (1892–1974) offered his services to California's Music Academy of the West in Montecito, California, founded to advance the cause of modern music in America in 1947. At the end of his second year at McGill, Bacharach attended a summer program with Milhaud at the Academy of the West, shortly before service call-up during the Korean War.* Bacharach was one of five others in the class, studying composition.

Fig. 17.3. Bohuslav Martinů (1890–1959).

---

*While serving, Bacharach would play piano to entertain troops, "pulling things" out of his hat, passed off as "unpublished works by Debussy." (Burt Bacharach, with Robert Greenfield, *Anyone Who Had a Heart,* 26).

Fig. 17.4. Composer Darius Milhaud (1892–1974).

In Paris, during World War I and subsequently, Darius Milhaud had been one of "Les Six": six French composers inspired by Erik Satie to go beyond the musical grip of Debussy and Ravel, but who, nonetheless were profoundly influenced by those composers. When Satie left the young group to "get on with it," they came directly under Jean Cocteau's aegis and applied themselves to avant-garde musical experiments in tune with Cocteau's romantic, symbolist-surrealism and Picasso's outrageous visual daring.

When Bacharach had the good fortune to encounter Milhaud, he was into the twelve-tone music of Schoenberg and pupils Berg and Webern, so when showing his "Sonatina for Violin, Oboe and Piano" to Milhaud, Bacharach was concerned it might fall under the modernist bar since its midsection was very, perhaps too *melodic,* a patent sin in avant-garde circles embracing Schoenberg's tonal experiments as a crux and starting point of modern music. Milhaud reassured Bacharach he should never be afraid of writing a melody he could whistle. Thank God for Milhaud! A true child of Debussy and Ravel, Milhaud could not resist conveying that love to Bacharach with lasting results for the ears and souls of the world.

When Bacharach was discharged from the army he went to live with his parents in Manhattan. He attended concerts given by avant-garde,

Fluxus musician John Cage, and studied at the New School under Henry Cowell, an avant-garde composer who had taught Gershwin when he was young. Bacharach also studied further at the Mannes School of Music, on the Upper East Side, under Bohuslav Martinů.

Like Milhaud, Bohuslav Martinů was also drawn to Debussy and to French modernism. Having been inspired by the spiritual hymns of the Bohemian Brethren, to which mystical Christianity he was inwardly affiliated (as, incidentally, was William Blake's mother), Martinů sought out teacher Albert Roussel (1869–1937), himself inspired to leave a naval career attracted by the symbolist music of the Satie-inspired Debussy and Debussy's follower, Maurice Ravel (1875–1937). Roussel even taught the mature Satie when Satie changed musical course and signed up for traditional studies at the Schola Cantorum of Paris. Roussel was much admired by Les Six.

One thing that united Les Six, Bohuslav Martinů, and Roussel, was an ear to the developmental potential of American jazz, and it is to the mutual influence of French modernism that we can trace much of the tonal development that spurred jazz on to the heights from its original roots in New Orleans, Louis Armstrong, blues, minstrelsy, ragtime, and Negro spirituals at the turn of the twentieth century. The French influence can be clearly heard on Bacharach-favorite Dizzy Gillespie's "Dizzy's Business" (1956), which ends with a major seventh with a root on G. While Bacharach's repeated employment of the aching major seventh, which takes us into richer and deeper melancholy romantic territory than the usual dominant sevenths of blues, was less frequently heard in jazz, Bacharach embraced it, along with other experiments in chord structure pioneered and developed by Erik Satie (whose famous *Gymnopédies* represents an apotheosis of the major seventh), Claude Debussy, and Maurice Ravel. Without detracting from the rhythmic essence of jazz and pop by embracing all of Debussy's experiments in pentatonic modes, medieval chants, inexact harmonic parallelism, tempo, and transposition techniques, one nonetheless feels a background echo of their presence in the way Bacharach's songs create a world of feeling out of the *loss* experienced by those recounting their woes through Hal David's lyrics, which, like the troubadours, betoken

what my mother would call "the religion of the heart," and the troubadours themselves called the *fin'amor,* or fine love. The rebirth of this
great love is the keynote of the cream of Sixties popular music. Its special tonalities were redefined by Bacharach's genius in the inspired way
he combined his unforgettable melodies with his musical knowledge:
knowledge, for example, of the double harmonic scale,* major and
minor sixths, sevenths, and ninths, and from Ravel particularly, added
notes of major and minor seconds, fourths, and sixths. The effect in
Debussy and Ravel is one of evoking through music mysterious passages *without resolution.* The gnostic background to this unresolved
yearning sense involves penetrating a mystery, or exposing a symbol of
a hidden idea. We find in these composers and those they influenced a
factor of the life of the heart where love is the path to the heart, and the
heart is the elusive (and often unresolved) path to love, a path fragile,
close always to tragedy, as well as to exaltation recollected in melancholy. The loss of this path is deemed unbearable. The pain invokes a
mystery, hence Oscar Wilde could say: "Where there is sorrow, there
is holy ground." In Hal David's lyric for "Loneliness Remembers," for
example, we find the last note unresolved on the final line: "first came
the pleasure, then the pain. . . ." Unharmonic tones hanging unresolved
are frequent guests at the Debussy and Ravel symbolist table, and I suspect Bacharach is closer philosophically here to the symbolism of those
composers than those who still labor under the mistaken misapprehen-
sion that they were "impressionists." Bacharach is not giving us nature
paintings or nature descriptions, still less, landscapes. His territory is
the mystery of love and the life of the heart in its heights and depths,
and in its tendency to linger after the flame has been extinguished; only
loss is present in loss, but for the memory of what is lost.

One of the most well known and popular songs of Bacharach and
David is of course the very great "This Guy's in Love" (1968). First
brought to the top sensitively sung by Herb Alpert, there is luxuriant

---

*Tonic, minor second, major third, perfect fourth and fifth, minor sixth, *major seventh*:
pioneered in Debussy's *La Soirée dans Grenade* (from *Étampes,* 1903), suggestive of the
Moorish (Arab) heritage that influenced the music and character of the *cansos* of the
medieval troubadours.

use of the major seventh, with its hanging note, a note either a tone or semitone down from the root note of the chord, but heard as an unresolvable extra pang, suggesting the depth of the surrender to love, a sacrifice of false ego, the letting go that is not only the only way to rise in love, but is also a spiritual message: that in order to obtain the salvation of love, we must let go. Leap, as it were, into the void, unknowing. In musical terms, the extra tone of the major seventh also betokens an ascent beyond the ordinary harmony and formal stability of the world, a kind of breakthrough into the beyond that can work two ways, but that is somehow bound up with tragedy and elusive dream. In this world, love is lost. If not love, then the object of love must be lost, *unless.* . . . And on that unresolvable "unless" our deepest, pained hope may reside, that the spirit may go beyond the limits of this world and what is known. The true lover is thus necessarily *contra mundum,* and in understanding this mystery we can begin to grasp the sometimes-hidden Spirit in Sixties pop, even though its most audible aspects express to most people's ears a simple spirit of fun and freedom.

Hal David was always especially proud of his lyric to "Alfie," associated with the famous movie role incarnated in its quip-laden amorality by Michael Caine, who finds out the hard way the difference between love and sex, responsibility and sin, in the eponymous movie of 1966. Here the ethic of love finds its explicit moral, but above all, spiritual message based on spiritual values of eternal validity:

> *What's it all about, Alfie?*
> *Is it just for the moment we live?*
> *What's it all about when you sort it out, Alfie?*
> *Are we meant to take more than we give?*
> *Or are we meant to be kind?*
> *And if only fools are kind, Alfie,*
> *Then I guess it's wise to be cruel.*
>
> . . .
>
> *As sure as I believe there's a heaven above, Alfie,*
> *I know there's something much more,*

Something even non-believers can believe in.
I believe in love, Alfie.
Without true love we just exist, Alfie.

Something even non-believers can believe in . . . Sixties pop offered the gift of love to everyone. No mean feat. Some have been crucified for less.

Of course, one could say the same, if one wished to, about popular music in practically any decade of the twentieth century. Spiritual things are spiritually discerned, and discernment is not given to all in like, or necessarily any, measure. I asked two acquaintances recently over a pint what the Sixties meant to them (they were both in their twenties and thirties during the decade). The older one said it meant free availability of sex, a time when you could go to a particular pub in Sutton Coldfield on a Friday night and leave with someone else's wife while the wife's husband also took his pick, or was chosen, by someone else's wife. No strings. That happened in well-heeled provincial England, and one may be sure, in parts of the States and elsewhere too. But it wouldn't be what the decade evoked in memory to most people. The other acquaintance, asked the same question, said, "I suppose it would be Peace and Love. That really was new, and different from what went before. I grew my hair." *Beauty is in the eye of the beholder.* We see what we are.

I asked another friend, this time about the extraordinary range of good-to-great pop melodies that seem astounding in number and range for the period. He was at Eton College aged about fifteen in the mid-Sixties and the memory that sprang to his mind was the immensely enticing sight, caught through a college window, of a very striking, hippie-dressed Marianne Faithfull entering the college with ex-college member Jeremy Clyde, who, with Chad Stuart, formed the popular folk duo Chad & Jeremy. Anyhow, my friend, on the subject of spiritual meaning with regard to the decade, remarked that the technical standard of music experimentation rose so phenomenally quickly over the decade that it was difficult to explain unless one attributed it to some collective sense of something, well, something extraordinary, that seemed suddenly to turn rock 'n' roll strummers into experimental virtuosi, or something like, almost overnight: a surge of ambition, imagination, effort, and confidence. The case of the Beatles was a case in point. Every one of their singles represented some kind of step forward from the one previous to it, the same with their ten or so albums EMI-Capitol released between 1963 and 1969. In October 1965, the Who belted out a witty, pounding but sad-messaged, jangling, stormy rocker about what it was like to be of "My Generation." Four years later, they released a rock opera called *Tommy:* a double album with more songs than *Camelot.* Anyone can hear the difference in musical standards and melodic ambition of top group music, apparently ever rising in sophistication from year to year.

A great deal has been written about how such a perceived rise in quality occurred, not that everyone would agree that *pop* as pop needs to be anything more than popular. Some have bemoaned pretentiousness and grandiose ineptness entering the pop field as less talented performers and writers tried to compete with sophisticated exercises in complexity. There has always been cleverness and sophistication in pop music. The Thirties and Forties stand strongly out as a mine of brilliant songs that have their own passionate devotees fully justified in their choices.

There is a strong case for positing the influence of key arrivals that created and stimulated an intense competition for the top spot with all the rewards attendant thereon: money, girls and boys, social advancement, houses, cars, expensive holidays, new experiences, freedom to fly, fashionable clothes, media appearances, fame, personal fulfillment, and so on. No doubt Bob Dylan's extraordinary lyrical inventiveness, which he has recently attributed to some undefined, unrepeatable "penetrating magic"* that he no longer feels able to practice, had its effect on the Beatles. The group was already into Dylan's *Freewheelin'* album when they met, and got high with its composer in 1964, but the New York Hotel meeting seems to have struck a chord in Lennon and McCartney that *here* was the real competition. John started wearing Dylan's style

---

*2004 interview; YouTube "Whatever Happened to Bob Dylan?" CBS News interview with Ed Bradley (www.youtube.com/watch?v=2WENXCJqpDk).

of hat and his songs embarked on ever more personal themes than hitherto; writing them became more painful. McCartney's writing also shot forward in depth and range, and many have suspected that what Bob shared with the Boys in New York was not only his time and talent, but his potent stash of pot and perhaps an additional inspirational clue or two. Brian Wilson also attributed his breakthrough when working on the Beach Boys' *Pet Sounds* album in 1966—in particular the song "Caroline, No"*—to a potent ingestion of marijuana that let open the floodgates of a new sensation of creativity, combined with a released will to create and an openness to celestial melody. Cannabin (hemp resin smoked or digested) has long been linked to novel, even arguably mystical states of awareness, exaggerating the conscious mind's perception of its own presence and trains of logic, as well as of sights and sounds, that on uncultured or weakened soil can simply generate delusions, hallucination, and in worst cases, a root of mental disease. The problem, as with all stimulants, is one of diminishing returns, rise in tolerance, and eventually psychological addiction such that the "straight" world becomes burdensome, and the desire to retreat into the cocoon of hash-induced interiority becomes for many users all too irresistible. In initial stages of acquaintance, however, the drug can act as a turn-on to a sense of heightened being and creativity, *if the capacity exists in the first place.* Ingestion might make the mind become aware of the intricacies of banal, or even exalted thought process, or the wonder of formerly unperceived links of mind, which may seem a revelation to begin with, but the drug's active ingredient (THC, or tetrahydrocannabinol) reduces greatly the capacity for intricate physical accomplishments, like playing guitar, piano, or any other instrument, save, arguably, percussion, and that is debatable. Coherent speech may also run at a significant deficit. Intoxication can also render the mildly amusing into the heights of unrestrained hilarity verging on, or over, the delirious and absurd. Users rarely laugh at themselves, though, I've noticed.

When cultural and commercial competition heats up, and the gen-

---

*Written with Tony Asher, and originally a solo single released in March 1966, then put on the Beach Boys album *Pet Sounds* as a finale.

eral desire advances in a sense of "space" (which did exist in the Sixties), advances in mental and spiritual expression are surely inevitable. With greater success comes more financial support, and the snowball keeps rolling. Another leap in popular music occurred with the arrival from the United States in London in 1966 of Jimi Hendrix (1942–1970). When Eric Clapton first heard the Seattle-born freak genius play, he felt like giving up and locking his "axe" away. Luckily for Clapton, Hendrix was an admirer of Clapton's tough, tight, fluent, and attentive blues and R & B style and enjoyed jamming with the guitarist whose more idolatrous followers thought was "God," presumably because that's how they thought the high-speed playing made them feel in the heat, light, and sweat of a Yardbirds or Cream performance; rock was never closer to God perhaps than in this hothouse period of galloping dreams, delirium, and innocence.

And then there was acid (we'll come to it in more detail in due course), and its musical effects. Lennon and Harrison and their wives took it by accident, so the story goes, in 1965, and it was a while before the two astonished Beatles took it again, but by mid-1966 the men were well into it, as were some of the other groups. Psychedelia brought

Fig. 17.5. The Jimi Hendrix Experience, 1968.

new strangeness, color, excess, vision, occasional genius and surrealistic whimsy, and much else into the popular music scene. How could you express musically what you'd experienced on these apparently other-worldly stimulants? This challenge too would stoke creativity to new heights and down potholes, especially as the psychedelic highs were extremely close to what many users were led to think were spiritual experiences. Though there was a duality: hell might also open its dis-locating oblivion to the unwary and the unfortunate formerly unaccus-tomed to unadulterated mental terror. But there was the hint of heaven too. From that point, the sky was no longer the limit (nor the earth for that matter). Paul McCartney would say with regard to *Sgt. Pepper* that the group had discovered in process of its making that there were no rules, no limits. No Limits. Get that? Everything was possible. Freedom can be marvelous, and very risky if you lack experience to handle it. But then, did not the era have a magic card that made the impossible pos-sible? And was that not Love, coupled with a willed spirit of openness? You could get by, and high, with a little help from your friends, so long, that is, as they knew they were "beautiful people." For a season, a new, if yet exclusive, collective identity was insulating the psychic adventur-ing. And all you had to be, to join, was to be young, and to be hip to it all. If you were older and hip, you could join too, preferably with a few adjustments to clothing and hairline, lest you be seen as a reactionary. To the working classes of course, still in a realm of sweat and physical endurance, it could all look quite fay, as well as remote.

There is in the psychedelic movement, with its popular wing in flower power emerging suddenly in late '66 and '67, the semblance of a spiritual movement.

It is not simply the case that improvements in pop were only *perceived* to be occurring. Expert musicologists were noticing too. At the end of 1963, William Mann, in the pages of the highly conservative *Times*, heralded Lennon and McCartney as composers of songs as dynamic as Franz Schubert's. This was something, because there was much com-petition for the top spot where songwriting was concerned. Richard Rodgers was still going; so were Lerner and Loewe. So was Lionel Bart with his magnificent success in *Oliver*. And Bacharach and David, of course. Mann had noticed something. It was new. And he heard it first on the Beatles' second album, *With the Beatles*, with its state-of-the-art black-and-white cover (released November 1963, on EMI's Parlophhone label). So many more started to listen to those vaunted "Aeolian cadences" and "pandiatonic clusters" and started to try harder, and get into the swing of the new thing. The progressive drive forward propelled everything onward: surely this was Progress. No one knew where "it" was going, least of all the Beatles, who just kept on running and grinning as if they knew something. And they just kept getting better, with George Martin's deft encouragement and genial creative touches. Never too much, Martin never smothered "the Boys" but listened and suggested and helped, made wonders possible, because those boys were really so instinctively intelligent and had a natural gift for form and beauty, and truthfulness of expression—and sheer, patient-impatient hard work where the music was concerned.

After William Mann came Leonard Bernstein in 1967 as we saw in the last chapter. He singled out "Surf's Up" played by Brian Wilson in 1967 for his (then) unfinished masterpiece, *Smile,* just at the tragic point when a poor, bedevilled Brian was succumbing to surfeit of psychedelic substance in his system, coupled with longstanding personal problems, and perhaps most destructive of his sensitivity of all, the uncompreheding hostility shown to his latest music by several key figures in his entourage, themselves narrow-mindedly worried that the risk-taking new music and especially (to them) odd lyrics would lose them hard-earned cash and status. *Oh ye of little faith!* But Lenny Bernstein told America that pop was now a serious form of music—though not all of it, of course. One forgets how much really bad or banal, or thin, or stupid or second-rate music came out on vinyl throughout the decade, but the best was something else, no doubt of it. And Bernstein advised Americans to get ready for strange things, and do the artists the courtesy of a fair hearing and a graceful welcome. Genius was at work, and it had long hair and might look scruffy or unusual. Artistic Bohemia, which had always represented a refuge, or getaway from straight society, now seemed to be getting back *in*; here was the problem. Unprotestant-like

Bohemianism was seldom welcome; what had most hard-working, normal, conforming families really got to do with such things? Here was the question—and the outrage.

Dylan had brought poetry big-time into popular music, or one might say, *back* into popular music, and the originally folk-based input of meaningful lyrics had a massive galvanizing effect on creativity. Even bad songs tried to sound like they meant something. And the world got to hear of two quiet, or apparently quiet and obviously intense performers from New York, Paul Simon and Art Garfunkel, who listened to everything that was happening, and just started doing their own thing with the folk and the pop, and the poetry and the cold of winter and the rain on the windowpane, and came up with musical atmospheres to rival the *Four Last Songs* of Richard Strauss . . . "A Most Peculiar Man" . . . "The Sound of Silence" . . . "I Am a Rock" . . . "Kathy's Song" . . . "For Emily, Whenever I May Find Her" . . . "America" . . . Sheer, lasting magic.

And the West Coast of America seemed suddenly ablaze with new talent and opportunity. The Beatles and the Beach Boys opened the door for the Doors, hailing from UCLA and beatnik lifestyles in Venice; for the San Francisco groups, for Grace and Janis; for L.A. cool, for the Buffalo Springfield: "Broken Arrow" the first pop song that showed someone (a young Neil Young) knew what Marlon Brando knew about the reality of life for Native Americans. Then, in late 1966, "For What It's Worth": Steven Stills found himself noticing that the police in Hollywood wanted to stop young people with long hair from meeting together on the streets and doing their thing. And suddenly, this whole music and social thing began to find a cause, not just the war, and the antidote of Love, but a spiritual fight with the eternal powers of oppression, the music haters, the ones who wanted to put everything on earth in some kind of uniform, and suppress the free spirit and the color and the joy and all the things you need . . . like Love, Love, Love.

I used to hold to a theory that the previously unheard-of outpouring of so very many fine paeans to Love, with so many unforgettable and distinctive melodies (an original melody is a rarity, more so today, by God), so often sung with sincerity and simplicity and childlike charm, and energy and drive and musical magic, that it was a kind of great spiritual compensation for the sheer numbers, incalculable numbers of young people who had been killed in the mass slaughters of World War II, the lost millions whose unborn, unconceived children were perforce absent from the decade's struggles and festivities. To me, it was like a cloud of spiritual witnesses returning into the hearts and minds of men and women and boys and girls, and saying: "Don't forget us! Live, and Love! Live as we were not permitted to live, and love as we were not permitted to love! Let not our deaths be in vain. We can see you, though you cannot see us. We bring the gifts of heaven closer to you." *Why do birds suddenly appear, every time you are near? Just like me, they long to be, close to you.* . . . I felt this way, I think, because of what I perceived as the extraordinary, that is to say, the sheer *level* of perception and inspiration that was granted to young people, too much for some few, no doubt, who gate-crashed into the spiritual with drugs and found a long headache, or worse.

On further reflection, anyone studying closely the top hits of the *1950s* will see a vibrant, varied music-publishing business operating throughout the world with many wonderful songs that lit up the ordinary loves and wonderful moments of ordinary, wonderful lives. This may be the great function of the pop song. If two people are in love and have truly found one another, perhaps for life, it doesn't matter if they are huddled in a bus stop in a dull-looking city at dusk, or on Waikiki Beach, the feeling is magical, spiritual, and transcends the ordinary world. A great pop song can bring those feelings to life, magnify them even, or just celebrate them. The 1950s had its share of haunting love songs that conjure up those moments, even of lost, much loved, impossible-to-lose partners, friends, relatives. I think of beautiful songs like "You Are My Special Angel" (Jimmy Duncan, 1957) and "Ebb Tide" (Carl Sigman and Robert Maxwell, 1953), among many other gems that would, for example, grace Frank Sinatra's string of highly artistic, often sublime, mood-themed albums recorded for Capitol during that decade.

It is significant that Burt Bacharach first met lyricist Hal David at "Famous Music" in New York's even more famous Brill Building, a streamlined version of the traditional Tin Pan Alley provider of quick, ready-to-wear songs whose United Kingdom equivalent was Denmark Street, by Soho. Hits were, as they say, churned out by talented writers, often compelled to work in cramped conditions to a formula, following lines and fashions. What had worked for an artist last time was deemed a successful formula for the next one, and managers paid songwriters to come up with the goods according to what they thought was public expectation. In the business, a "great song" is a song that makes money. Excellent songs were often overlooked for quite trivial numbers with little or no inspiration, as is the case again today. Bacharach and David wrenched themselves out of this regulation, factorylike system. Bacharach managed to make the leap by getting into the position of producing his own songs. He had the advantage here because he had already worked as a musical arranger, and director, notably for the touring career of top entertainer Marlene Dietrich (1901–1992), and could easily take on the role (John Barry in the United Kingdom occupied a similar position). Once Bacharach started producing, adding his own arrangements and personal touches, the songs began to improve markedly; he could pour more of his own creative spirit into them, and by 1962 the songwriting was well on the way toward the golden era of highly distinctive, classy songs, all of them different, catchy, memorable, meaningful, innovatively arranged to suit the song and the writer, with queues of artists desiring to "cover" them. Once Bacharach and David had found the phenomenally subtle and versatile voice of conservatory-trained Dionne Warwick, they became an industry of their own, the trio releasing their first single "Don't Make Me Over" on Scepter Records in November 1962. It is not surprising that the Beatles first album, *Please Please Me* (March 1963) contained a favorite of John and Paul's, "Baby, It's You" by Bacharach, Luther Dixon, and Mack David, which the group had been performing on stage since it first appeared, sung by the Shirelles in 1961.

John Lennon and Paul McCartney were very aware of the power in America of songwriters who could control their own work, and being "Lennon and McCartney" mattered to them a great deal. It is fascinating to note that their first self-penned single "Love Me Do" was released on October 5, 1962, barely a month before "Don't Make Me Over."

This appears to have been the magic key that set the whole ball rolling. *Originality.* The Beatles went right against the grain of the usual commercial exploitation of groups and singers in the United Kingdom and the United States. They wrote and they performed, and because they could do both, and George Martin allowed them to do both, they did not need to produce their own songs, for they arranged them themselves, with the avuncular presence of George Martin to smooth and augment things from the technical side of studio work. *Originality.* You can't get enough of that word. Once the Beatles started to tap their already developed wellspring of music talent, they just found more and more of it, and with more and more love and success, the well kept filling up, despite the draw. As they received love, they gave love; as they gave love in the form of song, they received love, and the spirit just grew and grew and grew, sensitive to every new development around them, the Beatles had the power to go on. They drank the milk of paradise. Inevitably, once you let the genie of originality, poetry, free creative spirit, out of the bottle, you are going to get, or conjure the spiritual meaning this book is all about. Because the Spirit is within, and if we do not bring it forth, it destroys us. But if we do bring it forth, then you have a spiritual movement, and that is something few grasp, though its effects may be felt as real enough. And, of course as the Beatles, fed on ambrosial love, grew bigger (without succumbing to overwhelming egotism), and their music and lyrics got better, and often more personal, as well as more universal, their example lit up the ambitions of all around them. It is not that their music as such necessarily influenced other music (there was constant reciprocation of styles and technical ideas in the really hothouse period 1962–1967)—though aspects of their style and guitar format were imitated to greater and lesser extents—it was their example, their light, their volume of projection, and the power and success of their ambition that moved mountains and inspired others to create and break out. Even Mick Jagger and Keith Richards have acknowledged how it was the Beatles hit-making example that got them down to composing their own powerful, incisive, dance-stimulating, energy-stacked songs, creating new audiences and even greater international excitement. The competition was healthy and very creative. And that atmosphere affected everybody else in the music and show business worlds, and with the growing power of television, the world shimmered into a new life populated by bright and not-so-bright young things, that for the first time perhaps ever, a lot of older people found themselves wanting to be close to (if not look like), to share in the party and distinguish themselves from those who did not. The change was seismic and inescapable. By 1964 even the dull-looking Labor prime minister, Harold Wilson, wanted to get himself on the bandwagon, handing the Beatles awards, while the next year, on government recommendation, H.M. the Queen presented the group with MBE honors for services to exports. And what they were exporting was courage, energy, brilliance, and love. And love travels very far, especially with an amplifier.

I well remember feeling, when I first heard Bacharach and David's "Do You Know the Way to San José?" sung by Dionne Warwick in 1968, that a world that could produce such freshness, such airy modernity, such open, decent insight and warm sense of good life, that this was a world sensibility that had passed *well beyond* the bestiality of war, and the old ways and bad memories. This was *Music for a New World— How could we go back now?* That sense congealed around 1970–1971 with the assumption that the world had definitively changed, that it had been through something irrevocable. I remember in 1971 when I asked my father to teach me to box, so I could better take care of myself at school and on the street, he said it wouldn't be necessary anymore. The days of having to fight to survive with one's fists were over. Wars that were still occurring about the world seemed obscene, not inevitable; they seemed Neanderthal, not planned and paid for. Perhaps it took the Falklands War, and the Gulf War and the Bosnian War and the whole reactionary disgrace of myopic jihadism to suggest that that sense of a new world was temporary, a delusion perhaps. Even lost forever. And yet, I wonder, can we still hear in some of these songs at sundry moments, other voices, calling us on (not back) still, calling us forth, and forward with love songs, as we may yet march with time as soldiers of love in our imaginations to the tunes of "What a Wonderful World" . . . "A Whiter Shade of Pale" . . . "Feed the Birds" . . . "White Horses"

... "Bewitched" ... "Far from the Home I Love" ... "If Ever I Would Leave You" ... "Blowin' in the Wind" ... "Georgie Girl" ... "We Have All the Time in the World" ... "Like a Rolling Stone" ... "Born Free" ... "Dulcinea" ... "The Impossible Dream" ... "The Look of Love" ... "Raindrops Keep Fallin' on My Head" ... "Voodoo Chile" ... "Me and Bobby McGee" ... "Ferry Cross the Mersey" ... "By the Time I Get to Phoenix" ... "MacArthur Park" ... "Up, Up and Away" ... "Reach Out to Me" ... "Always Something There to Remind Me" ... "A House Is Not a Home" ... "Message to Michael" ... "The Windows of the World" ... "This Boy" ... "Happy Together" ... "Badge" ... "Try a Little Tenderness" ... "We Can Work It Out" ... "House of the Rising Sun" ... "You Only Live Twice" ... "Casino Royale" ... "Windmill in Old Amsterdam" ... "Strangers in the Night" ... "I've Been Good to You" ... "All I Wanna Do" ... "Anna (Go to Him)" ... "Eleanor Rigby" ... "Fool on the Hill" ... "Girl" ... "Those Were the Days" ... "Hey Jude" ... "Play with Fire" ... "As Tears Go By" ... "Sympathy for the Devil" ... "A Groovy Kind of Love" ... "A Day in the Life" ... "Dark Star" ... "White Rabbit" ... "Wives and Lovers" ... "We Love You" ... "Don't Worry, Baby" ... "Tambourine Man" ... "This Wheel's on Fire" ... "Just Like a Woman" ... "The Wind Cries Mary" ... "Both Sides Now" ... "You Don't Have to Say You Love Me" ... "Going Back" ... "Gimme Some Lovin'" ... "In the Ghetto" ... "When the Music's Over" ... "To Sir with Love" ... "Light My Fire" ... "Cabinessence" ... "The Inner Light" ... "On Days Like These" ... "Something" ... "It's Alright, Ma" ... "What's New, Pussycat?" ... "Can't Take My Eyes Off You" ... "Baby, It's You" ... "Music to Watch Girls By" ... "Little Green Apples" ... "For Once in My Life" ... "She Knows Me Too Well" ... "Didn't We?" ... "It's Love That Really Counts" ... "I Love How You Love Me" ...

To name but a few, filled with something even nonbelievers can believe in.

EIGHTEEN

Cinema

One is inclined to be skeptical when people tell you how much better things used to be, whether in the Sixties, or any other time. Sweet sentiment and nostalgia do blind us to things we choose not to remember, or that our minds have suppressed, and exaggerate the delightful fruits so elusively lodged in the past. Like Tantalus, we agonize over what is now out of reach and very naturally feel a deep longing to replace what we cannot return to.

There is another dimension to this whole issue of being placed at a time at any given moment. We are united by time with that from which we are separated. Time cannot be broken so long as it runs. Our deceased loved ones are never more present to us than when we think of them in the past and our presence there binds us to them. Even further than this, we may observe that humankind is always caught between two worlds. There is the world we know, with its comforting regularities and apparent solidity, and there is a less solid world, the world of the mind in its musings and the sense of a deeper world of the numinous and the spiritual of which we know little, and in some cases perhaps, nothing. Criticism of religion will always be at its strongest and most confident when the critic feels he or she can objectify religion, or the spiritual world on which religion subsists. Periods of religious skepticism, it will be noted from a close study of history, transpire when observers feel greater confidence in the material world about them; lodged optimistically in a fulsome *now,* we are loath to concern ourselves with the hereafter or what appear intangible promises and conceptions, and may even come to despise their persistence among others we may wish to dismiss as unworldly fantasists. Conversely, when the world seems less secure, and life upon it less intimately grasped, we are more open to the call of the spiritual, however exotic its manifestations might be. When man is desperate, he will believe in anything resembling a life raft; he may be lucky, it may be just that. Either way, we are influenced by our fundamental feelings of security, or the lack of it, in this world. Looking at one aspect of the issue, John Lennon opined in 1970 that the more pain we're in, the more God we need: a most inconclusive statement if I may say so, but it has its share of truth.

To the spiritual mind, the world appears flimsy, even as Buddhists claim to believe, illusory and is easily objectified and judged. From the worldly perspective, the reverse is the case. Given the two poles, which are unavoidable since we are beings both in the world and not in it, due to our psychological and spiritual nature, and of course the ever-present terrifying fact of our and our loved ones' deaths, the healthiest course must seem to be, on consideration, to steer a midcourse, or balanced path, through this life, offering to each power its due. We know we must surrender the unequal struggle some day.

Denied in some measure by both parties in this struggle, is death. The spiritual mind is inclined to deny ultimate and complete cessation since it is aware of dimensions beyond time and decay, while the materialist with his or her treasures and concerns securely (?) lodged in this world, doesn't like to think about death at all, considering it a baleful encumbrance best not thought about lest the merriment be tarnished at thought of its conclusion; we vainly hope fate will not be fatal. He or she is most likely concerned about some kind of continuity through disposition of goods and property (legacy) and, with today's scientific "excuse" of passing on those genes of which one is apparently made to future generations, a kind of biological "reincarnation" that might satisfy the unimaginative worldling. *Life* only exists this side of the gate, so to speak.

As a corrective to this I should simply like to repeat the conviction of spiritual religion. The Mandaean faith, for example, which seems to owe something of its origins or at least development to John the Baptist, refers to God as "Life" or "the Life," and Life is what counts most. It is God's breath of life (spirit) that is breathed into Adam's nostrils in Genesis, making him a living being. You can express these ideas in scientific, even biological terms if you so desire, but the ancient conviction of our wiser delegates in time is that Life encompasses *all* existence, physical, soulful, spiritual, psychological, temporal, and eternal, and the sole calamity to be feared is spiritual death, which amounts to a refusal of the breath of divine Life. Sadly, much of Western intellectual culture has decided to inflict this horror on itself out of a combination of a depressing interpretation of contemporary scientific theories (though not so to their exponents of course), and disappointment at evils done in this world, often in the name of God, but usually for perceived material or symbolic gains, such as revenge. And one should never forget that our unenlightened species has ever entertained a capacity for sheer antispiritual mischief, and plain, destructive malevolence.

This peroration is, believe me if you will, a necessary preamble to consider the spiritual meaning of cinema in the Sixties, which meaning it obviously shares with cinema as a phenomenon before it.

When we enter a cinematic experience, we do so in the dark, an initiation with kinship to birth: from darkness, light, and life. This is vital to the way cinema works, and is fundamentally different to the relatively lonely TV experience. Cinema belongs to the world of collective as well as individual dream, of the subconscious, even, at its highest phase, of the spirit. It is something that, when it seizes our attention, we surrender to: that strange mechanism defined by Samuel Taylor Coleridge as "suspension of disbelief," something surely akin to religious conviction, though very temporary, even vain, in the case of cinema. In the cinema theater, the screen is the source of light and it enters into us; it becomes the world to us, which is why cinema can be the great escape from problems in the "real world" that beset us. Cinema's world also inhabits our bodies, which are in the dark, suppressing our ordinary body awareness. We feel things that appear to happen on the screen, we forget: forget ourselves as we think ourselves to be, while other dimensions may open to us. In the best films, we meet them halfway as it were, giving and receiving perception, so in co-creating this temporary reality, we may say that we receive but what we give.

When I think of my life in the Sixties, a significant part of that "life" was spent in cinematic abandonment. This out-of-the-ego experience constituted one of the first moral attacks made against cinema when it began its march at the dawn of the twentieth century. Clergy could see that cinema generated congregations, sharing in common experiences, often evoking deep feelings and sensations of transport and ecstasy. It competed for attention, but offered a dream, not a spiritual or even moral and material reality; it distracted from the serious business of life and salvation. This attack is still very much alive in the way that awards are given to films with "improving messages" (often of the most banal, simplistic, and predictable kind when analyzed), even when the films fail to excite audiences. Once the cinema was identified as a devil's tool, it wasn't long before the giant stars on the screens were compared to idols, that is, false gods and goddesses, that when seen as idols, and adored in their unreal reality, obstructed, it was asserted, access to the invisible God whose own *projection* was in the light and darkness of the real world. This was perhaps an unsophisticated reaction to the draw of cinema to the hardworking masses, people longing for some "time out" and who did not want "God" (at least not of the "preachy" kind) following them into the cinema where, under cover of artificial night, one could indulge a fantasy or two, perhaps in company. At least temporarily, cinema permitted interiority of a special kind, the painless transport of the nighttime dreamer, a place of myths, where dreams came true, and joy of life won every time.

Now, it happens that I consider that the world of movies in the 1960s was especially remarkable in range of talent, scope, investment (to begin with), variety, liveliness, spirited experimentation and playfulness, humor, consciousness, and, yes, of meaning. If not entirely with what had passed before it, then certainly with what has passed since that time. But I should not want you to take my word for it.

In the process of thinking about this issue, I remembered my old tea chest, the one with which my family returned to England, after two years spent as immigrants in Australia between November 1966

*Fig. 18.1. Left to right: Jamie, Vic, and Toby at the
Lone Pine Koala Sanctuary, Queensland, Australia, early 1967.*

and November 1968. We arrived in the state of Queensland with $100 Aus., the minimum requirement, soon taken away by sharp salesmen for medical insurance. Dad finally got a job laboring in blistering heat on Queensland Railways (think of Paul Newman in *Cool Hand Luke,* without the chain gang), saving a bit of money for our next leap into the unknown.

In January 1967, we departed a depressed Queensland and headed south by Greyhound bus for Melbourne, in the happier southern-coast state of Victoria. We had nowhere to live and my father had no job. When the bus pulled up to unload us into the unfamiliar city center, early on a Saturday morning, my father said to my mother: "If you haven't found a place to live, and I haven't found a job, by four o'clock this afternoon, we'll go and sit on the bishop of Melbourne's doorstep!"

Dad found a job, and Mum found us a little flat, Eildon Court, in St. Kilda, adjacent to the red-light district, close to the sea, an area full of immigrants, many with concentration-camp numbers tattooed on their arms, and all but a tram ride away from Melbourne's fabulous city center. We were not thinking of the past. We had the spirit of the

Sixties, and very soon we were making memorable trips to Melbourne's (then) dozens of attractive old and new cinemas.

CINEMA AS IT WAS—IN JUST ONE DAY

In my tea chest, Mum had long ago stashed one copy of the the *Sun News Pictorial,* Melbourne, Tuesday, February 20, 1968. And this amazing, faded document, rediscovered so many years later, I'd like to share with you, for the on-the-spot insight it gives us of cinema in the Sixties *as it was really experienced,* not by critics of the nouvelle vague, or of Italian neorealism, or of the trendy avant-garde with confusing talk of cinematic tropes and semiotics so dear to film theorists, but to ordinary, bright-spirited people with high hopes and short pockets.

First, the paper's headline that day: "Night-long Battle in Dandenongs." No, we weren't at war on our doorstep. This was a grueling firefighters' battle against the terrible phenomenon of bushfire that haunts Australian memories. We ourselves lived in Dandenong, and I remember coming out of Dandenong North State School onto David Street the day before to see an immense miles-long plume of black smoke spreading over the Dandenong Ranges (or "Blue Dandenongs"), heading from Ferntree Gully in our direction. Terrifying, but interesting too. That would explain why Mum kept the newspaper, so you have a great, long-forgotten bushfire to thank for this information.

We turn to page 2 of the *Sun:* "4,000 Civilians Killed. Da Nang, Mon[day]. AAP [Australian Associated Press]. Four thousand civilians have been killed and 80,000 made homeless in the five northern provinces of South Vietnam in three weeks of heavy fighting. Military sources said 4,062 civilians had died since the Vietcong began their Tet (new year) offensive on January 30." Next to the story we see a large photo showing a seriously wounded Vietcong, asking for a cigarette from a South Vietnamese soldier: "A wounded Vietnamese looks into the barrel of a machine gun—and at death. Seconds after this picture was taken he was killed by a burst of fire from the machine gun. 'I'll give you death,' shouted the South Vietnamese Marine holding the gun." Australia had her troops in Vietnam, so there was much debate about the war. Page 9 featured photographs showing Australian troops giving water to a surrendered North Vietnamese defector.

We turn to page 5 and see a big, more attractive photograph next to the headline: "Mason in Film of Qld [Queensland state]." The picture shows movie star James Mason arriving at Sydney's airport with . . . Helen Mirren, smiling very brightly through long blond hair, sporting a tiny white miniskirt, suitable for the midsummer temperatures. "Actor James Mason arrived in Sydney yesterday to star in a $1 million film based on Norman Lindsay's novel *Age of Consent*. Here he arrives with his co-star Helen Mirren, 22." Shooting would begin in Queensland about March 12.

The film was about an artist living on the northern coast, and was directed by the late great Michael Powell. I had the honor and pleasure of working on movie scripts and generally having fun with Michael's son Columba, also an artist, for a decade, with opportunity to examine documentation about the picture's making: quite an experience. Helen Mirren you all know. This was her debut picture, and very good she was too. Nowadays it is held that *Age of Consent* reflected the "free love" era of the late Sixties sexual revolution. I don't know. That conclusion was doubtless drawn in retrospect because Helen swam as nature intended close to the perilous reefs. And why not? It was Art.

Fig. 18.2. British actress Helen Mirren, circa 1968.

▲ ▲ ▲

We now come to the entertainment pages. The first thing I notice is an advertisement for the air-conditioned pleasures of Her Majesty's Theatre where "The World's Greatest Musical" was being presented: the story of Tradition clashing with the ways of youth and their sense of the future in the context of the vibrant faith of a Russian Jewish peasant family before World War I, Jerry Bock and Sheldon Harnick's *Fiddler on the Roof*. American actor Hayes Gordon (1920–1999) played Tevye, the man who dreamt of being a rich man, if only God could arrange it. Gordon had long worked in Australia and specialized in teaching drama, establishing viable Australian theatrical companies, and had successfully funded his theater work with *Fiddler on the Roof* income since 1967. My favorite song was, and is, "Far from the Home I Love." I recall it with tears in my eyes just before being dispatched to boarding school in September 1969.

Meanwhile, back in '68, at the Comedy Theatre, Melbourne, theatergoers were invited to behold actor Alfred Marks starring "in London's Longest running Comedy"—*Spring and Port Wine* by Bill Naughton. Marks had brought the role from London the previous year.

Fig. 18.3. "Far from the Home I Love" in my ears as boarding school beckons, September 1969.

I'll never forget his rapturous arrival in Australia at the great "Moomba" Festival parade of floats through Melbourne's streets in 1967. We were among the crowds that lined those bright streets that sunny Saturday afternoon, with my dad, most uncharacteristically shouting to the passing open limousine containing Alfred Marks: "Hello Alfie!" Perhaps Dad'd had a few beers. Alfie waved; he knew what it was all about.

What I now have to convey, you may not quite believe. It certainly astonishes me. Here following are the movies you could go and see in Melbourne on Tuesday, February 20, 1968. This, please note, is just *one* ordinary weekday in the Australian summer of 1968. I shall omit the word *color* that accompanies most of the movies advertised. It was still the case that color films were an attraction purely by that virtue, as the Sixties saw gradual abandonment in American and then other nations' movies of traditional cinematic black-and-white.

At the Barclay cinema, James Coburn starred in Blake Edwards's *Waterhole #3,* a 1967 Western comedy, while the air-conditioned Metro in Collins Street showcased Tony Curtis and Claudia Cardinale in *Don't Make Waves* (X-rated), a 1967 U.S. sex farce that debuted actress newcomer Sharon Tate as Malibu, a seductive siren whose bikini'd lifesize image in cardboard was shipped around American cinemas to bring the punters into the orbit of abundant charms displayed to Tony Curtis on the Californian beach in the movie. We are prefeminist as far as Hollywood was concerned. The in-your-face movie poster advocated a spin on Timothy Leary's countercultural "Turn On, Tune In, Drop Out." It said: "Turn on! Stay loose! Make out!" All good fun, no doubt—still, films about Californian beach life and Californian metaphysical gurus were not as common as you'd think, and besides, the title song, performed by the Byrds, was written by Roger McGuinn, great admirer of George Harrison's countercultural, spiritual "Within You, Without You" whose plain-speaking lyrics McGuinn had inscribed in stone in his Californian garden, I believe. *Waterhole #3* is a forgotten film now—some might opine, deservedly so. Sharon Tate of course will not be forgotten.

By contrast, the Metro in Bourke Street showed David Lean's eternally compelling *Doctor Zhivago,* the magnificent film my family saw in

Fig. 18.4. Julie Christie as Lara in Doctor Zhivago, *1966.*

London the night before flying to a new life in Australia in 1966, having passed at night through a Piccadilly Circus enveloped with student hippies advocating by example the dreamy effects of pot. Lean's movie showed what "revolution" was really like, 1917-style at least. Klaus Kinski portrayed the spiritually "free-est" man in the movie. Chained to a Red Guard taking him to Outer Siberia for refusing to submit, a somewhat gnostic Kinski tells the other refugees in the smelly train from St. Petersburg that chained as he is, he is the only truly free person present, for he is free in his mind and the world's a fool, and his mind will not conform, thus he is free in spirit and not a "lickspittle" like the ignorant guard watching him.

Meanwhile, the Palladium in Bourke Street projected the big-budget 1967 musical, starring Richard Harris and Vanessa Redgrave, *Camelot.* This, it was hoped, would bring the fashionable myth and magic to the masses. Harris and Redgrave, the latter especially, made it a bit too obvious they felt smarter than the script and that signal fact detracted from the conviction required even in fantasy hokum to bring the magic off. Nevertheless, the movie had a beautiful romantic soundtrack to match its perhaps slightly overrich color photography, with Lancelot (Franco Nero) singing the dreamy "If Ever I Would Leave You" by Lerner and Loewe. It will be observed that movies went round the cinemas sometimes long after their initial releases, and sometimes played long seasons at the same cinema, like theater bookings. This is unheard of today, of course, where you may well see a film in a plastic box before you ever, if ever, see it on the much smaller, ineffective, often paltry, mean cinema screens of today. Cinema seemed grander and less disposable in those days, and if you wanted to see a new or newish film, you had to get out, and very often queue with the rest of the human race on the streets of life.

With no home-porn market to speak of (nobody complained of the absence I daresay), if you fancied something of a turn-on in the racier sense, though within limits for sure, the cinema was your destination. The Roma, also in Bourke Street, was educating audiences with *The Oldest Profession in the World,* starring Raquel Welch and Elsa Martinelli, among others. This was a 1967 European coproduction with separate features about prostitution through the ages, directed by six different directors. The last feature, titled *Anticipation,* was a typically avant-garde exercise in Brechtian distanciation by Jean-Luc Godard. It starred Anna Karina as Natasha, Eleanor Romeovich as Hostess 703, and Marilù Tolo as Marlene, Miss Physical Love. You had your kicks from much-stockinged pulchritude, but there was some political and artistic education too.

At the Australia cinema in Australia Arcade (or "Australia on Collins"), you could see the hugely entertaining, technically innovative, hauntingly scored (arrangements by Alfred Newman) Rodgers and Hammerstein musical *South Pacific* (1958). I well remember, aged seven or eight, running home alone from Dandenong town center across a shimmeringly hot park (now vanished beneath concrete) singing loudly to myself "Younger Than Springtime," as well as I recall seeing with my family, *The Bible* at the Australia's 359-seat cinema, as well as *The Dirty Dozen,* in 1967, despite the latter's being an X-film (the attitude seemed to be, "well, if the kids are with their father, he knows best"). Alas! The arcade that connected Collins and Little Collins Streets between Swanston and Elizabeth Streets is now a vast, shiny shopping mall (like all the others you've seen anywhere else). In the Seventies, the Australia became an exclusively porn-showing cinema, and like almost every other stylish Melbourne cinema you may read of here, has now gone forever, taking the substance of dearly held memories with it.

The Albany, on Collins Street, Melbourne's trendiest, leafy boulevard-like street, was proud to be exhibiting the "Best Film of the '67 Cannes Festival," Antonioni's *Blow-Up*. This was one of those "archetypal" Sixties movies that was really out on its own, despite its inconclusive, mystery ending. It was billed as "Adults Only." Yes, it had a topless beauty played by Vanessa Redgrave, a lovemaking scene with Sarah Miles and John Castle, and a two-girl romp including Mrs. John Barry (Jane Birkin), actor David Hemmings, and another girl who will do a lot to be photographed, all set in and around a wealthy photographer's studio in East London, with curious goings-on amid quiet public lawns shot at the Marion Park in Greenwich. The film is ostensibly about "the nature of reality" and one may ask whether film is the very best medium in which to explore this tricky question, which of course has its bearing on abstract issues of the spirit. The film had a kind of sassy amoralism coating the troubled characters who seem caught up in a modern experience they don't really understand, but which they can at least try to manipulate to suit themselves. When the photographer tries to get to the bottom of what he becomes convinced is premeditated murder, we're not sure if it's because he wants the guilty punished, or because of mere technical interest in a puzzle of conflicting or ambiguous images. John Lennon's line "Nothing is real" would have made a suitable rubric for the very well-made movie that had cultured Melbourne talking about it for a long time. A sexy, beautiful image really can bring a philosophical issue to compelling life. All you need is the right performer and the right director. The Sixties stacked both in ample measure.

Still with a European cultural feel, you could go to the Century in Swanston Street and see French director and photographer Claude Lelouche's very enticing color experience, enlivened with unforgettable music by Francis Lai, *A Man and a Woman*. For some reason that may elude comprehension, this romantic, split-screen punctuated, glossy but not at all vacuous movie was on a double bill with the French movie *Mein Kampf* (X) which was "Repeated by Public Demand." A lot of people wanted to see again Erwin Leiser and Maurice Croizat's 1960 documentary movie about the rise and fall of Hitler and his Third Reich. The title of course is taken from Hitler's literary declaration of intent, so dear to those who are determined to believe Hitler sane.

One of the outflows of Hitler's activities could be observed in fictional form at the Capitol, Swanston Street, where Robert Aldrich's brilliantly crafted, entertaining, and not unmeaningful WW2 movie, *The Dirty Dozen* (X) of 1967 was doing the rounds. Lee Marvin starred, but so did everybody else in it.

Fancy a bit more sex? Go to the Curzon, also in Australia Arcade, where you can gaze upon *The Queens,* starring the glorious patrician features of Capucine, ubiquitous beauty Claudia Cardinale, along with the no less alluring images of Monica Vitti and Raquel Welch in the December 1966 "Adults Only" flick, about, well, something to do with glamorous women doing something silly and looking pretty while they're doing it kind of "foreign" movie. But if it's "culture" you want, Sport, try the Embassy, Bourke Street, where they're showing the Academy Award Nomination Best Foreign Film of 1960, *Macario,* a product of Mexican cinematic artistry.

Owned by Hoyts City Theatres, the Paris, Bourke Street, was showing Rex Harrison and Tony Newley in the Bricusse-Newley film musical, *Dr. Dolittle,* which won an Oscar for a song about talking to animals, keeping more deserving movie songs from the coveted award. My brothers and I quite liked the movie, especially the giant pink snail that floats in at the end, but that's a long time to wait for the magic of a supposedly magical movie that never matched the original book, despite Rex Harrison's charming performance.

Rex Harrison crops up again, ever so debonair, at the Athenaeum, also in Collins Street where he stars in the 1967 comedy-thriller, with lots of sexy romance, *The Honeypot,* directed by Joseph L. Mankiewicz, starring Susan Hayward and Cliff Robertson, fighting over an inheritance, with lighthearted murder in the spirit of *How to Murder Your Wife* (1964). Capucine lent her beauty to this movie too, as she had to Peter O'Toole in the glorious box of cinematic chocolates *What's New Pussycat?* (1965) with its beautiful score by Burt Bacharach—his first.

My favorite Melbourne cinema was the magnificently massive Plaza, in Collins Street, where we all saw the worthy and exciting history epic *Khartoum,* about a determined jihadist "messiah" (the "Mahdi," played by Laurence Olivier) pitted against martyr-warrior, Christian general, Charles Gordon (superbly played by Charlton Heston). This

Fig. 18.5. *Fifty years later, in April 2018, the author (foreground) revisits what used to be the Plaza and Regent Cinemas, Collins Street, Melbourne. The mighty Regent and Plaza building was closed in November 1970 (last film shown:* Butch Cassidy and the Sundance Kid*), and practically destroyed by Melbourne City Council. Lovingly restored from photographs, it was reopened as the Regent Theatre and Plaza Ballroom in August 1996. Photograph by Mark Bennett, 2018.*

particular Tuesday, the Plaza was hosting the thrilling, technically astounding movie by John Frankenheimer, *Grand Prix* (1966), starring James Garner and the very dishy (so my wife tells me) Yves Montand. In fact, the cinema I remember as the Plaza was the first duplex cinema in Australia, the Plaza being a basement cinema, below the sumptuous Regent, opened in 1929. The lavish Regent originally had seating for 3,500, while in 1953, a massive curved screen was installed for Cinemascope. The Plaza, with 865 seats, was converted for Cinerama in 1958, which explains why *Grand Prix* was shown there in 1968.

Still doing the rounds, visitors to the Regent in Collins Street—I was one of them—could see (or see again, lucky people!) Sean Connery as 007 in *You Only Live Twice,* shot grandly amid the rising suns and sunsets of Japanese coasts and volcanoes, with a score "to die for" by John Barry, and sizzling theme song sung (eventually) by Nancy Sinatra, who'd had a hit with "These Boots Are Made for Walking," which I especially recall hearing on a remote bus-station radio on the Greyhound ride south to Melbourne in early 1967, because my little feet were in so much agony from the cheap red plastic Woolworths sandals I had to wear and that, in the heat of the bus and the very long journey were all sweaty, blistered, and bleeding. My boots were not made for walking, or anything else, but Nancy's were, no doubt of it. Did I say walking? *Are you ready, boots?*

Moral and spiritual lift was to be had, and had again and again at the Esquire, Bourke Street, which showed *The Sound of Music* for the entire time we lived in Australia. The Esquire had been showing it since 1965 and was still showing it when we left in 1968. I'd like to think they were still showing it now, but this cinema—like every single cinema I visited in Melbourne as a boy—has gone. The movie however, lives on. They probably watch it at the pearly gates to remind themselves how to build a bridge twixt earth and heaven made solely of celluloid.

The Esquire was also advertising matinée performances of *Love and Kisses* (Color) with singer Rick Nelson and Jerry Van Dyke in a 1965 U.S. comedy, redolent of the Elvis Sixties, somewhat forgettable movies, made according to contract not love of a great project.

Now here was a great project: the powerhouse of Elizabeth Taylor and Richard Burton joined financial forces to launch a company to bring their dream of Shakespeare to the screen. The result could be seen at the Bercy, Bourke Street. *The Taming of the Shrew* is a stupendous Franco Zeffirelli–directed movie in which Burton and Taylor give their all, or what was left of it, which, as it happened was a very great deal, as they, like the Beatles, seemed to feed on Sixties energy, money, and fame and booze and all the hype that they hated but were surrounded and fueled by nonetheless. Never mind the media image, their films after *Cleopatra* are always special, and *The Taming of the Shrew* is arguably the best of them all. It shines still, undimmed, undimmable. God bless you both for making the screen shake and quake into life, your life, our life. Life. There is divinity in Burton's lust, like God imparting breath to Adam and Eve. They weren't kicked out of Eden for kissing!

Julie Andrews had a problem with her film image and whenever she tried to shake off the virgin childminder, there was doubt in audiences' minds. Perhaps audiences don't really want to believe their favorite characters are actors trying to have a good life. At the Chelsea in Flinders Street, audiences got a chance to see Julie Andrews show what a great comedian she could be, not missing a beat with Mary Tyler Moore and urbane male beauty James Fox in *Thoroughly Modern Millie:* lively, entertaining, colorful, and very expensive, and therefore, very Sixties— even though it was set in the Roaring Twenties, when skirts also went up, before the Wall Street Crash brought them down again (prizes for those seeing the connection).

We have had cause earlier in this book to hear about Sidney Poitier in *To Sir, with Love.* In February 1968, Poitier sparred with British "bird" Suzy Kendall and her spirited friends at the Odeon, Bourke Street. It was an X-film, which seems odd when one knows the story was about educating youths to see the virtue in growing up. But the censorship system was somewhat single-minded.

Another X-film, this one perhaps deserved, could be seen gracing the screen or disgracing it, of the Forum, Flinders Street, where *The Ambushers* (X) joined Dean Martin as serial spy Matt Helm with Senta Berger in this now very dated 1967 comedy, the kind of glossy (at the

Fig. 18.6. Sidney Poitier in To Sir, with Love, *the film based on
E. R. Braithwaite's book.* (New York Times)

time) movie that inspired *Austin Powers* spoofing in 1997. You could
hardly move for spy films in the Sixties, numerous examples of them
being self-conscious spoofs and plays around Bondish themes with *Man
from U.N.C.L.E* budgets. They have not stood the test of time, but at
the time, they had the energy, whimsicality, and wackiness that made
the era so pleasant to wade in.

It was not all fun and frolics. Take a walk to the Grosvenor, Collins
Street, showing *The War Game* (Adults Only): "The Most Hard-hitting
Film of Our Time!" "judged too horrifying to show on TV." All true.
We heard about it in our chapter on Apocalypse. Banned in Britain,
here it is: turning up at a Melbourne cinema, billed as a horror movie—
not a bad way perhaps to think of nuclear war. Let us pray it remains
a fiction, and not, as here, documentary realism. Interesting to think
you would have emerged from this screening into a delightful, hot but
shady, boulevard-like Collins Street, surrounded by many clean-cut men
in light suits, some carrying umbrellas, and tidily coiffured, fresh-faced
women in neat, colorful cotton skirts with shiny handbags, all smart
and lively, and barely an overweight person in sight (really), in a street

where even the habitual drunks wore suits, ties, and hats, which they would doff in a lady's presence. And then you might imagine, what would a bomb do to all this?

Another rarity, surprise, surprise . . . ever seen the one about four hippies kidnapping a Mafia boss? No? Get thyself with all haste to the Rapallo, Russell Street, where you can feast your eyes on *The Happening* (X) with stars Anthony Quinn, Michael Parks, and an early performance by Faye Dunaway (1967). It's a crime comedy and you'll remember Dunaway from last year's shocking *Bonnie and Clyde* where she was shot to death by protracted machine-gun fire in the filmic definition of "overkill" (was it a metaphor for the bombing of North Vietnam, or just a plea for better violence?). Unusual in its use of hippies in a crime context, *The Happening* theme became a monster Motown hit for the Supremes. A "happening" was of course that hippie gathering pioneered in distant San Francisco where people came together (the important bit) and did something, or just had a "Be-In," which was nice too, and an antidote to being lonely, or remote and angry. Come together. In this case, the group had a coming together for purposes of profitable kidnap, not, if I recall correctly, that they knew their victim was in the Mafia, who did not, we might think, feel immediate sympathy with the voice of the Love Generation. The fact is that we can see even from this one-day sounding of the cinematic waters in Melbourne, that hippies were still seen, when they were seen at all (or heard), as fringe happenings, and really as being rather amusing, even ludicrous. Then again, the humor was also a defense, because things could get very difficult if you *did* take them seriously. Because yes, they did hope to change a lot of things, including all those nice, tidy, clean-cut, well-turned-out "ladies and gentlemen" walking busily and purposefully down Russell Street outside the cinema. You could safely giggle inside, in the dark.

The general upbeat, capitalism-plus-fun of the period found its peak with films like *How to Succeed in Business without Really Trying*, starring Robert Morse, Rudy Vallee, and Michele Lee, whose song-and-dance office routines were far from reality, but amusing and escapist all the same and could be enjoyed at Malvern's suburban Theatre, run by Hoyts Drive-in Theatres. The name "Hoyt" was as ubiquitous to

Melbourne's entertainment circuits as that of Mayor Richard J. Daley to Chicago's public works.

Hoyts drive-in in St. Kilda was showing Robert Wise's very moving film of devotion, *The Sand Pebbles,* starring Steve McQueen, Richard Attenborough, Richard Crenna, and Candice Bergen. It was set in China during the 1920s, with Communist insurgents threatening the U.S. naval crew of the U.S.S. *San Pablo.* The film looks at the conflict purely from the human angle. One interesting thing about the movie is that the Christian missionaries whom the ship must endeavor to save strike one generally as rather myopic in outlook, blind to the facts of history, and to their real place in it. In the end, Steve McQueen's character demonstrates to the missionaries what real sacrifice might consist of, with no theological gloss, just a case of a man coming to terms with himself, and with the hellish realism of an impossible situation. One loves McQueen's character for his courage in fighting a private inner war while doing his "duty" to those around him whom he can help. He may not save souls but he sure as hell does his best (which is not good enough) to save bodies, including his own. It's a tragic film and the ending is not a happy one, but the man who dies probably forgotten has spiritual stature to match any fine words from any big-mouthed speaker of "eternal truths" be they religious or political: "A plague on both your houses! You have made worms' meat!" could have been McQueen's last words, but his blankly astonished face at the end says it all. Was *that* my life? The eternal truth of life on Earth is laid bare, and how we respond to it makes us what we are. McQueen as Jake Holman lives in our hearts, and up on screen. I shall never forget this very fine adult film that even reached the heart of a seven-year-old one Saturday afternoon in Melbourne with my father, who had read and admired the book by Richard McKenna on which the movie was based.

It was not all meaning. Bob Hope, Phyllis Diller, Shirley Eaton, and Jill St. John starred in the comedy *Eight on the Lam* (1967) showing at the Coburg, Newlands Road, along with *The Seventh Dawn* (X), another war-set movie in the Far East first released in 1964, and starring William Holden, Susannah York, and Capucine as Holden's wife. Can we guess the rest?

The drive-in, Sandringham, was showing John Guillermin's 1967 movie of World War I German pilots, pitting survival against vain ambition on a "losing wicket" in *The Blue Max,* with George Peppard, Jeremy Kemp (excellent), and Ursula Andress doing what Ursula Andress was expected to do after her debut appearance in a bikini in *Dr. No* (1961). *The Blue Max* was billed as "Three Hours of Blistering Color Action!" which is all true, folks, and of course it said what a hell war really is, without offering an alternative. The "hero" is the manipulated manikin of powers above. There was a message or two there somewhere between the dogfights. The "Blue Max" incidentally was a German Empire award for exceptional success in the air (number of kills) for which Peppard will do practically everything, even if it means ignoring gentlemen's codes; this being his undoing—the war is run by gentlemen. "What profiteth it a man if he gain the Blue Max and lose his own soul." The trouble is the antihero in this case doesn't seem to have a soul; he appears to have lost it already in the trenches, being shot at day and night. Besides, as the officers conclude, he was always a low-class nobody. Agh! The dark stab of cynicism was not unknown in Sixties movies.

The cinema in Balwyn was showing the Sixties wonder film, *Born Free,* which probably did more for animal rights and awareness of conserving wildlife than any other film at any other time. Music was by John Barry, and he got the Oscar for it, deservedly so. I have heard that the theme song was wanted as a national anthem by an emerging state in Africa, but suspect this snippet might just be on the apocryphal side. Besides, the animal "born free" in the movie is somewhat at risk in all African states, be they called free or frightening. If man is born free, why can't the other freeborns let him alone? *You Must Be Joking* is not only an answer to this question but the title of a 1965 comedy on the double bill with Bill Travers, Virginia McKenna, and Elsa the lion. Directed by Michael Winner, *You Must Be Joking* starred Terry-Thomas, and is one of those many lost movies of the period worth a look at for atmosphere of abandonment and overall lively innocence plus shameless sexual innuendo.

More comedy was on offer at the Regent, Box Hill, where

Phil Silvers, Zero Mostel, and Michael Crawford enlivened the music and lyrics of Stephen Sondheim in the 1966 movie musical, *A Funny Thing Happened on the Way to the Forum,* a farce set in ancient Rome, like the murder of Julius Caesar. For some reason, the very serious movie *Pressure Point* accompanied it, starring Sidney Poitier and Bobby Darin. Poitier played a psychiatrist whose job is to assess for parole a model prisoner. It turns out the model prisoner is a Nazi-sympathizing white supremacist with the potential to cause real pain if released. Poitier faces a career decision because only he can see the danger the patient (Darin) poses: an unusual film that must have made for a curious night at the cinema when shown back to back with the musical.

Another curious double bill was that at the Esquire, Elsternwick, where the delightful musical *My Fair Lady* (1964) with Rex Harrison and Audrey Hepburn could, and did, dance all night to Lerner and Loewe's great tunes and lyrics. George Bernard Shaw's essay on class may have been muted by the romance of the movie, but audiences lost nothing, seeing that love might transcend class, so long as the girl spoke properly and was presentable to mother, at any rate. Along with this pleasure came an improving work: an award-winning Australian film documentary from 1967 that took a candid look at South Vietnam. The title rather gives the game away: *The Unlucky Country.* You could say that again, but by the time the musical had come to an end, you might have forgotten about it.

The Palais, St. Kilda was showing François Truffaut's interesting, if awkward movie, based on Ray Bradbury's sci-fi novel, *Fahrenheit 451* (X). The title referred to the temperature at which paper spontaneously burns, and the film, starring Julie Christie and Oskar Werner, concerns a very modern society where everybody watches very large-screen TV and only reads picture books. A familiar ring there . . . The government runs the whole thing by TV. Books are forbidden. Well, fancy that. Oskar Werner does not fancy it, and discovers to his amazement that when he reads a book, his mind begins to open. He must soon hide from authorities and informants. He discovers the "Book People" who try to memorize whole books so that the memory of the living book will not die despite the state's regular bonfires and murder of bibliophiles.

There's much true prophecy in this. I think of the iPhone and home entertainment and all the rest, and it seems now that the state does not need to destroy the books. I have heard of folk not far away who cannot bear having a book in the house, because they "collect dust." People pose a similar problem, if they do nothing, but I would not favor their permanent removal. Many are taught to read today at great expense, and then can't face the sight of a book, but I still go on. The entertainment people thought the age of vinyl was dead, too.

Another drive-in experience drawing in the punters from 1967 paired Australian Rod Taylor with Catherine Spaak in *Hotel* (X), which dramatized unsavory goings-on at a posh hotel; one is amazed they could find any guests at all had any of them known whom they would be sharing breakfast with.

And, to cap it all, the flatcap movie of the Sixties (at a time when very many working people in the North of England—men anyway—wore flat caps): *The Family Way* (X) starring Hywel Bennett, Hayley Mills, and her father, John Mills. Paul McCartney wrote the tunes orchestrated into film music for this movie and received an Ivor Novello award for his trouble. He knew the world described well enough. It wasn't a million miles from *Spring and Port Wine,* in that *The Family Way,* like the popular play starring Alfred Marks, tried to show ordinary people adjusting to the great changes going on in the world and in British society, perhaps the top subject of which list was *sex,* that is, premarital intercourse. *The Family Way* (a euphemism for pregnancy) supported traditional values. A little "give" and forbearance on the adults' side could still ensure that true love led to respectable marriage and another fine family, with, doubtless, new problems. This was quite a brave attempt to inject some realism in thematic material into a cinema still, though very happily, concerned with taking audiences as far out of themselves as the law, and tolerances of the time, would allow.

Now, do you remember when we came in? It's a while ago, isn't it? And we've seen quite a lot. Time for an intermission (remember them?)—and a reflection. You have just been introduced to the films available at cinemas in Melbourne, Australia, on *one single day* of February 1968.

"Look on these works, ye mighty, and despair!" Still think those who say some things were better in the Sixties are kidding themselves? And I haven't finished yet, but do please hurry for an ice cream or a soda pop while we reload the projector.

SPIRITUAL VALUES IN SIXTIES CINEMA

The late Michael Powell (1905–1990), whose best films with Emeric Pressburger (1902–1988) are permeated by a sometimes intensely spiritual sensibility, once made the point of saying that "spiritual values we can know" whereas what he called "religious values" we can "only guess at." This point of view made for an interesting departure from our first conversation in 1987. What I think Powell meant was that when we *experience* how spiritual values work, we recognize that there's more to the picture than either our own personal desires or what the visible world shows us. If we deny ourselves the obvious, often tempting, material prize, we may well find spiritual treasure, and such a treasure is love, for example; wisdom is another, lasting friendship too. We may have to make sacrifices, but as opposed to being told by a bishop or imam or rabbi about the subject, when we make a sacrifice on interior, spiritual prompting, we often experience results directly, intimately, that is, as real, not as objects of faith. We *know* them. We may uncover new dimensions we hardly knew, or only dimly suspected. This may join us to the realm of spiritual knowledge whose symbolic life organ is the heart that, when it beats healthily, does wonders for the mind as well.

What I think Michael meant by "religious values" were dogmatic teachings or official creeds and formularies sent down to us by religious authorities for reasons we may not know or understand. We can't be sure of them, and proof is not available; we become subject to persuasion, often by fear. As Kant maintained, existence is not a predicate; we need not assume the existence of the God we're told about, for instance. But we may know through living, inner experience something like it, or more.

As cinematic material is largely the dramatic exposure of human character through story, it is a sad deficiency to that exposure when we find spiritual values absent. That is not the case in many movies of the Sixties, where spiritual values and meaning may be discerned in even the most flagrantly commercial productions. There follow a number of movies that have struck this author as having brought, however slightly, spiritual content into, and from, the culture and consciousness of the Sixties, and that is still available to us today thanks to those who have preserved what has passed. You may well feel I should have included others, or that I have misjudged intentions, and you may well be right. On the other hand, it does no harm to look again at something through the eyes of another; it can be very illuminating. I omit movies I have referred to already.

The year 1960 opened the decade with four very different movies that all have something to say about the dimension of the spiritual, though that is by no means the theme or even subtext of any of them. *À Bout de Souffle* (*Breathless*) was image-analyst and film-critic Jean-Luc Godard's first full-length movie and set a fashion in spontaneous styles of story-telling, of playing with genres and established rules of editing and camera discipline, for artistic or emotional reasons, and made a tremendous impact by virtue of the director's personal freedom, establishing the French "new wave" as something that could not be ignored, though it could be sidestepped, and was.

The story has little but simplicity to commend it. In the heat of the moment, a likeable crook with a "Bogart complex," played engagingly by Jean-Paul Belmondo, kills a policeman without malice in pursuance of a casual robbery. A man who loves his freedom above all, he needs cash; he knows, or thinks he knows, the world he lives in. On the run in Paris, he chats up an American girl played by Jean Seberg selling the *Herald-Tribune* on the Champs-Élysées. She offers him comfort, but with the police net tightening, is persuaded to shop her exciting lover. He is shot in the street and dies betrayed by the girl he might have loved. The film ends with his last breath, having realized her betrayal, uttering his last words "That's really disgusting." "Out of breath" means death. *Fin.* His last words appear to sum up his sense of ultimate futility and blank meaningless of life. But his life has not been one of Sartrean "nausea"; it's been exciting and he's lived and died on his own terms. He did what he did; the police did what they do. The film is full of fatal logic. What a man is, decides what he will do. Killers kill; burglars burgle; lovers love, he tells the girl. That's what it is. Godard's world is the world he observes going on around him. It appears to be void of spiritual values, and Godard concludes that it is. That's the way it is. He has said famously that cinema is "truth at 24 frames per second," a statement affirming a radical materialist cinema. He's not interested in dreams. He wants to show what *is,* and tear away those tricks of cinema that deny reality. In his later attempts to construct a revolutionary cinema, he will observe of much of what we see: "It's not a *just* image; it's just an image." Godard tries to find the right (revolutionarily appropriate) image, sifting through the garbage dump of modern images for images that say something in his cinematic scrapbook. He is looking for something meaningful amid the nothingness, a new language, one that delivers real love and real life in terms of social justice. This is really a spiritual search, and where it would lead him is another story. However, for most viewers of his Sixties films, his unflinching, idiosyncratic portrayal of realities of the material world, and his belief in an uncompromisingly materialist cinema, meant that in reflecting materialism through his restless lens, he advocated a value-free world. He didn't, but from my observation could not see how to go beyond it, as things stood. His trajectory would lead him in 1967 to the apocalyptic *Weekend,* which we have discussed elsewhere, and then into theory-laden anti-films.

A no less terrifying response to a filmmaker's personal predicament is that explored in Michael Powell's very amusing and in parts profound "horror" film, *Peeping Tom,* whose premise, offered as a potential script to Powell by WW2 code breaker Leo Marks, was to make a film about a man who murders women with a camera. "Yes," said Powell, "That's for me!" Powell was tired of war movies and the late-Fifties pap J. Arthur Rank's film company was producing under accountant John Davis's control at Pinewood Studios.

The murderer in *Peeping Tom* is a fascinating mix of character traits laced with a menace the poor man cannot control. Abused by his experimental psychiatrist father who used his son for experiments in the psychology of fear (the father played by Powell; the boy by his son Columba!), the young man grows up with an intense sexual and psychotic perversion whereby he can only find relief by filming women screaming in their death throes as they are murdered by a spike on the camera tripod he's filming (and killing) them with in their throats. The movie has a fair bit to say about scopophilia, which is gaining pleasure from looking, or as the movie puts it, "the morbid urge to gaze"— morbid meaning a condition that can or has led to sickness. Well, of course, Powell is talking about the cinema, his life's work, his art, an obsession with making images, manipulating the desires of the audience to *keep looking*. He's talking about us getting our kicks.

The girl who tries to help the murderer has a blind mother, but she can see what's going on upstairs in her rented attic room where the killer watches his postmortem movies. "All this filmmaking," she says, "can't be healthy." Very funny. But her daughter is writing a story about a "magic camera," a camera that transforms, we may suppose, for purposes of white magic: something for children. The killer, very polite, very warm, very intelligent, knows that for *him* there is no such easy or comforting way to make films. His films must go all the way; he can only obtain sexual release from absolute fear, for the women he kills are presented with a mirror at the brink of death in which they can see themselves screaming, and like all mirrors, the victim is hooked on the image of their own death, unable to look away. The filmmaker "captures" this moment. Ah! We get to Powell and Marks's point. When we watch a horror film or films of others dying, whether we realize it or not, we are haunted by the image's relation to ourselves. Is this healthy? Well, no, obviously not, if we take our psychopathic filmmaker as an example of the extreme case, but Michael Powell is an image maker, and like the killer in the film, or like Alfred Hitchcock, or Godard for that matter, or any other cinéaste filmmaker, he just can't stop himself from making films, cannot be stopped from making films, and there are always people who cannot stop themselves from watching films: the pleasure that comes from looking, and furtive looking in darkness in particular, has gripped practically everybody.

And that is why Powell can pour so much sympathy into his portrayal of the lovable killer. I say lovable because he is played that way by German actor Carl Boehm, but also because the girl who lives downstairs really loves him, and understands, and takes pity on what has become of the young boy for whom the camera should have been a magical gift, but whose father, with scientific intentions (cold logic), ignorant or blind to the spiritual value of his son's mind and life, has turned the lad into a mad person, who must be stopped. In the end, such love as she offers him makes the killer ultimately turn the camera upon himself, so that he does not, as he is sore tempted, turn it on the girl who loves him, and whom he loves. He dies with the words "I'm afraid. And I'm glad I'm afraid!" He does not know where he's going for his sins, but he has made the ultimate sacrifice for love. He has given his life for his friend; the only moral problem here being, perhaps, that he may, in the end, have enjoyed it.

Well, Powell launched this explosive movie on an unsuspecting world, and described the psychology not only of the narrow-minded executives he had come to know at Rank (the British film conglomerate that is parodied in the film), but also of the fundamental appeal of the "golden age" of British horror movies that was in the process of beginning, with the famous "Hammer" productions of blood and gore and the highly lucrative pleasure of being frightened. Ahead of his time, and far too subtle for the critics, the movie was treated the way the prosecution counsel in the Lady Chatterley case looked at D. H. Lawrence. It was, said critics, "filth" to be poured down the nearest sewer. It was said that the once-great Michael Powell had sunk beneath contempt, and Rank determined he would never make a film in England again. Powell went to Australia and spent the decade with only two Australian movies to show for his genius (though his name appears as producer on the credits to the Dirk Bogarde and Susannah York vehicle *Sebastian* (1968), based on another idea of former code-breaker, Leo Marks).

Powell's conclusion seems to be that cinema can only redeem itself from its inherent "unhealthiness" when it embraces again the magic that existed in the first promise of cinema, when the machine of cogs and switches was transformed into a magic camera that took the imagination to places no other art form could. I know that Powell dreamt of one day making an epic on the theme of the spiritual transformation of man, and might have done, had he not laid out his store of anguish and frustration in the form of *Peeping Tom.*

The third film of 1960 that captured my interest was a big Hollywood commercial picture, starring Elizabeth Taylor, Eddie Fisher (Taylor's husband before meeting Richard Burton on *Cleopatra*), and Lawrence Harvey. The movie was *Butterfield 8,* and it earned for Taylor a surprising Oscar. Surprising because in the movie she played an unmarried woman who slept with men she cared for. The first scene is a very long one of Taylor getting out of bed, naked, and preparing herself for the day. It is clearly exploitative of Taylor's remarkable beauty and acting talent, the latter redeeming the scene's obvious prurience. We get pleasure from looking. While dressing, Taylor discovers she has been left a wad of notes. Not realizing that this is what the lover (who has left for business) has given her to pay for the dress he had ripped the night before, and that lies discarded on the carpet, she takes it as a payment "for services rendered" and, horrified at being considered a prostitute, she quits the apartment of the married man (the wife is away), leaving the money and scrawling a message to the lover in lipstick on the mirror to show her contempt for the gesture.

The movie explores the relationship between her and the troubled lover in quite some depth, "Butterfield 8" being the number he must call if he wants her services as a professional escort (her job is adding glamour to product promotion—not unlike being a movie star today). The ambiguity of the role, that she is offering her personality, beauty, and glamour to the company, not her body as such, gives the film an unusual tension and, given Taylor and Harvey's compelling performances, much humanity. The movie does not judge Taylor, rather Taylor judges herself, and she wants to be clean of the whole distressing business of business, and start a new life, one that is morally respectable and spiritually clean. We do get inside the Taylor character's personal dilemma, and can only admire her courage when she finally decides to leave an appalling situation that can only bring heartbreak to someone (Harvey's wife, for example). She is prepared to sacrifice her love, for the new beginning. In the end, something of movie fatalism gets the better of the script, and she dies in a car crash, caused by Harvey's inability to let the object of his gaze, lust, and love go away from him. He chases after her, making her drive too fast. Losing control of the car, she loses her life. In her death, she vindicates her values at the cost of her life. Harvey, we can be sure, will spend his life trying to make up for his ruinous egotism. One might argue that Hollywood has had its cake and has eaten it: sex plus redemption; keep watching, folks, but the movie is nonetheless powerful on the side of the individuals concerned being able to respond to interior promptings of a self-sacrificial and elevated kind. Hooray for Hollywood! Sick as it is.

Another film that came out in 1960 (December) was Fred Zimmerman's wonderfully spacious, lyrical, and contemporary tale set in the Australian Outback, *The Sundowners,* starring Deborah Kerr, Robert Mitchum, Peter Ustinov, and Glynis Johns. I cannot recommend this highly enough as a movie that really shows what spiritual beings are like. They're not odd or adorned in nimbus and wings; they're like you and I could be if we just lived the best life we could and loved the people we loved, and made the appropriate sacrifices, developed our sense of humor, and worked to keep it all together. We are presented with a married couple raising their son in a traveling wagon that goes from job to job in the Australian Outback. They live beneath the stars; they watch the sun go down; they sleep in their tents and makeshift lodgings; they rib one another; and, when they've got a bit of money when they're in town, they take a room in the local hotel, and the father enjoys a drink, and the wife tells him off; he sobers up quickly and gets on with it, and they all get on with it and harm no one.

The challenge to the lifestyle comes when Deborah Kerr sees a little farm, and dreams of "settling down," something her husband has been trying to avoid (it would mean bills, lawyers, regular jobs, bosses, insecurity, material values, and the whole damn world). The teenage son likes the idea too. It would be different, he thinks, so mother and son encourage their father, usually a jobbing sheep drover, to work in a shearing shed for a whole season in extremely tough, regular conditions, to earn regular wages long enough to put a deposit down. And that, you can say, is when the fun starts. I'm not sure I want to spoil the ending for you if you haven't seen it, even for the sake of this book, because it's a story that brings real tears of joy to the eyes that come straight out of that "spiritual thing" in ourselves that movies can touch better than philosophers or most theologians of my experience. I must add that this movie helped to inspire my family's migration to Australia, and if that was not a transformation of the spirit, nothing was. Sadly, we did not meet Deborah Kerr or Robert Mitchum. Another time, another place . . . perhaps.

A movie with a kindred feel to *The Sundowners* was made from Arthur Miller's script for his then wife Marilyn Monroe, *The Misfits* (1961). Even the titles resonate, the one set in Australia, the other in the deserted hills near Fresno in Northern California. It starred Marilyn Monroe (never better in my view), Clark Gable, Thelma Ritter, Montgomery Clift, and Eli Wallach. The film explores a number of dilemmas and dichotomies as it traces the relationship and jealousies ignited when three very different men encounter recently divorced Marilyn Monroe. The main drama is played out through the symbolic encounter of the men around the task of roping in the last wild stallions in the hills, for money. The horses will be processed as pet food, such is the modern world the men are all desirous of escaping from, in their own ways. The most soulful of the men are Clift's devil-may-care cowboy, who is looking for a maternal light in his life (his mother lives with a man who is not his father and who kicked him out), and, above all, Clark Gable's character, who is a good man, spiritual but a realist also, and lonely with it. Eli Wallach is selfish and quite materialistic. He lusts after Monroe without understanding (though he has a dim sense of something), whereas the other two love her, but in different ways. And here we come to the nub of Miller's cleverness. Monroe is the divine, but wild, Sophia; she is fecund, creative, beautiful, sexual, free, wise about Nature, and a bit unbalanced, a creator of situations and attractions that conflict. She is the woman all real men, and perhaps women, seek, and she does not ask for it. She loves beauty of spirit. That's why she loves Gable.

Fig. 18.7. Marilyn Monroe and Clark Gable in The Misfits, *1961.*

When the penny drops, you realize that the three men represent the three types of human being in the gnostic scheme: spiritual (Gable); psychic (soulful Montgomery Clift with his bedroom eyes and gentleness); and hylic, that is, material—Eli Wallach who sees only his ego and Monroe's flesh, and wants to have his kicks and his cash before fearsome death takes him back to the meaninglessness he feels he's sprung from. Gable pulls in the horses, nearly killing himself in the process (the actor himself died of a heart attack at the end of 1960 undoubtedly exacerbated by the conditions of filming), but then, he gives the horses as a gift to Monroe, knowing what will happen; she sets them free, and with the horses goes the money. The two drive away in a truck, clean of heart, Gable and Monroe. Where are they going? Gable sees a shining star amid the sea of stars in the windscreen. He says they'll just keep heading for that "big star" up there: great stuff, and thoroughly spiritual—not that the pope noticed. After all, wasn't the film about a divorcée who sleeps with a cowboy? That's the difference between religious values and spiritual values, I guess.

I remember my family was on holiday at Colwyn Bay's seaside resort in North Wales in summer 1965, when we entered the local cinema not far from the promenade to see Richard Brooks's *Lord Jim*. Being a British summer, and being Wales, it rained and rained, so the old Colwyn Theatre was a welcome respite as all the sand for which I'd brought my red plastic bucket and spade was as wet as semolina. Watching Peter O'Toole's intense portrayal of Joseph Conrad's anti-hero soon made one forget the rain and dark clouds as we were wafted to high adventure on the high seas about Indonesia. The film is about what it takes for a man to recover his own soul after an understandable act he knows in his heart was cowardice. At that moment, having saved himself because frozen with fear, he is haunted by the shadow of a guilt that leaves him in spiritual distress. From being carefree and confident, he becomes a haunted man, and lets go of his promising career in the merchant navy in the late nineteenth-century days of expansion, mortal danger, and endless opportunity, and seeks to hide himself. Eventually becoming friendly with Malay and Bugis tribespeople, and saving them from an oppressor—played by Curt Jürgens with assistance from the sadistic Eli Wallach (the materialist again!)—Jim is finally brought to face his fear again when an evil, crooked trader played by James Mason tries to rob the village of the gold in their Buddhist temple. Somewhat carrying on the part of T. E. Lawrence that brought him fame and for-tune with *Lawrence of Arabia,* O'Toole portrays the man whose soul is riven asunder by inner, spiritual conflict. In Jim's case, he finds, in the end, his only path to wholeness is through ultimate conquest of fear by an act of voluntary death. The ending is deeply sad for those who like happy endings, and very meaningful for those who like meaning-ful endings. Despite sundry scenes of action and adventure, *Lord Jim* is really a play in which Jim's soul is on trial for its life. Eventually, he passes the test, and in passing, departs this life of shadows and strife, but the price is very high. He has found love, and he feels he must leave it to save his soul. Not a very profitable sounding idea, from the mate-rial point of view, and the film received desultory reviews, but still clawed back $5 million in rentals. It has its longeurs, but is there to be savored. Bronislaw Kaper's score, including traditional gamelans, is magnificently deep, sweeping, romantic, and haunting. Not a great film, but a very good and brave one, exclusively concerned with spiritual values in conflict with human nature.

The year 1964 saw Richard Burton establish a fresh vein of Sixties movies distinguished by spiritual meanings, that vein we may call one of spiritual nonconformity. Sometimes we are dealing with an individual who is a spiritual nonconformist; sometimes the movie itself is by its nature, attitude, and priorities spiritually nonconformist. In the first category must come *Becket* (1964), directed by Peter Glenville with great dignity, so giving Peter O'Toole as King Henry II and Richard Burton as Henry's chancellor-turned-archbishop Thomas à Becket free space to show off their contrasting characters, given powerful dialogue by Jean Anouilh who wrote the original play. Henry thinks he's pulled off a masterstroke when he thinks he can bring the church under his law by making his closest friend Becket head of the Church in England. But Becket surprises himself, and outrages the king, when, for the first time in his life he finds something he can wholly love, and serve, something he calls "the honor of God."

One interesting facet of the two friends' fatal conflict is that it is not Becket who is riven within by his spiritual discovery of the freedom and pain of God, but his king, the worldly Henry, who is cleft in heart by his love for his friend who has found something to love more than himself. The ensuing drama is compelling, but strangely, there is no scene of epiphany, no blinding light, no Damascus Road moment. Becket's embrace of God appears coldly intellectual, even the passion it evokes in him seems cold, and Becket and the king's last meeting on the beach of Normandy is cold. The theme of coldness runs right through the film, if you'll forgive the pun, from the moment we see them riding on a cold morning after a lustful adventure, to the two men discussing state policy while Henry endures a cold shower on his chancellor's advice: "Fight the cold with the cold's weapons." In the end, poor Becket must die under cold steel plunged coldheartedly through his martyr spine. And Henry must be stripped, cold after walking from London to Canterbury, in penance to be whipped by cold Saxon monks for encouraging his barons to murder the arch-bishop in cold blood because he could no longer stand the coldness of Becket's denying him his love. At the end, we have not much more sense of the spiritual than that it can easily become the sin of pride, and *that* goes before a fall: both men lose, but God's church wins. As archbishop, Becket conforms to God's will as he sees it, but in doing so, upsets the pope who expects his minions to make effective political compromises with earthly powers, not generate dangerous confronta-tions. Even the pope can't really control Becket, who appears to one of His Holiness's cardinals simply as a man seething with ambition and conceit. The cynical cardinal just may be right; alternatively, Becket may be God's unwitting instrument. At the end of the movie, we feel cold, but the coldness one might feel inside a great cathedral in a fro-zen waste: impressive but we're not sure why.

Very different is the nonconformist clergyman portrayed by Burton so brilliantly and vividly in John Huston's compelling film of the Tennessee Williams play, *Night of the Iguana*. This man, Rev. Dr. T. Lawrence Shannon, is hot. His passion has got him into trouble. He can't quite tell the difference between human and divine love when confronted by true passion for a woman. He has been rejected by his congregation and though still ordained, is without a parish to preach to, so has become a tour guide for bored middle-aged American women exploring the nether territories of Mexico by rickety old bus, prone like everyone else in the party, to some kind of breakdown—a scenario clearly as pocked with metaphors as the Mexican roads are pep-pered with potholes. Shannon's conduct is watched apprehensively by a miserable closet lesbian played superbly, venomously, by Grayson Hall, who seems sent by the devil or his opposite to taunt the poor Shannon, being slow-griddled on the trident of his dilemma. She is chaperone for a little Lolita-type played appropriately by Sue Lyon who takes a fancy to the older man who needs all his willpower to resist her very advanced advances.

Eventually he seeks refuge, bringing the tourists with him, to an obscure part-jungle, part-beachside little hotel run by a marvelously eccentric Ava Gardner, who knows Shannon and obviously loves him, and more so perhaps now her husband is dead. To the hotel come Deborah Kerr and her grandfather Ninno, both also eccentric, though vulnerable, apparently, and not a little angelic. She draws portraits; her very old grandfather composes poetry, and so they journey living on the goodwill of those with whom they come into contact. Shannon feels himself caught in a curious triangle, all the time taunted by the chaperone and her charge, and dreams of being reinstated, and controlled by church discipline. In the end, Kerr teaches him a spiritual lesson. Ava Gardner mistakes Kerr (Hannah) for a rival, but Kerr gets the better of the situation, even as her grandfather finishes his last poem he's been writing for years, before abruptly expiring in his chair, relieved at last. The tourists depart, threatening to ruin Shannon's life! It has been ruined for longer than they know. Now there just may be a chance of redemption. Shannon stays with Ava Gardner in her terraced paradise that none of the tourists realized was a potential paradise, and, we may hope, spiritual nonconformity leads to an Edenic return to love and grace. Fine picture.*

Burton would bring spiritual nonconformity to the screen again in a much-neglected Sixties classic, *Boom!* Directed by Joseph Losey, from another excellent play by Tennessee Williams, high, high up on a sunlit Italian coast where Elizabeth Taylor plays a dying millionairess (Sissy Goforth) living in extreme, self-indulgent luxury, to which Burton, playing Chris Flanders, a poet and a bit of a roué, mysteriously arrives like a figure of Greek myth. Noël Coward, in an effete performance to beat them all, warns friend Sissy that Flanders is known as the "Angel of Death" arriving just before the end to sever wealthy women from their fortunes. Taylor tries to rid herself of the "intruder" who is treated with great scorn and cruelty, but he persists.

At the end, Burton helps the cynical lady to die peacefully, with love, with compassion. He is an angel of death, not the cause of death but its divine grace: human sympathy and courage, born of a life lived

---

*The movie was shot at, and a few miles from, Puerto Vallarta, Mexico, where director Huston, as well as Burton and Taylor would buy retreat homes. Then unspoiled, it now seems the "tourists" have regained the upper hand, its residual beauties today ringed by high-rise hotels, which Ava Gardner's character wouldn't have been seen dead in.

off-the-road of expectation, a crazy artist misjudged by the world but sustained by some conviction whose root we know not.

It is difficult to know where to "place" the almost unworldly, magisterial excellence of Orson Welles's sublime portrayal of Falstaff in his 1966 movie of that name (original title: *Chimes at Midnight*). Rotund gentleman Sir John Falstaff appears in a number of Shakespeare's plays, and while he has sympathetic elements to his character, is generally used by Shakespeare as a comic fool and foil, at least, that is what a superficial reading of *Henry IV,* part 2, and *Henry V,* for example, might suggest. Welles has dug deeper into the soul of the character and by reconstructing Shakespeare's plays into a single drama centered on Falstaff has almost given us a new Shakespeare character, and, effectively, a new play-movie. Cleverly combining the Shakespearean dialogue with Holinshed's histories of late fourteenth-century and early fifteenth-century English history, Orson Welles creates a revelatory world that only his agile cinema could take to the heights. Welles's direction, acting, and wondrous editing are unmatched by any movie of the period. Furthermore, he makes his spiritual values clear as a bell, and without ambiguities evident in other movies of his such as *Touch of Evil* (1956) and *The Lady from Shanghai* (1946). We see Falstaff's soul, and find

Fig. 18.8. Orson Welles as Falstaff in Chimes at Midnight, *1966.*

that it is Welles's too. They are so intertwined that the movie comes over as a kind of personal confession, or rather *apologia pro vita sua*. Yes, Falstaff is a fool, yes, he is a bit dangerous, yes, he plays with the rules; but what a Great Man he is! And *great* in the best senses. We see a full-blooded *mahatma*, a great soul, shining through his large, laughing, penetrating eyes and in his true motives. We see innocence, and to see it, is almost to recover it.

Welles said on numerous occasions that he stood against the "modern world": the world where children did not honor their parents; where women were treated as sex objects; where beauty was despised in favor of profit; where nobility of character counted for nothing; where ugliness of mind and creation were praised as clever, where art meant artlessness and political power meant the quick fix and the lie with a smile. Above all, Welles loathed materialism and aggressive mindlessness. He favored the individual against the mob. Welles projected similar concerns onto Shakespeare's character of Falstaff. For Welles, at least, Falstaff stands for an older, merrier England, where the air was sweeter, where the warm meadows hummed with joy, where the humor was rich and the punch was hot; the world of old hospitality, of chivalry, of romantic love, of wild spontaneity and impossible dreams: a world where Arthur was hero, and the Lady was to be served, where life was a rich and varied feast to be enjoyed to the full, by gourmet or by drunkard. He is aware that something had happened with the end of the hot-blooded Plantagenets, when the "beady-eyed Tudor" Henry VII, the regal accountant, stood in waiting for a crack to get into, and instigate the new Tudor machine, the ironclad, pitiless juggernaut. Welles felt Shakespeare labored under this powerful, cruel establishment, and was only able to flourish briefly, while Elizabeth I chose for a season not to look into her subjects' souls, and took kindly to poetry and theater for a while, and invoked the spirit of old England to fight the Spanish threat.

Falstaff embodies the old world, with its twinkle in the eye of the old "fool" who knows how to love, is impetuous, merry, and above all, good. For Falstaff is an innocent in a world of eyes being gouged out, and uncompromising violence. This is demonstrated with tragic, comic elements in the unbelievable recreation of the Battle of Shrewsbury, which is like a mad rugby match on a wet Saturday afternoon in the mud, except that all the players have daggers and broadswords and axes and hack and cut and tear asunder with impunity and wild, inhuman, grizzly, and choking, squelching abandon. The cutting of this scene is so passionate, one feels the beat of Welles's heart in every frame, knowing that he has made, surely the finest testimony to the truly good, innocent Man, the only thing worth saving, and cherishing in this mad, bad world gone almost hopelessly wrong.

The last scene shows the enormous coffin of Falstaff, who has died of a broken heart at being publicly rebuked and rejected by the king he has loved and tried to bring forth the best from, being trundled on the back of a wagon, unheralded to its wet grave. It is the grave of innocence, and now the modern world covers it like heavy soil on the casket of an all but forgotten memory of what once was, and it seems, can never be again. Damn the king! The Falstaffs of this world are its kings, and are made to die like paupers. It is, truly, Welles's own story, and one for every man and woman to take heed of. See *Falstaff*, and see life.

It is hard to find a movie more spiritually nonconformist than Kenneth Anger's 1963 self-made movie, *Scorpio Rising,* which cooks up much heat with its blend of motorcycle mania, leather jacket and stud fetishism, the "star" (on the principle "Every man and every woman is a star")* Bruce Byron—an object presumably of the director's gay desire—Nazi imagery, Brando and James Dean fascination, and the music of Ricky Nelson, Bobby Vinton, the Angels, the Crystals, and other teen-dream pop-and-roll gems. Add to this, images of Christianity and the occult, astrology and the odd flash of nudity, and you have another Kenneth Anger alchemical recipe that will be much imitated by *cinéphiles* ever since it was first shown at the Grammercy Arts Theatre ahead of its time in '63. My favorite thing in it, besides the marvelous, over-the-top intro on the theme of the quasi divinity of chrome and leather, is the crosscutting between the arrival of heavy-clad bikers at an exclusive rendezvous and shots from an old Sunday school black-and-white silent

---

*From the Crowleyan gospel *Liber Legis,* "The Book of the Law," 1904.

film of Jesus and his entourage turning up in Jerusalem. *Scorpio Rising* gets under the skin and breathes not only the sweaty insides of leather trousers and shiny boots but an ambivalent spirituality that we know comes from Anger's love for bold outsiders and for one of the boldest ever: English occult scholar, adventurer, and magician, Aleister Crowley (1875–1947) whose religion of Thelema is Anger's brand.

Something of the spirit of Anger's movie seems to permeate the inimitable, original masterpiece that is Nicholas Roeg and Donald Cammell's *Performance*, made in Notting Hill in 1968 and 1969, starring Mick Jagger (who recorded a soundtrack for Anger's film, *Invocation of My Demon Brother*, 1969), Anita Pallenberg, and the devastatingly brilliant James Fox, who plays a man who begins a magicmushroom trip as an East London "heavy" of mordant wit and perverse charm, and ends it as a free-loving hippie turned psychopath. Jagger is the spiritual nonconformist who has abandoned his top-flight rock career to recover his lost mojo through a long exercise in the school of French decadent poet Rimbaud's protracted disorder of the senses. In this he is aided by his faithful(!) bisexual lover Pherber and her French friend Lucy, who take a fancy to the visiting gangster, despite his bizarre appearance, since, on the run from his outfit after a murder, he has painted his hair rust red with domestic paint. The girls can see through the makeup; after all, Jagger (Turner) is often caked in it, and then the alchemy begins. Chas, the villain, needs a new identity. Boy! Does he get one! Turner and the girls set to work on him as if he were a college exam in the high science of head fuck. In the process, Chas learns "a thing or two about performance," and at the end we are not entirely sure whether Turner has become Chas or the other way round. The only evidence left for the police is the dead body of Turner whom Chas has shot through the forehead as a parting gift before being led to his presumed slaughter by the gang who pick him up in what looks like John Lennon's Rolls Royce, but could be Jagger's.

It is illuminating to see both "Chas" and "Turner" evincing two sides (creative and destructive) of Blake's classic figure called "Orc" or "red Orc," fiery youth of Freedom and Rebellion, who appears when spiritual feeling is repressed. In Blake's myths, Orc first appears as Jesus, and again at the American and French revolutions. He is certainly a vital mythic archetype of the Sixties, and Chas's painting his hair red may well be a sign of the Chas + Turner = ORC alchemy of the movie. Turner-Jagger cannot "perform" without Chas's violence, while Chas's violence is balanced by Turner's feminine sensitivity. This is a quintessential component of the decade's spiritual meaning.

There are references to the Hashischim ("Assassins") and the Old Man of the Mountains, and many entertaining quips of the high-stoned variety, and an amazing, dramatized performance of "Memo from Turner" where the sideburned spirit of Elvis '56 meets Francis Bacon's tortured or torturing canvases in a part-naked romp with highly credible London gangsters, and the whole thing is played out with such an eye for pace and detail, and not a little genius, that one is left at the film's end wondering what magic has been effected upon the participants, the directors (who also photographed the picture), and us, the willing accomplices in the morbid urge to gaze.

We have been witnessing evil in *Performance* though it is difficult to see whose side the devil is on. That is not the case in either *Quatermass and the Pit* (1967), which is a sci-fi film of high technical and imaginative order, or *The Devil Rides Out* (1968), a superior Hammer production based on Dennis Wheatley's novel of upper-class Satanists. In both movies, one sci-fi horror, the other, well just horror, the devil is presented as an object, if very hazy or distant, and as something or someone whose power can be broken. That is because both films show the evil of the devil as working on the mind, as a means of delusion, of causing hallucinations, that is, preventing a clear sight of reality. The spirit of the victim is held in bondage and therefore love becomes impossible. In the traditional Christianity of *The Devil Rides Out,* the sign of the cross is the sign of love, whereas Satan can only handle lust. Evil is shown as real in both shock movies, but Satan's medium is psychology. The one film, where Christopher Lee plays a white magician dedicated to freeing persons involved in Satan-worshipping ritual, presents Satan in conventional imagery of horns and Pan-like features who is conjured by nude dancing and surrender to beat and magical incantation, whereas in *Quatermass and the Pit,* the vast horned devil that hovers in the haze over a collapsing London, is a kind of egrigore that achieves manifestation through harnessing the negative energy of all those who come under the influence of a spaceship that crashed beneath a London Underground station at the dawn of humanoid creatures, and whose influence has been generating occult phenomena ever since, now let out of low-level activity thanks to archaeology. One could say it all amounts to the same thing. The devil is the manifestation of the results of human weaknesses. In *Quatermass and the Pit,* this devil is neutralized by curiously nonspiritual means. An iron crane falling into the blackness of the evil being ("earthing" it), plus a simultaneous act of voluntary sacrifice, does the trick as surely as a stake to the heart of Count Dracula. Whereas, in *The Devil Rides Out,* the conjuror, Macata, evil black magician (played coldly but engagingly by Charles Gray), must be killed by fire in a conflagration of all his wicked works. It all sounds very medieval, and one must accept that in the 1960s, as today, our ideas about evil have not changed as much as our ideas about human heredity, whence our weakness comes to us.

One intriguing comedy that did take a completely fresh look at the devil and all his works was Peter Cook's script turned into movie *Bedazzled* (1967) by director Stanley Donen, starring Peter Cook, Dudley Moore, and versatile, sharp-as-a-pin Cambridge graduate Eleanor Bron, with very effective music by Dudley Moore, whose comedic timing is top-notch as well. It is obvious for the sympathy shown to "Beelzebub" by Peter Cook that he had thought a great deal about traditional theology concerning the role of rebel angel Lucifer and found the contradictions of religious mythology about him fit material for satire. In Cook's story, Lucifer fell out of heaven on account of boredom! Having to sing the praises of the Almighty perpetually would naturally bore any natural, human being, especially an ambitious one! Besides, as he makes clear, temptation gives human life its drama and interest, and, were it to cease, there would be no basis for a redemptive scheme, so, as the script makes clear: don't blame the devil! He's just doing his job, and as played by Cook, may not at all be devoid of human sympathy. The seven deadly sins are in everyone's nature, and it's our being what we are that makes the traditional devil's task a piece of cake! The script cleverly shows up the difficulty of anthropomorphizing theological or metaphysical concepts. Follow the logic of the anthropomorphism and you wind up with the contradictory absurdity that the Almighty may appear more cruel and unapproachably arrogant than the rebel angel. In the end, poor Satan is not allowed back into heaven because he has shown a capacity for goodness, which was not part of *his* contract! The argument is that if "God" is *that* almighty (omnipotence means he can do *anything*), he's ultimately responsible for everything that happens, and it's no good just keeping the bad bits for Satan with all the good bits being God's. It would make a reasonable theology or philosophy essay and Cook's genius has turned it into a super script with many original comedic elements. Its spirit of challenge, humanity, openness to the conclusion of logic, and sheer audacious cheek is fundamentally intellectual-meets-artistic Sixties at its core, and when Brendan Fraser starred in the remake with Elizabeth Hurley (2000), the whole axis of the story had to be changed to suit new sensibilities unable to take, I presume, the full-frontal, unsentimental challenge of Peter Cook's devil-may-care-a-bit analysis. The "meaning" in the end of Cook's scenario is that life with belief in the integrity of the soul is, regardless of argument, going to be practically and emotionally better than life without one, where at least there is hope and some room for freedom, both to succeed, and to fail honorably. The risk of damnation is worth the risk of living at all. The hapless Dudley Moore character's problems stem from his desires (for Eleanor Bron who works with him at a Wimpy hamburger bar). By looking outside himself for help (to the devil who offers seven wishes, all barbed), he fails to rely on the capacities of his own immortal soul (which he bargains away in the process), and winds up in a mess that, in the end, only Satan's uncharacteristic generosity redeems him from!

While *Performance* was undoubtedly the best film of the decade to harness to something like mainstream commercial cinema the spiritual nonconformity lurking in the Sixties upper-end rock scene, that scene itself generated its own movie effusions testifying to spiritual qualities within its bloom. Among these we may mention D. A. Pennebaker's *Monterey Pop* (1968), an account of the world's first festival of pop, held at Monterey, California, in the Summer of Love, so-called, of 1967. The

a   b

Fig. 18.9. (a) *Janis Joplin (1943–1970),*
(b) *Grace Slick of the Jefferson Airplane (1939–).*

spirit of the time comes over very strongly in the performances and the positively glowing reaction to those performances given for top dollar by the Mamas and the Papas, Simon & Garfunkel, the Animals, Hugh Masekela, Janis Joplin, the Who, Country Joe and the Fish, Ravi Shankar, Otis Redding (arguably the best performance), Jefferson Airplane, and Jimi Hendrix's triumphant return to the States from former obscurity in the company of English sidemen Mitch Mitchell and Noel Redding. He burnt his guitar, which might have meant something. He said it was to "sacrifice" something he really loved, but one suspects the stunt was simply to get one over Pete Townshend, who had smashed his guitar against his amplifier. Hmm. . . . Imitation masturbation while pouring lighter fuel on an unoffending Stratocaster was not the best introduction to Jimi Hendrix's spiritualized imagination, but nobody seemed to mind too much at the time. Monterey was a great success and its spirit traveled far—but who needs burning guitars? I daresay Richard Nixon would have liked to have set fire to all of them!

The Beatles did not have at their disposal the resources entrusted by MGM to Stanley Kubrick. Had they been so vouchsafed a movie

Fig. 18.10. A press photo of the Beatles during the filming of
A Magical Mystery Tour, *1967.*

budget, their Christmas 1967 TV film *A Magical Mystery Tour* might
have lived up more to the promise of its fecund ideation. One suspects
they received some inadequate advice about what could be achieved
with ordinary 16mm film without a proper production basis, and without a sympathetic director. But then, the exercise was Paul's way of trying to get the group to focus on something other than the ugly trauma
of losing manager Brian Epstein to barbiturate overdose in August of
1967 while they were taking lessons in T.M. from the yogi of Rishikesh
who had come up with a Western-oriented mantra-yoga program. It was
also something of a miscalculation that they shot the film with color in
mind when English and most world audiences, with the exception of

the United States, were only familiar with black-and-white TV. They were thinking ahead, but not very clearly. That probably had a lot to do with what they'd been taking in their spare time when not in the studio working on their many extraordinary songs of that very special year. Still, *A Magical Mystery Tour* is what it is, and what it is, my seventeen-year-old daughter thinks, is "very spiritual." I asked her which parts, and she said "all of it," though we did agree that the ending was something of a letdown, after some very fine, and some very interesting and amusing segments in this imaginative, and according to Martin Scorsese, pioneering and influential, potpourri.

For myself, I disagree with the idea that the picture is "ahead of its time" on the basis that it may be seen as preempting MTV or the "pop video" especially now MTV is already a thing of the past, and who really would want to claim parenthood of the pop video, whose diminished stock decreases further with the years? This was a poor excuse. No, damn it, *A Magical Mystery Tour* is a *film*, not a collection of promos. It is a film made, directed, produced, and written by the greatest group of all time, so it deserves respect for being what it is: a genuine moment of Sixties enthusiasm for doing something different, anticonformist, and imaginative. Despite the relatively weak nature of the 16mm color stock and the hasty editing, undershooting, and often uninspired camerawork, we have a concept, not entirely realized, of some merit, in many places very well realized. And the music is of course peerless. Pity most speakers in television sets had all the sonic fidelity of a biscuit tin.

Taking a tip one suspects from Ken Kesey and the Merry Prankster's multicolored bus and Kesey's "Electric Kool-Aid Acid Test" tours round the States, Paul McCartney reckoned the Beatles could do a kind of homely English version that would start on familiar ground with some minor stock characters from English comedy, and end-of-the-pier shows, before becoming more psychedelic as the magic (the Beatles' own) started to transform the experience like the onset of a mind trip, an experience at least three of the band were now more than familiar with. No matter that LSD trips can barely be recalled as experienced nor can be adequately described, the group put their faith in the magic of film and music to do the business. Besides, they had the notion of an inclusive tour, not an exclusive or élite experience. The spirituality behind this ambition is most evident in a very moving scene where the most miserable man on the bus, Mr. Bloodvessel (Buster Bloodvessel, an eccentric Scottish humorist) declares his real heartfelt love for Ringo's Auntie (played by Jessie Robins) who is very far from being the most obviously glamorous person on the bus (that honor going to a blond starlet who engages Paul's attention). The couple kiss and hold hands like two pensioners celebrating their golden anniversary, and walk on a British beach (Newquay) spelling out their love with sticks in the sand to a florid George Martin orchestral arrangement of the Lennon-McCartney credited song "All My Loving" from 1963. What is so moving is not only the love between these two characters but the fact that the Beatles reached out to all people of all ages, whatever they looked like. They were looking beneath the surface and seeing the lonely and gifted souls of people whose characters can make them lonely, and they were seen as whole people, worthy of love and good things. This was an attitude almost unknown in the world of showbusiness, where "love" was almost always the province of either young, healthy, good-looking, mostly white, photogenic boys and girls, or of smart married adults with loving families. The Beatles showed an inclusive love, and like Jesus's parable about going into the hedgerows to find guests for the real messianic banquet, the Beatles favored the outsiders, the people normally overlooked or frowned on. This was a spiritually Christian gesture in the real sense and shines on today, and will tomorrow.

There are poetic flourishes in the film that also merit appreciation and praise. Paul McCartney took a cameraman down to Provence in Southern France with him one day to shoot some material of Paul as "The Fool on the Hill" of his magical, spiritual song of that name. The sequence is a dream and works well. There is a moment when the mask falls from Paul's face and we see something of his soul, a sort of hapless, wide-eyed, perhaps suspiciously reddened look (around the windows to his soul), maybe not quite the holy fool of the song's imagining, but someone of that order nonetheless, someone who has surrendered his defenses at least momentarily to vision. John always

Fig. 18.11. The Fool.
Tarot trump card designed
by Frieda, Lady Harris,
for Aleister Crowley.
Courtesy of the OTO.

knew Paul had it in him, but his loved partner tended crassly and carelessly to suppress it. The Fool of the song is the one the world is blind to, but who sees; the one who hears but is not heard. He is invisible because his pitch is not material, but spiritual, essential not temporal. This is a completely traditional spiritual figure of hundreds of years of Western spiritual culture (we find him as a tarot trump with the number 0), and the song encapsulates the idea with lyrical contributions from John, I believe, that keep this song off the ground and forever in the air, timeless.

John's greatest contribution to the exercise, "I Am the Walrus," is almost opposite in tone because it is all about masks, about illusion, about change and disintegration, and about pain behind the mask: a familiar theme of John's, and of spiritual imagery of all time. "I'm crying," he sings through the cacophony of layered effects. No doubt many of the lyrics are just a bit of mischievous fun to confuse deliberately those who would see, as he put it in 1980, "depths of whatever" in the song. We would be foolish to interpret lines about "semolina pilchard climbing up the Eiffel Tower," but the overall effect of the song is one nonetheless of laying bare a desperate state of mind, an asphyxiated spirit by obscuring it deliberately. Its author, like Ken Kesey's hero in *One Flew Over the Cuckoo's Nest* expects to be "taken away" by "the van" to an insane asylum for thinking the way he does. He's suffering, sitting precipitously on his own in the rain in an English garden. John made this fear of his quite explicit in an interview with the BBC's *Release* arts program in 1968 when he said that the leaders of the world were "insane" and people didn't realize it, and that he was likely to be "put away" as insane for saying so, with just a hint of the tortured genius/ Christ complex there. You had to be mad to be sane in the Sixties, would be one way of expressing John's spiritual challenge, so easily garbled and misunderstood. Maybe the weakness of *A Magical Mystery Tour* is, in fact, its long-term strength. It will continue to garner the enthusiasm of young people who can still see the peak of the hill on which the Fool stands.

One cannot leave the Beatles' semichaotic ventures into independent filmmaking without mentioning a film the Beatles themselves were uneasy about. *Let It Be* began at the end of 1968 as another idea of Paul's, but this time they brought in Michael Lindsay Hogg to direct it. Perhaps it's a pity nobody realized at the time that the director was the son of Orson Welles, for they might perhaps have listened more to what he had to suggest—but I doubt it. As it was, the director was the instrument of the collective will of the group. Unfortunately they had difficulty agreeing on the best way forward. Perhaps the members of the group were all just very, very tired, with perhaps the exception of Paul, who never seemed to lack energy. Anyhow, after some desultory sessions in Twickenham Studios—I'm not surprised they were disconcerted; I've worked among its cavernous looms myself—they moved into the basement of their offices at Apple in Savile Row in London's Mayfair and, thanks to George, enjoyed the assistance on organ of the warm, incisive presence of fab fifth Billy Preston. Then things started to cook, and from the moment they all jam on an unfinished potential masterpiece called "Dig It" the rocket takes off, culminating in one of the finest, if not *the* finest, live rock performances ever given on this planet, when the group cast care aside, troop up to the roof of the building, and in blisteringly cold January winds perform a repertoire of new songs rehearsed to living perfection downstairs. The spirit of this performance tells us more about the vast energies available in the Sixties than anything else one might see. The band is mind-blowingly superb. The reaction from everyone who happened to be about Savile Row that lunchtime says it all. Nobody is indifferent. The high priests of commerce of course call the police to stop the rot before the genie gets right out of the bottle and takes over London, stopping capital flow and reminding money that money isn't everything, but before the official "black maria" (police wagon) turns up with its nervous young police, we see middle-aged men in trilbies with pipes, making their way in an orderly but slightly hurried fashion up to the rooftops to join excited office workers with a kind of "I do this everyday, don't you know" look about them—not to see Dick Van Dyke and the chimney sweeps "Step in Time" with Mary Poppins, but to see John and Paul and George and Ringo and Billy on the rooftops of London do what should have been done long before: be free before the world. They had gone as musicians where no man had gone before, and the people, all the people, responded, from a taxi driver who said he was "all in favor of it" to the passing vicar who said how nice it was to "have something free in this country for a change" to the war veteran who so eloquently, despite advanced years, expressed his genuine, even acute understanding of why the Beatles were "all out on their own" and unlike anything before or since, to the excited miniskirted girls who whooped and giggled with intense excitement, and *it* just might have happened that day. . . . But it did. And we can see it in *Let It Be.* It's time we saw the cleaned-up DVD, Paul and Ringo. Come on, men! Everybody understands those niggles twixt thee and George, Paul; it was all part of the mix, and the result of it all is what counts. Let it be free. Why not give the perfected copies away?

A last thought: The spirit of nonconformity generated within the rock and pop scene had its effects on the style of movies that were made independent of the music or any of its protagonists. I should name the following as examples of movies touched by that spirit: *The Knack* (Richard Lester, 1965); *What's New, Pussycat?* (Clive Donner, Richard Talmadge, 1965); *Modesty Blaise* (Joseph Losey, 1966); *Casino Royale* (John Huston, Ken Hughes, Val Guest, Joseph McGrath, Robert Parrish, Richard Talmadge, 1967); *Petulia* (Richard Lester, 1968); *Barbarella* (Roger Vadim, 1968); *Staircase* (Stanley Donen, 1968); *Castle Keep* (Sydney Pollack, 1969); *Goodbye, Mr. Chips* (Herbert Ross, 1969); *Cactus Flower* (Gene Saks, 1969); *On Her Majesty's Secret Service* (Peter Hunt, 1969); *Butch Cassidy and the Sundance Kid* (George Roy Hill, 1969); *The Italian Job* (Peter Collinson, 1969); *The Magic Christian* (Joseph McGrath, 1969).

There may be something in the fact that of this selection of fourteen movies, seven of them were made in the last year of the decade. Did they know something was ending, or was it that the money had finally, if briefly, caught up with the spirit?

NINETEEN

Television

Readers will recall my mentioning the arrival of my family in Melbourne by bus at the end of January 1967 with nowhere to live and no job and very little money. So we arrived, and while Dad went off to find a subsidiary of a toolmaking firm he'd worked for in England in hope of work, Mum took us round cash-eager estate agents, then furniture rental stores, and finally a supermarket, in hot streets very strange to us. By seven o'clock in the evening, we were leaning against the kitchen window of first-floor Flat 2, Eildon Court, St. Kilda—a place we'd never seen before in our lives—waiting for Dad to reappear among us. Then the kitchen furniture and bedtime mattresses arrived. The furniture was minimal, cheap Sixties tubular rubbish but preferable to sitting on the floor. We could now eat cornflakes on a table. We three brothers still felt a bit glum and shell-shocked, despite the sunshine outside. Then the door knocked: our first visitor. We all looked at each other—who could it be? In walked a deliveryman with a small portable rented TV. With mounting excitement we watched him place the white plastic, portable object on the formica-topped kitchen table and plug in its little aerial. Document signed, man departed and we hurriedly switched on. The first image to appear in crisp black-and-white was Roger Moore as Ivanhoe, the medieval English hero in chainmail, doing chivalrous things to rousing music in English forests. We all cheered. At last, we were *home*.

That is how important TV was to us in the Sixties. We were connected, and we were happy. TV provided anchorage and a rich, parallel world.

Fig. 19.1. Family gathered around the television.

By 1967, most of the world was connected to some kind of television service. No government was likely to miss the opportunity of speaking and being seen and *believed* right inside the intimate homes of their populations. From the late Twenties, the United States had led the way in TV development, quickly followed by the United Kingdom, Germany, Australia, France, Canada, and the Soviet Union. The biggest period of TV service development was undoubtedly the 1950s when relatively limited services began to resemble what we are familiar with today in terms of programming of news, entertainment (music, comedy, drama), quiz games, educational programs, and old films—and not forgetting, cheery advertising. By 1955 half of American households were accessible to TV advertising, the vast majority of sets being black-and-white, with color only coming into its own in the mid-Sixties when more American shows were made in color. The 1960s and 1970s saw central and most of southern Africa connected to their state-controlled broadcasts.

The year 1967 marked a new consciousness of what television could do. Not only could countries receive their own programs, but new satellite technology opened up the idea that we now all take for granted, that most of the world can receive simultaneous broadcasts, and any country can broadcast identical pictures and sound to other countries willing to receive the material (or immaterial). Suddenly it seemed the whole world was *in the air*. The psychological registration of this experience can hardly be appreciated today. This was godlike communication.

The fact was brought home, literally and directly, to somewhere between 400 and 700 million people (I was one of them) on June 25, 1967 (Greenwich Mean Time), when a special program optimistically called *Our World,* first sponsored by the BBC, was broadcast live to fourteen countries, and for which each country provided a segment of live programming. The countries concerned in the final broadcast were the United Kingdom, the United States, Australia, Austria, Canada, Denmark, France, Italy, Japan, Mexico, Spain, Sweden, Tunisia, and West Germany. Behind the Iron Curtain, Hungary, East Germany, Poland, Czechoslovakia, and the USSR all pulled out of the *Our World* project in a pointless protest against Western support for Israel in the Arab-Israeli Six-Day War (June 5–10, 1967). It's easy to bury your head in the sand when sand is all you've got.

The *Our World* program was made possible thanks to the launch into terrestrial orbit of the satellites Intelsat I, Intelsat 2-2, Intelsat 2-3, and NASA's ATS-1. Participating countries got to see some rather dull, frosty programming from the various countries, with a few highlights, such as painter Picasso and opera singer Maria Callas, but the excitement of the program was not, for once, the content of the broadcast but the phenomenon of the broadcast itself. Suddenly a large part of the world was looking collectively at the same thing, hearing the same message, *listening to one another.* An important project rule stipulated that no politician or world leader was permitted to speak, which must say something about organizers' understanding of the risks of such ventures even then. Most people saw live shots of pretty places such as Kitsilano Beach, Vancouver, or places of pride, like the Tokyo subway system. I can't remember whether I was up at 5:22 a.m. on what was for us by then June 26 to see live shots from Melbourne of trams leaving from the Hanna Street Depot, broadcast to the "world." Hanna Street was only about a mile up the road from where we lived in St. Kilda! So that certainly brought next door to our doorstep, so to speak, and our next door to the wide world. But I do remember being up at 6:54 a.m. to see the Beatles performing live (at what to them was 8:54 p.m. the previous night in London!) their only-just-in-time finished song, "All You Need Is Love." This was probably the only specifically spiritually meaningful content in the global broadcast, if one omits the fact that the program's special theme was sung in many languages by the Vienna Boys' Choir, famous for Christmas renderings of "Silent Night."

John Lennon had been eager to accept the invitation to provide a song message for the world, and in the spirit of the time, and genius of the moment, he summed up the Beatles' message, and the feelings of many of his and other generations, faced with a terrible war raging in Vietnam, and hate-filled conflict in the Middle East and elsewhere. "There's nothing you can do that can't be done," sang John meditatively, with his eyes closed. It wasn't enough to say, "Well we can't do anything about it; it's not up to us." Every person is capable of love. The message was, "We can do it if we put our hearts into it. But without love, forget it." And love is *free*.

For many people of my father's generation, this utterly Christian, and indeed universal, that is, nondenominational, spiritual message was obscured by the *image* of the Beatles, and by the preconceived image of them the newspapers were now beginning to promote, with barely concealed glee. Only one week earlier, the U.K.'s ITN News had shown an interview with Paul McCartney where, pressed by persistent journalists to answer honestly the question as to whether he had *ever* taken LSD, Paul had given the press a mighty morsel of prosecution evidence. Ignoring other interesting things Paul had to say, the message was quickly spread by telex around the world that the Beatles were "on drugs." Consequently, when John sang his song on *Our World,* the fact that the Beatles were seated, swung gently, heads bobbing slowly to the beat of their music, were chewing gum for concentration, had eyes intermittently closed, and were wearing very strange psychedelic costumes (pity nobody could see their amazing colors!), and unusual hairstyles, the conclusion reached by all but the Beatle-initiated young was that the Beatles were stoned, as were the oddly dressed young men and women squatting around them (including Mick Jagger and Marianne Faithfull) and were therefore advocating a kind of collective "loose living" ethic of "free love" (premarital sex) and were, arguably "not man enough" to do a "patriotic chore" (as Kenny Rogers and others would describe Vietnam conscription), and were therefore hostile to the values of responsible, right-thinking people, up against evil Commies. *What was going on in England?* came the cry, that the head of a once-great world empire that had given the world Winston Churchill and thrashed barbaric Germany twice was allowing itself to be represented by young men who were clearly(!) going astray, and would lead others astray in their apparently narcoleptic wake? The Beatles, it was observed widely, had gone *strange*.

Poor John! He had come to terms with Jesus's continued popularity and was now singing from the same hymn sheet—and he was *still* in the dock! It's funny for me today to see this clip of the Beatles in modern documentaries. The impression always seems to be given that this pop-musical soirée was some kind of countercultural triumph of mass communication, that the Summer of Love was shared by the (non-Communist) world. It *was* a triumph in a sense of course, in that it happened at all, but to imagine the world opened its arms to this new image of the Beatles and their message would be a great error. The Beatles, in their courageous innocence, had set themselves up. From being the world's darlings at the start of 1966, the Beatles' countercultural, spiritual stance was now making them appear obscure and possibly a perilous risk to the minds of youth about the world: an abyss of mutual noncomprehension had opened up between the generations, like the sharp expanses of the Grand Canyon. My dad looked dimly on the Monkees bubblegum cards I showed him soon after. I, like most boys that I knew, had "short-back-and-sides" haircuts at the time, and the only flowers were on tea towels or curtains. And Dad had risked his life fighting Communism in Malaysia in the Forties and early Fifties, and knew what the game was.

The *One World* show in fact revealed there were still many worlds of conflicting discourse and understanding, and only the blandest images

*Fig. 19.2. My father on active service circa 1948–1949
during the Malayan Emergency.*

imaginable were acceptable to all. And yet, something did happen that morning (or night). We became aware of an electronic global reality that could lift us from where we were. I don't recall myself feeling any particular foreboding about this at the time; we were quite ready to be entranced by science and the wonder of the technology, and many who were alive then did experience something like a spiritual frisson, a palpable uplift of being extraordinarily lucky to be living at such a time, such a moment, *live,* right now, in history as history was being made. TV was an all-seeing eye. . . . Despite the sour grapes of the Soviets (we were used to that), it all looked like things were, as Paul McCartney sang on *Sgt. Pepper* (released that June), "Getting Better," and would and could and should get better still. Alleluia! And TV would be plugged right into the center of the change. And we were plugged into *it.*

SPIRITUAL TELEVISION?

It's strange, isn't it? You'd think with a name like tele*vision* that the aspect of "vision" might have made producers think in terms of the visionary. A visionary is someone who sees, a *seer,* someone who sees through the obvious, and beyond the limits to glimpse essential reality, and we usually call that reality something on the lines of "spiritual reality" because it's a kind of ultimate. True mystics do not see misty or hazy visions but see things clear-cut and clean, crisp, true, and without obscurity, or to use a modernism "in high-def." A visionary has the full spiritual capacity of the mind balanced and working. He or she sees not with what Blake would call the "vegetable" eye but with the spiritual eye, with reason, intuition, feeling, and sensation in dynamic harmony and in a state of high receptivity. Well, that proved too much for the business! No, m'dear, "vision" in TV just means plain old seeing of objects as they appear, that is, the visible world, the measurable world, what materialists insist is "the real world" (though what could be less real than TV, which travels invisibly through air!). Whenever we get a bit further is because someone has used their imagination, and that can open up a few doors, though they tend to be into well-visited rooms.

I know what I'm talking about here because when I left university, I determined to go into religious TV. I don't mean evangelical channels trying to convert people or get money from them. In England there used to be the occasional documentary that investigated aspects of religion. I didn't want to make programs about church services. I wanted (*a*) to *investigate* religion and religious experience, and (*b*) somehow to *show* spiritual experience, reveal and explain it. In fact, it was difficult to know precisely what I wanted to do because as far as I could see there never had *been* any truly religious TV, by which I meant, I suppose, *spiritual* TV or tele*vision:* TV that would open up the inner eye. I said I wanted to put the *vision* back in the tele. This effort, you may not be surprised to hear, encountered considerable resistance in the business, though not from the viewing public, who were, as ever, eager to look!

So you can imagine it's quite difficult to locate spiritual meaning in Sixties television when outlets for investigation of spiritual meaning were rare to nonexistent. There was the odd documentary in the late Sixties in the United Kingdom about archaeology of Stonehenge, or witchcraft, or the odd thing about flying saucers, but nothing very serious or mind changing. Religion meant either services of religion or clergy debating public morals and condemning films and TV they thought bad for us. However, there was a spiritual vibe around TV during the Sixties, though hard to define or locate purely, a problem that need not deter us. First, there was some pretty good science fiction.

One of my earliest memories is that of seeing the second episode of the brand new *Doctor Who* TV series. This really was new, and to many, shocking and exciting. The series was not bought in the United States until 1972 and even then, syndicators Time-Life TV omitted all episodes from the series starring the first two actors who played the part: William Hartnell and Patrick Troughton, covering the years 1963–1969, so America missed the experience (Canada showed one series in 1965). The second episode of the first series was broadcast just after teatime on Saturday, November 30, 1963 (it was well dark outside and winter cold), and I can recall being scared to death as the light in the living room was switched off, and we had this huge TV with small screen that produced a shivering glow of wavy gray-and-white, pearly images because there was something wrong with the valves that ran the old sets. So it had a ghostly feel already! Anyway, the "Doctor" was a kindly, irascible old man who had a time machine because he was not really of this world, and the time machine looked like an ordinary London police box. In the second episode, he took a pair of young Londoners (as I recall) back in time to the Stone Age. I remember the scene in the caves where the cavemen lived in skins, with bones everywhere. It was very dark, and ever after I was fascinated by the word *cavemen* and looked for pictures about them in every book I could find. It might even have marked the start of my lifelong fascination with history.

Well, it was a great idea to have a character that could traverse time and space. The Tardis (the Doctor's time machine) could move through time (future or past), and thereby effectively traverse distances of space. However, it still operated in some sense within time and space, though his great-looking control station suggested *another dimension*. Now, a spiritual experience of the highest order must transcend the categories of created space and time altogether. However, with the freedom to break ordinary (to us) boundaries of space and time, the *Doctor Who* idea seemed to be heading somewhere very interesting, and the very varied and original stories (well before *Star Trek*) definitely stimulated the imagination in such a way as to make the notion that "anything is possible" quite acceptable, especially to the mind of a receptive and reasonably intelligent child. The sky was not the limit, and it would no longer be true to say "tomorrow never comes." *Doctor Who* could hop over many tomorrows.

Doctor Who proved immensely popular in England, and for quite a while, the Doctor and his semimechanical enemies, the Daleks, were probably as famous as the hairy group from Liverpool, who had a year's head start (no pun intended) in hitting the national imagination.

My own personal love of television really got off the ground when we moved to Australia, and moving there gives me a slight advantage in discussing Sixties TV, because Australia, unlike England, obtained perhaps the largest proportion of its broadcast material from the United States, as well as getting cartoons from Japan and many tie-in products from Hong Kong. So it was an opportunity to see the best of British and of American TV (European TV really didn't count as it was either very provincial or poor-imitation stuff), and the homegrown Australian television, all on the same bill as it were, and one could feel them interacting. One felt on the crossroads of the Western world, with the advantage of a very open, confident, optimistic, no-nonsense society around one. Australia was conscious of itself as being a young country, and Australia was proud, and as an Australian (we saluted the flag regularly on parade at school), one walked tall and felt entitled to whatever was available to be enjoyed.

Unlike England, which only had two channels when we arrived Down Under, the state of Victoria had four: GTV9, HSV7, Channel 0, and ABC2 (the latter being the national broadcaster, equivalent of the BBC with no adverts). As I recall, Channel 0 showed strange things like moral or religious discussions, and the other two were commercial channels, with loads of lively advertisements and program sponsors butting into shows to push products, which for an English observer was very amusing.

I must say that I found the American shows the most enjoyable to watch. I think we had arrived at a kind of golden age of wacky American comedy. Many shows were repeats of shows from the early Sixties, or even the Fifties, so one could see that there had been some change and development of theme and attitude, and things were moving fast. American producers were clearly aware of a brisk change in the air that clearly had something to do with the popularity of the madcap humor associated with the Beatles and with young people in general, but there was quite a bit more, I think.

Clearly, there was a great deal of competition between networks, and much copying of essential ideas, a lot of cashing in on established successes, and with all that cash came the hubris (perhaps) to be willing to give almost anything a try, and not always within reason either. As the mid-Sixties became the later and late Sixties, there were definite trends toward a kind of comedic appeasement of hippiedom. There was also a growing tendency toward satire, with a small dose of occasional surrealism, both strains of TV already well pioneered and developed in the United Kingdom. With satire comes cynicism, and this was nearly always aimed at authority figures and establishment areas where ultimate control seemed remote or alien from the ordinary person. And while we're on the subject of aliens, the growing UFOlogy and sci-fi interest fueled some curious programs, very much of their time, and often, as one might suspect, rather unworldly and obviously unearthly. Popular occultism also got a good splash of humor with a few way-out and very well-written shows.

Overall, however, there was a rollicking good-humoredness in the air, and the scriptwriters worked hard to come up with quips that had an edge and could sound wholesome at the same time. This was certainly a golden age of family TV. It was widely presumed that two or even three generations were sitting together watching the "box" at the same time, so offense was not something you wanted to give. American shows were certainly fundamentally more conservative morally and politically than U.K. material, but there was some clever subterfuge in getting risqué material through in double entendres and a hint to those who got the point. A feature of U.S. TV humor is the waiting for an audience to get, or even make the joke that's coming before it comes, or not. Let the audience appear to lead is a good trick and allows for much pleasant innuendo: that "*You* know what I'm thinking" thing.

I certainly got a huge buzz off the following programs during this mid- to late Sixties period, and though some are so much of their time as to be inaccessible in the main, there are some classics here that still lighten the heart, stimulate the imagination, and encourage a healthy sense of something other than the daily material round of things.

These were some of my favorite TV shows. We all loved *Gomer Pyle,* a sitcom about a hapless, rather stupid soldier, who is always being told to "Move it, Pyle!" It became a catchphrase of my father's when getting us to do chores. *F-Troop* with Forrest Tucker and Larry Storch ran from 1965–67 and I didn't miss many of the adventures of a U.S. bluecoat cavalry troop at a fort during the Indian wars. I daresay there wasn't a PC word in it, but it all seemed uplifting at the time. *McHale's Navy* was a rather old-fashioned comedy with overall upbeat feel set on a U.S. Navy vessel (similar things had been done as movies). There were lots of shows about imaginative couples and families finding their own way to stay clean, happy, and healthy through the modern experience. I loved *Green Acres* with Eddie Albert and Eva Gabor, which used to be shown on Sunday afternoons from 1965 in England, and concerned a couple who leave the New York rat race for a farm in the country, if memory serves. So many ladies wore gingham dresses in those days—extensions, it seemed, of spotlessly clean tablecloths! The series had a lovely theme song: "Green Acres is the place to be!" it went. I had to agree, and doubtless did millions of others who shared the couple's harmless adventures in search of a really good life of love and liberty. For fairly obvious reasons I always think of this show in relation to *Mister Ed,* which featured a talking horse. Why not? If you thought that was weird, there was *Mister Terrific,* a government agent who could fly, without a plane. You'd have thought the president would have had first benefit of such an advantage. That came out in 1967, and seemed to be going quite a long way into very offbeat territory. My brothers and I would look forward to it on Friday nights when Mum and Dad went out together to the Southern Aurora Hotel, Dandenong, for a well-earned drink and break from us, the family, the joys of which

Fig. 19.3. My favorite photo of Mum and Dad at the Southern Aurora Hotel, Dandenong, a Friday night in mid-1968 (we brothers were probably at home watching Mr. Terrific *with bottles of root beer).*

were celebrated bizarrely in both *The Addams Family* and *The Munsters* who seemed to be close cousins. The premise of both loveable series was far-out but they always kept their (lead) feet on the ground. Great fun and opened one's mind to other ways one might live if one *had* to live in California!

The first *Monkees* TV shows were pretty good too. They seemed to be first cousins of the fabulous *Batman* TV series that I adored: similar colors, very opaque. Adam West played it just right, and everyone played it *as if* it was serious, which was why it worked. My dad adored the sly humor while I, an innocent boy, thought it was for real! *Pow! Zap!* And it was very original in spirit. It was always interesting to see the Boy Wonder chatting with girls of his age group who seemed to be beatniks on a fast track to full San Francisco hippiedom, and it was clear Bruce and Alfred's clean-cut ward of stately Wayne Manor was

*Fig. 19.4. Adam West
in the television series*
Batman, *1966.*

not going to "skin up" and join them. Still, Dick Grayson couldn't have been completely square, to go out in green knickers and a yellow cape, hanging out with a man in shiny blue underwear sporting patent leather boots and gloves! Neal Hefti knew the score and gave it to us straight: the theme tune, that is. *Kepow! Wham!* A superior show, it was all very smart, and *Get Smart* with Don Adams and Barbara Feldon was also a gas—not surprising when you consider the series' devisors were comic luminary Mel Brooks, and Buck Henry.

Being children we tolerated most cartoons, though there were two cartoon series that rightly appealed to adults as well, thanks to the collective genius of Hanna-Barbera and Co. *Top Cat* and his feline sidekicks could have been played straight, such was the quality of the dialogue twixt the ever-ingenious rogue T.C. and the sentimental mug who upholds law and order in the back alley, Officer Dibble. *Top Cat* had a lot in common with Phil Silvers's Fifties creation Sgt. Bilko, a combination of egotism, sympathy, sentiment, generosity, fast-talking gags, and soft villainy. One feels he'd make it past Saint Peter as T.C.'s confession would make a saint giggle.

The Flintstones was a marvelous skit on so many aspects of then-modern U.S. family life—and Western working life in general—very

Fig. 19.5. Young Toby, aged six (1966). Note the Batman badge (my favorite TV show).

friendly, but cutting too, if you understood the pressures on families to be perfect examples of Americana and to make ends meet, with time and cash for some labor-saving entertainment. *Yabadabadoo!* is an appropriate cry of joy of a temporarily freed spirit at the close of a long working day in the capital machine—and back home to a wife who wants the latest gadget. One feels feminism may have sprouted from the thought that the "wife back home" had *become* the latest gadget. Though while an analysis of life amid the Flintstones might have inspired a feminist critique, such was not to be found in Sixties presentations of the "ordinary family"; roles were clearly defined and reveled in. At the bottom of the heap were the creature underdogs, running the "labor-saving" devices: "It's a living!" they'd sigh, resigned to the treadmill that went on and on. "Bedrock" meant reality, the backbone of the system that even had dinosaurs in harness—save the irritating house pet Dino, of course. Like so many among the best shows of the period, *The Flintstones* could be read on several levels. We writers like to make our point, one way or another.

By comparison, the Japanese imported (or exported, depending on point of view) cartoons such as *Kimba the White Lion, Marine Boy* ("Get that Kid!"), and *Space Ace,* while engaging to children's love of narrative, had no humorous dimension, and gave a curious insight into Japanese psychology and sensibility some twenty years or so after Hiroshima, Nagasaki, and Iwo Jima. American cartoons tended to be more in the spirit of Marvel comic books, usually with absurdly muscular masculine heroes—and in the case of the *Incredible Hulk* (Grantray-Lawrence Animation), nothing *but* muscle: "Doc Bruce Banner, belted by gamma rays turns into the Hulk!" went the song. One suggests if Bruce had been indeed "belted by gamma rays" he would in due course have wilted to a pulp like a wet leaf; but in the Cold War, radiation had to mean *power*. Then there was Captain America, wedded to the flag, who threw his "mighty shield," a subtextual metaphor one presumes for U.S. foreign policy: it might look like an attack, but really we're in the *protection* game. Many a boy in Vietnam would have liked Captain America's advantages. Why were soldiers sent into battle against bullets and shells with less armor than a medieval knight? In 1969, Peter Fonda would come up with a very different idea of Captain America: that of a chopper-mounted free spirit with the heart of a pioneer out for faraway gold, in *Easy Rider*.

The two U.S. series that went well out of this world for subject matter were the now legendary *Star Trek* created by Gene Roddenberry in 1964, which started going where no man had gone before in 1966—and kept returning, to this day—and a curiously morbid series that compelled our youthful attention called *The Invaders* (a Quinn Martin Production, 1967). Both have their interest for this book.

Apart from the obviously Hellenistic mythological nature of *Star Trek* narratives, there appears to be a kind of gnostic dimension to some of them as well. From the perspective of psychological observation, Spock represents pure rationality in the logical or scientific sense, being data reliant (nothing personal, Data, old boy), whereas Kirk (the old church?) is the emotional, instinctive, active principle. Other characters offer intuition combined with science (Dr. McCoy, for example), and the circumstances provide realms of sensation, much of it deceptive or wholly delusory. We thus have the four components of gnostic mind, or Jung's "quaternity," if you will: reason, feeling, intuition, and sensation. This is what it takes to face the "final frontier" in the age of space.

The "devil" or evil principle is usually in the mind, and there is a regular play on hallucinations. In early episodes, you even have enemies called archons (something *Gnostic Gospels* author Elaine Pagels reminded me of once) who, in classic Gnostic mythology indicate the dark, material-obsessed, spiritually myopic angels who govern the abortive universe in which divine light is trapped. "Beam me up, Scottie!" Being trapped is the perennial experience of the crew of the *Enterprise,* where "enterprise" speaks for itself. Don't expect to explore infinity without good ol' U.S. greenbacks! You can cash an Amex check anywhere! (Can't think why they've never used this gag in their self-promotion). Not only dollars, of course: you need faith, hope, and Old Glory! It's all very imaginative and frequently charming, as you can tell from the dialogue excerpts on Randy California's Spirit album *Future Games: A Magical Kahauna Dream* (Mercury, 1977), my favorite excerpt having traveled with me through life and runs as follows: "Though they are on opposite sides, both captains are in fact very much alike, and the captain of the Romulan vessel would have to admit that, *in another reality,* Kirk could have been his friend." Delivered deadpan, it gets me every time I hear it! Superb and hilarious at the same time. The best drama walks a razor-edge between genius and bathos. *Star Trek* does the business, and it was very nearly axed at birth. One needs vision, for from it comes faith.

The Invaders, on the other hand, despite its very effective typography and color schemes, was not a well-balanced meal, in my view at least. It managed to encapsulate, and even manipulate, a distinct paranoia that lurked just beneath the surface of the boiling, bubbling American geyser pool, which occasionally spouts forth a real turkey without Old Faithful's Yellowstone grandeur. The premise of *The Invaders* was interesting, though certainly not original. Aliens from a hostile world beyond this one have infiltrated "our," that is, American government agencies and society. Guess who they are! Apparently, not that easy. They are very difficult to tell apart from genuine Americans. Yes— except, one might jest, for the hammer and sickle tattooed on their scrotum! These "aliens" ain't really human; they lack something. You mean . . . they're *un-American?* Sure. You got it. *The Invaders,* in this context, is a shameless example of persistent McCarthyism in the Sixties, dressed up as sci-fi. Aliens = Communists = aliens. No one ever admitted it, of course, to my knowledge anyway. Indeed, my brothers and I, innocent imbibers of this hokum, really believed it had something to say about aliens infiltrating our planetary paradise for ends malevolent. We needed little convincing that UFOs existed. We'd all seen strange lights (unidentified flying craft to all our eyes) hovering in formation over the Churchill National Park near Dandenong—and Victor and James (my brothers) told me they'd seen a cigar-shaped light in the sky with points of light darting to and from it on another evening. Area 51, Nevada, okay—but this was (and I mean *was*) the Australian Outback, or near it! Mine eyes have seen and I'm damned if I know *what* it was we saw. I certainly doubt it was a Soviet plot to infiltrate our vital fluids! The trouble with *The Invaders* was that it sowed the seeds of unreasoned paranoia and of conspiracy in young minds. This is playing with fire, as we now realize, or should do, I think.

A DAY OF TV IN 1968

Now here is a rundown of shows you could see on *just one day* of any given week in the year 1968 in Victoria, Australia, that fascinating fulcrum of four cultures: domestic, American, British, and Pacific. I have mostly omitted shows I've already referred to.

Starting with children's TV in the late afternoon, we have *The New Adventures of Superman,* a Filmation cartoon from 1966. Man: powerful, flies. Woman: watches, adores; flies if invited.

Cheyenne: a TV Western series (1955–56) with Clint Walker as Cheyenne Bodie: Man with gun, doing right.

Sea Hunt: exploring undersea nature and adventures on the ocean about Hawaii (recently made a full U.S. state), starring Lloyd Bridges as Mike Nelson: like *Cheyenne,* a black-and-white series (1958–61), as were all pre-1966 dramas here. Note the man is the adventurer-hero, and the scientist and source of wisdom.

Whiplash: an unusual Western series, in that it was an Australian-British coproduction filmed in Australia (1959–60), starring Christopher Cobb: male-dominant of course.

Doctor Who: BBC drama series starring Patrick Troughton as the "Doctor," a "Time Lord."

Troughton's part (assumed in 1966 after the Doctor's first incarnation, veteran actor William Hartnell, could no longer take the pressure of learning lines), was in no wise a conventional hero, or muscular, heroic type; he is an emotional scientist with flaws, often reliant on the judgment and assistance of a young, modern girl called Zoë, and a young Scotsman called Jamie. Indeed, the way Troughton played it, the good Doctor appeared troubled, sometimes a little ill-tempered, but considerate, mystical, zany, even somewhat psychedelic. He had hidden abilities and features, and tended to see beyond appearances. He had *full-time* or trans-temporal perspective you might say, and so stimulated the imagination to go to outer limits, and beyond, for he himself was always fascinated by what he saw; he did not "know it all" but tried to understand. I recall one episode where such was the imaginative build-up of studio and dramatic elements that I was convinced I had "seen God" on screen. Strange, but true. And in those days, perhaps, one would not have been surprised. Sadly, I think the BBC wiped that particular episode to save money on reusable videotape. Dear old England!

The Littlest Hobo: This was a 1963–1965 Canadian TV series for children about a helpful German shepherd dog, treated like *Lassie*. It encouraged love of animals.

We now move into time when it was presumed parents would be watching, father (and in our case, mother) having returned from work.

Marshal Dillon was the title for early episodes of *Gunsmoke;* James Arness played the part in black-and-white. It was written for adults.

The Donna Reed Show was a very successful U.S. sitcom that ran from 1958 to 1966 and reflected changes in fashion and hairstyles, but not much change in terms of the model family portrayed. We follow the home-based adventures of Donna Stone, her pediatrician husband, and kids. The emphasis here is on the attractive, but not over-glamorous wife played by Donna Reed, and the conception of wife and family is about as straight as you could imagine. Anybody who has seen the brilliant movie *Pleasantville* (Gary Ross, 1998) about a young man obsessed with a Fifties black-and-white TV series where everything is "nice" and secure, and no one ever suffers or gives offense, and it's all clean and perfect but also sexless, unadventurous, with hidden spectra of intolerances, will get the picture projected in the undoubtedly compellingly

Fig. 19.6. The "ideal" American family:
cast members of The Donna Reed Show, *1960.*

entertaining *Donna Reed Show*. It is thoroughly materialistic, reflecting the ideal home of the time, and soothingly good natured. Problems are never insuperable and despair or anything like it is unknown. This is a life of conformity where spiritual crisis simply is unimaginable. *He* goes off to work, *she* looks perfect in gingham frock; kids kiss charming Mom goodbye, and she gets a visit from a nice neighbor where they can discuss their pleasant lives over coffee. Oh happy days! My mother, incidentally, worked full-time as a research lab technician attached to the Queen Victoria (women's) Hospital, Melbourne, so the idea of mother being at home was for us a dream unrealized. But then, our dad wasn't a pediatrician, and middle-class life was then, and is still now, practically everyone's ideal: a life we would not wish to put at risk for the sake of, say, space exploration, or even a "just war." Home is where the heart, and the money, is. And the access to it was television.

There was an awareness of the potential for parody of Fifties sci-fi series and films like *The Day the Earth Stood Still*, *This Island Earth*, and *Forbidden Planet* (which may have influenced the 1965–1967 series *Lost in Space*), and others. *My Favorite Martian* ran originally from 1963 to 1966 but was syndicated and repeated around the world, like all these shows here mentioned. Ray Walston played the crashed Martian, taken in by Tim O'Hara, a young reporter. This was a new vein of sci-fi comedy, sitcoms with extraordinary things going on and extraordinary and absurd characters doing them; the sky was the limit, but sometimes one felt one could, like Icarus, fly too high for the jackpot and come crashing down with the wax of one's wings melted in the heat of enthusiasm. *I Dream of Jeannie* and *Bewitched* were two of the most successful far-out shows with magical elements, whereas *Mister Terrific* (1967) and *The Flying Nun* (who, absurdly, can fly because she "only weighs 90 pounds" and doubtless subsists on Catholic faith, 1968) were arguably a step too far into space.

The Dick Van Dyke Show ran originally from 1961 to 1966, and, like today's *Frasier* (I catch the repeats!), concerns the middle-class home and work life of Robert Petrie (Van Dyke), head writer of a Manhattan TV show. It was very enjoyable, especially as the writers knew from experience what they were writing about, for once perhaps.

Garrison's Gorillas was unusual, insofar as it was a popularish TV series inspired by a "restricted" movie, in this case, *The Dirty Dozen*. Its last episode was aired in the States in March 1968. First Lt. Craig Garrison was played by Ron Harper who must get hardened criminals to perform covert feats of daring for the Allies in World War II. The series was hardly alone in this period for portraying that war in thoroughly anachronistic terms. Movies like *Kelly's Heroes* (shot in Yugoslavia in 1969) did the same, as of course did TV's *Hogan's Heroes*, which ran from 1965 to 1971—almost as long as World War II. The war had become a source of story and casual heroism, not sacrifice and tragedy; it was a superficial aspect of Sixties culture of which there is no cause for pride, though the programs themselves were undoubtedly entertaining, but money and fame are not everything.

Till Death Us Do Part was a BBC sitcom of uncompromising

realism in subject matter, written by Johnny Speight and starring Warren Mitchell as an East End working-class character of London whose daughter and her boyfriend (played by former British P.M. Tony Blair's father-in-law, as it happens) consistently taunt the father and father-in-law (Mitchell) for being out of touch, square, racist, imperialist, reactionary, conservative, hypocritical, and so on. Being well observed in fact, it was often painfully true to reality, but its frequent swearing gave opponents ample opportunity to accuse it of "lowering standards" in TV and corrupting the country, especially the working classes. American TV took the idea and came up with Archie Bunker, and if you've seen that, you'll get the idea. Alf Garnett, the would-be dominant male who is constantly reduced by wife, daughter, and son-in-law, is sentimental about queen, religion, and country and is at a loss to understand why the young people who feed off his work belittle everything he stands for, and are unremittingly so antiestablishment. The series is still hard-hitting, and its many issues are still, for many, largely unresolved, merely bulldozed over because uncomfortable for liberal and reactionary alike.

While *Till Death Us Do Part* amused and shocked Australian and British audiences, Americans could savor less controversial material. *Family Affair* was a U.S. sitcom that ran from September 1966, starring Brian Keith as Uncle Bill Davis, Sebastian Cabot as Mr. Giles French (the English-style butler), and Kathy Garver as Cissy Patterson-Davis. The leading male has a new and interesting dimension. Life presents him with the task of raising his late brother's children, though he is an "important" civil engineer with projects worldwide, living in Manhattan near 5th Avenue. Interesting, but one must observe, not quite as realistic as a similar scenario set in a government housing project in Harlem, but then, you would never have the five-star charm of Sebastian Cabot as the butler beset by the unpredictable.

The High Chaparral had started in 1967, and its color Western adventures mimicked many Western movies as far as 1971. Good, solid American values were reinforced with every episode, and the baddies always got what they deserved. It starred Leif Erickson and Cameron Mitchell, and is probably being screened somewhere right now.

More interesting to my eyes was *Court Martial,* a brief 1966 series set in the unusual World War II setting of a judge advocate general's office. It starred Peter Graves and Bradford Dillman in a series that did well to explore challenging moral dilemmas in the context of crisis.

And all that gives us some idea of what you got from Sixties TV, English language–style anyhow (these shows were dubbed into many world languages and became part of global culture, being so superior technically to most TV generated in the world at the time). One may ask what spiritual meaning can be discerned among them as an aggregate, and I think most would conclude "very little," at least explicitly. When we put them in the context of news and documentary programs about real events, the overall impression is that Sixties TV was a wall-to-wall entertainment barrage with little time left to catch its breath, so devoted to filling time and fulfilling schedules that it had little moment to ask what it was really saying or doing, or for whom. On the other hand, the atmosphere generated by these shows en masse was by and large tremendously positive and very frequently emotionally uplifting. The view of the world was a place where goodness is rewarded, where bad "comes a cropper," and the imaginative, strong, and resourceful win out. Life was full of opportunities, and individual character really mattered. Furthermore, the imagination had no formal limits and one could reach for the sky with impunity. TV was mainly conceived as entertaining distraction from life, and as such, due to the privilege of entering the private homes of millions, showed respect for tradition, and social attitudes were rarely challenged; spiritual issues were not regarded as suitable material for entertainment. It was generally presumed that the universe of TV operated in a shared world of meaning, though that assumption did start to flake somewhat after 1967, where storylines became less solid and more satirical, and artifice began to arch over solid drama values.

I have to say that few programs in the above schedule appealed to me personally all that much. What did greatly appeal to me were entertainment series that had a considerable high bar of imaginative and technical input and originality, and that did not rely on gag after gag, or jokes for the sake of it, like a nervous loudmouth. Some of the most outstanding examples of television in the higher category were written and produced in England, though they could not have been so conceived had it not been for the potential reward of an American market for the best products. In some senses, America "rediscovered" England in the Sixties, and it was a fecund, two-way relationship to which we all owe a great deal, if we count thoughtful pleasure as a serious matter.

Gerry and Sylvia Anderson's astonishing run of automated, advanced puppetry ("Supermarionation"), and model extravaganzas are difficult to assess in terms of spiritual meaning, for sure, as their intention was simply to delight and entertain all involved in creation or reception, but the "spirit" of them was buoyant, optimistic, generous, humane, and scientifically positive. All dominant characters tried to do good, from the Western-oriented *Four Feather Falls* (1959–60), to *Supercar* (1961), to *Fireball XL5* (1962), to *Stingray* (1964), to the magnificent *Thunderbirds* (based on the globally charitable, self-sacrificial "Tracy" principle of "International Rescue," which operated from 1965), to *Captain Scarlet* (Spectrum Organisation, a "rainbow" of world cooperation vs. the Mysterons—evil archons infiltrating the mind again!), to the ultrarefreshing 1968 series *Joe 90,* and *The Secret Service* (1969), which was a charming idea about a parish priest (played by inimitable comedian Stanley Unwin) who is also a government secret agent. Father Unwin, the priest, speaks in a gobbledegook that Unwin the comedian had made famous; it was not meant to be understood, but Lew Grade, who financed *The Secret Service,* cancelled it, believing Americans would be unable to cope with the "Unwinese" language, which amounted to asserting Americans could not cope with some English styles of humor (*all* Americans? I wonder). To say the motives of the heroes and heroines of these shows were permeated by spiritual values—goodness—goes without saying. We miss them only when they've gone.

Whenever people talk about Sixties TV, it doesn't take long before someone starts sighing over the long-running drama series *The Avengers:* Patrick Macnee as gentleman-agent John Steed, and his equally dynamic female assistants (British TV had more dynamic women roles per square foot of TV than American, it might be noted): first Honor Blackman (1962–64) who did wonders for leather gear and "kinky boots" and female karate, then the ultra girl-woman-judo mistress, Emma Peel (that is, *M-appeal; M* for "male"), played to perfection by (now) Dame Diana Rigg, and in 1968, Canadian Linda Thorson as the no-less dynamic and delightful, Tara King. Okay, that said; *why?* What's so special? Answer: style, flair, class, music, originality, eccentricity, daring, literacy, sophistication, imagination: nothing too absurd, nothing too evil, nothing too strange for the team to take on—'twas all grist to the Avengers' mill. And it was never *too much;* it knew its own bounds, which was fine, for the audience could not see them. Sure, there are fraying elements visible now in the fifty-plus-year-old fabric, but the aforementioned qualities still shine. One must remember one only had the chance to look into this world once a week; shown in succession, the shows lose a great deal. But to wait a week, knowing you're in for something completely different, well, it added much to quality of life. Its style gave us hope. You could be charming, old-fashioned, smart, beautiful, witty, and probably wealthy, or at least eccentric, and the world was an adventure, and you could be its star on your own terms, so long as you observe one rule: *Never be boring.*

As for spiritual values, well, there was plenty of old-world chivalry from Steed, but was not Emma Peel somewhat callous when presented with another prematurely slaughtered victim? The pair made jokes and plans over still-warm corpses. Of course; it's not serious! It was never meant to be more than the rising bubbles of the champagne whose happy clink initiated Laurie Johnson's top-flight, airy, stylish, Mayfair-at-its-best series theme, complete with harpsichord riff, tuba pulse, and rural-meets-city-sophisticate strings. It just worked and took us off planet Earth week after week and was more effective than psychedelics on the young thinking mind. A confession: the first girl I remember kissing was Diana Rigg as Emma Peel. I was seven, and she was an image in the Australian *TV Times* magazine. This was true love, though certainly enhanced by Mrs. Peel's zip-up one-piece jumpsuits whose varied colors were lost on us black-and-white viewers. Did she not possess the greatest smile since the Mona Lisa sat for Leonardo? I thought so.

The Avengers, older brother to the more earthbound *The Saint,* plus the angry-young-man grit of *Danger Man,* opened the doors to the

Fig. 19.7. Author returns to 9 Robe Street, St. Kilda, Melbourne, in 2018. In mid-1967 I would hide under my parents' bed in the sitting room of our rented first-floor apartment, to watch The Avengers *after my bedtime, in love with Emma Peel. Photo by Mark Bennett, 2018.*

greatest TV series of the Sixties, and for my money, of all time (to date anyway)—and you may be ahead of me here; yes, I'm talking about executive producer Lew Grade's great gamble begun in 1966 and broadcast in 1967 and 1968 (Oh blessed years!), *The Prisoner:* George Markstein and Patrick McGoohan's masterpiece series, a legacy for all, for all time.

If you're with me thus far, you'll probably know the basic story pursued through its seventeen episodes, shot largely on location at Sir Bertram Clough Williams-Ellis's coastal village masterpiece, Portmeiron, in North Wales: Secret agent wakes up in strange village; everyone takes his presence for granted, 'cept himself. This is

"The Village"—and there's no escape. But why would you wish to? Everything is provided, everything except freedom. There's a kind of democracy, lots of banal things to do: just like life, really. And they're by the seaside: many people's idea of a perfect holiday, with no work to speak of. But the Village is designed by some power to "break" everyone in it, to process and neutralize them.

I believe the original idea came from Markstein's perception of the socialist "welfare state," a society where if you did as you were told, the State would take care of you from cradle to grave. Of course, the State owned everything and had absolute power. Still, you could enjoy yourself, so long as real freedom meant nothing to you. The best thing was to conform, settle down, moderate all differences in line with the collective non-will, administered from above: "A still tongue is a happy life" as one of the ubiquitous Village nostrums goes.

Many adventures pass as Number Six (everyone is a number) does his best to escape. But he's trying to escape from a nightmare, and nightmares don't end until you wake up. The wake-up is reserved for the last apocalyptic episode (appropriately titled "Fall Out"). TV company switchboards were jammed when it was first broadcast in the U.K. on February 4, 1968. I watched it, agog, and knew I had seen, for the first time on the glass pulpit, T-R-U-T-H: the truth of self and identity and the way of the world—and the way to deal with it.

People have scratched their heads and moaned about the fact that the last episode was allegorical, not conventional narrative—but to me at least, it made perfect, ecstatic sense. Space does not permit a complete rundown of the drama and its points. But this much I can say. All through the series, Number Six has struggled to locate the power behind the solid illusion: Number One. At a grand trial of himself, he repeats the question: "Who is Number One?" Then, at last, he is taken to Number One.

Yes, Number One is himself. He must look momentarily into the hidden horror of his own nature. The duality of man is exposed: we as a species imprison ourselves, and always have done. Until we realize we *are* Number One, we will live in fear, and impose our dual mentality on everything around us. There will always be an enemy until we all know who and what we are. There is just a hint at the end that Number One is in some sense extraterrestrial—not rooted in the "world." A rocket with Number One on it is launched into space as the Village system falls apart and panic ensues. But the man, *the form* Number Six escapes with his two new friends (representing establishment, crushed but now awoken, and antiestablishment, now free) from the Village that seems to dissolve like a false vision of the world before our eyes.

Spiritually refreshed, he returns ("no longer a number" but an *individual*) to London, to the system, but we see from a little jig he dances to himself outside the Houses of Parliament that he is now inwardly free, lighthearted, generous, spiritually whole—above the world—and ready to enter the corridors of "power" that he has seen through, and to take them to task at last.

Ron Grainer's music of resolution, release, and fantastic Sixties optimism takes us all the way to the spiritual resolution of the absolute prisoner's dilemma. The "prisoner" is man, and we can, self-realized, break the mental chains and be ourselves: the "mad," the unpredictable, the sometimes wayward, the creative and unique self, the only God we'll ever know—that will not be chained, will not be "stamped, indexed, briefed, debriefed, or numbered." Rather, like the God who reveals himself to Moses in Exodus: I AM THAT I AM.

Patrick McGoohan had to flee the reaction, and eventually settled in the States. He left for all a divine gift that, but for television in the Sixties, and all that went before it, would never have happened. Thank God it did.

No one really knew where to go after that. In heaven, there is no space and no time. The decade had peaked. Ahead of Time.

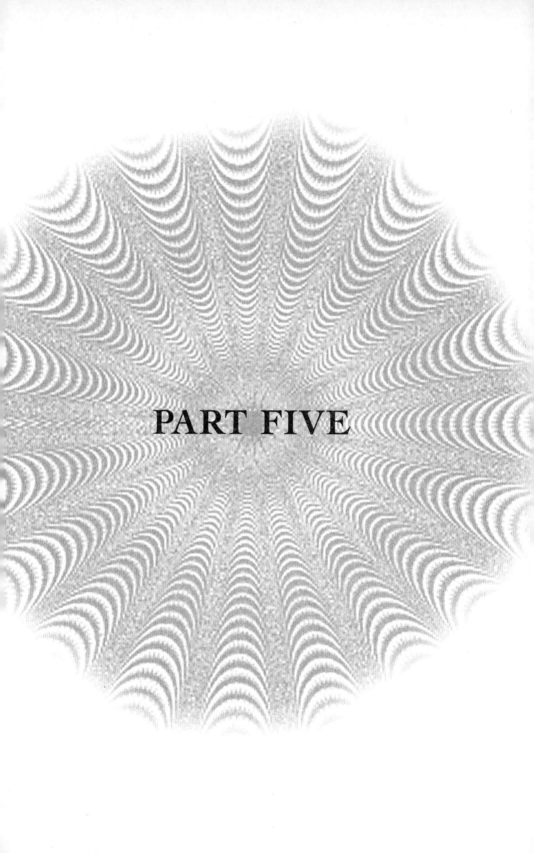

PART FIVE

TWENTY

Woman

What do we know of women in the Sixties? I think of city streets on work days, filled with men and women in the mid-Sixties: men in smart suits, women in smart knee-length dresses or twinsets, hair bobbed or curled neatly, symmetrically, or sometimes piled high and secured into conformity by hairspray and pins. It all looked so clean and orderly, even alluring, and running like clockwork; everybody knowing the rules, not showing too much, and any kind of scruffiness deplored. It might sound almost utopian, but what if we cut across the image and wonder what was happening inside?

Only one film director in the period attempted this task systematically. In a series of movies marked by a novel combination of objectivity and dramatic and psychological intuition, Jean-Luc Godard (b. 1930) attempted to examine the life of modern women. Though all the subjects of his major films on the theme were European, and specifically French, one feels the director imagined his analyses had a measure of universal application, and I think he was correct.

Vivre sa Vie (*My Life to Live,* 1962) starred Danish model and actress Anna Karina as Nana, a very sympathetic Parisienne whose severe money troubles make her vulnerable to exploitation by a pimp-boyfriend, through whose malignant agency she enters a life of prostitution. Nana's unhappy downfall is shown in a series of beautifully photographed tableaux (the cameraman was Raoul Coutard who always came up with exemplary work for Godard). Her ultimate death in the street is shown

Fig. 20.1. Actress Anna Karina in Godard's Vivre sa vie, *1963.*

as the casual act of gangsters shooting her out of careless spite in a trade-off of her flesh that goes wrong. Godard has shown the close, even intimate link between capital exchange, profit, male power, and prostitution, and its effect on one young woman. This was bold work, for it was not normal to think of prostitution as an economic issue, but as a moral and social one. Either way, woman finds her destiny in the grip of men operating their own schemes with indifference to her happiness. The title *My Life to Live,* suggests the woman has a will, but free will is what the system denies, while outside of it, she is threatened with extinction.

Godard was not writing a feminist tract. He was perhaps too involved in the issue for that. Indeed, the actress Karina was his wife, and he was employing her. He was aware of his own romanticism, evident in the affecting way Karina was presented in all his films. She is an object of mystery, fatal beauty, innocence, strength, vulnerability, adventure. Anna had a face that could launch a thousand novels. Godard was interested in the image and what images have constituted the image. This was an innovative approach, though not easily accommodated by cinema audiences used to established genres and obvious, culturally unchallenging representations of female roles in life and drama.

Godard was familiar with the fact that in the French language, when writers attempted to convey ideas, they tended to personify them as a woman. So many words in French to convey concepts and ideas were feminine. The image of woman had to carry a great deal of men's unconscious projections, fears, and ideological freight. This is brought out in every Godard film, where his restless camera will linger on a portrait on a wall; nearly always of a woman. Godard inherited the romantic notion of women as obscure objects of desire, as symbols, and as fatal and even castrating influences, traps. One thinks of the Symbolist movement's late nineteenth-century interest in *La belle dame sans merci,* in whose gorgeous hair the knight-errant becomes entwined as in a web, so losing his will and grip on his quest. Godard used this idea in several films, most notably, *Pierrot le Fou* ("Pierrot the madman," 1965), where Jean Paul Belmondo leaves his bourgeoise wife for a free-spirited, darkly mysterious girl (Karina again) called Marianne, whose name is linked to all the traditional fundamental ideas of femininity from Mother to the eternal presence of the fecund, fatal, and overwhelming sea. "Marianne" is also the French Republican symbol of liberty and reason. In her red Phrygian cap she is effectively a goddess, and is presented as a leader, but France has never had a female president. It is the *idea* that is feminine, and the idea is generally presented *in art* as bare breasted. Karina's character's surname is Renoir, which evokes the many impressionist portraits by Jean Renoir of compelling female beauties, whom we also encounter mute, breasts exposed, and wall-mounted in the film.

In 1964, Godard made *La Femme Mariée* ("The married woman")— at least that was *his* title for the movie. The state censor insisted on a change of title before he would permit the film's public release. It was changed to *Une Femme Mariée: A Married Woman,* also the title of its English release. The life lived by the female lead character (played by Macha Méril) must not, insisted the state censor, be taken as indicating *all* married women. God forbid! But Godard was not making a film about all married women, but of the *idea* of "the married woman" as seen objectively by those who intended to exploit her, consciously or otherwise. First of those, of course, was now the censor of the state

Fig. 20.2. Godard's La Femme Mariée *starring Macha Méril, 1964.*

machine, suspicious of "subversion" of sacred French middle-class womanhood. Note the double standard. You could portray a single woman as a whore, but the married woman was social bedrock. The second exploiter is of course business, which pays for the imaging of woman.

The movie dissects aspects of one fictional middle-class woman's life. She is, as it were, portrayed in pieces, her life sliced. The presentation is so crisply objective, in fact, that we feel we are almost watching a fly-on-the-wall documentary; Godard wants us to think about realities. Furthermore, when we first encounter her in bed with her lover, an actor—*aren't they all?*—her naked body is shown in almost abstract segments, as if she has been dissected, the images then pared by the editor. Partly, we may presume this has been for editorial objectivity, but also so that the censor would not cut the scene as a whole for being too revealing or sexually arousing. Images of skin stand in for the missing whole body (a sensibility the woman herself lacks, thinking of herself in parts that must be cosmeticized with alluring "products"). This idea of corporal disintegration is even echoed in the deliberately flat, but telling, dialogue between the lovers. *He* says he likes Italian films where the women have hairy armpits; *she* says she prefers American films because "they're prettier." *Maybe,* asserts the lover, but the Italian ones are more "arousing." It is as though the dialogue is suggesting the idea of what the censor would otherwise cut, while also making the important point that men and women see the same images differently, because they are looking for different things. Godard is actually interested in what the woman might be really looking for. He does not presume that her authentic dreams are to fulfill the man's.

However, the very fact that she prefers prettiness over certain unsightly (to her) realities is already opening us to the fundamental critique the movie offers its audience. In short, "the married woman" is shown as a person practically asphyxiated by images outside of herself that she has assimilated and that have become, literally, part of her own skin. She does not will; she is willed. We see her looking through magazines that tell her about this bra, or those knickers, or this mascara, or that lipstick. When she goes out, great advertising hoardings loom over her, godlike, promoting the "Triumph" bra that will give women "confidence." She is the target consumer and everywhere she goes, the telescopic sight is focused on her every "need" or whim that can be satisfied with cash. The image of the married woman has had to be constructed, and the price can be high, both in terms of cash expended (which comes through the husband in this case, and what he expects) and in terms of identity. We know there might be *another woman* beneath the cosmetic artifice of her social identity, because at one moment, she steps through a skylight onto the apartment roof and walks about in her underwear, covering her naked breasts with her crossed arms. When the lover objects to her thus exposing herself to the outside world, she says, quite properly, that she thought he liked her like that! Both profound, and a good joke on her part, made against the timidity of the male lover faced with the prospect of sharing what he desires to possess exclusively. In a later scene, the woman is shown entertaining the husband's business associate. She is, as we say, "immaculately turned out" (like a valeted car) with perfect hair, dress, shoes, make up, and when she speaks about the room's furniture and furnishings it is in the precise, but absurd mode of advertising copy. The couple is, you could say, literally "living the dream." But whose dream is it, really?

It may be supposed that ordinary(!) middle-class women seeing this film in 1964 would have felt discomfited somewhat, even alienated, by the presentation of the movie, and they would have wanted to know why the drama did not involve itself "properly" with the dramatic potential of the jealous husband and lover, with a proper, moral, or comprehensible conclusion at the end. She may not have been equipped with the means to see the director was trying to stimulate her own awareness of her complicity in her own suppression. Younger audiences, particularly students, not yet locked in wholly to the social fabric, would probably have been more aware to varying degrees of what the director was getting at.

In Godard's 1966 film *Deux ou Trois choses que je sais d'elle* (*Two or three things I know about her*), Godard went a step further, and starred Marina Vlady as a working-class mother in a new block of flats on the outskirts of Paris. This is the Paris that the Gaullist state was building, far from the "pretty" center that visitors would see and marvel at, intoxicated by its apparent romance. There was nothing romantic about the new concrete developments. Godard begins the movie by making it clear that these new developments would precisely segregate the classes, and tie the inhabitants into a system of work-for-capital, which they would spend on fulfilling what they were trained to imagine were their personal dreams. Yet again we find a woman, and this time her friend too, willing to perform sexual favors to obtain material goods, so that they could have at least a taste of a "high life" that they were almost certainly never going to have access to, for they were to be conditioned

Fig. 20.3. Godard directing actress Marina Vlady in
Deux ou Trois choses que je sais d'elle, *1966.*

to the expectations of their class, defined by where they were living and their role in the system. Godard showed it, he exposed the system that exposed itself for those with the eyes (or camera) to see. The camera endeavored to show what the ordinary eye, prejudiced, did not.

The "her" of the title of which he knows only two or three things, is in part, the situation of the real woman in the Sixties, and also, the new Paris being constructed without representation or consultation of the people who are going to live in it, and be shaped fundamentally by that experience. Even the idea of Paris is a woman, so we find woman as symbol again, despite the attempt at realism!

By 1967, when Godard made *La Chinoise* about a cell of French Maoist students, he seems to have reached the conclusion that it was probably only through a neo-socialist, communistic revolution that a society could be shaped where the images of women would be true to themselves.

Here he would encounter some profound difficulties of theory and practice, as well as losing touch with a great many of the women in the world who did not, could not, or would not "buy in" to proposed revolutionary "solutions." One problem was that of the role given to women in existing revolutionary systems. While in *Pierrot le Fou,* and in *La Chinoise* ("The Chinese girl"), and also in *Weekend* (1967), Godard had made the point that one should not imagine that because women had soft breasts and warm faces, and could show love, that they would not be prepared to pull the triggers of automatic weapons, or plant deadly explosives, if they believed they shared in the "cause," nevertheless, he had also made the point that the modern woman was already very much subjugated in the world of *consumption,* rather than the male, who was subjugated in the world of *production.* To conform to the world of consumption, there can be little doubt that women were oversexualized, even hypersexualized to the extent where they could begin to resemble commodities themselves. The only way to be visible, even to be treated kindly, was to be seen as pretty, as sexually open, as desirable.

In the Soviet Union, China, North Korea, Cuba, and North Vietnam, where women were not engaged in military roles, they were to significant extents *desexualized* into production roles, and, as mothers, were themselves means of production, providing future workers and soldiers for the "struggle." Such roles also constituted images of women, images that just might not be fulfilling their dreams. As the title of the first film we looked at stated: "My life to live." Nana had dared to try to find a way to live her life as she pleased by the means available. She was not permitted to do so because of the system she relied on (prostitution), and because of being a woman. Would she have found her own, authentic life in a revolutionary state? She might well have been persuaded to take up arms and fight for such a life, but what were the chances of getting such an existence when the fight was done? No female president of China . . . nor of the Soviet Union . . . and so on. Wives of presidents are set up as symbols for the people, and praised for their charm and abilities to entertain visiting dignitaries and are just as forced into roles by the roles themselves, and of course by their will to participate in those roles. (Look how "modern" West Germany fawned over Raisa Gorbachev in the mid- to late Eighties!) There are countless examples of the exploitation of images of women in politics. Once you notice, you'll see how brazen the show is, and how universal.

For all the brilliant and creative dissection of the problems of "imaging" women in the Sixties, Godard was unable during the decade to arrive at an approach to image making that accommodated what women, or any individual woman, might have liked for herself. Indeed, was it a man's task to accomplish such a thing anyhow? Until women took up their own path, could their own wishes ever be articulated to the degree where they might be broadly understood? *That* realization came very late in the decade, as we shall see.

Now, what can we say of the spiritual meaning of Woman in the Sixties? First, as far as the above discourse is concerned, there was precious little, if any, attention given to the spiritual nature of women in Godard's films made in the Sixties at all.* The entire approach was born of Godard's education as a student of ethnology and social anthropology.

---

*He approached the subject in a most original manner in his and Anne Marie Miéville's film *Je vous salue Marie* (*Hail Mary*) in 1985.

Categories for examining society and social roles were of the scientific kind with a long history of categorizations made by academic intellectuals, predominantly male, with fairly fixed ideas about social evolution. The basic framework was materialist, though allowing for some interest in biology and psychology. It was presumed that spirituality was or would be entirely subsumed within the category of the psychological. Man, according to the theory, adapted to nature progressively through experience and development of the brain, from the simple to the more complex. The history of culture was seen as a progression from myth to scientific "reality." This academic background presented a thought world of inexorable logic, only savored by elements of philosophy, thus Nana is encouraged by Godardian sympathy to construct the meaning of her own life, for that is what Jean-Paul Sartre permitted her to do; such was her existential freedom, and all she could do, and any "spirit" was simply the experience of so doing (no wonder she is so dreadfully sad throughout the film!). But of course, every revolutionary imperative devalues the freedom of individuals to find their own meaning. The collective struggle must always come first. Personal emotions are regarded as luxuries. I recall Tony Blair's speech to the latest batch of New Labor female MPs in 1997, many of whom were young women. They were not to think as individuals, but to put themselves behind the "movement" that had put them where they were. The movement may as well have been the party's kitchen. It was all deeply sickening to these ears; what did the "party leader" ever know about the dreams of these women, whether politicized or not? They were there to be used. The presumption was fit for exasperation. What is it that makes male dictatorial or manipulative types so ugly, however ingratiating the smiles? Conceit and egotistic presumption, for a start: the big "I am."

The spiritual meaning of women in the Sixties? Let us start with the spiritual meaning of women. We may take it that Marxist-Leninist societies had no official conception of women owning any spiritual meaning, as there was for Marxist-Leninists no spiritual meaning to anything. Meaning derived solely from correct revolutionary practice, as defined by those in power, and women, though technically "equal" (whatever that might mean), were not given or able to take power *over themselves as women,* but had to submit to the collective, and where they submitted, some fe-males [*sic*] might find constrained roles in the executive. As stated, women were means of production of workers, and as such "heroes of the state." Marriage was the State's—not personal or family business alone.

In animist or so-called primitive societies, women's roles and status could vary widely depending on the traditional experience and religion of tribes. Women certainly have a spiritual role in animist societies as there is usually great respect given to the mystery of birth and reproduction, so the woman can symbolize the spiritual power of creation, though this dignity is generally shared with the male. Both males and females have a spiritual essence that drives or "animates" them and that exists beyond the body and the duration of a life; so the female has a value independent of conditions of life in the created world.

The spiritual position of women in Buddhist societies will vary according to the brand of the religion operated in a given area. Technically, in Buddhism, reproduction is a misfortune, to say the least, but one born into this world may be treated with compassion and encouraged in the adoption or continuance of the path to enlightenment. Motherhood then has no doctrinally significant role, and insofar as women are seen as encouraging procreation, their ethical role may be suspected, and female "nuns" undertaking Buddhist vows may be exceptional in traditional societies.

Technically speaking, the Buddhist teaching of *anatta,* that is, no-soul, or continual essence, would deprive any organism from having spiritual meaning ultimately, but in practice such a meaning may be defined as the progress obtained on the path to extinction and permanent effacement from the wheel of destiny. The principle of harmlessness protects women and all living beings. There is nothing to be gained from oppression, and male and female distinctions are only conditions of the supposed general illusion that appears to make visible existence real. But duality is a sign of relative, not real existence.

Islamic societies, as is well known, recognize that men and women may, subject to God's grace, be resurrected in a final judgment, but so long as they exist in this world, women are positively subject to the will of men (first fathers, then husbands) and must serve them, and remain essentially subservient. How these basic ideas function in practice depends on the tribal, national, legal, and sectarian background of any given area, and the degree of social and ethical development reached in that vicinity. The more spiritual in outlook is the community, the greater the spiritual meaning may be experienced by individual females. Sufi communities may hold to a belief in spiritual complementarity between males and females when both parties are dedicated to knowledge of God.

In Western Judaeo-Christian societies, a grown woman's spiritual meaning may generally be found by individual preference or assumed from upbringing. During the Sixties, most Western "Christian" countries were legally secular from the judicial and governing point of view, but with some laws in conformity with Christian tradition. France was the most secular country in Europe, followed by West Germany (which had strong anti-Sunday trading laws, with restrictions for the main Christian festivals). Ireland was highly Catholicized politically. The United Kingdom had national churches but freedom of confession nonetheless. However, laws were subjected to Christian observation and recommendation. Spain was highly Catholic; Greece's society was dominated spiritually by the Orthodox Church, with the Left being generally anticlerical. Italy had strong secular movements in culture but was largely Catholic in practice. The United States was secular for the most part in outlook, but largely theist and Christian in Sunday practice. South America was generally speaking Catholic in confession, with animist tribespeople surviving, especially in Brazil.

The Christian conception of a woman's spiritual meaning varies. Jesus, the founder, is reported to have been someone to whom women came for understanding, kindness, and to offer service. Jesus was apparently criticized for having the regular company of women as disciples and helpers. He deplored hypocrisy and shocked traditional Jewish practice by exposing hypocrisy with regard to adulterers and, apparently, prostitutes. There is nothing to suppose that he did not hold the spiritual nature of women as being as significant to God's care and interest as men's. His follower Saint Paul left writings (his epistles), however, that expressed specific recommendations for women that appear derived from synagogue norms among patriarchally minded Jewish men. Paul stated that women should have their heads covered in religious services, and that they should not be too talkative. Men should marry rather than be tempted to have sex, and thereby bring women into shame. Husbands should treat their wives with love and dignity. The impression is that women were of equal value before God but in society were secondary, for their own good and that of families. However, women did have spiritual roles in early Christian societies; they could be prophetesses. By and large, early Christian communities offered safety and dignity to women, including widows.

Catholic dogma developed over time, and by the twentieth century, women's roles were strictly defined. They had no role in church services, other than as worshippers. They could, to obtain spiritual blessings, become nuns and renounce their sexual natures. They could become dutiful wives and mothers, and look to the Virgin Mary as an example of motherhood (however contradictory this might appear). As girls, their task was to remain physically pure and morally unsullied so that they might enter the bridal chamber as virgins. Enjoyment of sex was not acceptable to Catholic doctrine, and sex for enjoyment was morally on a par with adultery. Sex had one single purpose: the stocking of the church with saved souls, and the parents' first duty was to see their children saved and incorporated into the Catholic body or family. Poverty was a blessed spiritual state, and ambition was probably a form of temptation. The idea of a self-financing independent woman was anathema to Catholic dogma. Catholic dogma set the "high bar" that most Christian denominations followed to different degrees. There was in some Protestant churches greater liberty of interpretation, but not in all. Sex was a religious problem in all denominations, and so the Sixties continuity of postwar (and prewar) sexual liberation, or liberalization of proscriptions on sexual behavior, was deemed a threat to all Christian denominations, since by the fundamental teaching of the Christian communities, sex was the means by which Satan tempts the believer from the path to righteousness and unless it be redeemed by Christian marriage, it will lead to the spiritual ruin of the participants, women, it seems, especially. The role of Eve in the Genesis myth of the Fall of Man was regarded as emblematic of a persistent threat to salvation offered by the woman who used attraction to persuade.

When we take all this into account and ponder for a moment to imagine what this all meant to individual women living in the world in the Sixties, we might begin to feel the almost unspeakable enormity of the plight of women in the world, so great indeed that it could hardly be comprehended by mortal mind. When Juliet warned the amorous Romeo that "the orchard walls are high and hard to climb," with death the penalty if "any of thy kinsmen find thee here," she could well have been speaking of what women have been faced with, and in so many places today, still are. It may be a mystery how women have tolerated so much oppression and cruelty for so very long. But, as is well known, the child generally accepts the reality it is born into, and unless it is presented with the stable alternative of another reality, it will stick with what it knows best, for fear of oblivion. Nobody likes being cut off, and the church had a handy weapon in its power of excommunication, as families had when they would put women into nunneries or unhappy marriages or today in those Islamic societies where nonconformist women may suffer what are distastefully, outrageously called "honor killings," having in many cases first been genitally mutilated.

In fact, to my knowledge, there was only one skein of spiritual tradition that not only had a clear grasp of the spiritual meaning of women, but also a profound realization of the spiritual freedom proper to women in an oppressive, patriarchal empire of control and intimidation.

FREEING HELEN

Gnostic groups of the second and third centuries claimed the Samaritan magus Simon and his consort Helen as their progenitors, while the orthodox churches, for very different reasons believed that Simon Magus was the father of all heresies in the church. The story is told in the works of church father Justin that Simon of Gittho in Samaria led a sect of followers into the "supreme power" of which he was the first liberated exemplar. According to the Acts of the Apostles, Simon was a contemporary of the first apostles, and in that account, offered cash to Peter for the "trick" of passing on the Holy Spirit. Anyhow, this was not a story his followers held to his credit, rather that he had gone to the Phoenician city of Tyre where he had found the cosmic love of his life—and that he had found Helen, or Helena (whose name means "torch"), in a *brothel*. From there he had redeemed her (paid off her "debt"), and made her his equal consort. She, he said, was the same Helena over whom the war with Troy had been anciently fought. She was the reflection of God's Wisdom, Sophia, who had fallen into the lesser world of matter, there to be imprisoned by the Demiurge and tortured through time, incarnated again and again, to be suppressed and put to bestial service at the will of the false God and his dark-angel archons, and generations of men, of course. Goodness! Do we not here have a kind of Gnostic proto-feminist myth, or tract, for by identifying themselves with Simon and Helen, followers could be redeemed from the oppression of the antispiritual world and reign in eternity? The means, as I uncovered when I came to write my book *Gnostic Mysteries of Sex,* was a form of sexual magic, practiced in Simon and Helen's name, by followers.

The Simonian myth is practically the same in meaning as the signal myth of Gnostic groups. The spiritual equality, or, I should say, "dynamic complementarity," of the sexes comes from the realization of the fallen Sophia. Restoration of the wound of the world requires the spiritual reunion of the sexes in oneness and wholeness, thus restoring Sophia as the reflection of the divine mystery.

Conventional monotheistic religions date the division of Adam and Eve to the fall from Eden, with Eve as guilty protagonist. In the Gnostic double-Fall scheme, the primal fall begins in eternity. Therefore, the female spiritual meaning and identity goes directly back to God, not to the created woman of earth. Woman then may participate sacramentally in the redemption from the fall of divine Wisdom into the grip of demiurgically controlled men, themselves unconsciously bullied by dark angels, jealous of the divine Spirit of Sophia. In the Simonian system, Simon redeems the lost Queen of Heaven by his recognition of gnosis in himself and in his awakening of divine pneuma in her, for she had been transmigrated from body to body so much she had become amnesiac as to her true identity. Such is the plight of woman in Simonian gnosis! Thus, the freeing of women from oppression is a parergon of the release of Sophia from the grip of the archons, and the restoration of the harmony of the fullness of God is the redemption of men and women through sacramental sexual union. The freeing of woman from darkness and ignorance *is* the freeing of men. This is the traditional, suppressed gnostic doctrine that grants spiritual meaning, and the highest freedom, to Woman, maintaining her dignity and respect for her nature, sometimes described as "virgin-whore," for she gives herself freely but remains ever pure, as does the Wisdom that is divine celebrated in the literature of the wise.

We may then note how it is the heterodox form of "love" that is to be found within the outflow of the beat and hippie ethos, when combined with a political movement open to the oppression of women, that promotes a new feminist polemic toward the end of the Sixties. What may be regretted is that the spiritual dimension of this transformation was quickly overlooked both by the media and by self-appointed feminist pundits whose names would adorn hosts of paperbacks and magazine articles.

We may also note interesting parallels between the spiritual dimension of Sixties counterculture, built around the new singing groups, with the movement of Languedoc troubadours in the twelfth and thirteenth centuries. Among them appears to have been transplanted a heterodoxy of the equal spiritual role of women, perhaps from Catharism, perhaps from Sufi poets of ecstatic divine love—and probably both—that, coupled with the union of poet and Lady in the "fine love," generates a renewed spiritual identity granted to the Lady, or projected into or through her to the archangel Wisdom herself.

We may also note in this respect how, after the Beatles' example, a certain visual (though not sexless) androgyny becomes evident in the hippie movement that many young women recognized instantly as interesting if not necessarily spiritually liberating, and attractive to themselves. Femininity was treated affirmatively, with values of caring and loving and openness. Perhaps many would find that, as ever, looks can deceive, and the adoption of long hair and psychedelic clothing might have been for most simply following fashion (even in hope of "scoring" as men so unpleasantly euphemize), so the genuine Helen may have been at a loss to find her authentic Simon in the mêlée. Androgyny was for Péladan and the Parisian Gnostics of the 1890s a sign of the age of the Holy Spirit, and of the spiritual liberation of woman.

Perhaps a problem of the period was that the gnostic mythology, which would have explained so much, was very little known, and even when known, scarcely applied to the largely unconscious phenomena of Sixties enthusiasms. The protagonists and players of the spiritual movement of the time were largely in the dark as to what they were really doing, and what the dynamic was that they were, perhaps instinctively, involved with. And there were very few guides. The occult movements had fallen, by the Sixties, largely into sectarian quiescence or total obscurity and could not provide the ideological leadership required to harness the new energies. Instead, it may be regretted that the ideology of the time tended to be dominated by disparate points of view that, while they had a temporary wish to walk together as a rainbow coalition, were bound in due course (without guidance) to bifurcate and turn against one another. Thus, when feminism emerged to public view, it did so largely in a theoretical form closely tied to left-wing political priorities, and applied to issues of social discontent, such as industrial disputes and social welfare, tending to obsess over image issues, "man is the enemy" polemics, and abstract ideology. The path of spiritual meaning was lost or even spat upon.

But let us not forget that it was the unique and fresh emphasis on the power of Love, linked to flower power, that is, the unregarded regenerative powers of the planet, that brought women to the neotroubadours—the Beatles, the Stones—in search of a communion of spirit that was free, creative, sexy, and loving.

"BIRDS"

Much of the confusion and crossed lines of the time may be seen in a curious but compelling free-form documentary film made by

Peter Whitehead in 1967, *Tonite Let's All Make Love in London*. The film features the early Pink Floyd with Syd Barrett (performing "Interstellar Overdrive" at the UFO Club, 31 Tottenham Court Road, London), the Animals, the Stones, along with much psychedelic fast-cutting and light-show material, intercut with interviews with Mick Jagger, actors Michael Caine and Julie Christie, evangelist Billy Graham, author Edna O'Brien, a pop music producer, artist David Hockney, and visiting movie star Lee Marvin, interviewed on location for *The Dirty Dozen* (1967). Scenes of conventional London in conventional haircuts and clothes are crosscut with scenes of young people dancing in discothèques. All of the interviews are interesting and some seem ready-made for this chapter.

Writer Edna O'Brien, talking about changing sexual mores being explored in London, opined that it was a good thing now that "the woman doesn't have to disguise her libidinousness, or sexuality. That's a freedom!" She recognized the importance of the fact that women now had money and could work, and the dependence of women on men for money would always, and had always made women, unfree. She liked the honesty of new sexual mores, but noted that men and women were still different, with different expectations: "A woman likes to be with one man," she said, "even if it's only for three months, rather than going from bed to bed." A man, on the other hand, she noted without criticism, was prepared to shack up for an evening. Edna was suspicious of what happened with "this thing of falling in love," and noted how women were more devoted to, more committed to the notion of falling in love, and recognized that falling in love was the one great territory of adventure for women.

When the interviewer asked actress and movie star Julie Christie about what was new in London, and what had happened there that made it so different from anywhere else, she said it began with the Beatles. "We were lucky that they were cool and hip, and there weren't many people at the time who were cool and hip." She thought it had worked because people of that caliber had become idols, and therefore had been copied. And so London was "now cool and hip." She felt that everyone was having a good time, but maybe it was only a minority. Maybe it was just the circles she was familiar with. But whether that was the case or not, a good time was now being had much easier than before. "Pleasure is terrific," she said, and if that's all you've got, at least then you have something! "What do you love?" Christie was asked. "The sun," she replied. "I'm terribly superficial . . . sunflowers, good books, cats. I love strong relationships; there you are." Julie seemed embarrassed that when it came to it, all she could come up with was that she wanted strong relationships. One felt the pressure of those days to be clever, not to be shown up by the intellectual attitude of so many TV interviewers who tended to be looking for big words and macromeanings for everything. She felt a little uncomfortable at not coming out with something profound, or terribly, terribly witty. The interviewer tried to reassure her that that did not mean at all that she was superficial, to which she replied: "I think everybody likes strong relationships, don't they?" She seemed perhaps a little surprised to see herself, or to be seen, as someone without a remarkable opinion. She may have been reflecting on a tendency in her own circles to eschew superficiality and go for deeper meanings. Julie Christie had always tried to be in tune with nature, and perhaps, for a second, wondered whether that was enough, or whether being seen to be "hip" might now require more. One senses a cultural change in the air.

The short interview with Lee Marvin (in U.S. colonel's uniform) was surprising, as Marvin was himself a war veteran known for his tough, uncompromising image and attitude. He seemed very happy with the London of 1967, remarking that there seemed more room in a Mini (car) than in a Cadillac! He didn't mind short skirts and saw what was happening as "a healthy breakaway from all that was stoic and staid" that went before.

Short skirts did seem to pose a problem for the more conservative-natured Michael Caine, who, while being opinionated, seemed a trifle contradictory at times. He bemoaned the early closing of pubs in Britain and correctly observed that closing times had come in to keep working-class people from drinking so they wouldn't be late showing up, or still drunk, when working at munitions factories in World War I, whereas the upper classes could go to private clubs and drink if they wanted. He said it wasn't that he wanted to go out all the time and do things for pleasure that pleased him, but that when he *did* want to go out at any particular time of the day or night, he should have the freedom to do so. "I'm not a puritan," he said, or "a moralist," but "we seem to be selling our morals for a mess of cultural pottage." His view was that short skirts were an obviously sexual thing. He seems to have felt they demeaned women and encouraged men to look at women primarily as physical beings to be had. He reckoned society had lost "moral fiber." Looking back from today, it seems odd that Caine saw the fault in the skirt, not the mind of the onlooker, and seemed to think ogling girls was probably inescapable for a man presented with sexual attractions, whereas a woman should perhaps have the sense to cover up, rather for her own good, and to preserve the men's "moral fiber." On the other hand, he wanted the freedom to go out and drink and enjoy himself when he felt like it. Apparently, when Caine was living with John Barry in Knightsbridge in the mid-Sixties their flat was a thoroughfare of girls—or as they used to say in those days, "birds"—brought in and let out at sundry times. One wonders if it was spiritual meaning they sought through devotion to that other euphemism of the day, "skirt."

Nobody at the time seemed to have anything but the remotest idea of how to combine sexuality with spiritual meaning, though one feels there was perhaps something of the sort figuring somewhere in Julie Christie's love of "strong relationships," but the idea seems to have been most prevalent that "free love" was enough of a step in the direction of freedom for the time being. Spiritual meaning was probably going to have to wait.

The phenomenon of young women dressed only in swimwear being paraded before a panel of judges, not for the purpose of swimming in the sea, but so that fully dressed persons might judge the "beauty" of their bodies seems a fairly absurd way to treat women to our eyes today, but back in the Sixties, there seems to have been a difficulty in establishing a distinction between a beauty contest and an agricultural show. One wonders what the purpose of it all was. Was it simply innocence? Had women been dreaming of such an event? I don't know. There was no shortage of willing participants either to perform or to observe such gatherings. Nor, until September 1968, was there much objection to the existence of such entertainments.

On September 7, 1968, the Miss America 1969 Contest in Atlantic City received unexpected attention when some four hundred feminists of New Left persuasion (the New York Radical Women) chose the event as a good way to get over their view that the pageant had no idea what female beauty consisted of, and rejected stereotyped images of girls with large breasts who seemed to be rewarded for a superficial girliness more associated with dolls, that is, playthings, than young American women, who were already objects of capitalist exploitation. The event, in their opinion, gave women a standardized view to which they were expected to conform if they wished their beauty to be recognized. Demonstrating on the boardwalk outside the pageant, the demonstrators made a symbolic show of throwing heavily advertised products into a "Freedom Trash Can" to show their contempt for the commoditization of women, and the occupation of their lives by profiteers and chauvinists. To symbolize the change of priorities, the contents were going to be set alight, but the police would not permit it on the boardwalk. Into the deposit nevertheless were cast underwear items (including the body-distorting corset), bras, stilettos, kitchen items, cosmetics, and magazines such as *Playboy* and *Cosmopolitan*. Demonstrators furthermore observed the racism of the event since "beauty" allegedly only came in Caucasian white, as had been established in 1921. Organizers of the protest recognized clearly that the beauty of woman had been enslaved by the powers of consumption and that images of women were not chosen by women, but *for* the women they were aimed at. They also decried the prejudice against brains and assertiveness in chosen candidates, and distributed effective pamphlets to those who gathered with interest to hear what they were demonstrating about.

One reporter noticed how the trashcan resembled the principle of military draft resistors burning their draft cards, and so began the originally baseless idea promulgated in the global press that feminists advocated bra burning by individuals, an image that was turned against feminists as chauvinists regarded the idea as sexually provocative.

Feminists were parodied and frequently accused of defeminizing the feminine. As one protestor commented, had they advocated "girdle burning" they would have attracted great support from many of those who found such "supports" costly and physically onerous. Nevertheless, the bra-burning idea became a kind of shorthand symbol of refusing to appear as other people's images of women's beauty demanded, but the ambiguity of meaning in the image persisted through the Seventies.

Clearly, in retrospect, there was simply a justifiable need to swing the pendulum of oversexualized representations back to a level that was consistent with what women themselves wanted. The problem of course was that many women had been so inured to the prevailing system, assembled over many decades, if not from time immemorial, that they were unsure how to answer for themselves what it was that they wanted as an alternative to those catering to consumption. Feminist writers attempted to provide the rationales for resistance, but the whole issue was easily trivialized, and in the rush to assert themselves, various uniforms and stock attitudes appeared that could be imitated and identified as associated with feminist resistance to "male oppression."

Whatever the shortcomings stemming from the original misunderstanding, the demonstration marked a distinctive resurgence of feminism in global culture and the movement known familiarly as Female Liberation. The concept of liberation will always have an element of spiritual meaning because it is, generally speaking, a new spirit that is freed. However, liberation movements without serious spiritual meaning may initiate change, but not necessarily growth, for true growth comes from liberation within, when the demons of matter, so to speak, release the captured, unconscious goddess toward that wholeness that constitutes source of life. Sophia—the wild one—must be free!

In this process, ongoing, the Sixties marked only a beginning, but a beginning is where you start from, and without it, nothing.

TWENTY-ONE

Sexual Revolution

Perhaps some of the contradictory character of actor Michael Caine's 1967 recorded opinion in the documentary *Tonite Let's All Make Love in London,* that is, that we might have sold our morals "for a mess of cultural pottage" in the Sixties (he was referring to the U.K. principally), is understandable considering he had not long since starred in *Alfie.* The movie shows the path of an irresponsible, overly self-assured, rakish but somewhat winning character through a succession of primarily sexual liaisons until Alfie is finally brought face-to-face with the real consequences of his "laddish" attitude. He has to witness an illegal abortion performed in squalid circumstances that shield him neither from the lifeless fetus, for which he shared responsibility, nor its shattered mother-not-to-be. His career of selfish sexual opportunism appears to hit the skids with the film's close, as he himself suffers humiliation at the hands of an equally two-timing sugar mummy played venomously by Shelley Winters. The movie was not the decade's last word on the morality of changing sexual attitudes in the West. No less powerful was Richard Lester's *Petulia* (1968), which, appropriately, starred Julie Christie in the title role. Set in Swinging London's city cousin, San Francisco, the movie shows a free-loving, two-timing self-oriented girl, Petulia, involving herself with an emotionally and sexually vulnerable divorced middle-aged doctor, played movingly by George C. Scott. At the same time as she pursues her middle-aged beau, Petulia is suffering vicious physical abuse by her husband (pretty-boy Richard Chamberlain, as nasty as can be), supported by his corrupt and wealthy family. In the end, self-interest (and a curiously unexplored psychological-social dependency) sends her back to her husband, though for how long we may only guess. The lonely doctor (Scott) finds himself understanding better the value of what he lost when he divorced his rather conventional wife. *Petulia* failed to strike a chord with the public. Its approach was too advanced, ambiguous, even perhaps too prophetic. Most ordinary people had not had much opportunity yet to delve into a free-love lifestyle and would feel little sympathy or identity with wealthy Californian jet-setters. *Alfie* was a bit nearer the mark for most people in 1966, and in 1968 too.

It is something of a cliché to assert that it was the availability of birth control pills to women in the Western world from 1960 that, in giving control of fertility to women, kick-started an alleged sexual revolution in the Sixties. Pregnancy, it is true, could no longer be touted as the perilous recompense for premarital intercourse. However, the pill was not generally given out lightly, and was handled by many doctors as an adjunct to married people's family planning. Many unmarried young women would have found going to a doctor on an errand in favor of free love, embarrassing or impossible. Besides, pregnancy was not the only reason why a young woman might choose to keep a boyfriend's lust under a tight leash.

The freedom to indulge in sexual affairs of a serious kind was largely the preserve of financially independent people. As for the libidinous members of the upper classes, they needed little further stimulus to continue lives of liberty cushioned by financial security. There were factors other than the pill, equally powerful: financial status of working women gave more freedom of choice; changing attitudes to divorce loosened marriage bonds; young people with earning power, experiencing relationships as fun and pleasurable rather than scenarios of social duty, all played a part in raising the profile of sex. And of course, the whole subject was repeatedly glamorized in movies and advertising. But to have something like what people imagine by the phrase "sexual revolution" you need a more positive endorsement of sex itself. Someone has to say, and be believed, that sex is *good,* not just potentially pleasurable, whether the participant was married or not. And here the choir of Sixties opinion was exceedingly disharmonious. People (those who feared it) began to speak of a "permissive" society, in Britain at least, especially with some liberalizing, or humane legislation appearing in Britain in 1967 with regard to marriage and homosexuality, but *who* was giving permission? In the end, people have to permit *themselves,* and if determined, need little encouragement from outside, save freedom from fear. Besides, sexual allure had always been the currency by which partners secured a desired union, so it is fallacious to suppose that sex offended social morals. Sexual allure may be employed for many things, as movie after movie, risqué or otherwise, had been saying for decades. Sex was not invented as a means in the Sixties.

What perhaps *was* new was greater public awareness of the paradoxical idea that sex was not necessarily anything special, or that its naturalness ought to preclude its being loaded with guilt and prohibition, that is to say, that sex was *innocent.* Such an idea (influenced by popular psychology) clearly undermined centuries of Catholic and Protestant dogma. In that sense, perhaps the real revolution being slowly effected during the Sixties was toward greater secularization, the reduction of scriptural authority, for example, to the sphere of opinion. One suspects that what Michael Caine was getting at was the possible loss of *moral absolutes,* exchanged dangerously for a temporary feeling of being culturally right-on and apparently "free" (a very relative term). Without religious sanction, without a spiritual basis to morality, what compelling reason (other than fear of law) was there to hold any practice as good or bad, save whether you liked it nor not? Western law was ultimately based on Roman law, canon law, common law, and precedent, and the dominant proscriptions of these legal bases for civilization derived, in popular thought at least, from the Ten Commandments, combined with some Christian understanding of forgiveness for the willing penitent after suitable punishment, or relaxation of punishment out of considered charity in the face of regretful confession, contrition, and manifest respect for law. The issue of sex in the Sixties was fundamentally a spiritual issue, though it was not generally perceived that way, being strongly linked to the idea of personal freedom, something that was supposed to distinguish the "free world" from Communist tyranny. The politics undoubtedly complicated the issues.

Shortly before my mother died, at the age of seventy-eight, I asked her whether she felt she had missed anything being brought up in the Thirties, and growing up quickly in the Forties and Fifties. She told me she would like to have had more freedom to explore the sexual side of life as that kind of thing was not an option for someone who married in 1955 to begin a family. She had obviously witnessed the freedoms that became available to people in the Sixties and Seventies and thought she might like to have had the option of more experience. I said that she hadn't missed all that much, and that in some ways I would like to have experienced aspects of the life she had lived before I was born, though not, I think, with regard to dress, and the lack of color of the postwar world. It was an interesting conversation, and I still wonder whether she really did miss something that would have made her life a better experience. It's not like she did not participate in adult life in the Sixties!

Certainly, there was a general sexiness about the Sixties that was stimulating, even to a boy. I was not blind, nor without my own kind of sexual, romantic interest; being precocious, I was very fond of girls, more than was the norm for most of my age I think! Movies reflected a delight in the *idea* of sex and sexiness: more the latter. British comedies were ruder and cruder, and perhaps a bit more honest, than American ones, as I recall.

There was a persistent barrage of bright images of smart men and very pretty girls, with "tarts" or "loose women" clearly delineated from proper "gels." Sixties models looked younger than Fifties models, by and large. I happen to like Sixties dress and hairstyles, and I liked them then, though I draw a line at the beehive hairdo, which lasted long after its sell-by date! There was a freshness and innocence about the actual faces in consumer-oriented images that you very rarely see these days—and men did not look so self-consciously masculine, without today's de rigueur self-absorption in roughness and meanness of texture, cheekbone, facial hair, and eye, while one was never in doubt they were men. The projection of freshness was evident on record covers, magazines, photograph wallets, advertisements, film posters, some TV shows. A lot of people seemed to be having a good, easier time, and the swing and beat and brassiness of the music all added and reinforced that sensibility: work hard, play often. The emphasis was perhaps not so much on overt sexiness (though there was plenty of that in men and women), but a new accent on naturalness, lightness, almost fairylike qualities (in women), which is probably what I mean by *sexiness:* lightness of body, glowing flesh, availability. However, the images of women in particular were not without a major cosmetic enhancement factor: colored mascara became more noticeable as the decade wore on, false eyelashes, a fair amount of hairspray, but the faces still looked less faux aristocratic or doll-like than was customary in the Fifties, however refined the models' faces often then were. Eyes were made up to look more alert, aware, *bright to the world,* rather than demure, subtly seductive, aristocratic, and cunningly alluring, as you often saw hinted in Fifties imagery. The faculty of vision was emphasized over that of feminine mystery. Innocence was the setting for enchantment, rather than the magic spell of seductive glamour.

The long hair, loose and wild style that Roger Vadim's worship of Brigitte Bardot brought to the fore was immensely feminine and free at the same time, and was popular with the Bohemian, relaxed look favored by British stars like Julie Christie, Nanette Newman, Susan George, Suzy Kendall, Judy Geeson, among others whose look seems to have influenced Goldie Hawn in the States, though Jane Fonda's Sixties styles seem to be in a class of their own—Jane too had been under the guiding hand of Frenchman Roger Vadim for a while (he directed her in the stylish *Barbarella* in 1968). Overall, with looser fitting dresses with bright colors and floral and abstract designs, there was a greater naturalness in appearance. Of course if women did not possess de rigueur long, slim legs, they could find it hard to match the new "looks," which could be uncompromisingly overdominant, with few fashionable alternatives. There were also more self-consciously futuristic, beyond-this-time looks: plastic, sharp-cut capes, for example, and curious glossy hats and shiny, patent leather or plastic variants on the cap, some of which looked rather helmetlike, even robotic, abstract. Many girls wore

Fig. 21.1. French actress Brigitte Bardot (b. 1934).

narrow slacks in any number of colors, a style that also came from Left Bank Paris student chic, and that left bare ankles exposed and feet clad in sneakers rather than high or tight shoes that dictated gait.

The miniskirt enjoyed a long reign for a fashion item, circa 1964–1971, but the majority of women in Western countries wore skirts and dresses generally just above the knee. There was a moderate form of the mini that was almost universal by the end of 1967. Men's fashions could be as boring and uniform as ever, but from the early Sixties, there was much imitation of Beatle-style jackets, sometimes in colored suede, with tight hipster trousers coming in, often in anachronistic stripes. Groins received little material protection, and the visual gap between young and middle-aged men grew greater with the less fabric expended on trousers, jackets, and overcoats. From 1967, men's fashions really began to flourish in luxuriance, with the return of late Victorian and Edwardian "dandy" sensibilities, with exotic floral ties, Indian-patterned cravats, large, rounded collars, rich colors and fabrics, and frilly shirts of bright colors.

How can one say whether men and women were more attractive to one another than at any other time? The clothes doubtless encouraged contact, and that was a plus for many people. What people look for depends on so many factors, but there was a burgeoning sense of freedom and optimism that was palpable, and was reflected in dress, and the reduction of fear that came with freedom meant that people felt easier about exposing more personal body flesh. As a child, I must say I observed all the changes with great interest and enjoyment, and liked the more artistic, sometimes mid-Victorian style direction things seemed to be moving in (sideburns and velvet), and looked forward to joining the colorful cavalcade in due course.

When I refer to the greater naturalness, and frequently warmth, that entered the visual frame of how the sexes presented themselves to one another, one cannot of course underestimate the extraordinarily widespread effect on the era of flower power as advocated by what were at first called the "flower children."

FLOWER POWER

As far as is known, the origin of the flower initiative may be laid, gratefully or otherwise, at the door of beat poet Allen Ginsburg, who, in November 1965, wrote an essay while at Berkeley, California, called "How to Make a March/Spectacle," in which he advocated the view that the nature of a peace demonstration could be transformed positively by surprising the opponent with a fructifying gesture of generous, symbolic value, undercutting expectation of predictable confrontation strategies. He recommended distributing flowers (as was done in India, Hawaii, and elsewhere), a sign of the powers of the earth, of growth and life, and a reminder of what was essential and beautiful in life. Just over a year later, in January 1967, the flower children—usually identified by the media as one and the same with hippies—appeared at the Human Be-In in San Francisco. From there, the idea spread quickly of giving flowers as a gesture of "love" and of wearing floral costume. A hit record sung by Scott McKenzie spread the idea: "If you're going to San Francisco, Be sure to wear some flowers in your hair." On August 24, 1967, British Pathé News reported that the "cult" of flower children had reached Henrietta Park in Bath, England, where a "Love-In" was held, at which a local Church of England vicar engaged the flower children in discussion about what they stood for (though most sat, picnic-like, on the grass). Young men and women all dressed in floral shirts and sported flowers in their hair: a familiar sight once both to Renaissance artists and Edwardian Bohemia.

Between August 26 and 28, "By permission of His Grace, the Duke of Bedford," flower children descended on stately home Woburn Abbey for a "3-Day Non-Stop Happening," called in psychedelic-style poster, the "Festival of the Flower Children," with "Flowers and Fireworks," and where between 12,000 and 20,000 people, some more committed than others, came to sit on the grass (close to the earth nourishment) and listen to groups and singers such as the Move, Eric Burdon, Jeff Beck, the Bee Gees, Allan Price, Denny Laine, and the Small Faces. This was the Summer of Love, British-style, and the flower children bloomed, delicate in the soft breeze of the time. They were not so noticeable as a body the following year (1968), but the floral principle by then was combined with the psychedelic countercultural hippie explosion that would make governments about the world nervous and often violently reactionary. Fashions in mainstream dress very soon adopted floral patterns and paisley patterns into the most fashionable garments for men and women of all classes, and the whole effect was one of spreading "peace and love" across Western culture like seedy jam on dry bread.

The romantic and spiritual vibe of the flower children was based on a sense of pacific properties in Nature and the needs of growth. Much that was objectionable in global politics stood against these principles. The rush for capital left no time for spiritual development, and Nature was trampled over in the process, or crudely exploited without any sense of a reciprocal, living relationship with Nature. And this brings us very directly to the great paradox of Sixties free love. The issue turns upon this whole idea of *fertility*.

All ancient festivals involving flowers were related to the growth cycles of nature, and their integral relationship with the wonder and promise of human fertility, of life, of newborn children, of spring and summer languor, of time to love and celebrate peace: God's peace for all his children, symbolized by the rainbow gift to Noah after the flood. Now, what happens when we posit this very proper glorification of human and earthly fertility next to the idea of the freedom to control fertility, which very often simply meant the decision to thwart fertility in pursuit of something else, namely, personal gratification or earning a living? In attempting to consider this question in terms of the spiritual meaning of the Sixties, we are brought face to face with one of the greatest long-term tragedies of the decade, whose baleful effects are still with us: namely, the attempted removal of sex from the life expressed in the natural cycles of fertility.

First, what is the relation of sex to spirituality? According to the canonical Gospels, sex has no part to play in the life of beings proper to the "kingdom of heaven." Jesus says that the resurrected, like angels, "neither marry nor are given in marriage" (Luke 20:34–36). There may be a hint here of angelic androgyny, for it is females who are "given in marriage." Saint Paul was clear that marriage should be avoided among his followers unless the men could not contain their ardor. Then it was better for unions to be solemnized in marriage and resultant children baptized. This is the orthodox Christian line on spiritual, eternal life and sex. Sex is of this world, and this world will one day end when eternal life becomes sole reality for the redeemed, and eternal life has no need of reproduction, and therefore no need of sex. As for pleasure, spiritual joy will far exceed the temporal and fleeting character of earthly enjoyment.

The gnostic, so-called heretical tradition did not follow this reasoning though it might accept its conclusion. For Gnostics, becoming human on earth entailed a division of a primal Man (called "Anthropos") who was both male and female, *as God is,* for Man is made in God's reflection, or image. With the primal rupture from the pleroma ("fullness"), which Gnostics believed had been effected by Sophia's excessive ardor for knowledge, the primal principle whose image Sophia had absorbed split into duality, which is the nature of a temporal and spatial system. What ensued was both Sophia's "Fall" with the divine seeds (of pneuma = spirit) within her, and simultaneous creation of the universe according to a binary principle. That which has a start, has an end, and the two principles divided enable "time" to exist.

In Gnostic sexual sacraments, the joining of the male and the female with their minds on eternity becomes both symbol and sacrament of the Return to the One principle that obtained before the Fall into matter. So sacramentalized sex has spiritual meaning and may be a spiritual sacrament. As the friar puts it in *Romeo and Juliet* at the lovers' private, secret wedding: "We incorporate two in one." There should be joy and exceeding pleasure in this sacrament of what Valentinian Gnostics called "the Bridal Chamber." The resulting fertility was either consumed as a sacrament or, if children were born, they would be raised in the *gnosis* for reunion with the pleroma. Fertility for the Gnostic was the glorification of the spirit in life; its archangel was Sophia, divine Wisdom.

Students of comparative religion will recognize in this sacrament a direct parallel with tantric ideas where the man and the woman incarnate gods Shiva and Shakti, whose infinite sexual communion is believed to sustain the universe, which reproduces itself in cycles infinitely. It is little wonder then that Western counterculture began to find in Hindu philosophies an apparently amenable spiritual outlook missing from orthodox religion in the West. The Christian gnostic tradition had practically no voice at the time, a pity perhaps.

If the Western woman (and man by extension) was "freed" to avoid fertility purely for the exercise of personal pleasure, and it was *that* freedom that constituted sexual revolution, then there was a profound problem, from the spiritual point of view. You have the potential opposites of sex as pleasure *versus* sex as creation (fertility). There is a parallel here with the dichotomy of production and consumption. If sex finds its fulfillment in pleasure, where is the fulfillment of sex in creation? The natural order is plainly that sex finds its fulfillment in creation (production). Flower power is not on the side of free love for pleasure alone (consumption), and if it is, it is self-contradictory.

This debate becomes even more interesting, and acute, when we bring in the idea of commoditization of the image of woman. The self-gratifying unit is the "unit" of humanity that commerce likes to engage in for profit. The selling of products through the image of woman, especially available woman, especially woman who wants pleasure, who wants to give pleasure, and be pleasured (the pleasured and pleasure-seeking woman—and man), is central to the advertisers' dictum that "sex sells." This entire principle, as we have seen, encourages the idea that women come to resemble commodities in a consumer-based capitalism.

The hidden price of the commoditization of women (which of course can easily accommodate the idea of the "free woman," for she has money to spend) is that the sexual nature is ultimately divided. Sex has become a consumer product, a pleasure to be consumed at will, even a "good" *because a pleasure,* a right, an object of freedom. When the product is not available for consumption, frustration may result, and as modern consumerism knows, gratification must be as instantaneous as possible, lest the sale be lost. Thus, "silly" impedimenta such as the traditional courtship process may be jumped over. We are on the fast track to the "zipless fuck" of Erica Jong's *Fear of Flying* (1973), which perhaps inadvertently played further into the hands of further exploitation of women by the mechanics and economics of desire. Frustration may lead to regular masturbation, and the products will become available for this dimension of free consumption as well. Besides, what need for man hath the satisfied woman? The sexual revolution turned out to be a capitalist daydream.

The sexual nature stood in ultimate peril of being divided, thwarted, and disintegrated from its whole place in the natural world. To understand what is meant here, we need to understand sex as part of the spiritual integrity of our species. According to Blake, Jung, and any number of Eastern philosophical traditions, the spiritual integrity of man consists of four balanced principles we may name as reason, intuition, feeling, and sensation. To abstract sex from the realm of fertility in which it has its proper place in nature, we identify it primarily with only one of the four principles, that is: *sensation.* The bodily stimulus is primary, even all. It is the sensation that establishes the craving. Other aspects of the human mind may of course soon find themselves frustrated in their own manner. The result will be a division in the subject's mind, which may manifest in physical symptoms or in a discomfiting state of mind, perhaps guilt, or a sense of emptiness, for where fertility is absent, futility soon replaces it. You can deal with futility? Welcome to our world.

The separation of sensation from the other aspects of human spiritual integrity renders the satisfaction of the principle vulnerable directly to commercialization, whose aims frequently require the deformation of human nature, and the imposition of false needs and false identities. Sensation divorced from its integral life must ultimately be infertile, and that means one thing in nature: death. In this regard we may understand the central gnostic principle that the fall of Man is due to the "love of the body." When Man sees himself reflected solely in his image, he falls, such is the ultimate and obvious vanity, or the vain objective.

Unfortunately, the dominant Christian churches have not been able to help to resolve fully matters with regard to this paradox of infertile freedom. Catholic morals already have themselves tended to separate sex from human spiritual integrity, for in a twist of the gnostic observation, Catholic teaching has traditionally associated the female body with sin, and has tended to condemn both flesh and Nature herself. While it has approved of sex for birthing children in the spirit of Saint Paul (it's a step better than concupiscence), it has insisted that holiness is incompatible with sexual practice, and so the teaching has come down to Catholics that basically, however you look at it, sex is sinful, and pleasurable sex and impure thoughts particularly so.

While I accept that this question may be cut up and sliced very differently, I hope readers will recognize that there is an important issue here, and may perhaps agree that it is something of a pity that while the flower-child ethos seems to have eventually found a blossom within the environmental and planetary consciousness movement, there was also a proper place for it in the consideration of the spirituality of human sexuality, an issue that cuts across the rather too easy idea that the alleged sexual revolution of the Sixties was an unalloyed gift of joyous freedom, (though liberty, certainly) and therefore, an unmitigated "good." It wasn't. Important lines emerged that *could* have taken the movement in considerably more positive, less futile directions.

PORNOGRAPHY

Pornography (literally, pictures of prostitutes) has always existed and doubtless always will, for reasons not unrelated to issues discussed above. There is a widely held view in the United States particularly that the pornographic empire of today can be laid at the door of the liberties of the Sixties, which liberties may then be questioned.

There was a lot of sexual suggestion and titillation in Sixties movies and advertising, much of it harmlessly acceptable to many people within the context of a cinema outing or magazine intended for adults. Overt acts of sexual intercourse were however practically nonexistent in public cinemas, and very few were sorry about that at the time. Then in October 1967 Swedish director Vilgot Sjöman's film *I Am Curious (Yellow)* was released. The film was a serious drama with documentary elements (including an interview with Martin Luther King filmed in Stockholm in 1966) and would have sunk without trace outside of its country of origin were it not for the fact that it had scenes of candid nudity, simulated but apparently plain sexual intercourse between male and female and oral contact with a flaccid penis. By 1969, the movie was the twelfth most popular movie in America. Johnny Carson had been to see it. And, of course, it was Art. And Art had always been an acceptable justification for artistic license. This, however, was perceived as taking license too far, and the movie became hugely controversial. That it was tolerated in the main undoubtedly emboldened enthusiasm to make and see explicit sex films. For this author, a full consideration of this phenomenon lies outside the scope of this book, as the explosion of motion-picture pornography is principally a phenomenon of the Seventies.

Fig. 21.2. Director Vilgot Sjöman with actress Lena Nyman during the filming of I Am Curious (Yellow), *1967.*

Commercial cinema had from its beginnings recognized the pleasure many adults took in sex as entertainment; the difference in the Sixties was that the energies pushing through the years as a moving aggregate made the degree of potential expansion of the idea inevitable, as tolerances were inured to change and there was by the end of the decade considerable questioning about first principles of right and wrong, with the dominant mainstream becoming broadly suspicious of controls on expression, as freedom had become the essential progressive principle. This thrust gained force from the general view of clinical psychologists that exposure to sexual material among adults was not in itself corrupting and some degree of liberalization of attitudes might well prove positively healthy on the basis that repression of natural instincts encouraged neurosis, as well as crime. Where, or even if, there was a line to be drawn as to the limits of any freedom was not an issue that the decade was capable of reaching a conclusion about; the sole guiding principle to emerge was that so long as a pleasure could be related to "love" (which essentially sanctified a practice) then it might be good, and if not positively good, then probably harmless, and if it could be shown to be harmful, then it would be a matter either for private discretion, or, if there was a strong social dimension to the issue, for the law, after public debate.

HOMOSEXUALITY

One area to benefit long term from this changed attitude toward what was socially tolerable was that of the right (in some places) of homosexuals to be homosexuals.

In 1962, the state of Illinois adopted the Model Penal Code, which permitted consensual homosexual acts between males, though soliciting was prohibited. Nearly a decade would pass before any other U.S. state approved similar measures. Idaho and Michigan exercised particularly harsh penalties, with persons found guilty sentenced to many years in prison. The national government regarded homosexuals as liable to blackmail and therefore as security risks, so there was a steady expulsion from state administration and the armed services of homosexuals.

In the United Kingdom, Home Secretary Roy Jenkins succeeded in getting his Sexual Offences Act through Parliament in 1967, and many considered it the end of the world. The act did not make homosexual acts among adults in themselves legal but established that if adults were accused of consensual sexual acts in private, immediate cessation of prosecution must follow. The hope was to remove threat of criminal blackmail from homosexual men's lives, but it emphatically did not establish homosexuality as an acceptable practice in law, only that it was not the law's task to invade private space and interfere with adults' privacy. The same idea was not extended to the smoking of cannabis, as the Rolling Stones found to their cost later in the year. With regard to the passing of Jenkins's act, any public show of enthusiasm was discretely discouraged by ministers. *Keep it private* was the rule.

On June 28, 1969, New York police raided the Mafia-owned Stonewall Inn in Greenwich Village, a haven for gay people's entertainment. The results of the raid are now celebrated in gay lore throughout the world. Persons offended by the police action got together and decided they would no longer tolerate being treated differently from other people living and enjoying themselves. They'd had enough of all the "shit" they'd been taking, and mobilized support for what became in the next decade the gay liberation movement that spread from New York to many parts of the world. What is significant is that again we see that by 1969 a fundamental shift in consciousness had occurred whereby there was expectation that organized protest could bring about real amelioration of oppression among a "free people," along with a belief that change was inevitable simply by flagging up an issue with sufficient conviction.

Whatever the word *freedom* might have meant to the writers of the Constitution of the United States of America, there can be little doubt whatsoever that the Sixties oversaw a significant expansion of that idea, and its saints go marching on.

True freedom, like reason, I believe, is a gift of the spirit.

TWENTY-TWO

Psychedelics

Psychedelic: *English compound adjective,*
from the Greek noun psychē *(mind, psyche, soul, spirit),*
and the verb deloō *(I make manifest, show, reveal,*
make clear, make visible; noun: delōsis*)*

The first time my senses were assaulted by, or alerted to the existence
of the psychedelic was on my way home from Dandenong North State
School in the second half of 1967, which daily walk led past a psychiatric clinic on David Street. Stunning manifestations occurred after a
patient equipped him- or herself with ample tins of purple, pink, yellow,
and red paint and proceeded to daub the entirety of the brick facade
of the modern single-story building with huge colorful flowers and the
words *FLOWER POWER* and *LOVE* emblazoned big and bubbly for
all passersby to see. The work bore the stamp of an artist's execution,
perhaps seizing the role of herald, though naturally, the association of
florid colors, untamed graffiti, and presumed lunacy struck somewhat:
was something breaking out that might best be kept in? Reported to my
parents, their reaction was that some poor soul must have escaped from
psychiatric custody. Was this a sign of the times?

Shortly after this manifestation one became aware from disapprov-
ing news stories and from Mum and Dad's conversation that something was "going wrong" with the Beatles, back in England, and that

something first involved drugs, then the suspected suicide of manager Brian Epstein (in August) and to cap it all, Swami-ism: exposure to exotic Oriental practices of doubtful religious value to the Christian. Suddenly my Monkees bubblegum cards, featuring wacky TV-created California Beatle imitators, did not look quite so innocent. Dad was determined his three healthy, outgoing young boys were not going to join this strange tide of disturbance whose vibratory waves approached the Southern Hemisphere (and Melbourne, Australia, in particular) like the fatal cloud of "fall-out" in Nevil Shute's *On the Beach*, released as a movie, in timely fashion, in December 1959.

Without any doubt, some of the key moments of the Sixties were experienced in altered states of consciousness. That means that some of the key modulations of consciousness, revelation realizations, and even decision making, belonged to what were in fact new states of mind, inaccessible in essence to those who knew nothing of the peculiar consciousness states induced by chemical stimulants. That also means that the substance of what might have been experienced, cannot be accurately or in any way minutely recorded in words. The psychedelic trip experience is frequently in essence indescribable, though one can use simile and metaphor, whose value for communication will depend on the range of experience of the listener or reader. More than this, intense psychedelic experience does not imprint clearly or adequately on memory, whose lineaments and categories are dependent on ordinary experiences of sense, space, and time, developed from childhood, shaped by experience. Philosophers of the empirical school have long dismissed spiritual categories of experience precisely for not conforming to these terrestrial categories.

We can reflect on the imprint of *presence* of psychedelic experience, that is, we can know with certainty "it's happened." We can even see products of it, but we cannot properly see the experience itself without sharing it, and while such caveats are true to other forms of personal experience, it is especially, even acutely the case when trying to render psychedelic vision with our earthbound vocabulary. Such experience belongs to psychic and arguably in some cases, spiritual being, and "spiritual things are spiritually discerned." We might therefore conclude that a substantial proportion of Sixties experience is effectively missing, and yet none of the counterculture makes sense without the mightily influential presence of psychedelic experience, which frequently contained pristine, ultraclear awareness simply not capturable or even suggestible in the fading celluloid of contemporary 16mm documentary footage.

Many psychedelically experienced people recognize that these experiences of perception, often accompanied by elation or afflatus, mean most when communicated in terms of spiritual categories. In perhaps crude terms, "God" was in some sense experienced, or something that seemed to point in that mysterious but transcendent direction (hardly surprising perhaps, given our species experience and education), that is, what some users became aware of at the highest phases of psychedelic experience *could* only be described in such terms. This is not always the case. The psychoactive chemicals stimulate brain receptors, but the processing of effects depends on what kind of mind is being stimulated. As leading exponent of psychedelic experience Professor Timothy Leary enjoined—often quoted as a warning to potential users: "Don't take acid [LSD] unless you know you're a beautiful person." To reveal or manifest the psyche of a disturbed person, or one with deep-seated psychoses or instabilities, could be to exacerbate suffering, or stimulate mental illness, temporary or long lasting. More generally, a very dull mind is most likely to hallucinate, that is, see things created by misperception, or flummoxed imagination, as though drunk, or to self-deceive about real conditions, which can be either foolish or dangerous in impact. A spiritual mind, on the other hand, is already capable of elevation, and for such a one, a chemically induced experience *of moderate dosage* will, or can, enhance that capacity, or to intensify, deepen, broaden, or add perspective and awareness to it. Vaunted benefits on the properly prepared mind include cleansing of perception, restoration of clarity to vision and meaning, and therefore, help to open consciousness to pristine perceptions of the nature of truth and reality, leading to the rational or suprarational conclusion that ordinary terrestrial consciousness is better comprehended from a transcendent level than can ever be the case of the reverse. The earthbound cannot judge the heavenly. The sense-experience empiricist is a cripple in the spiritual dimension. The biologist is in no position to judge the vision of enlightened mind, or as Saint Paul would put it, flesh and blood cannot inherit the "kingdom of the heavens." The body is a temple of the spirit, or else it is a tomb. God cannot exist to those who cannot see God.

Another important aspect of psychedelic vision on the receptive mind is an instantaneous capacity to envision correspondences between different areas of being, or levels and categories of experience. This principle of correspondence, seeing links and connections, all points to the familiar mystical category of seeing "All as One," promoting enthusiasm for universalisms, for having seen the "end." The path to it may appear as simple as appeared to be the leap of consciousness that led to the liberating insight—namely, "We're all one, aren't we?" This enthusiasm can frequently find itself out of step with real, that is, ordinary conditions, of earthbound men and women, apt to fear change rather than embrace it without sufficient promise. Yes, we'd all "like to teach the world to sing," but it will take considerably more than a gathering of different, youthful race representatives on a cliff top each sipping Coca-Cola, as the memorable 1970 advert (and pop song) had it!

The category of correspondence is also, it should be noted, a familiar aspect of "esotericism" or esoteric systems, and it is the case that persons of lively intellectual curiosity who have undergone psychedelic experience find themselves later with a door into understanding and appreciating the esoteric traditions of East and West. Moreover, those very traditions seem to explain most clearly the nature of psychedelic vision and its potential. I am reminded that a poster for the London Free School initiative, active in 1967 in Notting Hill, West London, featured a famous nineteenth-century engraving, made deceptively in a style of medieval and Renaissance emblems that depicted an old sage crawling from Earth through spheres of celestial being surrounding Earth, with his head poking through the planets and stars surrounding Earth into the esoteric, supercelestial realm of the spiritual heavens. He has been shown that he's "everywhere," but can presumably get back in time for tea! This same engraving was used when my late colleague, Professor Nicholas Goodrick-Clarke, who founded the Exeter

University Center for Esoteric Studies in 2004, issued a leaflet to advertise the M.A. course on Western Esotericism to which I had the honor of contributing structure and teaching during the professor's lifetime.

HASHISH

An afflated sense of meaningful *correspondence* seems to have occurred to Paul McCartney the first time he smoked marijuana at the Del Monico Hotel at Park Avenue and East 59th Street, Manhattan, in August 1964. According to Beatles press officer Derek Taylor,* it was Bob Dylan and friends Al Aronovitz and Victor Mamudas who turned the Beatles on to marijuana in a smoky hotel room behind closed curtains far from home.[1] Dylan presumed the Beatles' familiarity with the effects of smoking the herb, having heard the line "I can't hide" in "I Wanna Hold Your Hand" (1963) as "I get high." This was an intriguing basis for a new relationship in the Beatles' lives. They had no illusions about Dylan's talent, having been mightily impressed by his *Freewheelin'* album, and they recognized a culture peer, a switched-on musician who seemed to have aborbed the entire spirit of American folk music traditions and transmuted their essences, through an eclectic ear for popular music, and lyric flair, into something distinctive, original, spiritually sincere and widely accessible, beyond established circles of folk music enthusiasts. Meeting Bob Dylan, the Beatles got very high indeed, and at one point, when Derek Taylor entered the private proceedings to try to arrange other introductions to the band, Paul grabbed Derek's arm and gleefully told him it felt like they were "up there," that is at ceiling level, looking down on themselves.

---

*I had the privilege of getting to know Derek Taylor (1932–1997) in 1985 when I was researcher/cowriter on a Yoko Ono–approved BBC TV drama-documentary titled *John Lennon: A Journey in the Life,* directed by Ken Howard and starring Bernard Hill (as Lennon), Roy Orbison, Roger Waters, Peter Cook, Helen Shapiro, G. B. Zoot Money, Andy Fairweather-Low, Stanley Unwin, John Gustafson, Screaming Lord Sutch, Carl Wayne, Edwin Starr, Linda Thompson, and numerous other talented performers and authoritative interviewees. The experience of conversing deeply, mind-to-mind on the subject with Derek over numerous occasions in person and by phone gave me an insight into the overall spirit, feeling, perspective, and attitude of the group that could not be obtained from books alone; it was a great, enlightening, affecting experience.

Paul began to feel a revelatory experience such that, when trying to put it into words, he asked roadie Mal Evans to note down what he said, lest it be forgotten. The next day, Paul was somewhat disappointed to see that his vision had coalesced in the apparently bare, simplistic statement, "There are seven levels." That, however, is a very meaningful statement in esoteric lore, and I can imagine Paul's mind, under the influence, seeing at once how such an insight could connect whole strata of integrated knowledge relating to the relativity of consciousness. That is, what you see depends on where you are, and what you are, and what level of consciousness you are observing from. Apart from anything else, what Paul had experienced was *being conscious* of being conscious. Naturally he would have felt "above" the newly and temporarily objectified ego. To be "turned on" was to be made open. As to his intuited numerology, the structure of seven-level initiation is not only evident in the seven liberal arts of classical education, and in the seven "signs" of Saint John's "spiritual gospel," but also adumbrated in numerous initiatory systems of the West, and in parallel schemes of alchemical transformation and initiatory ascent. Paul's was in fact a pure insight of esoteric meaning, grasped apparently without prior knowledge, by that sometimes startling intuition that set the Beatles so far apart from competitors. The experience of mutual reflection with Bob Dylan seems to have plugged them into another dimension of themselves. George Harrison also subsequently testified to the extraordinary nature of the experience. Something had definitely happened; they had experienced transcendence, and it would mark the beginning of a shift in the dynamics of the group's lyrics and music that would first flower in 1965 with the release of *Rubber Soul,* an unadulterated work of universally accessible art, and vinyl herald of psychedelia to come.

As to the varied effects of smoking or eating cannabis (some of which are quite banal), I can do no better than point readers eager for more in-depth knowledge in the direction of one of the first scientific analyses of the "psychology of hashish." Aleister Crowley's informed essay "The Herb Dangerous" (attributed to Oliver Haddo, fictional villain of Somerset Maugham's novel *The Magician*) was written in August 1908, in Madrid, fifty-four years before the Beatles' meeting with Bob Dylan.

With pipe, peshtin, and purity.

Fig. 22.1. Aleister Crowley (1875–1947).

Crowley first speaks of traditional circumstances that might surround the discovery of the herb's peculiar powers:

Through the ages we [Crowley and friend Allan Bennett in 1898–99] found this one constant story. Stripped of its local and chronological accidents, it usually came to this—the writer would tell of a young man, a seeker after the Hidden Wisdom, who, in one circumstance or another, meets an adept; who, after sundry ordeals, obtains from the said adept, for good or ill, a certain mysterious drug or potion, with the result (at least) of opening the gate of the Other-world. This potion was identified with the *Elixir Vitae* of the physical Alchemists, or one of their "Tinctures," most likely the

"White Tincture" which transforms the base metal (normal perception of life) to silver (poetic conception), and we sought it by fruitless attempts to poison ourselves with every drug in (and out of) the Pharmacopoeia.

Crowley went on to describe immediate effects:

1. "The volatile aromatic effect" (A)

This, the first evanescent symptom, gives the "thrill" described by Ludlow,* as of a new pulse of power pervading one. Psychologically, the result is that one is thrown into an absolutely perfect state of introspection. One perceives one's thoughts and nothing but one's thoughts, and it is as thoughts that one perceives them. Material objects are only perceived as thoughts; in other words, in this respect, one possesses the direct consciousness of Berkeleyan idealism† The Ego and the Will are not involved; there is introspection of an almost if not quite purely impersonal type; that, and nothing more.

I am not to be understood as asserting that the results of this introspection are psychologically valid.

2. "The toxic hallucinative effect" (B)

With a sufficiently large dose—for it is possible to get effect (A) only as a transient phenomenon—the images of thought pass more rapidly through the brain, at last vertiginously fast. They are no longer recognized as thoughts, but imagined as exterior. The Will and the Ego become alarmed, and may be attacked and overwhelmed. This constitutes the main horror of the drug; it is to be combated by a highly—may I say magically?—trained will.

I trust my readers will concede that the practice of

The Hasheesh Eater (1857): autobiographical treatment of the subject of hashish by Fitz Hugh Ludlow (1836–1870). Crowley probably bought the book in New York in 1906 when returning from India.

†The Idealist philosophy of Irishman Bishop George Berkeley (1685–1753), briefly that objects are primarily ideas of the mind; the mind is creative of reality.

ceremonial magic and meditation, all occult theories apart, do lead the mind to immense power over its own imaginations.

The fear of being swept away in the tide of relentless images is a terrible experience. Woe to who yields!

3. "The narcotic effect" (C)

One simply goes off to sleep. This is not necessarily due to the brain fatigue induced by (A) and (B); for with one sample of Cannabis, I found it to occur independently.

Crowley found for himself that after experiencing "dryness" in his raja yoga meditative practices in India 1901–1903, he found that combining small doses of cannabis with meditation increased speed and effectiveness of obtaining "Samadhi, that oneness with the Universe, or with the Nothingness, which is the feeble expression by which alone we can shadow that supreme trance." Oddly perhaps, the Beatles "came in" the other way round, first with *cannabis indica,* then LSD, and *then* mantra yoga, practiced as a "pure" alternative to chemical stimulants, particularly LSD. One presumes John Lennon had read something of Crowley's work on hashish and its value for understanding mental processes and mystical states of consciousness, as he was keen to put Crowley's image among people the group liked on the cover of the June 1967 album release of *Sgt. Pepper's Lonely Hearts Club Band.*

LSD-25

Usually administered as a colorless liquid or in "tabs" soaked in same, LSD already had a checkered history before a dentist put some in Lennon and Harrison's coffee at a dinner party in London in the late spring of 1965, apparently in an effort to loosen things up for some sexual games, something the Beatles and wives Cynthia and Patti were keen to avoid. It was Dr. Albert Hofmann of Sandoz pharmaceuticals, Switzerland, who made the first synthesis for medical purposes in 1938.

Lysergic acid diethylamide got its technical acronym LSD-25 from the fact that the synthesis was from the twenty-fifth variation in an experimental series aimed at finding circulatory stimulants for use in

Fig. 22.2. Albert Hofmann (1906–2008), discoverer of LSD.

obstetrics derived from ergot, a fungus that grows on rye.* In 1943, while World War II raged outside neutral Switzerland, Hofmann returned to his earlier synthesis and absorbed some through his finger-tips. He became conscious of "an intense stimulation of the imagination and an altered state of awareness of the world." He had some difficulty cycling home; his sense of time and space became increasingly disorga-nized and he occasionally felt he was outside his body. "I thought I had died," he remarked of one point of acute awareness on this, the world's first (hopefully) humanity-benefiting LSD trip.[2]

In fact, symptoms of intoxication were not so very far from expe-riences first detailed by Havelock Ellis[†] and subsequently developed by Aleister Crowley with regard to mescaline, a psychoactive alka-loid found naturally in the *Lophophora williamsi,* a spineless cactus (phenethylamine class) commonly known as peyote.

Interestingly, Crowley had played host to novelist and science writer Aldous Huxley when the latter visited Berlin in late 1930 with Crowley's friend, *Times* science correspondent J. W. N. Sullivan to

---

*Ethnomycologist R. Gordon Wasson (1898–1986), executive of the J. P. Morgan Bank, who pioneered research into peyote-ingesting tribes in Mexico, also wrote on the sup-posed foaming-wine stimulant employed at ancient Greek rites at Eleusis that gave visi-tors the spiritual experience of a lifetime in his book *The Road to Eleusis: Unveiling the Secret of the Mysteries* (1978), based on the theory that ergot grew on the rye that flour-ished on the Phrygian Plain, and that by combining its derivatives with wine produced a powerful entheogen. I was party in 1985 to an attempted documentary to be made by Philip Black, who interviewed Wasson.

†Havelock Ellis (1859–1939) published "Mescal: A New Artificial Paradise" in *The Contemporary Review* in 1898, following his investigation of ingestion practices of the Kiowa Indians of New Mexico.

Fig. 22.3. Havelock Ellis (1859–1939).

interview Crowley and Einstein on new scientific frontiers (see my book *Aleister Crowley: The Beast in Berlin,* 2015). Perhaps Crowley whetted Huxley's appetite for more knowledge of the drug's relation to new scientific paradigms and mystical experience, for during research Huxley undertook in 1931 for his book *Brave New World* (1932) into chemical means governments might use to control populations, he found himself drawn to research into mescaline. Rather than control behavior, however, mescaline also had the potential to liberate people from rigid mentalities, neurotic character armor, class mores and prejudices, and conditioned reflexes. This would be found to be true in part also of LSD, which could, for periods of time, "bliss" people out, making the idea of violence abhorrent, even absurd, since one was aware of a more refined sense of "body being," a spiritual sensibility, that required no external justification. It felt good to be good.

In the early 1950s, Huxley met young psychiatrist Dr. Humphry Ormond while researching the book that became a Sixties manual, *The Doors of Perception* (1954), the title of which came from Blake's dictum: "When the doors of perception are cleans'd, we shall see all things as they are, infinite,"* which confluence of interests and contrasting time periods would give us the great Sixties poetic band, the Doors. Anyhow, Huxley asked Ormond to supervise him on a mescaline trip, or experi-

---

*William Blake quotation from his *The Marriage of Heaven and Hell,* composed between 1790 and 1793.

ment. Huxley gave a glowing, though probably quite selective, report in his book of what he had experienced. When gazing as if for eternity on a vase of infinite interest, pulsing with hitherto unobserved energy of formal and interior beauty, Huxley was driven to describe the experience thus: "I was seeing what Adam had seen on the morning of his creation—the miracle, moment by moment, of naked existence."[3] The reference to the "morning of his creation" almost certainly shows Huxley's indebtedness to William Blake for his vocabulary and gnostic framework, as the expression is so reminiscent of Blake's famous engraving for the book of Job of angels choiring the Almighty, titled: "When the morning stars sang together, and all the sons of God shouted for joy," at the divine creation. The implication was that a new world, a much braver new world than dreamt of hitherto, could emerge, or even explode from this experience, a new sense of an *en-Godded* world. God was *not* dead then, but about to be reborn in the perceiving mind when the doors of perception were cleansed!

Huxley looked for a simple couplet to get the idea over *in seed,* so to speak, and sent the following to Ormond:

> *To make this trivial world sublime*
> *Take half a gramme of phanerothyme.*

To which Ormond replied with epoch-marking appropriateness:

> *To fathom hell or soar angelic,*
> *Just take a pinch of psychedelic.*

And there comes the origin of our word *psychedelic* from the young psychiatrist who would write in 1973, a decade after Huxley's death (Huxley died on the same day as J. F. Kennedy): "Let us hope that we will learn to use hallucinogens wisely and well rather than as trivial entertainments."[4] The press, typically, made a banality of Ormond's observation by persistently referring to LSD as "the heaven and hell drug," with the emphasis on hell, and the implication that the heaven was fraudulent, or artificial.

Nevertheless, as Derek Taylor observed, the spread of entheogen use—LSD, psilocybin, peyote—was often undertaken recklessly in the Sixties, with false expectations and occasionally catastrophic results. One wonders, for example, what a person without experience could make of Huxley's words: "I was seeing what Adam had seen on the morning of his creation—the miracle, moment by moment, of naked existence." Huxley was a highly cultured individual, with a good place in the world to come back to after the trip, and with intellectual equipment able to contain if not exhaust the meaning of what had been experienced. He had a framework, whereas many people have lacked those advantages and have frequently simply been turned on by the sensory aspects of the stimuli, and when confronted by the "infinite" have panicked with sometimes disastrous results. But one can overstress the very real risks to the point of obscuring possible benefits.

In 1967, Paul McCartney recognized the potential: "It opened my eyes. We only use one tenth of our brain. Just think what we could accomplish if we could only tap that hidden part. It would mean a whole new world."[5] George Harrison remarked for Derek Taylor's immensely valuable, but unfortunately exceedingly rare, autobiography *Fifty Years Adrift:* "It's shattering [LSD] because it's as though someone suddenly wipes away all you were taught or brought up to believe as a child and says: 'That's not it.' You've gone so far, your thoughts have become so lofty and there's no way of getting back."[6] We see here the confluence of entheogen experience or "drug" experience as people called it then, with the apocalyptic "new world" undercurrents of the period. The attitude was: "If we can see it; we can have it." These were demand-fed children growing up, seeing a new world, and expecting it to happen.

A gradual disenchantment with LSD among the Beatles sank in with the fading of 1967's Summer of Love. Harrison had flown over to the epicenter of the counterculture movement in San Francisco with Derek Taylor on August 8, 1967, shortly before embarking on the Beatles *Magical Mystery Tour* film. What he saw depressed him. He felt what had been a stimulating "hippie" haven, Haight-Ashbury, in late 1966 and early 1967 had become, on account of too many young people arriving with unreal expectations, something akin to the Bowery, or alcoholics' dive in New York. The kids seemed drunk, spiritually unmoved and largely unaware. Harrison and his wife Patti were followed on a walkabout with Taylor through the area strumming a guitar while fending off innumerable offers of drugs. The "new world" Harrison had expected to see being born in the city seemed unspiritual, unsightly, and psychologically disturbing. There was a kindly Free Clinic on the Haight dealing with some thirty bad trips a day from people who could not cope with the immense psychological power of LSD to obliterate ego and to bombard the panicked mind with successions of unstoppable images.

Harrison, shortly after, was shown what LSD looked like under the microscope. It resembled, he told an interviewer for Granada TV's 1987 documentary *It Was 20 Years Ago Today,* "old rope." *Old rope.* And old rope was what he had been regularly putting in his head all through that summer that never seemed to end, of 1967, with his friend John too, taking what Lennon would recall, doubtless exaggerating, as "thousands of trips," many good, some bad. But the spiritual impetus that seemed like the initial promise began to fade. It was doubtless reflected on that there had always been a cunning duality in LSD-25.

On the one hand, the drug had been tested by the CIA in the Fifties and early Sixties as a means of mind control, but, paradoxically, had given people freedom instead. On the other, it was worth noting why the CIA, and doubtless other intelligence branches worldwide, found the drug so useful. It could be used to induce anxiety: a helpful stimulant when subjecting persons to torture of the mind, or a mighty tool in "breaking" a subject who, under its influence, was more likely to give in to interrogation when exposed to stresses applied while under LSD's mind-disorienting effects. Worse still, a bad trip can cause lasting mental disorders, including bouts of paranoia, hyperanxiety, and in the worst cases, loss of familiar personality and degrees of ego dissolution and dissociation from once familiar bonds.

Warnings against reckless use (or rather abuse) of psychoactive stimulants will by some persons go unheeded. Persons driven to do something seldom have the will to listen. A proponent of LSD during the Sixties, Allen Ginsberg recognized several important aspects of the experience. The first was positive: metaphysical discovery, but that can cover a lot of ground. In one experiment, Ginsberg agreed to taking LSD while a stroboscope blinked synchronously with his "alpha rhythms." It was only when he felt the entire electrical network grid of the United States was absorbing him through the plug socket that he, intrepid as he was, called for the experiment to cease immediately before he disappeared into an electric abyss of no return.

On the other hand, Ginsberg could also see that part of the problem was the status the substance gained by its being made illegal. If someone tells you that kissing will give you VD (or STD as is now commonly called), and you do so, and such consequences do not ensue, your respect for the proscriber will diminish sharply. "People seeing it illegalized," commented Ginsberg, "having had their own experience of it, mind-manifesting and metaphysical, realized that the government had no business intruding, getting on our backs, and that they were trying to repress an alteration of perception—not merely behavior but perception itself!—and it became a classical situation that the government was outlawing an elixir that had some real scientific usefulness as well as general democratic usefulness for those who were interested."[7] I daresay government would reply to that with a plea of its duty to protect the vulnerable. But surely there needs to be an enlightened balance found in attitudes, now that the shock of the new has passed. As Derek Taylor liked to quote from the Anglican *Book of Common Prayer:* "There was never anything by the wit of man so well devised or so sure established which in continuance of time hath not been corrupted." Man himself is a plain example of a dangerous substance that can go very wrong. Would we have humankind's creator destroy us all out of perpetual disappointment? For even the righteous can fall from grace, dear friends.

Speaking solely for myself and without any intention of making a recommendation of any kind at any level, I can only say that while I very much regret a very bad trip I experienced alone on LSD in Oxford in 1980, and another, even worse, in Korbach, Germany, in 1985, and a very disturbing psilocybin trip I experienced on a wet Sunday afternoon in Islington in November 1987, I do not regret some very good experiences I enjoyed under excellent circumstances on other occasions during those times of inner and outer adventure in equally excellent company. But enough was enough, and too much may be too late, and I got the message, such as it was, and had you asked me during a bad trip whether I wished I had never heard of such things, or been shown a path to them, I should certainly have answered with the wish, perhaps uncharitable, that Albert Hofmann had better fallen off his bicycle in 1943 and forgotten all about the subject.

HIP GNOSIS

When brave John "Hoppy" Hopkins and American libertarian Suzy Creamcheese demonstrated for the legalization of "pot" with attractively written placards at Piccadilly Circus, London, in spring 1967, the message they held high was "You Don't Know." What the policemen who eventually dispersed the gathering didn't know—nor many of the passersby for that matter—was a knowledge (gnosis) that opened up an inner kingdom of perception to psychedelic drug users. How much of this liberating knowledge, that separated them from the "false world" of the unimaginative materialist even as it dissolved the separation of man from nature, was in the stimulant, or in the stimulated must be settled in favor of the preparedness of the user to being enlightened.

"The kingdom of heaven is nigh and within you" was a gospel message John Lennon was fond of quoting before entering that period of overt leftist political radicalism that imbued the early seventies; the sense of the gospel message returned to him in later years with renewed sense and meaning. No drug can put *that* in anyone, but many may not realize how close they are to seeing it in themselves, and sometimes a gentle push of some kind may assist.

When it comes down to it, a lot of the value of psychoactive stimulants, or entheogens, comes down to sheer energy, as much as, or in combination with, sensory adjustment. From my and others' experience one can quickly deduce that one of the effects appears to be the sudden access to stored adrenalin or other perceptual energies we may understand little of, during the period of consciousness of the stimulant. This helped myself, for example, to realize that a great deal of perception subsists in energy: energy of perception. In perception, "we receive but what we give." The mind is creative of reality; imagination is, in gnostic understanding, the light of God in us: the creative life that moves from "in the beginning" to seeing "it was good" (the creation, that is). Quite rightly, even God rests after sufficient work. Projection of imagination takes great energy and at high range too, or what people have been wont to call "higher vibrations." Vibrations are energy. So in meditation also—what may look like a state close to sleep has this in common with sleep, that in deep meditation, one stores up energy and is able to draw on deeper energies. The process may well end with a burst of perceptual energy and experience of sudden "enlightenment." Beneficiaries of the late Mahesh Yogi's transcendental meditation testify to the great energy enhancement after even quite short periods of mantra-centered meditation. Enlightenment means a light going on, and a light needs energy. After a trip, a user ought to rest very well for a day or two, and eat and drink well, so that stores of adrenalin can build up, and the body can recover natural balance and peace of mind.

One of the extraordinary things involved in taking LSD or "magic mushrooms" is the elated sense of energy release. One can walk for miles and miles with no pain, little sensation of effort at all, and what sensation there might be, seems delightful, full of color and depth, and greatest clarity. Breathing feels good, the air truly divine, for it is the giver of life. I recall cycling through the beauties of north Oxfordshire while stimulated aged twenty-three in an experience of ease and movement akin to flying, so one imagines that many an ancient "miracle" was a miracle of perception. This ties in with our understanding of spiritual meaning in relation to pneuma, spirit, or breath, life, mind. In high states of awareness life and mind seem to breathe as one, and the sense of isolation in the ego from the universe around one disappears. One feels the presence of nature's presence in a considerably more harmonious way than is the norm. Air seems clearer, the natural world infinite in depth, spiritual in source, its focus pin sharp. One also sees with absolute clarity the unwisdom of the soulless cretins who despoil the world's beauty and inner order. Odor of car or truck exhaust, for example, seems particularly invasive, out of place, and repellent to sense.

I myself recall realizing how very, very thin is the crust of beauteous life on this planet, and how delicately thin is its coating of living atmosphere, how precious it all is, how spiritual. And what does ordinary humankind do the moment it feels a bit of power? *We know.* We show power first by destroying things. What is the power of an army: destructive power. Do what we want, or we destroy you, or something else! No shame is felt by the ego-encompassed powerful, and they call it the *real world,* governed by smartasses with talk of realpolitik, as if the rest of us were stupid, or missing something. No, son, you have *lost* something. *What profiteth it a man to gain the whole world, and lose his own soul?* One quickly perceives a deep moral and spiritual dimension to human stupidity when one is in a state of heightened awareness, or enlightenment. This can be no bad thing, and was once properly considered the privilege of sainthood, those who bear the nimbus of the beyond.

Energy: we waste it.

Paul McCartney informed us earlier that we only use 10 percent of our brains. I suspect if we used much more we should expire from exhaustion. We have the divine potential, but we are human bodies, and so long as we live in the physical, we shall be aware of, or rather *unaware of,* our very real limitations in actualizing our spiritual potential. Entheogens give us more than a clue as to what we are capable of. The essence of magic ought to be developing skills to actualize on this plane the spiritual potential we hold. It is not an automatic process, nor does it achieve results by wishing alone.

The temporary experience of enhanced or intense perceptual energy during the Sixties was bound to have a great effect on creative minds, and who can deny that some of the greatest artistic achievements of the Sixties were in part stimulated by the perceptual boundary move induced by entheogen ingestion? The music of the Beatles, Dylan, Hendrix, the Doors, the Stones, the Floyd, the Beach Boys under Brian Wilson's aegis, the Grateful Dead, and so on, all received perceptual boosting from the high perceptual energy input available to entheogen users for the restricted honeymoon period before (note!) the mind starts to lose its acquired sense of form and duration, along with other elements of acquired practical wisdom, that make its products accessible.

It is a small step from the sublime to the ridiculous, and many artists in the Sixties happily walked over the edge piping wildly. Any derangement of the senses should be temporary once we realize that our brains and general constitution already represent an extraordinary degree of chemical sophistication and organic complexity. Don't insult the work of the centuries! Keep your temple clean!

And it was not only in music that psychedelic insights bore creative fruit. Image making too received a boost in imaginative range, many of the ensuing works still popular. People still thrill at many different kinds of occasions to elaborate light shows. Much of this technology was pioneered by people attempting to create environments conducive to happy tripping, dancing, and listening. There was already an overlap with surrealist art, hardly surprising since surrealism looked into the unconscious, and there was already a quiet, discrete tradition of drug use to promote ideas and stimulate creativity throughout the world of modern art, while in jazz music, marijuana had long been used by musicians to relax or to "get into" listening to the music. Few would be stoned while playing, but some performers might take a little nudge from herbal smoke to shut out the world enough to let out the feeling into fresh mental space.

San Francisco dominated, to begin with, the production of the overtly psychedelic art poster, and names like Stanley Mouse, Wes Wilson, Rick Griffin, Alton Kelley, and others dominated the production of new art forms that drew on Art Nouveau, Pop Art, and Dada, as well, occasionally, as nineteenth-century engraving and surrealist juxtapositions. The important aspect was working out how to manipulate color in such a way as to imitate visual derangements of a fun kind associated with the freedom of the music and human gathering together that psychedelic art was primarily promoting.

In Britain, the needs of Pink Floyd at the UFO Club not only stimulated the electronic light show projection, but also album cover design, and it was no accident that Storm Thurgerson chose the name *Hipgnosis* for his famous sleeve design company that gave us some of the most powerful creative images in domestic settings the world had ever seen. Also in Britain, Bridget Riley's op-art paintings and optic-deluding psychedelic patterns attracted great interest and were oft imitated by anyone seeking modern perspectives. In cinema, the use of disorienting perspectives and cutting came in with Stanley Furie's *Ipcress File* (with a super, brooding John Barry score) and got wilder and wilder as time went on; the apotheosis probably being Stanley Kubrick's delight in close-corridor, perspective-enhancing unshakable advancing shots and other tricks of the eye exhibited in the service of great themes in *2001*. Nearly every movie of the late Sixties and early Seventies had some psychedelic element somewhere, even if it was only an obligatory lovemaking scene with colored lights, or a shot of stereotyped youth in the ubiquitous discothèque. Psychedelia was everywhere for some years, and became almost a parody of itself. No accident that the Beatles' most colorful period came to a sudden close in 1968 with their double album, known as the "white" album, as there was no other way of describing it. Smart and always out ahead! The floral trousers were thrown in for jeans, while T-shirts replaced floral shirts. It took a long time for everybody else to catch up with what the Beatles were getting at. It's not what you looked like, man, it was where your head was at, and if it was stock-still for too long, it meant the tree inside wasn't growing. Or as the gospel has it: *a tree is known by its fruits*.

In fact, psychedelia continues in ever more bewildering and stimulating forms, such as computer fractal art, whereas in music, the influence is always somewhere to be found, for new generations want to recover lost territory before time obscures memory, and the new world that seemed to open in the Sixties becomes a legend unbelievers will deny ever happened—like those people who now seem to *want* to believe that NASA never put men on the moon. NASA succeeded, and perhaps the reason the effort stopped was because it had become *normal*. No wonder; no interest. The Sixties was full of wonders; that's why we're still interested. Crazy, of a kind, is not always bad, and I wonder what became of the person who slapped the brick walls of that psychiatric clinic in faraway Dandenong with a timely message of flowers and love. I hope it marked a great new beginning, or at least one of the best days of his or her life. It was certainly one of the more memorable of mine.

TWENTY-THREE

India

Every day we are confronted by the ugly facts of wayward, destructive human nature through scattered news reports from around the world. On a more microcosmic level, many parents of teenage children are confronted by irresponsible self-centeredness, inattention, and aggressive behavior exhibited by "young adults" in their care. These are two levels of the human problem. Let's get above these two. How might things look to the parent or parents of humankind itself?

The book of Genesis relates how the Father of our species was so disappointed at the way things turned out among Adam and Eve's progeny that a mass destruction was enacted, though finding goodness in one, Noah, God left a chance for Noah's race or family to restock a cleansed planet.

The Judeo-Christian tradition, of which the Flood story is a part, has different strands of conception of the progress of humankind. The orthodox tradition has tended to be both static and catastrophic in nature as regards our "end" or ultimate purpose. Man is, and will be as he is, until God destroys the world and his Son tries the culprits in low expectation of many acquittals.

Another more spiritual strand of apocalyptic interpretation sees a coming "Age of the Holy Spirit" occurring before a final rolling up of the material scroll: a period of revelation of God's spiritual and natural secrets, offering massive increases in knowledge, the which epiphany would constitute a Golden Age. The Rosicrucian tradition, for example, was constructed on this expectation.

Expectations that such an age was imminent have erupted in the West and elsewhere since at least the Middle Ages. Belief in a coming age of spiritual freedom and spiritual evolution gained fresh impulse from the beginnings of the Theosophical Society (TS), founded in 1875 in New York by Henry Steel Olcott and H. P. Blavatsky. What was peculiar to their esoteric outlook was a desire to show common ground within spiritual traditions of the East (mainly from India) and West (mainly Hermetic-esoteric) in a scheme promoting integration of spiritual *and* scientific knowledge, characterized by belief in spiritual evolution of the species through progressive initiation on a path of truth seeking. When the Theosophical Society moved its headquarters to Adyar, India, in 1882, it went against the colonialist grain and actively encouraged Indian natives to value their inherited shastras (scriptures) on a par with the respect missionaries asserted in favor of the Bible. The belief advocated by TS members in the United States, Europe, and throughout the British Empire was that the East had not exhausted its spiritual treasures in Christianity and had much to teach us still. The Western "Jesus" had been largely cut off from his roots, so to speak, and co-opted into materialism by spiritual blindness and political corruption of the churches.

Not everyone in the TS favored wholesale importation to the West of Hindu and Buddhist philosophy, believing the West possessed sufficient spiritual meat of its own (Christianity understood in the light of Western esotericism), suspecting that Blavatsky and her closest followers were at best diluting Christian tradition while failing to estimate properly differences between Eastern and Western mentalities. The movement bifurcated into competing strands. By the time World War I began to tear up the old map of Europe and the world (1914–1918), the chief strands representing schemes of humankind's progressive initiation into spiritual being consisted chiefly of Theosophists who followed Annie Besant and Bishop C. W. Leadbeater's advocacy of Indian youth Jiddu Krishnamurti as the coming "world teacher"; Theosophists who did not accept Krishnamurti; the Martinist and Synarchic movements in France; the Anthroposophical Society of Rudolf Steiner; various Rosicrucian societies; Golden Dawn continuity "Western Hermetic magic" organizations (following a major split in 1900); and, as a further result of that split, a neo-Rosicrucian and a parallel "High Masonic" order led by Theodor Reuss and Aleister Crowley, respectively (OTO).

Influenced both by Western esotericism and by Shaivite (Shiva-oriented) interpretations of Hindu Vedanta (late Vedic) traditions, Crowley identified a new age as having begun in April 1904 when he believed divine child Horus (of Graeco-Egyptian lore) became the god-force who would progressively clear the way for a succeeding age of justice and harmony over ensuing centuries. His reign would, if resisted, be characterized by bloodshed and catastrophic upheaval of the old world.

All these schemes of progressive spiritual evolution favored a universalist outlook, taking the globe in terms of its position in the entire cosmos, and they all took serious notice of the need to integrate scientific and spiritual knowledge. For example, Steiner called his system "spiritual science," while Crowley gave his system's rubric as "The Method of Science. The Aim of Religion," but science would have to "grow out" of its inherited materialism, which, by the end of the twenties, seemed likely with the experimental theories of Einstein and Heisenberg appearing to shatter eighteenth- and nineteenth-century Newtonianism. Spiritual understanding, for its part, would need to be shorn of inherited accretions of superstition, religious taboos favoring vested denominational interests, and general philosophical muddiness and obfuscation, and become scientific in the demonstrable, experimental sense (i.e: if you do x, then y will happen).

The surprising effect of the Theosophical Society's glowing evaluation of Vedic, late-Vedic, and post-Vedic philosophical traditions on members of Hindu lines of disciplic succession would directly affect the spiritual meaning of the Sixties. Confident of a hearing outside of India, mindful that the late nineteenth century's newfound respect for Indian culture would also help to secure degrees of independence from British dominance of the subcontinent, Indian missionaries began visiting the United States, Europe, and Great Britain, usually armed with some demonstrable exhibitions of hatha and raja yoga's ability to affect body and mind, together with an accommodating neo-Vedantist message from one strain of Indian Vedantist tradition or another, though chiefly

Shaivite (Shiva-worshipping) or Vaishnavite (Vishnu-worshipping) in origin. Decades of experience in dealing with Western listeners sharpened up Indian missionaries' ability to engage with Western intellects and enthusiasms, the usual key being the assertion that their spiritual knowledge was science, an assertion that calmed Western agnostics' fear of the word *religion.*

The 1960s marked a new era in willingness of large numbers of Westerners to listen to, and even adhere religiously to teachings emanating from India. By far the greater part of that influential teaching came from the Vedanta tradition of Hindu philosophical speculation, and from its sub-school, the Advaita tradition. These words often appear in treatments of the subject but are seldom understood clearly, so let's get a hold briefly on what they mean.

VEDANTA AND ADVAITA

The Sanskrit word *veda* means "knowledge"; it is etymologically related to the Latin *video,* that is, "I see." We are talking about recognition of facts, truths. The greater components of early Indian religious writings are called Vedas, scriptures of "knowledge," copied down over centuries, whose latest texts are usually dated 600–500 BCE by most scholars. The latest substantial Vedic texts are called Upanishads (meaning "at the feet of . . ."). *Vedanta* means the "end of the Vedas." The Upanishads comment on and encapsulate Vedic knowledge written before them in the light of initiated experience of the Spirit.

The "knowledge" that interests the Upanishads primarily is called *jñāna,* to be found in *jñānakāṇḍa* (knowledge books). The Sanskrit *jñāna,* like *veda,* also means knowledge, but it is a special knowledge: knowledge of the Spirit, knowledge that *liberates,* that is, that takes the aspirant from the impermanent world of manifestation to experience of ultimate, unchanging reality, the source: Brahman. The Western equivalent to jñāna is gnosis, and there are clear parallels between Hindu Vedanta philosophies, and schools of Western gnosis (gnostics). While originally concerned with the Upanishads, Vedanta also speculates on the Brahma Sutras (attempts to systematize Upanishadic ideas), and the Bhagavad Gita (chapters 23–40 of the sixth book of the Hindu epic, the Mahabharata; *gita* means "song").

Degrees of speculation over time have stimulated the existence of over ten schools of Vedanta, itself one of six orthodox schools of Hindu philosophy (these schools include the now familiar designation *yoga,* that is: "union"). We should be surprised to find any two unacquainted Vedanta missionaries agreeing on all points of doctrine.

Wherever two or three concepts are gathered together, there will be argument. The three primary concepts of Vedantist philosophy are, first, the individual soul or spirit *Ātman* (sometimes *jivātman,* where *jiva* is an entity with a life force), second, *Prakriti,* meaning the changing world of matter, and third, *Brahman,* the metaphysical source of reality ("Brahma" when that principle is personified as a deity). The basic idea is that every being has soul or spirit, which is of the nature of the ultimate unchanging reality. Therefore, the means to traverse or escape the flux of matter is to realize the soul's identity with beyond-the-physical Brahman, to adjust conduct accordingly, and thus be able to let go of the body, its desires and attachments, in life by degrees, and altogether at death. Such liberation (*moksha*) constitutes salvation, for it not only brings peace of mind through meditation in this life but enables the soul to avoid reembodiment, that is, incarceration, in another form after the body's death, the soul's status decided by "natural law" (karma) according to one's nature or conduct. You might not go to a "hell" but you might find the experience of being a housefly unwelcome (though in the "great scheme of things" salutary and correctional). Brahman is the best bet.

If we number the three concepts as 1, 2, and 3, then 1 gets to 3 by getting out of 2. This basically logical conception of salvation is, it ought to be said, incompatible with orthodox Christian doctrine that does not in theory accept birth as imprisonment, and that regards individuals as more or less permanent identities without capacity for transmigration into other physical bodies. Catholic dogmatists believed recompense for imperfection before salvation was solved by the doctrine of purgatory. One might argue that reincarnation and purgatory are in the same family of essential idea. Both ideas are based on the idea that sin merits punishment as the means to influence will.

In Hinduism, different schools disagree over the relative status of Ātman in relation to the ultimate reality. For example, the school most familiar to Westerners is that of Advaita. As in other languages, to put an *a* before a noun negatives it, meaning: "not" or "without," so *a*-dvaita, means "not two" in the sense of "no difference," where *dvaita* means the distinction of two (dualism, from *dvi* = two).

Advaita (no division) schools emphasize that there is no essential difference in substance between the spirit animating the living being and Brahman; there is unity of essence. The Spirit is, as it were, Brahman in us, but not fully realized on account of its proximity to matter. As one might expect, there are schools within schools, and some Advaitists may say that the Ātman is *to some degree* different from the absolute, for the absolute itself could not abide contact with changing matter, on grounds that Brahman is unchanging, and matter has no absolute reality. Some sages would then counter that it would be incorrect to say that there is no spirit in the world of matter, and so on. Advaitist principles lend themselves to pantheism.

Then there is the Dvaita school (founded by Madhvacharya, 1238–1317 CE), which would say that Ātman is different in kind from Brahman's supreme, unfathomable being. He considered the idea that souls could differ in degrees from Brahman, and thus knowledge could also be different in degrees. We find precisely the same philosophical problems producing different schools not only in Western gnostic traditions (the distinction between psychē and pneuma for example), but also in early patristic debates over Jesus's relation to God the Father in the formation of orthodox Christology in the first five centuries of Christianity. That is, if Jesus is of "one substance with the Father," for example, does that mean that the Father suffered on the cross (a heresy called patripassianism)? If the kingdom of heaven is within us, and we can experience Christ within us, and if Christ is the "Lord" and Son of God, then do we not have God in us on that basis, and if so, what gives a bishop authority over a believer? Old theological contests that lead to real violence seem odd to many Westerners today, but when philosophical satisfaction is bound up with salvation, the stakes can be high. It is fascinating therefore to see these disputes reoccur in English gardens in the Sixties!

I refer to a fascinating little book titled *Search for Liberation* (1981) that gives what appears to be a verbatim account of a discussion conducted September 14, 1969, in London between John Lennon, George Harrison, and Swami Bhaktivedanta, founder of the International Society for Krishna Consciousness.[1] His Divine Grace Śrīla Prabhupāda (the swami's other title) is at pains at one point to denigrate the teaching of Maharishi Mahesh Yogi on the grounds that the yogi allegedly used the Bhagavad Gita to further his *own* teaching, teaching that furthermore ignored the public Hare Krishna mantra swami Prabhupāda had been offering to the West—Mahesh Yogi offering instead a secret, individualized mantra to his devotees.* We are seeing the schools in conflict!

Śrīla Prabhupāda's title "Bhaktivedanta" tells us that it is a *bhakti* school of Vedanta that the swami represents, that is, it follows the path of *personal devotion and piety* to the personality of the supreme Brahman, called "Krishna." Rāmānuja (1017–1137 CE) is the name most associated with formulating the bhakti Advaita path, through devotion to a personal god (in his case, Vishnu, the preserver). Swami Bhaktivedanta believed his school gave direct access to supreme truth through a simple means of chanting. Mahesh Yogi, known generally as "the Maharishi" (or Great Seer) on the other hand, was not advocating the bhakti tradition of piety and devotion, often emotional in manifestation, but valued a tradition more attuned to the *impersonal* aspect of Brahman, through internally uttered mantra yoga. The latter yogi, having attained a degree in physics in his youth, felt the Western world was more likely to accept a simple practice without a theogony attached to it, than for skeptical Westerners to be persuaded to dance to Krishna's flute, so to say. As it turned out, Westerners would take fruit from both trees. There are people who like devotional methods,

---

*Lennon apparently revealed his mantra as "Jai guru deva Om" in the Beatles' song "Across the Universe," first released on the *No One's Gonna Change Our World* charity album for the World Wildlife Fund in December 1969.

and there are those who prefer paths of intellectual understanding. In general, Westerners have been more open to Advaita Vedanta because in its most ideal formulation it appears to remove longstanding theological problems of the Christian churches and, when rather too simply expressed, suggests awareness of God is itself sufficient for salvation.* Of course, the idea comes bound up with reincarnation as a required belief, though many have found this version of eternal life a more natural, less intimidating alternative to heaven and hell.

MAHARISHI MAHESH YOGI
(CA. 1918–2008)

The guru to gain most widespread attention in the Sixties was undoubtedly Mahesh Prasad Varma, disciple of Swami Brahmananda ("bliss of Brahman") Saraswati. Mahesh (a common name for boys, meaning "great ruler") is recorded as a 1942 physics graduate of Allahabad University under the name M. C. Srivastava, and there has been biographical dispute over his precise birth name, place, and date of birth. No one seems to disagree, however, that his family was of the Kayastha caste, engaged in learned work, but not of the Brahmin caste upon whose members spiritual authority normatively rests in India.

Before graduating, Mahesh served as secretary to the new *Shankaracharya,* that is spiritual leader of the line of Adi Shankara (eighth century CE), based at the Jyotir Math Himalayan monastery. Shankara was an important proponent of the Advaita Vedanta school. His poetry included Shaivite and Vaishnavi (Krishna-devoted) points of view (usually considered separate schools). Mahesh always claimed that it was Swami Brahmananda Saraswati who inspired him to write his own works and to advocate meditation as a lifetime's work. Wherever Maharishi taught, there was a portrait of his mentor framed nearby.

An honorific meaning "great sage," the name *Maharishi* was

---

*What Moravian-raised theologian Friedrich Schleiermacher (1768–1834) would call "basking in God-consciousness" rather than responding to, and engaging with, Christian ethical and practical duties in this world.

given to him, the story goes, by listeners to his lectures in India; *yogi* means he was an exponent of yoga ("union"), in his case, mantra yoga, that is, the vibration of a phrase of power to make manifest spiritual energy, usually containing seed syllables (*bijas*) related to potent deities or aspects of divine beings. After the Shankaracharya's death in 1954, "Brahmachari Mahesh" pursued his studies at Uttarkashi in the Himalayas before beginning a tour of India in 1955 as exponent of the "Spiritual Development Movement," renamed the "Spiritual Regeneration Movement" in 1957.

He had promised his master he would promote the goodness of meditation and this he did, in journeys that took him around the world from 1959 through the next decade. By then he had formulated what he called transcendental meditation. Its theory was neo-Vedantist in that he distinguished the changing world of matter from the unchanging world of ultimate reality. The path from one to another could be greatly stimulated by a method that effectively interrupted the ordinary process of thought and mind noise by internal utterance of the mantra, the meditator then riding on that mantra, identifying all consciousness with it until the mantra continued as it were of its own, and the subject experienced a pregnant nothingness, wherefrom much energy, and in theory limitless energy, could be drawn. Adumbrated in his book *Science of Being and Art of Living,* audiotaped in 1963 for subsequent successful publication, the method had therapeutic value, while the book proved comprehensible to Western philosophy and science of mind.

According to Maharishi, the world of the senses is the world of relative being, but that world is not the source of underlying order and reality; that must be unchanging, as laws are unchanging and reliable, working through relative changes. Harnessing the word *relativity* gave the presentation a pleasant twentieth-century cachet. It was all a question of point of view, of awareness. Relativity of awareness was already an obvious principle to thinking users of psychedelics. Furthermore, there was no obvious denominational aspect to the Maharishi's principles. John Lennon informed inquirers when he undertook his researches into the method in 1967 and early 1968 that it worked for Christians,

Jews, followers of Muhammad, anyone.* You do the practice—you get the result. What dismayed some teachers back in India was that the Maharishi did not ask his followers to renounce the world; he did not make a frontal assault on Western ways of living by advocating traditional ascetic practices, rather he accommodated them. This proviso was of course one of the USPs of the system in Western terms. Maharishi did not say the method was a quick way to God, or of itself sufficient for spiritual perfection, but the suggestion was there that in the process one might become more aware of spiritual reality, and one might then choose to enter further into the religious and philosophical traditions of the yogis. Maharishi was reasonable, humorous, and logical. Transcendental meditation accomplished "what it said on the tin." Whether, in the last resort, that really counted for very much depends on the starting point of the inquirer. For some, it might be a beginning, a toe in the water so to speak; for others, it might appear ridiculous or inadequate. Nobody, to my knowledge, has died from transcendental meditation, though some may have thought there was more to it than there was.

Mahesh Yogi brought transcendental meditation to the States first in 1959, founding the International Meditation Society, from which his teaching could be disseminated from centers in San Francisco and London. By the end of 1963 he had been to Europe, Australia, New Zealand, the United Kingdom, Asia, Canada, and had run another course at Rishikesh by the Himalayas, to which venue the Beatles and devotees from the West Coast pop scene would come for instruction in early 1968.

It was George Harrison's wife's sister, Jenny, who first got Pattie and George Harrison to come to hear the Maharishi at Caxton Hall in London for the first time in 1967. John Lennon, Paul McCartney, and Mick Jagger were also keen to hear what secrets of life could be

---

*Lennon argued his case on the *David Frost Show* with George Harrison in a British TV debate of September 30, 1967, that pitted him and George Harrison against a studio audience of intellectuals, including skeptical author and lawyer, John Mortimer (1923–2009). Harrison maintained forcefully and impressively that people could not see the point because they wallowed in willful ignorance.

Fig. 23.1. Sitting: Maharishi Mahesh Yogi, (left to right) Michael Cooper, Mick Jagger, Marianne Faithfull, Al Vandenberg, Brian Jones, 1967.

gleaned from the laughing guru. John, Paul, and George together met Maharishi at the Hilton Hotel, London, on August 24. The next day, the Beatles and their wives joined a meditation course in Bangor, North Wales. Mick Jagger also attended the occasion. It was while attending that event that the Beatles were informed by pursuing journalists that friend and manager Brian Epstein had died from accidental barbiturate overdose. The guru's advice was that grief might inhibit Brian's soul on its path beyond the body, and that they should send him good thoughts. The Beatles began to lean on the Maharishi's optimistic message as they became aware of incoming business problems exacerbated by their manager's untimely, accidental death.

In February 1968, arriving and departing at different times, the four Beatles went to Rishikesh, along with their wives, Mia Farrow, her sister Prudence, Jane Asher, Mike Love of the Beach Boys, Donovan, and several other wealthy refugees from the tumults of the Western world. John and George stayed the longest, of the Beatles, but John was informed by Alexis Mardas (electrical engineer, and overly respected

Beatles favorite at the time) that the guru made a sexual play either for Mia Farrow or her sister (accounts vary) and when the Maharishi was presented with John's blunt statement that he was leaving, and that if Maharishi was really so cosmic and "knew everything" he would *know* why he was leaving, the good vibes that had passed between John and Maharishi vanished.

Taxis waiting, already ordered by "Magic Alex" (Mardas), John and wife Cynthia ignored the guru's polite attempts to discuss the crisis, and rushed out of Rishikesh in a state bordering on paranoia, thinking the wrath of the guru might follow them. It didn't, and subsequent corrections to the story by Cynthia Lennon, George, and Paul suggest that it was all a misunderstanding, exhibiting naïveté and hypersensitiveness on John's part, particularly. Cynthia suggested strongly in her book *A Twist of Lennon* (1978) that the rumor of Maharishi's alleged misdemeanor was cooked up by Magic Alex to wean the Beatles off the Maharishi's influence, which was taking them away from his.[2] Anyway, John returned to London in combative mood, and soon swung the orbit of his devotion directly to the art and person of Yoko Ono (who had been corresponding with him while he was in India), while George was not entirely sure of what to do next as regards his spiritual path.

The fact is that while the Maharishi clearly gained in the extent of his following by his association with the Beatles, and that to a very high degree, the Beatles had to suffer good and bad for the association. On the one hand, they were lampooned by elements of the press for being foolish enough to be "taken in" by the guru (which must have been hard to take), while secondly, they had learned a very useful technique for finding peace of mind amid the squalls of superstardom, that proved both harmless and beneficial, benefits many others have also spoken of. Cynthia Lennon was adamant that the Maharishi's influence was wholly positive and their quitting Rishikesh was a "very wrong" way of recompensing all the Maharishi's thoughtfulness had given them. Besides, we probably owe the *White Album* to the quietude enjoyed by the Beatles in the Himalayas in February 1968, for many of its thirty original compositions were inspired while in earshot of the holy Ganges, and of the Maharishi.

Maharishi Mahesh Yogi continued to do what he had always done. He brought therapeutic value through meditation to great numbers of people, got many out of addictive habits, and died at a great age, having accomplished the mission he promised his master he would undertake back in the early Fifties, to emphasize the spiritual benefits of Vedantist meditation. And practically everyone got to hear about an idea that has now become almost commonplace, that is, *raising consciousness,* raising consciousness from the illusory to the real. Not a bad result, on reflection.

RAVI SHANKAR (1920–2012)

Born Rabindra Shankar Chowdhury, Ravi Shankar began his working life as a dancer before moving on to master the sitar, excelling in proficiency on an instrument that through his dedication brought millions to acquaintance with the beauties of Indian music. Already recognized as a master of his art, George Harrison met him in June 1966 in London at a period when the Beatles had entered a transitional phase, giving up tours to concentrate on recording and individual interests. Harrison felt a spiritual call issuing from the music and later in the year journeyed to Srinagar in Kashmir to study sitar under Ravi Shankar's

Fig. 23.2. Sitar master Ravi Shankar (1920–2012)

tutelage. Six weeks of study and home exercises brought Harrison into an epoch-marking fascination with the religious world inseparable from Indian classical music.

When things went awry with the Maharishi, Harrison still was able to communicate with his music teacher who, despite serious misgivings about the pop-musical, now drug-saturated world in which Harrison operated, formed a close personal relationship with the young, ardent star of the world's leading musical group. Shankar was able to encourage Harrison's omnivorous desire to learn all he could about Indian spirituality, intertwined with music.

Shankar's personal avenue of mystical devotion came from the city of his upbringing, Varanasi, known also as Benares, dominated by Shiva worship, Shiva being one of the more famous trinities of Hinduism, where, broadly speaking, Brahman is creator, Vishnu preserver, and Shiva destroyer, in an eternal cycle that though separated as personal faces, are but aspects of one unfathomable transcendent reality, as the basic doctrine goes. Also in Varanasi stands a temple to Hanuman, known as the monkey god. Ravi Shankar was particularly devoted to Hanuman, a god devoted to Rama, seventh avatar of Vishnu. An avatar is a manifestation of a god who has appeared on earth, displaying characteristics recognizable to human beings, sometimes disruptive and surprising. Krishna also attracts worshippers as an important avatar of Vishnu. Devotees worship Krishna as the personal aspect of Brahman, and see Krishna as everything, that is, as the reality principle of everything that can be accessed through devotion and acts of sacrifice to God. Shankar's favorite god Hanuman is also in some texts an incarnation of Shiva, and a figure of the Hindu epic *Ramayana* in which Rama wars with Ravana, demon king.

No less metaphysical perhaps was Shankar's love for Ma ("Mother") Anandamayi, whom he met in Varanasi. Ravi held Mother as divine, a great spiritual soul, and regarded his meeting with her as one of the great miracles of his life. Captivated by the beauty of her face and mind, Shankar passed this awareness to George Harrison, who would write an unreleased song about her ("Mother Divine") as well as another unreleased song about the town where she died in 1982, "Dehradun."

Ananadamayi means one who embodied "bliss" or "joy" unalloyed, and Anandamayi (1896–1982) was credited with miracles of precognition and healing. She herself appeared to devotees as being continually enlivened by an unearthly joy beyond the scope of mortals to comprehend. She was born in what under British rule was Brahmanbaria District (now in Bangladesh), at Kheora, and named Nirmala Sundari ("Immaculate, Beautiful One") by a poor father noted for his Vaishnavite devotion through his gift of singing. Married, as was customary, but celibate, Nirmala and her husband moved to Shahbag in 1924. Soon after, the intensity of her devotional ecstasies drew admirers to her as an embodiment of divine joy. In 1929, at Ramna, an ashram was established about her. People who visited her experienced minds open to the liberated spirit, and she became a window of experience to the world of the Spirit, a living testimony to the reality of the divine, even in this world.

By all accounts her predominant theme was to see everything as a reflection of where one was, in relation to God, and the business of life was realization of the deepest nature of the self. Only actions that brought forth the flame of divinity in the self were worth the name of worthy actions; all else was delusion. At the same time, she insisted every path undertaken by individuals be considered unique. So long as people embarked on a path to realization of divinity, then those paths were hers also. People must work within the possibilities of their own nature and not be expected to do otherwise. God ordained infinite ways of finding him: he was not to be limited by people's ideas of him. She did not impose limitations of access on account of people's religious background and believed that women were not in any way secondary spiritual creatures to males. What she was, she had always been, though her family had treated her according to the body; she was always and forever the same, a consciousness in love with God.

Ravi Shankar enjoyed the honor of performing before Mother Ananadamayi, and it is clear that closeness to her gave devotees direct experience of intimacy with the spiritual reality of Brahman, expressed in the threefold traditional formula of Sat, Chit, and Ananda: Being (or Existence), Consciousness, and Bliss.

George Harrison also approached and enjoyed this awareness. His readings from texts of the Vedanta tradition had insisted that it was important not just to believe in God, but to know him, and to see him, and that without personal experience of God, one had no knowledge, and without knowledge of God one was reliant on others as on a mere picture. Through engaging with the practices of Vedanta-inspired yogis, Harrison came to know God, and the experience was one he tried to share with the world through his music. Through his example, and that of those who lit his path, he left a legacy of a Sixties that was not content unless it went "all the way" to the unchanging way, real for all time, and accessible now and tomorrow.

SWAMI BHAKTIVEDANTA (1896–1977)

There is an intriguing snippet of dialogue in the Beatles' film, *Let It Be,* shot in January 1969, wherein Paul McCartney tells John Lennon that the previous evening he watched a home movie of Maharishi at Rishikesh. In one shot, John enters the guru's helicopter for a private tour. Paul related how afterward John had said to him (Paul) that he'd gone up because he thought Maharishi just might "slip" him "the *Answer!*" The Answer, that is, to *everything.*

People expect too much from gurus, and devotees are all too prone to project onto their teachers their own ideals of perfection. Better to recall Saint Paul's quote from the psalmist: "None is righteous, no, not one" (Psalm 14:3; Romans 3:10). By autumn 1969, John, ever searching, was again entertaining a guru. He opened up what had been a chamber music hall on his estate at Tittenhurst Park, Ascot, for use by devotees of Śrīla Prabhupāda. They installed a small deity altar and a podium for the swami. On September 14, John and George went over to Swami Bhaktivedanta's quarters in a block of houses on the estate where he had come among disciples as the Lennons' houseguest.

Born Abhay Charan De in 1896, this bright son of devout Vaishnavites enjoyed a good education at Calcutta's Scottish Church College, near his home, making him fluent in English as well as Sanskrit, giving him the tools for translating the Bhagavad Gita in his maturity (published as *Bhagavad Gita as It Is* in 1968). Vaishnavi swami Bhaktisiddhanta Sarasvati Thakura took the twenty-six-year-old Abhay on as a disciple, urging him to transmit the Krishna-oriented teaching of Chaitana (or Caitanya) Mahāprabhu (1486–1534 CE), founder of Gaudiya Vaishnavism, in which line Abhay's swami stood. Gaudiya Vaishnavis regarded Caitanya as an incarnation of Krishna who by this means was able to teach the true bhakti yoga path to devotees. From Caitanya comes the famous Hare Krishna chant, regarded by Śrīla Prabhupāda as the best way for this age (the dark age of Kali) to gain access to Krishna.

In 1933 Adhay was formally initiated his master's disciple and by 1944 was publishing a magazine devoted to Caitanya's teaching. The Gaudiya Vaishnava Society, in recognition of his contribution, gave him the title "Bhaktivedanta" in 1947. Followers called him "Swamiji" until 1967–68 when he was addressed as "Prabhupāda," that is, one who took shelter in the Lord (Krishna) where *prabhu* means Lord, and *pāda,* "taking shelter."

Swami Bhaktivedanta devoted the 1940s, 1950s, and early 1960s to Vedic scholarship and to promoting the tradition of Caitanya. In that critical year of 1965 he felt spiritually compelled to undertake a missionary journey to the United States, taking spiritual refuge in the Lord Krishna whom he believed upheld him in a journey he had not considered altogether rationally. He was no official representative and he had not been invited. Nevertheless, the International Society for Krishna Consciousness was founded in New York City in 1966. For him, *Krishna* encompassed all words used for God. In response to the escalating war in Vietnam, he wrote a widely publicized leaflet, echoing the teaching of Caitanya that if the people of the world would chant the great mantra given for the age, then there would be world peace and global prosperity. That was the way to end the terrible war. He wanted to teach the world to sing a new song (new to them, at least).

In New York, Swami Bhaktivedanta got to know the ubiquitous Allen Ginsburg, who lent him and fifteen followers a harmonium on a December night in 1966, with which they entered a studio near Times Square to record an album, *Krishna Consciousness,* featuring chant-

Fig. 23.3.
His Divine Grace
A. C. Bhaktivedanta
Swami Srila Prabhupāda
(1896–1977).

ing and meditation. The album came to the ears of George Harrison, who played it to John Lennon. In July 1967, at Magic Alex's recommendation, the Beatles chartered a luxury yacht, the *M.V. Arvi,* that took them about the Greek coast in search of a dream paradise where they could do what they fancied. George and John sailed for days round Greek islands, singing the Hare Krishna mantra with ukuleles for hours and hours, because, as George recalled in 1980, once you started, it was impossible to stop, though if you did, it was "like the lights went out."[3] So, yet again, we find the Beatles playing a crucial role in disseminating Hindu philosophy and practice.

Once they'd established Apple Records, the Beatles oversaw the release of the London Radha Krishna Temple's single version of the mantra. Six San Francisco married devotees had founded the London "Temple" in 1968 (first sited in a Covent Garden warehouse), after the swami asked them to move to London. Following hard times, members were urged to approach Harrison at the Apple offices in Mayfair. George liked what he heard and produced a single version of the mantra, recorded at Abbey Road studios in July 1969. Released on August 29, it reached number twelve in the United Kingdom. George found the

"Maha mantra" (great mantra) personally very effective, bringing a sweetness into his life that stood in steep contrast with current problems with the Beatles' business and personal frictions.

John Lennon had also availed himself of devotees of Swami Bhaktivedanta. The swami's Montreal followers joined John (who had adopted a very swamilike look himself) and sang on the Plastic Ono Band hit single, "Give Peace a Chance" recorded in John and Yoko's hotel bedroom in Montreal, released in the United Kingdom on July 3, 1969, and in the States four days later. The lyrics announce that "everybody's talking"* about Hare Krishna, and then John briefly chants an element of the mantra. Thus, the fifteenth-century Indian saint reached the Billboard Top Twenty! And all because the swami had followed his call to the United States in *1965* . . .

Postscript: I am not myself a devotee of the Krishna Consciousness Movement (that I am aware of anyway), but I must recount a little true story of something that happened to me some years back.

I was making haste down London's Oxford Street one morning, feeling very tense and none too happy in anticipation of a publisher's meeting near Soho Square. A devotee of the Radha Krishna Temple approached me rhythmically with the familiar robe, sandals, bells, and shaved head, pigtail, and nose marking. He started saying to me, unprovoked: "Hare Krishna, Hare Krishna, Krishna"—at which I spontaneously continued—"Krishna, Hare, Hare, Hare Rama, Hare Rama, Rama, Rama, Hare Hare." And the young man's face lit up beautifully and he said in wonderment "Hey!" as if to say: "You know!" I smiled, and from that second I had the most gloriously inspired day, overflowing with good vibes and good ideas, tension-free. I daresay this phenomenon could not be reproduced in strictly experimental conditions. However, if you think of life as something of a laboratory . . .

---

*The phrase "everybody's talking" may have been inspired by Harry Nilsson's version of Fred Neil's song "Everybody's Talkin' (At Me)," recorded by Harry on his 1968 album *Aerial Ballet,* which was a great favorite of John and Paul. It was Derek Taylor who recommended the song to John Schlesinger, director of *Midnight Cowboy,* who used it as the main theme song for the 1969 hit film.

TWENTY-FOUR

Shiva

The Destroyer, the Uniter, the Transformer

There is a nice story told to Aleister Crowley by his friend Allan Bennett. Civil engineer's son Charles Henry Allan Bennett (1872–1923) would study raja yoga under Shaivite solicitor general of Ceylon, P. Ramanathan, before becoming a Buddhist bikkhu of the Theravada tradition, and afterward responsible for the Buddhist *sangha*'s first arrival in the West in 1908. Having a particular devotion to Shiva (also written as *Śiva*), Bennett took exception to something Golden Dawn leader Samuel Mathers said regarding the myth whereby it was held that were Shiva to open his third eye, the universe would be destroyed. Irritated by Mathers's skepticism, Bennett assumed an asana on the floor and relentlessly began chanting: "Shiva! Shiva! Shiva!" Mathers, annoyed, then seriously afraid, begged him to stop. Bennett continued. Nearly out of his wits, Mathers threatened to shoot Bennett dead with a revolver if he did not cease chanting at once. Bennett continued, reducing Mathers to bare pleading. Bennett made his point, and Mathers was suitably humbled, a rare experience.

It will be noted that most of our Sixties Indian spiritual influences have emerged from Vaishnavi traditions. Vishnu and avatar Krishna are considered personable ways of attracting devotion and piety to God.

Shiva's reputation and surrounding mythology is rather different from Krishna's and seems to have a distinctly wilder aspect.

There are many things that can be said of Shiva. He is the Destroyer aspect of the "Trimurti" where Brahman creates, and Vishnu preserves, but these roles of divine activity all interact and interpenetrate, being manifestations of an ultimate dynamic, unfathomable unity, though that unity may be so unfathomable that to call it a unity may be inadequate, for its absolute meaning is known only to itself. Shiva is also the transforming power, that is, an end is necessary for a beginning: forms are transformed but essence may remain.

Fig. 24.1. Shiva

Traditionally, Shiva has a number of associations and iconographical features that occur regularly, though Shaivite worship in Hinduism is far from uniform. Depictions of Shiva show him with long, matted hair, which hair is the source of the holy river Ganges. He delights in forest life, with animals. Bhang (or cannabis) is sacred to him. In his temples, people (women especially) come to make offerings to the "Shivalingam" or Shiva-mark, or symbol, associated with fertility. It is pillarlike, fully rounded or domed, and naturally has come to be seen as a phallic symbol, but equally it is seedlike, and devotees resent the crudity of regarding the lingam as a word for the male organ. It is a symbol of creative energy for sure. Cells are round, and living things that acquire dimensions begin as round.

However, for all his colorful attributes, Shiva is properly speaking not to be anthropomorphized 'cept for accommodation to ordinary minds. His image is not what he is. Shiva is formless, and *in* everything, that is, Shiva *is* everything in its essential aspect. All things that rise and live rise out of him (hence perhaps the rising dome symbol). The forms that appear thanks to his life do not encompass him.

After winter, which appears like death, while the seed sits in earth apparently lifeless, there is Shiva, and the rising destroys what precedes it, as time advances and all is transformed. Who can say how it is that life returns transformed each year, how men and women die and return? Shiva has *gunas,* that is, qualities or properties, but he is not those qualities; they do not encompass Shiva, they appear to man as expressions of the life he generates. Shiva transcends thought.

It is widely held that his devotees ingest cannabis (bhang), but if they understand the idea of devotion to Shiva, they should know that to make the offering (*prasad*) of the sacred bhang is to offer the intoxication to Shiva, the intoxication of illusion (maya), sex obsession, impure thought. This is offered to the transformer so that the mind may be cleansed. Furthermore, bhang, correctly administered, was essential to Vedic medicine, having many healing properties recognized for millennia, healing skin complaints, depressions, mental problems, digestion, epilepsy, and of value to profound meditation. Alcohol is not sacred to Shiva; Shiva is not a license to "lose one's mind," but to lose one's impurity of mind, confusion. Shaivite devotees are abstemious, vegetarian, and restrain appetites. Bhang has been overused for entertainment in India as elsewhere, and taking too much of things makes us sick. Offerings of milk, yogurt, ghee, honey, and sugar to Shiva are for the moral perfecting of lives, to become closer to the Spirit.

In Shaktism, which holds that Brahma is feminine, whose power is "Shakti," the goddess nonetheless has Shiva for spouse, whose spiritual power is equal and complementary. In the Shaiva Upanishads, Shiva is identified with the unchanging Brahman and Ātman.

So, having absorbed as much of these ideas as might be easy for you, you may be as surprised as was I at first to hear the hypothesis that in searching for the spiritual meaning of the Sixties, one might well entertain the view that the era witnessed a kind of collective incarnation of Shiva in the world.

This at first startling, somewhat off-the-wall idea came to my ear from Ehud Sperling (b. 1949), founder and publisher of Inner Traditions International. The idea found temporary form in a rich conversation in December 2016 about the subject of this book.

Born in Israel, Ehud grew up from the age of four in Washington Heights, Manhattan, to be confronted in his teens with radical changes apparently going on everywhere. Not that it happened all at once. A science major and blues fan, Ehud Sperling ran the gauntlet with local toughs who objected to his long hair; he got beaten up for it. He remembers in the early Sixties how there was only one disc jockey specializing in rock on FM radio, and the show was on at midnight. There were a lot of people who were dead set against rock music. But rock 'n' roll, as Ehud noted, was *the* medium of communication. What in due course went with rock was first the ecstasy that came through sex, then the transcendence that came through psychedelics. The question he asked was: *how did it come to be that a whole generation, or at least a very substantial proportion of it, came this way?* What was going on?

Ehud reflected on the nature of Shiva.

Now at this point I just want to butt in and say that if we're talking about an "incarnation" of Shiva in every person who responded to this or that aspect of Sixties counterculture, we may be at a loss to understand what is implied here, especially to one like myself who enjoyed a highly rational education and who still holds firmly to the conviction that reason is a gift of the spirit. If, however, we remember that when we talk of gods, be it Shiva or Vishnu or another, we are talking in a context of the spiritual nature of reality, which, to employ a picture, means we're talking about energies of immeasurable nature pulsating, billowing, as it were, behind everything we see (like wind in a sail)—not literally "behind," as though if you lifted up the skin of the sky, you'd find God. That is too materialistic a conception. We're talking about powers that manifest themselves to our senses and our thoughts and states of mind on earth at particular times, to which we are free to respond or not. Of course, if you a priori deny any spiritual realities you'll find all of this utter meaningless nonsense, and any attempt I make to express the essential idea will be in vain. That being the case, I shall continue, or rather, let Ehud's hypothesis continue, as I am not disposed to suppress it. I should just add that one way of understanding the idea here put forward in more Jungian terms would be to see "Shiva," in this context, as the spiritual energy of the "collective unconscious" in this period.

Ehud considered the traditional power of Shiva to destroy hierarchies, establishments, ruling bodies, or states of mind, for the making of new worlds. He considered Shiva's association with dancing, with bhang, with a divine state of mind, with transcendence of appearances, with transformation of matter and of mind. Vulgarly, one might think of Shiva as getting stoned or high on his own being, or on the offerings of mind made by those devoted to what Shiva represents. Devotion is a reciprocal process. We receive but what we give. Go with your deity, your deity goes with you, enlightening you to the energies encompassed in that conception.

The *ecstatic* element (literally, to move out of stillness, to be out of one's ego, or simply to know transcending joy) of the Sixties, that is, its extreme characteristics in finding joys, may also be seen as analogous or expressive of Shiva's traditional representation. Shiva has to be "calmed down" traditionally, because like the Gnostic Sophia, he can get so worked up and hot as to become unbalanced and dangerous for those around him. His ardor is cooled with offerings of yogurt, milk, and honey. This ecstatic element is very close to Dionysus, the Greek god so dear to Jim Morrison, the Latin Bacchus, god of ecstatic ritual, of drunken transport, of letting loose the girders of the soul, of abandonment of formal constraints in excess of wine unto dreaming, loving, and spiritual release. German philosopher Nietzsche related Dionysus to chthonic powers of the underworld, or unconscious, opposed to the solar imperium of Apollo, the rational, orderly, predictable, external order.

Ehud became friendly with, and eventually published the writings of, distinguished French Orientalist and musicologist Alain Daniélou whose book *Shiva and Dionysus* makes this parallel explicit. Daniélou provided evidence for the view that there was a "universal empire of Ram" that extended from the Indus Valley to the shores of Portugal. During this time the cult of Shiva spread through the Mediterranean, eventually metamorphosing into the cult of Dionysus.

The point is that a generation may be said to have responded to Shiva, spiritual energy and god of destruction and transformation. Shiva destroys the world, the world established—*all systems must go,* so to speak—to build something better; corruption does not go unheeded in the world. Vishnu receives the gunas (qualities) to seed the new world. Brahma puts the seeds into the earth—or into the mind. Inspiration comes from spiritual sources. Think of the Sixties emphasis, a novel emphasis, on drugs, dance, and music. Shiva has long hair in the forest where he dances; he is fond of animals; living things respond to him, and he to them. One thinks of the movie *Born Free* and the care for animals that insisted on changes to laws protecting animals in movies and elsewhere. A new consciousness of animal welfare appeared along with the new environmentalism. When that welfare is transgressed, we feel something is wrong; our ancestors did not. We think of the ecological movement, the whole idea of an economy of "recycling," which could almost be a Hindu word or concept in itself, for in Hinduism, time is cyclic, and the trinity of creator, preserver, and destroyer we recognize as the whole concept of renewable energy, holistic theory, and call what Hindus have known as religion, "science." In the Sixties, people became more aware of the creation and the universe itself, of the powers of the earth, of the powers of regeneration, of the sun, and the moon that turns the tides, and the idea of tidal energy and solar power, and earth energy, and a growing frustration with pollution, uncleanliness, carbon-burnt offerings instead of living ones. We became aware of organics.

Look at the implications for *health* that came out of the Sixties, many of which bore an Indian flavor. Who now knows nothing of yoga, of meditation, of organic food, of natural healing, of spiritual medicine, of the benefits of brown rice, macrobiotic diets, and the righteousness of "you are what you eat"? Hip people said goodbye to the Texas war diet, protein stuffed and full of chemical, carcinogenic preservatives that preserved rottenness. Health and freshness came with a taste for the exotic, and Ehud Sperling, being young, curious, and passionate about these new ideas figured out a way to be an innovator in these monumental changes.

Ehud found himself working at Weiser's Bookstore in Manhattan, a magnet for spiritually seeking people. Many interesting people came there, such as André VandenBroeck, a student of R. A. Schwaller de Lubicz, Robert Lawlor, one of the founders of Auroville and later a prominent author of Inner Traditions, Mantak Chia, Cheng Man Ching, and many magicians, occultists, Hermeticists, alchemists, psychics, and spiritualists.

Fig. 24.2. Ehud Sperling working at Weiser's Bookstore.

Ehud began his publishing career after leaving Weiser's to work for Maurice Girodias (1919–1990) who published otherwise "forbidden" books such as erotic novel *The Story of O* by Pauline Réage, and works by William S. Borroughs, Nabokov (*Lolita*), and Henry Miller. French president de Gaulle banned Girodias. Ehud was put in charge of publishing the works of Sri Aurobino and the Mother, as well as pursuing his own interest in publishing the complete works on Egypt by R. A. Schwaller de Lubicz.

As part of this new spiritual awareness people took LSD to expand their consciousness. What LSD could do, thinks Ehud, depended on the content of consciousness in the individual. Some people didn't become really interesting until they'd taken LSD. Steve Jobs, who made Apple such a success, was turned on by LSD. It is possible for god-forces to materialize; some people became spontaneous *siddhas*—that is ascetics who achieved enlightenment. Through LSD, some people became fully aware that there was more going on than what they'd known as ordinary life. Minds were expanded; people got to enter a bigger, more interesting, sometimes more joyful world.

People have remarked that at the height of the Sixties, there was a sense that you could get up in the morning, and really get to do something. You could achieve with imagination, and it was good to get out and about as soon as possible, and perform the dance of daily ecstasy, creating life, turning away from the old, erecting the new. And there was a new communication: *music*. In those days music was the internet, the Web. New thoughts and ideas were being put out in the form of new songs with different lyrics combined with new sounds. A new album could turn you on to a whole new world, or just keep you buoyant and floating.

The Sixties was, Ehud believes, determinative. It was like a great river, where a stream has come off it, and gone another way. Many of the hashish smokers who eschewed hard liquor and went organic are often the ones surviving, enjoying health and youth into old age: those who learned to give and take. The reactionary society is getting ill with stress and mental illnesses, losing themselves and, being close to despair, try to shore up their sense of mortality with oblivion, aggressivity not

Fig. 24.3. Ehud as Horus.

joy. In the Sixties, there was just one farmer, a local farmer in New York who espoused organic farming, against the might of a multimillion-dollar industry. That was the seed. Now there's a whole organic movement (the Ono-Lennons were early patrons of the movement in the Seventies). Seeds planted then are bearing fruit, and will continue to bear fruit, those seeds planted by the spiritual power and love of preservation, and life and growth, and preparedness to change, radically if necessary, powers who don't keep looking back all the time, afraid of the now and the future. The Sixties, Ehud believes, represents the real dominant growth force in the world, and it will dominate. The reactionaries, on the other hand, have nothing to offer but illusions, maya, that kind of destruction that does not prepare the ground for growth, but tries to destroy life and mind and spirit.

The Tribe that gathered in the Sixties exists now all over the world, and its representatives, some rich, some not, are aware of responsibility to society as a whole, and to the future. The future is unfolding, and though it may yet take generations to see the best fruits, a great unfolding proceeds nonetheless. The seed contains the future within it. From the seed, the power grows high, like the Shiva symbol; it flowers, it radiates, it gives forth fruit, and so grows the forest and garden of the paradise to come, within and without.

Now say that Shiva has nothing to do with it!

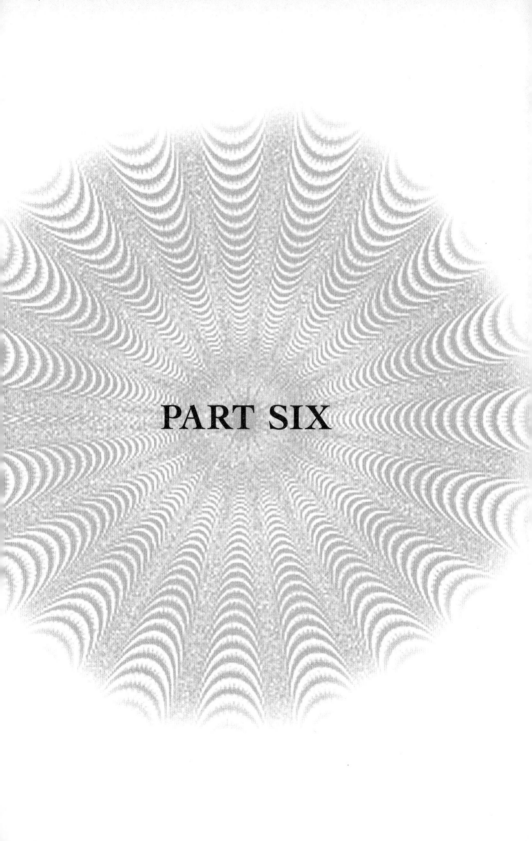

PART SIX

TWENTY-FIVE

The Turning Point— 1965: The Aeon of the Child Made Manifest

If readers are disposed to consider some of the more remarkable phenomena of the Sixties as manifest forms of spiritual agencies or energies, there are arguably competing conceptions of powers "behind" inward and manifest changes.

One of the more extraordinary events of the twentieth century was the appearance of a new religion in April 1904 when British poet, mountaineer, and magician Aleister Crowley (1875–1947) received *The Book of the Law* by direct voice dictation in a rented Cairo apartment. It took Crowley many years to come to terms with what he had written down, and to make the words of the three-chapter work he received over three days the cornerstone of his life and teaching. As his extraordinary life moved on, the conviction grew to interior certainty that the message of the gods determining the destiny of the human race had been communicated to him by an angel his clairaudient wife Rose informed him was called "Aiwass." The source of the message came, Crowley believed, from high spiritual powers concerned with governance of the planet. Yes, I know what you're thinking—*he* thought it was a tough one to swallow too, at least to start with.

In autumn 1938 Crowley distributed a limited number of copies of *The Book of the Law* to individuals chosen to represent the world's races. The world was going through tumultuous upheavals, he declared in the publication's covering document, because a new Aeon had come into force in 1904, with a new set of spiritual determinants. Whereas the Lord of the past Aeon was characterized by Egyptian god Osiris, with associations of suffering, sacrifice, sorrow, and salvation through death, the new Aeon had, as its "crowned and conquering Lord," the child Horus, "the avenger" whose word was "Force and Fire." Horus is an image of the sun and is associated with the light of revelation, of a casting aside of past obscurity—and also of youth and naïveté. Until humankind accepted what had been a latent spiritual current, *The Book of the Law* implied, the world would be embroiled in vast bloody conflicts until the planet was fit for a restored humanity.

On consideration, the reign of Horus the Avenger sounds very close to the conception of Shiva adumbrated in the previous chapter. There also we see an overturning, a transformation of a fiery, solar nature, in order to establish a future civilization of balance and justice. Students of comparative symbolism may be content to observe that Shiva has been compared to the Egyptian Seth, both in character and etymology, and in the Graeco-Egyptian form of the Horus myth, it is Seth's murder of father Osiris that impels Horus to rise and subdue "evil" Seth. Crowley of course was familiar with the fact that many of these characterizations of Egyptian gods reflected historic rivalries between solar priests, and could not be taken literally. Seth, formerly the sun god favored by pharaohs such as Rameses II for his powers of victory in war, was afterward denigrated, with the rise of rival priesthoods representing Amun and Osiris. The withering power of the sun in the south (Seth) came in time to be regarded as fatal, deadly, and therefore evil. Seth's color is red.

The name Shiva has been associated by scholars with the Tamil word *śivappu*, meaning "red," while Shiva is linked to the sun (*śivan* = "the red one"), and we note that Shaivite worship is strong in Sri Lanka, among Tamils, and that Crowley was himself in Sri Lanka (for the second time) shortly before he received *The Book of the Law*. It was there he contracted a lesion of the tongue that put him in an intermittently hallucinatory state when he arrived in Cairo with his wife in

March 1904, and which he later suspected had rendered his mind open to subsequent discarnate communication.[1]

The later Horus received qualities hitherto the preserve of solar deity Seth, so we may justly ascribe either name to the kind of divine energies imagined by Crowley to be at work in the world, energies which in fact he'd been writing about since 1900. Crowley was also very much aware that the forces concerned were not themselves new, but had, as it were, been brewing, though suppressed by human ignorance, for at least two millennia. In that sense, Crowley, as prophet, announced a religion that was rather a syncretic formulation of what already existed unfocused in essence, and whose coming into the human realm was now sufficiently acute to be stated directly.

The new aeon would be characterized by the qualities or properties of Horus, usually portrayed in late antiquity as a boy sucking his finger and seated on the lap of his mother, Isis, and known to Greeks as Harpokratēs, associated with initiated knowledge, occult secrets, and initiation in general. Crowley advised people to take stock of child psychology, its willfulness, directness, energy, violence, impatience, wisdom, sensitivity, creativity, innocence-ignorance, unrestrained reconnaissance, curiosity, affections, kindness to animals, simplicity, naïveté, love of laughter, unruliness, and so on, to form a picture of the characteristics of the new aeon. The spiritual emphasis would be on the will to discover the "true will," or divine orbit of one's life, and to brook no opposition. Crowley saw the old patriarchal religions as suffering a long death agony as they gave up—oh but so painfully, so reluctantly, so violently—their rule over "the Child." But the Child would conquer, and in course of time, perhaps a thousand years hence, the wine would again be fit to drink, to foam and restore the correct balance of man and "God," that is, his own potential, coming being.

And what does all of this have to do with the spiritual meaning of the Sixties? Well, I'm sure the penny will have dropped for some readers already, but to bring the issue into focus, let's read the following letter sent by Crowley on November 2, 1944, from the Bell Inn, Aston Clinton, Buckinghamshire, to Crowley devotee Grady Louis McMurtry,

Fig. 25.1. Lt. Grady Louis McMurtry, circa 1941.

serving officer in the U.S. Army in Europe against Nazi Germany, in which Crowley once more urged Lt. McMurtry to consider seriously his future career as Outer Head of the OTO (Ordo Templi Orientis). Crowley employed the term "caliph." By Oriental precedent, as Crowley was Thelema's prophet, his successors could be considered caliphs, with the prophet's authority vested in a caliphate. Crowley saw McMurtry as his post-mortem "alter ego," functioning with Crowley's authority in Crowley's absence.

> Frater Saturnus [Karl Germer, Crowley's agent in the U.S.] is of course the natural Caliph; but there are many details concerning the actual policy or working which would hit his blind spots. In any case, he can only be a stopgap, because of his age; I have to look for *his* successor. It has been hell; so many have come up with amazing promise, only to go on the rocks. . . . I do not think of you as lying on a grassy hillside with a lot of dear sweet woolly lambs, capering to your flute! On the contrary. Your actual life, or "blooding," is the *sort* of initiation which I regard as the first essential for a Caliph. [Allied forces in Europe were about to be sucked into what would be called the Battle of the Bulge] For—say 20 years hence—the Outer Head of the Order must, among other things, have had the experience of war as it is in actual fact today. 1965 e.v. should be a critical period in the development of the Child Horus![2]

This little note sent out during one of the bloodiest periods in world history, that nine months later would see the dropping of two atom bombs on Japan, using the nuclear "power of the sun," can only look in retrospect, something like prophecy. Crowley is quite specific: 1965 e.v. (*era vulgari* = the common era). He sees the year as a critical period in the Child's development, the Child being the spiritual character of the aeon. *Critical,* in this context, means a point where decisions become necessary, where choices must be made, commitments must be struck, and paths must separate.

Seen from this perspective, 1965 does acquire indeed the characteristic of a turning point in terms of the spiritual meaning of the decade. If we need a little reminding, just look at the following events that took place in that year, taken fairly at random.

The year got off to a psychedelic start when the Byrds, led by Roger McGuinn and David Crosby entered Columbia Studios on January 20 to record Bob Dylan's "Mr. Tambourine Man," a clarion song of the folk-rock, psychedelic, neotroubadour ethic. This was the same day that Lyndon B. Johnson announced the Great Society at his second inauguration ceremony. There was going to be justice and opportunity for all!

The Byrds started playing at Ciro's on the Sunset Strip attracting a new spectrum of costumed youth. California, and then national, favorites the Mamas and the Papas got together in 1965. In July, keyboard player Ray Manzarek got to know Blake- and Nietzsche-inspired poet and student filmmaker, James Douglas Morrison (1943–1971), about whom so much has been written, but arguably little of worth. By the year's end, the Doors had begun their extraordinarily imaginative and anarchic career, whose reverberations show no sign of fading, despite having been split up for nearly fifty years.

On August 24, in the company of the Byrds and Peter Fonda in Los Angeles, John Lennon and George Harrison took LSD for the second time in their lives (having taken it in London in late spring by accident). Ringo took it too. A curious but revelatory occasion, John turned it into a psychedelic classic called "She Said She Said," which referred to Peter Fonda's conversation about how he had shot himself by accident in his youth and nearly died. Lennon's comment: "Who put all that shit in your head?"

Paisley shirts began to appear on fashionably dressed men (performers to begin with): a first step toward androgynous styles that would threaten traditional Western notions of masculinity and division of sexes. Long hair became noticeably more common among young people who could cope with sometimes hysterical opposition to it. Being "adult" wasn't too cool. Janis Ian wrote and recorded "Society's Child" or "Baby, I've Been Thinking" in . . . 1965.

In October the Beatles started recording their turning-point album, *Rubber Soul*. Among its numerous highlights was a song called "The Word" that announced that its chief composer John Lennon had found a "word" in the "good and the bad books" that he'd read—and the word was *love*. Saying the word *love* made you free, the group sang. Through love, you could resemble the state of mind of the group. The world was invited to share in the saying of this word. And the impression given was that this word *love* was not quite the same in meaning or scope and depth as the same word *love* of commercial girl-meets-boy songs, or of the Beatles' own earlier repertoire such as "She Loves You." This was a sermon from Rev. Lennon, addressing the emerging flock. Hearing the whole album, Beach Boys producer, member, and songwriter Brian Wilson was stunned, knocked out, concerned that he would have to "up his game" considerably. Taking psychedelics for additional stimulus as if they were the bread of life from the master's table, Brian got his group to record an album that was intentionally made to convey what he called "spiritual love." The group prayed before sessions, seeking active divine inspiration. What they recorded was a message of spiritual love to everyone who heard it. It was intended to communicate spiritual love. It was called *Pet Sounds* and reached the public in May 1966. It would inspire the Beatles to go even further to remain ahead, resulting in *Sgt. Pepper*. But the turning point in consciousness was 1965. Many heard the word.

Burt Bacharach wrote "My Little Red Book" recorded by Manfred Mann for the movie *What's New, Pussycat?* whose title song was another lasting love song from Burt Bacharach and Hal David; the movie seemed drenched in incipient free love. It advocated free love, it screamed and shouted it from the chateau rooftops of the City of Light. "What's New, Pussycat?" *Love* was new, that's what.

On June 3, Ed White took a walk in space, in the vacuous footsteps of USSR cosmonaut Leonov, who'd been outside his craft on March 18 (were we surprised the Russians *let* him out?). Yves Klein would have loved to have lived to see it, or to do it himself. The age of space was real. Meanwhile, Robert Charroux wrote a book advocating that ancient astronauts, not content with space, had landed on Earth and mated with human women in prehistory inspiring Genesis's account of the Nephilim or "Watcher" angels. Charroux inspired the whole "Chariots of the Gods" idea that shows no sign of disappearing. The idea of course was also Indian: *avatars* manifesting on earth to guide mankind.

"Force and Fire" were in visible evidence (though denied to the British public) with the completion of Peter Watkins's *The War Game,* showing what a nuclear war would really be like for civilians.

The Second Vatican Council ended in December 1965 giving many Catholics the idea that the Catholic Church was finally making contact with planet Earth as it was, rather than how the church believed it should be. Hell was no longer such a viable concept, unless of course one came to see it as man-made. And John Lennon in 1965 released his book *A Spaniard in the Works* parodying organized religion's inability to answer the question of innocent suffering. Lennon was looking for an answer, a true and honest one. Meanwhile, Hugh Schonfield's book *The Passover Plot* was published and began a line of "alternative history of religion" books that continue to this day.

In 1965 John "Hoppy" Hopkins got his London underground counterculture career going, organizing the London Free School with John Michell, while getting the Indica Bookshop together with Barry Miles and sundry colleagues, while also becoming a one-man London internet for art and communication and all things new. On June 11, 1965, Hoppy, Barry Miles, and friends organized the International Poetry Incarnation. Allen Ginsberg came over from the States along with Lawrence Ferlighetti. The counterculture, hippy movement had begun. Young people were prophesying, seeing visions, and dreaming dreams.

And George Harrison, busy with Dick Lester's movie *Help!* had seen a sitar and heard one and liked what he heard. And Beatles fan Roger McGuinn showed George how he'd taken lines from Ravi Shankar's music and set them to guitar. . . . A sound revolution was underway. And the Beatles loved the Byrds too and took a few tips from them, and messages were crossing the Atlantic that turned people on.

And unknown to the pop crowd, 1965 saw Renaissance-scholar Frances Yates go on a U.S. lecture tour to give voice to her personal rediscovery of Hermetic philosophy and philosophical magic in the Renaissance, conscious of its links with early sproutings of modern science and the ancient gnosis.

And I was taken to see *The Greatest Story Ever Told* and wondered what it was all about. Mark Rothko also wondered what it was all about, for in 1965 he began work on his fourteen black paintings for the Rothko Chapel in Texas, while in West Germany, Joseph Beuys performed *How to Explain Pictures to a Dead Hare,* bringing ideas of spiritual alchemy into revolutionary performance art.

And there was childlike magic and children galore rocketing to the top of the album charts and movie ratings. Both *The Sound of Music* and *Mary Poppins* were released in 1965, affecting consciousness, inspiring people everywhere with a fresh sense of life. She was sixteen, going on seventeen, and *knew* she was naïve. . . .

And Bob Dylan switched from his folkie image to electric guitar, attracting the famous but solitary cry of "Judas!" from an offended fan who would not see what was blowin' in the wind. Earlier in the year, fresh wind blew into jazz with John Coltrane's spiritual statement, *A Love Supreme.* Even Benjamin Britten composed a song cycle in 1965, inspired directly by William Blake's poetry of imagination, childlike simplicity, mystical depth, and metaphysical challenge, the *Songs of Innocence and Experience.* It wasn't the Jimi Hendrix Experience, but that would not be long now in coming from behind the trash cans of Greenwich Village.

And spiritual music revivalist John Tavener composed his first cantata, *Cain and Abel* in 1965, while the Who shouted about what it was to be young, and defiant, in "My Generation," released in October, slaying the past as sure as Cain slew Abel. In France, Jean-Luc Godard's *Pierrot le Fou* had the antihero leaving his bourgeois wife for a life of uncertainty and existential adventure, chased by the police into the oblivion of romance and gunrunning before finding the answer by the sea at the moment of explosive death, followed by peace and a poem by Rimbaud about eternity.

And it was of course in November 1965 that flower power as neo-political, positive strategy began when Allen Ginsberg wrote "How to Make a March/Spectacle," bringing flowers to the global debate for peace, justice, love, and understanding.

On January 30, 1965, Sir Winston Churchill, who had cut his teeth fighting for the Raj in India in the late nineteenth century, had died. The great guardian of liberal Edwardian values left this world. I saw his soul rise while on the way to the shops down Mere Green Road. Later in the year, former British subject Swami Bhaktivedanta felt the call to embark on a spiritual mission to bring peace to the world through Krishna consciousness, and sailed to the United States.

On August 15, 1965, the largest number of people ever in the history of our species to gather for a music performance responded to it in Dionysiac frenzy. The band: the Beatles, of course. The place: Shea Stadium, New York. Over 55,000 devotees worshipped the four "boys" from England, while at the same moment race riots stormed through Watts, Los Angeles, leaving thirty dead after five days following complaints against police brutality toward black people. "Every man and every woman is a star" (*The Book of the Law*).

Back in England, on October 26, the Queen of England presented the Beatles with medals at Buckingham Palace. They became "Members of the British Empire," which Empire was now a past dream. They were building a new empire; perhaps that is why they were "pinned down" with medals. On November 30 several people set fire to themselves in protest against U.S. involvement in Vietnam. Operation "Rolling Thunder" got underway shortly after regardless, and by the end of 1965, U.S. casualties in the war passed 1,500 for that year.

And it was some time that year, at 15 Gibbons Road, Four Oaks, Warwickshire, that I had an experience in the garden. I was by Dad's workshop, standing in the sunshine, gazing toward the tall hedge at the garden's end. I had a complete revelation. My spirit spoke: "I cannot die." Suddenly, the idea of death withdrew into utter remoteness. I was in my real being. I *was* my real being. I knew this fact as well as I had ever known anything, more so, much more so. I *knew*. It was without doubt an unbridled experience of myself as spiritual being. I was not, as my mother would call me "Toby boy" at all, and yet I was, and more so, happily so. I was no age; I had never been an age, and I never would be. There was no question, and it was like the whole world quietly exploded into something else entirely before me. It didn't change, but everything had changed. I rushed into the kitchen to tell Mummy but I don't recall any reaction, or even if I *was* able to tell her, or really wanted to. I was ecstatic, and for a while not at all a five-year-old.

Shortly after, I remember when the family would go to the cinema on a Friday night, we'd be sitting on the S71 bus (I think), and James and Victor would laugh, and ask me to do my "face": it was a kind of immense gleeful smile with a strange nodding, affirmative bobbing of the head, a sign, I am quite sure, of pure interior gnosis, with no particular intellectual component: a quiet joy. But I did become aware that there was nothing I could not know or understand if I felt so inclined. The essence of the moment has been around at sundry times ever since in different shades, but there's nothing like the first time, if this was the first time.

I found this quote from Professor R. C. Zaehner in his book *Our Savage God,* where he writes about what Zen Buddhists call "satori":

. . . enlightenment, the supreme lightning flash of which shatters the time barrier, and through which one is reborn in eternity, where time does not exist and death is an almost laughable possibility. All things are fused into one and one can sing, as the boy poet Rimbaud sang:

> *Elle est retrouvée.*
> *Quoi?–L'Éternité.*
> *C'est la mer allée*
> *Avec le soleil.*[3]

Yes. 1965 was a "critical year in the development of the Child."

TWENTY-SIX

Feeling Groovy: The West Coast

Why so much political and social ferment emerged during the Sixties from the West Coast of the Unites States is a question infrequently asked. In particular, the radical spiritual shift from established spiritual beliefs toward New Age or adapted Oriental philosophies warrants explanation.

There seems little doubt that the Beatles' arrival in the United States in 1964 galvanized an existing potential for innovative lifestyle changes and fresh political consciousness, providing a vital arena of humor, physical stimulus, and psychological soundtrack. Psychedelia would be a strong component of the change, perhaps the strongest. Another vital element lay in the existence already in California of alternative spiritual movements long established. For example, Katherine Tingley's Theosophical Society had been operating at Point Loma near San Diego since 1900. Magus Aleister Crowley had visited the establishment in 1915, and received a cold shoulder for his trouble. Crowley lectured to at least one Theosophical gathering in San Francisco that same year, and after 1919 Crowley's magical religion of Thelema reached Los Angeles through connections in Chicago. By 1930 Crowley's OTO was established in small on the West Coast and attracted members of the L.A. science-fiction reading scene.

While meditation, Hinduism, and Buddhist philosophies were taught at Point Loma, there was also a flourishing Rosicrucian community based at San José (AMORC) and at Oceanside, where Max Heindel's Rosicrucian Fellowship flourished, about forty-four miles north of San Diego.

People usually came to California to live, not only in expectation of endless sunshine, space, and healthy sea breezes, but also because its position at the farthest extremity from Washington suggested independent thought, belief, and action. It would, furthermore, be impossible to understand the Californian hippie movement without taking into account the proximity to Native American cultures that impacted on people living in the Portland area (Yakama Reservation), some 375 miles north of San Francisco. We only have to think about the tassels that waved beneath the arms of suede jackets or vibrated similarly from the breast pockets of waistcoats to feel the Oregon breezes of the wind gods of the indigenous tribes. As for the ubiquitous bandana that adorned heads from Jimi Hendrix to the "Seine-et-Oise Liberation Front" of Jean-Luc Godard's *Weekend,* and on to Vanessa Redgrave marching against the Vietnam War in Grosvenor Square in 1968, its provenance is obvious to anyone who has seen a Western.

In 1962, Dick Price and Michael Murphy founded the Esalen Institute at Big Sur, about twenty-eight miles south of Monterey, in order to explore the furthest outreaches of Indian tantra for purposes of integrating Hindu spirituality into Western free lifestyles. So we can see how California hosted a heady mix of transcendentalism, experimental lifestyles, and when we take into account political liberties explored by students at the University of California–Berkeley and San Francisco's Art Institute, we begin to see outlines of the movement that would explode into public consciousness in 1967.

We may now add the word *hippie.* The word *hip* was used in the 1930s and 1940s by African Americans to suggest awareness of things sophisticated, fashionable, and up-to-date. In 1963, Dorothy Killgallen wrote a syndicated article about New York hippies baking marijuana in cookies. The term quickly acquired cross-reference to the beatnik scene of the East and West Coasts. Inspired readers of Jack Kerouac in San Francisco and Venice (a coastal residential area of Los Angeles) were keen to differentiate their sense of individuality from a mainstream

Fig. 26.1. An example of a Persian paisley design, 1963.

society obsessed with material values. What began as self-expression was soon copied by people who liked the idea.*

By 1965, the paisley shirt began to appear more frequently as the mark of Bohemian freethinking; it later distinguished openness to psychedelic experience. The famous paisley design, derived originally from Persia, became a nineteenth-century Victorian must-have when shawls were manufactured by textile factories in Paisley, Glasgow. Originally valued for intricate floral patterns, by the mid-60s the patterns suggested free love, colorful or Bohemian thinking, psychology awareness, more relaxed sexuality, and spiritual philosophies, set amid awareness of constituting a new community of feeling. Meanwhile, "King of Carnaby Street" John Stephen hooked into underground fashion and incorpo-

---

*Fascinating aspects of communities of artists and beatniks on California's coast at this time can be seen in sober light in Vincente Minnelli's remarkable, contemporary movie, *The Sandpiper*. Shot beautifully by Milton Krasner at Big Sur, and starring Richard Burton and Elizabeth Taylor—she plays a freethinking, free-spirited artist, he plays a thoughtful Episcopalian priest and teacher—it concerns the educational destiny of the artist's child, assisted by the philosophically challenged priest. Little known, but not forgotten, *The Sandpiper* was released in June 1965.

rated it into cutting edge designs that distinguished the trendy from the square. In 1965 the Dave Clark Five, hugely popular in the States, appeared in paisley shirts as a fashion add-on. On the West Coast, additions of beads and flowers and other Oriental trinkets carried across the Pacific by merchant ship conjoined with the flower-power guerilla tactics of Allen Ginsberg to add the finishing touches to the classic image of the hippie. The Beatles, of course, contributed the socially risky allure of long hair, a fashion extended beyond fashion when devotees of mediation desired to imitate Indian gurus with their straggly, dust-encrusted, Shiva-suggestive locks, so very distant from militaristic, bullet-headed shaven conformity.

THE HUMAN BE-IN AND GATHERING OF THE TRIBES

Critical to the West Coast scene, were the new bands that with the success of the Beatles, the Stones, and others found some U.S. record companies willing to give them a chance. On Sunset Strip, Hollywood, a famous old club called Ciro's welcomed the Byrds, who started playing there in 1965, attracting strangely dressed young people who came to hear the twelve-string folk rhythms of a band friendly with the Beatles. Like the Beatles, the Byrds were heavily turned on to Bob Dylan and a shared commitment to new consciousness. From New York came the Lovin' Spoonful, soon joined by the Buffalo Springfield, the Mamas and the Papas, the Turtles, the Seeds and other new bands, who all brought exciting new vibes to West Hollywood's Whisky a Go Go club on the Strip. The Doors, from Venice, were always somewhat apart from the rest, with their long, intense, keyboard-high workouts and overt reliance on poetry and symbolism.

By late 1966, large numbers of young people appearing on city streets invited savage police repression. Hair had gotten longer over the summer, and some kids walked about barefoot. Disquiet about their presence spread from San Francisco south to Los Angeles and Hollywood. There seemed to be a lot of concern about real estate on Sunset Strip, and the police effectively represented developers' plans to turn the Strip into a high-rise financial district. For some reason, description of the kids as "political" encouraged local politicians' anger, and armed police physically bullied the teenagers to clear the streets.

One night, about three hundred people were arrested by platoons of police in helmets armed with clubs; this was itself extraordinary. What appeared even more sinister was that nothing of the arrests appeared in the *Los Angeles Times*. Jim Dixon, a contemporary of James Coburn, James Dean, Marlon Brando, and an old fan of the beat poets formed a citizens group, Community Action for Facts and Freedom (CAFF). Its committee included Derek Taylor, Sonny and Cher, the management of the Beach Boys and Buffalo Springfield, and Elmer Valentine who owned the Whisky a Go Go. Peter Fonda, Dennis Hopper, and Jill St. John also joined to help monitor police activity. Fonda would himself be arrested on the Strip, an event that helped shape his cultural orientation for the rest of the decade and beyond. A concert to help raise funds joined Peter, Paul and Mary, the Byrds, Buffalo Springfield, and the Doors to common social purpose. The music welded together the gathering new consciousness. At the end of the year Stephen Stills wrote "For What It's Worth," played by Buffalo Springfield (including Neil Young) to protest the phenomenon of suspicious attacks on young people that made many of them feel understandably paranoid. The rise in public interest saved the Strip from the development machine. Similar protests some years earlier in San Francisco had preserved Haight-Ashbury and the Panhandle from omnivorous developers who own the collective distinction of producing an omniform globe of oppressive, repetitive, environment-insensitive "architecture" with no sense of human proportion and every sense of accountant speak. Wealthy they may be, but what dullards! What a legacy!

All of this took place as London saw Joe Boyd establish the UFO club with Hoppy Hopkins (September 1966), which kick-started London's psychedelic scene. In January 1967 San Francisco manager of the Avalon concert venue, Chet Helms, was in London to assess the European counterculture. Meeting Hoppy, Joe McGrath, and Barry Miles of *International Times,* they showed Helms the UFO where he saw Pink Floyd play amid feedback and an innovative projection and light show. The UFO accent on free improvisation was nothing new. In San Francisco, Chet Helms's Avalon ballroom was a place where jazz improvisation entered the rock mainstream. Chet Helms's family background included Christian evangelism, and Chet told Derek Taylor in 1987 that he felt the ballroom was in a sense his church, and he was its minister, keen to espouse the virtues of turning on, understood as achieving spiritual realization.

Corresponding to the circle around the *International Times* in London, San Francisco's "Diggers" were the counterculture's cutting edge. The world of the Diggers, inspired by the seventeenth-century English social revolutionaries of that name, advocated a world of "free." Free girl. Free boy. Free food and, especially, free love. Anarchic in spirit, they were also principled, truth telling, and compassionate, eager to offer irrefutable advice and practical assistance. Peter Coyote, now a Hollywood star, was a leader of the group that had no leaders. In the early Sixties he took peyote and, seeing himself as a creature of the wild, performed in a San Francisco mime troupe dedicated to the principle of *free*.

> We didn't stand *for* anything but we were about personal authenticity and taking responsibility for your own visions. There was a commitment to total radical overthrow of the culture, and that aim was shared by everyone. Everyone's response to it was different but it was the common denominator that made a person's behavior meaningful and separated young people from the generation that preceded them, because if they didn't share that premise, then everything we were doing was nuts![1]

The Diggers, whose members also included Emmett Grogan and Peter Berg, were instrumental in organizing and overseeing the ethics of many key activities and happenings in San Francisco of this period. The influence of the beats on the ethic of the Diggers was fundamental. Alan Ginsberg's *Howl* poetry collection and of course Kerouac's novels communicated loud and clear a spiritual void within postwar consumer society that was to be countered with spiritually enlivened people stimulated by their own spontaneity, by free-range intellect, by jazz, by rock 'n' roll, by art, by Indian philosophy, by suspicion of authority, and by creative psychedelia.

The Diggers were by no means alone in sharing a sense that anything could be done. Allen Cohen, for example, had had a dream of seeing a newspaper covered in rainbows that was read all round the world. He turned his dream into reality with the *San Francisco Oracle*. In early October 1966 he and artist friend Michael Bowen, in the midst of LSD elation and revelation, observed a group of hippies descend on the Haight Street police station making violent and angry gestures as their commune had been busted. Cohen and Bowen thought there must be a better way of carrying on than just baiting perceived opponents. Opting for celebration over demonstration, they organized the first outdoor rock concert of local bands in Golden Gate Park in the Panhandle while gifting the mayor's office with flowers and mushrooms. Attracting an audience of some twenty thousand, as well as national coverage, they contemplated the next step. Beat poet Gary Snyder joined the group that coalesced about the idea of a Human Be-In. Ginsberg maintained it bore no hyperrational purpose though it was about spirituality, about coming out of isolated consciousness into a sense of belonging, seeing beyond the ego to what could be achieved through presence of numbers and good intent, with good memories of the poetic renaissance of San Francisco beat enthusiasts a decade before.[2]

The event took place on January 14, 1967. Addressing the Human Be-In and "Gathering of the Tribes," Chet Helms announced with warm delight that he had just come back from Europe and London, and *it* was happening there too! The Tribes were gathering; people were *coming together*. It was all clearly *a sign*. What did it signify? It signified a generation awakening from international sleep.

Guests were allotted specific time slots to address the Be-In. Timothy Leary—who had lost his Harvard professor's seat in 1963 for overt advocacy of LSD—was there, as was East Coast politico Jerry Rubin, looking for fun ways to present a left-wing agenda. Suzuki Roshi meditated on stage throughout. And the bands played on.

Imitated across the Atlantic, the idea was contagious: a collective realization of living *now,* and it had a spiritual effect. The flow of the inevitable stopped slightly, and there was opportunity to innovate, think the unthinkable, do the undoable, be the un*be*able: break the bonds of expectation, the chains of authority, and to do it peacefully, confidently, with love and generosity. And it lacked all the heaviness of established means of protest and violent or noisy political activity. It was about *communication,* posing questions, existing, seeing. Interestingly, the purist Diggers were critical, sensing it was a way of promoting Haight-Ashbury merchandizing! They clearly foresaw what would happen to so much of the innovation and energy of the time. It was wide open to being co-opted by corporate powers that be. Sign a record deal, and you might just have sold your soul, your image, and your future.

The Diggers loathed copycat activity as not reflecting the authentic individual. Not everyone agreed with the Diggers. Enthusiast for spiritual enlightenment Ron Thelin, who ran the turned-on, tuned-in Psychedelic Shop on Haight Street, regarded the Diggers' criticism of the Be-In as "bullshit," finding a beautiful event to which the beautiful came, and asked for no more justification than that.[3]

In fact, the event served as a membership magnet to the counterculture, which was acquiring an identity, an image exportable and potent. It was fun, and the alternative to fun is boredom. It changed minds, such as that of middle-aged social scientist Helen Perry, who joined the twenty thousand-odd Be-In participants and went on to write a sympathetic account, *The Human Be-In* (1968). Two days before the event she went into a shop in Haight Street, bought a chain with a bell at each end. The wide-eyed assistant told her that it came from India, and Helen felt immediately she had made a significant step.[4] Critical perhaps, but aloof, no, the Diggers had their stall at the Be-In distributing free turkey sandwiches with turkey donated by the prime synthesizer of high-grade LSD, Owsley Stanley, whose latest synthesis, "White Lightning," circulated in the crowd. And this was no ordinary crowd. Testimonies from those present indicated that this event, in all its simplicity, enacted on a warm midwinter's day below clear skies, was super special for those who arrived to "be." Even the mainstream *San Francisco Chronicle* offered a fair report of the event: "They came,

Fig. 26.2. Jerry Rubin speaking at the University of Buffalo.

they Saw, they Stared." Soon the whole world would be staring. What they were staring at was not just the result of a chemical synthesis but a social-alchemical synthesis of differing minds finding themselves able to pool their active existences.

Jerry Rubin had just been bailed from a Berkeley jail. As a leftist agitator, he might have had little in common, politically speaking, with many attracted to the scene, but a positive energy of caring brought the tribes together. Helen Perry compared the event to another curious happening that took place in Palestine nearly 2,000 years earlier when "free food" appeared as if from nowhere as people gathered to hear wise words. It seemed like a great beginning. Roll on summer! Wow!

It wasn't going to be that easy. The night of the Be-In, police aggressively dispersed participants returning home. Hostility was obvious. Conscious of what had happened on Sunset Strip the previous year, Allen Cohen organized resistance. Activists as far apart as San Francisco and L.A. joined in common purpose: asserting a right to be in the streets. To Be-In. Opposition was palpable, and crossed national barriers, like the ideals of the movement itself. On February 12, police raided Keith Richards' house in West Wittering, Sussex, England, for drugs. In March, as spring freakouts took place in Los Angeles and New York, the London office of the *International Times* was raided. In April, Paul McCartney visited San Francisco, Denver, and Los Angeles, garnering ideas for the *Sgt. Pepper* album, such as the long name, based on West Coast names like Quicksilver Messenger Service, and Country Joe and the Fish. On the day he left (April 12), Ken Kesey was arrested on drug charges. Three days later, 400,000 marched on the United Nations Building in New York to demand an end to the war in Vietnam. On the thirtieth a "Love-In" in Detroit ended in a police riot. On May 10, as Mick Jagger and Keith Richards faced a Chichester court on drug charges, Brian Jones was arrested at home. Nine days later, on the day the Beatles held a party to launch *Sgt. Pepper* at Brian Epstein's flat, the BBC banned the great song that climaxed the album, *A Day in the Life,* insisting it promoted drug use by the words: "I'd love to turn you on." Despite the ban, the album began to turn people on across the free world after its release in the United Kingdom and the United States on June 1 and 2.

Soon after, a world already adjusted to huge public international events like the 1967 Expo '67 exhibition in Montreal, Canada, got to hear of the world's first international pop festival (June 16–18), the like of which was new and came straight out of the ferment in Los Angeles and San Francisco and London. The man to thank for this was Alan Pariser who had attended the 1966 Monterey Jazz Festival held at a fairground. Pariser booked the Monterey fairground, signed up performers, and raised some $60,000 to get the stone rolling. Pariser had become friendly with Derek Taylor after the latter emceed a benefit gig with the Doors, Hugh Masekela, Buffalo Springfield, the Byrds, and Peter, Paul and Mary at Los Angeles's Carousel Ballroom in late 1966, and his enthusiasm for the project saved Derek from dropping out. Pariser turned it into a charity event with codirectorship provided by the Mamas and Papas' producer Lou Adler and star, John Phillips. The festival's simple motto was: "Music, Love, and Flowers." Before the event, Pariser was edged out, and original investors had their money returned. The lineup had to attract big names. The Mamas and the Papas were about as big in pop as you could get in the States before June 1967, though the Doors, whom Pariser had booked, had had their first album released in January, eventually spawning the U.S. number one single, "Light My Fire" (July 29). Simon and Garfunkel came aboard on the basis that it would be a charity gig.

While San Francisco had always been somewhat aloof from the L.A. money scene, the effect of Monterey was to pull San Francisco's bands into the orbit of pop-for-money. Country Joe Macdonald, for example, who made a great impression at the festival, was scathing about the appearance of Scott McKenzie who'd had a hit with coproducers Adler and Phillips's "San Francisco (Be Sure to Wear Some Flowers in Your Hair)." The song had simply brought a lot of disoriented kids to the Haight imagining the streets were paved with fairy dust, and realists like Country Joe thought his appearance was an ethical sellout. Derek Taylor maintained it was a "pop festival," and pop had never in history been more diverse or so inwardly influential, and McKenzie's song was pop, and that was that. Besides, it was all to a "good cause." In retrospect, McDonald realized the Monterey Pop Festival did the San Francisco bands some good in confronting them with the realities of the business and what it could do for them if they played along on their own terms. Paul Kantner of San Francisco's Jefferson Airplane reckoned the festival was ruined by L.A. capital interests, but could not deny that it was still a great show of human brotherhood regardless. The festival opened the American door to Seattle-born Jimi Hendrix (introduced by Brian Jones), who only got in because Paul McCartney was on the advisory board and had seen and been blown away by Hendrix in London.

The event was a huge success from the music point of view (thirty acts showcased, including Ravi Shankar), from the good vibes, and even from the PR perspective, with a previously alarmed Police Chief Marinello who'd expected an orgy of drugs and abandonment having to send his underused and unneeded over-the-top force home with nothing to take offense to. Derek Taylor put a necklace round the chief's head and hoped it would make them "one." Taylor was now a thoroughgoing initiate to the counterculture. *What was there not to like?*—as we are tempted to ask these days. D. A. Pennebaker's film *Monterey Pop* reveals the magic of an event that brought so much diversity together in harmony. I remember seeing the film in a prewar Berlin cinema in 1987 and coming out into Kreuzberg (twenty years after the event) floating from the contact high with a past that seemed more futuristic than what 1987's yuppiedom seemed to be offering a spiritually battered world.

On June 23, 1967, Lyndon Johnson visited Los Angeles, to be greeted by a peace march at Century City. All that energy for peace and love now had a clear objective beyond the mists of the present. War was the sickness that excited people who had not "turned on"—such was the collective suspicion of the counterculture. Those not turned-on would need to be turned *off* the idea of war, so the war in Vietnam, killing young Americans, Vietnamese, and the people of Laos every day, became the target that brought hippies and New Leftists together, up to a point. Two days after the march, Muhammad Ali received a five-year sentence and lost his heavyweight title for refusing the draft. "Make Love, not War," cried the buttons that spread from the Panhandle across the free world. On June 19, the Stones received a prison sentence that even the conservative London *Times* thought excessive, its editor William Rees-Mogg suspecting the Stones were being persecuted for their antiestablishment image rather than the crime of possession of cannabis. In fact, the *News of the World,* first with the story, had been informing police of the Stones's party locations. In July the paper was targeted by a demonstration. On July 7 the Beatles' "All You Need Is Love" was released, and on July 31 so was Mick Jagger, on appeal.

Looking for a way beyond LSD, John, Paul, and George had their first meeting with Maharishi Mahesh Yogi at London's Hilton Hotel. The Maharishi declared the Beatles could lead the youth of the world to a new era of inner understanding and the world in general to a great change, with himself, the modest "great sage" to guide the way.

Meanwhile in San Francisco, things began to turn a bit sour. The Grateful Dead got busted on October 2, and four days later, fed up with the *image* of the hippie, and the glare of the media spotlight on the Haight, and concerned that what they believed in was being co-opted and utterly distorted by the media—and to show it was the *spirit* not the image that needed to be attended to—the hard core of San Francisco activists organized the "Death of Hippie" procession. It was the first anniversary of LSD being made illegal in America.

A great coffin was carried from the Haight to the Panhandle and ceremoniously burnt. Before it got there, people could throw into it hippie symbols, beads, trinkets, whatever they might want to get off their chests. Ron Thelin opened the Psychedelic Shop all night as they gave their stock away to the tunes of *Sgt. Pepper,* and Thelin announced to the *Chronicle* his intention of being free of possessions, and free of all images, and that he would no longer stand being looked at by visitors like an animal behind the bars of a media zoo. He accepted the media created the false idea of hippie and it was time to be rid of false ideas and false images, and be reborn. But of course, you cannot always get the media to accept the loss of an image they are very attached to, one that served such a useful purpose as a tool of ridicule, condescension, and suppression. Indeed, the image is still with us. One may ask: "Where is the meaning?" Similar ideas to those given voice to on the West Coast in 1967 are now stepped over like dirty puddles by the media and dismissed as New Age, as if the mere utterance served as sufficient condemnation. A pseudowizened cynicism is de rigueur in the media where anything of spiritual meaning is concerned (while conventional religious officials are accorded formal though empty "respect"). You might imagine the media was aware of something we are not! Don't kid yourself. I worked in TV for a decade and it was rare to find a free mind where spirituality was concerned, though not entirely impossible. You don't *get on* that way, you see. In 1997 the British media staged a long "Death of Diana" festival but they just couldn't let go of the image, could they?

So where did all those ex-hippies go after Death of Hippie? Why, they went to Washington, D.C., for the "Exorcism of the Pentagon" on October 21, which quite extraordinary march brought together many strange and diverse beings, and not only human specimens like Norman Mailer and The Fugs.

THE LEVITATION OF THE PENTAGON

New York activists like Abbie Hoffman had recognized the power of the theatrical hippie happening in terms of combining it with political

Fig. 26.3. Abbie Hoffman visiting the University of Oklahoma, 1969.

thrust. By Easter 1967, forty thousand gathered for a "Peace Parade" in Central Park's Sheep Meadow while only a third of that number assembled for the regular 5th Avenue Easter Parade, where Cardinal Spellman, who offered blessings on soldiers headed for Vietnam, posed by a machine gun, whereas, as Hoffman put it in 1987: "We had the freaks in the park for peace."[5]

Berkeley activists had been talking to Allen Cohen of the *Oracle* since the first Be-Ins; there'd been much talk of a big demo against the war. Cohen had read in Lewis Mumford's book *The City in History* that the Pentagon was an anachronistic structure whose existence obstructed a peaceful new world. Reading this to Michael Bowen and Jerry Rubin, Cohen suggested focusing on the Pentagon. Could they not project magical energies onto it and exorcise the evil? Bowen envisaged a magic ceremony as grand political theater, where Cohen saw a demonstration of the magic of living. It would be combined with a march, set for October 1967, on the pentagonal "heart" of what Eisenhower long before had called the "military-industrial complex." The leading lights would be Ed Sanders of the Fugs, Hoffman, Ginsberg, Cohen, and Keith Lampe, former soldier and newsman (afterward known as Ponderosa Pine, d. 2014). East Coast initiator of media projects, Lampe was surprised when Bowen turned up from Mexico having consulted shamans regarding levitation. Lampe reflected that the West Coast was different in basic approach, being concerned with lifestyle, whereas the East was more concerned with media events. Lampe also noticed that in other demonstrations, the leftists had controlled the rhetoric while the hippies got their skulls busted by police batons. Out of this thought emerged the "yippies" who attempted to fuse the attitudes with a creative combination of humorous theater plus political meaning.

Ed Sanders cottoned to the levitation-exorcism idea, modeled on ancient church exorcism practice combined with ancient Near Eastern practices and Graeco-Roman magic spells, while the whole event was conceived as "East Village meets Haight and has a Ball." Playfulness, inspired by Beatle attitudes, Ginsberg, and the San Francisco experience was building to a new political format with spiritual meaning, in the most literal sense. Sanders produced a ritual for the Fugs: poets, musicians, performing anarchists. It opened with a magic spell from a Greek manuscript: "*Chabrach Phneschēr Phikro phnurō phōchō bōch,*" after which followed the "Magic rite to exorcize the Spirits of murder, violence, and creephood from the Pentagon."

First, purification rites were enacted for for participants: cleansing of eye, hearts, and minds with a Hittite spell. Then a prayer was offered for the soldiers and their violent karma in Vietnam. Consecration of the four directions would follow, and afterward the creation of a magic circle for the protection of the rites. A trail of cornmeal was to be made around the Pentagon by an Indian. Point five indicated the invocation of powers and spirits of exorcism; this to be followed by placing of love articles and clothing onto the Pentagon: beads, feathers, rock 'n' roll records, books, and the "sacred Grope relic."

The exorcism ceremony involved the four traditional elements: Earth, that is, physical contact with the Pentagon. Air involved conjuration of "Malevolent Creep Powers." Water meant cleansing the object with water. Fire meant "destruction by fire." Whether the fire was presumed actual or spiritual would be a matter of wait and see. The rising of the Pentagon, anyway, should ensue as a result of these preparations, whereupon the exorcism could be pronounced, the banishment of the evil spirit amid "singing and shrieking." Ceremonies would conclude with a peace mantra.

"Out, demons, out. Out, demons, out!" was cried out to the pentagonal symbol of evil accompanied by bells, symbols, drums, and brass instruments, while Kenneth Anger, who had joined the motley crew from San Francisco, worked his own magic somewhere in the mêlée. The Pentagon did not rise in the physical sense, but the Pentagon was very successfully abstracted as an entity. A young man the same age as the nervous soldiers put outside to guard the sacred confines very bravely placed flowers in the barrels of the guards' M16s with calmness and dignity, while an officer followed, pulling the harmless flowers from the harmful barrels. The real powers involved were indeed made visible to anyone with the eyes to see. It was clear that government forces did not display the spirit of love fostered by the Christ they prayed to. Those flowers were originally going to be scattered over the Pentagon by plane but the FBI got wind of the plan and turned back the participants on the way to the airport. This was a blessing; the image of the young man with the flowers on the steps to America's "security" was worth more perhaps than the sight of flowers falling on an unwelcoming structure.

Fig. 26.4. Young protester puts a flower into a soldier's M16, 1967.

Marchers and demonstrators suffered the physical wrath of marshals and soldiers who beat demonstrators hard with billy clubs, young women included. There were over a thousand arrests, including writer Norman Mailer. Twelve demonstrators were charged with assault but there was no redress for injured demonstrators. *Had they not asked for it?*—such was the view of authority. As the sun went down about the Pentagon, amid incantations, there were agonizing cries from girls, weeping for a new world they longed to see. What had they done wrong? Ginsberg commented in 1987 that there was a kind of levitation insofar as the demonstration "demystified" the Pentagon, taking it away from its former grounding in public approval. Such was an achievement of directed human imagination, and quite a lot of spiritual courage of the kind that Republicans chose to associate only with the founding of the republic, but was alive in the good character of the very people they were now deeming enemies of the country. As Ginsberg put it: "The Pentagon was not the absolute authority of the universe. *The human spirit is the ultimate authority.*"[6]

In the event, while the demonstration had temporarily united different points of view, the violence made many people move apart from the kind of organized engagement face-to-face with political opponents that yippies deemed vital to win their war against what they saw as concrete sources of oppression and injustice. At least the violence came from the expected side of the argument. However, the subtleties were lost in the general media response to "no politics" style events. It was generally presumed in conservative press outlets that if there was violence, it was provoked. Passive-positive demonstrations had worked for Gandhi in India, up to a point, but then his demonstrations were not humorous and his spiritual stance was not theatrical. But then, neither was Martin Luther King's, and we know what happened to him.

The demonstration galvanized antiwar demonstrations in London and Amsterdam, and Abbie Hoffman was content that the government should conclude that if they were going to continue pursuing the war in Vietnam they were going to have to do it in a state of siege by a panoply of varied public opinion who considered it was not the United States government's task to wage aggressive wars with the blood of its young

Fig. 26.5. A demonstrator offers a flower to military police at an anti–Vietnam War protest at the Pentagon, 1967.

and the financial security of its people, unless they had the very full and honest backing of the whole country, which as further events would prove, was not the case.

Another thought: While the Summer of Love had been announced in San Francisco earlier in the year, and whilst a goodly number of young people and others had enjoyed some very nice music shows here and there, and many fine dreams of the utopian kind, the media image still perpetrated of the "summer of love" is an error. The Summer of Love was an ideal, a hope, and for many no doubt, a heightened reality, but in retrospect, it was a drawing of lines between directions Western culture might have taken, and there was much bitterness that would overflow in the year of 1968. Ed Sanders might have recalled Jesus's exorcism of the madman of Gadara. Having exorcised the "legion" from the violent wretch, the demons had to go somewhere. In the Gospels, they fled into a herd of pigs whose members promptly jumped off a cliff to their death like zealot suicides. As to the exorcism and levitation of the Pentagon, the question might have been asked: Where were the demons to go? As Jean-Luc Godard commented on Che Guevara's desire to set up three or four Vietnams, he forgot to realize that if you do, you are going to establish three or four capitalist armies.

For many, the event about the Pentagon was a wake-up call to reality, and that the dream of the gateway to a new world held aloft at the Human Be-In in January 1967 was perhaps childish, though on the side of the angels. However, as Ron Thelin (1939–1996) saw it, the vision that almost attained visible reality in that extraordinary year was not going to go away so easily, not because people remain foolishly committed to the unreal, but because there was within that vision, perennial truth for the future of humankind. The late Ron Thelin's summing up of the ideals of that year's imagining twenty years later is worth serious reflection:

> There was this door that was blown open by God, and light shone in on the world, huge amounts of light, at first blinding; and then a vision of the beautiful world started to be realized, and for about a year and a half the world felt it was really true. *Sgt. Pepper* . . . Hey, it's really going to happen. And then fear and habit and inertia and doubt started to push the door closed. They're still pushing. Reagan is pushing hard now [1987]. "No, no, let's keep to what we know about. No drugs! Oh God! No smoke. Close the door." But there's still a light under the door. And a friend of mine told me: "You know, a door can always be opened again."[7]

TWENTY-SEVEN

The Beast and the Six Six Sixties

We last encountered filmmaker Kenneth Anger (b. 1927) contributing his magick to the Levitation of the Pentagon ritual, along with Ed Sanders and the Fugs. Let's backtrack a bit. If we invert the *ts* of the *beats* we get *beast*, and beat poets can identify with Aleister Crowley, the hyperindividualist whose number was 666, indicating the solar principle. As we saw in chapter 15 on art, Crowley devotee Harry Smith was a friend of Allen Ginsberg, but even before Harry Smith got to meet Jonas Mekas and make a splash on New York's avant-garde film scene, there had been another man "out there." In the 1950s, Kenneth Anger had lived with artist-witch Marjorie Cameron, formerly intimate with rocket-fuel expert Jack Parsons, dominant member of the OTO Agape Lodge in Pasadena until a laboratory explosion in 1952 prematurely ended Jack's life. Fascinated by Crowley, Anger had even made the journey to the ruined "Abbey" Crowley inhabited with his Scarlet Woman Leah Hirsig from 1920 to 1923 at Cefalù, Sicily. In 1955 Anger removed whitewash to reveal Crowley's paintings à la Gauguin that once decorated every inch of the compact Villa Santa Barbara, a journey Anger undertook with sex-obsessed Professor Kinsey of the famous report that proved what many had long suspected, that Americans liked sex a lot, and many experimented when opportunity afforded them freedom so to do.

Anger came to England in search of the Beast's hunting ground and made friendly contact with the handful of people in Britain in the 1950s who still cared about the "Beast" who'd died in Hastings in December 1947. He met Frieda, Lady Harris (1872–1962), "artist-executant" of Crowley's now-famous Thoth Tarot pack, who had subvented the Beast on a stipend from her own pocket from the late 1930s through the war, and who had bravely gone through thick and thin in her complex dealings with him. Anger met Gerald Yorke (1901–1983), landowning gentleman of Forthampton Court, Tewkesbury, sometime disciple of Crowley from 1927 and, even after formal rupture in the early Thirties, friend to the end of the Beast's life: the man who saved the majority of Crowley's extant manuscripts for posterity.

Also operating in England under Crowley's inspiration during the Fifties was Kenneth Grant (1924–2011) who had served as Crowley's secretary for a brief time in 1944–45, and had studied under Crowley's tutelage. After Crowley's death, Grant established an OTO "camp" to pursue magick on Crowleyan principles and on idiosyncratic lines of his own, but when Crowley's successor Karl Germer found Grant was apparently looking on himself as OTO head in England, relations soured, resulting in Germer expelling Grant from the OTO. Grant persisted with his renegade OTO nonetheless into the Sixties, and its orbit would eventually interest guitarist Jimmy Page in that decade, for whom Crowley became a focus in his spiritual, philosophical life, as Page too pursued an independent path inspired by the Beast's magical religion.

Anger had been living in San Francisco when he decided to return to England in 1967, becoming familiar with the circle around art gallery owner Robert Fraser (whose Duke Street gallery would host John Lennon's first art exhibition in 1968). Through Fraser, Anger met pop singer and Rolling Stones intimate Marianne Faithfull, recently divorced from John Dunbar, owner of the Indica Gallery, just off Duke Street, St James's, at 6 Mason's Yard. Marianne would play Lilith in Anger's long-running film project *Lucifer Rising*, which also featured *Performance* director Donald Cammell as Osiris. Following a meeting with Anger in 1973, the music was originally scored by Jimmy Page of Led Zeppelin. Owner of a London occult bookshop, Page was attracted to a project that venerated Crowley's image and that attempted to realign the image of "Lucifer" not as utterly evil horror-villain "Satan," but as angelic Bringer of Light, archetypal rebel. Back in the late Sixties, Anger had wanted Mick Jagger to play Lucifer, but Jagger resisted, though he did let Anger use a bit of his synthesizer experimental music for his art-film *Invocation of My Demon Brother* (1969).

Written between 1928 and 1940, Mikhail Bulgakov's novel *The Master and Margarita* was finally published in 1967. A surreal story, it involved the devil playing fast and loose with events in Moscow after the Russian Revolution. Anger recommended it to Marianne Faithfull, who encouraged her then-boyfriend and lover Mick Jagger to get into it.[1] Such ruminations inspired by Crowley and Anger resulted in the title to the Stones' 1967 psychedelic album *Their Satanic Majesty's Request,* which had hashish, flower power, and magic written all over it, and of course, the following year, the extraordinary song "Sympathy for the Devil" (1968) whose abiding power was evident when the Stones hit giddy heights once more at the Glastonbury Festival of 2013. There might have been sympathy for Lucifer when the song begins but by the time his satanic majesty is making "traps for troubadours, who get killed before they reach Bombay," we may wonder whether sympathy has not been exhausted. It was of course Crowley who wrote how the devil is traditionally the god of any religious group another religious group is opposed to. Kenneth Grant went further than Crowley's generally more cautious remit and declared not only Lucifer's identity with the Graeco-Egyptian god Set (or Seth)-Typhon, but even asserted, without Crowley's warrant, that Set was also to be identified with Crowley's holy guardian angel, Aiwass. This whole string of ambiguities, tendentious interpretations, and errors has left an awful trail of misunderstanding and risk-laden confusion that persists. Lucifer never asked for sympathy, only mercy from the "Father of Lights," according to the book of Enoch (first century BCE to the first century CE, where the fallen angel is called "Azazel"). One might go so far as to suggest one spiritual meaning of the Sixties involves some reassessment of the role of the devil in the formation of religious mythology, for we are generally more doubtful, and perhaps more curious, about his nature now than our forebears were, for whom black was black and white was white. Of those forebears, we must exclude the Decadents, friends and followers of French Symbolist pioneer Baudelaire, who also found light in "Satan-Trisemgistus" (see my book, *Occult Paris: The Lost Magic of the Belle Époque*). For French followers of the Stones, at the time, they must have seemed something of an electric reincarnation of the visionary Decadent and Symbolist movements of the 1880s and 1890s. Association with Decadents was made abundantly clear in Peter Whitehead's film made to accompany the Stones's "We Love You" (1967), where Marianne Faithfull appears as Oscar Wilde and Keith Richards plays a very evil-looking judge, whose wig is comprised of rolled newspaper reports (a fairly subtle reference to the *News of the World*'s informant role in Mick and Keith's arrest for "possession"). The BBC's *Top of the Pops* refused to show the film in August 1967.

Anger got about while in England, visiting ancient sacred sites and performing little rituals. He was a visitor to Keith Richards and Anita Pallenberg's love nest at Redlands in Sussex where Anger made a magic circle on the lawn at dawn. A few years ago, I had the pleasure of meeting Gerald Yorke's son John, and his wife, at Forthampton Court. John Yorke described the Rolling Stones' visit to his father's house, following up on Anger's Crowley leads. Mick apparently asked patrician Gerald if he could "smoke," and was somewhat surprised, after lighting up a shared joint, by Gerald's reminiscence of hemp being a commonplace when he toured the Far East in the 1930s.

And through all this time, we should not forget that as from June 1967, Aleister Crowley was apparently a member of "Sergeant Pepper's" extended nimbus of favorites, if we may take those gathered around the Beatles on Peter Blake and Jan Howarth's unforgettable cover design in that light. There he is, against the blue on the top left in a somewhat touched-up, tinted, colored, and apparently vertically constrained photolithographic copy of Hector Murchison's 1913 photograph made for Crowley's magazine, the *Equinox*. The original was hardly flattering—Crowley had had his head shaved at the time and posed as a guru who meant business—and the copy on the album cover was even less so. The Beast appears to be wearing lipstick, a pop-art Warholian device used at the time for rendering some life, irony, and humor into the fashionable vogue for Victoriana, especially eccentric Victoriana, in which Crowley was perhaps mistakenly classed at the time (his halcyon days were Edwardian, with continued intense work throughout the second, third, and fourth decades of the century).

It may have been Paul McCartney who got Crowley into the act. He was at the time an habitué of Timothy d'Arch Smith's rare-bookselling business in St. John's Wood, where McCartney lived with Jane Asher until July 1968, and Timothy specialized in occult rarities for the cognoscenti, being involved in a "continuing" Hermetic Order of the Golden Dawn group in London, whose members included dear friend of mine, Western esotericist and fountain of lore on London's Sixties magical scene, Dr. Christopher McIntosh. McCartney was at the time tuned in to the counterculture, aspects of which nursed Crowley's memory, though somewhat hampered by paucity of adequate published Crowley material at the time, which itself gave rise to much confusion as to Crowley's life, doctrines, and practices.

When John Lennon left his house at St. George's Hill, Weybridge, in 1968, after divorcing wife Cynthia, a reporter gained access to the house as a prospective buyer, and noted the quantity of books on magic piled up ready for dispatch to new quarters. In one of his last ever interviews (*Newsweek,* 1980) John Lennon paraphrased the Crowleyan doctrine as being his own ethic: "Do what thou wilst, but don't hurt anybody" (the latter injunction being, as far as I can tell, a condensation of the Thelemic "Love is the law, love under will"). Lennon also found it politic to refer to Crowley's influence on his developing thoughts indirectly, a common enough attitude among people who admire the Beast but are unwilling to be tarnished by association by unscrupulous journalism with Crowley's ever controversial reputation. Crowley's work really shakes the establishment to its root, and they will not forgive, only hoping he will be forgotten; he won't be, but they will.

THE BEAST IN SIXTIES AMERICA

By the end of the decade, a *New York Times* review of Crowley's recently published *Confessions* (1969) described Crowley as "the unsung hero of the hippies." This was most unkind to Crowley in several respects.

He believed in orderliness and self-discipline (though not automatic conformity). He loathed laxity, sexual "filth" (that is, manipulative sensual indulgence and libidinous surrender for its own sake), and excessive intoxication in the observance of mystical or magical practices. Presumably the link between the Beast and hippies came with the primary watchword of Crowley's "Thelema" religious system. "Do what thou wilt shall be the whole of the Law." Often shortened to "Do what thou wilt," superficial, skewed hearing renders the injunction as "Do *as* thou wilt" (or "do as you want"). The *what* of "Do what thou wilt" rather refers to the aspirant's duty to discern his or her "True Will," on the basis that the core of the human star is divine, and therefore endowed with will, and the proper destiny of the individual is to live freely in accordance with that highest source. The Thelemite should find in the experience of True Will a "perfect freedom," for that is, according to the theory, authentic realization of the being, and of being itself. "Be yourself" is close. "Love, and do what thou wilt" (Saint Augustine) is perfectly Thelemite. It has been said that artists are natural Thelemites, often quite eligible candidates for François Rabelais's "Abbey of Thelema" in the French Renaissance physician's early sixteenth-century novel, *Gargantua and Pantagruel.* "Thy will be done on earth as it is in heaven" (the Paternoster) is consistent and precise, understood in the light of the gnosis. The doctrine insists that True Wills cannot conflict as "Thou hast no right but to do thy will," not to do others' wills for them, nor dictate what others' true wills should be.

On the other hand, hippie behavior in some respects might be considered to conform to those positive attributes of "child psychology" Crowley regarded as typifying tendencies of the "New Aeon of Horus," and may be seen as developments in the growth of the "Child." Horus is not fully mature, but is arguably no worse for that!

It is a shame that Crowley's legacy was not better organized in the Sixties, for many pitfalls of the "hippie trail" could have been avoided, and perhaps a great deal of the energy accrued through the decade would not have been wasted in a *fin-de-décennie* splurge of often mindless excess. Crowley had a plan for the future. On the other hand, one should recall that freedom lovers of the time were faced with a concrete opposition of extensive repressive systems, not imaginary ones, and it is also true to say that for a significant number of inner space travelers, the road of excess did eventually lead to the palace of wisdom, as Blake promised, for one rarely knows what is enough until one has had too much.

Crowley had died in 1947, strongly desiring—as preserved correspondence makes clear—that Grady Louis McMurtry participate in an authoritative capacity in his OTO affairs in the United States, subject to agreement with Crowley's immediate successor Karl Johannes Germer, and in any case McMurtry was to succeed Germer as O.H.O. (Outer Head of the Order). The German Iron Cross–decorated Germer proved inadequate to the task he inherited, being prone to aridity of interpretation, paranoia (exacerbated by FBI observation), and a gift for alienating people. Having little respect for America or its inhabitants, he was neither a peacemaker nor a negotiator, and by the time of his painful demise in West Point, California, in 1962, the OTO was hardly functioning at all. What is more, he had, predictably, fallen out with Crowley's intended caliph (after Germer), McMurtry, who involved himself in other matters, including his U.S. Army career (McMurtry served in Korea), and subsequent teaching posts at UCLA and elsewhere. Germer had, however, found a willing acolyte in Brazilian Thelemite Marcelo Ramos Motta (1931–1987), whose subsequent opinion of Californian Thelemites would show every sign of his master's acute paranoia. Motta determined to take a cue from a letter sent to him by Germer's distraught widow, Sascha, on October 30, 1962:

To Marcelo Motta,

Our Beloved Master is Dead

He Succumbed October 25. 8:55 p.m. under horrifying Circumstances

You are the Follower

Please take it from me, as he died in My Arms and it was his last wishes! [*sic*]

Who The Heir of the Library is [Crowley's collection and other OTO archives], I do not know up to now.[2]

McMurtry was not made aware of Germer's death and the OTO was practically nonexistent. Motta was certainly not recognized as O.H.O. by the few Californian members.

In 1967, Sascha Germer's home was robbed by members of a "pirate" lodge known as the "Solar Lodge." This group resulted from Geraldine "Jean" Brayton's having been initiated into the OTO's Minerval Degree in late 1962—just after Germer's death—by Agape Lodge members Ray and Mildred Burlingame, without any OTO authority whatsoever. Ray had never been chartered to initiate, and Brayton's "Solar Lodge" enjoyed no valid affiliation to the OTO. It was, according to James Wasserman, "as invalid as her gang's behavior was corrupt."[3] Solar Lodge members had stolen much of the OTO archive, Crowley's Golden Dawn robes, several of Crowley's original diaries, and much else of great value that had been sent to Germer when he and wife Sascha lived in the Hamptons, after Crowley's estate was settled in England by Louis Wilkinson and Gerald Yorke.

McMurtry was alerted to the 1967 burglary and drugging of Sascha. Brayton's group secreted material at their ranch in the Sonoran Desert, California, which attracted members from the hippie belt between San Francisco and L.A. (urban myths persist in repeating uninformed journalistic accounts that Charles Manson spent time there, leading to utterly erroneous statements in several works intent on confusing Manson, and the Solar Lodge, with the OTO).[4] McMurtry's investigation pinned the archive robbery on Brayton's group, despite police concern that Sascha Germer seemed so unbalanced she might have done the whole thing herself. Most of the stolen material was destroyed in a fire at the Solar Lodge ranch in 1969.

Fortunately, the original manuscript of *The Book of the Law* escaped that fate. The Brayton group had overlooked it when they rifled the shelves of Sascha's home. It had been kept in either a desk drawer or small filing cabinet with other personal and business documents. When McMurtry obtained court authorization to go to Sascha's house in pursuance of Germer's will that OTO property be restored to the order, McMurtry didn't find the box containing *The Book of the Law*. It might still have been held by the county administrator, for most of the box's contents related to the kinds of documents used by an administrator in winding up an intestate individual's estate, and was probably returned to Sascha's house later. Somehow, this box wound up in a basement in Oakland, where by something like a miracle the material was discovered and, most remarkably, restored to the Order, so that the prophetic writings written down by Crowley in April 1904 today survive in proper care.

At one of Grady McMurty's remarkable meetings in London with Crowley in 1944, Crowley told his intended "caliph" that when Grady saw young people living in tents and dressing in oriental garb, he would know his work was to begin.

Realizing the depths of near extinction into which the OTO had sunk, Grady McMurtry assumed the long task of restoring life and health to the OTO. He formally accepted the grade of O.H.O. in 1971, supported by the few remaining members of the order, as well as by Gerald Yorke in England.

The personal transformation of Grady McMurtry into active O.H.O. is told in one of its aspects in a remarkable story vouchsafed to me personally at a Manhattan restaurant in 2012 by his successor in

Fig. 27.1. Grady McMurtry circa 1971.

that role, William Breeze. Though the events described here following did not take place in the 1960s, they belong to the story of the consciousness shift of that era among many young people.

At the time Grady moved back to the Bay Area to investigate the robbery of the OTO Archive from Sasha Germer, he was an instructor at Georgetown University working at the U.S. Department of Labor. Clean cut, black horn-rims, military bearing and speech patterns, crease in the trousers, and shined shoes. When he arrived in the Haight he was an alien—and they had wall hangings and dressed in loose oriental clothing, which took him back to what Crowley had said.

He had not tried LSD but had heard about it and asked his host, Chuck (one of the Level Press people, with Llee Heflin), if he could take some. He was given a tab which he took, and sat and waited. Time passed, and he got impatient when nothing happened, so he asked for more, remarking that he was a large man. So they gave him another tab. And left the bag on the table. After more time passed, with nothing happening, he got impatient again and without asking anyone, shook out the content of the bag and swallowed the lot. Grady said the bag had many more LSD tabs plus at least one hit of STP that he didn't know about. He took all of them. He later recalled eleven tabs total according to one person who heard the story from him (Bill Heidrick).

One of his hosts came in and noticed that he was on the floor writhing around. No doubt the empty bag was noticed as well. It seems that Grady was trying without much success to take off his clothes. Whether they helped him change or not, I'm not sure, but it was suggested that they take him down to the Pacific (reportedly the area where Playland used to be) for a walk, set and setting and all that, where he could cool out.

The Pacific is deceptively named—pacific at times but given to sudden freak waves of some size. Grady was walking along the beach, with his friend tagging along nearby, when a huge wave came in and covered him, and the undertow dragged him out to sea. His friend looked for him, walking down the beach, calling his name, with no results, and after some time had passed another big wave came in and deposited Grady on the beach, blue from cold and not breathing. An ambulance was called and he was taken to hospital. He was admitted dead on arrival, taken to the basement morgue, and put on an exam slab with his toe tag filled out.

An unknown amount of time later, he woke up alone in the morgue on the slab—peaking on who knows how many micrograms of acid. If there had been ten tabs and they were Orange Sunshine or similar, then maybe 3,500 micrograms—about three times the typical max dose of a very experienced LSD user, the threshold being about 80 micrograms and the typical dose being about 350. Plus he apparently took STP, a rare psychedelic, and one in which the trip lasts for several days.

But however the experience ended in the hospital—probably he was given thorazine and so on—he suffered terrible aftereffects from this, including memory loss, profound personality change, and a complete overnight change in appearance—the hair and beard of course grew to give the Grady we know. He struggled with depression and made at least one suicide attempt in the months following this. His marriage—not good to start with—disintegrated. But the Grady that had arrived from Washington, D.C., would have gotten precisely nowhere in rebuilding the OTO. It is only because Grady underwent his transformation that he succeeded in reaching and relating to the young people in the new counterculture, the people who made the OTO renaissance a reality. Grady had had a very powerful ego structure and a strong personality to match—even Crowley would be left exhausted by his company after a few hours, and the few recorded accounts of his early meetings with some of the young people out there were not encouraging—to them he was an old guy with old books but sort of without a clue as to what was going on. That changed, and he became a countercultural icon in his way.

Aside from the obvious *Egyptian Book of the Dead* theme of all this, it changed Grady fundamentally. Where before his letters to

Yorke were written in clipped, military staccato, businesslike in his way, they changed to rambling missives loaded with counter-cultural slang and mystical references. Yorke became alarmed and suggested politely that Grady should take it easy with the drug experimentation.

Crowley's rather vague prophecy carried quite a sting. But he rose to the occasion, as you British probably still say!

Aspects of the tangled story of what happened to Crowley's Order in the Sixties are revealed by James Wasserman, now a respected, leading OTO member, in his important record *In the Center of the Fire: A Memoir of the Occult 1966–1989* (2012). Indeed, of most interest to us is that to look at Wasserman's life in the Sixties gives us intimate insight into the spiritual meaning of the Sixties as it happened on the ground, so to speak, for James Wasserman's spiritual quest brought him into proximity to several of the key figures referred to in this book—artist Harry Smith, Allen Ginsburg, the Fugs, Jerry Garcia, and Weiser's Bookstore, Manhattan—and Jim's progress exhibits some of the deeper contradictions of the era. Wasserman was also witness to the Woodstock Festival, but quite properly, cannot remember much about it! His life at the time encapsulates what is almost an object lesson in the contradictions and the largely unrecognized spiritually positive thrust of the era.

WASSERMAN'S QUEST

Born in 1948, James Wasserman was taken as a boy to the Café Figaro on Bleecker and Macdougal Streets in Greenwich Village where he told his parents he wanted to be a beatnik. Graduating from high school and looking for a college, he chose Antioch College, 1 Morgan Place, Yellow Springs, Ohio, because the students had long hair and the girls were as "cool" looking as those he'd seen in the Village.

Founded in 1850 by the interdenominational Unitarian and evangelical-backed "Christian Connection," Antioch College is still a progressive liberal-arts institution operating a cooperative curriculum whereby lessons are interspersed with work on social-improvement programs. On his first visit there, Wasserman met his cousin Paul, whose parents Wasserman's disapproved of as they were Communists, whereas his own were first Depression-era socialists, and afterward, Roosevelt/Stevenson Democrats. Paul, on the other hand, was campus leader of the Students for a Democratic Society (SDS), founded in 1960 and the decade's most successful New Left group, in Wasserman's view. Through Paul, James met Jeff Jones who in time would join the violent hard-left "Weather Underground,"* emerging from hiding decades later as environmental activist and consultant to the New York State governor's office![5]

James Wasserman entered Antioch, aged eighteen, in June 1966, taking a class from civil rights activist, Larry Rubin, who'd suffered beatings from Southern sheriffs. The system he enrolled in was a five-year alternating work-study program, so in fall '66, he went to work with civil rights attorney Bill Higgs, last white attorney still working for the SNCC (the Student Non-Violent Coordinating Committee), Stokely Carmichael having proclaimed Black Power in the spring. Higgs too had suffered from white reactionaries in Mississippi before leaving for the capital around 1963.

Wasserman smoked pot for the first time that summer. A practice then enveloped in transcendental mystique, James recalls people's naïveté, referring to a lyric he'd heard from Jesse Colin Young and the Youngbloods: "Come on people now, smile on your brother, everybody get together, try to love one another right now." Within a few years, three "Weathermen" were killed in an explosion at a Greenwich Village bomb-making factory, following which, Wasserman's acquaintance Jeff Jones fled into the real underground.

Wasserman's experience with Bill Higgs proved decisive. Many of the people he met coming to Higgs "should have been in a zoo."[6] Why, he reflected, replace one gang of sociopaths with another? When he asked Higgs whether opposing the Vietnam War meant supporting communism, Higgs replied that he did not necessarily reject Communism. Similar sentiments would be found among associates of activist Tariq

---

*The name "Weathermen" comes from Bob Dylan: "You don't need a weatherman to know which way the wind blows" in his song "Subterranean Homesick Blues" (1965).

Ali who organized anti-U.S. government demonstrations in London in '67 and '68; Ali wanted the Vietcong to win so as to inflict a defeat on "capitalism."

By the end of 1966, Wasserman informed his parents that "the only true means of redeeming humanity and ending suffering was through individual spiritual development with meditation and inner-directed awareness."[7] In early '67, while studying Existentialism and "Absurdist Morality" with SDS past-president Carl Oglesby, Wasserman took LSD, while reading Alan Watts's *The Joyous Cosmology:* "I did make continuous progress in self-awareness," reflected Wasserman over forty years later, "but often at the cost of considerable agony."[8]

During spring and summer 1967 he worked at Wiltwyck School for Boys, specializing in psychologically disturbed pupils ("delinquents") aged eight to fourteen. One of Eleanor Roosevelt's favorite charities, it had moved from Esopus (very close to Esopus Island on the Hudson in upper New York State where Crowley had undergone a "Great Magical Retirement" in 1918) to Eleanor Roosevelt Campus, Yorktown Heights, New York. One of Wasserman's coworkers there shared digs on Jones Street and West 4th Street, Greenwich Village. Of the other two Antioch students living there, one worked for *Time,* the other *Newsweek.* While living in the Village, Wasserman saw the Fugs, "one of the all time great bands" at the Players Theatre, Macdougal Street, whom we last saw at the levitation of the Pentagon in the previous chapter. According to Wasserman: "They [the Fugs] represented a transition between the beat and hippie phenomena." Fugs spokesman Ed Sanders and Tuli Kupferberg ran the Peace Eye Bookstore on the Lower East Side and assisted the *East Village Other* underground paper. In 1992, Ed and Tuli joined Allen Ginsberg, Peter Orlovsky, and other "Bohemian luminaries" in attending the Gnostic Mass the OTO performed for Harry Smith at Saint Mark's church.

Only a year earlier, you could have seen an unknown Jimi Hendrix (then "Jimmy James") jamming at the Café Wha and other places in the Village, and booked him for a few bucks or a hot meal. Since July's Monterey Festival, Jimi was now a U.S. overnight sensation, and had given new hope to Steve Paul, manager of the Scene Club in the Village when Jimi played a special-request gig for him on July 3, 1967, blowing hip band the Seeds off the stage with his stratoclastic brilliance. That same summer, Wasserman, was but fifteen feet from hero Jerry Garcia and the Grateful Dead when they played a small club called the Bitter End on Bleecker Street. The poor Dead had received a pasting at the Monterey Pop Festival, having to follow Jimi Hendrix, who'd given a total knock 'em dead performance, setting fire to his guitar at the climax of "Wild Thing" to mixed consternation and delight.

After a bad trip, Wasserman moved to an apartment on 7th Street on the seedy Lower East Side, not at all fashionable in those days. He encountered the "smack scene" and some way-out and way-down characters, shooting amphetamines and God knows what else. Wasserman, despite a hatred for needles, injected himself in the interests of "experimentation." A shared interest in such habits brought him into contact with a girl entwined with the Warhol Factory on Saint Mark's Place. Her name was Barbara, and she was heavily into speed.

In fall 1967, James moved off campus with good friend Brian Crawford into a college dormitory, "laced with drugs, women, and spiritual seeking." Brian was an atheist, James was not, but both were committed "to the psychedelic lifestyle."[9] Joining psychedelics to sexuality gave Wasserman an insight into Crowley's "sexual magick" whose first key was to expand consciousness beyond "the boundaries of the ego."[10] Someone called Jesse introduced Wasserman to vegetarianism, and he's been one ever since. Meanwhile, friend Dennis Deems, whom he'd met in February 1967, made his time at Yellow Springs more engaging by sharing information on Aleister Crowley, yoga, and Kabbalah. Wasserman didn't think he'd ever heard of Crowley until that meeting. There was little possibility of people finding anything. There was Castle's edition of Crowley's *Magick in Theory and Practice* (first published in 1929), but for anything else you had to have funds and access to Weiser's Bookstore in New York. As Wasserman explained to me recently: "It wasn't so much that the books were so expensive (they were). It's more that they were so rare, so obscure, so unknown, with no sources or references pointing people anywhere. It was only a couple of years later when the blossoming of published reprints and new editions began that a person could begin to make sense of Crowley's literary corpus."

In 1967, Jerry Kay of Xeno Publications printed *The Book of the Law,* but the floodgates didn't open till John Symonds and Kenneth Grant's edited version of *The Confessions of Aleister Crowley* appeared in 1969, when people got a taste of what they'd been missing, or what mainstream culture had been trying to avoid since it was written during the Twenties. That year Weiser also published Crowley's study of the tarot, *The Book of Thoth,* but the pack of cards to which it referred was still not available, despite its images having been completed and exhibited in 1944!

James was obsessed at the time with the idea of becoming a Catholic priest, especially absurd as he was Jewish and not a believer in Christianity. A dozen years later, he did become a priest, in the Gnostic Catholic Church (E.G.C.) and has been "passionately involved" ever since.[11]

Back in Yellow Springs, over thirty students were arrested after a "narc" infiltrated students digs at Yellow Springs. "What part of private nonviolent behavior do these busybodies not understand?" comments Wasserman today.[12] It was enough to make any young person involved paranoid. Privacy should be private.

Down from heroin abuse, James dropped out of fall 1967 classes, and, on his way back east, suddenly saw his life whole, but in the third person singular. Years later, on Grady McMurtry's suggestion, Wasserman compared that experience with a similar one associated with Jack Parsons's mental breakdown in Agape Lodge.

In the winter of '67–'68, Wasserman contracted hepatitis from needles while trying to hold down a job working at an Antioch bookstore. The physician called to attend him called his patient a "dirty hippie" and wrote to his draft board "assuming it was his patriotic duty to keep me out of the army and I received a 1Y classification."[13]

By spring 1968, James had a new girlfriend, Mary, whose kindly parents lived in New Jersey. The couple decided on a trip to Boulder, Colorado. Near Boulder in a small mountain town lived a dealer Wasserman had known on the Lower East Side. Visiting him, James and Mary were astonished to find folk singer Judy Collins and musician Steven Stills of the Buffalo Springfield there, both Laurel Canyon residents, and central to the scene that had raved over Hendrix at Monterey the previous July, dreaming, for a while, that maybe anything was possible. They "smoked some excellent grass" but Wasserman to his regret felt he was rude to Judy Collins, as he was trying too hard to be cool about meeting her, instead of honestly showing how honored he was to meet the lady in person. "Cool" is not always cool.

By the summer of '68, student rebellion had almost become a global cliché, following the "Prague Spring" when Czech premier Dubček relaxed Communist rule in Czechoslovakia, bringing democracy and hope to the people, who felt a profound need for spiritual, and by extension, practical, freedom.

Meanwhile in Germany, student revolutionary leader Rudi Dutschke (1940–1979) survived an assassination attempt on April 11 at the hands of a young anti-Communist. Student supporters blamed the act on Axel Springer's conservative newspaper publishing empire, which was running a vociferous anti-student campaign. Influenced by Marxism, Dutschke was in fact of pious Lutheran background, his democratic socialism rooted in a vivid spiritual sense of what he saw as Jesus's real message to liberate people within and without. For Dutschke, Jesus was the true exemplar of committed revolutionary, attempting profound change from within. Dutschke advocated the democratization of Communist countries. The effect of his being shot in the head only radicalized student positions further, and as in the States, there were factions now advocating violent overthrow of what they perceived was an irredeemably wicked system of manipulation and public mind control, exemplified by the reality of the Vietnam War.

Before the Prague Spring ended, the events of May '68 shook the world when students in Paris nearly succeeded in overthrowing the government of Charles de Gaulle in the name of a heady mix of socialism, anarchism, and hippie ideals—so near, and yet so far!

On August 22, Soviet tanks crushed, if not the hopes of Czech youth, then certainly those hopes' immediate realization. Some thirty

Czech demonstrators against the invasion died, and 300 were injured. The Soviet Union understood that much of the New Left posed as much of a problem to hard-line authoritarian Communism as did the Politburo's traditional enemies. They weren't going to tolerate a "May '69" in Moscow or any other part of the Soviet Empire. Western reactionary press tended to see New Left factions as being but a few steps from being effectively, if not intentionally, Soviet collaborators.

Wasserman found himself with Mary in San Francisco that summer. In particular, he remembers standing amid a Black Power Rally in Golden Gate Park. Things had certainly changed in tone from the previous year's summer of love. Wasserman suddenly realized in his stoned state it was "a violent Maoist Communist" movement he was observing, but nonetheless found himself joining in with their mimicking of a Nazi salute, yelling "Fuck you, Alioto!"—Alioto being San Francisco's mayor. Then he realized with a start that a Jew had no business mimicking

Fig. 27.2. James Wasserman in the Sixties.
Photo courtesy of James Wasserman.

Nazi salutes, and besides, why ever should he insult a mayor of a city he'd only just come to visit? Things got no better for James. By the end of his visit, he heard that Nixon was elected and became "aware of a sense of complete alienation."[14]

Between fall 1968 and the end of winter 1969, he experienced repeated dreams that he was an apostle of a new revolution to help humanity. The dreams persisted for months; he also had a bad experience with mescaline. Dennis Deems and his new wife and baby girl, now living in Portland, Oregon, confirmed his dreams, insisting "there was a group of people charged with altering consciousness, and I was one of them."[15] Mary did not accept the messianic calling, and the two agreed their intimate relationship was over. James returned with Mary to her parents in New Jersey, at which time he realized there was something seriously wrong with his mind function. His mental state was awry. "I underwent a complete mental breakdown."[16] He was paranoid, hallucinating he was being followed by federal agents. Paranoia seemed contagious in the States for young people engaged in searching America for truth at this time, especially if the search involved drugs, whether their own or the "narcs.'" To be seen with long hair was as much a target for harassment in some places as being black in the "wrong place" in another.

James's parents did not send him to a hospital but cared for him at home. In spring 1969, he was working in his father's plastics factory, and things began to improve. However, a visit to Dennis and Claire's in New Rochelle again confirmed that his dreams about participating in a group whose duty was to change consciousness were valid. Dennis advised James to obtain from Weiser's Bookstore Aleister Crowley's *777*, a book of kabbalistic, astrological, and mythological correspondences that showed an esoteric unity behind Eastern and Western systems of thought and magic. Wasserman went to New York to see a girlfriend, and to see the Band at the Fillmore East. He took too much mescaline and imagined Garth Hudson with his bushy beard behind his organ surrounded by lights as no less a personage than God Almighty. This kind of thing should worry rock stars, because what is seen as God one day can turn very black the next, to minds unseated by chemistry or psychosis, or both.

In summer 1969, Wasserman read Crowley's *Magick in Theory and Practice* from cover to cover, and then read it again, something he'd never done before. The book, he was convinced, had "extraordinary value," though the reader understood little of what he was reading, so allusive was Crowley's prose, so extensive the referents and knowledge the Beast took for granted in his readers. Then, Wasserman felt, having grasped the meaning of the pentagrammaton (the Hebrew name of God with Hebrew letter *Schin* in the middle, making the name audible as "Yeheschevah": Hebrew name of Jesus), that he was entitled to a vision of Crowley, which duly occurred, as Crowley was to him suddenly as vivid as "the keys on my typewriter," though he was also taking speed at the time, he admitted. Wasserman went to Weiser's, and obtained their new editions of *The Book of Thoth* and *The Equinox of the Gods*. Bookshop founder Samuel Weiser had worked with Germer in the Fifties on binding some of Crowley's printed sheets.

In August, Wasserman and friend Claus drove up to Woodstock for the rock festival. "For my part, I got so high circulating among the crowd of psychedelic revelers that I did not remember Mary having been there with me until she told me when we met again some twenty years later."[17] This anecdote of Jim's is of some interest to me personally, for back in my college days at Oxford in 1980, I had an idea for making a movie about Crowley. I saw the first scene as taking place on the early Monday morning, as Hendrix closed Woodstock with his shredded version of "The Star-Spangled Banner," and people had already started to leave, and a cold breeze was blowing refuse about. And the camera, at soil level, comes up close to an open book, discarded amid the garbage, whose leaves are blowing in the wind. It is *The Book of the Law,* and the pages stop blowing a moment, and we see the words: "Love is the law, love under will." CUT.

James Wasserman has spent years between then and now developing his magical and spiritual knowledge, committing his life and energy to reestablishing the OTO after a long hiatus, with Grady McMurtry, William Breeze, and a band of generally loveable, hard-working well-wishers in New York, California, and elsewhere. Though he had for a long time operated in association with Germer's somewhat demented "follower" (as a grief-stricken Sascha called him) Marcelo Motta, and occasionally represented Motta's views in negotiation with publisher Donald Weiser (Wasserman worked at Weiser's, learning the book trade), the passage of time and mounting evidence led to his definitive move to the McMurtry side of the argument, realizing Motta was not only paranoid, and armed with a very weak argument for supremacy, but had attempted to incite at least one of his own representatives to arson and murder. Wasserman describes Motta now as "a fallen adept." It happens.

James Wasserman has also managed to overcome completely his destructive drug habits and wishes his example would deter others from getting involved, or at least urge them to face up to what they're doing, but doubts his experience will have any effect. Truth is as much a casualty of drug abuse as it is of war. There is, he believes, after as much experience as a still-living person might claim, no way of successfully combining hard drug use with spiritual attainment, or a life well lived, a conclusion Crowley came to in 1924 after terrible ordeals with cocaine and heroin, but still found himself unable to kick heroin for long, for all his very exceptional willpower. In his case, there is some excuse, in that his family doctor, Dr. Batty-Shaw of Harley Street, in 1919 prescribed heroin quite legally to combat debilitating asthma, and Crowley found his severe bouts were only relieved by this drug and one other available only in Germany when he lived there 1930–32, but impossible to obtain in England thereafter. Nevertheless, an experienced junkie might smile at this reasoning as another example of an addicted person's perennial self-deception.

Being philosophical, Wasserman is inclined to justify some degree of stimulant use on the basis of what it took for his generation to escape from the materialist vacuum of postwar false consciousness, and expects today's youth not to require extreme measures, for in most of the West they are now at liberty to embrace spiritual paths of individual expression, in thought, dress, and hairstyle, but if they can, let them bear in mind that the freedom that has become available is owed to many hard battles faced and fought in the Sixties and Seventies. Now young people have the freedom, what are they going to do with it? Repeat the errors of the past? Make even more catastrophically stupid choices, such as extremist Islamic brainwash? It's no good just blaming the establishment this time.

Do what thou wilt shall be the whole of the Law. It's not so far off now from *being* the Law, is it? For those who understand it.

I recently asked James Wasserman to give his own personal answer to the question: *What is the spiritual meaning of the 1960s?* This is his answer to my question:

> The spiritual meaning of the Sixties is a mixed bag for me. I see elements of optimism, spirituality, and idealism in contrast with hypocrisy, childishness, and cynicism. Sorry: "turn on, tune in, and drop out" is not a legitimate interpretation of the bodhisattva vow. On the other hand, few Westerners even knew what the B.V. was before the Sixties. America, at least, was a different place in the Fifties. A rigid repressive conformity and cookie-cutter aspiration seemed the norm. The horrors of World War II encouraged families to seek security. Men traded their uniforms and military discipline for the regimentation and adherence to authority that was familiar to them. There was little room for rebellion among a generation that literally had the hell scared out of it by a fight for survival against gigantic odds and faced the very real specter of nuclear annihilation.
>
> *Father Knows Best* may have had a universal appeal, but *Rebel without a Cause* lurked in the dark underbelly of our culture. Bill Haley and the Comets rocked us all. But when Elvis leapt onto the scene, the world went nuts. Shaking and seducing, bringing a black soul beat to white rock 'n' roll, the King flayed the nerves of the Establishment, serenading the young like the Pied Piper. Buddy Holly followed, dragging the reminder of mortality in his wake. I remember the Beatles on the Ed Sullivan Show in 1964. The next day, one of the kids in our high school combed his hair down in dangerous imitation of the Fab Four. It was a time of awakening.
>
> Then LSD literally blew the lid off, and we never looked back.

The collective unconscious was rocketed into the fifth dimension overnight. Tie-dye and hippie beads, psychedelic rock and sexual liberation, the peace movement and antiauthoritarian ethics, native ethnic culture and holistic consciousness, communes and crash pads. Zen Buddhism and Indian gurus replaced whatever remained of Sunday school. Acid was like a cultural nuclear explosion with the youth as Ground Zero. Acid decimated the last vestiges of the Fifties. We, who had hidden under our desks in countless drills of nuclear war preparation, woke up to the fact that we'd have been fried crouching with our heads between arms under our desks just as easily as if we had been standing about or sitting in our chairs. It was a chilling insight into the phoniness of the world we knew.

But I also can't shake the corruption of "our" side. I read the House Committee on Un-American Activities transcripts of the antiwar hearings of 1967 at the time and was nauseated by Jerry Rubin and his self-aggrandizing behavior. He went on to become an overweight stockbroker who got killed jaywalking in front of his penthouse apartment. Abbie Hoffman, who I found more interesting, committed suicide—not exactly the behavior of an enlightened adept whose path I should be following. Leftist hero Eldridge Cleaver "practiced" his rape skills on black women before graduating to white women. Even in 1968 when I read his *Soul on Ice,* I thought he should go fuck himself. Carl Oglesby, cofounder and past president of SDS, told us in class at Antioch in 1967 that he had punched his mother. Maybe I am revealing myself as a bourgeois, but I was mortified. He described himself as a Marxist and I still fail to understand how that works with the Bill of Rights. When I reconnected with him briefly in the 1990s to suggest a book collaboration, I found a bitter man.

The Berkeley Free Speech Movement was "before my time," in 1962, but it is depressing to see it morph into the modern, politically correct Speech Code Movement. Today, Berkeley fascists run around campus with sledge hammers, tire irons, and boxes of matches. The peace and love generation with flowers in their hair raising the Safe Space Snowflakes. No thank you! Maybe it's because Uranus and

Pluto are in square today rather than the conjunction they formed during the Sixties.

Three people who were sincere shining examples of the Sixties to me were older than the rest of us. I was close to Harry Smith and Don Snyder, and ran into Tuli Kupferberg from time to time in New York City. All seemed like real non-sellouts. Harry was a true magical adept in every sense of the word. Don was the quintessential artist, a photographic genius whose work demands preservation and exhibition. Tuli Kupferberg struck me then and now as a true rebel, a poet who maintained his integrity in the face of much suffering and temptation. And I frankly love the commitment to art, growth, and survival shown by the more popular Leonard Cohen, Bob Dylan, and the Rolling Stones. None of them ever stopped doing what they loved best, Cohen nearly to the day of his death. Many other Sixties folks have also not stopped, despite the process of "growing up." I have a couple of precious friends who survived those days. They are as beloved today as they were then. We aren't as close as we used to be, the consequence of loss of proximity and adulthood, and we have our disagreements (mainly on politics), but we have never lost the affection and enthusiasm we shared half a century ago.

The Sixties lightened the girders of the soul of the West. As Crowley wrote to Grady McMurtry in 1944, "1965 e.v. should be a critical period in the development of the Child Horus!" I hope we can get beyond the Collectivist Qliphoth of the period to the Immortal goal of human Liberty—which I believe to be the true spiritual message of the Sixties.[18]

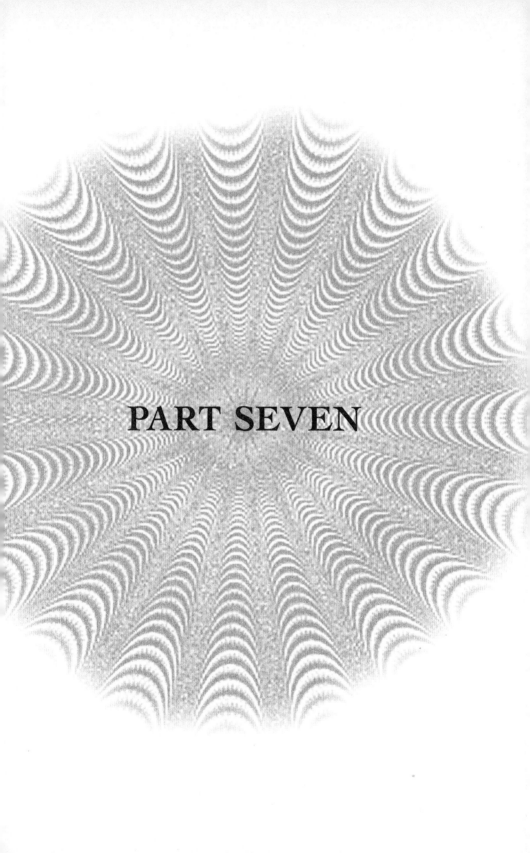

PART SEVEN

TWENTY-EIGHT

New York

He took me past the outskirts of infinity
And when he brought me back, he gave me Venus witch's
ring

FROM "VOODOO CHILE" BY JIMI HENDRIX, 1968

Badly run, frequently run down, ragged at the edges and often dirty, New York still had character and some glamour in 1968–69, and despite social tremors was still churning change in the midst of a hurricane decade that had seen its street-arteries run with the crosstown traffic of any number of contradictory expectations and fears. Manhattan kept them all bottled up nicely, until the corks popped.

Publisher Ehud Sperling, then aged eighteen to nineteen, remembers it as a tough place that nonetheless had fingers black and white on the pulse of spiritual energy. Ehud started going to Steve Paul's nightclub the Scene on a regular basis. He became friendly with Steve Paul who took him under his wing. Steve Paul would invite Ehud to Max's Kansas City's back room where all the celebrities would hang out. Ehud has particularly fond memories of Max's Kansas City, a late-running club and restaurant at 213 Park Avenue South that hosted space for poets, artists, politicos, theatricals, and above all, in this period, rock 'n' rollers. Opened in 1965(!) by Mickey Ruskin (1933–1983), Andy Warhol held court there, and "anybody who was anybody" in the underground art scene would be dropping in at some time or other, lest they missed something. Ehud remembers meeting Lou Reed upstairs (the Velvet Underground performed there regularly).

Along with Lou Reed, Ehud says, he met many other luminaries of the underground rock and arts scene. Steve would come to Max's as well as visit with radio-company executives in his signature blue terry-cloth robe. He wore this bathrobe wherever he went. That was distinctive Steve, and everyone who knew him recognized him by his robe.

When Steve had to close the Scene because of extortion pressure from the mob he became a full-time talent agent. In Texas he discovered Johnny and Edgar Winter. When Steve brought Johnny and Edgar Winter to New York he asked Ehud to help them find an apartment and assist them with moving in.

Ehud would often drive up on weekends to an estate on the Hudson, which was rented for Johnny and Edgar, where there would be jam sessions and get togethers with other people in the underground art scene at that time. In 1968 Johnny Winter jammed with Hendrix (and a drunken, rambling, foul-mouthed Jim Morrison) at Steve Paul's Scene club in the Village, with Randy Hobbs on bass, and Randy Z on drums, with Hendrix improvising a version of Lennon-McCartney's psychedelic "Tomorrow Never Knows" amid other wild numbers. Winter became known as one of the greatest contemporary blues musicians, right up there on the scale of guitar god Eric Clapton. Edgar was an equally good musician who played the saxophone. Steve Paul became Johnny and Edgar Winter's manager, and after their careers took off, he would eventually patronize a young Patti Smith in the early Seventies.

In the late Sixties, a then-prominent FM rock DJ invited Ehud to bacchanalian orgies in the area of New York later known as Soho—at the time a ghost town of lofts amid light industry. Like many underground artists of the era, Ehud had a loft there. The Chelsea Hotel was another venue Ehud visited for late-night parties with Johnny Winter and Steve Paul, meeting Tinkerbell (Jeni Lee Veronica Visser), Ultra Violet (Isabelle Collin Dufresne), Viva (Janet Susan Mary Hoffman), and other members of the Andy Warhol film scene.

During this period, rock got considerably "harder," its mood darker.

Ehud saw protopunk band, the MC5, fresh and radical bursting out of Detroit in 1968 with a contract with Elektra Records, sacrificed to principle and industry paranoia. Their 1968 live album *Kick out the Jams* originally opened with lead vocalist Rob Tyner hurling this injunction at the audience: "Kick out the Jams, motherfucker!" This was too much for Elektra Records. Most who heard at least the first part of the battle cry took it to indicate a desire to break free from establishment constraints, to confront authority, and hit back in general. Reflecting on the phrase in subsequent years, Tyner opined that the original context was a reference to bands that hogged Detroit stages with longwinded jam sessions, as well as to a perceived laziness in British bands on tour in the States who didn't put in the exhausting raw energy demanded of a committed rock 'n' roller. In other words, the MC5 were ahead of punk by some eight years!

As for the kind of commitment demanded by the MC5, it was pretty radical, to say the least. Manager John Sinclair (about whom John Lennon would pen a rather uninspired, if generous, campaign song in 1972) would be busted by the feds for possession of two joints after it became known he'd struck a deal with Huey P. Newton of the Black Panthers to establish a White Panther Party dedicated to militant leftism and confrontation with the establishment in the name of all the people. That put Sinclair high on J. Edgar Hoover's target list for FBI suppression.*

When the MC5 performed at the 1968 Democratic National Convention, the gig erupted into chaos when police "rioted," incensed by the band's incessant stance of aggressive, rasping rock, unnerved by the radical vibes in general. Hoover was determined to keep Panther influence adrift from white antiwar and New Left movements, fearing revolution. Such fear was a factor in the election of Republican Richard Nixon in November '68.

---

*John Lennon would put out a song in defense of Sinclair on his and Yoko's *Sometime in New York City* album (Apple, 1972), entitled "John Sinclair," a brave move at a time when Lennon himself had been targeted as an undesirable radical by the FBI.

NEW YORK'S ART AND LITERATURE SCENE

It was not all rock 'n' roll. Spiritual movement was evident in the worlds of literature and avant-garde art in the city. Ehud Sperling enjoyed hanging out at the Gotham Book Mart at 41 West 47th Street, a bookstore that functioned as a permanent literary salon where anybody with a mind who read books in Manhattan could be found at some time or other. The James Joyce Society held its assemblies there, and many famous people—including comedian Woody Allen—regarded it as an intellectual mecca. John Held Jr.'s sign above the door declared "Wise Men Fish Here," a rubric reminiscent of the colophon of Edmond Bailly's publishing wing of his "Independent Art" bookshop in Paris's rue de la Chaussée d'Antin that was such a magnet for the French Symbolist movement in Paris in the late 1880s and early 1890s.*

The Gotham hosted readings, held art exhibitions, and sold books old, new, rare, and popular. Ehud met George Gurdjieff's follower John Godolphin Bennett (1897–1974) there, as well as novelist Fritz Peters (1913–1979) who had known Gurdjieff personally as a boy. Another figure who made an impression on Ehud around this time was Zen roshi Bernie Glassman (b. 1939), whose reading of Alan Watts, D. T. Suzuki, and Christmas Humphreys led him, after meditating under Taizan Maezumi's direction, to cofound the Zen Center of Los Angeles, and to advocate socially engaged Buddhism, going on to found the Zen Community of New York in 1980.

We have already observed the art collecting and philanthropic work of Dominque de Menil, who gave the world the octagonal Rothko Chapel, opened in 1971 as a "no man's land for God" as Dominique put it for the *New York Times* in 1986.[1] Increasingly spiritualized by dedication to art, philanthropy, and civil rights–oriented arts projects during the Sixties, Dominique developed a fondness not only for a universalist Catholic spirituality, but also for the whirling dervishes who perform the Sufi dance for the purposes of *dhikr*, remembrance, that is, of God, and therefore of the essentially spiritual nature of human beings. Sufism

---

*"Not here the fish of everyone."

is the gnosis of Islam, holding to an inner spiritual and universal core of mystery, of divine revelation.

Dominique's spirituality has flowered most perhaps in daughter Philippa (b. 1947), though it did not happen all at once. Philippa spent much of the Sixties running away from the art world. "I couldn't run far enough. Because when you have parents doing something, you don't want to repeat it."[2] Having attended the Brearley private school for girls on the Upper East Side, she went to Barnard College, the private women's liberal arts college in New York City, thence to UCLA and finally, Harvard, where she received her B.A. (after eight years). Already moved by teachings of Buddhism and of Sufism, the Sixties influence would really coalesce in 1973 when she met Heiner Friedrich in New York.

Born in 1938, Friedrich spent seven hard years in Berlin right through the war, and the experience gave him, he believes, a grounded sanity and desire to accomplish things that benefit humanity. A visit to the fourteenth-century Arena Chapel in Padua in 1957, decorated entirely by Giotto's frescoes, had a tremendous impact on nineteen-year-old Friedrich. It was the seed for what became in 1974, his and Philippa's dream child: the Dia Foundation, whose works have since transformed parts of New York and vast areas elsewhere. The credo for Dia (from the Greek for "through," with the sense of catalyst) was: "One artist, one space, forever."

A philosophy graduate of Munich, Friedrich opened his first gallery in Munich in 1963 with minimal whiteness of wall and gray cement floors, to exhibit Warhol, Twombly, Judd, Flavin, Turrell, and La Monte Young as the decade advanced. An artist who made a particularly strong impression was Walter De Maria when in 1968 he created his shocking *Earth Room,* formed from hundreds of tons of soil. Other German giants of the period exhibited at the gallery too, and included Joseph Beuys, Georg Baselitz, Gerhard Richter, and Sigmar Polke.

Friedrich would never have met Philippa but for the Menil Foundation, as it was Helen Winkler, who worked for the foundation who introduced them, but it was that Sixties permission for the "crazy," or what the unfeeling world calls crazy, that got her into a world that she had till then considered her parents' domain: "The funny thing is, how it came out in me after my parents' collecting. I was interested in art, but shy and out of contact with the art world. I never really wanted to collect, but the idea of a foundation that would help artists build excited me. You were sharing in the great adventure of making a work of art that was maybe too crazy to realize in any other way. He [Heiner Friedrich] reminds me of my father, with his strong idealism and willingness to undertake certain things that others wouldn't. Heiner has helped me step out into life."[3]

One of the finest collections of works by artists in the Sixties and Seventies in the United States today is held by the Dia Foundation at Dia: Beacon, opened in the Hudson Valley in 2003. Perhaps the most striking of the many gifts of art made possible by Dia today is Walter De Maria's *The Lightning Field* (1977), a beautiful work of "land art" sited at Quemado in New Mexico's Catron County where four hundred steel poles have been erected in a grid pattern covering a rectangular mile, recommended to be walked about and seen at sunrise and sundown for the full meditative and cosmic experience. It shows one way human beings can work with Nature directly, harmlessly, yet spiritually powerfully. It makes you think, or if necessary, stop thinking, and start feeling. It is very Sixties, in the best sense of that epithet: simple, striking, cosmic, and lasting.

Dia's founders married in 1979. And no ordinary marriage either, for both were devotees of Sufi guru Sheik Muzaffer Ozak, for whom Dia converted a firehouse at 155 Mercer Street into a Sufi mosque, the Masjid Al-Fara, enhanced by Dan Flavin's fluorescent light works. In the light of Sufi initiation, Philippa changed her name to Fariha, and it is as Fariha Friedrich that she runs a Sufi community in New York City to this day.

AXIS BOLD AS LOVE

Nevertheless, however Sixties this may appear to be, the pacific nature of a settlement of Sufism in New York in subsequent decades seems far removed from the years of turmoil in which its seeds were first planted. When musical avatar Jimi Hendrix made temporary, sporadic home in

New York in 1968 and 1969, the atmosphere was very different. A sense of agitation was palpable. In Manhattan it seemed at least three worlds were coexistent, just avoiding one another on the sidewalks. There were smart people in fashionable, but not excessively flamboyant clothes (most women had shorter—but not necessarily mini—skirts), with hip-length, angular women's jackets, while men, if not in gray suits, still looked like country-club committee members with dreadfully unappealing broad-checked jackets and mismatched ties with large collars. Men's hair was generally short, but the crew cuts had largely gone. Then there were the others who were not doing so well, or who wore workmen's clothes. And there were black people, mostly poor, still waiting for the Promised Land, or who had given up on it altogether, most content among their own.

Just occasionally, if one was at the right spot, you might see a bevy of people in particularly trendy garments from London, fashionable hipsters (though not hippies), more in the Edwardian "dandy" line with velvet jackets, bell-bottomed slacks, cravats, and hair touching the shoulder. Sideburns of Victorian type, moustaches, and floral shirts were now fashionable, though the counterculture was moving slowly toward a sartorial austerity, caught among images, somewhere in the hinterland between the Beach Boys and the MC5.

Jimi Hendrix and his entourage of chicks and freaks would still have stuck out like a sore thumb in most places. "White-collared conservative flashing down the street pointing their plastic finger at me—they're hoping soon my kind will drop and die."* But then, Jimi Hendrix had always stuck out; it made some women want to take care of him. He was never short of domestic helpers, something he had in common with oriental "holy men."

Another thing Jimi had in common with peripatetics and solitaries from the East, was a truly exotic belief system, impregnated from top to bottom, or from infinity to infinity with a most colorful, imaginative spirituality, illuminated by otherworldly occultism of eclectic composition, and, as I have written elsewhere, quintessentially gnostic

---

*Jimi's spoken rap in "If Six Was Nine" (1967).

in orientation. Along his difficult road, Hendrix seems to have been touched deeply, for example, by certain conceptions of Sufi and neo-Sufi provenance he had made his own, even turned into lyrical song. Such a state of mind juxtaposed with New York streets was bound to make a complex musician feel lonesome, and inspire blues of a remarkable kind, which blues were Jimi's speciality.

The Jimi Hendrix Experience began their first proper tour of the United States in February 1968 (an earlier tour with the Monkees had been aborted midway). Fellow tour members were the Soft Machine (fresh from London's UFO Club), Eric Burdon and the New Animals, the Alan Price Set, and Nova Express. Jimi's bassist was Noel Redding, and drumming was in the care of Mitch Mitchell. After a press conference at the 'Copter Club of the PanAm building, Al Aronowitz of the *New York Post,* a friend of Brian Jones, took Jimi for soul food at the Pink Teacup on Seventh and Bleecker, the best soul food below Harlem. They doubtless talked about the Experience's latest album, *Axis Bold as Love,* which reached Billboard's number three that month, and which the long tour would promote.

Hendrix biographer David Henderson took it that what Hendrix meant by the "Axis" was "like a Christian cross or the voodoo peristyle," a link between the heavens and the earth.[4] It was related to the earth's axis, which, if altered would *change everything.* It related to the electromagnetic nature of the earth's constitution, something Jimi felt instinctively close to through the strings of his guitar, magnetized over electromagnetic pickup coils. Could the earth receive his music through the Axis? Could people feel the Axis? Could he pick up on astral vibes governing planetary destiny? He likened a vinyl disc spinning to the earth's axis. He felt the earth was on the cusp of a great axial change, and he was here to spread the vibe.

In neo-Rosicrucianism, and in the esoteric formulation of St. Yves d'Alveydre (1842–1909) in particular, the Sufi Axis was linked to the appearance of a Golden Age, age of Spirit. St. Yves wrote of a place called "Agarttha," revealed to him as located somewhere underground in the Tibetan Himalayas. In this place, the "Tradition" of Ram, patriarch of enlightened religious awareness, held sway through a "king of the world," a conception fundamentally akin to neo-Rosicrucian ideas of the secret direction of the world by "Secret Chiefs," analogous to the Sufi idea of the Axis—the *Qutb,* or perfect, universal human being who leads the saintly hierarchy and brings to each generation the desired knowledge of God. On the new album, Jimi Hendrix sang a song of how the "Axis" was "Bold as Love" and knew everything. So the Axis was also an identity, a perfected human identity. Jimi often spoke as if that was his orientation. On the microcosmic level, this change could be compared to someone falling in love, an event that could really change a life, so this was something everyone could feel from their experience. That was what the experience was: you had to know what it is to fall in love. That was the key, the first step, then you start, or may start, to see how the principle of love changing works at the macrocosmic level too. So while the changes could appear violent, scary, shaky, they had a focus. Yeah, that was like love, wasn't it? And that's why we resist it. And fear it. But real love is the gift. As Jimi said from the stage count-less times: "The best thing that can happen to a man is a woman, and don't you ever forget it."

While James Wasserman was on the West Coast in '68, he went to hear a lecture by Manly P. Hall, author of the classic *The Secret Teachings of All Ages: An Encyclopedia Outline of Masonic, Hermetic, Qabbalistic and Rosicrucian Symbolic Philosophy* (1928). Of the Axis, Manly Hall wrote: "The Axis is a mysterious individual who, unknown and unsuspected, mingles with mankind and who, according to tradi-tion has his favorite seat on the roof of the Kaaba. . . . When an 'Axis' quits this earthly existence, he is succeeded by the 'Faithful One,' who has occupied the place at his right hand. . . . For to these holy men, who also bear the collective titles of 'Lords of Souls' and 'Directors,' is committed a spiritual supremacy over mankind far exceeding the tem-poral authority of earthly rulers."[5] Jimi was taking the blues beyond the stratosphere, and at the same time trying to absorb the higher rays the cosmos was directing at and through the planet. This was what his music was all about, at least in its highest phase, where he liked it to be. But he could party too, for sure, and get the mood going, and play the crowds. But as time went by, he got more frustrated with the management that was content to milk that raw ability for all it was worth, even if it meant the lifeblood of Jimi's spiritual existence, the music, was sacrificed—for money. Such was the anguish of Jimi's "star" status. His music was for the giving, not the taking.

The new album contained another gem, this one about his guardian angel, called "Little Wing." She was usually feminine and could be incarnated in a lover or friend at a particular time. Jimi lived in a world of shifting images, but the spiritual patterns were the same, and he didn't want to get tied down to one image; he wanted to stay pure, true to the spirit. The Angel gave him everything, and one day she would accompany him away from everything, from the noise and the war, and he would then go through his own spiritual change and be another form in the molten lava of spiritual evolution in which the pure spirit could swim.

In the meantime he would play, and show the world the power of the music. On February 7, 1968, twenty thousand attended the Experience's concert at Arizona State University's Union. March 15 saw *Life* magazine dub Jimi the "Most Spectacular Electric Guitarist in the World." Did they know what was driving him, that yearning of sound, that reaching out, always beyond, to the yonder, yonder where the train was comin' in. . . . He gave a fabulous party at New York's Waldorf-Astoria that night. The psychedelic hippie crowd trooped in to stunned looks from staff. And it wasn't just hippies; it seemed all New York's movers and shakers wanted a piece of the action that night. Truman Capote, Eric Clapton, Mike Bloomfield, Eric Burdon: they were all rapping about what made Hendrix such a trip. Many tried to analyze it all in terms of technique. He did this with the Delta blues; he did that with soul rhythm; he did this with the toggle switch, and that with the tremolo bar; and his fingers were so strong and long; and . . . Jimi played the sounds of the heavens, as he heard them, and as they came through him, and it was a sweet song of love, and pain, and change and restless energies in transformation and crisis, and spiritual resolution: far out, on the blue horizon. He would look away, and see *Her* there, waiting.

Jimi had various pads in different parts of New York, each with a young lady looking after everything for him. In '68, Devon Wilson did most of his, what we now call P.A. work, and there was Monique, of North African ancestry, who inspired him some, but she was married. He got his own place at 12th Street off University Place, short distance to the clubs and studios where he was now crafting his next album, one he would truly make his own, *Electric Ladyland*. When he had time to kill, he would join Monique on the Lower East Side at a dress shop owned by two friends of hers. He'd sit and enjoy the three women doing their selling thing at 321 East Ninth Street and sometimes leap forward to play salesman himself, shocking customers by his presence. And some presence! He'd buy presents for customers if the whim took him, and tried to live a few hours of normal life, with Monique decorating his apartment in North African styles.

Jimi went back to the Scene club, which soon became a late-night haven, with its tiny stage that compressed the Doors in '67, and which, thanks to Hendrix, became a place visiting bands like Pink Floyd wanted to be seen in. It was the Scene. Jimi would bring in his Teac recorders and jam with those willing or able to jam with the magician. At the Scene, he got to know psychology major Ray Warner of the Chambers Brothers, from Mississippi. And they talked about the Axis for days and days, when they could. Ray was astonished by Jimi's mind, and realized he could be saying two opposite things at the same time, and used an ironic dualism indicating that his real mind was floating above the straight plane of yes and no. For "Jimi's concept of the axis was hooked up like a freeway from Earth to space to infinity. The axis was like a bridge or crossing over a threshold from one reality to a deeper reality, or from one dimension to another. He looked upon the earth as a single creature. Jimi wanted to help the whole world, the whole universe. The wars and the bloodshed were terrible to behold—the wounds and the swords and the poverty. . . . It was like the axis itself was a living form of energy music, a mass of love and creativity all rolled up into one thing that came out positive. The axis was like a stepping stone to a greater understanding. [Jimi would write a song in 1969 called "Stepping Stone"] He was trying to say that he could take you to a holy place without even moving your body—and he wanted to do that. It was not about LSD or any hallucinogenic—he was the drug, he was the high. . . . Warner began getting the distinct feeling that Jimi Hendrix was not of this Earth."[6]

What is especially fascinating is that while a hostile critic might think it was "fame and drugs" that led to these unusual states of mind and depths of perception, the fact was Jimi was like this all along. He'd got this concept together before British manager Chas Chandler ever sat up and noticed the crazy, near-penniless guitarist and took him to England for a spot of fashion grooming. Indeed, it was the pressures of stardom to conform to ordinary expectations that drove a wedge into Jimi's soul and made him lonelier than he was naturally already. When he had a free hand, he chose to speak of his work as that of a missionary.

As he neared completion of his double-album masterpiece *Electric Ladyland,* he gave an interview, and let the cat out of the bag:

> The background of our music is a spiritual-blues thing. Blues is part of America. We're making our music into electric church music—a new kind of Bible, not like in a hotel, but a Bible you carry in your hearts, one that will give you a physical feeling. We try to make our music so loose and hard hitting so that it hits your soul hard enough to make it open. . . . We want them ["black kids"] to realize that our music is just as spiritual as going to church. . . . The content of the old blues was singing about sex—problems with their old ladies— and booze. Now people are saying so much more with music; music is such an important thing now; people have to realize that.[7]

One of the things that really bugged Jimi's management was his interest in the Black Panthers and black self-determination. This was politics, and management feared it could wreck the reputation of the group with the mainly white audience, as well as bringing authority down on them, especially if Nixon got in. A month before Nixon was elected, New York magazine *Circus* interviewed Jimi. Jimi told them one of his new songs was dedicated to the Panthers. He didn't say what its message was, but at no time did Jimi ever use his music to advocate negative or destructive messages. He was becoming aware of all kinds of evils and wasn't looking to add to the host. Jimi added that who-ever might be elected, he was going to be making a "whole new thing *regardless.*" He was against a passive response to intimidation; that's what authority wanted, the feeling of passivity and weakness. You had to believe in yourself and fight fire with fire when necessary. Had he contacted the Panthers? "Not much. They come to the concerts, and I sort of feel them there—it's not a physical thing but a mental ray, you know. It's a spiritual thing."[8]

On November 2, 1968, *Electric Ladyland* entered the charts and went straight to number one. And Richard Nixon was elected. Meanwhile, on the album: "And the Gods Made Love"—the first track laid out the Bigger Picture. Nixon's now gone; Hendrix still enchants.

In February 1969, Jimi was in London for a gig at the Albert Hall, featuring conga player Rocki (Kwasi Dzidzornu), whose father was a voodoo priest, chief drummer at a Ghanaian village. Rocki was agog at Jimi's rhythms. He told him they were the same as ancient tribal rhythms he'd been raised on. Jimi dug Rocki too. At one point when jamming at Jimi's pad, Jimi turned to Rocki: "You communicate with God, do you?" "Yes," replied Rocki, "I communicate with God."

Jane de Mendelssohn was working as a reporter for Barry Miles and friends' *International Times.* She came to Jimi's London pad to ask about his Cherokee heritage. Cherokees traditionally came from southeastern America—Georgia and Mississippi—but Jimi's Cherokee grandmother was living in a nice flat with TV and all things modern in Vancouver, British Columbia, not too far from Jimi's dad's place in Seattle. His own family had already traveled a lot before Jimi began his own traveling on inner planes and airplanes. Jane asked him about the Indian heritage. Did they still take peyote, for example? "Oh yes, it's all over the place," replied Jimi, "But you know all Indians have differ-ent ways of stimulants, their own step toward God, spiritual forms, or whatever . . . which should be kept as nothing but a step, mind you . . ." Jimi wanted to get the message across that drug abuse was an abuse of the soul.[9]

In the course of the interview, he let out a clue on what would become his last great unfinished project: "A really nice piece of music that I'm getting together for this late-summer LP that I'd like to do with this cat named Al Brown [a musician friend who offered Hendrix his 57th Street apartment when he was in town], in America. It's called 'The First Ray of the New Rising Sun,' and it gives my own solution."[10] The tracks that gathered over the next eighteen months or so are, in my personal opinion, profoundly underrated. Jimi was trying to bring the above and the below into a groove and a harmony, maybe the world was not ready for, despite the deliberate simplicity of the lyrics he was now composing: simple messages about "living together," overcoming differences, and finding your true will, and accepting one was a child of God with a freedom that could move mountains with love and understanding.

In April 1969, Jimi leased a house with grounds at Boiceville on the Esopus Creek, Ulster County, upstate New York, just fifteen miles west of Esopus Island in the Hudson where Aleister Crowley had spent the summer of 1918 and contemplated his spiritual destiny, past and future (see my book *Aleister Crowley in America,* 2017) fifty-one years previously. That summer, Crowley had bought paint and painted the words: DO WHAT THOU WILT SHALL BE THE WHOLE OF THE LAW in red on the little cliffs of the island. Jimi would be singing with his new bands Gypsy Sun and Rainbows, or simply the Band of Gypsys, that year: "Find yourself first, and then your talent. It's all in your mind."

At Boiceville, Jimi would get into a whole new range of music, with Juma Sultan and Larry Lee, with more than a mind on the idea of jazz and Afro-fusion, just a mind's blink away from what Miles Davis was doing in New York, the ambitious jazzman mindful of Hendrix. On the day Woodstock opened (which Jimi would close), Miles Davis assembled an ambitious body of shit-hot musicians, including Chick Corea, Joe Zawinul of the Cannonball Adderley band, and Larry Young, who'd come straight from amazing jam sessions with Hendrix out at Boiceville. Miles Davis's New York Columbia Records sessions made *Bitches Brew,* suitable to drink, and drink deep.

Meanwhile at Woodstock, Jimi's own ambitious soundscape couldn't get over the limitations of the sound system at Max Yasgur's farm, and most of the depth he'd been working into his sound was lost on the airwaves, dominated by his searing, pain-racked, intense guitar. If you see the film, you can tell Hendrix is not happy with the sound. Most of the crowd was too tired to notice; Jimi had come on at sunup after a grueling weekend of excess and sometimes near panic.

As the Sixties were sucked down the plughole of their own inevitable end, Jimi was increasingly ambivalent about many issues. Poet Jim Brodey interviewed him for the *Los Angeles Free Press* and pressed Jimi on rumors that he intended to go into some sort of seclusion. No, said Jimi, that wasn't what was happening, but he was going "toward a spiritual level through music," which, to many minds, meant seclusion from political issues.[11] Brodey pressed him on the Black Panthers. He (Jimi) did think the Panthers were necessary though? "Yeah, only to the word necessary. You know, in the back of their minds they should be working toward their own thing. They should be a symbol only to the establishment's eyes. It should only be a legendary thing. . . ." I think he was saying that standing up against oppression was a symbol of conviction and had to be done, but it was not the be-all-and-end-all of life. You had to live beyond the political frame and transcend it in your soul, and see what was going on above that dimension, otherwise you were simply being pushed into positions and states of mind by the powers that be, that in the end, would use your stance against you, so you ended up doubly defeated; you had to stand really tall. Really tall, above the expected. You had to be what God meant you to be, despite the opposition. That of course was the moot point. Because as the decade drew to a close, Jimi was having trouble being taken seriously by people who were supposed to be his management, and he felt reduced by the pressures, and was really crying out for someone to save him.

At the end of the year, he looked for some support from a band of brothers, an all black band, going on stage with friends Buddy Miles (drums) and Billy Cox (bass) at New York's Fillmore East on New Years' Eve 1969, playing two sets into New Year's Day 1970. After the first show, he asked the venue's manager Bill Graham what he thought, so Graham, up front, gave him the "works," telling Jimi that while the audience obviously loved it, and were entertained by his physical gyrations, gimmicks, and peerless showmanship, *great artists* had a duty to perform beyond the populist approval, and show all of themselves, and make music that would be unmatchable and unassailable and as great as they could make it.

On the next show, Jimi Hendrix stood stock still, and just played, and played, and *by God* he played: "Message of Love" . . . "Changes" . . . "Power to Love" . . . "Machine Gun" . . . "Who Knows" . . . "We Gotta Live Together." His performance was beyond compare. You can hear it on the *Band of Gypsys* album. Nobody has been *there* since. And when it was all over, on the morning of January 1, 1970, so were the Sixties.

TWENTY-NINE

1969 I

No Peace for the Wicked

At precisely the time Jimi Hendrix was giving his all at the Fillmore East, on New Year's Eve / New Year's Day 1969–1970, John and Yoko Lennon were lying in the Scandinavian winter darkness at a remote farmhouse, at Ellidsbølvej 37, near Vust in the Hanherred area of North Jutland, Denmark, its bleak grassy flatlands within sight of the cold North Sea. After spending Christmas at home at Tittenhurst Park, Berkshire, they had flown to the small city of Aalborg on December 29, some twenty-eight miles east of their destination, in order to meet up with Yoko's daughter, Kyoko, and to stay with her and Kyoko's father, Tony Cox and Tony's new wife Melinda for a New Year "retreat." There were no phones at the farmhouse.

Events at the farmhouse became a little strange, even by John Lennon's extensive experience of strangeness. Tony Cox, who back in 1966 and 1967 had been Yoko's husband while managing or assisting her artistic career in England and elsewhere, had involved himself with Donald James Hamrick, lately of Nova Scotia, Canada, and Northern California. In 1967, Hamrick had founded "Harbinger," a well-organized commune for working, learning, and conferences hosted by Hamrick's Frontiers of Science Fellowship. Water therapies, hypnosis, and meditation were practiced alongside conventional science and arts lessons for members' children. The facility could be found four miles off the track at Harbin Hot Springs, Lake County, Northern California, in an area formerly lived in by Pomo Indians, who still used to drop in on the site, as did many other waifs and strays strung out in late Sixties West Coast hippie fallout. Hamrick was an eccentric combination of physicist, artist, architect, and social visionary who believed he was in telepathic contact with extraterrestrials, contact with whom he believed had furnished him with the name "Zee." Hamrick was particularly committed to lifestyles free of cigarettes and drugs.

A frontier of science conference called the Celestial Synapse began at Harbinger on February 19, 1969, but next day, the commune was raided and Hamrick's fifth child was murdered, a tragedy that led to Hamrick's leaving the commune and the breakup of his marriage. A new commune was established in Nova Scotia, but a group of people arrived who had already created mayhem in California, and insisted on taking drugs. Hamrick departed "Harbinger II." Now he was in Denmark, at this time a country with some of the most permissive laws in Europe.

When the Lennons arrived, a nervous Cox insisted cigarettes and any other stimulants be deposited in his care to protect Kyoko from harmful influences. Hamrick and a colleague called Leonard were on hand to advise. This seemed apposite since the Lennons had recently returned from a remarkable fifty-minute meeting with Canada's prime minister Pierre Trudeau, during which the Lennons had mooted the idea of mounting a peace festival rock concert at Mosport Park, forty-four miles east of Toronto, to match or exceed Woodstock's in August. Trudeau offered tacit support, subject to proper organization, and over-pitched hopes for some apocalyptic new beginning for the human race reached a zenith in Canada with the onset of Christmas 1969.

In the meantime, Lennon had discussed the planned event with musician Ronnie Hawkins (on whose farm the Lennons had stayed during their historic Canadian visit), Toronto-based *Rolling Stone* journalist Ritchie Yorke, and with John Brower (who had produced the Toronto Rock 'n' Roll Revival Festival that John and Yoko's "Plastic Ono Band" had performed at "for peace" in September). Brower made all kinds of assurances, but with Lennon out of phone contact, made

*Fig. 29.1. Canadian prime minister Pierre Trudeau
with John Lennon and Yoko Ono, 1969.
(Photo by Duncan Cameron, Library and Archives Canada)*

some arrangements without the Lennons' approval. Brower meanwhile was involved in subterfuges against the involvement of Beatles' manager, Allen Klein, which complicated matters further.

An odd strain now enters the end-of-decade events. Cox urged Lennon to take advantage of on-hand Harbinger-style hypnosis to conquer nicotine addiction, while Hamrick suggested the possibility of arranging John and Yoko's arrival at the planned peace concert in an "air car," specially built at his instigation, which wondrous craft would be powered by psychic energy, rather than conventional fuel. This proposed phenomenon would certainly kick off the new decade, a decade that Lennon wanted renamed as Year 1 AP (After Peace), conventional history having ended with the Sixties (an idea that has gained some unattributed currency perhaps with the academic conception of postmodernism and sundry related novel classifications of history, and its alleged end). According to the Lennons' personal assistant Anthony Fawcett—with whom I had opportunity to discuss these events over summer 1985—shortly after further bizarre discussions in Denmark, the Harbingers announced at a San Francisco press conference that flying saucers would be landing at the planned festival, such was its significance to beings beyond our world![1] This seems a trifle bold for Year 1 AP, or any other time in the near future, and even open-minded Lennon could see his simple original idea (as he saw it) of rock for peace heading in a preposterous direction, so overwhelmed did proponents seem by the thought of millions ($$) being attracted to the junket. The nature of John's thoughts on the issue he revealed in an article he issued to print called "Have We All Forgotten What Vibes Are?" dated Monday April 16, 1970, wherein he vainly asserted that despite disappointments, he had not altogether abandoned the idea of some kind of peace festival (though it now resembled a forlorn hope):

> Someone said, "Do we need a festival?" Yoko and I still think we need it—not just to show that we can gather peacefully and groove to rock bands, but to change the balance of energy power. On Earth and, therefore, in the universe. Have we all forgotten what vibes are? Can you imagine what we could do together in the one spot—thinking, singing, and praying for peace—one million souls apart from any TV linkups, etc. to the rest of the planet? If we came together for one reason, we could make it together! We need help! It is out of our control.

A trail of bitterness would undoubtedly follow. What effect hypnosis really had on John at the time is now impossible to determine. He would be smoking again soon anyhow. One thing that is peculiar is that while at the farm both John and Yoko agreed to have their hair cut by a lady in a barn, their locks being bagged for later use at a charity auction. That is, not just cut, but positively shorn, hacked off without style. Most of the year they had been advocating with great frequency the idea of "Hair Peace," or "Grow Your Hair (for Peace)," and their appearance was deemed a political and ideological statement that could be shared in literal terms by every person sympathetic to it. Hair did get even longer among youth in 1969. When John attended the mass festival at the Isle of Wight to see Bob Dylan in August, he was in some respects (but for his specs) indistinguishable from many of Britain's hippies present. Why now, at the cusp of the new decade were acknowledged leaders of the peace campaign severing its most recognizable symbol, indeed—and this is more telling perhaps—the outward symbol of the decade itself? The idea of *renunciation* seems very strong in the act of cutting, and, in being cut, of a curious passivity, or novitiate-like preparation for a stripped-down new phase, as yet undetermined. Just as the Maharishi and other rishis *grew* their hair as a symbol of renouncing worldly involvement and bodily affections, now the world would be confronted by figures the media could hardly help comparing to the "skinhead" movement that had swept disaffected working-class youth in Britain, with a hint of muddy, even bloody, reactionary realism. A reversal had begun. However one looks at it, one determines that John Lennon felt the need, probably a painful one, to draw a line.

When John Brower turned up at the farmhouse in January 1970, he was confronted by some of his own promotional blurb that read: "Free (for one dollar) John Lennon Peace Festival."[2] While in the States the commercial conceit that one dollar was tantamount to "free" was accepted, such was definitely not the case in England, where it looked like sheer, brazen exploitative deception. Lennon insisted, somewhat contrary to earlier suggestions on the issue—where he had considered payment for performing rock stars)—that he was only interested in an absolutely free festival, with Klein's participation, and *that* idea was now firm in his deliberations, and he insisted that nothing further be brought into effect regarding the festival without his prior approval. Dismayed, Brower left the meeting with Anthony Fawcett, and with that, John and Yoko's peace campaign, which had reached its dizzy peak only weeks before, slowly began to fade. Though sentiments remained, the Lennons' lives would take a very different, more personalized, course. The 1970s were going to be markedly different. A significant aspect of the spiritual meaning of the Sixties thus ended in an austere Nordic farmhouse, with the decade's confused end.

How had John and Yoko's global peace campaign begun in the first place?

THE AMSTERDAM BED-IN

Perhaps one of the greatest successes of the Beatles was to convey the fruit of a relatively tiny counterculture to a massive public. They made its divers options of vision and attitude attractive and accessible, and while overt interest in countercultural messages and lifestyles with spiritual meaning would lose them more conservative fans (while gaining others), generating a hostile reaction that began with the Christ controversy in 1966 and grew with the LSD revelations, they still managed to keep the ship of hope afloat, such was the accumulated respect, reinforced by astonishing capacity to produce great music at a furiously progressive and inspired pace. As Lennon would opine in 1969, the Beatles were treated as "Britain's children," and while they could be naughty, and needed (in the "parents'" eyes) to have their faces slapped [*sic*] from time to time, they were given some license to play nonetheless.

By 1968, however, events were in large part getting ahead of the Beatles' ideals of nonviolent change, with a lurch in that year to violent confrontation with the Establishment, somewhat glorified by Mick Jagger and Keith Richards's stirring song "Street Fighting Man," from their *Beggars Banquet* album, released in December 1968, banned by the BBC. The Beatles' own white double album, released the previous month nodded in a revolutionary direction, while looking equally the other way. Its revolutionary character lay in its ability to stir the inner life of listeners, arguably more effective in both short and long term than lashing out with aggressive posturing. John's "Revolution No. 1" said you could "count me [John] out, in" when it came to "destruction," but his soundscape "Revolution No. 9" depicted a violent, painful, revolutionary breakdown of society, though, it must be said, as *a nightmare,* followed by a poetic-ironic "Goodnight" kiss, John's tender dream song sung amid soothing strings and angelic voices by cuddly uncle Ringo.*

---

*I think the idea for this ironic juxtaposition may have come from episode fifteen of *The Prisoner* TV series ("The Girl Who Was Death," broadcast January 21, 1968) where, after Number Six (Patrick McGoohan) fights a nightmarish battle over a deadly missile disguised as a lighthouse, and aimed at London, with a mad scientist dressed as Napoleon (Kenneth Griffith as Schnipps), we cut from the battle's dénouement to see the Prisoner

Whether John wished the nightmare to come true in the morning was not something he could make his mind up about definitively. Was it coming anyway? It might seem so. But his acquired wisdom was that passive-positive protest of the Gandhi type plus art values and humor (like the yippie-meets-hippie Pentagon Levitation) was probably the best approach. However, he was concerned at the physical sufferings inflicted on even quite peaceful protestors, and wondered if he could do anything to save their heads and limbs from being bashed in by establishment forces that took the streets as *theirs*.

An opportunity to make an original contribution to committed action, and the vocabulary of committed protest, came after John married Yoko secretly in Gibraltar on March 20, 1969. Since they knew the moment the press got wind of them marrying, they'd be hounded, they decided to turn the publicity into a Yoko-style art "event." They didn't turn the wedding into a stunt, but its honeymoon was effectively sacrificed on the altar of press interest and artistic ideals. Taking the name from the Human Be-In idea of 1967 San Francisco, they gave it an amusing twist as the "Bed-In for Peace," with the happy, suggestive pun that people could "stay in bed for peace." This was about as passive a means of protesting as could be imagined or wished for, and was undoubtedly intended as humorous, a kind of "sketch" for, if you like, an "Unfinished Protest" in the conceptual mode: a species of performance art. Again, it was inclusive, and generated headline after headline across the world, and for a while captured the globe's anxious attention as the world's press made their way to room 902 of the Amsterdam Hilton.

As Lennon said many times during what afterward became a con-

---

(cont. from p. 583) close a children's storybook (the whole episode transpires to have been a children's tale) and address the eager, listening children, hanging on his words: "And that is how I saved London from the mad scientist." He then says, warmly, "Goodnight children . . ." and pauses (addressing both his listening-in *captors,* and the TV audience) "—*everywhere.*" Prison bars then hit the screen and the story (and principal narrative of the series) ends. The Beatles were keen *Prisoner* fans. Their "All You Need Is Love" played a critical part in the climax to the final episode (shown a fortnight later), "Fall Out," broadcast on February 4, eleven days before the Beatles arrived in Delhi to begin their sojourn with the Maharishi at Rishikesh, where much of the *White Album* was written.

certed campaign, wasn't it better to see the word *Peace* on the headlines than more news of war, napalm, dismembered bodies, and untrustworthy statements of politicians? Have a laugh at John and Yoko, by all means. They were willing to be the world's clowns, because all the "serious" people like Kennedy, and Gandhi and Martin Luther King "got shot." If the Establishment could (and did) persistently manipulate the media, then so should the "Peace Movement." John and Yoko's method was peaceful and invitational, political and artistic. People who were interested could come to the bedside, a place incarnating human love, and in that context they could see and report to others what "peace" was about. It was about people, just living, being allowed to live and love. What was stopping this from happening? Maybe people only needed to show just a bit of courage, and if enough people got an idea, then collectively, the collective unconscious could become the collective conscious. It was all on a par with the Krishna consciousness idea, of setting up rhythms and vibrations of positive action backed by spiritual prayer and "soul power." Lennon's awareness was that the movement for change was fighting an essentially *spiritual* war. Of this he was most explicit—and this performance art (for that is what it was effectively) was a weapon in that war, a truly peaceful weapon. The idea of a spiritual war behind the appearances of this life was an important component of John's thinking on the matter, and the concept was obviously present in Christian tradition, but massively understated.

John referred to his opponents as "manifest forms" of darker spiritual forces that assailed the consciousness of humanity, whose interest prevented spiritual light and awareness from getting through. Jesus spoke about the "lord of this world" in the same light, the "Satan" that shadowed him and even had a grip on the minds of his followers. The people who crucified Jesus did not really know what they were doing; they were tools gripped by the shadow of evil, of which they were unconscious. People say and do terrible things because they are not aware fully of what they are doing, for they do not realize *who they are,* and are thus vulnerable to manipulation by what Jung called the "shadow." When the formerly overwhelmed *do* become aware, often by shock or bitter experience, they experience sorrow and often repent, or cry or both; anyhow, the mask falls off and we see the human heart. Lennon's thinking on the matter was extremely close to the Gnostic idea of a material consciousness dominated by dark archons (rulers) who serve the Demiurge, a conception with which he exhibited great familiarity in his book *Skywriting by Word of Mouth* published after his death in 1981.

Anyone could be a Christ or a Hitler; they had to make a choice; "we all have everything within us." "We're all God and we're all potentially divine, and potentially evil." He told interviewers who would listen that he wanted "Christ to win."* The battle was fought in every individual soul. "Christ," the "anointed" or light principle in this context, was the real light of humanity (an Advaitist and gnostic position), the divine that we have within us that we don't draw on, rather we act out of fear, and in the shadow of fear. John was prepared to be a fool because, as he said, the spiritual opposition could not handle humor (or negation, for the number of the tarot fool is 0). But the opposition could certainly handle violence, their métier! Violence speaks their language, so to speak (and *ours*, were we honest to ourselves and others). So the "Establishment" (the manifest Demiurge) wants to get a rise out of the kids so they can repress them the more. Once you realize the spiritual nature of the game, you can see the manifest forms of evil, and laugh at their stupidity. John spoke of what he and Yoko represented as a spiritual force, echoing Yoko's artistic ideas about wind: "John and Yoko are like the wind," he said, "You can't see it, but when it passes the trees bend."

---

*Here we see another idea implicit in the final episode of the TV series *The Prisoner,* where at the climax of Number Six's escape from the grip of the Village and its ruler Number Two, he tears a mask off Number One, whom he has won the right to confront by demonstrating he is a true "individual." Beneath the mask of a face divided into black and white (dualism) is first revealed the face of an ape. Ripping that mask off, Number Six finally reveals *Number One:* it is Number Six, the Prisoner himself. That is where the evil lies in the first instance, in ourselves, and that evil constitutes the condition of our own imprisonment. As Christ said: "And why beholdest thou the mote that is in thy brother's eye, but considerest not the beam that is in thine own eye? Or how wilt thou say to thy brother, Let me pull out the mote out of thine eye; and, behold, a beam is in thine own eye? Thou hypocrite, first cast out the beam out of thine own eye; and then shalt thou see clearly to cast out the mote out of thy brother's eye" (Matthew 7:3–5).

Yoko's song "Who Has Seen the Wind?" would dignify the B-side of Lennon's spiritual-positive song "Instant Karma" (1970). He was going very far when he said such things, and though he reckoned that so long as he wasn't too serious, he'd avoid assassination, his song "The Ballad of John and Yoko," recorded with Paul McCartney at Abbey Road Studios after the Amsterdam Bed-In, nonetheless posited the idea that he might yet be "crucified," if only figuratively. He told a hostile Al Kapp (political cartoonist) in Montreal later in the year that *everyone* was open to being crucified in this world, the dark powers got at every person, including Al Kapp. Conversely, "Imagine if the whole world stayed in bed," he said, tongue in cheek, "They'd have peace for a week and they'd get an idea of what it was like; the tension would be released."

One of John's problems in communication that year was that he had a genius for simplifying abstract and (to some) difficult or unfamiliar concepts. The price to be paid was that his views could be presented as simplistic by limited minds that did not share the spirit of the utterances, apparent to many who hear, rather than read his public discourse.

AMSTERDAM

We rather take the locus of the first Bed-In for granted these days. Why did John choose *Amsterdam* to initiate the peace campaign?

In 1967, London's *Daily Mirror* fashion editor Felicity Green posted an article "Where Did Pattie Get That Gear?" about Pattie Harrison's latest psychedelic wear. The source was revealed as a workshop off Montagu Square run by The Fool. The Fool consisted of twenty-three-year-old Amsterdam girls Marijke Koge and Josje Leeger, Marijke's husband Simon Posthuma, and business manager Barry Finch. Having helped with Brian Epstein's Savile Theatre in Charlotte Street, they went on in 1967 not only to design clothes donned by all the Beatles and their wives, but also a painted piano for John, an entire wall of the Baker Street Apple shop, and furnishings for the Harrisons' home in Esher. They received credit on the *Sgt. Pepper* cover for their contribution. Their aim to make beautiful clothes so beautiful that people could not resist them had all begun around the time the Beatles first visited Amsterdam as conquering heroes in 1964 when three of the group sailed down the canals on a special boat surrounded by ecstatic fans. Simon and Marijke got married and got high, and saw a barge called *The Beatles* that, taken as a sign, sped them off to North Africa for inspiration that brought them to design a poster for Bob Dylan, then friendship with Donovan, and subsequently to the Beatles. From The Fool alone, Lennon had a good vibe about the city of tulips and canals.

In an interview included on John and Yoko's *Wedding Album* (1969) an interviewer informs the couple that Amsterdam was known as the "center of Europe," a somewhat implausible assumption geographically speaking but one that delighted the tulip-holding newlyweds, who ascribed this revelation to "magic." The reputation John took note of regarding Amsterdam was informed by knowledge that it had already played a special role in the interpenetration of countercultural values into the life of the continent.

When I lived in Amsterdam myself in the late '80s I spoke to a Dutch professor of Gnostic history who informed me that many parents after the war were so relieved to be free of the Nazi yoke and the horror of war that they permitted their children more personal freedom than they had been permitted themselves. Young people were valued, especially in a relatively small country like Holland, and rather indulged. If young people had a vision of the future, then their vision should be heeded: it was *their* future after all, and their grandparents' generation hadn't made such a great job of it.

In 1965, Robert Jasper Grootvelt (1932–2009) started the Dutch "Provos" (short for *provocateurs*) with a campaign against a statue of a street urchin placed in the newspaper district by the tobacco industry. Grootvelt recognized a corrupting image, as the papers were full of stories about cigarettes causing cancer, while the papers' biggest source of advertising was what Grootvelt called "the legalized dope syndicate" (cigarettes). Grootvelt was imprisoned for sixty days after producing a poster with a girl smoking on it, slapped with the word *cancer*. Freed, Grootvelt motivated young street-oriented people, who'd been thought little more than "yobs," to become a kind of public alert system. The police had a special part to play in the proceedings.

Amsterdam's mayor gave an order there were to be no more "happenings." The police using loudspeakers went round saying "no more happenings!" so people in pubs said: "Ah, where's the happening?" Let's go find it! So the police did the public address job! Having had fun with the police, Grootvelt looked for another symbol the kids could have a go at, and came upon the "holy automobile" as a target for fun, anarchist plans. They invented the "white bicycle." You could use it, but not own it. You left it when you were done, and someone else could use it. This seemed a good symbol, and made lines between good and bad. And being white, you could see it at night: good symbol.

Fig. 29.2. Dutch artist Robert Jasper Grootveld, 1964.

Provo was the first group to make a stink about pollution, and other ideas have been taken from them into the mainstream. Provo stimulated what later became Holland's reputation for openhearted liberalism, which John and Yoko were also tapping in to. Before Provo, only official views on anything were heard, and people just accepted what was happening, as there was thought "nothing you could do," and religion seemed to say, oh, just accept this world as it's heaven that matters.

Jasper pioneered political street theater in Amsterdam. Provo mounted protests at Dutch royal weddings in 1966 and 1967. When Crown Princess Beatrix met Claus, who'd been in the German army, Provo protested the wedding, playing on the traditional message of Dutch Saint Nicholas day when children would say "Klaus (Nicholas) is coming." "Klaus" turned out to be Claus. There were symbolic smoke bombs in the streets when Beatrix chose to wed in Amsterdam. There were no real bombs or violence. Grootvelt kept the thing "white" (the equivalent of the San Francisco Diggers' "Free") and symbolic, but nonetheless got points across.

One can see the ideological tie-in with John and Yoko's white honeymoon for peace. Grootvelt spoke about his activities in 1987:

> Magic only means power. We were in need of power or strength to do our thing. My friends Roel and Rob called themselves anarchists. They called me the Magician. I thought: Yes, that's the word for me. A magician is someone who makes things happen.
>
> Provo lasted two years. It was an idea, a state of mind, a happening. We had Provo printing, Provo cinema, we were provoking. But by the end we had people who were afraid of being called Provos.[3]

Around the summer of 1967, American hippies started turning up in Amsterdam, having heard about the happenings. By the end of the year Amsterdam joined the list of cities to host large anti–Vietnam War demonstrations. From that time on, Amsterdam's reputation as a city favoring liberal progress, rock 'n' roll, spiritual freedom, and tolerance was sealed, and it became a haven for good vibes, as well as drug self-abuse, for many years, run very effectively on rational and profitable lines, as only the Dutch seem to be able to bring off so well. It was the right place to launch a peace movement, and was perhaps, all things considered, a magical choice.

At the end of March 1969, John and Yoko went to Vienna for the world premiere of their 73-minute film *Rape* on Austrian National TV, before which they appeared to the press in a bag, labeled BAGISM, to show that it was possible to have "communication without prejudice," if, that is, you didn't see the skin color or other aspects of the person you were communicating with. The label Bagism probably didn't do much to allay prejudice, and people are likely to take exception to anything, including accent, aroma, or anything, but they had a point. On the other hand, it was because they knew (or thought they knew) it was the famous couple that the presspack were prepared to point mikes at a bag—but a brave thing to do in the country that gave the world Adolf Hitler (as well as *The Sound of Music*), no doubt. Returning, the "peaceniks" revealed they were sending acorns to world leaders to plant for peace. I believe Israel's prime minister Golda Meir planted hers.

On May 16, the Lennons planned to join Ringo Starr and Peter Sellers on the QE2 where they were filming Terry Southern's story *The Magic Christian,* a superbly funny spiritual and surreal commentary on liberty, greed, and materialism. Unfortunately, the Lennons were unable to join their luggage on board as the United States delayed the visa process, presumably for fear the Lennons would stage a Bed-In there and upset Nixon's administration, which regarded student protestors as "college bums" in that ever-generous spirit that characterizes unnerved people taking safety amid their own kind.

Unable to bed down in the States, the Lennons first tried the Bahamas but it proved too hot and inhospitable. They headed first to Toronto, then established themselves at Montreal's Queen Elizabeth Hotel, where they could, and did, make many telephone calls over the border to the States, including pleas to student radicals not to walk into the firing line or baton charges of National Guardsmen and police.

On May 31 a mobile sound recorder was brought to the hotel suite and John, Yoko, and everyone present joined in with John's new anthem

"Give Peace a Chance." The Plastic Ono Band this time included Derek Taylor, Rosemary and Timothy Leary, Tommy Smothers, Rabbi Abraham L. Feinberg, and members of the Canadian temple of the Krishna Consciousness movement. The song was intended as a chant that could serve as a collective mantra. It was released on July 7, and went to the top of the U.S. charts. We still hear politicians today saying they're going to "give peace a chance." Not a bad legacy by any means.

In September, Canadian promoter John Brower invited John to perform at the Toronto Rock 'n' Roll Revival Festival beside Chuck Berry, Little Richard, Jerry Lee Lewis, and Bo Diddley. John and Yoko took drummer Allan White, bassist and old friend from Hamburg Klaus Voorman, along with Eric Clapton to perform "Give Peace a Chance" and some old and new rock favorites before the appreciative audience who lit matches at the end of a performance that showed off the old rocker beneath the manifest off-white suit and guru hair. The experience of rocking without the other Beatles, and its reception, made a strong impression on John, which filtered through as the year began to run out.

In October, John had a notable row with Paul at Apple. Paul was trying to get John to agree to a tour or TV show, but John wasn't in the mood to listen to the idea. Something was bugging him, and had been bugging him over the year about the Beatles simply meaning "pressure," and far too often, *boredom,* and he had pressure coming from all sides already with the peace campaign that was occupying many of his spare hours, giving interview after interview at the Apple offices where he was in danger of suffering media overexposure, as well as public disapprobation of Yoko. He just couldn't take the idea of "something else" piled on yet again, coming not from his own creativity but from Paul's frustration. As far as John was concerned, he'd forced himself through the *Let It Be* film nine or so months earlier; he'd devoted love and care to the recording of *Abbey Road* in July and August, and there was still unfinished work around over the unreleased *Let It Be* material, and plenty of ongoing business and financial problems, and so much else to do. Blowing his top, he told Paul he was leaving the Beatles, that he wanted "a divorce," and stormed off, leaving his musical partner shell-shocked.

Later Klein persuaded John it was not in his own interest to make any public announcement of his feelings, but to wait till it *was* at least in his own interest. John complied. One suspects something in him didn't *really* want to end completely something he had created, not acrimoniously anyhow. Paul's well-intentioned insistence had just felt like the last straw that broke the back of his patience. The Beatles had power as a communications medium; he knew that. He probably hoped the pressures might fade and Paul would cool down, back well off for as long as it took, and let things be one way or another; but there was also a sense that something was ending, but no one wanted to utter the final, fateful words. This inner crisis may well have played a part in the complex feelings that led to the haircut and massive turnabout over the New Year '69–'70 discussed above. If the game *was* going to change, then he wanted to be ahead of it, whatever it took. The Beatles had an image; the image would have to change.

In the meantime, the peace campaign ground on with good days and bad days, with apposite record releases, endless, often crazy Apple office activity, and more interviews. The effort would culminate in December with billboards plastered all over the world with posters declaring: WAR IS OVER (IF YOU WANT IT) HAPPY XMAS FROM JOHN AND YOKO. Then, the icing on the cake: on December 16, John and Yoko flew to Toronto for a high-powered series of peace-oriented activities. John Brower and Ritchie Yorke had already been to Apple to discuss a Mosport Park Peace Festival for July 1970 and the possible establishment of a Peace Foundation, and it was beginning to look like a meeting with Pierre Trudeau, Canada's premier, was in the cards. Excitement and anticipation grew apace.

Ontario's Science Center hosted the first press conference. John announced an international peace referendum. Everyone could vote for peace, or war. When they'd got, say, twenty million votes, they'd be handed to the United States. John seemed to have forgotten about Nixon's trump card, his arguably imaginary "great silent majority." Nixon didn't listen to any alleged vocal majority; they were college bums, weren't they? But he knew many were voters too.

Extra phones were installed at Ronnie Hawkins's farm, and Lennon spoke to radio stations all over the States. Here was Marshall McLuhan's nascent "global village" at work, and John was spinning round its electromagnetic core, part perhaps of Jimi's Axis.

Shortly before Christmas, media guru Marshall McLuhan hosted a meeting with the visiting Beatle at Toronto's Department of Culture and Technology, filmed by CBS TV. They spoke about the essence of language and the nature of song. Lennon must have felt elated, being taken seriously, at last, after years at school and college as the bad boy, the bum, here he was with his words hung on to like oracles in the presence of high-grade media pundits. Waving goodbye after an intense forty-five minutes talking, McLuhan said the portals had been honored by John's presence.

During the week, John's representatives met with government aides, and then it was communicated a meeting with the Top Man had been agreed, but the task of media management was to be strictly the government's. John was excited. A train left Toronto Union Station on Monday, December 21, for Ottawa. Inside a specially hired, spacious observation car with dining and sleeping facilities, John, Yoko, Anthony Fawcett, John Brower, Ritchie Yorke, Ronnie Hawkins and wife Wanda, spread themselves out like an Oriental caravan on the way to a date with destiny. This was the closest John was going to get to a flying saucer ride in Canada. Never before had such a hirsute collection made its way to the pinnacle of a national establishment. At Montreal, limousines took the party to the Chateau Champlain Hotel for another press conference. Returning to the train, a hole was specially drilled in the carriage for installation of a telephone. At the top, you can have it all, even your own phone on a train—incredible in 1969! Later a secret meeting occurred by Platform 18 with the Le Dain Drug Commission, interested in Lennon's views on marijuana legalization.

At 2:00 a.m. on Tuesday, the historic train arrived at Ottawa with temperatures at 10 degrees below freezing. John hadn't slept for nerves. Then he dressed in his best Pierre Cardin suit and black silk tie, and looked a picture of stately elegance and eccentricity combined.

Running the gauntlet of press alerted by the government, John and his party entered Center Block on Ottawa's Parliament Hill. Photos were taken in Trudeau's oak-paneled office, with the P.M. giving Yoko a warm hug, before doors were closed and an unusually long fifty-minute meeting got underway, with nervous opening, then noticeable warming, as Anthony Fawcett noted in his written account of the meeting.⁴ John's writings were discussed before conversation turned toward the generation gap—John was, or was taken as, representing his generation—and then the peace festival idea. Trudeau recognized the quality of John's arguments for a "young Canada" PR coup if the festival were held in his country, and offered government assistance, which must have made John's heart leap, with maybe just a niggling fear of "cozying-up" to the establishment he'd always thought he despised.

Trudeau talked about his recent visit to a totally authoritarian Maoist China, and asked if Beatle John had a private life now he was so famous. Before the meeting ended, Trudeau said he'd hope they could meet in less formal circumstances in the future, and that he'd do all he could to help with the peace initiative. John, buoyant on afflatus, announced to the press: "If there were more leaders like Mr. Trudeau, the world would have peace," adding that Canada didn't know how lucky it was to have such a man at the top. "It was a beautiful meeting."⁵ From there John and Yoko took a meeting with Health Minister John Munro, who wanted to know how best to communicate with disaffected youth. John offered sage advice. If the youth hit you with message-laden placards, get your own, and show them back. In other words, try to speak in the same language.

It must have felt very strange coming back to England where the press generally treated John and Yoko's peace campaign as one of the jokes of the year and John himself as having gone off his rocker (Yoko was widely presumed barmy already). He and Yoko spent Christmas at Tittenhurst Park and then flew to Aalborg, Denmark. And the rest, is it not history?

THIRTY

1969 II
So Near and Yet So Far, or . . .
What the Hell Went Wrong?

Walking on water wasn't built in a day.
JACK KEROUAC, ABOUT TO TAKE
PSILOCYBIN MUSHROOMS IN THE COMPANY OF
ALLEN GINSBERG AND TIMOTHY LEARY, 1961

Decades of course don't just end on a schedule. The Chinese New Year is different from the West's, so is the Orthodox Church's New Year's Day. In most Islamic countries, strictly speaking, the dating system does not respect the Christian calendar at all, and even in the West, Australia entered 1970 nine hours earlier than Greenwich, England. The sun rises the same, the weather doesn't change because of the date, the moon is indifferent, and the stars continue to look down. So what's new under the sun?

The difference in our case, I suppose, is that the Sixties was a decade conscious of itself as such. As stated at the beginning of this book, President Kennedy defined it quite openly by declaring that America would put a man on the moon before the decade was out; that promise immediately gave the decade a shape, a character, and a pace (see page 106). There is no doubt that *after* that miracle of science, fortitude, and determination had taken place on July 24, 1969, there was no "decade" left, but it went on, and all too soon, the headlines would be filled with other things, including all-too-familiar things like the Vietnam War, though on July 8 the first U.S. combat unit left Saigon, marking initiation of Nixon's vaunted "Vietnamization" program, with painfully gradual disengagement and shifting of the military burden onto South Vietnamese forces, which scheme played well with voters. Yes, they were told, the president wanted out just as much as anybody else; American boys *were* finally being brought home alive (while secret orders had been given for intense new bombing of eastern Cambodia, beginning March 1969).

Just before Woodstock sent out a hopeful sign of peaceful coexistence on a mass scale (maybe hippies weren't so bad after all), the first announcement of the Manson Family murders occurred on August 9, when the bodies of pregnant Sharon Tate and her friends were revealed to have been found savagely lacerated by female Manson followers arrested on December 1, 1969. By the new year, LAPD detectives became aware of Charles Manson's instrumental role in the murders and of his apocalyptic plot to initiate a war between whites and blacks, the which plot's key phrases Manson and the Family had taken from the Beatles' *White Album* released a year previously: "Helter Skelter," *pigs* (from George Harrison's "Piggies"), and *rise* from Paul's "Blackbird," while "Revolution No. 9" provided what Manson considered a "prophetic" soundtrack of a grand showdown that would tear the "illusion" apart and truly blow the minds of perceived conceited "rich pigs."

As an ingratiatingly long-haired Manson, before the multiple homicides, had availed himself of the hospitality of an innocent Dennis Wilson (of the Beach Boys), and thereby of a recording opportunity gained through Doris Day's son Terry Melcher, Manson's and his followers' crimes hit the L.A music scene hard, sending very un-Pepperlike reverberations across the world; but how much of the fallout might have influenced Lennon's decision in 1970 to remove, as a policy, all further poetic, symbolic or quasi-symbolic, surrealist ambiguities, or implications of personal responsibility or ideas of leadership, from his future songwriting, is impossible to tell. Minimalism had been Yoko's style for years, and John's lyricism had been increasingly influenced by it, as his writing would also be influenced by the psyche-baring, religious "myth-killing" experience of "primal scream therapy" administered by psychotherapist Arthur Janov (1924–2017) at Tittenhurst Park and at the Janov Institute, Los Angeles, beginning in spring 1970.

While playing allusive word games was fun, and could prove interesting for a songwriter, such innocent, if occasionally mischievous modes might yet trigger psychotic episodes in very rare cases of the obsessed and dangerously paranoid. But was there a wider dimension to consider? *Had the era become unhinged?* Flying saucers? Air-cars run on psychic energy? The Manson murders were so unspeakably horrific that it is completely comprehensible that there would be no public discussion by the Beatles on possible links between symbolically potent song lyrics and possible consequences among a tiny minority of the deranged.

Nevertheless, it had certainly been brought home sharply by the end of the decade, that in some quarters the Beatles were being taken *too* seriously. Not only had Timothy Leary personally, and perhaps foolishly, elevated the Beatles to "avatar" status in his cheerful psychedelic rhetoric, but 1969 had also seen the "Paul is dead" controversy, a kind of proto viral-tale that went around the world, wherein it was alleged Paul McCartney was in fact dead. Paul's mysterious "death" was apparently conveyed by symbolic messages in Beatles' songs and record cover images, culminating in 1969's *Abbey Road* where an allegedly spectral McCartney crosses the road in bare feet!—to be seen as a sign of "mourning" in some country or other; bass-wielding "McCartney" on the album was a double!—though a remarkably gifted one, we might think. Whatever the absurdity of this "fake news," it was noticeably dark in nature and import, and disturbingly foreboding.

In 1970, Lennon would task himself with systematically debunking and destroying what he would eventually crushingly dismiss as the Beatles "myth," continuing to do so over the early, embittered, yet psychologically revealing years of the 1970s. Any suggestion of spiritual meaning in the music could now expect short shrift, at least from him. Religion was rejected as a myth employed to cover, transmute, or avoid authentic personal pain. The vaunted (Janovian) cure for the world's sorrow was *reality*, experienced when repressed pains were therapeutically exorcised. The sole hopeful option was to improve reality by authentic efforts to establish love and peace, personally and politically: a social projection of the womb state where the new being had experienced nourishment and protection unalloyed. It is curious how the phenomenon of painful birth was seen as determinative of future miseries both in Janov's therapies and in Vedanta and Buddhism. Psychology here replaces religion with an analogous itinerary of suffering and redemption. In what was a painful shift of perspective for Krishna-conscious George Harrison to witness, "spirituality," to put it bluntly, was now seen to involve a high rate of nutter attraction, and was dangerous. As Lennon had himself informed David Wigg of the *Daily Express* in a June 1969 interview, "God" was, in his estimation (at the time), a "power," and, *like* electricity, people could use him to light a room, or to kill people in a chair. The idea of a morally neutral, or rather ethically transcending "ultimate deity" is a perennial of Vedantist speculation deriving from the Upanishads, in which Brahman is ultimately neither good nor bad, but everything and nothing, and as John opined, we use him to our best ability. History might suggest our perverted ability in this regard.

Obviously, something as hideous as the Manson murders could not have been further from John's or anybody else's mind at the time. John presumed, in tune with the idealism of the period, that most people were, unless "got at," or brainwashed by aspects of the "system," fundamentally well intentioned, good willed, so the idea of using "God" to murder innocent people would have seemed positively medieval, something from the Dark Ages (like the death camps of Hitler and his followers?). Despite stark evidence from World War II, few at the time considered the possibility that medieval frames of mind and reference could enter an ever-progressive modern world. This fatal optimism would prove a dangerous assumption of the liberal belief system, as we now can see all too clearly.

John Lennon was not a person who either welcomed or courted taking responsibility for other people's lives, quite understandably finding it sufficient a task in any given day to take responsibility for his own and close loved ones' existence and problems. One can only speculate what the effect might have been on John, given the direction things were moving in at the end of the Sixties, of having been taken into the bosom of the Canadian government, with the implication of responsibility for peace in the world, or as a generation's representative: an awful role in any sensible person's view. Trudeau would soon be expecting to hear from him and his associates what they intended to do. That expectation suggested obligation plus responsibility. The unfolding debacle in Denmark with John Brower over the part-planned Mosport Park Festival must have emphasized this problem further. Had he (Lennon) been "taken in" by Trudeau's state establishment on a subtle or perhaps unforeseen level? If the *government* would assist with the festival, just *whose* cause would it serve? And who, ultimately, would be responsible for it? John must have wished he still had Brian Epstein to lean on. Allen Klein, though out for John's best interest (and his own) wasn't all that much help.

What had started in March 1969 with an inspired performance-art event for peace, with the *concept* of John and Yoko *representing*, or symbolizing in an artistic sense the people of the world's desire for peace, looked rather different by the end of the year. By meeting Trudeau, in suit and tie to boot, did it not look like John and Yoko had become, as it were, *leaders* of a peace faction, or mass youth lobby? So must it have appeared to Trudeau and his aides. John had long since taken to heart Bob Dylan's line "Don't follow leaders, watch the parking meters," and therefore must, on reflection, have felt extremely uncomfortable with any suggestion he had willingly taken on any such conformist role, which position carried with it a weight of awesome responsibility—and very great personal danger to himself and his family. Did he even have backup and protection for such a role? Having fallen out with Paul in October, he couldn't hide behind or within the Beatles' collective power any more, and he could see that his Canadian associates were soon going to get into a mess, and were, anyway, dependent on his status. Besides, responsibility for what could happen when a free concert goes wrong would, and if not, *should* have been brought home to him even more forcefully after December 6, 1969, when at the

Jefferson Airplane–Grateful Dead–Rolling Stones–organized "free" rock festival at Altamont Speedway, thirty miles to the east of San Francisco, Meredith Hunter was stabbed to death at the front of the stage before a staggered Mick Jagger while the Stones played "Sympathy for the Devil," in a festival that came to a halt with increased violence (the Stones had approved Hells Angels for "security"—one of whom punched Jefferson Airplane's guitarist)—and that by the event's grotesque end also involved the accidental deaths of three others. When I first saw the film *Gimme Shelter,* about the Altamont catastrophe, at a university film-society showing aged eighteen, it made me physically ill, so disturbing was it in its gathering, churning mood of dark, uncontrollable, sinister, and sickly forces.

NOT SO EASY RIDER

Peter Fonda's experience of being bundled unceremoniously into a police wagon after the "fuzz" weighed in to the Sunset Strip to arrest and disperse young people gathered there in late 1966 doubtless confirmed the actor's nascent commitment to the counterculture. Having made a less than successful effort to turn that experience into a film with 1967's *The Trip,* written with Jack Nicholson, as well as several formulaic motorcycle movies, Fonda got together with Dennis Hopper and brilliant writer Terry Southern (1924–1995; who gave us not only the marvelous novel and spiritually aware movie script *The Magic Christian* [1969], but also contributed to the script of Kubrick's 1964 movie *Dr. Strangelove*) to create the unexpected hit of 1969–70, *Easy Rider.* First released in June 1969, the film was epoch marking and significant in many ways, influencing young minds for years to come. First, it showed an authentic contemporary American experience, seen not only through Laszlo Kovacs's objective but richly observant Panavision-Technicolor lens, but also through the uninhibited point of view of the counterculture itself. It presented psychedelic experiences in authentic settings where they made some kind of real sense to the characters. It showed hippie commune life as members felt their life to be, and indeed, showed that manner of life somewhat in the raw. And it showed, in a series of "signs," an America few who saw it

Fig. 30.1. Movie poster for Easy Rider, *1969.*

had any direct experience of. And it did all this to an innovative musical soundtrack of counterculture rock songs, without any further musical accompaniment.

While it did have strong elements of cinema-verité, with a nod toward Godard and other new-wave directors, it also featured a directorial style built up from the elements of the script rather than imposed, and was perhaps one of the first mainstream commercial successes to be made "under the influence," at least some of the time. But for all that, it was loaded with heavy symbolism, and a background message of some, if arguably overblown, power.

The movie posed an interesting question. Its two leads Captain America (Fonda) and Billy, (presumably "the Kid," played by Hopper) taking their profits from a sale of "junk" (or some narcotic powder passed over in a New Mexican junkyard) south to "freedom" in the bodywork of their custom-built chopper motorcycles—highly cool at the time and subsequently—encounter hostility, of ascending degrees of menace, in most places they stop. The question is: Who was more in the spirit of the white pioneers of America, the men and women who scratched the land with their hopes and hard work and their dreams of personal freedom to live as they thought best? Was it the two longhairs on motorbikes, or was it the sundry rednecks they encounter on the way, full of McCarthyite, Klanlike paranoia at anything different from postwar imagery of all-white, clean-cut, straight, square, liquor-laced, God-fearin' America? There's no doubt how the directors and writers of a movie saturated with paranoid introspection would answer that question.

Yes, the bikers were to a degree outlaws by dint of their task, and lifestyles, but was not the myth of the West built on legendary outlaws, and on long-haired individualists and cultural outsiders who escaped town and city prejudice to make their own way in the mountains and across the plains, to find some peace of mind, dressed in the skins of hand-caught wild beasts, and fed without benefit of supermarket or tinned produce, with ideas of their own? The *freedom* of the open plains and mountain passes . . . *Easy Rider* was a *Western*.

"Don't you know who this is?" Billy asks a policeman who is locking them up for "parading without a license" (the law serves established powers). "This is Captain America, man!" The Stars and Stripes, sewn onto Fonda's leather jacket, were not simply ironic; the flag is intentionally patriotic. Making *Easy Rider* was an act of love for the country Fonda and his friends wanted to believe in, needed to believe in.

Nowadays, when we see the movie and we see the pair take off from the rather dull commune for a blissful afternoon with some commune girls at a natural rock pool, to the beautiful tune of the Byrds' psychedelic take on the "Paradise" dreamt by poet Samuel Taylor Coleridge in revolutionary Nether Stowey, England, in 1797, while he was on opium ("I Wasn't Born to Follow"), we're rather glad Billy and his friend have left the seriousness of the hippie idealists' almost certainly vain attempt to make desert sand bloom. We share the boys' brief moment of Edenic joy, before they find themselves arrested for breaking some no-law in a no-good, dumb town of apparently largely dumb people, seemingly brainwashed by years of boredom and crushing independence from any original thought or culture. Fortunately, they meet Jack Nicholson, a loveable roué lawyer (George Hanson) who knows how to play both sides, and is himself desperate for a better life beyond court appearances and sensitivity-insulating hooch.

The boys turn him on to grass, and he takes it all in good spirit, without judgment, that is, prejudice. His favoring the boys with his friendship costs him his life in a harrowing scene of casual viciousness undertaken by friends of a Texas sheriff.

After another excoriating scene of a "bad trip" undertaken by the men and their girlfriends in Mardi Gras celebrating New Orleans, we know pretty well what the stakes are, and what is likely to happen. Even so, when it does, it's a shock. I daresay at the time, there were people who would have said, "Come on, things like this wouldn't really happen in America!" The two men on their bikes are passed by a goitered redneck and good ol' boy. They consider the bikers targets, first for laughter, then worse. The man takes a shotgun and, smiling like a dork, casually blows Billy off his bike after telling his victim to get a haircut. Captain America tends to a bleeding, dying Billy then takes off for help. Returning, the rednecks in the pickup blow him away too, and Captain America's gleaming chopper and Stars and Stripes explode apocalyptically from a God's eye view as Roger McGuinn's "Ballad of Easy Rider" whines plaintively: "All they wanted, was to be free, and that's the way it turned out to be. . . ." We see a road, and a river; the one made by man, the other nature. One brings death, the other life. They had taken the road.

It could be taken as an epitaph on the Sixties, or the history of the country. The only freedom from the "hell of other people" would be death. And in this graphic depiction of Nixon's end-of-decade America, that death would be sudden, violent, and cruel. Did Fonda and Hopper go too far? Was this a paranoid bad trip, a fear of what might happen to freedom in America? No, I don't think so. I don't think *Easy Rider* was journalese, a mere allegory of the political scene. It was born of a spiritual experience, a half-crazed shooting process intensified by hallucinogenic and countercultural experience. Its legacy to the future is undoubtedly a sense of either paranoia, or real fear that if you stand too far across the line, for too long, you will get hit, and hit hard. Behind the charade of democracy, the filmmakers saw something quite evil, and very real.

Sixties hip terminology typified the patriarchal, "square," bullet-headed, controlling, capitalist-materialist opponent, as "the Man." The Man ran the military-industrial complex; the Man pulled the strings. The Man made the War, and the Man made the things. The Man could take many forms, but the truly hip could sense the vibes of those who were effectively, even and probably *unconsciously,* agents of the Man. The Man is the equivalent of the Demiurge of the Gnostic myth. As the Man is necessarily an egoist, pure ego, or false self, so the Gnostic Demiurge is the ego of the universe: the Big I AM, blind. He sets bounds of law and reason to the infinite universe of the imagination and is continually mistaken for God by the unenlightened, those without the gnosis or spiritual knowledge. His universe is the material universe, the laws of which, and only the laws of which, this "idiot" (another Gnostic epithet for him) understands. The Demiurge recognizes something has entered that universe, something the Gnostic knows as spirit (pneuma). The Demiurge (or Craftsman) only knows it comes from a higher realm whose existence he denies. He wishes the mysterious spirit for himself and tries to trick humankind into surrendering it to him, so that he can equal the power of the "unknown" or transcendent deity, beyond the material hell that the Demiurge and his archons control. He will torture the soul till he gets what he wants.

We're all crucified.

As the spirit enters the dark world, falling by a primal catastrophe into the grip of material powers, so we see Billy and Captain America on their inspirited machines, dropping in to the dark worlds of the southern states of America "where black is the color and none is the number" (Dylan). They are targets. As Jack Nicholson corrects the two men's conceit: "They ain't afraid of *you*. They're afraid of what you *represent*." George tells the boys that while such people talk on and on about "individual freedom," look what happens when they actually *see* a free individual! This, Billy and Wyatt (after "Earp," known as Captain America) have just experienced in a small-town café, provocatively taunted by a group of men who agree the longhairs won't make it across the parish line. The two boys represent the freedom, the spiritual liberty, that the spiritually moribund have long since surrendered or bartered away to join the Machine, even though if they could see how pitiable their lives were, they'd do anything to get back what they were presumably born with. And that is why they'll surrender themselves again to any passing preacher who offers a glimmer, and be sure, that glimmer will never take them out of town, only into the show tent of "Jayzus," the born-agains who stay the same, but know they're guilty.

Easy Rider planted seeds, or tried to, and has much to say about the spiritual meaning of the Sixties, which spiritual meaning of course can never be anything substantially different from what has ever been thought of as meaningfully spiritual. The spiritual meaning of the Sixties must in the end be found to be the meaning of the spiritual.

AND SUDDENLY, IT WAS THE SEVENTIES

For me, the newly self-conscious Seventies as a definable changeover experience came in a TV advert for Cadbury's milk chocolate, broadcast in 1970. The images showed a "modern" young couple, moderately hippie-like in terms of personal fashion, but clearly a young couple in off-the-rack contemporary dress struggling in the mainstream of the system, except they are not really struggling; they are indulging themselves for a few sweet seconds. They embrace and eat chocolate in the context of a frantic, fast-movin' London, with cars, and buses, and traffic signals a-changin' (like Dylan's "Times"), while a very effective song is played in fast-chompin' U.S. West Coast style. The song declares in a lyric very similar to the lip-smackin' and thirst-quenchin' Pepsi ad of later in the decade, that even in the fast-paced, concrete, image-saturated, traffic-dominated, motorway-speedin' techno-Seventies, "isn't it nice to know, that there's *still* Cadbury's chocolate: *One of the World's Great Tastes.*" Ah, the world that wants to be taught to sing!

What is so interesting about this ad, apart from the clever marriage of image and sound, plus message, is that the "hippie" voice, sung in that emotionally intense Yvonne Elliman, breathless, hippie-country style of the time, with a hint of Grace Slick laid-back cred and hipness, represents a *reactionary voice,* of youth pitted against the *real* character of the times. The voice is saying that despite "progress" (clearly controlled by others, controlled by technology, controlled by other people, remote controllers of a blindingly fast overwhelming, ugly *machine*), despite all that, there are still some things that are good and natural and tasty, and linked with love and intimacy and romance. Yes, the hippie thing has been thoroughly co-opted into the materialist system. Even its sense of reaction to materialism becomes itself reassuring. The new hippies are harping about how things *used to be,* and don't we all agree? There is even a hint of nostalgia *for the Sixties!* While yet we know, don't we that, well, progress must go on! And yes, there will still be times for a little carefree, innocent, harmless, winsome wishin', and there will still be mist-laden countryside to walk in, and wear pastel costumes, and look tastefully and sexually pre-Raphaelite at the weekends (Kapital's gift of "freedom"), and imagine romance as one sucks on a Cadbury's "Flake" like a Shivalingam! In the Seventies, counterculture represents a *withdrawal* into Nature, and to an advertiser, that can look very romantic, and above all, profitably harmless, so long as you don't want to stop the new freeway they're building through the valley.

The Man could reemerge from hiding, and go about his business without too much opposition, so long as his hair was a bit longer, and his lapels a bit wider, his tie or cravat less old school, and he still cultivated occasional sympathy for the dreams of youth. But the world was *tough* and needed toughness and money, and good things like dressing up and getting privately stoned, were for noncollective weekends and holidays when and if one had the money to pay for them. If you wanted the good old homely things, and the thatched cottage in the country, and the country kitchen, and the Laura Ashley dream, you were going to have to work jolly hard, or shall we say: tune out, turn off, and drop in. And those very nice, hip people at the record companies would be only too happy to bliss you out of reality with some nice progressive, laid-back, country-rock music you could play anywhere, but most of all at home in your stereophonic cocoon, when not at work.

In late 1970, after undergoing a proportion of Arthur Janov's "primal scream therapy" in California (an experience that seems to have precipitated a period of atheism), Lennon would bitterly opine to *Rolling Stone* editor Jann Wenner that the only thing that *really* happened in the Sixties was that a lot of people grew their hair, leaving the "same bastards" still running everything. Is that why he'd cut his peace locks? As though to say: "don't blame *Me!*" Renunciation has many phases, as does exhaustion.

I can't say, speaking for myself, that the Beatles' imminent demise was high on the things that registered with me at St. Chad's Cathedral School, Lichfield, where I was a gently rebellious boarder from September 1969. This school could not have been further from the times. In those days, Lichfield was still a quiet cathedral city the industrial revolution had passed by, leaving intact the lineaments of what had been an eighteenth-century horse-drawn coaching center and what Dr. Samuel Johnson called a "city of philosophers," intact on an island of civilization surrounded by sandstone-supported lush countryside, with no class hatred or social bitterness at all. Our school operated in the shadow and light of a cathedral whose oldest visible parts went back to the time of the Crusades. The headmaster wore knickerbockers and had side-whiskers a Victorian would have been proud of. He wrote with a quill pen, and he administered five strokes of the cane on my tender backside in two terms in 1969–70 for trifling misdemeanors, whose coldhearted administration left me feeling lonely and isolated. We had cold showers inflicted by a stern matron at 7:00 a.m. every day, after which we had to run round the cathedral in the dark—a task that, if unperformed in two minutes, led to further punitive measures. Yes, for a surviving Victorian, it would have been a nostalgic experience, but even there, in the bosom of High Anglicanism and arresting ritual, we were very aware, as the Sixties came to a close, that there was a terrible war going on in West Africa, and that in November 1969 the Nigerian Army would not permit the Red Cross to feed the thousands of starving Biafran men, women, and little children, whose faces pleaded from the covers of newspapers. Little Biafra was being starved to death, its leader exhausted with fighting. We were also aware that horrible things had started to happen in a far distant place (to us), that was really very close, called Northern Ireland, where in August 1969 British troops had at first been cheered when their arrival brought a temporary end to weeks of sectarian fighting in Belfast. But battle lines were now drawn that would in due course explode again into bitterest hatred and mutual, bloodsoaked incomprehension, a stalemate of opposites.

I had a fabulous Action Man Space Capsule for Christmas that year, and the biggest hit was "Two Little Boys," a song written and sung by (then) popular entertainer Rolf Harris, set in the American Civil War (Margaret Thatcher would claim it as a favored song many years later). Returning to boarding school in January 1970, I noticed no obvious difference. I recall that I was glad that *Rowan & Martin's Laugh-In* was still on TV, along with *Henry VIII and His Six Wives*. There was no immediate discernible difference anywhere, and the snow was as thick on Beacon Street in January as it had been in December. The general outlook, despite ugly, and mercifully brief, bulletins, was that there were powers in the world that cared about these disasters and that would try to improve things where possible. We did know what the proper way to live was, and cold-blooded violence was not it, and ought to be avoided. The "conquest of space" idea still seemed to point in the direction of a global perspective, and the possibility of a much bigger picture to open minds to come. The outlook was cloudy, with sunny spells.

Fig. 30.2.
Dick Martin, Judy Carne,
and Dan Rowen, cast
members of the popular
comedy show Laugh-In,
1967.

In short, what had been perceived as good in the Sixties was still perceived as good, and few at the time had succumbed to what would later become a permeating fashion for cynicism, which is ordinary intelligence taken to the limit of its comfort, and no further.

There was of course, and had been for a while, a burgeoning reaction to the direction the culture seemed to be taking in the late Sixties. As people were still effectively "in" that culture, or very close to it, and perhaps unconscious of much of it, they had not had time to miss it, or rue the loss of its special and irretrievable glamours.

Several aspects of the reaction may be mentioned here, other than that of the political opposition in the West to antiwar and pacifist demonstrations.

It was widely perceived by quite reasonable people that while it might make sense to knock institutions that already existed, and while criticism can be creative if offered in the right spirit, the question about revolution was: "What are you going to erect in place of what is destroyed?" And here of course lay the problem, for few could agree on much more than on some principles, such as equality (whatever that may mean given the nonequal nature of nature), fairness, and so on, in the direction of justice, honesty, and accountability. After that, one group would tend to break with another. Without authority, who can decide? Well, the pat answer is "the people." But people are individuals and disagree through superior knowledge or ignorance, with one another. Who makes the decision? A lot of people are going to be disappointed in a democracy. In the end, most people under crisis will go for the tried if not entirely trusted option, and hope wise heads can make an orderly best of the system, and perhaps reform some of it before too many people's lives are destroyed.

By the late Sixties, there was a countercultural quasi-Christian move toward living together, that is, abolition of the nuclear family toward shared lives in a commune following the example either of the early church in Jerusalem where people pooled their material resources, and distributed alms to the poor, and so on, or what was happening in Israel or California, or even China. This communistic ideal then found various political forms, most of whom argued over theory, and tended to attract demigods, egomaniacs, and extremists to whom compromise was some kind of mortal sin, such was their defensive-aggressive conviction in their self-erected purist best thoughts.

People in general were not open to the partial rhetoric of Black Panthers any more than most English people would join the skinheads. There had been a kind of social hyperventilation, with "too much too soon" for people caught in the currents. Everyone could see the sad sight of drug casualties, homeless young people, and an oncoming gaudiness as commercial interests tried to harness psychedelia in ever-gaudier mass-produced forms, with tasteless mismatched colors and inept clothing innovations made for the sake of it. People were getting head sick of the *image* of the Sixties-modern, and there would be a conservative, even romantic reaction. In Britain, trade-union unrest was not something "beautiful people" wanted to have much to do with, on the whole, and that itself indicated that much of the distinctive Sixties experience was a middle-class experience.

To most comfortable observers, the commune was hardly a step forward, more resembling a state of being one might perforce have to adapt to in the event of a nuclear war, and there was little afterward to live on. If a young person had endured conditions of student life, it was not such a big step, initially, to think of more sharing, but there comes a point when sheer boredom kicks in and the ideologically novel becomes the experientially boring, and people do what they've always done. They quit. Those who have tried commune life may tell their own tale of what it means to have limited privacy, and many other, mounting irritants that come from the fact that people always resemble . . . people, whatever their ideals, under the skin.

By 1970, there were more materially satisfied people in many parts of the world than there were in 1960. Living standards in many places, though by no means all, had improved somewhat (though less in America), but living standards were still vulnerable. Many reflected that the work of the Sixties, as they saw it, was in many respects "done." There had been a wholesale attack on the class system, and wages had risen a bit. Modernity, as in the advertisement referred to above, was everywhere to be encountered, and much of it still looked shiny and new, though it was beginning to show its slender basis in profit over value. Amazing how materialism tends to favor poor materials! Certainly, in the West, young people had the enjoyment of freedoms alien to many of their parents and grandparents. Schools were loosening up, and corporal punishment was on the decline. The fact that *Easy Rider* made the screens of local cinemas *at all* showed liberalization had occurred to the benefit of free artistic expression. Sexy and risqué books and pornography had become commonplace. Rock music and long hair were more acceptable too, in many, though not all places.

Of course, to many around the world, the Sixties had never happened in terms of the cultural and spiritual changes discussed in this book. A lot of the world's population was quite oblivious to much that had passed, and were, as it were, left behind. With the oil crisis of 1973, the balloon of increasing Western prosperity burst, and the conditions that had allowed the Sixties to inflate in the first place, ceased to operate.

Despite the space race, there had been no shortage of inward-lookingness in the Sixties, as we discovered when we examined the exported-imported "Indian" experience in the Sixties. This was rather ironic for many educated Indians, as was apparent from several books published subsequently, such as Gita Mehta's *Karma Cola,* as well as Joyce Collin-Smith's *Call No Man Master,* a revisionist view of Maharishi Mahesh Yogi. Many bright Indian intellectuals were aghast to see so many intelligent Westerners embracing what they had themselves come to see as past obscurantism! Many Indians wanted to be *modern,* and to embrace social ideals, philosophies, and material improvements that had been developed and taken for granted in the West. Materialism wasn't all bad when you were raised in a culture where spiritual ideas were used to justify everything from extreme poverty to physical diseases. The Westerner's fascinating "karma" discovery meant for an Indian villager that there was no need for a proper hospital, as he or she might come back healthy in the next life if they accepted their position gracefully in this one.

This all indicates a certain departure from reality that went hand in hand with Sixties embrace of Hindu mysticism. It felt like a healthy, even bracing draft of *reality* for many in the Seventies who abandoned "the dream" or the dream state. John Lennon would receive praise for his courageous(?) stance on his first solo album of finished songs that declared that God was a concept whose value was relative to the amount of pain one was suffering (the old "crutch" argument restated), while he announced in song he no longer believed in magic, Gita, Jesus, tarot, Buddha, and practically every other lineament of the countercultural Sixties bookshelf, ending the litany with his nonbelief in Elvis, Dylan, and the *Beatles*. He said he believed in "reality," which boiled down to himself and Yoko, and in a famously bitter *Rolling Stone* interview of 1970 confirmed to Jann Wenner his newfound solipsism with the statement that he wasn't veering away from reality for anything. The dream was over. For the time being anyway. The dream was back a year later in "Imagine," (though stripped down and atheistically politicized) and in Yoko Ono's song "Now or Never," (1972) which cleverly fused dream and reality: "Dream we dream alone is only a dream; dream we dream together is reality." So the dream wasn't entirely over, after all. Different dream, perhaps.

A different kind of inward-lookingness would dominate the new decade: psychological self-obsession. For many observers, the space race had really led nowhere. Everyone agreed America had won the race, but what then? There was no epiphany, no mystical revelation—no real change in the predicament of man. Unlike the Man in the Moon, the man *on* the moon had feet of clay, and returned to Earth. Putting man on the moon only delivered a man on the moon, but the moon was still cried for, because it would remain forever distant, turning the tides. And yet, paradoxically, by putting a man on the moon, we had not so much taken man into infinite space, but brought the moon down to Earth. We had "earthed" it, and robbed it of its historic magic. Someone said it was the utmost impiety to walk on the moon. I don't know about that, but the taste for any more planet hopping declined quickly. Anyone could see they'd rather live in the Yellowstone Park than in space. The earth became, inevitably perhaps, inward looking, and rather narrow-minded again. People thought about themselves a lot, and psychological therapies took off big-time. The thrust outward of the previous decade had lost its trajectory, rather like the Renaissance, dissolving into the Reformation, with its hideous extremities of religious righteousness.

Something else had gone with the Sixties, other than the fairy dust of positive dreaming, shared magic, and desire. Western societies had lost much of their cohesion, their comforting wholeness. They all were rather raw, as though overexposed. America, particularly, was bitterly divided. I remember meeting a Worshipful Master of Iowan Freemasonry and discussing Masonic recruitment there in the Nineties. He told me that they had "lost a generation to the hippies." That was quite a statement when you think about it. Odd how all the talk of unity, of the human Be-In, of mystical oneness, may have proved in the end to be shatteringly divisive, generating new levels of intolerance and competing self-righteousness. This is a dualistic world; do one thing, expect the opposite as well. Look how the more the European Union pushes to unite, the more it splits apart. They never learn.

It might be argued then that the Sixties was a victim of its success. Perhaps there was too much pushing, and the forces of reaction grew alarmed and decided "it" had to stop.

It was a hell of a show, while it lasted, and if it was rather in fact a new beginning, or the beginning of a beginning, then it was a hell of a way to start!

THIRTY-ONE

The Spiritual Meaning
of the 1960s

Seek and ye shall find.

MATTHEW 7:7

The imagination is the spiritual part of humanity that possesses the vision of all things. Through imagination we grasp the spiritual unity of the universe.

LOUIS CLAUDE DE SAINT-MARTIN

In such a conflict I stand neuter.
But oh! mistake not gold for pewter!
The plain fact is: materialise
What spiritual fact you choose,
And all such turn to folly—lose
The subtle splendour, and the wise
Love and dear bliss of truth. Beware
Lest your lewd laughter set a snare
For any! Thus and only thus
Will I admit a difference
'Twixt spirit and the things of sense.

What is the quarrel between us?
Why do our thoughts so idly clatter?
I do not care one jot for matter,
One jot for spirit, while you say
One is pure ether, one pure clay.

ALEISTER CROWLEY, FROM "PENTECOST"
IN *THE SWORD OF SONG: CALLED BY CHRISTIANS*
THE BOOK OF THE BEAST, 1904

I have said elsewhere that hope and tragedy were the pillars of the Sixties.

In what lay the tragedy? Certain persons were, at the decade's end, already aware of a tragedy inherent to the decade itself, while most of us are of course aware of many well-known tragedies that scarred that decade with ill omen, beginning most famously with the murder of J. F. Kennedy, then mounting with assassinations of his brother Robert, Malcolm X, Martin Luther King (all four involved with freeing black people from legal and social penalties). Then there were the sudden deaths of three American and at least one Russian astro/cosmonauts, the untimely deaths of Marilyn Monroe, Otis Redding, Brian Jones, and all of the Manson Family's poor victims. We remember the mass deaths by starvation and conflict in Nigeria and Biafra, the bloody Russian invasion of Prague in 1968, the beginning of the Troubles in Northern Ireland, the My Lai massacre, and many other atrocities committed in the names of two ideologies in the Vietnam War, the persecution and silencing of individuals in the USSR and Cuba, the killings at Sharpeville, South Africa, the continued conflict between Israel and her neighbors, the 1966 Aberfan disaster in Wales, political murders in Germany, Italy, Spain, the genocide of Chinese ordered by Mao Zedong—the list might seem endless on the global scale. Only the astronauts it might seem "came in peace for all mankind" before plunging a national flag into the moon's apolitical, anational, mysterious surface.

It might be objected that tragedy is endemic to life, and the Sixties were no different from any other decade in this regard. Certainly, one can see at a glance that the popular myth of the Sixties is very far from accurate: peace, love, freedom, sex, drugs, and rock 'n' roll—this scrapbook image of wishful thinking (or moral outrage), or convenient media manipulation, or just poor memory, is a travesty.

No, but what if the age *itself* was a tragedy, implicated in something lost irretrievably, lost and gone, destroyed, through a tragic flaw in the character of the times, and the times of its characters? Such seems to be the import of Peter Fonda, Dennis Hopper, and Terry Southern's prophetic movie *Easy Rider*—and by *prophetic* I mean forthtelling, rather than foretelling, for the prophecy concerns most what had already happened, and was happening.

The night before the tragic murders of Billy and Wyatt, there is a kind of "last supper" by a campfire. You don't see the motorcycles this time; never to be seen again, they'd just been stolen from the production and dismembered by thieves: a betrayal symbolically and sinisterly at one with the story's climactic narrative.

Warmed by the fire, Billy tries to put aside the fact that their civil rights lawyer friend George Hanson (Jack Nicholson) has been clubbed to death by rednecks filled with ungoverned, or malevolently directed hatred for the boys' nonconformity, perhaps banally jealous of their sexual attractiveness to local girls. Certainly, the lovely George's murder is tragic, a slaughter whose stark horror has not been assuaged by a harrowingly intense—arguably "bad"—LSD trip in a New Orleans cemetery, provided courtesy of George's membership card (or invitation) to the city's finest whorehouse: "and these ain't pork chops," a now dead George informed his two friends regarding the hookers there— "These are U.S. *Prime!*" Despite the girls' charm, we have seen Captain America take them out of the purgatorial brothel and into the Mardi Gras outside, thence to the cemetery where the "acid" is shared among them like a eucharist. In the surreally shot and edited necropolis, we have been privileged to see the "real" Peter Fonda actually weeping and wailing at a funerary statue, its female head chosen for its resemblance to the Statue of Liberty. Fonda cries and moans with revisited horror, begging for an answer as to how his (real) mother could have killed herself by slashing her own throat. *Liberty* (mother) *dies in Fonda's arms.* Where has Liberty gone? Why has she done this to herself? How could she? Yes, this is part of the symbolic tragedy attended to at the last campfire before the young men are "crucified" by those "who know not what they do"—more rednecked ignoramuses salivating in the arrogance of their numerical ascendancy in the state. You can see the snarl of their minds: *if the nigger's got his freedom, it's thanks to white trash liberal lawyers and longhairs like these motherfuckers.* Nothing's been learned, only bitterness, and revenge, more revenge.

But Billy seems unaware of any impending darkness. He thinks he's "got away with it" and, the night before, tries to put a shine on the situation. After all, they've got the money from selling the junk (evidently cocaine) they'd acquired in the junkyard (the world) at the beginning of the story, unloaded on Phil Spector (the Connection) in his own Rolls Royce, beneath incoming aircraft and by a railway line that was actually carrying tanks to Vietnam: visible to all the crew but omitted from the shots in the movie—and all to the tune thumping forth from Steppenwolf's lines: "The Pusher is a Monster! Goddamn the Pusher Man!" And the money, Billy believes, guarantees their freedom: the good times are comin'. Billy smiles at thoughts of the happiness they're heading toward: the dream they have dreamed of. Freedom. But all Wyatt can say is: "We blew it." Billy is incredulous: *Blew what?* Fonda repeats the line: "We blew it."

WE BLEW IT

The next day the boys meet their fated deaths *on the road:* was there a hint of Jack Kerouac there?—the Kerouac who'd written *On the Road* (1957) whose fourth part sends its characters off happy after a party at a bordello in Gregoria, Mexico, having crossed the Texas border? The Kerouac introduced to psilocybin mushrooms by Allen Ginsberg as the Sixties opened? Whither the dream?

On the road . . . the locus of the end of the dream was the literary place where the dream of freedom first began. But unlike the book, our boys don't make it across the parish line. The road is where the dream ends. Why?

It is clear that here, on the road, is the import of the movie, and the tragic message it has unfolded. We may recall Nicholson's earlier lines about the vile taunters in the Texas café-bar: that these types did not fear the young men themselves (having violence *and the law* to help them), but rather "what they represent." As we noted earlier—and the lines bear repetition—he went on to say that "sure," people like to *talk* a lot about "individual freedom" as a virtue of the "American dream" (or everyone's really), *but,* warns Nicholson, just see what happens when they actually, physically meet a "free individual!" They can't bear it, because it shows them up for the unfree, ungainly, unbeautiful bits of the machine they really are, and pride in their abject, bought-and-sold wretchedness makes them not frightened, but *dangerous.* Subconsciously, these creatures know they're not free, and they ain't gonna let anyone else show 'em what real freedom means. Like the tool-discovering representative of ape-humanoids in *2001: A Space Odyssey,* the first chance they get to exercise the "liberty" the new weapon affords them, and once they find an object to oppose, they resort immediately to violence and murder. "Crucify him!" they cry, *en masse.* And being a mass, they're proud of it! We find the same message in Patrick McGoohan's *The Prisoner* TV series: "You," the Prisoner—and only truly free man in the prison— is told, "are *Number Six.*" He is *not,* say the governors, the rulers, the *archons,* "a Free Man." We can't be having "free men," can we? No, indeed. Such a man would be a king, and it was as a *king* that Jesus was crucified, an example to all the other would-be free Jews or any other troublesome subjects of the state preaching new kingdoms, new ages.

What has the Free Man got? What makes him different? He has *Spirit,* and the spirit of freedom is the spirit of God on earth. And that is why we recognize in a symbol that when the mob demanded "the King of the Jews" crucified, they were, not knowing what they were doing, attempting to crucify *God,* but failed, for *God is Free.* And the unfree kill themselves. God is life. God is breath. The Free Wind: the eternal life within life, within breath, within freedom. And ask not who "He" is, for He is You. And that was a discovery of the Sixties, and for all I know, may represent its spiritual meaning, still unrecognized in its import. *Advaita*: not two.

△ △ △

Are we getting closer to the spiritual meaning of the 1960s?

We blew it. "Blew" . . . to breathe. . . . One might think the "we" is self-condemnatory, and perhaps it is. After all, it's not the "free" motorcyclists shooting the breeze who commit the atrocities; they are victims, not crucifiers. "All they wanted," as Roger McGuinn's final song goes, "was to be free"—and for that the forces of Fate, and of Will, destroy the children of what Fabre d'Olivet called "Providence," those who take what is provided, who live in faith of divine foresight, who have put their faith in the God (or Goddess) of Freedom. Perhaps we understand better the meaning of "We" when we realize the true meaning of the movie's title.

EASY RIDER

Most people have not stopped to ask the meaning of "Easy Rider." Little wonder when the name was blazoned across epic images of libertine joys astride chromium bikes. They were riders and made it all look easy; a bit like "easy listening," these were "easy riders." That seems to have been the sense Hendrix took "easy rider" when in '69 he wrote his song "Ezy Rider" about "riding on the highways of desire." But according to Dennis Hopper's late admission, the phrase "easy rider" is in fact slang for a man who lives off the (suggested immoral) earnings of a woman. He's a guy flying easy on the back and buck of a whore's labor, not a pimp but the guy she loves to care for. While she does the work, he can take it easy. Now I presume the use of this expression was meaningful to Dennis Hopper, and he had reason to keep it unrevealed in the script. Apart from the obvious pleasantly appropriate pun with the images of Billy and Captain America "laid-back" on their bikes traversing the continent, the symbol of the man living off the profit of the whore suggests to me two distinct ideas.

The first idea is that the "whore" is the capitalist system that means that freedom can only be bought after a visit to the junkyard where contact is made with the underworld (unadulterated materialism), providing, through intermediaries, rich men with their kicks (it is clear throughout that neither Billy nor his friend are into hard drugs). The system invites prostitution of self: to work only *for money*. They have to (they think) prostitute themselves a little to earn sufficient to be "free." What price then, freedom? And if bought at such a price, were they ever as free, or would they ever be, as free as they imagined in their dream? And look at the terrible price! The good young man they offered to take away from the sins of his world was murdered under their very noses, and they proved helpless to prevent it. Had they then "blown it" by *relying on the system* for their freedom, rather than challenging the system directly, or even trying to change or subdue it? Was not the truth that they were *running away* from something, albeit in pursuit of the very thing the country was allegedly founded to foster, namely liberty—who herself has been sacrificed for cash?

The second, perhaps more interesting idea (at least in my mind), has more to do with the sense of freedom the young men breathe in as the "free winds take them higher" (as Hendrix expressed the spiritual experience in his musical-poetic take on the subject). If we take the "whore" as the Gnostic whore, or "virgin-whore" (Wisdom = *Sophia*) found in a brothel and redeemed by magus Simon as a vehicle of revelation, then we may see that what has made them free, what has given them the spirit of the pioneer, the one who travels further, who breaks beyond the line, who chooses not to conform, but who in his spiritual wholeness embodies freedom, is the divine blessing of pneuma, or holy spirit, that which in Gnostic myths is to be rescued from this world, and its false values. In this context we can immediately grasp an interesting parallel between the Gnostic Sophia whose desire to know the unknowable abyss of the divine leads to her instability and the loss of her "seeds" (pneuma), which fall into the lower world (the brothel), and the wildness of Shiva. In some myths about Shiva, he is presented as being so passionately unstable, boiling over with hot energy, ecstatic, and freaking out with explosive tendencies, he has to be taken to high places where the cold will "cool" him down to levels that can be dealt with. Sometimes, yogurt is administered to his volcanic head as you would to a flaming hot curry! Sophia, likewise, was described by Gnostics as so filled with ardor for the unknowable Father, so foolishly passionate that she is literally lopsided, losing control of her divine seeds of spirit, which, unbalanced, fall from the perfection of the divine pleroma into the imperfection of its material parody. Wisdom's fruit for humankind is *gnosis,* and that is the profit of the whore Wisdom, what she gives for nothing, while remaining ever pure.

The point is that, had they but realized it, the young easy riders *already* had freedom, for that was the "easy ride" wisdom granted them, planting it in their souls: the knowledge of the spirit is the freedom from the world. She who gave freely was the virtuous woman whose price is "far above rubies" (Proverbs 31:10). That is what they "blew," and while they breathed it, or Her (the free wind) into their lungs, they lived and saw, and by exchanging that for the wages of the world, their true freedom blew away. Billy thought the transaction in the junkyard was a simple matter, like paying a tax, buying off at last the grip of the world in the world's currency (junk). In fact he was turning his back on what he had already, but could not see. As a representative of the age, he blew it, and becomes subject to fate through his willfulness. When the boys take the New Orleans hookers out of the brothel, they have nowhere to take them but the cemetery, where Fonda weeps real tears for the death of liberty. They take acid, but find not freedom, only a nightmare.

And that too is the spiritual meaning of the Sixties: the knowledge so near, its fulfillment, so far away. But as we began this story with the words of artist-filmmaker Harry Smith, we might consider them again. When William Breeze asked Smith about the Sixties, he said they were "great," with the caveat, "if only we'd known what we were doing." The spiritual life of the decade was involved in a spiritual drama the lineaments of which were not grasped and systematically applied. The temptations of the world proved, as ever, very strong, and while the word *freedom* was spoken often enough, how often was it understood?

Many felt that the precipitous decline of awareness and positive energy began when hard drugs started to take the place of "soft" stimulants with, briefly, revelatory potential. Soon the *sensation* was all ("I Feel Free" as Cream sang in a hit single of 1966), and the nature of addiction is the loss of will, judgment, and ultimately, virtue, which is the life force. Who can say such a thing did not take place, and take with it that vital aspect of the "providential" man or woman, *innocence?* Eden is for the innocent, not the smartass, or the cool fool. Orson Welles understood this, in *Falstaff* (also 1966); Falstaff's personal freedom is a function of his innocence. He is a flower child, born of an English rose, when the hay smelled sweeter and the dawn glowed brightly on the fields of green.

We had it all, but did not see it.

I hope readers have recognized by now that the Sixties embodied a transnational spiritual movement—and that is why many of us collectively miss it. No "feel-good" factor artificially stimulated by mere cash can match the pulse of the heart beating to the vibe of eternity! Spiritual things are spiritually discerned. The carnal mind is enmity against God.

If the spiritual movement had had more cohesion, had even been aware of itself as such, it could have achieved greater things than were accomplished in the period, and there might have been a genuine sense of progress beyond the seedtime, rather than attempt after attempt since to re-create it, or raise it by sympathetic magic of imitation. People really did believe during the Seventies that if the individual Beatles "got together" again, the whole thing would revive and the party could get going again. But John, some time over the cusp of the decades seems to have concluded consciously or otherwise that he could stand the mantle of leadership not at all. In some respects he switched from being a "providential man" (reliant on the divine) to a "will man." Trying to resist the passivity of the one who accepts Fate, he arguably tried through science, or knowledge, to free himself. The battle between Will and Fate, as d'Olivet argued, means a humanity bound to destroy every step of progress he makes, bound to try and try and try again, with the "Satanic" willfulness continually destroying. Besides, had the Beatles not led, by not leading? Had they not *commanded* respect, rather than demanded it? Was it not absurd to expect the future to depend on the Beatles staying together? Lennon made an investment in the New Left, with "Power to the People," but in a democracy, the people cannot achieve power, only confer it. The individual, the true locus of sovereignty, is politically neutered in the mass.

The fact was that by the end of the decade many communities were even more divided than they had been at the start of it. There was more rancor, more bitterness in many places. Prosperity had altered appearances, but also created envy and impatience for wealth. The forces of deformation were there already, and the youth movements were reactionary but not decisive; there was no real Plan. Doubtless, important aspects of the counterculture have come through in terms of some individual freedoms, care for the environment, health issues, spiritual eclecticism, but these seem in relative terms like trinkets, or at the most, little buds, compared to the potential of the era.

Aleister Crowley prophesied in 1943 that 1965 would mark an important stage in the growth of the Child, that is, the Aeon, or Age in the largest sense. He would have had no truck with the "Age of Aquarius" color scheme. In fact he wrote that if there really was a new constellation in which the vernal equinox appeared of significance (astrological calculations differ greatly), then the obvious sign Aquarius would more likely mean its opposite, and Leo would be more dominant. The year 1965 was certainly a period when minds opened and new light came in, giving birth to a new aesthetic and attitude. And if we think of the times as being in a sense a growth of an archetypal child with enormous potential, then we may understand better why there was a failure of youth (expressing the energies of that child) *to take control,* and "to blow" the chances of taking power away from the spiritually ignorant and morally corrupt whose numbers secured power over the will of the child. Was it deep troubling of this kind that took Lennon away so suddenly from the vaunted "triumph" of meeting Trudeau as though on a state visit, or summit, into introspection and withdrawal? One may imagine how, on reflection, it might have felt like he had gone "cap in hand" to authority, almost being co-opted into a state-sponsored youth-control program similar to that when Harold Wilson said he'd approved of giving the Beatles MBEs because they kept "the kids off the streets"—how convenient, for social countries have special problems in suppressing the intelligence and energy of youth.

One important aspect of the spiritual meaning of the Sixties must be the appearance of individualistic tendencies in various acute forms, of which social rebelliousness is just one. One thinks of the power of the "child" Krishna, or fierce Shiva, intolerant and assertive, hard to control. Dr. Spock had seen the star rise of the child as new being, not to be beaten into shape but brought forth in its own terms. Whatever else this might mean, it must stand as the long death knell of socialism. The old appeal to the barbed fruit of socialism is still made, but it is plainly old, not the modern thing it appeared to so many for so much of the twentieth century. New bribes have to be found to keep youth and individualism in check. Money, jobs, the usual promises of freedom, of fast cars jetting round misty mountains with pretty girls and filed-faced boys with five o'clock shadows pretending to be men! The same old bribe!

In retrospect, most thinking people now recognize the utter ruinousness of Timothy Leary's injunction to "turn on, tune in, and drop out." Apart from the patronizing nature of this interference with other true wills (and Leary claimed to be Crowleyan in orientation!), its baselessness in realizable practicality would soon be felt by first the Diggers—trying to deal with dropouts descending on San Francisco— then by society at large. We may be in, but not *of* the world. As Derek Taylor wryly observed, one needs to know where the next meal is coming from, even if that does make one appear as an "easy rider." Leary's idea to avoid contact with the wicked world lacked holism. Love your enemies; you don't have to *like* them. Frankly, the renouncing "sannyasi" system will not work in the West, for our mentality is of an active, ego-led and realist kind, not passive, resigned, or dreamlike. And though one needs a harmony of both principles, one is not to be sacrificed to the other, except in love, the which word will, I hope, always be regarded as the key word of the decade, for its virtue is eternal and may keep all that was good about the Sixties alive. We are not to submit ourselves to "God," which in this context only means fate, abrogating responsibility, but rather to rise in love.

Billy and Wyatt die, in one sense, because they haven't got control of the situation; the road, in fact, is not *theirs*. They have spent their energy rebelling in a rather obvious way, while allowing the enemy to maintain complete control of their destinies; their freedom is illusory. They are easy riding on bitches' brew. However much they drop out, they won't find a free rock to fall on; they will go on paying. In the end, following their path, their only redemption seems to come with death, when we see the road and the river and hear a sad song when we should have heard a hymn of triumph as the men come Home. Their fatality was to withdraw, to head "south." Vulnerable, they could easily be picked off. They had no control.

Moderation and discipline get better results, but one also needs spiritual strength and knowledge and the wisdom to apply it. In this regard, the Sixties marked a seedtime; the fruits are to come. You don't have to reinvent the wheel. I like to think then that Billy and Wyatt did not die in vain, and we shall see wiser, freer radicals take what the mystics have called "the Royal Road," one of whose characteristics is neither to favor the right, nor the left, neither to accept unadulterated communism, nor unadulterated capitalism, but to head *straight on* with great faith. The gnosis was there in seed in the Sixties. Embraced with moderation, determination, and self-discipline, it works wonders, and when the seeds truly flower, as they must, we may look forward to another astonishing—well, not a mere decade, but a historic era.

The Sixties was the Herald, the *kerux;* the main show has not yet begun, but book me a seat when it does! I'm in for the ride; how about you?

Fig. 31.1. The burning motorcycle at the climax of Easy Rider.

Notes

CHAPTER 1.
THE SIXTIES—*PHEW!*—AND ME

1. Email from William Breeze to the author, January 22, 2017.

CHAPTER 5. WATERTOWN

1. *Frank Sinatra, Watertown,* interview of Jake Holmes by Ed O'Brien in booklet accompanying 1995 CD rerelease, Reprise Records, 13.
2. *Frank Sinatra, Watertown,* 13.
3. *Frank Sinatra, Watertown,* 14.

CHAPTER 8.
PSYCHOLOGY

1. Feuerbach, *The Essence of Christianity,* chapter 2: 29–30; chapter 16: 158.
2. Nietzsche, "God Is Dead," in *The Gay Science* (Sections 108, 125, and 343); Nietzsche, *Thus Spoke Zarathustra,* prologue and section 25.

CHAPTER 11.
DISCOMFITING CHANGES IN THEOLOGY

1. Acquaviva, *The Decline of the Sacred in Industrial Society,* 201–2.
2. John Lennon, *A Spaniard in the Works,* 89

CHAPTER 12.
THE PERSISTENCE OF THE BIBLE

1. Fawcett, *John Lennon: One Day at a Time,* 15–25.
2. Churton, "My Life in the Sixties," unpublished manuscript.

CHAPTER 13.
CIVIL RIGHTS

1. Winston, "Blacks Say Atheists Were Unseen Civil Rights Heroes."

CHAPTER 15.
THE SPIRITUAL IN ART IN THE SIXTIES:
THE AGE OF SPACE

1. Kuspit, "Concerning the Spiritual in Contemporary Art," 313.
2. Kandinsky, *Concerning the Spiritual in Art,* 17.
3. Kandinsky, *Concerning the Spiritual in Art,* 2.
4. Kandinsky, *Concerning the Spiritual in Art,* 4.
5. Lipsey, *An Art of Our Own,* 360.
6. Hess, *Abstract Expressionism,* 40.
7. Tuchman, *The Spiritual in Art: Abstract Painting 1890–1985,* 416.
8. Raymond Foye, "Harry Smith: The Alchemical Image," in Raymond Foye, "Hanuman Books" website: www.raymondfoye.info (accessed April 3, 2018). Foye's essay originally appeared in the "The Heavenly Tree Grows Downward" catalog (2002), and can now be read in its entirety, fully illustrated, on the official site of Harry Smith's fellow artist, Philip Taaffe, maintained by Raymond Foye Ltd. Fine Art Services.
9. Foye, "Harry Smith: The Alchemical Image."
10. Foye, "Harry Smith: The Alchemical Image."
11. Foye, "Harry Smith: The Alchemical Image."
12. Foye, "Harry Smith: The Alchemical Image."
13. Foye, "Harry Smith: The Alchemical Image."
14. Garcia and Higashi, *Jerry Garcia: The Collected Artwork,* xviii.
15. McEvilly, "Origins of Anti-Art," 63–64.
16. McEvilly, "Origins of Anti-Art," 63–64.
17. McEvilly, "Origins of Anti-Art," 63–64.

18. For some interesting thoughts on Klein's works' analogy with alchemy, see Seegers, "Metabolic Processes: On Great Works and Invisible Values in Contemporary Art," in Dupré, von Kerssenbrock-Krosigk, and Wismer, *Art and Alchemy: The Mystery of Transformation*, 186, 195, 201.

CHAPTER 16.
THE SPIRITUAL IN ORCHESTRAL, FILM, AND JAZZ MUSIC

1. Rózsa, *Double Life: The Autobiography of Miklós Rózsa*, 11.
2. Rózsa, *Double Life: The Autobiography of Miklós Rózsa*, 11.
3. Rózsa, *Double Life: The Autobiography of Miklós Rózsa*, 11.
4. Rózsa, *Double Life: The Autobiography of Miklós Rózsa*, 190.
5. Rózsa, *Double Life: The Autobiography of Miklós Rózsa*, 190.
6. Rózsa, *Double Life: The Autobiography of Miklós Rózsa*, 180.
7. Rózsa, *Double Life: The Autobiography of Miklós Rózsa*, 181–82.
8. Rózsa, *Double Life: The Autobiography of Miklós Rózsa*, 186.
9. Burlingame, *The Music of James Bond*, 33.
10. Fiegel, *John Barry: A Sixties Theme*, 14–15.

CHAPTER 22.
PSYCHEDELICS

1. Taylor, *It Was Twenty Years Ago Today*, 91.
2. Taylor, *It Was Twenty Years Ago Today*, 97.
3. Taylor, *It Was Twenty Years Ago Today*, 98.
4. Taylor, *It Was Twenty Years Ago Today*, 99.
5. Taylor, *It Was Twenty Years Ago Today*, 99.
6. Taylor, *It Was Twenty Years Ago Today*, 99.
7. Taylor, *It Was Twenty Years Ago Today*, 105.

CHAPTER 23.
INDIA

1. John Lennon and A. C. Bhaktivedanta, *Search for Liberation*, 34–39.
2. Cynthia Lennon, *A Twist of Lennon*, 160–62.
3. John Lennon and A. C. Bhaktivedanta, *Search for Liberation*, v.

CHAPTER 25.
THE TURNING POINT—1965:
THE AEON OF THE CHILD MADE MANIFEST

1. Churton, *Aleister Crowley: The Biography,* 91–97.
2. OTO Archives, courtesy of William Breeze, OHO, OTO.
3. Zaehner, *Our Savage God,* 63. The poem is "L'Éternité," in Rimbaud's *Oeuvres completes*: "It is found again. What? Eternity. It is the sea mingling with the sun." (The lines are also heard over the final shot of Godard's 1965 *Pierrot le Fou* after the final suicide, and the camera pans out from the island to the sea, as the smoke of the explosion wafts gently away.)

CHAPTER 26.
FEELING GROOVY: THE WEST COAST

1. Taylor, *It Was Twenty Years Ago Today,* 205.
2. Taylor, *It Was Twenty Years Ago Today,* 179.
3. Taylor, *It Was Twenty Years Ago Today,* 180.
4. Taylor, *It Was Twenty Years Ago Today,* 180.
5. Taylor, *It Was Twenty Years Ago Today,* 249.
6. Taylor, *It Was Twenty Years Ago Today,* 251.
7. Taylor, *It Was Twenty Years Ago Today,* 258.

CHAPTER 27.
THE BEAST AND THE SIX SIX SIXTIES

1. Brown, "Kenneth Anger: Where the Bodies Are Buried," interview with Kenneth Anger.
2. Wasserman, *In the Center of the Fire,* 253.
3. Wasserman, *In the Center of the Fire,* 84.
4. Wasserman, *In the Center of the Fire.* See also the admission of the Solar Lodge's role in Frater Shiva, *Inside Solar Lodge, Outside the Law,* 2007.
5. Wasserman, *In the Center of the Fire,* 16.
6. Wasserman, *In the Center of the Fire,* 17.
7. Wasserman, *In the Center of the Fire,* 17.
8. Wasserman, *In the Center of the Fire,* 19.
9. Wasserman, *In the Center of the Fire,* 23.

10. Wasserman, *In the Center of the Fire,* 23.

11. Wasserman, *In the Center of the Fire,* 25.

12. Wasserman, *In the Center of the Fire,* 26.

13. Wasserman, *In the Center of the Fire,* 26.

14. Wasserman, *In the Center of the Fire,* 29.

15. Wasserman, *In the Center of the Fire,* 30.

16. Wasserman, *In the Center of the Fire,* 32.

17. Wasserman, *In the Center of the Fire,* 35.

18. Personal interview of Wasserman by Tobias Churton, Spring 2017.

CHAPTER 28.
NEW YORK

1. Glueck, "The De Menil Family," interview with Dominique de Menil.

2. Colacello, "Remains of the Dia" (interview and article).

3. Glueck, "The De Menil Family," interview with Dominique de Menil.

4. Henderson, *'Scuse Me While I Kiss the Sky,* 167.

5. Henderson, *'Scuse Me While I Kiss the Sky,* 170. Henderson gives the source as Manly Hall, "An Encyclopaedic Outline of Secret Tradition."

6. Henderson, *'Scuse Me While I Kiss the Sky,* 197–98.

7. Henderson, *'Scuse Me While I Kiss the Sky,* 206–7.

8. Henderson, *'Scuse Me While I Kiss the Sky,* 219.

9. Henderson, *'Scuse Me While I Kiss the Sky,* 241.

10. Henderson, *'Scuse Me While I Kiss the Sky,* 241.

11. Henderson, *'Scuse Me While I Kiss the Sky,* 272.

CHAPTER 29.
1969 I: NO PEACE FOR THE WICKED

1. Fawcett, *John Lennon: One Day at a Time,* 69–70.

2. Fawcett, *John Lennon: One Day at a Time,* 69.

3. Taylor, *It Was Twenty Years Ago Today,* 214.

4. Fawcett, *John Lennon: One Day at a Time,* 66–68.

5. Fawcett, *John Lennon: One Day at a Time,* 67.

Bibliography

Acquaviva, Sabino Samele. *The Decline of the Sacred in Industrial Society.* Oxford: Blackwell, 1977.

Bacharach, Burt, with Robert Greenfield. *Anyone Who Had a Heart.* London: Atlantic Books, 2013.

Baldwin, James. *No Name in the Street.* New York: Dial Press, 1972.

Booker, Christopher. *The Neophiliacs: A Study of the Revolution in English Life in the Fifties and Sixties.* London: Collins, 1969.

Brown, Mick. "Kenneth Anger: Where the Bodies Are Buried." *Esquire,* January 2014. esquire.co.uk/culture/news/a5483/kenneth-anger.

Burgess, Anthony. *A Clockwork Orange.* London: Heinemann, 1962.

Burlingame, Jon. *The Music of James Bond.* Oxford: Oxford University Press, 2014.

Charroux, Robert. *Le livre des secrets trahis.* Paris: Laffont, 1965.

The Children's Bible in Color. London: Paul Hamlyn, 1964.

Churton, Tobias. *Aleister Crowley: The Biography.* London: Watkins Publishing, 2011.

———. *Gnostic Mysteries of Sex.* Rochester, Vt.: Inner Traditions, 2015.

———. *The Invisible History of the Rosicrucians.* Rochester, Vt.: Inner Traditions, 2009.

———. *Jerusalem! The Real Life of William Blake.* London: Watkins Publishing, 2015.

———. "My Life in the Sixties." Unpublished manuscript.

———. *Occult Paris.* Rochester, Vt.: Inner Traditions, 2016.

Clarke, Arthur C. *2001: A Space Odyssey.* New York: New American Library, 1968.

Colacello, Bob. "Remains of the Dia." *Vanity Fair,* April 30, 2008. www
.vanityfair.com/magazine/1996/09/colacello199609.

Crowley, Aleister. *The Confessions of Aleister Crowley.* New York: Hill & Wang,
1969.

———. "The Herb Dangerous." Series of essays on hashish in Crowley's peri-
odical, *The Equinox.* Volume 1. London: Simpkin Marshall, Hamilton,
Kent & Co., 1909.

d'Olivet, Antoine Fabre. *Histoire philosophique du genre humain* [The
Philosophical History of the Human Type]. 2 vols. Paris: Chez J. L. J. Brière
Libraire, 1824.

Fawcett, Anthony. *John Lennon: One Day at a Time; A Personal Biography of the
Seventies.* London: New English Library, 1976.

Feuerbach, Ludwig. *The Essence of Christianity.* Translated from the second German edition by Marian Evans ("George Eliot"). London: John
Chapman, 1854.

Fiegel, Eddi. *John Barry: A Sixties Theme.* London: Constable, 1998.

Frater Shiva. *Inside Solar Lodge, Outside the Law.* York Beach, Maine: Teitan
Press, 2007.

Gans, David, and Peter Simon. *Playing in the Band: An Oral and Visual Portrait
of the Grateful Dead.* New York: St. Martin's Press, 1985.

Garcia, Dylan, and Hart Higashi. *Jerry Garcia: The Collected Artwork.*
New York: Thunder's Mouth Press, 2005.

Gleason, Ralph J. *The Jefferson Airplane and the San Francisco Sound.* New York:
Ballantine Books, 1969.

Glueck, Grace. "The De Menil Family: The Medici of Modern Art." Interview
with Dominique de Menil. *New York Times,* May 18, 1986.

Godard, Jean-Luc. *Three Films: Une Femme est une Femme, Une Femme Mariée,
and Deux ou Trois Choses Que Je Sais d'Elle.* London: Lorrimer Classical
Film Scripts, 1975.

Hegel, Georg Wilhelm Friedrich. *The Phenomenology of Mind.* 1807. In
Phenomenology of Spirit. Translated by Arnold V. Miller. New York: Oxford
University Press, 1977.

Heindel, Max. *The Rosicrucian Cosmo-Conception.* North Yakima, Wash.:
Rosicrucian Fellowship, 1909.

Henderson, David. *'Scuse Me While I Kiss the Sky: The Life of Jimi Hendrix.*
London: Bantam, 1981.

Hergé (Georges Remi). *Vol 714 pour Sydney.* Tournai, Belgium: Casterman, 1968.

Hess, Barbara. *Abstract Expressionism.* Cologne: Taschen, 2005.

Hesse, Hermann. *Siddhartha: An Indian Tale.* New York: New Directions, 1951.

The Holy Bible. King James Version. Oxford: Oxford University Press, 1969.

Huxley, Aldous. *The Doors of Perception.* Harmondsworth, U.K.: Penguin, 1968.

Jung, Carl. *Man and His Symbols.* London: Aldus Books and W. H. Allen, 1974.

Kandinsky, Wassily. *Concerning the Spiritual in Art.* 1912. Translated by M. T. H. Sadler. Reprint, New York: Dover, 1977.

Kerouac, Jack. *On the Road.* New York: Viking, 1957.

Kesey, Ken. *One Flew Over the Cuckoo's Nest.* New York: New American Library, 1962.

Kuspit, Donald. "Concerning the Spiritual in Contemporary Art." In *The Spiritual in Art: Abstract Painting 1890–1985,* edited by Maurice Tuchman. New York: Abbeville Press, 1987.

Laing, Ronald D. *The Politics of Experience and the Bird of Paradise.* Harmondsworth, U.K.: Penguin, 1967.

Lennon, Cynthia. *A Twist of Lennon.* London: Star Book W. H. Allen, 1978.

Lennon, John. *A Spaniard in the Works.* London: Jonathan Cape, 1965.

———. *Skywriting by Word of Mouth.* London: Jonathan Cape, 1981.

Lennon, John, and A. C. Bhaktivedanta. *Search for Liberation.* Worcester, U.K.: Bhaktivedanta Book Trust, 1981.

Leonard, Geoff, Pete Walker, and Gareth Bramley. *John Barry: The Man with the Midas Touch.* Bristol, U.K.: Redcliffe Press, 2008.

Lipsey, Roger. *An Art of Our Own: The Spiritual in Twentieth Century Art.* Boston: Shambhala, 1989.

MacDonald, Ian. *Revolution in the Head: The Beatles' Records and the Sixties.* London: Random House, 1994.

Macquarrie, John. *Principles of Christian Theology.* London: SCM Press, 1977.

Maugham, Somerset. *The Razor's Edge.* London: Heinemann, 1944.

McEvilly, Thomas. "Origins of Anti-Art." In *The Triumph of Anti-Art: Conceptual and Performance Art in the Formation of Post-Modernism.* Kingston, N.Y.: McPherson & Co, 2012.

Melly, George. *Revolt into Style.* London: Allen Lane, 1970.

Michell, John. *The Dimensions of Paradise: Sacred Geometry, Ancient Science, and the Heavenly Order on Earth.* Rochester, Vt.: Inner Traditions, 2008.

———. *View over Atlantis.* New York: Ballantine Books, 1973.

Morris, Desmond. *The Naked Ape*. New York: McGraw-Hill Publishing, 1967.

Mumford, Lewis. *The City in History: Its Origins, Its Transformations, and Its Prospects*. New York: Harcourt, Brace & World, 1961.

Nietzsche, Friedrich. *The Gay Science (The Joyful Wisdom)*. Digireads, 2009.

———. *Thus Spoke Zarathustra*. London: Penguin Classics, 1961.

Ono, Yoko. *Grapefruit*. London: Peter Owen, 1970. First published Tokyo: Wunternaum Press, 1964.

Perry, Helen. *The Human Be-In*. London: Allen Lane, 1968.

Powell, Michael. *Million Dollar Movie*. London: Heinemann, 1990.

Robinson, John. *Honest to God*. London: SCM Press, 1963.

Rózsa, Miklós. *Double Life: The Autobiography of Miklós Rózsa*. Tunbridge Wells, U.K.: Baton Press, 1994.

Saint-Martin, Lous Claude de. *Des erreurs et de la vérité, ou les hommes rappelés au principe universel de la science* [Of errors and of truth, or men recalled to the universal principle of science]. Edimbourg: par un philosophe inconnu, 1775. [Edinburgh: Anonymous; in fact: Lyon, chez Jean-André Périsse-Duluc].

Sanders, Ed. *The Family: The Story of Charles Manson's Dune Buggy Attack Battalion*. New York: Dutton, 1971.

Schonfield, Hugh J. *The Passover Plot: A New Interpretation on the Life and Death of Jesus*. London: Bernard Geis Associates, 1965.

Scott, Walter, ed. *Hermetica*. Vol. 1. Boston: Shambhala Press, 1987.

Seegers, Ulli. "Metabolic Processes: On Great Works and Invisible Values in Contemporary Art." In *Art and Alchemy: The Mystery of Transformation*, edited by Sven Dupré, Dedo von Kerssenbrock-Krosigk, and Beat Wismer. Düsseldorf: Hirmer Publishers, 2014.

Shotton, Pete, and Nicholas Schaffner. *John Lennon: In My Life*. London: Coronet Books, 1983.

Slaughter, Frank G. *The Crown and the Cross: The Life of Christ*. London: Jarrolds, 1959.

Spock, Benjamin McLane. *The Common Sense Book of Baby and Child Care*. New York: Pocket Books, 1946.

Taylor, Derek. *It Was Twenty Years Ago Today*. London: Bantam Press, 1987.

———. *Fifty Years Adrift (in an Open-Necked Shirt)*. Guildford, U.K.: Genesis Publications, 1984.

Thompson, Alan. *The Day before Yesterday: An Illustrated History of Britain from Attlee to Macmillan*. London: Granada Publishing, 1971.

Tuchman, Maurice, ed. *The Spiritual in Art: Abstract Painting 1890–1986.* New York: Abbeville Press, 1986.

Vahanian, Gabriel. *The Death of God: The Culture of Our Post-Christian Era.* New York: George Braziller, 1961.

Vitz, Paul C. *Psychology as Religion: The Cult of Self-Worship.* Grand Rapids, Mich.: Eerdman's Publishing, 1977.

Von Däniken, Erich. *Chariots of the Gods?* New York: Bantam Books, 1971.

Vonnegut, Kurt. *Cat's Cradle.* New York: Dial Press, 1963.

Wasserman, James. *In the Center of the Fire: A Memoir of the Occult 1966–1989.* Lake Worth, Fla.: Ibis Press, 2012.

Wasson, R. Gordon. *The Road to Eleusis: Unveiling the Secret of the Mysteries.* New York: Harcourt, 1978.

Watts, Alan. *The Joyous Cosmology: Adventures in the Chemistry of Consciousness.* New York: Pantheon, 1962.

Wells, Brian. *Psychedelic Drugs: Psychological, Medical and Social Issues.* Harmondsworth, U.K.: Penguin, 1973.

Wiener, Jon. *Come Together: John Lennon in His Time.* Champaign: University of Illinois Press, 1984.

Winston, Kimberly. "Blacks Say Atheists Were Unseen Civil Rights Heroes." *USA Today,* February 23, 2012.

Zaehner, Robert Charles. *Our Savage God.* London: Collins, 1974.

Index

INNER TRADITIONS • BEAR & COMPANY
P.O. Box 388
Rochester, VT 05767
1-800-246-8648
www.InnerTraditions.com

Or contact your local bookseller